NATIONAL ACADEMY PRESS

The National Academy Press was created by the National Academy of Sciences to publish the reports issued by the Academy and by the National Academy of Engineering, the Institute of Medicine, and the National Research Council, all operating under the charter granted to the National Academy of Sciences by the Congress of the United States.

CRIMINAL CAREERS AND "CAREER CRIMINALS"

VOLUME I

Alfred Blumstein, Jacqueline Cohen,
Jeffrey A. Roth, and Christy A. Visher, *editors*

Panel on Research on Criminal Careers

Committee on Research on Law Enforcement and the
   Administration of Justice

Commission on Behavioral and Social Sciences and
   Education

National Research Council

NATIONAL ACADEMY PRESS
Washington, D.C.   1986

NATIONAL ACADEMY PRESS   2101 CONSTITUTION AVENUE NW   WASHINGTON, DC 20418

NOTICE: The project that is the subject of this report was approved by the Governing Board of the National Research Council, whose members are drawn from the councils of the National Academy of Sciences, the National Academy of Engineering, and the Institute of Medicine. The members of the committee responsible for the report were chosen for their special competences and with regard for appropriate balance.

This report has been reviewed by a group other than the authors according to procedures approved by a Report Review Committee consisting of members of the National Academy of Sciences, the National Academy of Engineering, and the Institute of Medicine.

The National Research Council was established by the National Academy of Sciences in 1916 to associate the broad community of science and technology with the Academy's purposes of furthering knowledge and of advising the federal government. The Council operates in accordance with general policies determined by the Academy under the authority of its congressional charter of 1863, which establishes the Academy as a private, nonprofit, self-governing membership corporation. The Council has become the principal operating agency of both the National Academy of Sciences and the National Academy of Engineering in the conduct of their services to the government, the public, and the scientific and engineering communities. It is administered jointly by both Academies and the Institute of Medicine. The National Academy of Engineering and the Institute of Medicine were established in 1964 and 1970, respectively, under the charter of the National Academy of Sciences.

This project was sponsored by the National Institute of Justice, U.S. Department of Justice, under Contract No. 83-IJ-CV-0010. The contents do not necessarily reflect the views or policies of the grantor agency.

Library of Congress Cataloging-in-Publication Data

Criminal careers and "career criminals."

Bibliography: v. 1, p.
Includes index.
1. Crime analysis—United States.   2. Crime and criminals—United States.   3. Criminal behavior, Prediction of.   I. Blumstein, Alfred. II. National Research Council (U.S.).   Panel on Research on Criminal Careers.
HV7936.C88C75   1986   364.3'0973   86-18282
ISBN 0-309-03684-4 (v. 1)
ISBN 0-309-03683-6 (v. 2)

Printed in the United States of America

Panel on Research on Criminal Careers

ALFRED BLUMSTEIN (*Chair*), School of Urban and Public Affairs, Carnegie-Mellon University

ALLEN H. ANDREWS, JR., Superintendent of Police, City of Peoria, Illinois

DELBERT S. ELLIOTT, Department of Sociology and Behavioral Research Institute, University of Colorado

DAVID P. FARRINGTON, Institute of Criminology, Cambridge University, England

JOHN KAPLAN, School of Law, Stanford University

ROLF LOEBER, Western Psychiatric Institute and Clinic, University of Pittsburgh

CHARLES F. MANSKI, Department of Economics, University of Wisconsin

NORVAL MORRIS, School of Law, University of Chicago

ALBERT J. REISS, JR., Department of Sociology, Yale University

LEE ROBINS, Washington University Medical School, St. Louis, Missouri

HAROLD ROSE, Department of Urban Affairs, University of Wisconsin at Milwaukee

DANIEL S. SMITH, Department of History, University of Illinois at Chicago

ANDREW L. SONNER, State's Attorney for Montgomery County, Maryland

REGGIE B. WALTON, Associate Judge, Superior Court of the District of Columbia

JAMES Q. WILSON, Department of Government, Harvard University, and Graduate School of Management, University of California at Los Angeles

MARVIN E. WOLFGANG, Sellin Center for Studies in Criminology and Criminal Law, University of Pennsylvania

JEFFREY A. ROTH, *Study Director*

CHRISTY A. VISHER, *Research Associate*

GAYLENE J. DUMOUCHEL, *Administrative Secretary*

JACQUELINE COHEN, *Consultant,* School of Urban and Public Affairs, Carnegie-Mellon University

Committee on Research on Law Enforcement and the Administration of Justice

Contents

Contents, Volume II

Preface

In 1983, when the Panel on Research on Criminal Careers was convened, the U.S. prison population had experienced a rapid growth—more than doubling from 196,000 in 1972 to 437,000 in 1983—and the crime rate had just passed its 1980 peak of 13 million reported index crimes, or almost 6,000 crimes per 100,000 population. There was strong policy interest in finding alternatives to rapidly escalating imprisonment costs and what was perceived as relatively ineffective crime control.

One approach that was widely considered was to direct attention at "career criminals," high-rate or long-duration offenders who contribute most to total crime rates. Research at the Rand Corporation had highlighted the extreme variability in individual rates of criminal activity: in surveys of prisoners, the worst 10 percent of offenders reported committing more than 50 robberies or 200 burglaries per year, but half the prisoners reported committing fewer than 5 burglaries or robberies per year. This extreme variation enhanced the appeal of being able to distinguish high-rate from low-rate offenders. To this end, a number of prediction scales have been proposed to distinguish the high-rate offenders from the more numerous ordinary offenders.

Any prediction of an individual's future offending must draw on research on criminal careers, the characterization of the sequence of individual criminal activity: initiation of criminal activity, variation over the career in the frequency of offending and in the kinds of crimes committed, and, finally, termination of criminal activity. Any attempt to identify the *career criminals* in a population requires examination of the *criminal careers* of all offenders to find the characteristics that distinguish the most serious offenders: those having the longest remaining careers, the highest frequencies of offending, and committing the most serious kinds of offenses.

The panel was convened at the request of the National Institute of Justice to evaluate the feasibility of predicting the future course of criminal careers, to assess the effects of prediction instruments in reducing crime through incapacitation (usually by incarceration), and to review the contribution of research on criminal careers to the development of fundamental knowledge about crime and criminals. Ultimately, such knowledge is necessary for understanding the dimensions of the crime problem, for isolating factors that contribute to criminality, and for developing effective crime control strategies. In particular, many commonly held perceptions of correlates of crime that derive from aggregate or macroanalysis do not hold at the individual or micro level. As knowledge about criminal careers develops, the insights into individual offending that emerge will certainly stimulate refinements to criminological theory. They will also lead to improved criminal justice decisions, both by drawing attention to some variables that are not adequately appreciated and by directing attention away from other variables that are incorrectly perceived as important. Criminal career information is also necessary for estimating the effects of changes in incarceration policy on crime and on prison populations.

In reviewing the scientific evidence on criminal careers, the panel members were in general agreement about the findings and conclusions, but there were, however, divergent views on the ethics of how such information should be used in dealing with offenders. At one end of a spectrum is the view that no actions taken by the criminal justice system should take any account of individual differences in anticipated future offending; from this perspective, any use of predictive information would be objectionable. At the other end of the spectrum is a desire to see even weak results put to use as quickly as possible; advocates of this position point to the shortcomings of current decisions and emphasize that any contribution could improve the quality of decisions and thereby reduce crime. In the middle, most panel members view prediction of future offending as a legitimate consideration in criminal justice decisions, particularly since it is currently being done implicitly at some level in practice. This view also maintains, however, that the role of prediction must be rigorously constrained and, in particular, that it not result in punishments or restraints that are unjust in terms of the offense committed. Although the panel viewed the making of pronouncements on ethical issues as outside its role, we did devote considerable attention to ethical considerations to be sure that our conclusions were sensitive to them. The scientific concern that is central to the panel's role is that any use of prediction be based on correct information intelligently used. We found a number of instances in which prediction rules were naively generated, with poor methods, or violated fundamental tenets of validity testing. Thus, it became important to call attention to more appropriate methods and to identify useful information—both information that contributes to identifying "career criminals" as well as information that is frequently used but should not be used.

Many aspects of the work of the panel can be viewed as a follow-up to earlier work by the Panel on Research on Deterrent and Incapacitative Effects, whose report was published in 1978. That report noted that any assessment of incapacitative effects or improvement of them was severely handicapped by the paucity of substantive research findings on individual offending patterns that could contribute to estimates of the magnitude of incapacitative effects. That panel thus recommended that priority be assigned to research on criminal careers and that "the most immediate empirical investigation should be directed at estimating the individual crime rate and the length of a criminal career."

Pursuit of these issues has been a major feature of the Crime Control Theory Research Program of the National Institute of Justice, directed by Richard Linster and Joel Garner. It is always disappointing to find that knowledge does not accumulate as fast as one would like and that the measurements of those criminal career parameters are still short of definitive. In the context of the earlier review, however, it is impressive how much additional research has accumulated that provides internally consistent measurement of the key dimensions of criminal careers and of their relationships to other relevant variables.

Criminal justice is a field of social science research that is heavily beset by ideological considerations. In such a setting, any individual study is properly met with some skepticism and concern about the author's particular ideological bent and the degree to which that perspective may have had an excessive influence in shaping the results. A panel such as this one, which brings together individuals with a full array of the requisite disciplinary perspectives and technical skills, and with a diversity of ideological stances, thus represents an important vehicle for assessing the current evidence in the field and for identifying promising research directions.

Given its charge to assess the evidence on criminal careers and to point to future research directions, the panel pursued two intensive efforts. First, the panel's staff reviewed the relevant literature, and these reviews are included as appendices in this volume: Appendix A by Christy Visher and Jeffrey Roth reviews the literature on participation in criminal careers; Appendix B by Jacqueline Cohen reviews the literature on the individual frequency of offending and on the mix of offense types by active offenders.

Second, the panel commissioned a number of papers that were presented and discussed at a workshop in Woods Hole, Massachusetts, on July 23–25, 1984 (see Appendix C for the program and list of participants). Several of the papers review major bodies of literature: on prediction and its uses (by Stephen and Don Gottfredson); on the influence on criminal careers of alcohol (by James Collins) and of drugs (by Eric Wish and Bruce Johnson); and on group patterns in offending (by Albert J. Reiss). Because of the considerable interest generated by the second Rand inmate survey, the panel also asked Christy Visher to undertake a reanalysis of the data from that survey. Two commissioned papers, one by Joseph Weis and another by John Copas and Roger Tarling, address methodological and measurement issues; a paper by Mark Moore addresses relevant normative issues; and two papers introduce new models of criminal careers that derive from recent advances in economics (by Christopher Flinn) and in stochastic processes (by John Lehoczky). These papers constitute Volume II. They are the responsibility of their authors and do not necessarily represent the views of the panel, but they were valuable resources for the panel in its discussions and represent important contributions to the literature on criminal careers.

The panel members represent a diverse group (see biographical sketches in Appendix D). The panel benefited particularly from the sensitivity, sophistication, and challenges offered by the practitioners, who conveyed insights about the current state of their professions—needs, strengths, shortcomings—and the operational constraints that limit the application of research findings. The academic members of the panel are all distinguished researchers. Some are working in areas related to criminal careers, while others brought specialized expertise in particular disciplines, methodologies, jurisprudence, or policy analysis. Discussions at panel meetings were always lively, full of interesting ideas; disagreements were consistently isolated and dealt with directly. It was indeed a pleasure working with so able and committed a group.

The dedicated efforts of the staff have been central to the work of the panel. Jeffrey Roth was the study director from the inception of the panel and contributed considerably in terms of managing the affairs of the panel, in drafting significant segments of the report, and in his careful review of all materials. Christy Visher began her association with the panel as a National Research Council Fellow, undertook the review of the second Rand inmate survey, and brought significant criminological background and experience to the work of the panel in its review of the literature and in drafting and editing major sections of the report. Jacqueline Cohen of Carnegie-Mellon University built on her experience as a consultant to the prior Panel on Research on Deterrent and Incapacitative Effects, her extensive research on criminal careers and incapacitation, and her extensive knowledge of the related literature; her diligent contributions to all aspects of the work of the panel, especially in reviewing the literature and in drafting major portions of the report, are very much appreciated. The task of editing the large volume of material assembled by the panel has been considerable. Eugenia Grohman, the associate director for reports of the Commission on Behavioral and Social Sciences and Education, not only sharpened our language but also challenged our assertions when they were insufficiently developed or documented, and in doing so made an excellent and important contribution to the report of the panel. Jean Shirhall was also very effective in editing the appendices to this volume and the papers in Volume II.

The panel has benefited considerably from the administrative and secretarial work of Gaylene Dumouchel at the National Research Council and Elizabeth Kiselev at Carnegie-Mellon University.

An important feature of the panel's work has been the support and encouragement of the sponsor, the National Institute of Justice. Richard Linster kept in close touch with the panel throughout its work, and James Stewart, the director of the National Institute of Justice, provided the kind of encouragement and support that has characterized his stewardship of the institute's research program.

ALFRED BLUMSTEIN, *Chair*
Panel on Research on Criminal Careers

CRIMINAL CAREERS AND "CAREER CRIMINALS"

VOLUME I

Summary

THE CRIMINAL CAREER APPROACH

Much research on crime has focused on aggregate crime rates, i.e., crimes per capita in the general population. In contrast, the criminal career approach seeks to analyze the activity—the careers—of the individuals who commit criminal offenses. In this approach, aggregate rates are partitioned into two primary components: the percentage of the population that commits crimes and the nature and extent of activity of those people who are actively engaging in crime (i.e., active offenders). This partitioning is important because the two components can be influenced by very different factors and call for quite different policy responses: the first—participation—is associated with efforts to prevent individuals from ever becoming involved in crime; the second—frequency, seriousness, and career length—is central to the decisions of the criminal justice system. Together, these four key dimensions characterize criminal careers:

1. *Participation*—the distinction between those who engage in crime and those who do not;

2. *Frequency*—the rate of criminal activity of those who are active;

3. *Seriousness* of offenses committed;

4. *Career length*—the length of time an offender is active.

Frequency, seriousness, and length of career may vary substantially across offenders. At one extreme are offenders whose careers consist of only one offense. At the other extreme are "career criminals"—also variously characterized as dangerous, habitual, or chronic offenders—who commit serious offenses with high frequency over extended periods of time. Both of these extreme career types are of policy interest. Offenders with short careers who commit very few offenses are of interest for identifying external factors that foster early termination of careers and that can be affected by public policy. Such knowledge will be especially useful in the design of crime control policies, including prevention achieved through the imposition of sanctions for deterrent or rehabilitative purposes. Career criminals are of interest for formulating policies that can identify these offenders early in their careers and selectively target criminal justice resources at preventing their crimes, primarily through incarceration.

Partitioning criminal activity enables research to focus more directly on the development and evolution of individuals' offending behaviors over time and their relationship to aggregate crime rates. For example, a drop in the aggregate index crime rate may reflect a decline in participation, a decrease in frequency, a shift to less serious crimes, or a shortening of career lengths. If a causal factor strongly affected only one of these career dimensions, variation in the others could mask that relationship when crime is measured in terms of the aggregate rate. Since different factors are likely to affect the different dimensions of criminal careers, it is important to isolate those dimensions to assess each factor's respective influence.

Measurement of the dimensions of criminal careers is inherently difficult. It would be easy, of course, if one could find a large representative sample of the population, each of whom would cooperate by maintaining and regularly submitting a daily log of any criminal activity. Since that option does not exist, criminology has developed two primary sources: retrospective self-reports from individuals about whether they have committed crimes and, if so, when, what kinds, and how often; and official arrest histories, which are viewed as a sample of crimes committed. Each of these approaches has its own flaws—nonresponse, distortion, and recall error in self-reports and variations in police arrest decisions or offender skill that lead to biases in the sampling process that generates official records. But the findings derived from one ap-

proach can and should be tested against the findings derived from the other to develop more reliable measures of the underlying crime process.

FINDINGS ON CRIMINAL CAREERS

Some of the factors most strongly associated with aggregate crime and arrest rates are the demographic factors of age, race, and sex. By separately analyzing the links of these factors to participation and frequency, one can begin to see the importance of the criminal career approach. The data show that these demographic variables are strongly associated with participation and only weakly associated with individual frequency. That is, teenagers, blacks, and males are most heavily represented in aggregate measures of offending because larger percentages of those populations than of other populations become involved in offending. But among all offenders, frequency of offending is much less related to the demographic variables. Because criminal justice system clients have already passed through the participation "filter," sanction decisions that invoke those demographic variables are likely to be seriously in error from a crime control perspective. Thus, separating the participation rate from the course of active offenders' criminal careers enables one to isolate influences on the initiation of offending from influences on the frequency or duration of a criminal career. In practical terms, prospective indicators of a high participation risk are useful in suggesting prevention strategies to reduce the fraction of offenders in the population.

Participation in Offending

Measures of Participation

Participation can be measured either cumulatively (the fraction of a given group ever committing at least one crime before attaining some age), or currently (the fraction committing at least one crime during a particular observation period). It is possible to tabulate participation rates based on either official records of arrests or convictions or self-reports of offending.

Scholars concerned with crime and delinquency have tended to study urban areas, where crime is most heavily concentrated, and males, who dominate aggregate arrest statistics. Therefore, knowledge is most complete concerning participation by urban males, and comparative participation data are most readily available for the racial groups in urban areas. Participation in criminal behavior, as measured by arrests, is higher than many people expect: 25–45 percent of urban males have been arrested by age 18 for a nontraffic offense; 12–18 percent for an FBI index offense (murder, rape, robbery, aggravated assault, burglary, larceny, and auto theft); and 4–8 percent for a crime involving personal injury. About half of those ever arrested during their lifetimes are first arrested before they reach 18.

The earliest criminal careers can begin before age 10; the rate of initiation rises to a maximum in the late teens and then drops off rapidly. At the peak age in the teenage years, the maximum probability of a first arrest for an index offense is about 6 percent for blacks and 2 percent for whites. Based on a number of studies, the black/white ratio of males ever arrested by age 18 is about 1.8 to 1 for nontraffic offenses. Other data suggest that the ratio is about 3 to 1 for FBI index offenses and at least 4 to 1 for offenses involving injury. The greatest demographic differential is that attributable to sex: even for all nontraffic offenses, male participation rates based on official records are 3 to 5 times those for females; the ratio is higher for more serious crimes.

Risk Factors in Criminal Participation

Research suggests that adverse family influences and early antisocial behaviors are major risk factors associated with participation in delinquency and crime. The family influences most strongly associated with subsequent participation include inadequate parenting, as manifested by inconsistent or sporadically violent discipline, poor parent-child communication, and poor supervision; parental delinquency or criminality; parental discord and family breakup; large family size, especially in poor families; and some indicators of low socioeconomic status (primarily for serious crimes).

High rates of delinquency participation have been found among children exhibiting the following antisocial behaviors at an early age: covert antisocial behavior (e.g., lying, stealing); overt antisocial behavior (e.g., aggression, fighting); poor school performance; abuse of hard drugs or alcohol; and association with delinquent peers. Of course, all of these behaviors occur frequently in many children who never begin criminal careers, but their chronic occurrence is correlated with a higher risk of participation in criminal activity.

Although these risk factors have been suspected "causes of crime" for some time, recognition of their links to participation could provide some basis for designing strategies to prevent the initiation of criminal careers. However, several considerations hamper efforts to do so:

• Difficulty in prospectively identifying offenders. Most youth who present any one of the precursors do not initiate serious criminal careers.
• Uncertainty about effective interventions. Attempts to remediate precursor behaviors associated with participation may not influence participation itself;

most evaluations of preventive programs carried out thus far have design problems that preclude definitive conclusions about effectiveness.

• Uncertainty about the optimal age for intervention. While the behavior of young children (e.g., ages 4–6) is more responsive to interventions, it is more difficult to correctly identify high-risk children at those young ages.

• Other concerns such as program cost, unintended undesirable consequences, and legal and ethical limitations on permissible interventions with youths who have not been charged with any offense.

While a few interventions have demonstrated effectiveness in well-designed experiments, they have involved small samples. Larger, more heterogeneous samples in multiple settings should be used to further explore Head Start preschool enrichment programs and programs to train parents and teachers in communication with and supervision of children and in behavioral methods for modifying children's antisocial behaviors.

Individual Frequencies for Active Offenders

Overall Rates

Individual offending frequency (λ) is measured by the number of crimes committed per year by an active offender. Despite differences in observation techniques (self-reports or arrest records), in the samples used (inmates, arrestees, or general population samples), and in the jurisdictions examined (with their different population characteristics and criminal justice system practices), there is considerable convergence in estimates of λ for any given offense type: averages of 2 to 4 violent crimes per year for active violent offenders and 5 to 10 property

crimes per year for active property offenders.

The average λ of inmates is higher than that of offenders not incarcerated, which is to be expected since the greater activity of high-rate offenders increases their exposure to arrest and because selectivity in criminal justice decisions increases the risk of incarceration of those offenders if arrested. Estimates derived from self-reports by inmates in California and Michigan indicate that, before being incarcerated, those who were active in robbery committed an average of 15 to 20 robberies per year and those active in burglary committed an average of 45 to 50 burglaries per year. Rates estimated for Texas inmates more closely resemble those of offenders in the community.

Most significantly, λ varies considerably across offenders so that the distribution of λ is highly skewed: the median offender commits only a handful of crimes per year, while a small percentage of offenders commit more than 100 crimes per year. This finding is obviously especially important in developing policies to reduce crime by concentrating on high-rate offenders, or "career criminals."

Demographic Differences in λ

Sex, age, and race data are routinely collected on offenders, primarily for operational identification purposes, and estimates of λ are often contrasted across demographic subgroups defined in those terms. In contrast to the large demographic differences observed in participation rates, average values of λ do not vary substantially with the demographic attributes of sex, age, or race.

Most notably, black/white ratios for λ range from about 1–1.3 to 1 for most crimes and are less than 2 to 1 even for robbery and other violent offenses that show very substantial race differences in aggregate population arrest rates. In other words, the large race difference observed in aggregate crime or arrest rates is due mostly to black/white differences in participation rather than differences in λ. Preliminary data also suggest that male/female frequency ratios are generally less than 2 to 1, even for the traditionally male offenses of assault and robbery. And, finally, λ is relatively insensitive to age.

Other Factors Related to λ

Differences in λ are associated with a number of nondemographic factors, including age of initiation of criminal careers, drug use, unemployment, and prior criminal record. Although their theoretical significance is sometimes ambiguous, these factors offer policy potential, especially as a basis for identifying high-rate offenders. Offenders who begin criminal careers at younger ages generally have higher values of λ than offenders who begin at older ages. High frequencies are found among active offenders who are currently using drugs, especially multiple drugs, and among those who used drugs as juveniles. The values of λ for drug users are at least twice those for other offenders and can be 6 times higher during periods of heavy drug use. The length of time spent unemployed is a significant factor associated with λ: offenders who are unemployed for substantial periods of time commit crimes at higher rates. Last, high frequencies in the past are a good indicator of high frequencies in the future for offenders who remain active.

Trends in Seriousness

Most active offenders engage in a considerable variety of crime types, with a somewhat greater tendency for offenders to repeat the same crime or to repeat within the group of property crimes or the group of violent crimes. For juveniles, offense seriousness generally escalates over successive arrests, but it is difficult to determine how much of that escalation is due to differences among offenders (with more persistent offenders also committing more serious crimes) or to a tendency of offenders generally to escalate the seriousness of their crimes as their careers progress. For adult offenders who are arrested more than once, the evidence suggests no clear trends in seriousness.

Career Length

Since participation in criminal activity is more widespread among teenage males than among adult males and λ is relatively stable over age for those offenders who remain active, many careers must be very short, ending after only brief ventures into crime as teenagers. This conclusion is consistent with the decline with age observed in aggregate arrest measures.

Research on duration of careers in fact suggests that adult careers average only about 5 years for offenders committing index offenses. However, this average hides major differences across offenders. Residual career length (the expected time still remaining in careers) is 5 years for 18-year-old index offenders, but it is 10 years for index offenders who are still active in their 30s, and it does not begin to decline for active offenders until they are in their 40s.

This finding—that residual career length increases through the 20s to reach a maximum in the 30s—contradicts the widely held view that the low arrest rates in the 30s reflect high rates of career termination at those ages. These low arrest rates result from the high termination rates at the earlier ages, but those few persistent offenders who continue to be active into their 30s display the lowest termination rates and the longest residual careers.

USE OF CRIMINAL CAREER INFORMATION IN CRIMINAL JUSTICE DECISION MAKING

The findings from research on criminal careers can play an important role in the decisions of the criminal justice system. Those decisions take place at five points: arrest, pretrial release, prosecution, sentencing, and parole. At each point, decision makers are motivated by different objectives—such as maintaining public order, ensuring appearance at trial, attaining convictions, imposing deserved punishment, and maintaining order in prisons—but each also shares in the objective of crime control. To further this objective, decision makers may attempt to modify criminal careers, either directly through behavioral or other individual therapies, or indirectly, by modifying substance abuse, employment prospects, or other characteristics associated with the frequency or residual duration of serious offending.

Career Modification

An earlier Panel on Research on Rehabilitative Techniques reported in 1980 that no particular technique had been found to be broadly effective in directly modifying criminal careers. For juvenile offenders, some community-based programs result in recidivism rates that are no higher than those for juveniles who were incarcerated. A few recently studied programs with behavior modification orientations are reported to have favorably modified the careers of small samples of delinquents during short (e.g., 1-year) follow-up periods; these warrant replications with longer follow-up periods and larger samples. Among indirect approaches to career modification, intensive drug abuse surveillance and treatment appear to reduce the frequency of serious offending by criminals addicted to hard drugs. Evaluations of interventions to upgrade employment skills or to assist the reentry of ex-inmates into the community have not documented success in modifying offenders' careers in the United States, although such programs have met with some success in the United Kingdom.

Given the dearth of interventions that have demonstrated general effectiveness in modifying careers, decision strategies focused on career criminals have recently become especially prominent, which has led to research on how criminal career information can be used to achieve greater crime control, especially through incapacitation of the most serious offenders.

Incapacitation

Under 1970 incarceration policies, incapacitation was estimated to have reduced the number of FBI index crimes by 10 to 20 percent. For robberies and burglaries, incapacitation is estimated to have reduced their number by 25–35 percent in 1973; in 1982, after the national inmate population had almost doubled, the incapacitative effect for these offenses is estimated to have increased to about 35–45 percent. For general increases in incarceration to reduce index crimes by an additional 10 to 20 percent from 1982 levels, inmate populations again would have to have more than doubled.

Since the increments to crime control from incapacitation are modest, even with very large general increases in inmate populations, and since considerable pressure on prison and jail resources exists, interest has been stimulated in developing policies that selectively target incapacitation on the most active offenders. Such policies have the potential of achieving the same, or even improved, crime reduction, with much smaller increases in inmate populations. Two forms of selective incapacitation policies have been considered: offender-based policies, which extend the time served for those predicted to be high-rate offenders among all those convicted of the same charge; and charge-based policies, which impose mandatory minimum terms on all offenders convicted of selected offense types in which high-rate offenders tend to engage.

Of the selective incapacitation policies that have been proposed, the estimated crime reduction effects through incapacitation are modest, ranging at most up to 10 percent. Compared with the 100 percent increase in inmate populations required to achieve this reduction through general increases in incarceration, however, selective incapacitation policies involve only 10 to 20 percent increases in total inmate populations. The achievable incapacitative effect will be lower, however, if the offenses of incarcerated offenders are continued by others or replaced by new recruits. The degree to which replacement occurs can be expected to vary by crime type (e.g., presumably higher for drug sales than for acts of personal violence), but there are no estimates of rates of replacement.

Furthermore, although selective incapacitation policies can offer an attractive tradeoff between crime reduction and inmate population increases, they raise a number of ethical and operational issues:

- the inevitable errors associated with any classification rule that distinguishes between high-risk and low-risk offenders;
- the proper balance in criminal justice decisions between deserved punishment and public protection (concern for future crimes);
- the degree to which the added crime control from selective incapacitation policies warrants sentence disparity in offender-based policies or mandatory sentences in charge-based policies; and

- the possibility that some selection rules might disproportionately penalize offenders who are from minority groups.

PREDICTION-BASED CLASSIFICATION RULES

There have been a number of recent developments in systems for classifying offenders on the basis of assessments of their criminal careers. These systems involve two components: a statistically derived prediction scale that relates offender characteristics to the course of the criminal career and a rule for classifying offenders as high risk or low risk on the basis of their prediction scale scores. In assessing such classification rules, the panel considered several factors:

- the extent to which existing decision practices already focus on offenders whose criminal careers tend to be the most serious;
- ethical limitations on the proper influence of predictions in decision making and on the choice of predictor variables;
- methodological issues in constructing and validating a prediction scale and classification rule; and
- the record-keeping implications of a criminal career orientation to decision making.

Existing Decision Practices

Because criminal justice decision makers do not routinely articulate their decision processes, it is difficult to know the extent to which predictions about offenders are incorporated into their decisions. However, using statistical techniques, studies have tested whether decision outcomes are consistent with variables associated with the criminal career: the instant offense; the adult criminal history, measured by the record of previous arrests or convictions; the juvenile record, including police contacts and adjudications; indicators of multiple illicit drug use; and employment history and current status.

The panel found that the instant offense has the dominant influence on decisions at all stages of the criminal justice process, from arrest through parole. The second most influential variable is the record of previous arrests or convictions. Use of the juvenile record is largely limited to sentencing and parole because laws in most jurisdictions separate juvenile records from adult records. Drug use is associated at the sentencing stage with higher probabilities for jail or prison sentences. Employment history and status is associated with decisions only at the stage of pretrial release.

On the basis of criminal career research, current decision practices could be improved, in terms of crime control through incapacitation, if more weight were given to the juvenile record and to serious drug use.

Ethical Limitations

Opinions differ on the extent to which it is ethically proper for predictive considerations to influence the choice of criminal justice sanctions. Strict adherents to a just-deserts philosophy exclude predictions altogether, arguing that the blameworthiness of the instant offense is the only permissible basis for sanctions. Alternative views are that while blameworthiness for the offense determines a presumptive range of acceptable sanctions, the appropriate sanction in a particular case may vary within that range and could be based on prediction-based classifications.

The weight one considers acceptable for prediction-based classification rules depends on the gravity of the harm one is trying to prevent by means of classification and the accuracy of the classifications in assessing risk. In assessing whether a potential predictor is ethically acceptable, its relationship to the blameworthiness of the offender and the empirical and logical relationship of the predictor to the behavior being predicted are commonly invoked criteria.

In light of these considerations, variables such as prior adult convictions are more widely accepted as predictors than behaviors or characteristics such as employment status, over which the offender is presumed to have less control. Characteristics such as race, ethnicity, and religion are especially unacceptable as candidate predictors because they have no relationship to blameworthiness, they have no logical relationship to offending patterns, and their use affronts basic social values.

Methodological Issues

Since offenders' behavior cannot be predicted perfectly, two types of classification error occur: false-positive classification of offenders as high risk when they are truly low risk, and false-negative classification of offenders as low risk when they are truly high risk. For any prediction scale, the number of false-positive errors can be reduced by raising the cut point to classify fewer offenders as high risk at the cost of more false-negative errors. Any final choice of a prediction-based classification rule should estimate and weigh both types of errors, in developing the final classification rule.

Because the criminal justice process consists of a series of decisions that result in the release of some offenders while others are confined, classification rules are frequently distorted by selection bias when a rule developed for use at one stage—parole, for example—is applied at another, such as sentencing or assignment to a career criminal unit for prosecution. Also, because the mix of offender characteristics at any given stage is likely to differ across jurisdictions, classification rules constructed and validated in one jurisdiction should be revalidated before use in another jurisdiction, even if they are to be applied at the same stage of the criminal justice system. Finally, even after a rule is implemented, its accuracy may change over time because of changes in offenders' underlying behavior patterns, changes in the composition of the offender population, or changes in criminal justice selection processes. Therefore, periodic revalidations should be performed to be certain that the classification rule is still effective.

Specific Classification Rules

Several prediction-based rules for classifying offenders have attracted sufficient attention to warrant assessment by the panel. Two have been applied in parole decision making and invoke similar variables: the Salient Factor Score of the United States Parole Commission and the Iowa Risk Assessment Instrument. Using a broad criterion variable with a large base rate (rearrest during follow-up periods of 3 years or more), the rate of false positives (offenders classified as high risks who were not arrested during the follow-up period) is less than 30 percent in construction samples and less than 40 percent in validation samples. The accuracy of these scales has generally been maintained in applications to new samples of offenders and after various personal attributes of questionable appropriateness have been eliminated from them.

A third scale has been proposed by INSLAW for use in selecting cases for high-priority federal prosecution. This scale is noteworthy for having focused on the continuous measure of time until recidivism rather than merely the dichotomous variable of the occurrence of recidivism. The accuracy of this scale in its construction sample is comparable with the parole scales, but it has not yet been tested in a validation sample. A fourth scale, developed from data collected in the Rand inmate survey, is unique in its use of offending frequency (λ) as the criterion variable. However, when the scale was used to classify the offenders as high λ, the false-positive rate was 60 percent for a sample of California inmates and 55 percent for the entire three-state sample.

Future scale development should be aimed at improving the classification of offenders in terms of their frequency of offending and their residual career length. While these career dimensions are not directly observable, their values can be inferred using statistical techniques that analyze time to recidivism.

Record-Keeping Implications

For criminal career knowledge to be helpful in decisions (whether formally or informally), the relevant information has to be accurate and available to decision makers on a timely basis. Much of this information is stored in the record systems of adult and juvenile justice agencies as well as social welfare agencies. While there is no universal agreement about what information should be permitted to influence criminal justice decisions (e.g., some people believe that only adult convictions should be used and neither arrests nor juvenile court actions), it is clear that full adult and juvenile arrest records do provide valuable information about criminal careers.

The improvement of arrest and disposition data should be a high-priority objective of criminal justice systems. Arrest records should be made more complete and accurate, and pertinent attributes of an offense should also be reported on the arrest history. Arrest records to be used in decisions should be augmented with corresponding dispositions. When an arrest is found to have been clearly unwarranted, as in a case of mistaken identity, there should be a prominent notation and an opportunity for expungement.

Adult justice system agencies should gain access to the juvenile record at the time of a person's first serious criminal involvement as an adult. In defining criteria for access, different jurisdictions might choose different thresholds of crime seriousness and different stages of criminal justice processing (e.g., arrest, indictment, or conviction). Requiring a high level of seriousness would reflect a desire to avoid opening a juvenile record in connection with only a minor offense. Precluding access until after conviction would reflect a belief in the principle that a juvenile record should not influence decisions in the adult system that are made before guilt is established with legal certainty. Alternatively, permitting prosecutors and judges to see a juvenile record when making charging, pretrial release, and plea bargaining decisions would allow them to become more fully informed of the public safety risks associated with their decisions. Different jurisdictions will weigh these concerns differently and so may choose different thresholds and stages. One choice that seems reasonable would be the first adult arrest for a felony. A juvenile record would be appended to an adult record only if the adult arrest leads to a conviction. The juvenile record, with appropriate safeguards against dissemination, would be retained in the juvenile repository at least as long as it retains value for decision making in the adult criminal justice system.

AN AGENDA FOR FUTURE RESEARCH

The area of criminal career research is sufficiently promising from both knowledge and policy perspectives to warrant a significant effort with a long-term commitment for support. Key features of the effort should be improved measurement of the dimensions of criminal careers; measurement of their distributions, which are still known only imprecisely; measurement of the variation of the dimensions over the course of a criminal career; and better identification of the factors that influence criminal careers.

The most important criminal career dimension is individual frequency, particularly of serious offenses. The two approaches now used to measure frequency—self-reports and official arrest records—provide reasonable measures, but estimates would be improved appreciably if the two methods were applied to the same samples. Particular attention should be directed at learning how the probability of arrest following a crime varies across subpopulations or crime types. More knowledge about the error structures of the two approaches, and their links to the underlying crime process, would increase the usefulness of the large number of official-record data sets that are available as primary record sources for estimating criminal career dimensions. Research should focus especially on the path of λ over time as offenders age, variation in λ with age for active offenders, the factors associated with intermittent spurts of high-rate and low-rate offending, and differences in λ by crime type.

While some correlates of career dimensions are reasonably well established (e.g., employment), it is still not clear whether the correlations reflect causal relationships that could be manipulated to facilitate earlier termination. For example, it would be desirable to follow up earlier experiments that provided postrelease subsidy payments to parolees to reduce their economic needs with a program designed to avoid the work disincentive effects observed in that experiment (perhaps by requiring the recipients to perform community service). Of particular policy significance is exploration of the factors most influential in terminating a criminal career. For example, little is known about the effect of time in prison on residual career length, especially about whether such time simply postpones career termination. Questions of effects of particular treatments on career dimensions are generally best addressed through an experimental approach.

Research activities that relate closely to incapacitation policy include the development of improved methods for classifying individuals in terms of their criminal career dimensions. Strong candidate classification variables include those that characterize prior juvenile and adult criminal activity—the age of initiation, the frequency and total number of arrests and convictions, and the mix of crime types. It is important to assess the degree to which an individual's record of juvenile and adult arrests provides significantly more predictive information than does the adult conviction record alone. Since active drug use is strongly associated with high offending frequencies, both the uses of this knowledge in decision making and the role of drug treatment in crime control should be further explored.

It is also important to refine and test theoretical explanations of initiation of delinquency or criminal activity and of continuation into serious adult careers. Better information is needed on particular behaviors, life events, and early career patterns that can be linked to subsequent career paths. One aspect of criminal careers, especially among juveniles, is the role of others in influencing initiation and continuation of offending. It would be particularly important to identify the degree to which some identifiable individual offenders serve as recruiters to offending and to what extent behavior can be explained as compliant responsiveness to recruitment efforts. Also with regard to initiation, it is important to explore more carefully the events that may influence the initiation of careers but that have not been sufficiently studied in a longitudinal context to establish causation. Such events include abuse at the hands of family members, parental alcohol or drug abuse, and divorce or other traumatic life events.

Many of these issues are best addressed through a longitudinal research design, especially in view of the inherently longitudinal and dynamic character of criminal careers. A major new longitudinal study that follows multiple cohorts of individuals, linking their criminal careers to personal characteristics and to other life events, would be very valuable. Such a major project should be undertaken in a way that reflects multiple disciplinary and theoretical perspectives relevant to understanding criminal careers. The project should also try to incorporate opportunities for experimental interventions that can be tested on the population being studied longitudinally. Such a program should be a major national priority as the next phase of research on criminal careers.

1

Introduction:
Studying Criminal Careers

THE CRIMINAL CAREERS CONCEPT

Although widely studied, crime is one of the most elusive subjects of social science research as well as a major public policy issue. It has been addressed by many scholars from a wide variety of disciplines; there has been extensive theorizing about its etiology; the public has consistently ranked crime as a serious problem; and there is intense public debate, even about facts, when considering alternative policies for dealing with crime. Yet, despite the importance of the issues and the amount of research, little definitive knowledge has been developed that could be applied to prevent crime or to develop efficient policies for reacting to crime. Over the past decade, however, some significant progress has been made, and much of that has focused on the "criminal career" paradigm.

A criminal career is the characterization of the longitudinal sequence of crimes committed by an individual offender. A previous National Research Council panel called for "research . . . directed at characterizing the patterns of individual criminal careers" (Blumstein, Cohen, and Nagin, 1978:78). This call was motivated in large part by the realization that crime is committed by individuals, even when they organize into groups, and that individuals are the focus of criminal justice decisions. Thus, a paradigm focusing attention on individuals might be most appropriate both for probing the causes of criminal behavior and for developing crime control policies intended to interrupt or modify criminal careers.

Much research on crime has been focused on aggregate crime rates, that is, crimes per capita in the general population. The criminal career approach partitions the aggregate rate into two primary components: participation, the distinction between those who commit crime and those who do not; and frequency, the rate of activity of active offenders. This partition is important not only because the two components may be subject to very different influences, but also because different authorities have different levels of responsibility for control of the two components. In particular, education, social service, and mental health profes-

12

sionals all provide services that may reduce participation in crime, while controlling the rate of criminal activity is more central to the decisions of the criminal justice system. A decision on imprisonment, for example, often involves some concern for incapacitating a convicted offender, and so it is a matter of prime interest to estimate how many crimes in the community might be avoided by the removal of that offender.

In addition to the primary components of participation and frequency, two other dimensions that affect aggregate crime rates can be incorporated in the criminal career approach: duration, the length of an individual career (the time from first to last offense), and seriousness, which includes both the offenses committed and patterns of switching among offenses.

Separate consideration of participation, frequency, duration, and seriousness provides a finer resolution in the search for the factors associated with crime than do other common approaches. Traditional research on criminal behavior has often relied on aggregate arrest rates or recidivism statistics to develop or to test various causal models. These conventional measures of criminality, however, confound different aspects of individual offending patterns. For example, a drop in the aggregate crime rate may reflect a drop in the proportion of the population engaging in crime (level of participation), in the average number of crimes committed by active offenders in a given time (individual frequency), or in the average number of years over which offenders commit crimes (duration of activity). A causal factor could strongly affect one of these dimensions, but variation in the others might mask that relationship if the aggregate crime rate is used as the primary measure of crime. Thus, as in most research, when different factors affect different dimensions of a phenomenon of interest, it is extremely important to iso-

late those dimensions in order to assess the influence of any factor.

Different sets of "causes" may influence individuals' decisions to initiate criminal (or delinquent) activity, the frequency with which they commit crimes, the types of crimes committed, and their decisions to stop committing crimes. Attention to these separate dimensions of the criminal career can thus help to refine theories of criminal behavior, since some theoretical explanations may account for the initiation of deviant acts by teenagers, while very different theories may be more relevant to the termination of serious criminality by adults or to fluctuations in rates of offending during an active criminal career. Thus, basic knowledge about each component of individual criminal careers is fundamental for an understanding of how various factors and government policies may encourage or inhibit criminal activity.

For example, past research on the impact of unemployment on crime has resulted in inconsistent conclusions. However, the inconsistent results may be a consequence of the use of aggregate crime rates as the dependent variable. If the relationship between unemployment and criminal behavior were to be studied at the individual level, the effects might become more focused and consistent. One might hypothesize, for example, that variation in unemployment is not likely to have much influence on the initiation of criminal activity, which usually occurs in the teenage years, before most people have begun working, but that the opportunity for full-time employment leads to early termination of teenagers' criminal activity. Separation of the dimensions of individual careers might permit more precise tests of these hypotheses.

Criminal careers may vary substantially among offenders. At one extreme are offenders whose careers consist of only one offense. At the other extreme are "career criminals"—also variously characterized as dangerous, habitual, or chronic offenders—who commit serious offenses with high frequency over extended periods of time. Both of these extreme career types are of policy interest. Offenders with short careers who commit very few offenses are of interest for identifying external factors that foster early termination of careers and that can be affected by public policy. Such knowledge will be especially useful in the design of crime control policies, including prevention achieved through the imposition of sanctions for deterrent or rehabilitative purposes. Career criminals are of interest for formulating policies that can identify these offenders early in their careers and selectively target criminal justice resources at preventing their crimes, primarily through incarceration.

Individual-level data are fundamental to the analysis of criminal careers. An ideal approach for collecting data on the individual offender would involve getting a representative sample of offenders to maintain accurate logs of their daily criminal activity. In light of the obvious difficulties in mounting such an effort, two principal approaches have evolved for estimating the information that might be derived from those logs. One approach uses retrospective self-reports, typified by the work of Short and Nye (1958), West and Farrington (1977), Chaiken and Chaiken (1982a), and Elliott et al. (1983, 1985), which involves asking individuals to report on their offenses over a recent period. The other approach uses official records, typified by the work of Wolfgang, Figlio, and Sellin (1972), Blumstein and Cohen (1979), and Shannon (1982a, b), in which arrests are viewed as a sample of the actual criminal activity that led to the arrests. Each of these approaches relies on different assumptions and introduces different distortions into the resulting descriptions of the underlying crime process.

In principle, offender self-reports could provide a complete picture of offending over time, but inaccuracies are introduced by respondents' selective nonresponse, intentional distortion, and inability to recall precise counts and sequences of previous crimes. In contrast, an offender's official arrest record provides counts and sequences of offenses, but only of those offenses recorded by police. The records therefore reflect only a sample of all the offenses committed by an individual and may occasionally include notations of crimes that did not occur as charged.[1] As a sample of the underlying crime process, arrest records are distorted by patterns in victims' willingness to report crimes to the police, by differential police attention to different crimes, and by police discretion in deciding which suspects to arrest, which arrests to record, and what charges to file. Arrest histories used in research may be incomplete because of failures to forward notations of all arrests or to include arrests recorded in jurisdictions other than the study site. Only recently has attention turned to-

---

[1]In addition to the distortion that may result from differences between actual offenses and arrests, the issue of false arrests is an important concern when inferring crimes from arrests. It is well established that a majority of arrests fail to end in conviction even for serious crimes. This differential raises questions about the validity of assuming that every arrest is properly associated with a crime and suggests using only those arrests that are followed by conviction. Two types of error are involved: using arrests as indicators of crimes probably involves some errors of commission because of false arrests; using only convictions is more likely to involve errors of omission. In adjudicating specific individuals, of course, the presumption of innocence makes the error of commission unacceptable. In assessing the relative validity of data for research purposes, however, there must be a relative weighing of these two types of error. Reports by criminal justice practitioners indicate that the errors of commission associated with using arrest records are far smaller than the errors of omission that would occur if only convictions were used.

ward synthesis of criminal career data from both self-reports and official records.

Because of the limitations on the data from both sources, models are needed to convert the observed information into estimates of the principal dimensions of criminal careers. Such models have emerged only in the last decade, largely stimulated by the stochastic-process approach introduced by Avi-Itzhak and Shinnar (1973), which was followed several years later by empirical estimates of various career dimensions. Later, attention shifted to modeling the distributions of those dimensions and identifying their covariates (Chaiken and Chaiken, 1982a; Greenwood, 1982). This panel has contributed to that body of work by commissioning extensions of the modeling from the perspectives of economics (Flinn, Volume II) and stochastic processes (Lehoczky, Volume II).

CRIME CONTROL POLICIES

The criminal justice system's efforts to control crime take three forms: deterrence, rehabilitation, and incapacitation. Deterrence is the symbolic threat broadcast to actual and potential offenders by imposing punishment on identified offenders. Incapacitation is the removal of a convicted offender from the community, usually through imprisonment, to prevent the offender from committing further crimes. Rehabilitation is the modification of an offender's criminal behavior. These efforts to control crime are carried out in conjunction with efforts to achieve other goals of the criminal justice system, such as imposing "deserved" punishment, enhancing public confidence in the justice system, and maintaining order in penal facilities.

Knowledge for Policy

Knowledge about criminal careers may be especially helpful in developing effective crime control policies. The appropriate response to crime will differ depending on whether the aggregate crime rate is the result of a small group of high-frequency offenders or a large group of offenders who commit crimes infrequently. In the former situation—low participation combined with high individual frequency—strategies of incapacitation or intensive supervision may well be effective and feasible. But if participation is high, incapacitating many offenders would be impractical, and other crime control strategies involving efforts to prevent participation would be more effective and feasible.

Distinguishing among the various dimensions of criminal careers may also serve to enhance the crime control potential of alternative strategies by more effectively targeting various crime control efforts. The effectiveness of incapacitation as a crime control strategy, for example, depends not only on how frequently offenders commit serious crimes, but also on the duration of an offender's career. From the perspective of incapacitation, prison capacity is used inefficiently if offenders are imprisoned beyond the time at which their criminal activity would have terminated if they were free on the street. Therefore, it is reasonable to ask whether "habitual-offender" laws, which mandate very long sentences, may result in incarceration of offenders well after they have ceased to be serious risks.

Effective policy strategies may also emerge from knowledge about individual offending patterns and the relationship of different attributes of offenders to the dimensions of their criminal careers. For example, early indicators of likely participation in criminal activity, such as educational difficulties or disruptive school behavior, suggest preventive strategies like preschool education or family-oriented treatment, which may reduce participation in crime. In contrast, career modification or rehabilitation strategies seek to terminate or reduce criminal activity through counseling, group therapy, job training, or similar programs. If heavy drinking and drug use are found disproportionately among high-rate offenders, intervention strategies might focus on treatment for substance abuse. If frequent, serious offenders can be identified by using characteristics of the offense or the offender, the criminal justice system could use incapacitation strategies effectively.

Knowledge of the factors that are associated with variations in criminal careers can also be helpful in assessing existing policies and practices. For example, if a particular criminal justice system routinely imposes long sentences on offenders who commit serious crimes at a high rate, then it is already enhancing crime control by using incarceration to incapacitate offenders. But if incapacitation decisions implicitly invoke characteristics that are irrelevant to offenders' careers or use characteristics inappropriately—such as imposing long sentences on all young black offenders—then wider use of career knowledge could contribute to incapacitative effectiveness.

At the aggregate level, relationships between criminal careers and demographic variables can be used to forecast changes in crime volume or in the size and composition of prison populations arising from demographic changes in the general population. When combined with data on criminal justice system performance (e.g., arrest probabilities, judge's time required per case, conviction-to-arrest ratios, average time served per incarceration), criminal justice system resource requirements can also be projected. Knowledge of crime-specific offending frequencies and their correlates could also be used to estimate the incapacitative crime-reduction effects of alternative incarceration policies. Thus, in a number of ways, knowledge of criminal careers and their correlates can refine the analysis of criminal justice policies.

Classification of Offenders

Selective treatment of offenders in the criminal justice system is one way to direct criminal justice discretion more effectively toward reducing the level of crime. Recent research findings have rekindled interest in basing selection explicitly on classifications derived from empirically demonstrated relationships between specific variables and criminal career dimensions, especially the frequency of serious criminal activity. In various ways, such information has long been used as a selection criterion: in formal ways in parole release decisions and in structuring prosecution priorities for "career criminal units" and more often informally in setting pretrial release conditions and sentencing. The recently discussed crime control strategy of "selective incapacitation" at sentencing (e.g., Greenwood, 1982) is based on selection rules defined explicitly in terms of frequency classifications. More generally, classifications defined in terms of available, reliable, and legally usable information about offenders and their offenses could be used as one of the bases for selection at such criminal justice decision points as arrest, pretrial release, prosecution, sentencing, and parole.

Selective treatment involves implicit or explicit use of classifications related to the frequency and duration of serious offending. Since those career dimensions cannot be directly observed for individuals in the context of high-volume criminal justice decision making, offender classifications are operationally defined in terms of other variables that are routinely measurable and that are correlated with the frequency, seriousness, or duration of the criminal career. Criminal justice processing based on these classifications is, in turn, subject to statutory and constitutional constraints. Within these constraints, classification and selection rules involve articulating a balance between the competing objectives of protecting the community against harm by offenders and protecting the presumed offender from unjust treatment by the state.

Ethical Considerations

Invoking prediction-based classifications in criminal justice decisions raises a number of important ethical concerns. When, if ever, is it appropriate to invoke predictions of future criminal activity in criminal justice decisions? Is a difference in predicted future criminal activity a legitimate basis for imposing different sanctions for the same crime? What level of predictive accuracy is necessary to justify using predictions? What balance is appropriate between the harm done to offenders and that done to the community by different types of prediction errors? Should some effective predictor variables be explicitly ignored for ethical reasons?

These ethical concerns have a direct bearing on the policy uses of scientific knowledge about criminal careers. For this reason, their implications for criminal justice policies are important considerations in both Chapters 5 and 6, in which the crime control uses of criminal career knowledge and the efficacy of prediction-based decisions are examined.

Many of the ethical issues considered are matters of long-standing legal and philosophical debate. The resolution of some issues may rest on absolute principles, but more often it involves a balancing of competing ethical concerns. It is thus reasonable to anticipate that the principles governing the use of prediction-based classification rules as an aid to criminal justice decision makers will evolve, changing as public concerns about crime ebb and flow and as im-

proved knowledge about individual criminal careers is developed.

DIMENSIONS OF CRIMINAL CAREERS

The panel's characterization of criminal careers partitions crime into four dimensions: one dimension describes the fraction of a population becoming offenders by virtue of participation in crime; three others describe active offenders in terms of the frequency, seriousness, and duration of their activity. The criminal career paradigm presumes that offending is not pervasive throughout a population, but is restricted to a subset of the population. This subset consists of active offenders—those who commit at least one crime during some observation period. It also presumes that the composition of active offenders varies over time as some criminal careers are initiated and others terminate.

Participation

The measurement of participation—the fraction of a population that is criminally active—depends on the scope of criminal acts considered and the length of observation periods.[2] Including minor infractions in the scope of crime types greatly increases the level of participation in of-

---

[2]In the literature reviewed by the panel, the term "prevalence" is often used to refer to the current involvement of some portion of a sample in criminal activity, but occasionally to other measures of participation. The term "incidence" is usually used to refer to the per capita crime rate for the sample but occasionally to refer to individual frequency. In short, these terms have been used inconsistently by many researchers for decades. To avoid confusion, the panel adopted the vocabulary being introduced here. The relationship between the panel's framework and other individual and aggregate statistics on criminal behavior is discussed in the section, "Basic Definitions and Symbols."

fending in a population. Longer observation periods also increase participation measures, since more offenders who commit offenses only rarely will be included as will more offenders who are initiating or terminating their criminal activity. Conversely, restricting the criteria to focus only on serious offenses and using short observation periods will result in lower measures of current participation.

In any observation period, active offenders include both new offenders whose first offense occurs during the observation period and persisting offenders who began criminal activity in an earlier period and continue to be active during the observation period. Participation in any observation period thus depends on the number of individuals who become offenders and on how long offenders remain active. The longer the duration of offending, the greater the contribution of persisters to measured participation in successive observation periods.

Individual Frequency Rates, Seriousness, and Duration

Individual frequency rates—the number of crimes per year per active offender—vary substantially among offenders, with some having very high rates and others low rates of offending. For any individual, frequency rates may vary over time. Because they commit more crimes per unit of time, high-rate offenders contribute disproportionately to the total measured number of crimes.

Many different offense types may contribute to an individual's frequency rate. The scope of offending for individual offenders may vary from "specialists" (who engage predominantly in only one offense or a group of closely related offense types) to "generalists" (who engage in

a wide variety of offense types). The degree of specialization may also vary across offense types, with some offense types committed predominantly by specialists and other types routinely committed by generalists. The mix of offense types committed by offenders may also vary over the course of their careers, with offenders becoming either more or less specialized, and with the mix of offense types escalating or de-escalating in seriousness.

The duration of criminal careers can also be expected to vary across individual offenders. It is likely that many criminal careers are very short, ending in the teenage years. However, some offenders continue to commit crimes into their 30s and even older ages. Thus, it is important to understand average *total* career length and the factors that distinguish offenders with long careers from offenders with short careers. But to understand the impact of decisions made about individual offenders, it is also extremely important to understand *residual* career length, the expected time remaining in an offender's criminal career at the time of the decision.

Basic Definitions and Symbols

To use these concepts to organize research results that have been developed in a variety of paradigms, the panel found it necessary to adopt consistent vocabulary and symbols for labeling the key dimensions that characterize individual criminal careers. This need arises from a confusion in the literature over specific terminology for individual and aggregate crime data. The confusion can be seen clearly, for example, in the variety of referents of the term "rate" in the literature: to a population (e.g., prevalence rate, the fraction of males ever participating in crime); to a time period (e.g., frequency rate, the individual's annual frequency of offending); or to both simultaneously (e.g., crime rate, the annual crime index per capita).[3]

The symbols and definitions adopted by the panel are displayed in Table 1-1. Symbols in the second column describe the crime process, i.e., the actual offending process; symbols in the third column describe the arrest process from which

_____

[3]Crime itself is a heterogeneous phenomenon, and a variety of terminology has developed to distinguish more serious or less serious crimes. This report is primarily concerned with serious crimes, which are classified herein in several ways. *Personal* crimes encompass homicide, aggravated assault, and rape. Rape and homicide are relatively infrequent, and data are not usually reported separately by researchers for these crimes. The FBI includes these three crimes and robbery in their definition of *violent* crimes. *Safety* crimes include violent crimes and burglary. The five safety crimes plus larceny and auto theft are frequently referred to as *index* crimes, because they are included in the Part I crime index reported in the FBI's annual *Uniform Crime Reports*. In 1981, arson was added to the FBI's crime index; however, because reporting of arson was sporadic before that year, it is rarely included in the research reviewed here. *Property* crimes typically include burglary, larceny, and auto theft. In addition to the Part I index crimes, the FBI also uses the category of Part II crimes, which are recorded separately, are less often reported to police (e.g., white-collar crimes), are less serious (e.g., public order crimes), and include "victimless" crimes (e.g., prostitution, drug use). Some researchers also distinguish between a *felony* and a *misdemeanor*: the former is usually defined in statutes as any crime carrying a sentence length of at least 1 year. *Delinquency* has a less precise definition: it can refer to traditional youth crimes, such as truancy or underage drinking (sometimes called status offenses because they are only offenses as a result of the status, i.e., age, of the offender), or it can refer to any crime committed by someone under the age of majority.

Virtually all the research discussed in this report is on male offenders; hence, the pronoun "he" is used exclusively in referring to offenders.

much of the available information about the underlying crime process is derived.

We begin with the aggregate annual crime rate per capita (C) that is normally reported to the public in the press, and partition it into its component parts: one that focuses on the individual offender and his *individual offending frequency* measured in terms of crimes per year, λ, and another that describes the *current participation rate* of offenders in the population at any time (d). These three key variables are linked by the relationship $C = \lambda d$. Thus, for example, an aggregate crime rate of 1,000 crimes in a population base of 100,000 people could be a consequence of 10 criminals each committing an average of 100 crimes ($d = 10/100,000$, and $\lambda = 100$) or 100 criminals committing 10 crimes each ($d = 100/100,000$, and $\lambda = 10$). The two situations present different problems in the development of crime control strategies.

Much of the literature is not concerned with the current rate of participation in crime (d) but with the question of what fraction of a population has *ever* been involved in crime. This is simply the accumulation of new participants over time. We denote *cumulative participation* by the related symbol D. (For further discussion of definitional issues relating to participation, see Appendix A.)

Comparable symbols are defined for the arrest process, which is often the only source of information about individual criminal careers. The counterpart to the crime rate (C) is the number of *arrests* per capita per year, A. The average number of arrests experienced per year by active offenders is denoted by μ. The percent of a population that is arrested (or "busted") within some observation period is denoted by b. A relationship similar to that in the crime process exists for the arrest process, $A = \mu b$. Finally, as an analogue

TABLE 1-1 Glossary of Basic Symbols and Relationships

Measure	Symbol and Definition	
Measure Based on		
Crimes and Arrests	*Crime Process*	*Arrest Process*
Aggregate crime rate per capita per year	C Crimes per capita per year	A Arrests per capita per year
Individual frequency per active offender	λ Crimes per year per active offender	μ Arrests per year per active offender
Current participation rate	d Percent of a population committing a crime within a year ("*doing*")	b Percent of a population arrested for crimes within a year ("*busted*")
Cumulative participation rate	D Percent of a population *ever* committing a crime	B Percent of a population *ever* arrested
Aggregate crime rate per capita: frequency per active offender times participation rate	$C = \lambda d$	$A = \mu b$
Other Measures		
Arrest probability	q = Probability of arrest following a crime ($q = \mu/\lambda$)	
Career length	T = Total criminal career length	
Residual career length	T_R = Average time remaining in a criminal career	
Career dropout rate	δ = Fraction of a criminal population whose careers terminate during an observation period	

to the cumulative participation rate in crime, we denote the fraction of a population that is *ever* arrested as B.[4]

The arrest process can be viewed as a sampling from the crime process, since not all crimes result in arrest. This linkage is reflected in the "sampling probability" or the probability that a crime will result in an arrest, denoted by q. The two key individual rates, μ and λ, are thus linked through q by the relationship $\mu = \lambda q$. Thus, for example, if an offender commits 8 crimes per year and there is a 10 percent chance that commission of a crime will lead to an arrest, then the average arrest rate, μ, should be 8(0.1) or 0.8 arrests per year.

The final principal construct for which we use symbols is the *total* criminal ca-

reer length, T, denoting the number of years over which an offender is criminally active. In many cases, we are more interested in the *residual* career length, the number of *future* years a currently active offender is expected to remain active, and we denote this length by T_R. The fraction of careers that terminate during an observation period is denoted by the career dropout rate, δ.

Obviously, estimates of the criminal career dimensions represented by these symbols will vary by crime type, across different population groups, and in different settings. In the text of the report, we occasionally distinguish these different variations of the basic criminal career dimensions. The glossary presented in Table 1-1 should therefore be helpful as a continuing reference in reading that material.

Basic Model of a Criminal Career

The basic criminal career paradigm provides a framework for organizing knowledge about the dimensions that describe

---

[4]Many studies use an alternative official-record indicator of an event, such as referral to juvenile court or conviction. For notational simplicity, we symbolize fractions involving all these events by B and b, but recognize in discussion the implications of these more stringent thresholds for empirical results.

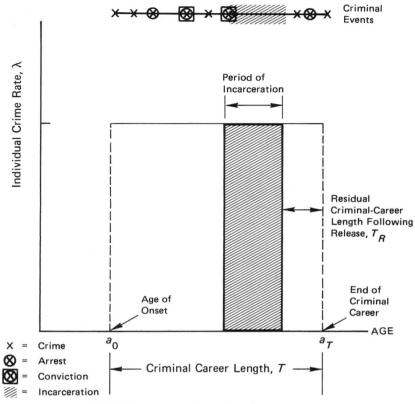

FIGURE 1-1 An individual criminal career.

individual criminal behavior. It permits specification of relationships among the dimensions and computation of statistics that describe offending in an observed sample, such as a cohort of individuals followed over time, a cross-section of active offenders arrested during some time interval, or matched control/experimental groups being studied to assess the impact of some intervention.

Figure 1-1 presents a highly simplified framework that introduces the essential concepts of the criminal career. The top of the figure represents a sequence of events during the criminal career of an active offender. On the line, the symbol × denotes the times at which the offender committed crimes. Symbols of crimes for which the offender was arrested are cir-

cled, and the crimes for which the arrest led to conviction are enclosed in a square. The shaded area indicates a period when the offender was incarcerated following conviction. In theory, all incidents marked × could be reported by the offender in a self-report survey, while only the circled ones could appear in an official arrest record.

A person initiates criminal activity at some time. That first offense may involve a conscious personal choice, it may follow from the development of a new set of associations developed, or it may be an inadvertent consequence of other changes in the individual's life. Once the offender has begun his criminal involvement, it continues for some period of time, perhaps increasing or decreasing in frequency. Finally, the person terminates his criminal career, possibly because of death, but more typically at a relatively young age, after which his probability of offending within any observation period is small enough to be ignored.

The minimum representation, which clearly omits many of the complexities of a real career, is represented in the lower portion of Figure 1-1. The offender is assumed to begin criminal activity at some "age of onset," a_O, but his official record does not reflect onset until some later time, at the point of his first arrest. Once begun, the offender continues to commit crimes at a constant rate λ during any time that he is not incarcerated. The career ends when the last crime is committed, represented at age a_T in Figure 1-1.

The representation in Figure 1-1 invokes three primary elements of information: the frequency or mean individual crime rate, λ, the age at career initiation, and the duration of the criminal career, T. Each of these three dimensions of a career varies across offenders. This variation may be influenced by personal events associated with the individual or by broader forces such as sanction levels or other community characteristics.

Extensions of the Basic Model

This simple representation can be extended to more richly describe a criminal career. Possibilities include a "start-up" time during which an offender's frequency increases, a decrease in frequency toward the end of a career, and sporadic spurts or intermittent recesses from criminal activity. If the intervals between spurts are much shorter than a typical sentence, the intermittent pattern may be ignored and the average λ used as a consideration in setting sentencing policy. But if the intervals of inactivity are long, then separate estimates are needed for high- and low-rate periods and for the duration of these periods, to adequately estimate average λ. In addition, spurts in activity make it difficult to obtain information from offenders for use in estimating average annual rates. Distinctions among different offense types can also be made, permitting attention to single offenses (e.g., "robbery careers") or to patterns of switching among offense types during a career. In this context, it is important to know whether offenders are more likely to be "specialists" (who engage in only one or a small group of offenses) or "generalists" (who switch more widely among a range of offenses). Last, extensions of the basic model can address whether offending patterns typically "escalate" in the seriousness of successive events so that crimes later in the career are more serious, or whether they peak in seriousness in mid-career and then begin to decline in seriousness as a career nears its end.

USING THE CRIMINAL CAREER PARADIGM

Interpreting Aggregate Crime Rates

The criminal career paradigm adopted here represents a departure from analyses that have focused on aggregate measures, such as incidence rates of crimes per capita or arrests per capita. Applying to active offenders and nonoffenders alike in a population, these aggregate measures confound the combined contribution of the extent of participation and the frequency of offending by active offenders. Despite this confounding of different aspects of individual offending, variations in aggregate measures have served as the basis for much of the broadly accepted current knowledge on the causes and correlates of crime.

Perhaps the most widely accepted view of crime is that it varies substantially

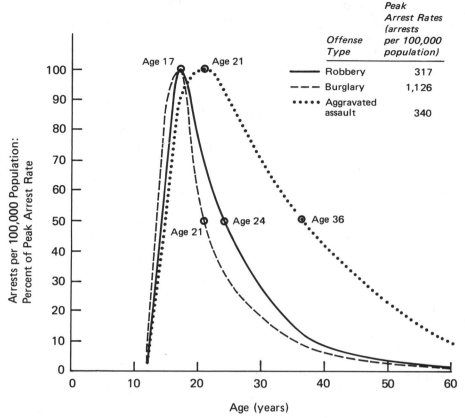

Offense Type	Peak Arrest Rates (arrests per 100,000 population)
—— Robbery	317
– – – Burglary	1,126
•••• Aggravated assault	340

FIGURE 1-2 1983 U.S. age-specific arrest rates (arrests per 100,000 population of each age). The curve for each offense type is displayed as a percentage of the peak arrest rate. The curves show the age at which the peak occurs (at 100 percent) and the age at which the rate falls to 50 percent of the peak rate. Source: Federal Bureau of Investigation (1984).

with age. While varying in absolute magnitude, aggregate population arrest rates display a very consistent pattern—increasing rapidly during the juvenile years to reach peak rates in the late teens and then steadily declining.[5] Figure 1-2 illustrates this pattern for the FBI index offenses of robbery, aggravated assault, and burglary in 1983. Analyses of recidivism rates for identified offenders have also found a decline in criminal involvement for older offenders.[6] The declines in offending observed in aggregate data and recidivism measures have been characterized as "maturing out of crime" and have been attributed to physiological and social changes with age that lead to gradual reductions in criminal involvement.

These analyses, however, do not tell the full story. The distinctive age patterns

[5]Historically, arrest rates peaked in an offender's early twenties. This pattern was observed as early as 1831 in France (Quetelet, 1984); recent reviews of this research can be found in Greenberg (1983), Hirschi and Gottfredson (1983), and Farrington (1986).

[6]See, for example, Glueck and Glueck (1937, 1940), Sellin (1958), and more recently, studies of differential success on parole release (e.g., Hoffman and Beck, 1980; Rhodes et al., 1982; Bureau of Justice Statistics, 1984c).

in aggregate measures may be due either to changes in participation or in individual frequency rates for active offenders. In the former case, the peak rates of criminal activity would result from growing participation in crime during the late teen years, followed by declining participation as increasing numbers of offenders end their criminal careers. In the latter case, peak rates would arise from variations in the intensity of offending by a fairly fixed group of active offenders, with individuals' frequency rates increasing during the juvenile years and then gradually declining with age.

Distinguishing between these alternative processes has both theoretical significance for understanding the causes of crime, as well as operational implications for efforts to control crime. From the theoretical perspective, the participation and frequency alternatives have implications for whether causes should be sought in broad social processes affecting the general population and people's movement into and out of criminal careers or in more isolated processes affecting only active offenders and their activity patterns. From a policy perspective, distinguishing between these alternatives has implications for the relative effectiveness of efforts to reduce peak levels of offending in the late teens by preventing participation by new offenders or by targeting intervention more narrowly at already active offenders.

Similar concerns about disentangling the relative contributions of participation, frequency, and duration emerge when considering other offender attributes. The sex of offenders is potentially an important factor in characterizing individual offending. Very large differences between males and females are observed both in aggregate arrest rates (see Table 1-2) and in recidivism rates (Bureau of Justice Statistics, 1984d), with substantially higher rates for males. Aggregate arrest rates also show large differences in levels of criminal activity between whites and blacks. As shown in Table 1-2, the differences between races increase as one focuses on more serious offense types, and have decreased in recent years. However, large differences between races are generally *not* found when recidivism rates for black and white offenders are compared (Wolfgang, Figlio, and Sellin, 1972:288–289; Blumstein and Graddy, 1982:283–284; Bureau of Justice Statistics, 1984d:Table 10). The differences in aggregate measures by sex and race reflect the combined contributions of differences in levels of participation in crime and differences in frequency for active offenders—distinct phenomena with very different policy implications.

Demographic Correlates of Criminal Careers

Demographic variables have received considerable attention, primarily because they are widely available in data on the general population, are easily observed by crime victims and police, and are routinely recorded for identification purposes in data from administrative and operational agencies. Data on dimensions of criminal careers are therefore widely available for different demographic subgroups defined in terms of age, sex, and race. The strong empirical associations observed between the demographic variables and aggregate arrest rates (see Table 1-2 and Figure 1-2, above) have generated substantial debate about the causes of subpopulation differences. But much ambiguity surrounds the underlying theoretical meaning of differences in criminal behavior between males and females (see Pollack, 1950; Adler, 1975; Nagel and Hagan, 1984), among racial and ethnic groups (e.g., Moynihan, 1965; Berger and Simon, 1974), and most recently, across age (Greenberg, 1983;

TABLE 1-2 U.S. Sex- and Race-Specific Arrest Rates in 1970 and 1980

Offense Type	Arrests per 1,000 Population				Ratios[a]	
Sex-Specific Arrest Rates						
	Males		Females		Male/Female	
	1970	1980	1970	1980	1970	1980
All (except traffic)	76	81	12	14	6.3	5.6
All index[b]	14	17	3	4	5.2	4.6
Property[c]	11	14	2	3	4.6	4.0
Violent[d]	2	3	0.2	0.3	8.0	8.3
Robbery	1	1	0.1	0.1	16.2	13.6
Race-Specific Arrest Rates						
	Whites		Blacks		Black/White	
	1970	1980	1970	1980	1970	1980
All (except traffic)	35	40	107	97	3.1	2.4
All index	6	8	28	29	4.7	3.7
Property	5	7	20	21	4.0	3.2
Violent	0.6	1	4	5	7.3	4.6
Robbery	0.2	0.3	3	3	15.4	10.3

NOTE: Rates are estimated from the number of reported arrests in 1980 (Federal Bureau of Investigation, 1981) and 1980 population figures (Bureau of the Census, 1983:Table 33). Similar data are available for adults and juveniles separately. Arrest rates for 1970 are estimated from the number of arrests reported in 1970 (Federal Bureau of Investigation, 1971) and 1970 population figures (Bureau of the Census, 1983:Table 33). To adjust for agencies not reporting to the FBI, reported arrests are increased by the ratio of total population available from the Bureau of the Census to the population covered by reporting agencies. This assumes that the arrest rates and population distribution in nonreporting agencies are similar to those available for reporting agencies.

[a]These ratios were computed before the arrest rates were rounded.

[b]Index rates include arrests for murder, rape, robbery, aggravated assault, burglary, larceny, and motor vehicle theft.

[c]Property rates include arrests for burglary, larceny, and motor vehicle theft.

[d]Violent rates include arrests for murder, rape, and aggravated assault.

Hirschi and Gottfredson, 1984; Greenberg, 1985; Wilson and Herrnstein, 1985; Farrington, 1986).

While demographic differences account for large portions of the variability in aggregate measures of criminal involvement, these differentials reflect relationships with other variables that are not yet well understood. For example, over the years, explanations offered for the differences between males and females have variously been biological differences, differences in moral training, differences in socialization experiences, and fewer criminal opportunities for girls because they are more closely supervised. These changes over time in interpreta-

tion of demographic differentials reflect the changing social contexts in which this research has been carried out.

Recently, Peterson and Hagan (1984) argued that criminal justice research on differences between racial and ethnic groups should be viewed in an historical context. In the first half of this century, American research on criminal behavior focused on the criminality of newly arrived ethnic groups, the Irish and Italian immigrants in large urban areas (e.g., Glueck and Glueck, 1940). Researchers associated high crime rates among urban ethnic groups with a vast array of social problems, including low-paying jobs, poor housing, and weak ties to the "dominant" culture. Slowly the emphasis in racial/ethnic studies of criminal behavior has shifted to comparisons of white and black Americans. This shift in attention probably reflects the changing demographic composition in large cities from a variety of ethnic minorities to blacks as the dominant minority and the most recent arrivals to large urban areas. Even more recently, other racial/ethnic groups—Hispanics and Southeast Asians—have begun to receive special attention (see Moore et al., 1978; Zatz, 1984; LaFree, 1985).

The panel did not attempt to resolve the theoretical debates concerning age, sex, and racial/ethnic differences in criminal behavior. Empirical relationships are reported because so much of the research results are presented in these terms, and because the differences are often large in bivariate comparisons, robust in multivariate analyses, and stable across a variety of geographical and temporal settings and data collection methods. However, by allowing for different causal structures for the initiation, persistence, and termination of offending, the partitioning of the aggregate differentials into separate career dimensions should facilitate better theoretical interpretation. As suggested above, one finding of research invoking the criminal career paradigm has been that the demographic differentials arise more from differences in criminal participation patterns, rather than in the frequency or duration of individual offending.

Incapacitation, Rehabilitation, and Deterrence

Analyses that partition the effects of sanctions among participation, frequency, and duration may provide valuable insights for improving the effectiveness of alternative crime control strategies. To date, for example, evaluations of deterrent effects have relied almost exclusively on aggregate crime rates, and evaluations

of rehabilitative interventions have relied primarily on recidivism rates. To the extent that participation, duration, and frequency are differentially affected by deterrence, rehabilitation, or incapacitation policies, important relationships may be obscured in aggregate measures. Analyses of the separate effects may provide valuable insights for improving the crime control effectiveness of deterrence and rehabilitation policies. Crime control effectiveness may be improved by targeting some strategies at reducing participation, very different ones at encouraging career termination among active offenders, and still others at reducing frequency among active offenders.

Incapacitation, which is usually achieved by incarcerating active offenders, is frequently presented in terms of the criminal career paradigm. In Figure 1-3, the shaded area indicating crimes prevented during the period of incarceration represents the "incapacitative effect." Crime control effects through incapacitation increase with the magnitude of individual frequency, with the length of incarceration, and with the expected duration of the criminal career. More specifically, higher frequency means more crimes averted for each unit of time incarcerated. And longer career duration means less likelihood of wasting incarceration on offenders who would have ended their careers during the time they were incarcerated and would therefore not be committing any additional crimes whether incarcerated or not.

The incapacitative effect actually achieved will depend on the effectiveness of the criminal justice system in identifying and incarcerating offenders, especially those with the highest rates of offending. The incapacitative effect is reduced if criminals are not arrested, if arrested criminals are not convicted, if convicted criminals are not incarcerated, if sentences are short, or if parole is early. The incapacitative effect is further reduced if the crimes of an incarcerated

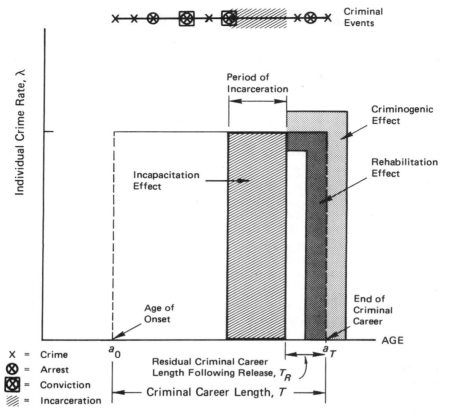

FIGURE 1-3 Incapacitation, rehabilitation, and criminogenic effects in an individual criminal career.

offender are replaced by crimes by other offenders. This might occur, for example, if the offender is part of an organized illegal economic activity, like drug sales or burglaries organized by a fence; in this event, a replacement might simply be recruited from the available "labor market" to continue the crimes that would otherwise be committed by the incarcerated offender. If the offender is part of a crime-committing group, the remaining members of the group might continue their crimes, with or without recruiting a replacement. Group offending and its implications for crime control are addressed by Reiss (Volume II).

The criminal career construct discussed in this section is most directly related to incapacitation, with its fundamental objective of interrupting a crimi-

nal career, but it also relates directly to the other two modes of crime control used by the criminal justice system, rehabilitation and deterrence. In most evaluations of rehabilitation programs, effectiveness is measured in terms of the recidivism rate. Recidivism is usually measured as the fraction of a release group that is rearrested, usually within an observation period of 1 to 5 years.[7] If the

---

[7]Recidivism is often also measured by reconviction or recommitment to an institution. Indeed, there is considerable debate over the "true" value of recidivism, which is unwarranted since measurement at these different stages will provide different *numerical* values, but usually not different *relative* values when all measure the same process (see Blumstein and Larson, 1971). This discussion focuses on arrest, but it applies equally to any other recidivism event.

offender depicted in Figure 1-3 received effective rehabilitative treatment in prison, its effect would be reflected as a change in his criminal career: as a reduction in his offending rate, as a shift to less serious crimes, or as a reduction in his career length. The crimes avoided by rehabilitation are depicted in Figure 1-3 by the dark gray area, "rehabilitation effect." These crimes are averted in addition to those averted through incapacitative effects during the period of imprisonment.

However, incarceration can also be counterproductive, criminogenic, if it leads to increases in postrelease criminality. This effect could be reflected by an increase in frequency or career length, depicted by the dotted area labeled "criminogenic effect," in Figure 1-3, or by an increase in the seriousness of crimes committed.[8] A criminogenic effect may result from an offender's enhanced identification as a "criminal," his learning new criminal techniques from fellow prisoners, or his strengthening ties to other offenders. The *net* rehabilitation effect is the rehabilitation effect less the criminogenic effect. No empirical comparison of these two effects has yet been carried out in the criminal career context. However, major reviews of evaluations of offender rehabilitation programs suggest that the net aggregate rehabilitation and criminogenic effect is small (Lipton, Martinson, and Wilks, 1975; Sechrest, White, and Brown, 1979).[9]

The third principal mode of crime control by the criminal justice system, in addition to incapacitation and rehabilitation, is deterrence. Deterrence is the crime-reduction effect achieved from the symbolic threat communicated to other offenders and to potential offenders by sanctions imposed on identified offenders.[10] The most common mode for examining the deterrent effect has been cross-sectional studies of jurisdictions with diverse sanction practices to examine the effect on aggregate crime rates of the sanction variation (controlling for other sources of variation in crime rate and in sanction policy). This research has yet to provide good estimates of the magnitude of deterrent effects (see Blumstein, Cohen, and Nagin, 1978). To determine the extent to which the deterrent effects of sanctions work by inhibiting career initiation, decreasing individual offending frequency, or encouraging career termination, it would be desirable for deterrence research to focus more specifically on the effects of community sanction levels on participation, and on the careers of active offenders.

SCOPE OF THE PANEL'S REPORT

The above discussion has presented the basic structural concepts involved in the criminal career paradigm. Aside from

---

[8]A special case of this effect would be a postponement of the offender's criminal career, so that the residual career length after release assumes the same value it had when incarceration began. Thus, the delay in the career is equal to the period of incarceration, and the crimes avoided through incapacitation are exactly offset by the same number of crimes committed after the career would otherwise have ended. If this effect occurs, incarceration would delay crimes, but not reduce their number.

[9]Sechrest, White, and Brown (1979:34) caution that the poor quality of the evaluations, and the

narrow range of options explored, militate against excessive pessimism concerning the potential of rehabilitation. But despite these qualifications, the failure of hundreds of evaluations to find demonstrable effects suggests that, given the current state of research methodology and correctional management, the net effect is fairly small.

[10]This effect is often characterized as "general deterrence" to distinguish it from "special deterrence," which refers to the effect of punishment on later behavior of the person punished. In this report special deterrence is considered an aspect of rehabilitation and the term deterrence refers to the broader crime-reduction effects achieved through general sanction policies.

its intrinsic value, knowledge about the dimensions of criminal careers, their distribution in the population, and the factors that affect them, is important for a variety of policy uses:

• identifying variables associated with the most serious offenders (in terms of their criminal careers) so that such information may be used by decision makers, within legal and ethical constraints, to anticipate future criminal activity by an offender about whom they must make a processing decision;

• identifying variables that are widely but erroneously viewed as predictors of offenders' future criminal activity;

• improving identification of high-risk offenders and designing programs likely to be effective for them;

• better assessment of the magnitude of incapacitative effects under current or proposed imprisonment policies, possibly leading to more efficient use of limited prison space; and

• planning research programs that will build on existing knowledge and provide more effective policy directions over the next decade.

In its work, the panel focused primarily, though not exclusively, on criminal careers that involve robbery, burglary, and aggravated assault, including incidents leading to the victim's death. This decision was motivated by the scarcity of research on careers that involve only other offense types, by the priority given to those crimes by policy makers, and by the fear of those crimes expressed by the public (see, for example, Research and Forecasts, Inc., 1980). The following crime types were excluded from the panel's primary focus: arson, "white-collar" crime (e.g., embezzlement, securities fraud, mail fraud), and organized crime, for which neither extensive prior empirical research nor the requisite data exist; "victimless" crimes (e.g., prostitution,

gambling, and drug use or possession); minor sex offenses and other deviant behaviors, for which offenders are commonly diverted from criminal justice to mental health or community treatment agencies; minor property offenses; and status offenses (acts that are illegal only when committed by juveniles). Although these types of offenses were not of primary interest, the panel did review studies that related them to the major crime types considered by the panel. For example, the panel was particularly interested in the relationship of minor delinquent acts to later adult careers involving robbery, burglary, and aggravated assault.

The panel also focused primarily, though not exclusively, on research that involved individual-level data on criminal careers of large samples representing clearly defined populations. Examples include analyses of arrest histories of an urban birth cohort, self-reports of offending by high school students, self-reports of incarcerated offenders, and arrest histories of criminals who are active during some observation period. Overall, the research reviewed by the panel represents most of the literature that is relevant to the study of individual criminal careers.

Several categories of research literature that study criminal behavior using paradigms other than the criminal career as defined in this report were not systematically included. Biographical and autobiographical case studies of individual offenders are excluded because the subjects are not generally representative of specific offender populations. Most ecological studies (jurisdiction-level analyses) generally relate aggregate crime measures to community or jurisdictional characteristics and do not include information about dimensions of individual criminal careers. Most recidivism studies lack sufficient detail on the number and timing of postrelease arrests that would be necessary for estimating annual offending frequencies and termination rates; hence, many research reports and program evaluations that used recidivism as the only measure of criminal behavior were not reviewed. Finally the research reviewed is primarily based on U.S. samples; a few studies of British and Danish populations are also included. The panel limited its review almost exclusively to studies published in English.

While much of the panel's work—as with all research—is concerned with the eventual development of causal theory, the panel did not pursue any particular theoretical tradition. This approach reflects the panel's recognition that synthesizing the available statistical descriptions of criminal careers will contribute to many theoretical approaches. However, development and refinement of causal theory about criminal careers should evolve from much more intensive investigation of the various dimensions of criminal careers than the literature now contains. Ideally, this investigation should proceed with a mixture of ethnographic studies to generate detailed hypotheses, longitudinal studies to explore temporal sequences, and field experiments to rigorously test hypotheses.

In considering the effect of influences possibly associated with reducing crime, the criminal career approach—with its focus on individual offenders—naturally suggests various influences that operate at the individual level to prevent initiation of a career, reduce the frequency of offending, interrupt the career, or encourage termination of a career. Individual-level influences on careers (e.g., maturation, family influences) and planned interventions grounded in knowledge

about those influences (e.g., substance abuse treatment, incapacitation through incarceration) were reviewed by the panel. However, they are not the only ways in which individual careers are influenced. Individual criminal careers are also influenced in broader ways, such as through planned community-level interventions and uncontrolled events in the community (e.g., a factory shutdown). These other influences may operate through the social, economic, political, or environmental structure of the community in which individuals grow up or live, the social networks with which they become involved, or the deterrence effects generated by local sanctioning practices. Over time, all of these may change and therefore alter the nature of criminal careers. Therefore, their relationships to careers should be objects of future research. But because so little research is currently available that links these community-level effects to individual criminal careers, the panel did not address these broader relationships.

With the framework developed in this chapter for characterizing individual criminal careers, Chapters 2 and 3 review the existing empirical knowledge about criminal careers, and Chapter 4 reviews the methodological problems in studying individual careers. Chapter 5 considers the uses of this information in assessing different types of interventions intended to modify criminal careers. Chapter 6 considers the effects of incorporating knowledge about criminal careers into explicit classification rules intended to aid criminal justice decision making. The last chapter presents an agenda for future research on criminal careers.

2

Participation in Criminal Careers

Efforts to develop effective crime control policies can be enhanced by an understanding of the ways in which individual criminal behavior contributes to total crime. The panel's approach to the study of criminal behavior rests fundamentally on a criminal career paradigm of individual offending, which disaggregates the various elements of individual offending into four key dimensions. This chapter summarizes the literature on one of those dimensions, the level of *participation* in crime and some demographic and social covariates of participation; Appendix A (Visher and Roth) of this report provides a detailed critical review of individual studies.[1]

Participation in offending is reflected in the fraction of a population *ever* committing (or "doing") at least one crime before some age a (D_a) or *currently* active during some observation period (d). Estimates of participation have been derived from self-report surveys of offending in cross-section samples. Commonly, these studies present respondents with descriptions of specific criminal acts that correspond to legal definitions of crimes. *Cumulative participation* (D_a) is computed from responses to questions of the form "Have you ever . . . ?" Questions of the form "Within the past year, have you . . . ?" provide the basis for estimates of *current participation* (d). Because the fraction of people who have committed any crime during the preceding year is smaller than the fraction who have ever committed a crime, estimates of D obvi-

---

[1]Gordon and Gleser (1974) formally defined "prevalence of delinquency" (referred to here as participation), and resolved some of the confusion surrounding its precise definition, computation, and terminology. In a later paper, Gordon (1976) reviewed several important studies of "prevalence" based on official-record data through the juvenile period (to age 18). The Visher and Roth review (Appendix A) of participation in offending, on which this chapter is based, updates the review by Gordon and also includes studies of adult participation and self-reported participation. While Gordon used ra-

cial differences as a defining variable and adjusted published participation rates to reconcile differences across studies, race is treated here as just one source of variation, and participation rates are reported as they appear in the published literature.

ously cannot be smaller than estimates of d for the same sample and crime type.

Estimates of the fraction of a population that is ever arrested, B, and the percent of a population arrested within some observation period, b, measure participation as reflected in arrest (or other official) records. Since many people who commit crimes are never arrested, estimates of arrest participation are obviously less than those of crime participation, that is, b is less than d. As careers continue, however, the chance of at least one arrest increases, so that the difference narrows between B and D.

Although studies based on official records vary widely in design details—nature of sample, criterion for identifying individuals who have participated, and length of observation period—b and B can be computed in only a limited number of ways. Agency statistics on the age distribution of arrestees within a year can be used to compare b for any age by dividing the number of arrestees of that age by the entire population of that age. Because researchers usually want to study influences on participation beyond the demographic and criminal history variables contained in agency records and because only a fraction of crimes result in arrest, current participation is usually studied in terms of self-reported d rather than officially recorded b.

To estimate officially recorded cumulative participation rates—for example, B_{18} (the fraction of a population arrested by age 18), three approaches are available. First, in prospective longitudinal studies, a cohort of individuals is selected and followed over time; notations of the ages at first arrest are used to compute B by each age. Second, in cross-section studies, agency files are searched to ascertain the fraction of any sample of 18-year-olds for whom official records exist. Third, if arrest or court referral records for first offenders are easily distinguishable, a

life-table approach similar to that used in mortality studies can be used: the distribution of age-specific *initiation rates*, I_a (i.e., the fraction of the population whose *first* arrest occurs at each age) can be computed and cumulated to age 18 to estimate B_{18}. This rate can be calculated from the age distribution of first arrestees in one year (T. Monahan, 1960, as corrected by Gordon and Gleser, 1974), or from arrest history data on members of a birth cohort (Wolfgang, Figlio, and Sellin, 1972). However, to understand the relationship between age and initiation rates, the conditional initiation rate, or *hazard rate* (h_a), may be more useful: this is the fraction that age-a initiators represent of the total a-year-olds who have not yet initiated their criminal activity.[2] Each of these three research designs has different implications for the measurement of B.

Designs of self-report and official-record participation studies vary in other details, such as the time period in which the data were collected; the seriousness of the behavior considered; and the threshold of contact with the criminal justice system, ranging from none (i.e., an undetected crime) to a police contact, a court referral, or conviction. Self-report studies of delinquent activity usually include a broader range of deviant behaviors and less serious crime types than studies based on official police or court records. The source of official records also affects estimates: juvenile court records, which record only incidents referred for formal adjudication, are likely to produce

---

[2]Thus, for example, in a cohort of 1,000 boys, if 200 have initiated their careers by age 16 and 100 more begin in their 17th year, then $I_{17} = 100/1,000 = 0.10$, and $h_{17} = 100/(1,000 - 200) = 0.125$. At later ages, more of the offenders in the sample have already begun offending and they are therefore no longer at risk of becoming offenders for the first time, so I_a is likely to decrease but h_a could well increase.

lower estimates of participation than are records of police contacts.

As inventories of all crimes committed by an individual, both official records and self-reports are subject to error. The probability that an individual's offense will be recorded by police depends on such factors as patrol allocations, victims' reporting behavior, offenders' success in avoiding police detection, and police discretion in recording offender contacts, which is especially wide for juveniles. Errors in self-reports of criminal involvement arise primarily from under- and overreporting of criminal behavior and differences between individual and legal definitions of crime. These variations in measurement and their effects on estimated participation rates are a central concern in the following discussion of empirical research on participation.

STUDY DESIGNS AND PARTICIPATION ESTIMATES

Criminal participation is an individually based phenomenon that typically cannot be derived from aggregate arrest statistics. However, early estimates of B were made using record systems that distinguish arrests or court referrals of first-time offenders from those of other offenders. Although such systems are rare in American agencies, one exception is the Philadelphia Juvenile Court. In one of the first studies of criminal participation, T. Monahan (1960) combined one year's age distribution of persons arrested or referred to court for the first time with data for the same year on the age distribution of the general population (see also Ball, Ross, and Simpson, 1964). British agencies routinely keep records of first offenders and this technique has also been used to estimate B in Britain (e.g., Little, 1965; Farrington, 1981). These data permit generalizations to contemporaneous subpopulations, but they only

approximate participation rates in any single birth cohort represented in the subpopulation. Record systems in most jurisdictions, moreover, do not collect the data needed to study nondemographic correlates of participation; these data must be collected through interviews or searches of other record systems for individuals being studied in cross-section samples or being tracked longitudinally.

Studies based on individuals' self-reports do permit study of the relationship between criminal participation (D and d) and a broader range of characteristics. Data are gathered from cross-section or prospective longitudinal studies of samples of persons representing some population of interest. Respondents are asked if they have committed specific criminal or delinquent acts, either ever (D) or during some defined preceding interval (d), and many other data are also collected. This method can generate detailed information on crime-specific participation and its relationship to family structure, group membership, other behaviors, and a wide variety of socioeconomic characteristics. But measuring criminal involvement through self-reports can introduce several sources of error. For example, underrepresentation of offenders is a problem in self-report surveys because youths who are at a higher risk of criminal involvement are often school dropouts or truants or otherwise difficult to locate. Some evidence also suggests that underreporting and poor recall of crimes is common in self-reports of criminal activity. However, some respondents may exaggerate their criminal involvement. Differences in question wording and method of administration also affect self-reported participation rates in ways that make it difficult to compare results across studies.

Official-record estimates of participation (B and b) are computed by using a sample of individuals selected on some basis other than status as an offender, such as a random sample of a population or of participants in a prior study, perhaps unrelated to crime. Searches of official records have been carried out in conjunction with prospective longitudinal or cross-section studies of demographic and social characteristics hypothesized to be related to participation. Some researchers have gathered both official-record and self-report data on the same individuals because of interest in comparing D with B (e.g., Gold, 1966; Hindelang, Hirschi, and Weis, 1981; Elliott et al., 1983).

Because juvenile and adult records are generally maintained in separate repositories, researchers concerned with cumulative participation estimates for adults—in particular, the lifetime risk of participation, B_L—have generally had to combine age distributions of participation rates from multiple sources and even multiple jurisdictions (Christensen, 1967; Belkin, Blumstein, and Glass, 1973; Blumstein and Graddy, 1982). To the extent that juvenile and adult participation behavior is similar across jurisdictions, this approach can yield reliable estimates of lifetime participation for different subpopulations. But since subpopulation composition may vary across jurisdictions, it is important that these subpopulations, which may differ systematically in terms of their participation (e.g., sex or race categories), be analyzed separately. Another concern in combining jurisdictions is that arrest recording thresholds and definitions may differ across the jurisdictions.

Official records are becoming more widely accessible as a source of sequential information about involvement in crime. However, since only a fraction (q) of all criminal acts lead to arrests that are recorded by the criminal justice system, official-record estimates of participation will always be lower than actual levels of involvement. In addition, crimes reported in an individual's official record may not be a representative sample of all crimes committed by that offender. Crimes of specific types (e.g., robbery relative to burglary) or of specific subpopulations (e.g., intoxicated offenders and inexperienced offenders) may be more likely to lead to arrest than others, thereby distorting comparisons of participation across different groups. In addition, police patrolling or investigation priorities defined in terms of location or crime type may also lead to over- or underrepresentation of particular subpopulations in official arrest records (see Wilson, 1968; Black and Reiss, 1970; Black, 1971; Smith and Visher, 1981). Information in arrest records, however, can be combined with other data to infer estimates about the likelihood of arrest for a given criminal event and for different subpopulations of offenders.

A crime victim, in reporting an event to the police, has an important role in generating an official arrest record. Reporting probabilities are known to differ by characteristics of the crime, the offender, and the victim (Hindelang, 1978b; Bureau of Justice Statistics, 1984a). Also, some reported crimes are "unfounded"—which usually means that the crime is not recorded—because the victim refuses to follow through with a complaint or because police conclude that the reported event does not constitute a crime.

The choice of data source also affects the type of criminal behaviors that are represented in any estimate of participation. Most self-report studies do not have large enough samples to reliably measure D and, especially, d for serious but less common offenses, such as burglary, large thefts, and robbery. Thus, self-report studies usually cover a much broader set of criminal or deviant acts, frequently including school-related infractions and minor delinquencies (e.g., fighting, trespassing, vandalism, alcohol use) in which a large proportion of all youth are involved. Official records generally include only behaviors that are serious enough for a crime to be reported to police and thereby brought to the attention of the juvenile or criminal justice system. Even when official records and self-reports capture the identical set of events, discrepancies are likely to exist because of differences between legal and public definitions of crimes.

PARTICIPATION AMONG MALES

Participation in offending is more often estimated for males than females. Female participation receives less research attention because female offenders account for a much smaller share of crime, as measured by official statistics on total arrests. Because of the large amount of research on males, the panel used estimates of D and B for males as a "baseline" for comparison with other subpopulations. Criminal participation among males has been estimated using the methods described above for vastly different samples and across several decades. Although few studies have attempted to produce national estimates of participation, consistent findings across jurisdictions increase the confidence with which generalizations can be made from local studies to subgroups regardless of their location. Our discussion focuses primarily on male participation before the 18th birthday, B_{18}, and lifetime participation, B_L, as derived from official-record estimates in published English-language research. Other measures of participation—current participation, d (e.g., within the year preceding the interview) and cumulative participation by high school age, D_{HS}—which are generally derived from self-reported data are also considered (for

more detail, see Visher and Roth, Appendix A).[3]

Official-Record Estimates

Wolfgang, Figlio, and Sellin (1972) reported that 35 percent of a sample of males born in 1945 and residing in the city of Philadelphia from ages 10 through 18 had at least one recorded police contact for a nontraffic offense by their 18th birthday (see Table 2-1).[4] This estimate has become the most widely cited estimate of criminal participation among U.S. males. Since not all juvenile police contacts result in court referral, it is not surprising that analyses of Philadelphia juvenile court statistics collected at about the same time (mid 1950s to mid 1960s) yield slightly smaller estimates of B_{18}. Those analyses found that 25 percent of males had a juvenile court record by age 18 (reanalysis of T. Monahan, 1960, by Gordon and Gleser, 1974). Findings in Kentucky and, more recently, in Oregon are consistent with the Philadelphia court statistics: by age 18, 21 percent (Ball, Ross, and Simpson, 1964) and 25 percent (Polk et al., 1981) of males had juvenile court records.

Table 2-1 presents estimates of participation by 18 (B_{18}) for all official-record studies reviewed by the panel. While some of the estimates differ substantially

---

[3]Not all types of data exist for these four measures of criminal participation. In fact, estimates of participation by age 18 and in a lifetime are exclusively based on studies with official-record data, with one exception (Porterfield, 1946). In contrast, active participation and participation by high school age are usually estimated from self-reported data (a few studies report B_{HS}). Estimates of D_{18}, D_L, and b do not generally appear in the published literature.

[4]"Nontraffic offenses" in the Philadelphia study encompass a very broad range of reasons for police contact, including many nonserious charges such as disorderly conduct, liquor violations, drunkenness, and investigation.

TABLE 2-1   Estimates of Male Participation Rates by Age 18 (official record data)

Crime Type and Level of Involvement	Participation Rates (percent)		
	White	Black	All Males
U.S. Studies			
Known to police or juvenile court	52	64	56
Nontraffic arrest or police contact	23, 29	42, 50	25, 33, 34, 35, 41, 44, 47
Juvenile arrest or court referral	13, 17, 18	31, 38, 38, 43, 50	17, 21, 25, 26
Juvenile court conviction	—	—	26, 28
Arrest for index offense	8, 8, 9	26, 27, 27	12, 14, 18
British Studies			
Conviction *or* police caution, indict- able offenses	—	—	15, 28, 29
Conviction for indictable offense	—	—	12, 15, 16, 17, 17, 26

NOTE: See Table 1 and discussion in Visher and Roth (Appendix A) for sources and analysis of these alternative estimates.

from Wolfgang et al.'s estimates, much of the variation can be explained in straightforward ways. Differences in the set of offenses included, in the threshold of involvement (e.g., police contact, arrest, or conviction), or in the composition of the base population lead to considerable variation across studies. A broad definition of criminal activity that includes disorderly conduct or suspicious behavior generates higher estimates of B_{18}, which may explain the high average estimates of 56 percent reported by Palmore and Hammond (1964) for a high-risk sample in New Haven, Connecticut. Similarly, the difference between Shannon's (1982a) estimates of B_{18} for nontraffic contacts (41, 44, and 47 percent) and those from the Philadelphia cohorts (33 and 35 percent) is likely due to the fact that in the Shannon study considerable emphasis was placed on recording police contacts for minor infractions of the law as well as for status offenses (L. W. Shannon, 1985, personal communication).

When the measure of participation is restricted to arrests or contacts for index offenses, B_{18} drops to 14 percent in the 1945 Philadelphia cohort and to 17 percent in Shannon's 1942 cohort (L. W. Shannon, 1985, personal communication). Thus, a narrower seriousness definition of criminal involvement substantially lowers B_{18}: according to four estimates, about 15 percent of all males participate in serious criminal activity, defined as an arrest for an index offense.

Estimates of participation for a specific time period and location are also vulnerable to changes over time in the scope of crimes and in population composition. For example, analysis of delinquency in a second Philadelphia cohort, born in 1958, was initially interpreted as implying that B_{18} was almost identical with B_{18} for males born 13 years earlier (for the same offense definition and threshold of involvement). In fact, participation rates actually decreased for both whites (from 29 to 23 percent) and blacks (from 50 to 41 percent); however, because of the large increase in the black population between 1945 and 1958, the overall rate appeared relatively unchanged. One possible explanation contributing to the race-specific declines in participation is that the range of crimes that prompted police to stop suspects or make arrests may have narrowed during this interval. If police in Philadelphia began to focus on more serious crime types in the 1960s, the participation estimates could have declined.

Other Philadelphia data and another cohort study do show an increase in participation rates for serious crimes over the period (Shannon, 1982a; Tracy, Wolfgang, and Figlio, 1985). For all Philadelphia males, B_{18} for violent index offenses (murder, rape, aggravated assault, robbery) increased from 4 to 10 percent. A similar pattern emerges from Shannon's cohort data: cumulative participation estimates, based on at least one felony arrest by age 18, were 9 percent, 10 percent, and 15 percent for males in the 1942, 1949, and 1955 cohorts, respectively. However, additional analyses are needed to partition this apparent increase in participation among effects of changes in population composition, of changes in participation behavior across successive cohorts in any subpopulation, and of changes in police arrest and recordkeeping practices.

Estimates of lifetime participation, B_L, are considerably more scarce—16 estimates, 10 of which are from two studies—and subject to some methodological concerns rooted in the imprecision of mortality adjustments and in the nature of the samples (see Table 2-2). In general, about half of all males have been projected to have at least one police arrest for nontraffic offenses by ages 40 to 50 (Robins, 1966; Christensen, 1967; Belkin, Blumstein, and Glass, 1973) and perhaps as many as 25 to 35 percent of U.S. males will have arrests for an index offense (Robins, 1966; Blumstein and Graddy, 1982).

As the threshold of criminal involvement narrows to a conviction record, estimates of B_L would be expected to drop. McCord (1979) reports that about 30 percent of a Massachusetts sample of males treated for childhood problems in the 1930s had a conviction record for any offense by age 50. A British projection based on aggregate statistics (Farrington, 1981) also concludes that 44 percent of British males will have a conviction record in their lifetime. These surprisingly high participation estimates reflect particular aspects of the studies' designs: broad definitions of crime were used, including serious misdemeanors (Farrington) and disorderly conduct (McCord); McCord's sample is generally acknowledged to have been at high risk of criminal participation; and the very high probability of conviction following arrest

TABLE 2-2 Estimates of Male Lifetime Participation Rates (official record data)

Crime Type and Level of Involvement	Participation Rates (percent)		
	White	Black	All Males
Nontraffic arrest	47	68	50, 60, 60
Arrest for index offense	15	52	23, 36
Conviction for serious offenses (unspecified)	—	—	6,[a] 29, 30, 35, 44
Conviction for property offense	—	—	26
Conviction for violent offense	—	—	17

NOTE: See Table 2 and discussion in Visher and Roth (Appendix A) for sources and analysis of these alternative estimates.

[a]This anomalous 6 percent applies to the adoptive fathers in Mednick, Gabrielli, and Hutchings (1984), who were presumably screened for absence of criminal records before being permitted to adopt.

in Britain makes the arrest and conviction thresholds more comparable there than in the United States.

Self-Report Estimates

Alternative estimates of cumulative participation in crime (D) are available from self-report studies of specific criminal activities (e.g., theft over $50, burglary, robbery) by cross-section samples of youth, usually those enrolled in high school. Since several grade levels are typically sampled, the reported measure is interpreted as participation by an age range (e.g., 13 to 18 years), or more simply, by "high school age," which we denote as D_{HS}. Considerable imprecision surrounds this measure since both D and d vary strongly with age during the teenage years. Nevertheless, the literature on these estimates provides much of the available information on relative crime-specific participation rates, and general consistency emerges from 10 studies conducted over the last 25 years.[5]

From these studies, a systematic pattern emerges in criminal participation across crime types. The two studies based on self-reports of high-school-age males during the 1950s and 1960s report that 13 percent have stolen autos and 5 to 6 percent admit having stolen items other than autos worth more than $50 (Short and Nye, 1958; Jensen and Eve, 1976). In more recent studies conducted in the 1970s and 1980s, D_{HS} for non-auto thefts over $50 has increased to around 15 percent, and similar recent estimates for auto

theft have decreased to 10 percent. These changes in crime-specific participation likely reflect the effects of inflation and enhanced security features on newer autos. Burglary appears to be a relatively common crime among high school males: in three different studies, 16 to 20 percent reported ever committing at least one burglary. For assault with injury, cumulative participation averages 13 percent in both the older and more recent studies. Last, participation rates for robbery are generally consistent across several studies, with about 6 percent of high-school-age males reporting commission of a robbery, although one study, using a constructed single cohort, reports D_{HS} for robbery of 15 percent.[6]

A few studies of high school males also measure participation rates through both self-reported and officially recorded involvement with the police or juvenile court. These estimates vary widely, probably because of differences in definitions of crime, in thoroughness of record searches, in year of survey, and in geographic area. One recent study (Hindelang, Hirschi, and Weis, 1981) permits a direct comparison of official-record and self-report estimates of the fraction of a single sample with police contacts. In that study, involving a sample of high school students in Seattle selected in 1978, one-third to one-half of the teenagers did not report their police contacts to interviewers, if the official records are accurate; the underreporting was highest among white females and black males. However, the findings from earlier studies comparing police contacts as mea-

---

[5]Many other studies have obtained self-reports of delinquent involvement among samples of high school youths, but the panel chose to focus on the subset of studies that reported involvement in serious crime types for which an adult could be arrested. In addition, many self-report studies of delinquency only report aggregate frequency measures or composite scales and not crime-specific individual participation rates.

[6]Estimates of cumulative participation by age 17 were calculated from data reported by Elliott and Huizinga (1984:62) for a synthetic cohort that was aggregated from three birth cohorts (1959, 1962, and 1965) to get cumulative participation rates at each age from 11 to 21 for the entire sample. The offense types used in their analysis are actually broad clusters of crimes, but some comparisons are possible.

sured by self-report and official-record data are inconsistent: some show higher rates on self-report than official-record data, and some show other differences by subgroup (see Visher and Roth, Appendix A:Table 3).

For white males in the Seattle study, about 27 percent had an official record of police contact, which is consistent with official-record estimates for white males of 26 percent for B_{HS} in a 1964 California sample and 29 percent for B_{18} in Philadelphia. The self-report estimate of police contact of 17 percent for the white males in the Seattle cohort (Hindelang, Hirschi, and Weis, 1981) is also similar to that reported in two other studies (Gold, 1966; Williams and Gold, 1972). In contrast, only 5 percent of one 1967 national sample of youths had official police records (Williams and Gold, 1972). This latter estimate may reflect both the difficulty of obtaining complete official records on a nationwide sample and lower participation rates among the rural youth that were more heavily represented in that sample. When participation is measured by the presence of a juvenile court record that includes adjudication, the estimates range from 2 percent for index offenses in a 1967 national sample to about 11 percent for a broader range of offenses in the recent Seattle study.

The three cumulative measures discussed thus far are the most common statistics on participation reported in the literature—either from official records or self-reports. But for many purposes, an annual measure of current participation by active offenders, d, is useful. (Estimates of b are not commonly reported in the literature.) As discussed earlier, d is computed as the fraction of some population committing at least one crime within a specified interval, usually one year. Estimates of d are less common in the literature than estimates of D or B, cumulative participation.

All estimates of d reported here were obtained by the self-report method through questions about involvement in specific offense types during a specific preceding reference period. In one study, reports of d were based on a 12-month reference period; for the other studies, 12-month estimates were interpolated from values based on reference periods of 18 months and 3 years. The panel reviewed four studies (Weis, 1976; Bachman, O'Malley, and Johnston, 1978; Tittle, 1980; Elliott et al., 1983) that used similar methods and reported d for five serious crime types: grand theft (over $50), breaking and entering, assault with a weapon or injury, robbery, and auto theft. Published statistics were annualized to provide comparable estimates across all studies.

In any given year, about 3 to 6 percent of teenage males steal items worth at least $50. Slightly more youths, 4 to 7 percent, report breaking and entering a building. Estimates of d for assault with a weapon (or causing injury) are less consistent across studies, with a range of 3 percent for younger adolescent males (12–14 years) to 13 percent for older males in high school (16–17 years). The age differences and personal definitions of "assault," even with injury or a weapon, are likely explanations of this variation. Last, d for robbery and auto theft among teenagers averages 5 percent and 2 percent, respectively, although some variation exists between studies and age categories. Few studies report d for adults, but some limited data suggest that current participation declines rapidly in the early 20s.

In summary, estimates of cumulative participation rates among males by high school age, by age 18, and by age 40–50 (lifetime) and current participation rates are influenced by: (1) the type of data used (aggregate statistics, official records, or self-reports); (2) the crimes in which participation is being measured; (3) level or threshold of involvement (police contact, arrest, court referral, or conviction); and (4) the characteristics and representativeness of the sample. These factors account for most of the variation in estimates of participation (see Visher and Roth, Appendix A, Tables 1–4, for more details).

PARTICIPATION ESTIMATES BY SEX, RACE, AND AGE

Differences in participation across demographic subgroups—defined in terms of sex, race, and age, are discussed because much available data on participation are reported in these terms. Furthermore, the often substantial bivariate relationships are robust in multivariate analyses and stable across a variety of temporal and geographic settings and data collection methods. The policy implications of these empirical associations and those of other covariates are discussed in later chapters.

Sex

Some of the research that reports participation rates for males also reports comparable measures for females. For females, 16 estimates of B_{18}, 5 estimates of B_L, and 11 estimates of D_{HS} were located in the literature reviewed by the panel; current participation, d, among females in specific crime types was also reported in three studies. In general, patterns of participation among females parallel those among males: higher estimates for broad crime domains (e.g., all nontraffic compared with index offenses) and low thresholds of involvement (e.g., police contacts or arrests compared with convictions). The most consistent pattern with respect to gender is the extent to which male criminal participation in serious crimes at any age greatly exceeds that of females, regardless of source of data,

crime type, level of involvement, or measure of participation.

With few exceptions, the ratio of male-to-female participation in U.S. samples ranges from less than 3:1 for broadly defined offense categories to 5:1 for index offenses and specific crime types. In the 1958 Philadelphia cohort study, which included females, 14 percent of females had a recorded nontraffic police contact by age 18, as compared with 31 percent of males. In the three Racine, Wisconsin, cohorts, the average B_{18} for males (with crime types broadly defined) was about 45 percent; for females, B_{18} averaged 19 percent (Shannon, 1982a). Juvenile court referral estimates of B, which average 25 percent for males, range from 5 to 14 percent for females in four studies. Lifetime participation estimates for females converge at 15 percent, compared with B_L for males of 50 percent based on any nontraffic offense. For specific crime types, corresponding male/female ratios of D_{HS} and d vary more across studies as a result of low reported participation values based on self-reports.

Race

Racial differences in criminal participation have been examined with both self-report and official-record data for cumulative participation measures, B_{18}, B_L, and D_{HS}, and for current participation, d. These differences reflect a number of social and economic factors that are correlated with both ethnicity and participation. Self-report studies that report participation rates separately for white and black male subgroups (e.g., Gold, 1966; Hirschi, 1969; Hindelang, Hirschi, and Weis, 1981; Elliott et al., 1983) generally find negligible differences for primarily minor delinquent acts. The few self-report studies that permit race comparisons for serious offenses show that the estimated ratio of black/white participation is only slightly above 1:1 for self-reported serious property offenses such as grand theft, auto theft, and burglary (see Hindelang, Hirschi, and Weis, 1981; Visher and Roth, Appendix A:Tables 3 and 4). For self-reports of robbery and assault and for scales limited to index offenses, this ratio increases, especially at younger ages. For example, in the National Youth Survey, annual current participation rates for robbery, d, for blacks and whites aged 11–17 were 9 and 4 percent, respectively, for a black/white ratio of 2.25:1. But in the fifth wave of interviews, when the age range was 15–21, d for black and white youth in the same sample was 3 and 2 percent, respectively, for a lesser ratio of only 1.5:1 (Elliott et al., 1983; see discussion in Visher and Roth, Appendix A:Table 4).

Studies using official data generally report greater black/white ratios and stronger associations between race and participation in crime as the seriousness of criminal behavior increases from nontraffic offenses to all index offenses to violent index offenses. Combining data from several studies with criminal participation broadly defined as nontraffic offenses, the black/white ratio averages 1.8:1; for index offenses, the ratio averages 3.2:1 (Visher and Roth, Appendix A:Table 8).

The Philadelphia cohort data are the only source of official-record participation estimates by racial group across several levels of offense seriousness (Tracy, Wolfgang, and Figlio, 1985:Tables 4a and 5a). For the cohort born in 1945, the black/white ratios for B_{18} were 1.8:1 for nontraffic offenses, 3.3:1 for UCR index crimes, and 4.5:1 for offenses with injury. For the cohort born in 1958, the ratios were very similar: 1.8:1, 2.9:1, and 3.2:1 for nontraffic offenses, UCR index crimes, and offenses with injury, respectively.

Analysis of all the data shows that racial differences in aggregate measures of criminal behavior appear to be largely a

function of differences in participation rather than offending frequencies. For example, the 1980 black/white ratios for *arrest rates* of males under age 18 were 1.6:1, 2.4:1, and 3.4:1 for nontraffic offenses, all index offenses, and violent index offenses, respectively.[7] These ratios are very consistent with the participation ratios just presented for the Philadelphia cohort born in 1958. Since aggregate arrest rates are a function of both participation rates and individual frequency rates ($A = \mu b$), the similarity in the black/white ratios suggests that racial differences in criminal behavior are largely a function of differences in participation. More black youth are arrested at least once, but black and white offenders tend to be rearrested at similar rates (see also Blumstein and Graddy, 1982; Tracy, Wolfgang, and Figlio, 1985).

Age

The relationship between age and participation in criminal behavior can be examined using several measures. Common measures are age-specific values of d and of the hazard rate for initiation (h), as discussed above. Often, hazard rates can be calculated from official records (e.g., Wolfgang, Figlio, and Sellin, 1972; Farrington, 1983a). Age distributions of current participation rates, d_a, are usually generated by studies that gather multiple waves of self-reported data on criminal involvement during recent intervals (e.g., Elliott et al., 1983).

Some patterns emerge from the studies that the panel reviewed. Even though only a small fraction of youth at risk begin criminal careers at any given age, a concentration of initiations among youth is

---

[7]These ratios were computed from 1980 race-specific arrest data (Federal Bureau of Investigation, 1981) and 1980 population figures (Bureau of the Census, 1983:Table 33).

evident (see Blumstein and Graddy, 1982). For both blacks and whites, about half those ever arrested during their lifetimes were first arrested before age 18. The initiation of officially recorded criminal activity for males is negligible only until age 8; it is 2 percent by age 15–16 for whites and 6 percent by age 17–18 for blacks and falls thereafter. Perhaps surprisingly, self-reported current participation rates peak at a slightly earlier age interval—14 to 17 years (see especially Elliott et al., 1983). The apparent inconsistency—participation peaking before initiation—may arise in part from different definitions of crime, different methods of observation, and different samples used in calculating the two measures of age-specific participation. However, taken together, they suggest that a substantial fraction of teenagers are active in crime for several years before their first arrest. To resolve the issue, data are needed for a common sample on crime-specific age distributions of initiation and current participation, according to both official records and self-reports.

Although demographic patterns of participation are apparent, they are of little use in explaining participation or providing a basis for policy intended to prevent the initiation of criminal careers. The next section discusses correlates of participation that are of more interest in terms of both theory and policy.

OTHER FACTORS ASSOCIATED WITH PARTICIPATION

Many studies in the criminological literature examine associations between a wide variety of social factors and some measure of "criminality." Frequently, these studies provide limited information about participation in criminal activity because the measures of criminality confound participation with diversity, frequency, and seriousness (e.g., Nye, 1958;

Hirschi, 1969; Williams and Gold, 1972; Polk et al., 1981; Ensminger, Kellam, and Rubin, 1983). Also, a large number of studies inappropriately infer individual relationships from aggregate data or ecological relationships and thus do not shed light on individual criminal careers. The precise nature of the relationship between social factors and criminality at the individual level is difficult to disentangle when different aspects of criminal careers are confounded. Despite this, many studies do focus on the factors associated with individual criminal career parameters, including participation. This information about demographic, social, familial, and individual covariates could be useful in identifying groups that are at a higher risk for future criminal behavior. If systematic relationships can be established between characteristics of adolescent children and subsequent adult offending, the relationships may be helpful in designing intervention policies to reduce criminal participation.

This section focuses on the empirical relationships of a small set of factors to participation. This discussion excludes studies that relate these factors to composite indices, seriousness scores, frequency measures, scales derived from factor analysis, or nonserious offenses, rather than participation rates for specific, serious crime types (for examples of specific studies excluded, see Visher and Roth, Appendix A). In addition, comparative studies of samples involving predetermined selection ratios of known offenders are omitted because they cannot yield estimates of participation (Hirschi and Selvin, 1973). Also excluded are samples in which the threshold for participation is incarceration, rather than self-reports or officially recorded arrest (e.g., Gordon, 1973): because the incarceration decision is correlated with λ, seriousness, and elapsed career length, use of incarceration as the participation measure would lead to a confounding of relationships involving those parameters with relationships to participation.

Finally, the factors associated with participation in the following discussion are not necessarily causally related to criminal involvement. They may be only correlates that need explanation through the use of other variables, or they may diminish or be eliminated in a multivariate analysis of criminal participation. Most of the empirical data supporting the following discussion are reported in Visher and Roth, Appendix A:Tables 11–17.

Family Influences

One group of variables showing strong and consistent effects on participation in juvenile delinquency and adult offending are aspects of family interaction and structure such as parenting skills, adult-child interaction, and parents' antisocial or criminal behavior. Many traditional theories of delinquency include some elements of family functioning in their explanations: poor attachment to parents and weak parental controls (social control theory); lack of value consensus within the family (anomie theory); an absence of law-abiding values in the family (differential association theory); and poor child-rearing practices (social learning theory).[8]

Parenting

In the panel's review of the existing literature on family influences, parental supervision, adult-child interaction, and other aspects of family management emerged as factors likely to be associated with participation in serious criminal behavior among children. The most important dimensions of parenting related to *low* rates of criminal participation appear to be consistent, strict discipline; close supervision; and strong parent-child relationships including communication, affection, and interest in the child's activities (e.g., McCord, 1979; Wadsworth, 1979; for discussion see Loeber and Dishion, 1983; Patterson and Stouthamer-Loeber, 1984). In one study using multivariate analysis to explain delinquency or criminal behavior at several different ages, indicators of poor parenting for children at age 8 (e.g., poor supervision, social worker's ratings of poor parental behavior) were strong predictors of "troublesome" behavior at ages 8–10 and of convictions at ages 10–13 (Farrington, 1983a).

Longitudinal studies that relate measures of parenting and family structure when a child is in elementary school to later official records or self-reports of that child's participation in serious delinquency or adult criminal behavior are particularly well suited to assess the impact of parenting on criminal involvement.[9] In a comparison of single-source and composite measures of parenting (i.e., those that invoke several observers' assessments), some evidence suggests that composite measures of parents' child-rearing practices are better predictors of future delinquency than single measures (Loeber and Dishion, 1983).

---

[8]For a more formal discussion of the role family influences play in various theories of delinquency, including those mentioned above and psychoanalytic, deterrence, and labeling theories, see Bahr (1979).

[9]Examples of such research include the Cambridge Study in Delinquent Development, a longitudinal study of 400 British males (West and Farrington, 1977; Farrington, 1983a); the British National Survey, another longitudinal study of over 5,000 British youngsters tracked since birth in 1946 (Douglas, Ross, and Simpson, 1968; Wadsworth, 1979), and the Cambridge-Somerville Youth Study, which has followed 500 American youngsters for 30 years (McCord and McCord, 1959; McCord, 1979).

One reason for this result may be that a single teacher's or parent's rating of child-rearing practices may be influenced by various subjective factors that affect the generalizability of the findings. Another explanation might be that the presence of multiple risk factors within a family (such as poor supervision, poor discipline) predicts delinquency better than single risk factors.

Recent studies of the effects of parenting techniques on pre-adolescent conduct disturbances as precursors to later criminal behavior have also pointed to the adverse effects of parents' lax supervision, passive attitudes, and ineffective discipline.[10] In addition, cross-section research has also found correlations between some family management variables—principally discipline and supervision—and criminal involvement, but many of these studies do not report criminal participation rates (e.g., Nye, 1958; Hirschi, 1969; Patterson and Stouthamer-Loeber, 1984).

Parental Criminality

A factor consistently associated with serious delinquency and adult criminal participation in many different studies is criminal behavior of parents. In one study, for example, twice as many children at age 10 with a convicted parent had a criminal conviction by age 25 as those without a convicted parent (Farrington, 1983a; see also Osborn and West, 1979). A multivariate analysis of these same data showed that having a convicted parent was a significant predictor of juvenile convictions and self-reported delinquency. This relationship persists in

studies of children whose parents, or even grandparents, have a history of juvenile delinquency, arrest, or other antisocial behavior, such as excessive drinking or a poor work record (see Robins and Lewis, 1966; Robins, West, and Herjanic, 1975).

The apparent association between parental criminality and participation of their children in delinquency is supported by studies that suggest that some offender characteristics (e.g., low arousal levels of the autonomic nervous system, certain EEG patterns, low intelligence) may arise from a mix of inherited and environmental factors. The strongest evidence for a partially genetic origin emerges from several studies conducted in Scandinavian countries, showing that adopted children with criminal biological parents are more likely to be criminals than those with noncriminal biological parents, even when the adopted children were separated at a fairly young age from biological parents (Hutchings and Mednick, 1975; Cadoret and Cain, 1980; Van Dusen et al., 1983). Although it is difficult to completely separate genetic and environmental influences, the findings do not appear to be attributable to correlation in social class between the biological and adoptive parents, class-related adverse perinatal events, age at adoption, or adverse labeling effects (see Van Dusen et al., 1983). However, Loeber and Dishion (1983) found that the predictive strength of parental criminality in accounting for later delinquent behavior in the child was weak in the studies of adopted children when compared with such other factors as parenting and early indicators of antisocial behavior in the child.[11]

---

[10]Recent discussions of this topic can be found in Hirschi (1983), Patterson (1982), and Rutter and Giller (1984:180–188). For reviews of studies relating nondelinquent but disturbing antisocial conduct to family functioning, see Rutter (1977), Hinde (1980), or Patterson (1980).

[11]Loeber and Dishion (1983) calculate a single measure of accuracy of early predictors of male delinquency for a large number of studies in which prediction tables could be reconstructed. Their measure, relative improvement over chance (RIOC), is intended to standardize for differences

Likely environmental explanations for the observed empirical association in unbroken families are that children who are raised in homes with criminal parents are exposed to aggressive behavior and antisocial attitudes (Rutter and Giller, 1984), poor child-rearing practices (Wilson, 1975), and adverse family conditions associated with lower-class upbringing (Van Dusen et al., 1983). Because the relationship exists even with respect to parental delinquency occurring before the child's birth, it is apparently not a consequence of direct involvement in the parents' criminal activity (Farrington, Gundry, and West, 1975). Last, parental antisocial behavior, including unstable work patterns, alcohol and drug use, and a record of delinquency, also appear to be significant in the genesis of serious delinquent behavior in their children.

Family Disruption

The impact of family disruption, especially divorce and separation, on the participation of youth in criminal behavior has been a popular topic in studies of juvenile delinquency (for reviews, see Hennessey, Richards, and Berk, 1978;

---

across studies in the base rate of delinquents and the selection ratio used by the researchers (for further discussion of RIOC, see Chapter 4 in this volume and Copas and Tarling in Volume II). Eight different predictors were examined for their association with male delinquency: composite measures of parenting; child problem behavior; stealing, lying, or truancy; criminality or antisocial behavior of family members; poor educational achievement; single measures of parenting; separation from parents; and socioeconomic status. Loeber and Dishion found that the median RIOC for these predictors (averaged over studies with data on a specific predictor) followed the above order. For parental criminality, the median RIOC was .24 with a range of 1.0 to .08. For example, the Hutchings and Mednick (1975) study of adoptees was used to calculate three RIOC measures: .11, .13, and .20; in addition, the false-positive rates for this study exceeded 70 percent.

Wilkinson, 1980). Family disruptions are consistently related to a record of conviction (Wadsworth, 1979; Farrington, 1983a) and to self-reported commission of index offenses or serious offense types (Farrington, 1979b; Elliott et al., 1983), with participation rates almost twice as high among youth from disrupted families as those from intact families.

However, self-report studies that use nonserious offenses or other measures of criminal behavior besides participation report small and inconsistent associations between family disruption and delinquency, perhaps because such minor acts are so widespread. For example, one study found a slight effect of family disruption on a six-item scale of self-reported criminal activity that included property damage and theft under $2 (Hirschi, 1969; see also Nye, 1958; Dentler and Monroe, 1961; Berger and Simon, 1974). It appears that "broken homes" may differentially affect males and females, urban and rural youth, and different ethnic groups (see Datesman and Scarpitti, 1975; Austin, 1978; Wilkinson, 1980), and these variables could account for some of the inconsistent results in research on family disruption and criminal participation. There is also some evidence that family disruption has a selective impact on delinquency, primarily affecting rebellious behavior such as running away and truancy.

In any case, it does not appear that family disruption per se is associated with delinquency. Rather, parental discord, which usually precedes a break-up, or other difficulties that follow a break-up apparently impair normal family functioning and increase the risk of delinquency. Marital conflict within intact homes is associated with participation in delinquency, perhaps to a greater extent than broken homes (Rutter, 1981; McCord, 1982). Evidence that parental death is unrelated to criminal involvement while parental divorce increases delinquency suggests that conflict between parents may account for the association between family disruption and delinquent behavior (see Rutter, 1981; see also, West and Farrington, 1973; Wadsworth, 1979; but see Rankin, 1983). When father absence was broadly defined to include death and other separations unrelated to divorce in two other studies, it was not a significant predictor of adult criminal behavior when multivariate analysis was used to sort out the importance of several variables (Farrington, 1983a). And, a recent empirical review of several studies found that separation from parents at an early age was only weakly predictive of delinquency as an adolescent (Loeber and Dishion, 1983).

A composite measure of parental behavior that includes parental conflict, however, does predict adult criminal participation (Farrington, 1983a) and juvenile convictions (McCord, 1979). As the operative factor, parental discord probably reduces the effectiveness of parental supervision and discipline, interferes with supportive parent-child relationships, and offers negative, antisocial models for a child. Moreover, the association between family conflict and criminal participation among children is probably a complex relationship affecting some youth but not others, depending on other family variables and the youth's characteristics.

Family Size and Structure

Family size appears related to delinquency, but explanations for this finding are not yet established. Large families—defined as those with at least four children—may handicap effective parenting and result in increased delinquency participation by children. However, the family size/delinquency relationship does not appear in a few studies of children

from large middle-class families, suggesting that the pertinent explanatory variable is the "disadvantages which tend to accompany family size in poorer sections of the community" (Rutter and Giller, 1984:186) and not simply family size. For example, the decreased control of children because of lack of resources for child care and overcrowding in homes are plausible intervening explanatory factors (see Hirschi, 1983; Rutter and Giller, 1984). In Farrington's (1983a) multivariate analysis, family size was not an independent predictor of criminal involvement in any of the four age groups examined; however, associated variables, such as low family income and poor housing, were significant predictors of delinquency by ages 8–10 and 10–13.

Other family structure characteristics that may increase participation through their influence on parenting skills include short intervals between first and second births, continued growth in family size after a child reaches age 6, younger mothers (under age 20), and short intervals between marriage and the first child's birth, especially less than 1 year (see Wadsworth, 1979). But these types of variables, including family size, have not been extensively studied with U.S. data (for an exception, see Hirschi, 1969).

Early Antisocial Behavior

Using various measures of antisocial behaviors in the elementary school or preadolescent years, many investigators have examined the association of early antisocial behavior with later serious delinquency and adult criminal activity. With few exceptions, the evidence indicates that such conduct as aggressive behavior, "troublesomeness" in school, dishonesty, and stealing are all related to a record of arrest or court conviction in later years (see Loeber and Dishion, 1983). For example, in one study, 62 percent of children who were rated by teachers, peers, or parents as troublesome at ages 8–10 had court convictions by age 25, compared with 26 percent of other children (Farrington, 1983a; see also Feldhusen, Thurston, and Benning, 1973). In addition, the panel found that more general measures of early antisocial behavior—referral to a child guidance clinic, teacher rating as "potentially delinquent" or "antisocial," and excessive elementary school absences—were similarly associated with criminal activity at older ages (Reckless, Dinitz, and Kay, 1957; Robins, 1966; Robins and Wish, 1977; Ouston, 1984).[12]

Further evidence of a strong association between preadolescent antisocial behavior and delinquency appears in some research that has examined the importance of various categories of variables in predicting delinquency. In a review of more than 20 studies, child problem behavior—including stealing, lying, and truancy—was second only to poor family management practices as a predictor of later juvenile and adult criminal involvement (Loeber and Dishion, 1983). Using several different techniques, Robins (1966; Robins and Wish, 1977) concluded that childhood deviance and adult antisocial behavior represented different stages of a single developmental process and that childhood behaviors were better predictors than family variables. Last, Farrington (1983a) also supports the view that criminal behavior is part of a developmental sequence usually initiated by troublesome, defiant, or aggressive behavior in children before the age of 12. In

his data, family influences and the child's antisocial behavior were equally important in predicting conviction by age 25.

Despite the apparent consistency of the relationship between early antisocial behavior and subsequent criminal participation, data are lacking on several significant points. First, while continuities between antisocial behavior and participation in crime have been found in studies of older children (ages 8–14) followed into adolescence or early adulthood, virtually no studies have followed children from ages 4 to 7, when antisocial behavior tends to begin, into young adulthood, when the risk of criminal career initiation has largely passed. Therefore, understanding of the relationship between early behavior and criminal participation is incomplete. Second, most children who exhibit antisocial behaviors do not become involved in criminal activity as teenagers or adults. There is little knowledge of the factors that reliably identify antisocial preadolescents who do not progress to offending patterns involving serious crimes. Furthermore, there is evidence that suggests it is even more difficult to predict eventual serious criminal behavior among persons who first become offenders in young adulthood.

Social Class

Social class is often discussed as an important correlate of criminal behavior, although there is substantial debate over the consistency of the relationship between low social class and involvement in criminal activity and about its underlying meaning. Most of the recent U.S. studies of this class/crime association have relied on self-report data, which tap nonserious criminal activity that is relatively common and does not necessarily attract justice system intervention.

In the panel's review of the research relating participation rates to individual-

---

[12]A large literature outside the scope of the panel's focus on criminal careers addresses the prevalence of antisocial behaviors (e.g., fighting, lying, stealing) in elementary school children and the evidence of continuities between these behaviors and various psychosocial problems in adulthood (Olweus, 1979; Loeber, 1982; Loeber and Dishion, 1983; Rutter and Giller, 1984:Chapter 2).

level measures of social class, no significant association emerges in self-report studies when the measure of criminal activity is primarily nonserious behavior, such as vandalism, fighting, or small thefts. This result probably reflects the fact that a large fraction of youths engage in that behavior regardless of their social class.[13] Also, in studies of the class/ participation relationship in which measures of official involvement (e.g., police contact, arrest record) encompass a wide range of delinquent behaviors, no association is usually found (e.g., Hathaway and Monachesi, 1963; Polk, Frease, and Richmond, 1974; Hindelang, Hirschi, and Weis, 1981).[14]

When criminal participation is restricted to serious offenses, social class differences emerge in one major study that used self-report measures (Elliott and Huizinga, 1983), and this association persists after controlling for race. With official data (e.g., juvenile court or police records), the class/serious crime relationship is fairly strong, especially in the pre-1970 studies (e.g., Reiss and Rhodes,

1961; Gold, 1966; for another review, see Tittle, Villemez, and Smith, 1978).[15] Recent evidence, however, is limited because individual official records usually do not include individual-level social class measures, and arrest statistics are not disaggregated by this variable. Some existing data sets presumably contain official-record data that would provide further information about the relationship between participation in serious offenses and social class (e.g., McCord, 1979; Hindelang, Hirschi, and Weis, 1981; Shannon, 1982a; Thornberry and Farnworth, 1982), but the appropriate analyses have not been reported in the literature.[16]

The strongest evidence for a negative association between social class and criminal participation appears in research using ecological (area) measures of social class (e.g., Lander, 1954; Chilton, 1964; Shaw and McKay, 1969; Wolfgang, Figlio, and Sellin, 1972). Indeed, until 1950, ecological correlations were the only basis for conclusions about social class and criminal behavior (Hindelang, Hirschi, and Weis, 1981:184). However, comparisons between these studies and those with individual social class indicators must be made cautiously. For one

---

[13]Many investigators have examined the class/ crime issue with self-report data (e.g., Nye, 1958; Akers, 1964; Hirschi, 1969; Williams and Gold, 1972; Johnson, 1980; Krohn et al., 1980). For a detailed review of studies considered by the panel, see Visher and Roth (Appendix A). However, some studies using other measures of criminal behavior, principally aggregate "incidence" rates, have reported differences by class group (e.g., Elliott and Voss, 1974; Hindelang, Hirschi, and Weis, 1981:194; Elliott and Huizinga, 1983). Other important reviews on this topic appear in Tittle, Villemez, and Smith (1978), Hindelang, Hirschi, and Weis (1979, 1981), and Clelland and Carter (1980).

[14]In the Racine, Wisconsin, cohort study, which had official data on broadly defined police contacts (including investigations, suspicion, and information-gathering), Shannon (1982a) found social status to be unrelated to number of police contacts; however, participation rates by social status could not be computed from published data.

[15]Hindelang, Hirschi, and Weis (1981) refer to Hirschi (1969) as another study with a moderate class/official-record relationship (correlation of −.21), but participation rates by social class are not reported in the original source. In three British studies (Wadsworth, 1979; Farrington, 1983a; Ouston, 1984) and one study with data from Denmark (Van Dusen et al., 1983) the class/crime relationship is particularly strong.

[16]Using regression analysis and follow-up data from the 1945 Philadelphia cohort initially collected by Wolfgang, Figlio, and Sellin (1972), Thornberry and Farnworth (1982) found a strong association between individual social status and both the frequency of officially recorded serious (e.g., index or violent arrests) and nonserious (e.g., total arrests) adult criminal behavior, but participation rates by social class were not reported.

thing, aggregate relationships do not necessarily permit valid inferences to individuals (see Robinson, 1950; Hannan, 1971). Urban areas that are defined as lower class may have higher crime rates because of a small group of very active criminals or because outsiders come into the area to commit crime. In addition, differential police surveillance and arrest practices in lower-class areas may contribute to ecological correlations between social status and crime. In discussing this issue, Tittle, Villemez, and Smith (1978) argued that census tracts—a common unit of analysis in ecological studies—are typically quite diverse with regard to family income, and especially so during the 1950s and 1960s when most of the ecological research was carried out.

In summary, individual social class may be empirically related to some types of serious delinquency and adult criminal behavior when participation is measured either by self-reports or official records, but relevant research is limited, especially that based on recent samples. In a review of socioeconomic class as a predictor of a child's later delinquency in seven studies, Loeber and Dishion (1983) concluded that social status was a poor predictor compared with early antisocial behavior or measures of family functioning. But low social class and low family income at age 14 significantly predicted convictions at ages 17–20 and 21–24 in a multivariate analysis that controlled for some family influences (Farrington, 1983a). The meaning of this association is far from clear, but it may be due in part to social class differentials in police detection, official recording of criminal behavior, or victim reporting. Indicators of social status may also overlap with unmeasured aspects of parental behavior and family structure that are consistently related to delinquency.

School Performance and Intelligence

The relationship between participation in delinquency or adult criminal activity and various measures of school performance or intelligence measured by school achievement test scores, standard IQ tests, vocabulary skills, and "school failure" has been examined in many studies. In the panel's review of eight studies (see Visher and Roth, Appendix A:Table 15), the empirical association between low intelligence or school achievement and criminal involvement was consistent in a wide variety of samples and with both self-report and official measures of delinquency.

In general, participation decreases with higher IQ scores, grade point averages, reading test scores, and other measures of academic achievement. Polk, Frease, and Richmond (1974) reported that 42 percent of a general high school sample with low grades had a juvenile court record compared with 22 and 9 percent of students in the sample with average and high grades, respectively. In some studies, the relationship between participation and intelligence/achievement is independent of race (e.g., Wolfgang, Figlio, and Sellin, 1972) and social class (e.g., Reiss and Rhodes, 1961; Polk, Frease, and Richmond, 1974); it also exists in research that relates school achievement or intelligence to other measures of criminal behavior, such as scales derived from factor analysis or aggregate frequency measures (Weis, 1973; data from Hirschi, 1969, cited in Hirschi and Hindelang, 1977; Menard and Morse, 1984). In addition, empirical links emerge between various nondelinquent conduct disorders, which may precede delinquency, and measures of intelligence (for a review, see Rutter and Giller, 1984).

While empirical results are consistent, the search for possible explanations of the association between delinquency and low intelligence/achievement continues (see discussions in Gordon, 1976:256–270; Hirschi and Hindelang, 1977; Wilson and Herrnstein, 1985). Hirschi and Hindelang argue that IQ influences delinquent behavior primarily through its correlation with school performance, although the empirical evidence for their hypothesis is weak and is contradicted by at least one recent study (Menard and Morse, 1984). Alternatively, low scores on IQ tests may reflect a predelinquent's resistance to authority and unwillingness to make the effort needed to do well on such tests. The association between school conduct disorders and IQ is fairly well established (see Rutter and Giller, 1984:163–168), but no study has successfully resolved the issue of how school performance, IQ, and early antisocial behavior might interact in predicting delinquency.

In two multivariate analyses, low IQ emerged as a strong predictor of juvenile convictions along with poor parenting and antisocial behavior (Farrington, 1983a), but was not significant in another study once school variables and social class were controlled (Wolfgang, Figlio, and Sellin, 1972). Thus, what we know at present is that low intelligence and weak school performance appear to be closely intertwined, and several studies have shown them to be strong predictors of serious delinquency and adult criminal behavior (Loeber and Dishion, 1983), but any causal structure among these factors is not yet established.

Substance Abuse

The relationship between substance abuse and criminal activity is widely thought to be firmly established, supported by empirical research as well as informal observations of criminal justice operations. But this relationship is much more complex than it initially appears, especially when "criminal activity" is defined in terms of criminal career dimensions. The distinction between participation in criminal behavior (D) and the frequency of that behavior (λ) is particularly important when discussing substance abuse. We examine here the relationship of criminal participation and substance abuse, that is, whether drug users are more likely to be involved in crime than non-users. In the next chapter, on active offenders, we review the research on whether drug-using criminals commit crimes more frequently than non-using criminals (see also Wish and Johnson, Volume II).

The panel did not consider much of the research on substance abuse and criminal participation, which has focused on juveniles, their use of marijuana or alcohol, and their involvement in relatively minor criminal behavior (e.g., small thefts, school crime, vandalism) (see Burkett and Jensen, 1975; Wechsler and McFadden, 1976; Kellam, Ensminger, and Simon, 1980). But the available evidence on participation in serious criminal activity suggests that drug users, especially multiple drug users, are much more likely to be involved than non-users (e.g., Johnston, O'Malley, and Eveland, 1978; Elliott and Huizinga, 1984). Table 2-3 presents data from a national sample of youths aged 11–17 in 1976 and 15–21 in 1980 (Elliott and Huizinga, 1984). The self-reported participation rates for felony assault, felony theft, and robbery increase dramatically as drug use becomes more serious, from no drug use to alcohol only, alcohol and marijuana, and multiple drugs.

Data of this type, however, cannot answer the frequent question whether substance abuse leads persons into crime. A longitudinal study of both criminal involvement and drug use is needed to sort

TABLE 2-3 Current Criminal Participation Rates, d, by Drug User Types (percent)

Crime Type[a]	Drug User Type[b]	11–17 years[c]	15–21 years[c]
Felony assault	No drugs	12.7	4.1
	Alcohol	18.3	5.2
	Alcohol/marijuana	33.8	13.5
	Multiple drugs	51.7	24.2
Felony theft	No drugs	6.3	2.3
	Alcohol	18.6	4.4
	Alcohol/marijuana	32.4	13.5
	Multiple drugs	55.2	27.3
Robbery	No drugs	4.0	0.8
	Alcohol	5.7	0.4
	Alcohol/marijuana	6.8	2.8
	Multiple drugs	22.4	6.4

[a]These crime types are actually clusters of related offenses. Felony assault is composed of aggravated assault, sexual assault, and gang fights; felony theft includes auto theft, theft over $50, breaking and entering, and bought stolen goods; robbery encompasses strong-arming students, teachers, and others.

[b]Based on self-reports of drug use in the preceding year. Since the researchers wished to focus on non-experimental drug use, use of the specific drug at least four times was a definitional requirement.

[c]Active participation rates for the preceding year, d.

SOURCE: Data from Elliott and Huizinga (1984:Tables 1 and 2), for first and fifth waves of longitudinal study.

out the causal relationship between substance use and criminal activity. Table 2-4 presents such data on youths aged 11–19 from the National Youth Survey (Elliott and Huizinga, 1984). Although the measure of criminal activity is not strictly based on participation, the data are relevant here. In this particular sample, the predominant pattern among drug users who are also delinquent was for initial drug use to follow delinquency or to occur simultaneously, rather than for drug use to precede delinquency. This study concluded that both substance abuse and criminal behavior may be a result of similar social and individual factors, principally ineffective socialization in the home, involvement with delinquent peers, and school-related difficulties (see also Elliott, Huizinga, and Ageton, 1985). In another study (Robins and Wish, 1977), the median age of initiation for serious alcohol problems and barbiturate and amphetamine use (16.3

years) was later than the median age at initiation for juvenile arrests (15.2 years). Studies of drug addicts, which show that a history of criminal behavior preceded addiction, also appear to support this view (see Wish and Johnson, Volume II; Robins, 1979; Friedman and Friedman, cited in Kaplan, 1983).

Employment

The relationship between unemployment and participation in criminal activity has been a source of considerable controversy. Presumably, a disorganized life-style is associated with both unstable employment and involvement in crime, but the specific causal relationships have not been fully explored (for one recent attempt, see Thornberry and Christensen, 1984). In a comprehensive review of 25 studies using aggregate data, Freeman (1982) concluded that there is no solid evidence that unemployment affects

TABLE 2-4   Temporal Order of Drug Use and Delinquency

Involvement in Drug Use and Delinquency	Percent of Total Sample (1976–1978)	
No drug use[a] and no delinquency[b]	46.0	
Drug use and no delinquency	26.5	
Alcohol		(18.6)
Alcohol and marijuana		(7.1)
Alcohol, marijuana, and other drugs		(0.6)
No drug use and delinquency	8.9	
Initial drug use *before* delinquency involvement	4.4	
Alcohol		(3.9)
Alcohol and marijuana		(0.5)
Alcohol, marijuana, and other drugs		(0.1)
Initial drug use *after* delinquency involvement	8.0	
Alcohol		(4.7)
Alcohol and marijuana		(2.1)
Alcohol, marijuana, and other drugs		(1.3)
Initial drug use and delinquency involvement occur in same year	3.7	
Alcohol		(1.6)
Alcohol and marijuana		(2.0)
Alcohol, marijuana, and other drugs		(0.1)
Other, not classifiable	4.3	

[a]Drug use is defined as use of the specific drug at least four times in the preceding year, or use of each drug at least four times for multiple drug use types.

[b]Delinquency involvement is defined as engaging in 12 or more self-reported delinquent offenses and at least 2 index offenses in the preceding year.

SOURCE: Elliott and Huizinga (1984:Table 9).

criminal behavior (see also Cantor and Land, 1985). However, the panel's review of research based on individual data did find some consistent patterns (see Visher and Roth, Appendix A).

In particular, the association of unemployment with criminal participation appears to be different for adults than for school-age youths, possibly because unemployment may have different mean-ings for the two age groups. Unemployed or erratically employed adults are more likely to be involved in criminal activity than those with stable employment, and in one study this relationship persisted even when controls were introduced for criminal history and drug use (Viscusi, 1983). An unstable work record at age 18 was also a significant predictor of a conviction record at age 21–24, even controlling for antisocial and delinquent behavior at earlier ages (Farrington, 1983a). In contrast, full-time employment appears to influence school-age youths adversely, with higher fractions of employed youths, especially at ages 15–17, than others currently participating in serious offenses (Elliott et al., 1983, 1985). Unfortunately, research on the effects of school-age employment is scarce, and some studies only report mean arrest data or seriousness measures, rather than participation rates.[17]

Taken together, analyses of unemployment and crime suggest that employment may inhibit criminal participation in adult years, while employment during adolescence may be associated with criminal activity, perhaps because it separates teenagers from parental supervision and gives them funds to buy drugs and alcohol. The research that shows different

[17]The studies reviewed by the panel vary in their measures of criminal behavior (e.g., active participation, cumulative participation to age 25), and the respondents in these studies range from a representative sample in the National Youth Survey (Elliott et al., 1983), to 2,000 young black men in three highly urban settings (Viscusi, 1983), to a study of 400 British youngsters followed for more than 15 years (Farrington, 1983a). The study by Viscusi used a broader definition of criminal activity than the others: respondents were asked whether they had participated in any of 10 specific criminal acts including the category "any other illegal activities" (1983:16). Three studies do not report participation rates by employment status (Bachman, O'Malley, and Johnston, 1978; Shannon, 1982a; Thornberry and Christensen, 1984), but their results are consistent with the findings discussed in the text.

directions of effects at different ages highlights the necessity of partitioning the population under study into separate groups within which observable factors have consistent theoretical meanings. Unless such partitioning is done, the underlying relationships may be masked by confounding effects. This possibility is particularly relevant to the relationship between employment and criminal behavior, and it may also have an impact on other factors associated with participation.

Peer Group Influences

Involvement with delinquent friends is widely believed to be positively related to juvenile criminal behavior. Indeed, this concept lies at the heart of one major theory of delinquency, differential association theory (Sutherland and Cressey, 1978). Several longitudinal studies report that association with delinquent friends is clearly related to participation in serious criminal behavior at later ages (Farrington, 1983a; Polk et al., 1981). In Farrington's British study, 59 percent of males who had extensive involvement with delinquent friends at age 14 had a conviction record at age 25, in comparison with only 25 percent of other children.

Unfortunately, few empirical tests of differential association theory present data on participation in serious criminal activity and negative peer influences. Many studies examine marijuana and drug use because these activities are often tied to peer contacts (e.g., Burkett and Jensen, 1975; Kandel, 1978; Akers et al., 1979), or focus on a delinquent population and their peer contacts (see especially, Reiss, Volume II; Hindelang, 1976; Morash, 1984). Other research has used multivariate modeling techniques. While some of these studies report significant direct effects of negative peer influences on delinquency (e.g., Jensen, 1972; Matsueda, 1982; Elliott, Huizinga, and Ageton, 1985), the delinquency measure is usually a composite index of minor and moderately serious behaviors (but see Johnstone, 1978).

Analyses of peer influences and criminal behavior indicate that involvement with many delinquent friends is a significant risk factor for participation in delinquency. These results are consistent across a wide variety of samples, measures of delinquency and peer influences, and estimation techniques. Some recent research (e.g., Matsueda, 1982; Elliott, Huizinga, and Ageton, 1985) is attempting to sort out the underlying causal relationships, including the possible mediating effects of parental supervision and attachment, involvement in conventional activities, and exposure to conventional attitudes.

SUMMARY

Perhaps the most striking observation about participation is the high rate at which males ever become involved in crime and even in arrest. Typically, about 15 percent of urban males are arrested for an index offense by age 18 and about 25 to 35 percent will be arrested for such an offense sometime in their lifetime. Demographic differences in participation, as measured by arrest, are large, most strikingly between the sexes and less so between the races.

The differences in participation among demographic groups vary considerably with offense seriousness. When the definition of criminal behavior is broadly defined, participation is widespread in all demographic groups and so relative differences in participation are small. For serious offenses, for which the base rates of participation are low, the demographic differences are considerably larger. This interaction of demographic variables with changes in the scope of criminal participation resolves only part of the discrepancy between some self-report studies (which indicate small and inconsistent black/white differences in "offending" when the offense threshold is extremely low) and official-record data for serious offenses, which show large differences between blacks and whites.

Of more theoretical and policy significance is the fact that research on other factors associated with participation in serious offending consistently points to the same variables that have long been associated with crime: ineffective parenting, poor school performance, low measured IQ, drug use, and parental criminal-

ity. It is extremely difficult, however, to develop reliable measures of the *relative* influence of each of these variables, largely because of the complexity of the underlying relationships among them and because different studies highlight only one or a few of the variables rather than all of them.

The factors that distinguish participants from nonparticipants could well be different from the factors that distinguish among participants, in terms of their offending frequency. The next chapter considers estimates of frequency and the factors associated with variation in frequency.

3

Dimensions of
Active Criminal Careers

Participation in criminal activity is obviously restricted to a subset of the population. For the subset who do become offenders, our focus turns to the frequency, seriousness, and duration of their criminal careers. This chapter provides some empirical estimates of those dimensions of active criminal careers and also examines some factors that may be associated with active offending, such as age of initiation, drug use, and employment history.

INDIVIDUAL FREQUENCY RATES

Individual offending frequencies are a fundamental feature of the criminal career. The offense rate for individual offenders, λ, reflects the frequency, or intensity, of offending by individuals who are actively engaging in crime (i.e., active offenders). Despite the importance of λ, research that statistically characterizes the intensity of offending for large numbers of offenders is relatively recent. Short of having offenders maintain daily logs of their criminal activity, two main approaches are available to measure fre-

quency rates for active offenders: retrospective self-reports of prior criminal activity and officially recorded arrest histories. Each approach has its own limitations and sources of error. The main problems with self-reports stem from selection biases in the subsample of offenders who are willing to provide self-reports and errors in responses arising from erroneous recall or intentional misrepresentation. The main problem in using official arrest records—aside from errors in the records themselves—is that arrests typically occur for only a small number of the crimes that are committed. The limitations of each approach require that various assumptions, albeit different ones, be made in order to draw inferences about individual crime rates from the available data. Because of the basic difference in the sources of error, however, the two approaches can serve as important tests and cross-validations for each other.

Two sources provide explicit estimates of individual offense rates for active offenders: self-report estimates developed at the Rand Corporation, and official-record estimates developed at Carnegie-Mellon University. Both estimates of λ are limited to samples of adult males who have committed serious offenses.

The Rand Corporation estimates are based on surveys of male inmates serving sentences in state prisons (Peterson and Braiker, 1980; Chaiken and Chaiken, 1982a), and the most recent survey also includes inmates serving sentences in local jails. The samples are thus restricted to offenders whose current offense or prior criminal record are serious enough to have warranted incarceration. The frequency estimates are based on inmate self-reports of counts of crimes they committed in an observation period preceding the current incarceration.

The Carnegie-Mellon studies using official arrest records are based on samples of adult arrestees selected because they had at least one arrest for an index offense (other than larceny) during the years sampled. Arrest frequency estimates are developed from the history of arrests recorded prior to the arrest leading to their selection. This design excludes offenders who engage exclusively in minor offenses. While females are not explicitly excluded, the arrestee samples are composed predominantly of adult males.

In addition to total rates, crime-specific frequencies can be estimated for specific offense types. In computing the mean frequency for a given crime type during any observation period, only "active" offenders—those who commit at least one offense or experience one arrest for that crime type—are included in the calculations. Therefore, mean frequencies differ from "incidence rates," which relate the total number of crimes to the size of the entire sample, including those with no crimes of that type.

The Rand and Carnegie-Mellon studies are different from the much larger body of research on participation in offending, which is based on self-reports or official records of offending or of deviance for juveniles sampled from a general population. Results from that body of research are therefore dominated by common minor offenses such as vandalism and simple assault. This difference in design reflects the different focus of the studies, in one case on the scope of deviance found in a broad population, and in the other case on the intensity of serious offending by more continuously active adult offenders. By focusing on subsets of offenders who are active in serious offense types, these studies can yield frequency estimates for serious offenses.

In addition to focusing on active offenders, the studies also restrict the calculation of λ to periods when offenders are at risk of committing offenses in the community. The time that an offender is incapacitated through incarceration or long-term hospitalization (e.g., more than a 1-month stay) is excluded from the time at risk. The resulting estimates of λ reflect the frequency of offending that occurs while an offender is criminally active in the community. It is the rate of offending that would be expected if the offender were not incarcerated.

While not reporting explicit estimates of frequency rates for active offenders, a number of other studies do report estimates of population incidence rates measured by offenses per capita (Wolfgang, Figlio, and Sellin, 1972; Elliott et al., 1983; Farrington, 1983b, 1984). These incidence rates reflect the frequency of offenses (or arrests) in a total population at risk of offending, while λ is calculated for active offenders only. Such reported incidence rates reflect the combined effects of participation in crime in a population and individual frequency rates for active offenders. An incidence rate measured by crimes per capita in a total sample can be partitioned between participation rates and frequency rates:

$$\text{Incidence rate } (C) = \frac{\text{Total number of crimes committed by sample}}{\text{Total number of persons in sample}}$$

$$= \frac{\text{Number of persons who commit crimes in sample}}{\text{Total number of persons in sample}}$$

$$\times \frac{\text{Total number of crimes committed by sample}}{\text{Number of persons who commit crimes in sample}}$$

$$= \text{Current participation rate } (d)$$
$$\times \text{Mean individual frequency rate } (\lambda)$$

This partition indicates that the commonly reported incidence rates, when combined with estimates of participation rates, can be used to develop estimates of individual frequency rates. The general strategy is to divide incidence rates by participation rates for the same measurement period to yield frequency rates for the active subset in the population. With this approach, frequency rates can be estimated for a broader range of offender samples, including juveniles. However, these estimates of frequency are inflated by the requirement of at least one event (offense or arrest) during the measurement period reflected in current participation rates, but adjustments for this upward bias are possible (see Cohen, Appendix B).[1] Also, values of λ estimated

from incidence rates typically do not distinguish between time incarcerated and time at risk of offending in the community, and so they understate frequency rates while offenders are free in the community. For the samples of juveniles that are the basis for most available incidence rate estimates, however, these underestimates are likely to be small because incarceration is infrequent, and when it occurs, the length of time served is usually shorter than found among adults.

Arrest Frequencies (μ) by Crime Type

The Carnegie-Mellon estimates of mean individual arrest frequencies for active adult offenders (μ) have been obtained directly from longitudinal official-record data (Blumstein and Cohen, 1979; Cohen, 1981). The analysis included only offenders whose first arrest as an adult occurred before age 21 and who had a subsequent arrest in the sampling period 7–10 years later. Arrest frequencies were estimated for the period between the two required arrests. This requirement of an arrest prior to and another arrest following the estimation period was intended to limit the analysis to arrestees who—with reasonable certainty—were active in criminal careers during the estimation period. Since inclusion of the required arrests would lead to artifactually inflating the estimate of μ, the required arrests were excluded from the analysis. Furthermore, when calculating arrest frequencies for any particular offense type, say, robbery, only offenders in the sample with at least one arrest for robbery are included.[2]

[1]Estimates obtained directly from data in the Rand and Carnegie-Mellon studies (Blumstein and Cohen, 1979; Peterson and Braiker, 1980; Chaiken and Chaiken, 1982a; Cohen, 1983) are also vulnerable to this upward bias: to be considered active in an offense type, offenders must have at least one event for that offense type. In the Carnegie-Mellon studies, this arrest may occur any time in a career; in the Rand studies the criterion event must occur within the observation period prior to the current incarceration. As indicated in Cohen (Appendix B), however, this upward bias is small when the length of time during which the required event may occur is long—as in the Carnegie-Mellon studies, or when frequency rates are high—as in the Rand studies.

[2]Since the required one arrest for an offense type may occur during the estimation period, the resulting crime-specific frequency estimates may be inflated somewhat. To have restricted the required arrest for each offense type to the bounding periods before and after the estimation period would have

TABLE 3-1 Mean Individual Arrests Rates from Official Arrest Histories (arrests per offender per year free)

	Mean Individual Arrest Rates (μ)			
Offense Type	Washington, D.C., Adults[a]	Detroit SMSA Adults[a]	Philadelphia Juveniles[b]	Brooklyn (New York City) Adults[c]
Robbery	.23	.20	.23	
Aggravated assault	.19	.18	.13 (violent	
Burglary	.26	.20	index)[b]	
Larceny	.27	.22	.41 (property	
Auto theft	.14	.14	index)[b]	
Index	.59[d]	.33		
Total (any type excluding traffic)	1.07[d]	.56	.84	1.2

NOTE: Reported arrest rates are based on samples of 100–300 active offenders per offense type, except for violent index offenses and robbery for Philadelphia juveniles, for which the samples number 49 and 29 active offenders, respectively.

[a]Arrest rates were estimated by offense type only for offenders with at least one arrest for an offense type some time during their arrest histories. Only arrests prior to the sampling years and after the first arrest were considered. When computing μ for 1973 arrestees in Washington, D.C., only the most serious charge was considered (Blumstein and Cohen, 1979); for 1974 to 1977 arrestees in the Detroit SMSA, all charges recorded for an arrest were counted (Cohen, 1981). This will inflate μ for individual offense types in Detroit somewhat relative to those estimated for Washington, D.C.

[b]Derived for the panel by Cohen (Appendix B) from data on juvenile arrest histories of males born in 1945 and residing in Philadelphia between ages 10 and 18 (Wolfgang, Figlio, and Sellin, 1972). Rates are not adjusted for time served and are thus not rates while free. Violent index offenses include murder, rape, aggravated assault; property offenses include burglary, larceny, and auto theft.

[c]Derived for the panel by Cohen (Appendix B) from data on the adult (16 or older) arrest histories of adults arrested in Brooklyn in 1979 (McGahey, 1982).

[d]Arrests for murder and rape are excluded from computation of individual index arrest rates in Washington, D. C.; in 1973 those crimes accounted for 7.3 percent of all adult arrests for index offenses. The reported rates in Washington, D.C., are simple averages of "index" rates and total rates found for the five offender types with at least one index arrest (i.e., robbers, aggravated assaulters, burglars, larcenists, and auto thieves).

The mean arrest rates for adult arrestees in their 20s between 1966 and 1973 in Washington, D.C., and in the Detroit Standard Metropolitan Statistical Area (SMSA) are reported in Table 3-1. The lowest values of μ are found for auto theft and aggravated assault, with active offenders in these offense types averaging about one arrest every 5 to 7 years. In Washington, active offenders in robbery and burglary experience about one arrest

so limited the sample sizes that estimating frequency rates would have been impractical. Furthermore, since the measurement period in which the required arrest may occur is long (ranging from 7 to 10 years), the upward bias will be very small.

for these offense types every 4 years; Detroit arrests for these same offense types occur about once every 5 years.

Individual arrest rates for active offenders are generally higher in Washington than in the Detroit SMSA. Including all crime types, adult arrestees in Washington experience just over 1 arrest per year, while the average for adult arrestees in Detroit is half that rate, only .56 arrest per year. A similar difference is found for index offenses: arrestees in Washington experience an average of .59 index arrest per year compared with only .33 index arrest per year for Detroit arrestees.

Very similar estimates of μ were obtained in an analysis by Cohen (Appendix

B) of the arrest histories of active juvenile offenders in a 1945 birth cohort of boys in Philadelphia (Wolfgang, Figlio, and Sellin, 1972). On the basis of reported incidence and participation rates, active male juvenile offenders are arrested at average annual frequencies of .23 for robbery, .13 for the other violent index offenses (murder, rape, and aggravated assault), and .41 for property index offenses (burglary, larceny, and auto theft). Active offenders among Philadelphia juveniles experience an average of .84 arrest per year. In another estimate from incidence and participation rates (Cohen, Appendix B), active offenders in a sample of adult arrestees in Brooklyn, New York (McGahey, 1982), are arrested for all offense types at a mean annual rate of 1.2 per year free.

The accuracy of the estimates of μ, especially in comparisons across jurisdictions, depends in large part on the completeness of the arrest history data. As indicated in Cohen (Appendix B), nonrecording rates vary substantially across jurisdictions: in the Detroit SMSA, less than half of all arrests reported in local police statistics are recorded in the arrest history data, while in Washington, D.C., recording in arrest histories is almost complete.[3]

The failure to record large numbers of arrests leads to two countervailing biases: an undercount of total arrests, which biases estimates of μ downward, and an undercount of low-rate active offenders, which biases estimates of μ upward (see Cohen, Appendix B). The accuracy of arrest frequency estimates thus depends on the relative strengths of the two biases. Incompleteness of the arrest history data

could be a factor contributing to the lower values of μ estimated for arrestees in the Detroit SMSA than for Washington, D.C., arrestees, especially for less serious offense types, which are more likely to be subject to greater discretion in terms of being recorded in the central repository.

Offending Frequencies (λ) by Crime Type

This section discusses estimates of λ that have been obtained in either of two ways: by adjusting estimates of μ to infer λ, using aggregate arrest probabilities, or by surveying samples of offenders to obtain self-reports of their offending frequencies.

Inferring λ from μ

Individual arrest rate estimates like those in Table 3-1 can be used in combination with assumptions about the arrest process to generate estimates of individual frequency rates for crimes committed. Assuming that the individual crime rate (λ) is independent of the probability of arrest for a crime (q), the individual arrest rate (μ) is just the product of the individual crime rate and the risk of arrest per crime, $\mu = \lambda q$. Therefore, some estimate of the probability of arrest for a crime is needed to estimate λ.

Assuming that all offenders face the same arrest risk, the probability of arrest per crime can be estimated using aggregate data: the needed probability is basically the ratio of the number of reported arrests for an offense type (A) divided by the number of reported crimes (C). The number of reported crimes, however, must be adjusted by the fraction of crimes reported to the police (r) to account for unreported crimes. Also, because many crimes are committed in groups, the number of arrests must be divided by the average number of offenders per criminal

---

[3]A major factor in the low recording rates for the Detroit SMSA is a policy in the city of Detroit to only forward arrest reports with known dispositions. However, this nonrecording of many arrests in Detroit does not affect the estimates of q, which are based on aggregate statistics.

TABLE 3-2 Estimates of Arrest Risk per Crime (q) by Offense

Offense Type	Estimates of q from Aggregate Data		Estimates of q from Self-Reports	
	Washington, D.C.[a]	Detroit SMSA[a]	California[b]	California, Michigan, and Texas Combined[c]
Robbery	.069	.043	.21 (armed robbery)	.21 (business) .16 (personal)
Aggravated assault	.111	.062	.10	.24
Burglary	.049	.038	.07	.06
Larceny	.026	.030		.02 (theft)
Auto theft	.047	.015		.11

[a]Probability of arrest per crime is estimated from aggregate data on reported arrests (A), reported crimes (C), the rate of victims reporting crimes to the police (r), and the average number of offenders per crime incident (O) (Blumstein and Cohen, 1979; Cohen, 1981). A, C, and r are based on data available from local police statistics and from victimization survey data for Washington, D.C., and the State of Michigan; O is estimated from national victimization data available in Reiss (1980a).

[b]The probability of arrest per crime is estimated from the ratio of self-reported arrests to self-reported crimes in a survey of inmates of California prisons in 1976. The estimates from inmates are weighted to reflect the estimated average probability of arrest per crime faced by street offenders (Peterson and Braiker, 1980:Table 2, 236–237).

[c]The probability of arrest per crime is estimated from the ratio of self-reported arrests to self-reported crimes in a survey of state prison inmates in California, Michigan, and Texas in 1978. The estimates reflect the arrest risk per crime faced by an incoming cohort of state prison inmates for respondents in the three states combined (Petersilia, 1983:Table 4.4).

event, O. The final estimate of the probability of arrest per crime of type i (as proposed by Blumstein and Cohen, 1979) is given by

$$q_i = \frac{A_i/O_i}{C_i/r_i}.$$

Table 3-2 presents estimates of the arrest risk per crime (q) derived from aggregate data in Washington, D.C., and the Detroit SMSA. The probability of arrest per crime is highest for aggravated assault in both jurisdictions, at about 1 arrest for every 10 to 20 offenses committed, or more than 5 percent; the risk of arrest for other offense types is generally less than 5 percent. The arrest probability is also generally higher in Washington than in Detroit. This higher arrest risk per crime in Washington contributes to the higher individual arrest rates found in that city (Table 3-1).

Alternative estimates of q from self-

reported arrests and self-reported crimes by inmates are also presented in Table 3-2. With the exception of larceny (theft), the arrest risk estimated from the inmate self-reports is somewhat higher than that from aggregate data. In part, this difference reflects the nature of the offenses surveyed: armed robbery and serious assaults were more likely to involve identifications by victims that would increase the risk of arrest for these crimes. Also, the arrest risk may have been inflated by the exclusion of individuals who reported no arrests (see Peterson and Braiker, 1980:237).

Table 3-3 presents individual offending frequencies estimated from arrest frequencies for adults. For most offense types, the individual frequency rates estimated in Washington and Detroit are comparable in magnitude, with mean individual rates of 3.5 to 4.5 robberies, 2 to 3 aggravated assaults, and 5 to 6 burglaries. The largest difference in λ between the two jurisdictions is found for auto theft, with a mean rate of only 3 auto thefts committed per year free by offenders in Washington compared with more than 9 by offenders in Detroit. Total frequency rates are lower in Detroit than in Washington: active adult offenders are estimated to commit from 9 to 13 index offenses per year free in the two jurisdictions.

The accuracy of these estimates of λ derived from official arrest histories depends fundamentally on the adequacy of estimates of the arrest risk per crime, q. In addition to concern about the accuracy of the average value of q that is used, the

TABLE 3-3 Mean Individual Offending Frequencies Estimated from Arrest Histories for Adult Arrestees (crimes committed per active offender per year free)

	Mean Individual Offending Frequencies, λ	
Offense Type	Washington, D.C., Adults[a]	Detroit SMSA Adults[b]
Robbery	3.4	4.7
Aggravated assault	1.7	2.9
Burglary	5.7	5.3
Larceny	10.9	7.3
Auto theft	3.0	9.3
All index	13.2	8.7

NOTES: Sample sizes for specific offense types range from 100 to 300 active offenders.

In computing λ for all index offenses, the arrest probabilities for individual offense types are weighted by the distribution of offense types found in the aggregate. Murder and rape are excluded from the computation of rates in Washington, D.C.; in 1973 those offenses accounted for 7.3 percent of all adult arrests for index offenses. The Washington, D.C., index rate reported here is a simple average of index rates computed for each of the five offender types with at least one index arrest (i.e., robbers, aggravated assaulters, burglars, larcenists, and auto thieves).

[a]Estimates from Blumstein and Cohen (1979).
[b]Derived from data of Cohen (1981, 1983).

estimates of λ may also be distorted by failure to adequately address variation in q among offenders. Even after controlling for offense type, this heterogeneity in q is especially problematic if λ and q for an offense are systematically related to one another. If λ and q are negatively related, with high-rate offenders less likely to be arrested for each crime, use of a single, homogeneous value of q for all offenders will result in an underestimate of λ. Correspondingly, if λ and q are positively related, λ will be overestimated. Such relationships might arise directly because the same offenders are skillful both at committing crimes and avoiding detection (a negative relationship) or because of police practices that target apprehension efforts at high-rate offenders (a positive relationship). Alternatively, λ and q might be related indirectly because they both vary systematically with other offender attributes. If λ and q are related, the failure to adequately control for variations in q will confound individual differences in λ with differential police practices reflected in q. While knowledge about the variation in q and its relationship to λ is crucial to developing improved estimates of λ from arrest histories, available results suggest that estimates of the average value of λ derived by assuming λ and q to be independent are not likely to be seriously in error.

The Rand Inmate Surveys

Two surveys of sentenced prisoners (in 1976 and in 1978) provide estimates of individual crime rates for active adult male offenders (Peterson and Braiker, 1980; Chaiken and Chaiken, 1982a). The estimated rates are based on self-reports of the number of offenses committed during an observation period prior to the start of the current incarceration. The most striking feature of these estimated frequency rates is the highly skewed distribution of rates across individuals. Figure 3-1 presents the distribution for robbery only, but it is illustrative of the distribution of frequency rates found for other offenses. The distribution is characterized by a large number of offenders committing offenses at low rates and a small number committing offenses at very high rates. In this example, among incoming prisoners who commit robbery (i.e., in-

mates who report at least one robbery during the 1 to 2 years prior to incarceration), the mean frequency rate per offender is 43.4 robberies committed per year of street time. Half of these offenders, however, committed fewer than 4 robberies each per year free, while about 5 percent committed more than 180 robberies per year free. A distinguishing feature of these skewed distributions is that

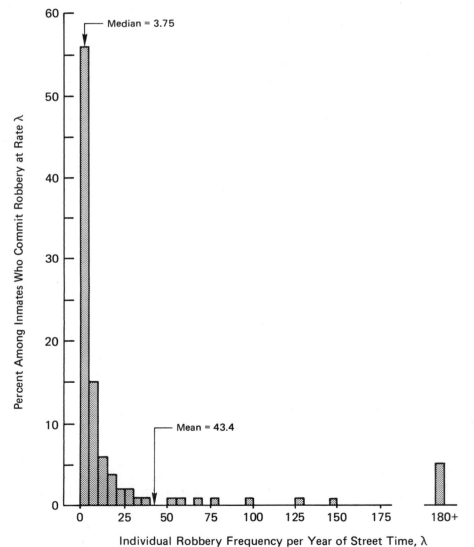

FIGURE 3-1 Distribution of robbery frequency among incoming inmates. Source: Derived from data in Visher (Volume II) reanalysis of Rand inmate survey data.

TABLE 3-4 Mean Individual Frequency Rates (λ) from Surveys of California Prison Inmates (offenses committed per person per year free)

Offense Type	First Inmate Survey, 1976[a] Resident Prisoners	Second Inmate Survey, 1978			
		Incoming Prisoners (Min-Max)[b]	Visher Reanalysis[c]	Chaiken/ Rolph Reanalysis[d]	Adjusted Rates[e]
Robbery	5.2	49–74	42.4	38.9	21.8
Assault		7.1–7.6	N.A.	7.5	N.A.
Shot/cut	2.0				
Threatened	3.2				
Aggravated	2.8				
Burglary	14.2	116–204	98.8	114.6	44.6
Motor vehicle theft	3.9	38–102	N.A.	28.7	N.A.
Forgery	4.9	62–94	N.A.	52.5	N.A.
Fraud	11.4	156–202	N.A.	48.1	N.A.
Drug deals	115.0	927–1681	N.A.	849.9	N.A.

NOTE: Sample sizes for specific offense types are generally in the range of 100–350 active offenders, except for fraud and motor vehicle theft in the second inmate survey of incoming prisoners, with 69 and 87 active offenders, respectively. In general, the offense type categories in the second survey were more inclusive than those in the first survey (except assault). For example, the first survey includes only armed robberies; the second survey includes all robberies.

[a]The first inmate sample was drawn randomly from the resident population at five California prisons (Peterson and Braiker, 1980:Table 10a).

[b]The second inmate sample was drawn to reflect cohorts of incoming prison and jail inmates in three states: California, Michigan, and Texas. Minimums and maximums for the mean frequency rates were estimated. These rates for California prison inmates are reported as a range in the table; from Chaiken and Chaiken (1982a:Tables A3–A14).

[c]The original data from the second inmate survey were reanalyzed for the panel as described in Visher (Volume II). The rates reported from this reanalysis include both prison and jail inmates in California; the rates for prisoners alone will be slightly higher.

[d]The rates are adjusted downward to reflect the offender's frequency averaged over spurts in activity and quiescent periods; from Chaiken and Rolph (1985:Appendix).

[e]Using the Visher estimates, high estimates of λ are truncated at the 90th percentile value before calculating the final adjusted means.

most offenders committed crimes at rates well below the mean.

The original frequency rates from the two surveys of inmates published by the Rand Corporation differ substantially in magnitude, with much higher values of λ estimated from the second inmate survey. Table 3-4 compares various estimates of mean frequency rates for selected offense types. Except for assault—the only offense that is not defined more broadly in the second survey—even the minimum mean rates estimated in the second survey are at least seven times higher than the mean rates for incoming prisoners estimated in the first survey. Many factors contribute to the substantial differences between the rates reported from the two surveys. For various methodological reasons—discussed in detail in Cohen (Appendix B) and summarized here—there is reason to believe that the originally published estimates from the second survey are inflated, while the rates from the first survey are underestimated.

The principal differences between the surveys relate to the length of the observation periods and the response formats used to elicit counts of the number of crimes committed during that observation period. In the first survey, the observation period was the 3 years preceding the current incarceration. In the second survey, the observation period ranged from 1 to 2 years depending on when in the calendar year the arrest leading to the current incarceration occurred: the later in the calendar year, the longer the available observation period preceding that arrest. The longer observation period in the first survey could contribute to underestimates of λ if memory recall problems led to greater underreporting of offenses in the more distant and longer observation period and if the time that offenders were active in an offense type was overestimated by a failure to account for possible initiation and termination of careers sometime during the longer observation period. Imprecision in the frequency response categories in the first survey, especially for high frequencies, could also contribute to underestimates.

Other factors could lead to possible overestimates of λ in the second survey. By directly requesting a respondent's own estimate of usual frequency rates, the question eliciting counts of crimes committed on the second survey is intended to provide greater precision for high rates of offending. The increased complexity of the rate response items—which required separate responses on (1) the most appropriate time interval for gauging their offending frequencies (e.g., monthly, weekly, or daily); (2) the number of crimes committed during that time period; (3) the number of months in which crimes were committed at this usual rate; and (4) total months free during the observation period—greatly increased respondent problems in answering these items. The resulting 35 to 40 percent ambiguous responses were likely to have been a factor in the computation

of minimum and maximum rates for each respondent in the original analysis of the second inmate survey. In a reanalysis of the survey data, Visher (Volume II) adopts an alternative to the extreme values represented by the minimum and maximum estimates: in cases with ambiguous responses, she relies on information available in the responses of unambiguous respondents to develop a single estimate for each respondent. As indicated in Table 3-4, Visher's estimates are close to Rand's minimum estimates for the second survey.

However, even Rand's minimum estimates and the alternative Visher estimates from the second survey are much higher than the estimates from the first survey. Certain structural features of response items, especially reliance on crime counts in small time intervals (e.g., monthly, weekly, or daily counts), could lead to overestimates of λ. When offending is irregular over the entire observation period with periods of high levels of activity interspersed with periods of low levels of activity, applying frequencies found in short high-activity periods to the entire observation period will overstate the frequency rate. In a reanalysis of the data from the second inmate survey, Chaiken and Rolph (1985) found evidence of such spurts in offending, with periods of high activity clustered just prior to the current incarceration. Respondents with short street times are thus especially vulnerable to overestimates since their observation periods are more likely to be limited to periods of spurts in activity. To account for these spurts in activity, the estimated rates were adjusted downward to reflect an estimate of an offender's frequency averaged over active and quiescent periods. As indicated in Table 3-4, this adjustment reduces the original minimum frequency by as much as 25 percent for some offense types; only burglary and assault are unaffected by the adjustment for short-term spurts in activity.

Even with the adjustment for spurts, a few individuals are estimated to commit crimes at very high rates—averaging one or more crimes every day. The mean frequency is very sensitive to these few very high-rate offenders, and thus vulnerable to serious overestimates arising from errors in the estimated rates for those offenders. To reduce the impact of the high-rate offenders, the mean λ can be reestimated by identifying a maximum limiting value of λ and assigning that value to all offenders whose estimated rates exceed it. Cohen (Appendix B: Table 16) uses the Visher estimates to illustrate the changes in mean value of λ when different upper limits are used: using the 90th percentile as a limit for robbery, for example, the maximum value of λ is 71.3 robberies for the three states combined. The 10 percent of active robbers with individual rates above that limit each commit an estimated average of 346.3 robberies per year. When the 90th percentile value of 71.3 is assigned to the high-rate robbers, the mean λ decreases from 43.4 to 14.3 per year. When the 90th percentile is used for burglary, the mean λ is similarly reduced by more than half, from 79.0 to 36.7 per year. A similar procedure was used to estimate the adjusted rates for California prison inmates that appear in Table 3-4.

The maximum limit adjustments to the estimates from the second survey reduce the mean frequency rates to values that are much closer to those estimated from the first survey. For incoming inmates, the mean rates for the various offense types (other than drugs and burglary) most likely fall in the range of 5 to 15 offenses committed per active offender per year free. The lower rates in this range are characteristic of violent crimes,

and the higher rates are characteristic of property crimes. The rates for burglary are even higher: between 15 and 40 burglaries per active offender per year free.

National Youth Survey

Individual offense frequencies are also estimated from self-reported offenses in the annual National Youth Survey. Incidence rates (offenses per capita) are combined with current participation rates (offenders per capita) reported by Elliott et al. (1983) to yield estimated offending frequencies for active offenders (see discussion by Cohen in Appendix B). Annual incidence rates for male youths are between .5 and 1.0 for serious offense types, while annual participation rates are between 5 and 20 percent over the 5 years of the annual survey. When estimates are restricted to male youths who are active, mean annual frequencies by offense type are 4.4 felony assaults, 8.4 robberies, and 7.1 felony thefts committed per year per active offender. Youthful male offenders who are active in index offenses are estimated to commit an average total of 7.6 index offenses per year.[4]

Estimates of λ

As shown in Table 3-5, there is reasonable convergence among various estimates of λ that are derived by applying different estimation techniques to data from different jurisdictions and with different offender attributes. The frequencies derived from the arrest histories of

---

[4]These rates are adjusted to remove the upward bias introduced by the requirement that all active offenders commit at least one crime of an offense type during the 1-year observation periods. The rates do not account for any time served by active offenders. However, if the amount of time served by youthful offenders is small, the underestimates of λ will also be small.

TABLE 3-5 Alternative Estimates of λ by Offense Type (crimes committed per active offender per year free)

Offense Type	Self-Reports of Incoming Inmates to Prison and Jail[a]			Arrest Histories of Adult Arrestees[b]		Self-Reports of U.S. Youths[c]
	California	Michigan	Texas	Washington	Detroit	
Robbery	21.8	15.8	4.8	3.4	4.7	8.4
Burglary	44.6	50.3	14.9	5.7	5.3	
Larceny	N.A.	N.A.	N.A.	10.9	7.3	7.1[d]
Auto theft	N.A.	N.A.	N.A.	3.0	9.3	
Aggravated assault	N.A.	N.A.	N.A.	1.7	2.9	4.4[e]

NOTE: Sample sizes for specific offense types number from 100 to 325 active offenders. The one exception is for robbery among U.S. youths, with an annual average of 59 active offenders.

[a]Mean rates based on estimates by Visher (Volume II) using the original data from the second Rand inmate survey (Chaiken and Chaiken, 1982a); means have been adjusted downward by assigning the 90th percentile value of λ to all active offenders with estimated rates above that value.

[b]Mean rates inferred from individual arrest frequencies estimated from arrest history data for active offenders; see text. This offending frequency is obtained by dividing the mean individual arrest frequency by an estimate of the arrest risk per crime for each offense type (Blumstein and Cohen, 1979; Cohen, 1983).

[c]Offending frequencies derived from incidence rates (crimes per capita) and participation rates (active offenders per capita) reported for a national sample of youths (ages 11 to 21) in the United States by Elliott et al. (1983) (see Cohen, Appendix B).

[d]Felony theft, includes burglary, larceny (over $50), auto theft, and receiving stolen goods.

[e]Felony assault, includes aggravated assault, sexual assault, and gang fights.

adult arrestees and those derived from self-reports of youths in a general population sample are most similar. Active offenders in various offense types are estimated to commit an average of 2 to 4 serious assaults each year and an average of 5 to 10 of the various property offenses. The rates from the self-report data are slightly higher than those from arrest histories. This difference may reflect underestimates in the rates from arrest data, due to incomplete arrest histories, or it may reflect age differences in offending frequencies with slightly higher rates for younger offenders.

The frequencies estimated from self-reports by inmate samples are generally higher than those for offenders who are free in the community. For California and Michigan inmates who were active in robbery or burglary before being incarcerated, annual frequencies were estimated at 15 to 20 for robbery and 45 to 50 for burglary. These higher mean rates for

inmates would be expected if higher-rate offenders are more vulnerable to incarceration. Even if the arrest risk per crime does not vary systematically with λ, offenders who commit more crimes in a year would be expected to experience more arrests: if the arrest risk per crime averages 10 percent for all offenders, for example, an offender who commits 10 crimes each year will be arrested on average once every year, while an offender who commits only one crime each year will be arrested on average only once every 10 years. Each arrest exposes the offender to the risk of incarceration, and so increases the representation of more frequently arrested high-rate offenders among inmates. The overrepresentation of high-rate offenders among inmates will be even larger if there is any selectivity in offender processing that increases the risk of incarceration after arrest for high-rate offenders. On the other hand, if high-rate offenders have a particularly low arrest risk for each offense, their representation will be diminished.

The differences in average values of λ among inmates in different states (see Table 3-5) could reflect either cross-state differences in general offender populations, with higher frequencies in California and Michigan than in Texas, or differences in offender processing, with greater selectivity in directing incarceration at high-rate offenders in California and Michigan while imposing incarceration more broadly in Texas. Further research estimating λ for different population groups (e.g., offenders in and out of prison in the same jurisdiction) and using different estimation techniques on the same samples (e.g., using arrest data and self-report data for the same sample of offenders) is required to resolve the sources of any important differences in estimates of λ.

Until recently, estimates of λ were available only for offenders generally, with little attention to distinguishing among offenders by demographic and other attributes. With varying degrees of richness, information is available on characteristics of the offenders used to generate estimates of λ. These data provide an opportunity to explore some of the variations in the magnitude of λ across different offender attributes. Accumulating knowledge on the patterns of variation in frequency rates is essential for understanding the factors contributing to individual criminal activity, and it may be useful in developing more effective crime control policies.

Variations in λ by Sex, Age, and Race

Sex, age, and race data are routinely collected on arrestees, primarily for agency identification purposes. Therefore, even though the relationship of these variables to λ is theoretically ambiguous, λ is frequently contrasted across

demographic subgroups defined in these terms.

Sex

Large differences are found in participation rates for males and females, with 5:1 ratios of male/female participation for UCR index crimes. Because the numbers of female offenders are generally small, especially for serious offense types, separate frequency rates are rarely reported for females. However, some preliminary indications of sex differences in offending frequencies are available in two estimates of λ obtained from reported incidence and participation rates (see Cohen, Appendix B). Both estimates are based on self-reports of crimes committed in the preceding year, in one case by active heroin users (Inciardi, 1979) and in the other by a nationally representative sample of U.S. youths surveyed at ages 11–21 (Elliott et al., 1983).

As indicated in Table 3-6, offending frequencies for females who are active in a crime type are reasonably close to those for active males; the male/female ratios are generally less than 2:1. The one major exception is burglary by active heroin users, for which males report committing almost five times as many burglaries as females. Another sex difference that might be expected is for prostitution, an alternative economic opportunity for females. The large differences between males and females found in aggregate population arrest rates appear to arise predominantly from differences in participation. If active in a crime type, females commit that crime at rates similar to those of active males.

Age

Several studies provide preliminary evidence on the nature of changes over age in individual frequency rates for active

TABLE 3-6 Individual Offending Frequencies (λ) by Sex

Offense Type	Self-Reports by Active Heroin Users		Self-Reports of U.S. Youths	
	Male	Female	Male	Female
Robbery	29.7	28.7	8.4	3.3[a]
Assault	3.3	2.7[a]	4.4[b]	2.6[b]
Burglary	24.8	4.9		
Vehicle theft	7.4	2.2[a]		
Theft from vehicle	12.5	8.3	7.1[c]	4.4[c]
Shoplifting	68.2	63.1		
Other theft	12.0	7.6		
Forgery/counterfeiting	17.8	25.4		
Con games	17.8	12.6		
Drug sales	186.7	118.8		

NOTE: Frequency rates were derived by Cohen (Appendix B) from incidence and participation rates reported for 356 active heroin users in Inciardi (1979) and for a national probability sample of 1,725 U.S. youths surveyed at ages 11 to 21 (Elliott et al., 1983). Sample sizes for specific offenses range from 20 to 95 active offenders for females and from 49 to 219 active offenders for males.

[a]Based on fewer than 20 active offenders in the offense type and thus subject to considerable sampling variation in the estimates.

[b]Felony assault, includes aggravated assault, sexual assault, and gang fights.

[c]Felony theft, includes burglary, larceny (over $50), auto theft, and receiving stolen goods.

offenders. Whether based on estimates of individual arrest frequencies (μ) from official arrest histories or individual offending frequencies (λ) from self-reports, the data provide little evidence of strong systematic changes with age in offense-specific frequency rates for active offenders. The strong opposite trends observed during the juvenile and adult periods in aggregate population arrest rates—increasing for teenagers and decreasing for adults—are not observed in individual frequency rates estimated by offense type and age for cohorts of juveniles or adults.

Within cohorts of arrestees first arrested as adults in the same year and at approximately the same age, Blumstein and Cohen (1979:576) find no evidence of downward trends in crime-specific arrest frequencies for young adults. Indeed, for burglary and narcotics offenses, arrest frequencies appear to increase with age, at least through the late 20s. Further support for general stability over age of λ is found in the first self-report survey of California prison inmates. After controlling for individual offenses, Peterson and Braiker (1980:54) found that among their inmate sample, the mean values of λ for older offenders active in an offense type were the same as those of younger active offenders. Similarly, in the second inmate survey, Chaiken and Chaiken (1982a: 82–124, see especially p. 105) report that while age is often a factor in identifying the type of offender in this sample of inmates (as indicated by the mix of offense types in which he participates), it is rarely a factor in distinguishing crime-specific offending frequencies for an offender.

There is also a general absence of strong increases with age for crime-specific frequencies among juveniles and youths, especially for violent index offenses (Table 3-7). With the notable exception of robbery in Philadelphia and in the U.S. sample (and much less so, burglary in London), frequency rates for separate offense types are much flatter over age than are aggregate arrest rates or participation rates for the same offense types.

TABLE 3-7 Individual Frequency Rates by Age

A. Annual Arrest Frequencies for Philadelphia Juveniles[a]

Offense Type	Age				
	13	14	15	16	17
Robbery	.1	.1	.4*	.4	.2
UCR property	.5	.5	.4	.4	.3
UCR persons (excluding robbery)	—	.1	.1	.2	.1
Total (any type)	.6	.7	.9	.9	.8

B. Annual Conviction Frequencies for London Youths[b]

Offense Type	Age			
	10–13	14–16	17–20	21–24
Burglary	.4	.6	.5	.3
Taking vehicles	.3	.4	.4	.4
Stealing from vehicles	.3	.4	.3	.3
Shoplifting	.4	.5	.4	.5
Assault	.3	.3	.3	.3
Damage	.3	.3	.3	.3
Total (any type)	.5	.8	.8	.7

C. Annual Offending Frequencies for U.S. Youths[c]

Offense Type	Age							
	13	14	15	16	17	18	19	20
Robbery	6.3	5.4	15.3	6.7	6.5	5.6	5.2	3.7
Felony theft	3.6	6.5	6.2	4.5	8.7	6.3	8.8	7.2
Felony assault	4.0	3.4	5.5	3.3	3.4	3.7	6.6	5.5
Any index	6.0	5.6	10.0	5.2	7.1	5.3	7.9	7.1

[a]Frequencies were derived by Cohen (Appendix B) from arrest incidence and participation rates at each age for a cohort of boys born in 1945 and residing in Philadelphia from ages 10 to 18 (Wolfgang, Figlio, and Sellin, 1972). The rate marked with an asterisk is based on a sample of less than 20 active offenders. Otherwise, samples include 24 to 32 active offenders for robbery, 197 to 356 active offenders for UCR property offenses, and 25 to 80 active offenders for UCR person offenses.

[b]Frequencies are convictions for indictable offenses experienced by a sample of male youths residing as children in a center-city neighborhood of London. Since conviction risk after arrest is very high in England and Wales, conviction frequencies are close to arrest frequencies in this sample. The rates were derived from the ratio of incidence rates to participation rates in Farrington (1983b:Table C-4). No adjustment for the required one conviction in each age category is made. However, since the age categories are at least 3 years long, the reported rates are not likely to be seriously overstated (see Cohen, Appendix B). These rates are based on samples of less than 30 active offenders per age category; also, half of the crime-specific rates are based on sample sizes of less than 10 active offenders.

[c]Offending frequencies were derived by Cohen (Appendix B) from incidence and participation rates of self-reported crimes for a national sample of youths (Elliott et al., 1983). These rates are based on samples of fewer than 30 active offenders annually per age category; for robbery, the sample sizes often fall below 10 active offenders.

This absence of strong opposite age effects for juveniles and adults in crime-specific frequencies, however, is still a preliminary result because of the generally small samples of active offenders (sometimes less than 35) used to generate age-specific rates and because the available analyses do not yet extend past ages in the 20s for adults.

Some evidence of a more systematic age effect is found, however, when separate offense types are aggregated to form

TABLE 3-8 Variations in Offending
Frequencies by Age (from self-reports
by California prison inmates)

Age[a]	Intensity Scale Score[b]	Total Offense Score[c]	Number of Active Crime Types[d]
Under 21	1.44	.64	4.61
21–25	1.42	.57	4.09
26–30	1.44	.49	3.29
Over 30	1.33	.35	2.70

[a]Age at the midpoint of 3-year observation
period preceding the current incarceration.

[b]Each offense that a respondent reported committing was assigned a score indicating whether
the respondent's frequency in that offense type
was below the median (score 1) or above the
median (score 2). Scores for the separate *active*
offense types were then averaged to yield an
"intensity scale score" for a respondent. The average intensity score across respondents was then
computed.

[c]Each of the 11 offense types studied was assigned a score reflecting the respondent's level of
activity in that offense. If the respondent reported
that he never committed the offense, he was
assigned a score of 0 for that offense. Respondents
committing the offense at a frequency below the
median were assigned a score of 1 for that offense;
if their frequency was above the median, they
were assigned a score of 2. Offense scores were
averaged over the 11 offense types to yield a total
offense score for a respondent. The average total
offense score across respondents was then computed.

[d]This is the mean number of separate offense
types that respondents reported committing out of
11 different offenses studied.

SOURCE: Peterson and Braiker (1980:Tables
27–29).

larger offense categories. During the juvenile years, mean total frequencies exhibit some tendency to increase with age
through the late teens (Table 3-7). During the adult years, mean total frequencies are reported to decline with age
(Peterson and Braiker, 1980; Cohen,
1983). One intriguing hypothesis is that
these opposite trends in total frequencies
for active offenders may be associated
with an increase with age in the number

of different offense types committed by
juvenile offenders, followed by a decline
with age in offense types committed by
adults. Evidence for such an effect was
suggested in the first Rand inmate survey: the number of active crime types
declines with age, while crime-specific
frequencies (reflected in the "intensity
scale score") are stable over age (Table
3-8). In summary, preliminary evidence
suggests that while mean individual frequencies appear to be relatively stable
over age for most single offense types,
total frequencies—reflecting the combination of all offense types committed—
vary more with age, increasing during the
juvenile years and decreasing during the
adult years.

Race

The frequency rates of active white and
black offenders are strikingly similar. As
indicated in Table 3-9, the ratio of
black/white arrest frequencies for adult
offenders who are active in a crime type
in the Detroit SMSA are very close to 1:1
for most offense types. The largest differences are found in arrest frequencies for
robbery with a ratio of 1.7:1, and larceny
with a ratio of just over 2:1. The adult
black/white ratios based on self-reported
crimes by respondents to the first Rand
inmate survey are even smaller. Using
self-reports by inmates in three states
from the second Rand inmate survey,
Petersilia (1983:40–43) also finds little
difference between races in crime-specific offending frequencies for those who
were active in a crime type prior to their
incarcerations. Similarly for estimates
from juvenile offenders in Philadelphia
and a sample of U.S. youths, the ratios are
all under 2:1. In contrast to the pattern
observed in aggregate population rates
and in participation rates, race differences
in μ for active juvenile offenders are
smaller if one focuses on more serious

TABLE 3-9 Individual Frequency Rates by Race

Offense Type	Whites	Blacks	Ratio of Black/White Rates[a]
Arrests per Year per Active Offender, μ[b]			
Adult Offenders in			
Detroit SMSA			
Robbery	.13	.23	1.74
Aggravated assault	.18	.18	.97
Burglary	.18	.22	1.19
Larceny	.13	.29	2.13
Auto theft	.13	.15	1.15
All index[c]	.25	.39	1.54
Total (any type)	.55	.56	1.01
Juvenile Offenders in Philadelphia			
Robbery	.27*	.23	.84
Violent index[d]	.11	.14	1.32
Property index[e]	.34	.46	1.34
Non-index	.46	.79	1.72
Total (any type excluding traffic)	.59	1.08	1.84
Crimes Committed per Year per Active Offender, λ[f]			
Estimates for Adult Street			
Offenders in California			
Armed robbery	2.3	1.7	.74
Assault	2.7	2.1	.78
Burglary	12.4	2.7	.22
Auto theft	5.0	2.8	.56
Forgery	5.4	4.8	.89
Drug sales	108	121	1.12
Self-Reported Offenders			
Among U.S. Youths			
Robbery	9.6	4.6*	.48
Felony theft	5.8	7.4*	1.28
Felony assault	3.4	3.9	1.15
Any index	6.4	6.3	.98

NOTE: Rates denoted by an asterisk are based on fewer than 20 active offenders in the offense type. Sample sizes for other offense types number at least 35 active offenders and, in most cases, more than 75 active offenders.

[a]The ratios were computed before the frequencies were rounded to the two significant decimal places reported in this table.

[b]Individual arrest frequencies were estimated for separate offense types only for offenders with at least one arrest for an offense type. For adult offenders in the Detroit SMSA, arrests any time in their arrest history prior to the sampling years were considered (Cohen, 1981). Arrest frequencies for juvenile offenders in Philadelphia are based on a reanalysis of the data from Wolfgang, Figlio, and Sellin (1972). The raw frequency rates computed by dividing incidence rates by participation rates, and which require at least one arrest in a year, were adjusted to reduce the impact of this criterion event (see Cohen, Appendix B).

[c]Index offenses include murder, rape, robbery, aggravated assault, burglary, larceny, and auto theft.

[d]Violent index offenses include murder, rape, and aggravated assault.

[e]Property index offenses include burglary, larceny, and auto theft.

[f]Offending frequencies for adults are based on self-reported counts of crimes committed by respondents to the first Rand survey of inmates in California prisons. By use of a model reflecting the likelihood of being in prison for a crime, the inmate responses were reweighted to reflect frequency estimates for a sample of street offenders (Peterson and Braiker, 1980:Table 35). The offending frequencies for youths (ages 11 to 21) were derived for the panel by Cohen (Appendix B) from annual incidence and participation rates for 1976 to 1980 reported for a national sample of U.S. youths by Elliott et al. (1983).

offense types. This same trend is also found for λ on the basis of self-reports by juveniles.[5]

The most striking finding in the comparisons in Table 3-9 is the general similarity in frequency rates for active white and black offenders. The race differences in arrest frequencies, which are based on official-record data, do not come close to the ratios of 10:1, or even 5:1, in aggregate population arrest rates and official-record participation rates for robbery and violent index offenses. And the black/white ratios for λ based on self-reported crimes by active offenders are even lower than ratios based on arrest data.

The black/white ratio for frequency rates based on self-reports is always lower than that for participation rates based on self-reports. Indeed, the black/white ratios for λ often fall below 1:1. For robbery, for example, self-reported participation rates among black respondents are about twice those of white respondents, but self-reported frequency rates for black offenders are only one-half to three-quarters those for white offenders. Thus, the sometimes substantial race differences in criminal activity found in aggregate population rates appear to result primarily from differences between blacks and whites in participation: there are more active offenders in the black population, but, when considering only active offenders, frequency rates are very similar for whites and blacks.

Other Factors Associated with Variations in Frequency Rates

Other factors have been studied in relation to frequency rates. Though their theoretical significance is not always clear, these variables often offer insights for policy, especially as they provide a basis for identifying high-rate offenders.

Age at Onset of Criminal Activity

Aside from any changes in frequency rates as offenders get older, age at criminal career initiation is another variable that may distinguish among offenders. Numerous studies have reported higher recidivism rates among offenders who have records of early criminal activity as juveniles. Estimates of recidivism rates during a follow-up period reflect the combined contribution of the fraction of offenders who persist in criminal activity and their frequency rates. The lower recidivism rates for offenders who started criminal activity at older ages thus may result either from a greater tendency for those relatively late starters to terminate their criminal activity early or from lower frequency rates for active offenders who begin their criminal activity at older ages.

Figure 3-2 presents annual total frequency rates for all offenses estimated for offenders who begin criminal careers at different ages (as indicated by age at the first detected criminal event). These estimates of frequency rates were derived from incidence and participation rates and then adjusted to reduce the upward bias introduced by the requirement that offenders have at least one event (see Cohen, Appendix B). The estimates of arrest frequencies for Philadelphia male juveniles are based on annual incidence and participation rates at every age for offenders who start at the same age. (The estimates were provided by Wolfgang, Figlio, and Sellin, personal communica-

---

[5]This finding contrasts with the finding reported by Elliott and Ageton (1980) of significant differences in 1976 between whites and blacks in incidence rates, but not in participation rates, for total crimes and predatory crimes against property. The differences in incidence rates for 1976 are not reflected in similar differences in frequency rates when the 5 years of data from 1976 to 1980 are combined.

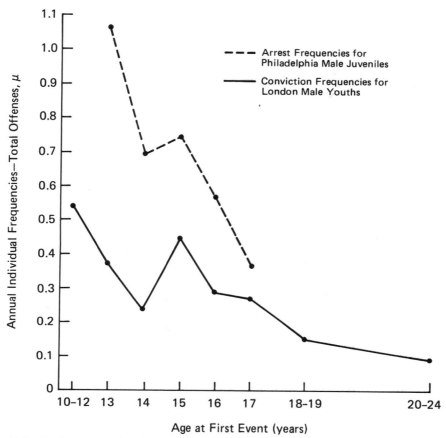

FIGURE 3-2 Annual individual frequency rates by age at first criminal event. Source: Frequency rates were derived by Cohen (Appendix B) from incidence and participation rates obtained from longitudinal data for Philadelphia males born in 1945 and residing in Philadelphia from ages 10 to 18 (Wolfgang, Figlio, and Sellin, 1972) and for a sample of London male youths aged 8 and 9 in 1961 and 1962 and residing in a center-city neighborhood of London (Farrington, 1983a).

tion.) Thus, only active offenders enter the estimates. The estimates of average conviction frequencies for London male youths are based on the total convictions per youth over the period between ages 10 and 24 for each starting age, as reported in Farrington (1983a:Table 3). The 19 offenders first convicted at age 14, for example, are reported to average a total of 2.82 convictions each from age 14 to 24. As a first approximation, the annual frequency rate can be estimated by dividing total convictions by the number of years observed (11) for 14-year-old starters and adjusting for the one required conviction. The resulting estimate shown in Figure 3-2, however, does not account for career termination before age 24 for some offenders. If the estimate were properly limited to include only active years for each offender (i.e., years in which they have at least one conviction), the estimates of annual conviction frequencies would be higher than reported in Figure 3-2.

Offenders who start careers at younger ages generally have higher annual frequency rates than older starters. The decline in conviction frequencies at older starting ages that is observed for London male youths would be even sharper if younger starters are also disproportionately more likely to terminate their careers before age 24. The same general pattern of a decline in frequency rates for older starting ages, illustrated in Figure 3-2, is also observed for separate offense types.

Drug Use

Offending frequencies vary with drug use for active offenders (Wish and Johnson, Volume II). Higher frequency rates are found both among active offenders currently using drugs and among those with histories of drug use, especially early drug use as juveniles, across a variety of offense types, and using both official-arrest and self-report data.

Annual incidence and participation rates from official arrest records reported in Sechrest (1979) were used to estimate μ and λ for active offenders in samples of participants in drug treatment programs (see Cohen, Appendix B). When estimates of the probability of arrest for a crime are applied to mean individual arrest frequencies, active offenders among participants in drug treatment programs are estimated to commit an annual average of 3 assaults, 6 to 8 robberies, and more than 20 property offenses. These rates are twice those found for adult arrestees generally (Table 3-3, above).

The offending frequencies derived from official records of arrests are comparable in magnitude to the mean annual offending frequencies estimated from the self-reported offenses of "irregular" drug users in another sample of street drug users (see Table 3-10). In general, λ increases as drug use increases. There are also increases in the number of offenders active in various property offenses (Table 3-10), suggesting increases in participation rates with increases in drug use.

TABLE 3-10 Individual Offending Frequencies (λ) by Drug Use for Street Drug Users (offenses committed per year per active offender)

| Offense Type | Drug Users[a] | | | |
	Irregular	Regular	Daily	All
Robbery	8.9	16.7	26.5	20.4
	(12)	(18)	(27)	(57)
Burglary	12.8	35.9	60.5	41.2
	(19)	(33)	(35)	(87)
Shoplifting (resale)	67.8	74.7	105.7	84.5
	(31)	(48)	(42)	(121)
Other larceny	14.8	40.4	32.4	32.1
	(22)	(41)	(37)	(100)
Forgery	6.8	11.4	18.4	13.4
	(6)	(7)	(8)	(21)
Con games	138.1	125.2	85.9	113.8
	(16)	(21)	(21)	(58)

NOTES: Derived by Cohen (Appendix B) from data on incidence and participation rates reported by Johnson et al. (1983:Tables VI.1 and VIII.2).

The number of active offenders in each offense type is noted in parentheses.

[a]Irregular drug users reported using heroin less than an average of 3 days per week; regular drug users reported using heroin an average of 3 to 5 days per week; daily drug users reported using heroin an average of 6 or 7 days per week (Johnson et al., 1983:42).

Drug use also distinguishes frequency rates estimated from self-reports by inmates (Chaiken and Chaiken, 1982a). Higher mean values of λ while free are estimated for drug users than for nondrug users, especially for armed robbery and burglary, while forgery is committed at higher rates by nondrug users. Offenders who commit robbery, burglary, and assaults at especially high rates ("violent predators") are characterized by extensive use of drugs as juveniles and use of multiple drug types as adults.

The differences between the rates reported for daily drug users in Table 3-10 and those for offenders generally in Table 3-3 (above) are consistent with the large differentials in λ between drug users during periods of heavy drug use and other offenders that are found in some self-report studies. During these periods, crime spurts with frequencies as much as 6 times as high as those for nonusing offenders have been reported (McGlothlin, Anglin, and Wilson, 1978; Ball, Shaffer, and Nurco, 1983; Gropper, 1985).

Employment

Only a few studies that examine the relationship between employment and λ for active offenders are available. Studies that rely on official-record data rarely include the necessary information on individual work experiences. When available, employment data are usually obtained from self-reports by study participants.

Time spent unemployed is a significant factor distinguishing the frequency rates of active offenders. Among inmates surveyed by the Rand Corporation, offenders who were employed less than half the time during the observation period prior to their incarceration reported committing property crimes at higher rates than other offenders (Chaiken and Chaiken, 1982a; Greenwood, 1982). Irregular employment is also a factor distinguishing those who committed robbery, burglary,

and assaults ("violent predators") at especially high rates.

These findings for λ are consistent with other results on the effect of time spent unemployed in increasing individual levels of criminal activity, but typically measured by aggregate incidence rates (e.g., crimes per capita) that confound λ and participation (Glaser and Rice, 1959; Glaser, 1964; Cook, 1975; Sickles, Schmidt, and Witte, 1979; Thornberry and Farnworth, 1982; McGahey, 1982; see also the interpretation of the potential intervening role of increased time unemployed in Rossi, Berk, and Lenihan (1980), and a critique of this approach in Zeisel, 1982a). Research has generally found that individual levels of crime, as measured by incidence rates, are not related to wage rates (e.g., Witte, 1980; McGahey, 1982).

Previous Criminal Involvement

High levels of criminal activity in the past are a good indicator of continued future offending at high frequencies. This relationship has been observed for various offense types, for both juveniles and adults, using frequency rates based on official-record and self-report data and using various indices of previous offending, including self-reported offenses, arrests, convictions, and incarcerations (Blumstein and Cohen, 1979; Peterson and Braiker, 1980; Chaiken and Chaiken, 1982a; Greenwood, 1982) and also using incidence rates that combine frequency and participation (see e.g., Farrington, 1984).

In most of these studies, past criminal activity has been measured crudely, using a simple count of events found in a prior criminal record (often referred to as an offender's record length) or a binary variable indicating the presence or absence of a prior record. A recent study reanalyzing data for persistent offenders among male juveniles in Philadelphia, however, finds that when past offending rates are used explicitly, the relationship between record length and subsequent frequency disappears: offenders with long prior records also tend to have high rates in the past, and, with age and the number of prior arrests held constant, arrest frequency in the past is predictive of subsequent arrest frequency for juveniles who remain active (Barnett and Lofaso, 1985).

Summary

In contrast to the patterns observed in aggregate data on population arrest rates and participation rates, individual frequency rates for active offenders do not vary substantially with the demographic attributes of sex, age, or race. Differences in frequency rates are observed with age of onset of careers, drug use, unemployment, and prior criminal involvement. Active offenders who begin criminal activity at young ages, use drugs heavily, are unemployed for long periods of time, and have extensive prior records of criminal activity generally commit crimes at higher rates than other offenders. These results suggest a general stability in the frequency of offending by active offenders. It thus appears to be reasonable to characterize individuals as high-rate or low-rate offenders, since these frequency rates generally are sustained during careers. These characteristics form the basis for several prediction-based classification rules, which are evaluated in Chapter 6.

SERIOUSNESS

In addition to individual frequency rates, which gauge the intensity of offending by active offenders, the mix of different offense types that are committed is a key dimension of individual criminal careers. Distinguishing offenders most likely to engage in serious predatory offenses is of particularly important policy interest. The patterns of change in offense types during individual criminal careers are also of concern, especially the extent of specialization in the same offense type by offenders and of escalation from less serious to more serious types of offenses. One can consider changes in the seriousness of offense types without regard to patterns in frequency rates.

Types of Studies

A number of studies have analyzed individual trends in the seriousness of offenses over a career. These studies share a common reliance on official-record data. Some use the broad category of police contacts, which may include police stops for questioning that do not lead to arrest or any formal charges but are recorded in police files. Analysis of police contacts is especially characteristic of research on juvenile offending. Other studies rely on arrests or convictions.

This research relies predominantly on official-record data because it represents the only recorded source of information on the sequence of offense types. The usual self-report interval of a year or more is too long to obtain reliable information on the sequence of offenses for individuals. Self-report data can be used, however, to explore patterns of offense mix by active offenders, as has been done by Chaiken and Chaiken (1982a), who used self-reports by inmates. Also, if repeated self-report surveys of the same sample are available, changes in offense mix during different reporting periods can be examined. Such analyses of self-reported offenses are part of the National Youth Survey (e.g., Dunford and Elliott, 1984).

It is important to stress that analyses relying on official data reflect patterns of official contacts with the criminal justice system, but they are not likely to be representative of switching among offenses actually committed. The distortion in official records arises from variation in the likelihood that different offense types will result in an official contact. Rare offenses generally have a high risk of arrest (like murder or aggravated assault), while common offenses like larceny or drug law violations have low risks of arrest and so are underrepresented in official record sequences. In addition, overcharging by police or erroneous arrests could further distort official records. Because of these differences in the probability that different offense types will appear on official records, the results of analyses based on official contacts do not generalize to offense-type sequences between crimes actually committed. Transitions from rarely reported events to frequently reported events will appear to be more common than they actually are because occurrences of the rarely reported events will often be missing from the record.

Since dynamic processes like "specialization" or "escalation" make sense only in the context of longitudinal data of individual event histories, all studies of crime type sequences necessarily involve longitudinal data on individual offenders. Because of the focus on transitions between events, these studies are dominated by more persistent offenders who accumulate larger numbers of events.

Two general approaches are used in analyzing the offense types found in individual offense histories. One approach attempts to characterize complete histories, summarizing offending patterns in terms of the mix of offense types found or using profiles of complete offense sequences. The usefulness of these summaries of complete histories depends on the extent to which large numbers of individual histories can be adequately represented by a relatively small number of distinctive patterns. If identifiable patterns cannot be found, analysis based on large numbers of complete histories can be quite cumbersome.

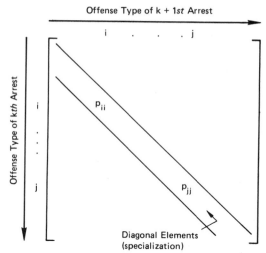

FIGURE 3-3 Simplified transition matrix for offense-type switches between successive arrests.

The other approach relies on transition matrices that focus more narrowly on pairs of successive events within histories. The term "switching" commonly refers to the sequence of crime types in a pair of successive arrests but also refers to repeating the same crime type. As shown in Figure 3-3, transition matrices characterize pairs of successive arrests in terms of the probability of a next arrest for type *j* after an arrest for type *i*. The diagonal elements in the transition matrix depicted in Figure 3-3 reflect transition probabilities between arrests for the same offense type. This approach has the advantage of being able to accommodate in a convenient analytic form both the mix of different offense types and the sequence in which those offense types occur for large numbers of offenders.

Changes in Offense Mix

Data on the changing mix of offense types at different stages of criminal careers are available from several sources. As illustrated in the first two studies in Table 3-11, comparing adult and juvenile offending patterns, property offenses are

TABLE 3-11 Changes in Mix of Offense Types (in percent)

A. 1,000 adjudicated delinquents[a]

Offense Type	Age at Arrest			
	11–15	16–20	21–25	26–30
Property	62.9	48.7	24.6 (34.6)	18.2 (31.9)
Disorderly conduct	21.7	22.2	30.3 (42.7)	22.5 (39.5)
Violence	2.5	4.4	7.3 (10.3)	6.8 (11.9)
Drunkenness	0.0	9.3	29.0 (—)	43.0 (—)
Family and children	0.0	0.5	1.6 (2.3)	3.3 (5.8)
Sex	0.3	1.6	2.4 (3.4)	2.6 (4.6)
Narcotics	0.0	0.1	0.3 (0.4)	0.6 (1.1)
Others	12.6	13.2	4.5 (6.3)	3.0 (5.3)
(Number of arrests)	(1,333)	(2,719)	(2,547)	(2,195)

B. Cambridge-Somerville Youth Study[b]

Offense Type	Age at Conviction			
	Under 13	13–18	19–22	Over 22
Property	91.4	80.9	44.8 (71.1)	40.7 (71.3)
Person	5.7	6.1	9.1 (14.4)	10.7 (18.7)
Sex	2.9	5.3	9.1 (14.4)	6.0 (10.5)
Drunkenness	0.0	7.7	37.0 (—)	42.9 (—)
(Number of convictions)	(35)	(131)	(143)	(84)

C. Juveniles with police contacts in Philadelphia birth cohort[c]

Offense Type	Sequence Number of Juvenile Police Contact			
	1	2–3	4–6	7–9
Non-index	65.5	63.3	61.6	57.8
Injury	7.6	8.1	9.1	11.2
Theft	13.9	16.5	18.1	17.5
Damage	7.3	3.9	3.1	3.2
Combination	5.8	8.2	8.1	10.2
(Number of juvenile police contacts)	(3,475)	(3,074)	(1,960)	(875)

D. Adults arrested in Washington, D.C.[d]

Offense Type	Sequence Number of Adult Arrest			
	1	2	3	4
Violent	21.3	24.0	20.9	19.4
Property	36.2	32.8	35.1	32.9
Robbery	13.3	13.1	10.6	11.6
Drugs	4.3	6.2	6.7	6.1
Others	24.9	23.9	26.6	29.8
(Number of adult arrests)	(2,968)	(2,968)	(2,431)	(1,952)

NOTE: The renormalized distribution for adults after excluding arrests for drunkenness is reported in parentheses.

[a]Adapted from Cline, 1980; Table 13.2 in Brim, O., and J. Kagan, eds., 1980, *Constancy and Change in Human Development*, Harvard University Press. Used by permission. Based on data from Glueck and Glueck, 1940.
[b]N = 506; adapted from Cline, 1980; Table 13.3 in Brim, O., and J. Kagan, eds., 1980, *Constancy and Change in Human Development*, Harvard University Press. Used by permission. Based on data from McCord and McCord, 1959.
[c]N = 3,475; adapted from Wolfgang, Figlio, and Sellin, 1972:Matrix 11.1, Tables 11.2 to 11.6.
[d]N = 5,338; adapted from Moitra, 1981:Table 2.1.

more common for juveniles and violent offenses are more common at older ages (Glueck and Glueck, 1940; McCord and McCord, 1959). The last two studies in Table 3-11 provide data on changes in offense mix on successive arrests for juveniles (Wolfgang, Figlio, and Sellin, 1972) and adults (Moitra, 1981). In contrast to the differences in offense mix of juveniles compared with adults, offense mix is rather stable over successive arrests within either age group. Overall, violent offenses are more common among adults than among juveniles.

The first two studies in Table 3-11 are distinguished by the heavy representation of drunkenness at adult ages, which comprises 43 percent of the arrests and convictions in the oldest age categories; a similar pattern is not observed in the final study for adults reported in the table. The studies cover different historical periods, with the Gluecks and McCords studying offending in the first half of this century, and the Moitra data including predominantly arrests in the 1960s and early 1970s. Much of the difference in the role of drunkenness for adults may lie in changes in arrest and police reporting practices over this period, not in changes in offending behavior. When drunkenness is removed in the first two studies, the distributions for adults are more comparable across the various studies, especially for violent offenses, which represent 10 to 20 percent of all arrests or convictions for adults.

These data on offense mix at different times during careers provide useful insights into the relative frequency of different offense types, especially highlighting which types are rare and which are commonplace. However, they do not necessarily reflect the dynamics of change during criminal careers. Because the distributions are not linked to the same offenders in each time period, comparisons across time periods may reflect changes

in the mix of offenders rather than changes in offense types during careers. Increases in violent offenses at older ages, for example, might result from offenders' changing to violent offenses as their careers progress or from earlier termination of careers by offenders who do not engage in violent offenses. In the latter case, violent offenders would contribute a larger share to offenses at older ages with little or no change in the offense mix for those who remain active in careers. Data on offense mix alone that are not linked to the sequence of offense types for individual offenders cannot distinguish between these processes.

General Offense-Switching Patterns

Transition matrices are often used to characterize the sequence of crime types over successive events for the same individuals. A number of studies examine directly or provide data that permit comparisons of offense-switching patterns across various demographic subgroups of individual offenders (see Cohen, Appendix B, for details).

Race

Significant differences in offense switching by race are found in all but one of the samples of offenders examined. These race differences are found for a variety of offense types and for both juveniles and adults. Nonwhite offenders are more likely than whites to switch to serious offense types, especially those involving violence and robbery, and less likely to switch to less serious offenses or to desist from offending (Wolfgang, Figlio, and Sellin, 1972; Bursik, 1980; Moitra, 1981; Blumstein, Cohen, and Das, 1985). Among male juveniles with police contacts in Philadelphia, for example, the likelihood of a next police contact for an offense involving injury is .09 for nonwhites and .04 for whites; the likelihood of no further contact is .23 for nonwhites and .37 for whites (derived from data in Wolfgang, Figlio, and Sellin, 1972:Tables 11.27 and 11.28). Among adults arrested in the Detroit SMSA, the likelihood of a next arrest for a robbery is .08 for whites and .13 for blacks (derived from data in Blumstein, Cohen, and Das, 1985).

The greater likelihood of switches to violence and robbery found among nonwhite offenders parallels the race differences observed in participation rates for these offense types. The only study that finds no evidence of differences in offense switching for black groups includes other ethnic groups in addition to blacks and is distinguished by its much lower representation of blacks and by its larger representation of females in the offender sample (Rojek and Erikson, 1982). These factors contribute to a greater representation of less serious offense types in the sample, which may obscure differences that are more prominent in serious offense types.

Sex

Only one sample includes a sufficient number of females to permit examination of differences in offense switching by sex (Rojek and Erikson, 1982). In this sample of juvenile offenders, offense switching is significantly different for male and female offenders, with female offenders much more likely than males to desist or to shift to runaway offenses. Switches to these two categories comprise 73 percent of offense transitions for females compared with only 36 percent for males.

Age

Adequate evidence is not available to assess changes in offense-switching patterns either with age of offender or with age of onset. While the basic data are generally available in sample data, appropriate analyses of these data have not yet been performed. Variations with age of onset could be evaluated by directly comparing transition matrices estimated for different starting age groups. To detect age effects, offenders could be characterized by age of the offender at a transition. Separate transition matrices could then be estimated and compared for each age at transition.

Offense Clusters

Offense-switching patterns also provide a basis for identifying clusters of related offense types. Clusters represent natural partitions of offense types: offenders display a stronger tendency to switch among offense types within a cluster and a correspondingly weaker tendency to switch to offense types outside a cluster. A cluster is defined by the fact that switching within it is higher than would be expected if the next crime type were independent of the previous crime type; switching between clusters is lower than would be expected under independence of crime types.

In three jurisdictions, two distinct clusters—one for violent offenses and the other for property offenses—were found for adult offenders in analyses done for the panel (see Cohen, Appendix B). This tendency for offense types to cluster varies somewhat by race, with a stronger partition between violent and property offenses evident among black than white offenders. In Detroit and the rest of Michigan, but not in Washington, D.C., there is some relationship between these clusters and other offense types: switching is elevated between the cluster of violent offenses and robbery and diminished between the cluster of property offenses and drugs.

Offense switching does not appear to

be independent of prior offense type. Instead, knowledge of prior offense type provides information that is useful in predicting the next offense type. The analysis of offense switching by adults provides behavioral support for the frequently used partition between violent and property offenses. Adults exhibit definite tendencies to switch among offenses within clusters of violent or property offenses and a tendency not to switch between these two clusters.

The clear tendency toward distinct clusters of violent (person) offenses and of property offenses provides empirical support for the use of these aggregate categories in other studies of offense switching. Not only are these offense types conceptually similar, they are also behaviorally related, with offenders more likely to switch among offenses within a cluster on successive arrests.

While a strong partition between violent and property offenses was found among adults, this partition is not as sharp among juveniles (see Cohen, Appendix B). Only incarcerated juveniles in New Jersey (Smith and Smith, 1984), nonwhite juvenile offenders in Philadelphia (from data in Wolfgang, Figlio, and Sellin, 1972), and white juvenile offenders in Cook County (from data in Bursik, 1980) display a tendency *not* to switch between injury and theft offense categories. Furthermore, there is some evidence of a tendency to switch between violent and property offenses among juveniles. Juvenile offenders of both races in Philadelphia exhibit higher-than-expected switching between theft and "combination" offenses (which include components of both harm to persons and property loss). Switching between persons and property categories is also elevated in the Pima County sample of juveniles (from data in Rojek and Erikson, 1982).

The Pima County study provides the only data that separately identify juvenile status offenses (runaway and "other status"). The observed switching patterns in this sample indicate a sharp partition between status offenses and other crimes. There is a tendency *not* to switch from status offenses to other crimes. Also, while there is a tendency not to switch to desistance (i.e., no further arrests in juvenile record) from other crimes, there is a tendency for desistance to follow a juvenile status offense.

Specialization

Specialization is the tendency to repeat the same offense type on successive arrests. This tendency has been reported in several studies of arrest data (Wolfgang, Figlio, and Sellin, 1972; Bursik, 1980; Moitra, 1981; Rojek and Erikson, 1982; Smith and Smith, 1984; Blumstein, Cohen, and Das, 1985). Specialization estimates based on arrest records could be inflated by police arresting and recording practices. For example, an arrest may be recorded redundantly by several police departments, or police may arrest suspects because of a recent history of similar offenses.

Table 3-12 illustrates this greater tendency of repeating the same offense type on successive arrests for juveniles with police contacts in Philadelphia and adults arrested in the Detroit SMSA. When white juvenile offenders in Philadelphia are arrested again, the overall probability is .17 of a next arrest for theft; among those rearrested after an arrest for theft, however, the probability that the next arrest also will be for theft is almost twice as high, .30. Similarly, among all blacks who are arrested again in the Detroit SMSA, the probability is .13 that the next arrest will be for robbery; for those arrested again after an arrest for robbery, the probability is .31 that the next arrest also will be for robbery. In general, arrests for any specific offense type are

TABLE 3-12 Specialization in Offender Samples: The Likelihood of Repeating the Same Offense Type on Next Arrest, by Race

Offense Type of Next Arrest Among Recidivists	Probability of Each Offense Type on Next Arrest Conditional on Offense Type of Prior Arrest			
	White Offenders		Black Offenders	
	Overall	Same	Overall	Same
Juveniles in Philadelphia[a]				
Non-index	.66	.70	.58	.62
Injury	.07	.13	.11	.14
Theft	.17	.30	.18	.25
Damage	.03	.14	.03	.05
Combination (e.g., robbery)	.07	.20	.10	.18
Adults in Detroit SMSA[b]				
Murder	.01	.15	.01	.14
Rape	.01	.15	.01	.17
Robbery	.08	.35	.13	.31
Aggravated assault	.07	.22	.08	.23
Drugs	.17	.50	.09	.34
Burglary	.27	.45	.20	.38
Larceny	.19	.31	.27	.45
Auto theft	.07	.24	.07	.28
Weapons	.05	.12	.07	.19
Fraud	.08	.40	.06	.32

NOTE: Among those arrested again, the *overall* rate is the likelihood of a next arrest of each offense type, regardless of the previous offense type; the repeat rate is the likelihood of a next arrest for the *same* type as the previous arrest type.

[a]Derived from data in Wolfgang, Figlio, and Sellin (1972:Matrices 11.11 to 11.26).

[b]Derived from data in Blumstein, Cohen, and Das (1985).

more likely to follow a previous arrest for the same type than they are to follow any other offense type.

As defined here, specialization does not imply that repeating the same offense type is very likely on the next arrest. Indeed, in the examples in Table 3-12, the likelihood of repeating the same type rarely exceeds one-third. However, repeating an offense type, say, aggravated assault, is more likely than the overall chance that a next arrest will be for aggravated assault. For white adults who are rearrested in Detroit, only 22 percent of aggravated assault arrests are followed by another aggravated assault arrest, but this number is more than three times the 7 percent chance of an aggravated assault arrest found generally among recidivists.

Age

Important differences in specialization are observed between adults and juveniles. While specialization is evident in some offense types for juvenile offenders, specialization is stronger in magnitude and found in all offense types for adult offenders (see Table 3-12, for example). This finding suggests a more exploratory approach to crime by juvenile offenders and a stronger commitment to particular offense types by adult offenders.

The difference between juvenile and adult offenders may reflect a developmental process in which more specialized offending patterns emerge gradually as offending continues over time. But it might also reflect a selection process in which juvenile samples include a mixture of casual offenders who desist from offending very quickly and a core of committed offenders who are more specialized in their offending. As the casual exploratory offenders leave offending in the juvenile years, adult samples would consist more heavily of the committed, specialized offenders.

Sorting out these rival hypotheses requires samples with data on both the juvenile and adult periods for the same individuals. Whether specialization changes or is stable over time could then be examined for the subset of offenders who begin as juveniles and persist into adulthood. Unfortunately, none of the available samples permit such an analysis. However, a sample in Cook County, Illinois, of very serious juvenile offenders—all had been adjudicated delinquent in juvenile court, and they all had at least five arrests as juveniles (Bursik, 1980)—exhibits widespread offense specialization like that found among adults. Significant specialization is found in all offenses and for both races, except personal injury by white offenders. The pervasiveness of specialization in this sample of persistent juvenile offenders suggests that the juvenile/adult differences in specialization found in the other juvenile samples may be due to sample selection, particularly the presence of large numbers of early desisters in other juvenile samples.

Offense Type

While specialization is pervasive among adults, it is not uniformly strong for all offense types. The most specialized offense types in all adult samples are drugs and fraud. Auto theft is also highly specialized among black offenders in the Detroit SMSA and among the predominantly black offender population in Washington, D.C. (Cohen, Appendix B).

Higher specialization in these offense types is consistent with the frequent role of these offenses as part of larger, organized illegal economic enterprises. The least specialized offenses among adult offenders are the violent and often impulsive offenses of murder, weapons, and rape (Cohen, Appendix B).

Specialization is more sporadic among juvenile offenders. A sample of Pima County juveniles exhibits the least specialization; only property and runaway offenses show a significantly greater tendency to be repeated on successive arrests than would be found if switching were independent of prior offense types. (For analysis of data from Rojek and Erikson, 1982, see Cohen, Appendix B.)

Sex

The only study of specialization to contrast sexes is a sample of juvenile offenders in Pima County (Rojek and Erikson, 1982). While specialization is in fact less frequent for female offenders, occurring only for runaway offenses, specialization is generally limited in this sample of juveniles. Even among male offenders, only property and runaway offenses show evidence of specialization.

Race

In a sample of Philadelphia juveniles, white offenders are more specialized than nonwhite offenders (Wolfgang, Figlio, and Sellin, 1972). No differences in specialization are observed between white and black adults. Interestingly, despite the greater tendency of nonwhites to switch to violent offense types discussed previously for Philadelphia juveniles, they do not exhibit specialization in either injury or damage offenses. While arrests for violent offenses are more likely for nonwhites than for whites, they are no more likely to follow previous arrests for violent offenses than to follow arrests for any other offense types.

Escalation

Escalation is the tendency for offenders to move to more serious offense types as offending continues. A belief in escalation is probably the most widely held view of the pattern of criminal careers. Data on offense transitions provide an opportunity to investigate escalation empirically.

The evidence shows that escalation is observed for juveniles: seriousness of offense types increases on successive events, especially for nonwhite offenders. Average seriousness scores increased on successive police contacts for Philadelphia juveniles (Wolfgang, Figlio, and Sellin, 1972), and analysis of successive transitions finds increases in switches to more serious offense types and decreases in switches to less serious offense types on later transitions (Cohen, Appendix B). Likewise, reanalysis (Cohen, Appendix B) of data for juveniles in Pima County (Rojek and Erikson, 1982) finds increases in switches from juvenile status offenses to more serious crimes on later transitions. In contrast, the evidence for adults from several studies shows that average seriousness measured by several seriousness scales declines on successive arrests (Moitra, 1981; Blumstein, Cohen, and Das, 1985). (See Cohen, Appendix B, for a discussion of seriousness measures.)

The apparent opposite seriousness trends for adults and juveniles, however, are confounded by a potentially important selection effect in the analyses. Because offenders have different numbers of arrests, the same offenders are not observed over the full sequence of arrests. For early arrests, average seriousness reflects the contributions of a mixture of offenders, some with only a few arrests

and some with long records of arrests. As the arrest number increases, however, average seriousness is increasingly restricted to offenders with large numbers of arrests. Thus, the trends in seriousness observed over successive arrests could reflect differences among offenders, rather than changes in seriousness over the course of individuals' criminal careers.

To control for this potential selection effect, offenders can be partitioned by their number of arrests, and the analysis of trends restricted to a common sequence of arrests found for a subset of offenders. Thus, for example, only offenders who have at least six arrests would be used in comparing average seriousness from the first to the sixth arrest. When record length is controlled in this way in adult samples, average seriousness appears to be generally stable over successive arrests within subgroups of offenders who have the same minimum number of arrests. When compared across various offender subgroups, however, average seriousness is lower for the subgroups of adults with larger numbers of arrests. In Washington, D.C., for example, including only adults who have at least six arrests, average seriousness over the first six arrests is stable. For offenders who have at least eight arrests, average seriousness is again stable over the first eight arrests, but with a lower average seriousness score.

Just as the apparent decline in seriousness for adult offenders results from differences in the mix of offenders available on successive arrests, differences among offenders may also be a factor in the increases in seriousness on successive police contacts for juveniles. As the number of police contacts increases, average seriousness measures depend increasingly on offenders with large numbers of contacts. If more serious offenses are more common in the records of the more active juvenile offenders, the changing mix of offenders alone could produce the observed increases in average seriousness on successive contacts. Appropriate controls for record length are needed to assess the role of selection effects in the observed escalation for juveniles.

TERMINATION AND LENGTH OF CRIMINAL CAREERS

The findings that participation in criminal activity is more widespread among teenage males than among adult males, that λ is relatively stable over age for offenders who do remain active, but that there is a decline with age in aggregate arrest measures suggest that many criminal careers must be very short, ending after only brief ventures into crime as teenagers. At the same time, however, many offenders do continue careers beyond the teenage years. Consequently, certain critical questions about the duration of criminal careers emerge, particularly about the length of typical careers and how to prospectively distinguish short careers from long careers. Also, for already active offenders, there are questions about the process of terminating their careers, especially about the expected time remaining in an offender's criminal career as of a particular time— the residual career length. Variations in career length with crime type and with attributes of offenders may be important factors in distinguishing persisters— those with long careers—from other offenders.

The answers to these questions have implications for attempts to modify criminal careers. A finding that career length is related to identifiable attributes of offenders, for example, may serve as a basis for distinguishing among offenders who have different career lengths. At one level, such variations in the base levels for duration across offenders should be

taken into account in evaluating treatment programs so that existing differences among offenders are not mistakenly interpreted as effects of treatment. At another level, the variations may be useful in selecting offenders for intervention programs. A strong relationship between legitimate employment and termination of criminal careers, for example, may suggest greater attention to employment facilitation as a useful policy intervention. Alternatively, the factors associated with longer residual careers might influence the selection of offenders for incarceration for reasons of incapacitation, since the effectiveness of incapacitation is diminished if an offender's career terminates while he is incarcerated.

Types of Studies

Depending on the attributes of the data used, analyses have addressed career termination at very different levels.[6] Partly because of the partition between juvenile and adult justice systems, much research on criminal careers has focused exclusively either on juveniles or on adults. These studies have of necessity taken the passage from juvenile to adult status as a partition for analysis, signaling the end of juvenile careers or the start of adult careers. Other researchers, recognizing the potential continuity in offending between juvenile and adult periods, have followed juvenile samples into the early adult periods and report data on the juvenile/adult

---

[6]Besides the analyses discussed here, earlier studies have reported termination rates for groups of subjects followed for long periods following juvenile court contact (e.g., Glueck and Glueck, 1940), release on parole (e.g., Glueck and Glueck, 1943), or other types of release (e.g., Christiansen et al., 1965; Soothill and Gibbens, 1978). Because of the wide range of ages in the samples and the methods used, those studies do not provide estimates of career length (measured in years), of the probability of persistence of juveniles into adult criminality, or of the probability of a "next" arrest.

link in participation between these two periods.

Other studies have examined the sequence of events in individual careers in more detail, providing estimates of termination probabilities after each arrest. In these analyses, career length is characterized by the number of arrests in a history. Important questions in these studies are how termination probabilities change with the accumulation of further arrests, what the expected number of future arrests is at any point in a career, and whether there are any bases for prospectively identifying the "persisters," who go on to have long records with large numbers of arrests or crimes.

The third approach to career length focuses on the actual duration of criminal careers, estimating the time that elapses between the first and last crimes committed. In analyzing incapacitative sentencing policies, variation in residual career lengths at the time of sentencing is especially important because incarceration that extends beyond the end of a career has no incapacitative effect.

Persistence by Delinquents into Adult Careers

Consistent evidence is available from various research settings that 30 to 60 percent of juvenile delinquents known to the police or juvenile courts persist as adult offenders with at least one arrest or conviction as an adult for an index or felony offense (McCord, 1978, 1982; Shannon, 1978, 1982a; Polk et al., 1981; Farrington, 1983a; Wolfgang, Thornberry, and Figlio, 1985; see also a review by Langan and Farrington, 1983). As shown in Table 3-13, follow-up studies of delinquent and nondelinquent juveniles indicate that a much smaller fraction of nondelinquents are arrested as adults.

The fraction classified as persisters into adult careers increases when the expo-

sure period is lengthened by observing adults to older ages, when broader domains of crime are used, and when the measures are based on arrests instead of convictions. For three birth cohorts in Racine, Wisconsin, for example, Shannon (1982a) reports that 31, 44, and 54 percent of males with police contacts for nontraffic offenses before age 20 were arrested again as adults by ages 21, 26, and 32, respectively. If the cohorts are in fact similar in terms of their tendency to persist into adult careers, the differences in persistence must reflect the effects of earlier cutoff ages for the more recent cohorts. Reflecting the relationship between persistence and domain of crime, a study by Shaw in 1947 (cited in Langan and Farrington, 1983) reports that, of 1,336 males appearing in Chicago juvenile court for the first time in 1930, 66 percent were arrested as adults by age 31 for a felony or misdemeanor but only 46 percent were arrested for a felony.

When comparable measures and procedures are available, demographic variations in juvenile-to-adult persistence mirror variations in overall participation rates. Among the male delinquents in the 1945 Philadelphia cohort followed from age 18 to 30, about twice as many nonwhites (54 percent) as whites (28 percent) were arrested for nontraffic offenses as adults. For young female offenders in the three Racine cohorts, Shannon (1982a) reports persistence rates after age 20 in nontraffic offenses of 20, 29, and 34 percent compared with rates of 31, 44, and 54 percent, respectively, for male offenders. One implication of these findings is that differences in sample composition with respect to these demographic attributes would substantially affect juvenile-to-adult persistence rates in different samples.

A juvenile record is a strong indicator of later adult offending, and the strength of this relationship increases as the juvenile

TABLE 3-13 Persistence of Delinquents into Adult Careers

Study	Sample	Offenses Examined	Criminal Event	Age Range for Adult Events	Delinquents with Adult Careers (percent)	Non-delinquents with Adult Careers (percent)
Shannon (1982a: Table 2)	356 males born in 1942 and "residing continuously"[a] in Racine, Wis., to 1974	All nontraffic (including suspicion and investigation)	Arrests (police contacts as juveniles)	21 to 32	54	36
As above	As above for 740 males born in 1949	(Same as above)	(Same as above)	21 to 26	44	15
	As above for 1,114 males born in 1955	(Same as above)	(Same as above)	21	31	3
Farrington (1983a)	Cohort of 411 London boys aged 25 in 1980	Indictable offenses	Conviction	18 to 25	71	16
McCord and McCord (1959:92)	506 boys from Cambridge and Somerville, Mass.; median age 10.5 in 1939	All nontraffic (adult and juvenile)	Conviction	18 to median age 28.5	52	18
McCord (1978:285)	(Same as above)	All nontraffic as juveniles; "serious crimes" against persons or property, as adults	Conviction	25 to median age 47	36	11
Polk et al. (1981)	1,227 boys from Marion County, Ore.; high school sophomores in 1964	All nontraffic	Arrests	18 to 30	49	22
Wolfgang, Thornberry, and Figlio (1985:348)	975 Philadelphia boys born in 1945	All nontraffic	Arrests (police contacts as juveniles)	18 to 30	51	18

[a]Never absent from Racine for a period exceeding 2 years.

record becomes longer. As shown in three cohort follow-up studies in Table 3-14, the fraction of members with adult criminal records is lowest—16 to 18 percent in the data of Farrington (1983a) and Wolfgang, Thornberry, and Figlio (1985)—for members with *no* juvenile records. This fraction rises sharply with the presence of just one police contact in a juvenile record and continues to rise

TABLE 3-14 Persistence into Adult Careers, by Length of Juvenile Record

Study	Sample	Criminal Event	Cutoff Age for Adult Offending	Juveniles Becoming Adult Offenders (%) Number of Juvenile Arrests					
				0	1	2	3	4	5+
Farrington (1983a)	Cohort of 411 London boys aged 25 in 1980	Convictions for indictable offense	25	16	64	71		92	—
Wolfgang, Thornberry, and Figlio (1985:348)	10% follow-up sample of cohort of boys born in 1945 and residents of Philadelphia from ages 10 to 18	Arrests for nontraffic offenses (police contacts as juveniles)	22	18	38	45	55	68	78
Shannon (1982a)	Males and females born in 1942 and residing continuously in Racine, Wis., to 1974	Arrests for any offense including traffic (police contacts as juveniles)	32	47	71	89	90	89	93
	Same as above for males and females born in 1949	(Same as above)	26	41	58	75	79	89	98
	Same as above for males and females born in 1955	(Same as above)	21	26	44	59	70	78	85

with each additional police contact in the juvenile record. Thus, while the precise fraction persisting into adult criminal careers varies by jurisdiction, by domain of crime, and by the criterion used for characterizing the adult record (e.g., arrests or convictions), there is strong evidence that the existence of a juvenile delinquency career foreshadows adult criminal careers.

Even though juvenile delinquents are far more likely than nondelinquents to become adult offenders, 40 to 50 percent of adult offenders do *not* have records of juvenile police contacts: because nondelinquent juveniles greatly outnumber delinquent juveniles, even though a smaller fraction of the nondelinquents become adult offenders, their great numbers lead to a substantial contribution of adult offenders. Thus, for a sample of the 1945 Philadelphia cohort followed to age 30, in which B_{18} was 35 percent, nondelin-

quents made up 65 percent of the entire sample and 41 percent of adult arrestees in the sample, even though only 18 percent of nondelinquents were arrested as adults, compared with 51 percent of the delinquents (see Table 3-13). Similarly, nondelinquents accounted for 47 percent of adult arrestees in the 1942 Racine cohort (followed to age 32) and 49 percent of adult offenders in the Cambridge study. These findings from prospective studies, based on official records, are consistent with studies of retrospective self-reports; of 755 incarcerated robbers and burglars providing usable responses in the second Rand inmate survey, 67 percent reported not having been convicted of any offense before age 16 (Greenwood, 1982:Table 4.4). This result, previously noted by Shannon (1982a) has significant policy implications for targeting crime control efforts on juvenile offenders: despite the much higher likelihood of continued offending as adults by juvenile delinquents, substantial proportions of adult offenders will not be prospectively identifiable as juvenile delinquents.

Measuring Career Length by Number of Arrests

Attention was initially drawn by Wolfgang, Figlio, and Sellin (1972) to analysis of career length as measured by number of arrests. They noted that "chronic" juvenile offenders—those who were arrested five or more times by age 18—made up only 6 percent of the Philadelphia 1945 cohort, or 18 percent of all arrestees in the cohort, but accounted for 52 percent of all arrests of cohort members. Thus, any social intervention that could reduce participation by the chronic offenders could have a significant crime control impact. In retrospective analyses comparing chronic offenders with those whose juvenile careers terminated with fewer arrests, Wolfgang, Figlio, and Sellin (1972) reported that chronics were more likely than others to be nonwhite; within each race category were more likely to be of low socioeconomic status; and within each race-status category were distinguished from other arrestees by more family moves, lower mean IQs, fewer school grades completed, and more school discipline problems. The authors reported that chronic offenders were arrested for more serious offense types than other offenders and began their delinquency careers earlier, as measured by the age of first arrest. Their longer period of exposure to risk before turning 18 artifactually creates greater opportunity for early starters to become chronics, but later analyses controlling for exposure time (Barnett and Lofaso, 1985; Cohen, Appendix B) suggest that the result is also attributable to a genuinely higher level of activity by early starters, as measured by annual arrest frequency, μ.

The basic finding—that a small number of extraordinarily active offenders account for a disproportionately large share of total arrests—attracted the interest of scholars and practitioners and stimulated efforts to understand offenders' termination patterns. This problem has often been pursued by examining persistence probabilities of at least one more event after each event in a criminal history.[7] As indicated in Table 3-15, between one-half and two-thirds of first offenders are rearrested (Philadelphia and Racine) or reconvicted (London). After each subsequent event, the persistence probability increases, reaching a plateau range of .7 to .9 by the fourth event. This same general pattern has been found in various settings, with only minor variations due to differences in the criminal event (arrest or conviction) and the domain of offenses (indictable offenses in London and all nontraffic offenses in Philadelphia and Racine).[8]

Blumstein and Moitra (1980) noted that the Philadelphia data are consistent with a constant persistence probability of .72

---

[7]Actually, the research has often computed termination probabilities following each arrest, usually in the context of analyses of crime-type switching between arrests. Following any arrest, however, persistence probability is simply the complement of the termination probability.

[8]Police contacts in the Racine cohorts include substantial numbers of contacts for investigation and suspicion involving nothing more than police stops for questioning. This broader domain of offense types accounts for the higher participation and persistence rates in those cohorts. Persistence probabilities have also been computed for two Columbus, Ohio, samples: juveniles arrested at least once for a violent offense before age 18 (Hamparian et al., 1978), and adults arrested at least once for robbery, murder, assault, or rape (Miller, Dinitz, and Conrad, 1982). Because the arrest causing inclusion in the sample may not have been the first arrest, persistence probabilities for those samples are not comparable to the probabilities for the other samples described in Table 3-15, and are therefore not reported there.

TABLE 3-15 Conditional Persistence Probabilities for Males from Contact $(k - 1)$ to Contact k

Contact Number (k)	Philadelphia Cohort I[a]	Philadelphia Cohort II[b]	London[c]	Racine, Wis., Cohorts[d]		
				1942	1949	1955
1	.35	—	.33	.70	.68	.59
2	.54	—	.63	.69	.72	.68
3	.65	.67	.74	.78	.77	.76
4	.72	.73	.69	.78	.81	.80
5	.72	.73	.76	.83	.81	.89
6	.74	.72	.69	.91	.83	.89
7	.79	.81	.91	.86	.84	.90
8	.77	.73	.90	.88	.88	.87
9	.80	—	.78	.92	.88	.87
10	.83	—	.86	.82	.92	.92
11	.79	—	—	.87	.94	.90
12	.80	—	—	.85	.93	.92
13	.73	—	—	.82	.90	.94
14	.88	—	—	.89	.90	.96
15	.70	—	—	.79	.94	.98

[a]Data from Wolfgang, Figlio, and Sellin (1972:163).
[b]Data from A. Barnett, 1985, personal communication.
[c]Data from Farrington (1983a).
[d]Data from Shannon (1981:169). Contacts for investigation and suspicion but not for traffic offenses are included in computation of the persistence probabilities reported here.

after the third arrest. All offenders with more than three arrests can be expected to have an average of 2.57 subsequent arrests $[.72/(1 - .72)]$ no matter how many prior arrests they have. Thus, the number of previous arrests alone would not be sufficient to prospectively distinguish chronic offenders from other offenders who have at least three arrests. There is a need for research on correlates of persistence probabilities.

The tendency for persistence probabilities to increase to a common limit as the number of arrests or convictions increases can be interpreted as reflecting a developmental process, in which persisters gradually become more strongly committed to illegal behavior (or less well suited for legal employment) as their criminal careers progress. An alternative account (Blumstein, Farrington, and Moitra, 1985) poses a model of offender heterogeneity in which some offenders are "desisters," with relatively low persistence probabil-

ities and others are "persisters," with relatively high persistence probabilities. As more careers of desisters end after each arrest, the remaining sample of offenders is increasingly composed of persisters with their higher persistence probabilities. This model of population heterogeneity represents a reasonable alternative to models of a homogeneous population in which career parameters change as individual offenders' careers progress.[9]

Another problem in interpreting the findings on desistance is the cutoff of observations at a specific age. Arrest-free

[9]In Blumstein, Farrington, and Moitra (1985), persisters were distinguished from desisters by the following characteristics observed at ages 8–10: "troublesomeness" as assessed by peers and teachers; "conduct disorder" and "acting out" as rated by teachers and social workers; a "deprived background" (in terms of income, social class, housing, family size, and neglect); criminal parents; low nonverbal IQ; and poor parental child-rearing practices.

intervals at the end of the observation period do not necessarily indicate termination of criminal careers. Offenders who are arrested at rate μ per year will have average time intervals of length $1/\mu$ years between successive arrests. Thus, crime-free intervals as long as $1/\mu$ years will not be uncommon for active offenders.[10] Erroneously attributing the absence of further events near the end of the observation period to career desistance rather than to the random time between events in a still active career will lead to overstatements of desistance, called "false desistance."

For example, in the case of the analysis by Wolfgang, Figlio, and Sellin (1972), some portion of arrestees who are not considered chronic offenders by age 18 would accumulate additional arrests if they were followed after age 18. Therefore, truncation of observations at age 18 undoubtedly biases downward the estimated proportion of cohort members with five or more arrests. Barnett and Lofaso (1985) attempted to measure this bias by estimating individual arrest rates for the 312 youths with five arrests by age 17. They estimated that even if there were no desistance in this group, 43 of these youths would be expected to have no further arrests between their fifth and the cutoff age of 18. That number is quite close to the 51 youths actually observed to have no more arrests. This similarity suggests that the true desistance rate is very small and that the desistance rate of 28 percent reported for the chronics probably exceeds the actual rate substantially. Similar false desistance among youths with less than five arrests by age 18 probably led to an understatement of the number of chronic offenders in the cohort.

The problem of false desistance highlights the ambiguity inherent in the characterization of chronic offenders in terms of numbers of arrests without reference to exposure time. For example, a cohort member first arrested at age 15 would have to be arrested at twice the annual rate of one first arrested at age 12 in order to accumulate five arrests by age 18. "Chronics" can be early starters, high-rate offenders, or offenders with especially long careers.

Measuring Career Length in Years

Analysis of career length measured in years is relatively rare. Estimates of total career length in three major studies range between 5 and 15 years (Shinnar and Shinnar, 1975; Greenberg, 1975; Greene, 1977). Shinnar and Shinnar (1975) estimated total careers to be 10 to 15 years based on aggregate data on the time between first and current adult arrests of 5 years for all offenders and 10 years for recidivists reported for a sample of offenders from the FBI computerized criminal history file. This estimate is dependent on the statistical assumptions made to infer total career length from the partial career length observed for active offenders. Also, because the data include only first arrests as adults, the 5- to 10-year arrest careers observed for adults were arbitrarily inflated to 10 to 15 years to include both juvenile careers and the active period before the first adult arrest (Shinnar and Shinnar, 1975:597). There is also some concern about the representativeness of the arrestee sample, which predominantly includes persons arrested for a federal offense.

Greenberg (1975:561–562) used a simple approximation to estimate the average length of careers for index offenses. If μ is the average number of index arrests per year for an offender and N is the total number of additional lifetime index ar-

---

[10]For example, under an assumption that arrests occur according to a Poisson process with annual rate μ, the chance of an arrest-free interval of at least $1/\mu$ years is given by $e^{-\mu(1/\mu)}$, or 37 percent.

rests experienced after the first arrest, then $T = N\mu$ is the average career length for index offenses. Using estimates of $\mu = .5$[11] and $N = 2.5$,[12] Greenberg calculated the average index career length to be 5 years.

Following a method outlined in Shinnar and Shinnar (1975), Greene (1977: Chapter 3) applied a life-table approach (derived from survival models) to the age distribution of arrestees in a single year to estimate the total length of adult criminal careers. Using data on adult index arrestees in Washington, D.C., in 1973 and assuming that they were all criminally active at age 18, he estimated the mean adult career length for index offenses to be 12 years. This career length estimate, however, was acknowledged to be quite sensitive to late starters who begin their careers after age 18; failure to exclude these late starters leads to overestimates of career length. This career length estimate includes only adult careers, so time as a juvenile offender would be added to estimate overall career length.

More recently, Blumstein and Cohen (1982) used life-table methods to provide estimates of residual career length—the expected time remaining in careers con-

ditional on the time already elapsed in careers. The analysis used data on the histories of individual arrestees to adjust the more conventionally reported age distribution of arrests and to estimate the relationship between residual career length and age. The pattern displayed in Figure 3-4 led Blumstein and Cohen (1982) to characterize the career in terms of three segments: a "break-in" period (I), a "stable" period (II), and a "wear-out" period (III). For adult careers beginning at age 18, the total adult career is estimated to average 5.6 years for index offenses. This is very close to the approximation for adult index careers provided by Greenberg (1975). As time in the career elapses, the pattern in residual career length is consistent with the heterogeneous population model of persistence in arrests. Over the first 10 to 12 years of the break-in period of index careers, mean residual career length increases from 5 to 10 years, a pattern consistent with increasing dropout of desisters from the offender population. After the 12th elapsed year (or around age 30 for 18-year-old starters), residual career length remains fairly stable at about 10 additional years for each of the next 10 years, perhaps representing the mean residual career length for persisters. Finally, perhaps reflecting "burnout" by persisters in the wear-out period, the residual career begins to decline at about age 41 (or after 23 years in active adult careers). Further research is needed to discover the extent to which this decline is due to greater mortality found among active offenders than among the general population, differential incarceration at older ages, physical "burnout," or other reasons.

The three-period pattern for residual career lengths has important implications for incapacitation policies applied to older, more established offenders. The sharp decline in aggregate arrest rates by age 30 has conventionally been inter-

---

[11]This crude estimate of μ, based on the total number of intervals between index arrests divided by the time between the first and most recent index arrests derived from the FBI report on criminal careers in 1965 (Federal Bureau of Investigation, 1966), is almost identical to the more recent estimates of μ for index offenses, reported earlier in this chapter, based on analysis of arrest histories for active offenders.

[12]In a simulation of criminal careers using crime-specific recidivism probabilities (which were held constant to some age and then declined to zero at some later age) and an empirically derived crime-type switch matrix for recidivists, Blumstein and Larson (1969:222–226) estimated the total number of subsequent index arrests after the first to be between 2.2 and 2.9 for different initial index offense types, which was Greenberg's source for his estimate of N.

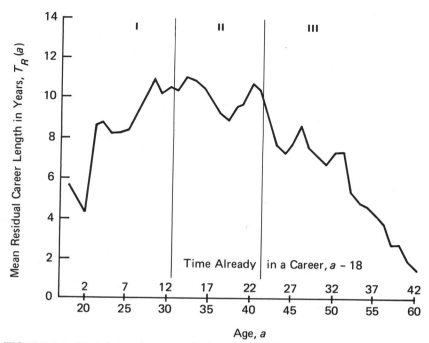

FIGURE 3-4 Variation in mean residual career length (T_R) with time already in a career (18- to 20-year-old starters only). Source: Blumstein and Cohen (1982:Figure 12).

preted to mean that incarceration would be wasted on 30-year-old offenders because they are about to terminate their careers. The findings for residual career lengths, however, suggest that such interpretations may be wrong. The few persistent offenders who begin their adult careers at 18 and remain criminally active into their 30s appear to represent prime candidates for incarceration.

There are also variations in residual career length by crime type. Estimates of crime-specific residual career lengths refer to the average period during which offenders engage in a particular crime type. For example, the residual career length for robbery refers to the remaining period during which a robber continues to commit robberies. The same offender could similarly have a residual burglary career or an index offense career. When the techniques laid out by Blumstein and Cohen (1982) are used, distinct career-

length patterns are evident for property and violent offenses. For the property crimes of burglary, auto theft, and robbery—analyzed separately and as a group—patterns of residual career length are similar to that shown in Figure 3-4 for all index offenses. In terms of career length, then, robbery is perhaps best viewed as a property crime from the perspective of the offender, even though it is a violent crime from the perspective of the victim. In contrast, for the serious violent offenses of murder, rape, and aggravated assault, residual career lengths are on average longer, and offenders who are arrested for these crime types are less likely than property offenders to drop out during the early years of their careers. Thus, older offenders often have long careers marked by arrests for violent offenses, especially aggravated assault. These crime-specific career length patterns suggest that persisters are found widely among violent offenders. Among property offenders, persisters are less widely found, but those who do remain active as adult property offenders in their 30s are likely to continue committing property crimes for another 10 years.

CONCLUSION

Some of the most important conclusions from the review of research on criminal careers relate to factors that are well known to be associated with aggregate crime rates (C) or aggregate arrest rates (A)—factors such as age, race, and sex. Most prior literature has not distinguished whether such factors are associated with participation in offending or with frequency, and the literature has implicitly suggested that the association is equally strong with both. As the last chapter showed, these demographic variables are associated with participation; however, results from research on active offenders indicate that those variables are only weakly related to individual frequency. Thus, the demographic groups most often found to be associated with offending—young, black, and male—differ predominantly in the fraction of their base population who become involved in offending. To the extent that criminal justice officials use their knowledge of the demographic correlates of aggregate rates to make judgments about the future criminality of individual offenders, those judgments are likely to be incorrect. Even though appreciably different fractions of the various demographic subgroups become involved in crime, those who do participate seem to be much more similar across the demographic categories.

The distribution of individual offending frequencies (λ) is highly skewed over the population of active offenders. The median offender engages in only a few crimes per year, but the most active 10 percent of offenders commit crimes at rates that may exceed 100 per year. At virtually all stages of criminal careers, the factors that distinguish the highest-rate offenders are still only incompletely known, but certainly include the following:

- high frequency of prior offending;
- early onset of delinquency as a juvenile;
- drug use, measured either currently or over time; and
- unstable employment in the recent past.

Offenders engage in a great diversity of crime types, with a somewhat greater tendency for offenders to repeat the same crime or to repeat within the group of property crimes or the group of violent crimes. For samples of juvenile offenders, later arrests tend to be for more serious offenses than earlier arrests, but it is difficult to determine how much of that tendency is a consequence of more serious offenders committing a larger number of offenses or of the same individuals escalating the seriousness of their offenses as their careers progress. Adult offenders who are arrested more than once do not, on average, escalate to more serious crimes as their criminal careers progress.

Research on the length of criminal careers indicates, first, that careers are reasonably short, averaging about 5 years for offenders who are active in index offenses as young adults. In the first 10 to 12 years of adult careers, residual careers (i.e., the time still remaining in careers) increase from 5 years for 18-year-olds who commit FBI index offenses to an expected 10 years for index offenders still active in their 30s. This increase probably occurs because of early career termination in the early years by many offenders, leaving the offender group more densely populated with offenders who have longer average career lengths. Offenders with the longest residual career length (T_R) are those who were active in careers at age 18 and who are still active in their 30s. T_R does not begin to decline rapidly until active offenders reach their 40s.

These insights into the structure of residual career length contradict a widely held view that derives from aggregate statistics. These show low aggregate arrest rates (A) by individuals in their 30s and have been assumed to reflect high termination rates in those years. Individual-level analysis of the variation in residual career length with age suggests that offenders who started young and who remain active into their 30s are few but have the lowest termination rates and so are probably the most confirmed offenders.

4

Methodological Issues in
Criminal Career Research

This chapter examines some methodological issues that affect research on criminal careers: of particular concern are various aspects of the observational approaches used to obtain data and the estimation techniques applied to those data. This chapter draws heavily on Cohen (Appendix B), who provides a more detailed review of these issues. On the basis of our examination, we propose various suggestions for improved research strategies to reduce potential biases arising from sampling and measurement problems.

OBSERVATIONAL APPROACHES: SELF-REPORTS AND OFFICIAL RECORDS

The two main observational approaches for obtaining data on individual criminal careers—self-reports and official records of contacts with the criminal justice system—invoke longitudinal data for individuals.[1] Each approach is vulnerable to various sources of error that may limit the accuracy of the derived estimates of criminal career dimensions.

Self-Reports

The sources of distortion in self-report surveys include problems in design of survey instruments, response errors, and analytic problems in inferring career dimensions from questionnaire responses. The role of analytic problems was illustrated in the Chapter 3 discussion of alternating spurts and quiescent periods in offending: recognition that offending frequencies during spurts are unlikely to persist over periods as long as a year led to downward revisions of as much as 25 percent in estimates of λ.

Response errors may arise from prob-

---

[1] Data on crimes committed could also be obtained from reports by victims, from direct observation by researchers, and from information provided by informants. Although such data might provide rich information on the nature of the offense and sometimes on the attributes of an offender, they are usually linked to particular crime events and not to individual offenders. Thus, it is often difficult if not impossible to use such data to trace the development of criminal careers for individual offenders.

lems in questionnaire design or administration procedures, from intentional misrepresentation by respondents, or from respondents' errors in the classification or recall of events.[2] An example of questionnaire design effects comes from the Rand inmate surveys: the open-ended queries about λ in the first survey may have yielded imprecise results for high-frequency offenders, but the alternative approach used in the second survey—a complex series of closed-ended questions—apparently increased the rate of ambiguous, unusable responses (see Chapter 3 for details).

One source of misclassification is respondent uncertainty about which events are to be counted as arrests or police contacts. The ambiguity for respondents may increase as the number of interactions with police increases and respondents are less able to distinguish which of the interactions involve an official charge or notation in police records. There is also ambiguity in classifying self-report items into official-record crime categories: discrepancies may arise because distinctions in the official categories reflect considerations of strength of evidence, criminal intent, and seriousness of the outcome, which are probably not considered in the self-report categories. For example, a self-reported burglary may be noted in the offender's official record as a burglary, a larceny, or possession of stolen property, depending on the circumstances of the arrest.

Memory recall is likely to be affected by the saliency of the events (with more salient events more likely to be remembered) and the recency of the events. Two factors potentially affecting the saliency of crimes are the seriousness and the frequency with which they are committed. In general, more serious crimes—with the greater risks they pose both for

victims and for offenders—are expected to be more salient. The more frequently that crimes are committed, however, the less salient any one of them is likely to be, and so there will probably be errors in counting the total number of crimes committed. These sources of memory errors are likely to be of greatest concern for high-rate, serious offenders.

Since recall is usually best for events that occurred most recently, memory problems are likely to increase with longer recall periods and with greater intervals between the recall period and the survey date. These problems are most typical of surveys that request reports of lifetime frequencies. To reduce those problems, most self-report surveys now limit the recall period, for example, to the year preceding the interview. But even this period is subject to potentially serious recall errors for frequent and low-saliency events. Further reducing the recall period to less than a year, however, could jeopardize precision in estimates of the number of reported criminal events, especially for more serious offense types that occur infrequently.

Defining the recall period in terms of the interview date (e.g., during the year preceding the interview)—although it will enhance the recency of recalled events—may make the data especially vulnerable to bounding errors: events that occurred before the designated recall period may be mistakenly attributed (or "telescoped") to the recall period. Bounding errors may be reduced by specifying a recall period with more salient boundaries for respondents, such as the calendar year or "age-year" (i.e., time between birthdays). A more effective but far more costly solution to the problem of telescoping is to administer two surveys, one at the start of a recall period and the other at the end of that period; events that are reported in both surveys are then removed from responses for the bounded

---

[2]This discussion of errors in self-reports draws heavily on material presented in Weis (Volume II).

period. Because of the extra cost and time required for this approach, however, bounding of this sort is not usually done for self-report surveys.

Even if a researcher exercises great care, there will be ambiguous responses that present difficulty in analyzing the data. For example, on the basis of a reanalysis of the data from the second Rand survey, Visher (Volume II:Table 11) indicates that 35 to 40 percent of the responses by inmates active in robbery or burglary were ambiguous. The Rand researchers tried to deal with that ambiguity by computing minimum and maximum estimates for each respondent (Chaiken and Chaiken, 1982a). Visher adopted an alternative strategy for dealing with ambiguous responses: rather than developing extreme estimates for all respondents, she formulated rules for deriving a single reasonable estimate for each individual and excluded from the analysis those few for whom no reasonable estimate could be computed. For example, individuals who indicated that they committed 1 to 10 crimes but did not report the exact number were assigned a single value in the range from 1 to 10 to match the distribution of the responses by the unambiguous respondents. She used similar estimating strategies for other ambiguous responses. As indicated in Tables 3-3 and 3-4 (in Chapter 3), Visher's estimates are much closer to Rand's original minimum estimates than to the maximums.

Various structural features in the administration of self-report surveys may potentially bias or limit the validity of responses. Such features include differences between responses to self-administered questionnaires and interviews, between anonymous and nonanonymous surveys, and the effects of differences in interviewer attributes. It is reassuring that the research that has examined these effects in self-reports of offending generally finds the reliability and validity of responses reasonably insensitive to these various administration conditions (Weis, Volume II). Rather, the response errors that are found in self-reports are due primarily to the saliency, frequency, and timing of criminal activities and to the structure of the survey items; further development of survey instruments to better address these aspects might reduce their effects significantly.

Official Records

Official records are also vulnerable to important, but very different, errors that affect the accuracy of estimates of individual offending. The main sources of error are the extent to which officially recorded criminal events are limited only to crimes that result in arrests or convictions, are unreliably recorded, and are selective in being more likely to record arrests or convictions for one population subgroup or crime type than for another. There are two main structural sources of recording errors: misclassification of events and nonrecording.

Classification errors can result from differences among local agencies in their classification of offense types, as in the ambiguity over whether a purse snatch is a larceny or a robbery. These classification differences can also occur when locally recorded criminal events, based on the crime categories found in local statutes, are transformed to some other crime classification scheme in centrally maintained official records. Within a single jurisdiction, classification is likely to be fairly consistent, but inconsistencies may be introduced in records that reflect classifications from multiple jurisdictions or in comparisons across jurisdictions. Thus, a high estimate of λ for some crime type in one jurisdiction might reflect a difference in classification rather than a difference in actual offending.

Nonrecording may occur because the event does not meet reporting standards, such as the requirement for a fingerprint or disposition data, which may not be available (Michigan State Police, 1983a, b). Nonrecording is also likely to vary across jurisdictions: jurisdictions that rely especially heavily on state criminal history files are likely to be more thorough in their reporting. Differences in the strength of administrative ties between local jurisdictions and the agencies maintaining central records may also affect recording.

Nonrecording of some events obviously understates the number of arrests by sample members and thus contributes to underestimates of arrest frequencies. However, nonrecording can also lead to overestimates when some arrestees are missing from the arrest history data. Since each subsequent arrest increases the chance that a record will be created, low-rate offenders with their smaller expected number of arrests are likely to be disproportionately missing from the arrest history data, contributing to overestimates of arrest frequencies.

But however complete the recording may be, officially recorded arrests still account for only a small portion of all crimes committed. In addition to the crimes directly associated with an arrest (or a conviction), offenders usually commit other crimes that do not result in arrest. Arrest records can be used to infer the volume of unobserved crimes committed. Such inferences require estimates of the probability of arrest for a crime q and assumptions about the nature of that process, along with direct estimates of individual arrest rates (μ) based on the number of recorded arrests and the length of time that an offender is free and so at risk of arrest. For individuals with arrest rate μ and probability of arrest for a crime q, λ is equal to μ/q.

One approach to estimating the probability of arrest for a crime was proposed by Blumstein and Cohen (1979). The estimate relies on readily available aggregate data and starts with the ratio of the reported per capita arrest rate, A, to the reported per capita crime rate, C, in a jurisdiction. The ratio A/C is then adjusted by the rate at which victims report crimes to the police, r, to reflect total crimes, including those not reported to the police. Data on reporting rates are available from annual victimization surveys, and the adjustment should use reporting rates for the jurisdictions being studied whenever possible. The estimate of q is further adjusted by the average number of offenders per crime incident, O, also available from victimization surveys. This correction adjusts for the fact that the estimated risk of arrest per crime for any individual offender is overstated when the arrest data include arrests of several different offenders who are involved in the same crime incident but the crime data do not. The resulting estimate of the probability of arrest for a crime, q, is $(A/O)/(C/r)$.

There are various potential sources of error in estimates of q and thus in the associated estimates of crimes actually committed. Reported numbers of arrests and crimes are subject to nonrecording, as discussed above. Both victims' reporting rates and the number of multiple offenders per crime are vulnerable to recall and other response errors by the respondents to victimization surveys. The multiple-offenders factor is also subject to biases arising from systematic differences between crimes for which victims know the number of offenders (and report it in victimization surveys) and those for which the number of offenders is not known or reported. The multiple-offenders factors estimated from the victimization surveys will overstate the number of offender-crime incidents ($C \times O$) and thus result in underestimates of q if the number of offenders is more likely to be known in crime incidents involving multiple offenders.

Because of possible errors in components involved in the estimation of q, it is useful to perform sensitivity analyses to assess the impact of those errors on estimates of λ. Based on available empirical estimates of the various component values—a range of A/C from .1 to .3 (Federal Bureau of Investigation Uniform Crime Reports, annual), values of O in the range of 1.25 to 2.50 (Reiss, 1980b), and values of r in the range of .25 to .75 (Bureau of Justice Statistics, 1982a, b)—the values of q calculated from $(A/O)/(C/r)$ range from .010 to .180. This broad range of estimates of q can be combined with a typical annual value of μ of .2 (Table 3-1) to generate estimates of λ ($\lambda = \mu/q$) ranging from 1 to 20 crimes committed annually. Because of the sensitivity of these λ estimates to variations in the factors comprising q, better estimates are needed of the range of error in the components of q.

Even if the average value of q is estimated accurately, estimates of both individual offending frequency (λ) and participation rates (d) may be biased by interactions between λ and q at the individual level. If individual crime rates and arrest risks are negatively related to one another, with high-rate offenders less likely to be arrested for each crime, application of a homogeneous q to all offenders results in an underestimate of λ. Correspondingly, λ will be overestimated if λ and q are positively related. If λ and q vary systematically with the attributes of offenders, failure to adequately represent that variation will also distort the estimates of λ associated with different offender subgroups. Without adequate controls for variations in q, any estimate of λ derived from official records will confound individual differences in λ with differential police practices reflected in q. The limited research available to date

generally fails to find systematic substantial variations in q with differences in λ or in the demographic attributes of offenders (see Cohen, Appendix B). Further research on this relationship should have high priority. However, while still preliminary, the available results suggest that the errors may be small in estimates of average values of λ that are derived from arrest records made on the assumption that λ and q are independent.

Even in the face of heterogeneity in q, estimates of individual crime rates would be unbiased if the arrest risk for a crime varied independently of individual crime rates. Nevertheless, the potential for bias in estimating dimensions of the crime process from official data of the observed arrest process highlights the importance of empirically investigating the nature of any variation in q, and especially in finding any systematic variation in q with changes in individual crime rates or with attributes of offenders. To date, homogeneous qs have been used because official records do not provide the information necessary to indicate how arrest risks vary across different offenders. Such information, however, can be derived by combining self-reports of individual crime and arrest experiences.

Potential for Synthesis of Observational Methods

Self-reports and official records are currently the best available methods for obtaining longitudinal data on individual criminal careers. Because of the fundamental differences between them and their sources of error, the two approaches are often posed as competing alternatives. This conflict between the methods has been fueled by apparently substantial differences in conclusions based on the two data sources: most notably, early findings based on official-record data showed important differences in criminal participation by social class and race that were not supported by data from self-reports. For the most part, these early differences are resolved when appropriate controls are included to ensure that the two data sources are comparable in sample composition and in the seriousness threshold used for criminal activities.

A more constructive approach is to view the alternative methods as complementary and to search for mutually beneficial ways of using them. The discussion above highlighted some of the more important sources of error in the two approaches: because their sources of error are very different, however, it is possible to use the two approaches in concert to ameliorate some of the error problems in each. For example, one can compare estimates of individual offending patterns that are derived independently from the two methods. If the estimates are similar, some confirmation of their accuracy is provided. Since it is unlikely that the two approaches would consistently result in the same wrong estimates, similar findings from independent analyses would suggest that the errors in each approach are not grossly distorting. The search for such convergent validity between results is one way of using analyses of self-reports and official records in concert.

The two approaches can also be used together at intermediate levels in research to try to deal explicitly with various sources of error. Official records of arrests or convictions are already used in combination with self-reports of these same officially recorded events as a means of validating the accuracy of self-reports. Official records might also be used to help reduce response errors by invoking events in the official record during self-report interviews, both as a means of triggering recall of events and time periods for respondents and of reducing respondent inclinations to intentionally misrepresent their criminal activities.

Self-reports of crimes committed are sometimes based on samples of inmates in order to increase the number of respondents who have a sufficient number of criminal events. While providing a usable number of reported events for analysis, such samples are not representative of the general offending population (see next section on sampling). In these samples, official records can be used to estimate various statistics (e.g., the probabilities of arrest for a crime, of conviction following arrest, and of incarceration following conviction, and the average time served once incarcerated) that describe the selection process that led to the respondents' incarceration. These statistics, which determine the chance that an offender with particular characteristics will be found among inmates, can be used to weight observations in the inmate sample in order to provide estimates applicable to offenders who are not incarcerated.

Data from self-reports can also be used to address one of the main sources of error in analyses of official records—the oversimplified characterization of the arrest process implied by the assumption of homogeneous q. Self-report data provide an opportunity to directly link self-reported crimes to both self-reported and official-record arrests for specific individuals with known attributes. With these data, it is possible to explicitly examine the variability in q both with individual crime rates and with various attributes of offenders. The patterns of variation that are found would provide a basis for introducing heterogeneous estimates of q into analyses of official-record data.

SAMPLING ISSUES

Analyses of criminal careers involve some important choices on the appropriate sample design for generating offender data. Central to problems of sample design are tradeoffs between the representativeness of offenders and obtaining a sufficient number of active offenders for analysis. The best sample choice in any study varies with the career dimension being measured.

At one extreme, a random sample of people can be drawn from the general population and their criminal careers followed through self-reports or official-record data. But since arrests and crimes occur relatively infrequently in the general population, the number of crime and arrest events will be low, especially for the more serious offense types. Therefore, samples from the general population are of value primarily for studying participation in offending. Only for very minor crime types, like truancy and smoking by juveniles, which occur in large numbers, do such samples permit analysis of active offenders' careers.

Stratified sample designs can increase the yield of active offenders by oversampling high-yield subpopulations, but at the cost of a reduced number of offenders drawn from low-yield subpopulations. Therefore, stratification increases the precision of estimates of the career dimensions of active offenders in the high-yield subpopulation and usually in the aggregate population, but decreases substantially the precision of estimates for the low-yield subpopulation. For example, oversampling teenaged males from low-income neighborhoods will improve the precision of λ estimates for that subpopulation, but with a substantial loss of precision in λ estimates for young adults, females, and residents of high-income neighborhoods.

Regardless of stratification, samples drawn from community-based sampling frames like schools and households are more likely to miss offenders than nonoffenders, and this problem is likely to be most severe for high-rate offenders, leading to their disproportionate underrepresentation in these samples. For example,

all community-based samples exclude offenders who are incarcerated at the time of sampling, who tend to be disproportionately high-rate offenders. If high-rate offenders are more likely to drop out of school, they will be underrepresented in school-based samples. High-rate offenders who are free in the community are hard for survey researchers to locate because they are likely to be "on the run" or otherwise trying to avoid detection; those with highly transient living arrangements tend to be missed in household-based samples. And high-rate offenders who are located may be more likely than others to be uncooperative, refusing to participate in research.

The principal alternative to general population samples is samples drawn from populations of presumed offenders, such as arrestees, convictees, or incarcerated people. The choice of a definition for sampling offenders involves a tradeoff between the degree of certainty about offender status and the degree to which the sample is representative of offenders more generally. Sampling from convicted offenders greatly reduces any uncertainty about the actual criminal involvement of sample members. However, convicted offenders in prison, for example, are not likely to be representative of all offenders: they are presumably the most serious, the oldest, and perhaps the most inept at avoiding detection.

The broadest sampling base among officially detected offenders is arrestees. But selecting a sample of arrestees involves potential errors of commission, since some falsely arrested persons are wrongly included among active offenders. Selecting convictees, by contrast, is more likely to involve errors of omission because active offenders in the arrestee population who are not convicted (and often not prosecuted; see below) are excluded from the sample. In dealing with dispositions for specific individuals, of course, the presumption of innocence makes errors of commission unacceptable. In dealing with the empirical characterization of criminal careers, however, there must be a relative weighing of these two types of errors. Fundamental to this consideration is some assessment of the factors contributing to the lack of a conviction after an arrest.

Empirical examinations of the reasons for nonconviction suggest that nonconviction is by no mean synonymous with innocence (Forst, Lucianovic, and Cox, 1977; Vera Institute of Justice, 1977; Brosi, 1979; Boland et al., 1983; Feeney, Dill, and Weir, 1983). The vast majority of nonconvictions are the result of diversions from adult criminal courts (to juvenile court or to pretrial diversion programs) and dismissals, rather than the result of acquittals. The reasons for dismissal frequently have little to do with the guilt or innocence of the defendant. Instead, many cases are dismissed because of noncooperation by witnesses (often arising from the existence of a prior relationship between the offender and victim), inadmissibility of critical evidence, and the lesser importance of the case compared with other cases. Many less serious cases are also diverted prior to trial. In view of the predominantly procedural reasons that many arrests do not result in a conviction, the errors of commission associated with truly innocent arrestees appear to be far less frequent than the errors of omission that would occur if the more stringent standard of conviction were used as a basis for sampling offenders.

An important consideration in using samples of identified active offenders is the degree to which those samples are biased toward high-rate offenders. High-rate offenders would be overrepresented among persons who have at least one detected event (a crime, arrest, conviction, or incarceration) during a sampling period, since they are more likely to incur the sampling event. This bias is greatest when the sampling period is short compared with the mean time between events.[3] These biases can be compensated analytically by accounting for the differential sampling probabilities associated with offenders having different event rates. Alternatively, one can include only offenders whose first recorded event occurs in a sampling period that is short compared with career length. This sample of starting offenders mirrors the distribution of λ among offenders.

There is also a greater concentration of more serious offense types in convictee and inmate samples than in other offender samples. Processing cases through the criminal justice system typically involves increased filtering and selectivity as many less serious cases are dropped. Thus, the further into the criminal justice system that samples are drawn, the less likely samples are to be representative of street offenders generally. From the perspective of ensuring greater representativeness, samples of self-reported offenders and arrestees are better than samples of inmates or even of convictees.

It is possible to correct for biases arising from the sampling process. The correction involves reweighting the sample to reflect the differences in the sampling probabilities of sample members. Such a weighting scheme would give greater weight to offender types who are underrepresented in a sample and less weight to those who are overrepresented. Successful correction of sample biases using

---

[3]If events follow a Poisson process, an offender with individual event rate μ has a probability of being sampled during a period of length t of $p_s = 1 - e^{-\mu t}$. If t is very short compared to $1/\mu$, then p_s is approximately μt, and so higher-rate offenders are seriously overrepresented. If t is very long compared with $1/\mu$, then p_s is close to unity, and the sample is reasonably representative of the offender sample.

this approach requires an adequate characterization of the sampling process and reasonable estimates of the sampling probabilities.

General population and offender-based sampling strategies, with their different flaws, are each suited for different purposes. General population samples, which include offenders and nonoffenders, are more appropriate for estimating participation rates. The undercount of high-rate offenders in such samples will understate participation, but this bias is not likely to be substantial because of the small numbers of high-rate offenders among total offenders. However, general population samples are inefficient for estimating frequency rates of active offenders because of the low yield of active offenders in such samples. The inefficiency is aggravated by the underrepresentation of high-rate offenders in those samples. Samples of arrestees or inmates are better suited for estimating λ, but corrections are required to adjust for the overrepresentation of high-rate and more serious offenders in these samples.

USE OF COHORT AND CROSS-SECTIONAL DATA

Research on criminal careers involves a study of the variation in an individual's criminal activity during his life, including the ages at initiation and termination and the pattern of offending between those two points. Thus, all such research is inherently longitudinal.

There are many ways in which such longitudinal research can be pursued. The most obvious would be to identify a cohort at birth and to follow that cohort prospectively for a long enough period of time to include the termination of most criminal careers of cohort members. The most important disadvantage of this approach is the long time required to develop results. In addition to the considerable cost involved, the historical environment in which the cohort is observed may no longer be relevant at the time the results become available. Thus, for example, a cohort that reached maturity before the sharp rise in drug use of the late 1960s would yield no information on the influence of drug use on involvement in other criminal activity.

A different approach to longitudinal research is a retrospective longitudinal design. This approach avoids the long delay associated with the prospective study by defining a cohort and reconstructing its prior criminal involvement. This is the approach pursued by Wolfgang, Figlio, and Sellin (1972), who first defined a cohort—all boys born in 1945 and residing in Philadelphia from ages 10 to 18—and then retrospectively collected their records of police contacts.

In the absence of longitudinal data, annual cross-sectional data can be used to synthesize a cohort by examining variations across age within a year as a proxy for longitudinal age variations of a cohort. However, the two may not be equivalent. If there are important cohort effects, then those cohort effects will be confounded with age effects in a synthesized cohort. If there is a positive association between career length and λ, for example, then a cross-section cohort will display a larger average λ and more high-rate offenders than a natural cohort; a negative association will lead to the opposite effects. Furthermore, a cross-section design precludes examining temporal sequences within individuals, which is a main feature of longitudinal cohort designs.

A major problem with single-cohort designs is that age effects are inextricably confounded with historical effects. Thus, a cohort that happened to reach the high-crime ages of the mid-teens at a time of considerable social turmoil would display an amplified age effect in involvement in crime compared with another cohort that reached those ages at a time of social tranquility. Analysis of a single cohort would not be able to isolate these effects. One way to overcome this problem is by drawing multiple cohorts and obtaining longitudinal data on them. A variant of this approach involves identifying a cross-section sample of the population (thus representing multiple cohorts) and collecting longitudinal data—either prospectively or retrospectively—on them. Because of residential migration, however, the members of the cross-section sample will differ from the birth cohorts within the jurisdiction studied. Also, if the cross-section sample is drawn from an arrestee population (or some other offender sample), then the older members of the cross-section sample will overrepresent individuals who have longer criminal careers, and any estimates of relationships with career length will be biased; for example, factors positively associated with career length will be overrepresented.

The relative strengths and weaknesses of the various design aspects considered here suggest that an appropriate compromise involves drawing samples from multiple jurisdictions and developing multiple overlapping cohorts, each observed for a limited time through certain key developmental age periods. For each of these periods, prospective longitudinal data on criminal activity and other related events should be collected on cohort members. Those data can and should be augmented by retrospective longitudinal data whenever available.

PROBLEMS OF CONFOUNDED EFFECTS

A number of factors may confound estimates of criminal career dimensions. In some cases, there are interactions among various dimensions, which result in possible distortions in the separate estimates for each dimension. The possibility of career termination during a follow-up period, for example, distorts estimates of λ for offenders who remain active, since some offenders will end their criminal activity during the follow-up period. If λ is calculated by assuming that all offenders are active throughout the follow-up period, failure to account for this shortened duration for some offenders will result in a downward bias in the estimate of λ.

Many criminal career analyses focus on changes in offender behavior as their criminal careers progress. For example, such studies include analyses of trends in offense seriousness or in λ as offenders age or accumulate arrests. When such trends are established they are often attributed to developmental changes as offenders mature, to growth in criminality as the career unfolds, or to consequences of offenders' interactions with the criminal justice system. Another interpretation of observed trends that is rarely invoked, however, involves none of these causal explanations but derives from offender heterogeneity. Under this interpretation, different offender groups will display differential persistence in their criminal careers. In such a situation, the more persistent groups and their characteristics increasingly dominate samples of offenders who are observed at later stages of criminal careers. To the extent that offender heterogeneity is a factor in generating the observed trends and is not adequately controlled in the analysis of them, the changing composition of the offender population over the course of careers will be incorrectly interpreted as changes in the behavior of offenders.

Measurements of career dimensions often differ across studies and are sometimes characterized as presenting conflicting information. In many cases, however, the differences in measurements are attributable to differences in the scope of offenses considered or to the composition of the population studied. For example, participation rates will be higher for all offenses than for violent offenses, for cumulative lifetime participation (B_L) than for participation by age 18 (B_{18}), and for samples of males alone than for samples of males and females. Therefore, any reporting of criminal career measurements must indicate the basis of the measurements.

Variations in exposure time can also affect measurements of criminal career dimensions. For example, if an individual initiates or terminates a career midway through an observation period, then the estimate of his offending frequency, when distributed over the entire period, would be only half his true rate during his active period. A similar distortion could occur in analyzing the effects of covariates on criminal career dimensions. Consider, for example, the relationships between precursor behaviors, such as alcohol or marijuana use, and criminal participation: alcohol use generally begins at an earlier age than marijuana use, and thus alcohol users have a longer exposure time within any independently established observation period than do marijuana users. Thus, even if both substances had the same influence in initiating delinquent careers, more of the alcohol users would have had the opportunity to begin offending within the observation period than would marijuana users. Isolating the relative influence of these two covariates on participation requires adequate controls for the differences in times at risk (Robins and Wish, 1977).

Identifying the covariates of criminal careers is especially important both for improving theory on the causes of individual criminality and for distinguishing among offenders for various policy purposes. The proportional hazards method is a statistical technique that permits simultaneous control for variations across individuals in covariates of criminal careers and for variations in exposure times. Its primary application in criminology has been to data on time to recidivism (Barton and Turnbull, 1981). By relying on time to a first recidivist event as the dependent variable, however, these models cannot distinguish the separate effects of covariates on the career dimensions of frequency and termination.

Maltz (1984) explores one approach to disentangling the relationship of independent covariates to separate career dimensions. He proposes a model that partitions recidivism between the probability of ever recidivating (which is related to career termination) and the failure rate of recidivists (a direct measure of offending frequency for active offenders). To examine the role of covariates on those career dimensions, the data are partitioned into groups that are reasonably homogeneous with respect to the covariates of interest, and the two dimensions of recidivism are estimated separately for each group. In an illustrative analysis of the effects of one covariate—age at release—the estimated probability of ever recidivating decreases as age at release increases in three of four jurisdictions examined, but there appears to be no effect of age at release on failure rates for those who do recidivate (Maltz, 1984: 131–133). This approach, however, is still preliminary, and considerable development and testing are required to identify the statistical properties of the technique. The problem of identifying and controlling for the effects of independent covariates on the various career dimensions remains an important area for further research development.

EXPLICIT MODELS OF OFFENDING

Virtually all estimates of criminal career dimensions invoke some kind of implicit model of individual offending. Because of the inherent difficulties in obtaining direct observations of crimes committed by individual offenders, estimates of career dimensions rest on other observable data, like arrests and self-reported crimes, as indirect indicators of the underlying crime process. The various estimation strategies that are applied to these data rest fundamentally on models that characterize both individual offending and the processes that give rise to the observable data. The accuracy of the estimates of criminal careers that emerge depends on the adequacy of the assumptions in the models, which are usually unstated.

Because the available observable data are only indirect indicators of actual crimes committed, improving the precision of measurement of those data is only one part of needed work; estimates for the underlying, but unobserved, crime process must also be improved. This second step requires explicit models that link the unobserved crime process with the observed data. With explicit models, the adequacy of estimates can be assessed in terms of the reasonableness of the assumptions and the sensitivity of results to those assumptions.

Models of individual offending have moved from treatments of offending based on traditional aggregate measures such as per capita crime rates and recidivism rates to more detailed characterizations that partition offending levels among the various aspects of a criminal career. The initial models of criminal careers have relied on a number of simplifying assumptions, principally that individual careers are stationary over time and homogeneous across offenders. This simplest characterization underlies most currently available estimates of career dimensions. More recent developments have begun to enrich the basic model to better accommodate the complexities of real careers. One issue of concern has

been possible nonstationarities in offending frequencies during individual careers. Two forms of nonstationarity have been addressed in recent research: spurts in criminal activity as offenders move between active and quiescent periods and changes in frequencies as offenders age.

Two approaches to addressing spurts in criminal activity during a career are available. In reanalyzing the data from the second Rand inmate survey, Chaiken and Rolph (1985) found evidence that periods of criminal activity during the observation period tended to be clustered near the arrest that led to the current incarceration. The observation periods for respondents with short street times are thus only slightly longer than the periods of spurts in activity. When offending rates during these periods are treated as if they applied to both active and quiescent periods, they lead to overestimates of offenders' average annual frequency, λ. Chaiken and Rolph propose a model to reflect this mixture of active and quiescent periods during a career and adjust individual frequencies downward to reflect this mixture. Lehoczky (Volume II) proposes an alternative model to accommodate spurts in criminal activity: individuals alternate between active and quiescent periods, and they commit crimes and are arrested only during the active periods. After each arrest, an offender faces a possible transition—to move into a quiescent period (with probability a) or to continue in the active state (with probability $1 - a$). In the Lehoczky model, sanctions may also have an inhibiting effect on future crimes as each arrest triggers a possible move to a quiescent period.

Other model refinements address possible changes in λ with age, like those observed in aggregate per capita arrest rates, which increase rapidly into the late teens and then decrease steadily for older ages (see Figure 1-2). Similar declines with age for adults have been observed in recidivism rates and in frequency rates for broad aggregate offense categories, such as "all offenses," or "all index offenses" (see, for example, Peterson and Braiker, 1980).

Two different approaches to modeling these age effects are presented in papers commissioned by the panel. Flinn (Volume II) models individual allocations of time to criminal activity as a rational choice based on the net expected returns from legitimate and criminal activities. In this model, declines in criminal activity with age result when wage rates from legitimate activity increase as individuals accumulate more work experience and when the expected cost per crime, measured by expected time spent incarcerated, increases with the number of prior incarcerations. The model by Lehoczky (Volume II) captures the distinction between aging effects for individual crime types and for the aggregate of several crime types. An individual offender is modeled as having multiple careers, one for each crime type. The careers in each crime type are separate and operate independently of one another. For any single crime type i, an individual's frequency rate (λ_i) is fixed during his career in that crime type, and that crime-specific career terminates with some probability β after each crime committed. In this formulation, the total value of λ for an individual—reflecting the sum over all crime types—declines with age as active crime types are gradually eliminated.

The Lehoczky model also incorporates other refinements to the model of criminal careers, including variation across offenders in their career dimensions. It also permits covariates of the dimensions reflecting both fixed background characteristics (such as sex, race, juvenile record, and age at first encounter with the criminal justice system) and dynamic attributes (such as drug use and employment status). While the model has not been applied to data, various techniques for estimating the model parameters from empirical data have been proposed.

The model developments by Flinn (Volume II), Lehoczky (Volume II), and Chaiken and Rolph (1985) represent conceptual advances over the simple model of criminal careers represented in Figure 1-2 that underlies most available estimates of the various career dimensions. As models of criminal careers are extended to better reflect the underlying behavioral and observational processes, the estimates derived from those models should be more valid. Application of the enriched models to improve estimates of the distributions of career dimensions is still necessary. It will also be useful to compare the resulting estimates with similar estimates derived using the simple model. Such comparisons will permit an assessment of the error introduced by the assumptions in the simpler models (e.g., homogeneous frequency rates across offenders or the use of a single uniform arrest probability per crime across offenders). Such comparisons may indicate that the assumptions of the simple model are reasonable approximations that yield satisfactory estimates and that adequately account for important effects, or more detailed sensitivity analyses may indicate which assumptions of the more elaborate models are most important.

5

Crime Control Strategies Using Criminal Career Knowledge

The criminal career paradigm suggests three general orientations for crime control strategies: prevention, career modification, and incapacitation. This chapter first presents the evidence and conclusions on programs intended to prevent young children from becoming offenders. It then reviews efforts to modify ongoing criminal careers through interventions with the family and efforts to change substance abuse behavior and employment status, both of which are associated with a high frequency of serious offending. This chapter also updates the work of the National Research Council Panel on Deterrent and Incapacitative Effects (Blumstein, Cohen, and Nagin, 1978) by examining the crime control effects of different sentencing policies from an incarceration perspective.

Preventive strategies are intended to reduce the number of nonoffenders who become offenders. Two types of knowledge are needed to design effective preventive strategies: prospective indicators of subpopulations having high participation rates and identified interventions that reduce participation in targeted sub-

populations. Although the panel's review of experimental findings on the effectiveness of various interventions in reducing participation found little evidence supporting specific interventions as preventive mechanisms, it did find a few candidates sufficiently promising to warrant a call for experimental replications.

Career modification strategies are focused on persons already known to be criminals and seek to reduce the frequency or seriousness of their crimes. Also, modification strategies usually attempt to encourage the termination of ongoing criminal careers by creating fear of punishment, by modifying offenders' values, or by expanding opportunities for legitimate alternatives to crime. Career modification strategies, such as counseling or behavioral therapies, intervene directly in the life of the offender to change criminal behavior. The panel was particularly interested in the substantial body of research relating recidivism rates to various interventions, including community-based supervision as an alternative to incarceration, verbal and behavioral therapies intended to inhibit aggressive and antisocial behavior, substance abuse treatment programs, and programs to improve employment prospects. Some of these interventions might also effectively inhibit future participation among nonoffenders. Methodological problems limit the knowledge that most of these studies provide about the effectiveness of those interventions in modifying the criminal career, but several studies in which large samples were randomly assigned to alternative treatments provide evidence about the relative effectiveness of some intervention programs.

Incapacitation strategies focus on the crime reduced as a result of removing offenders from society during their criminal careers. While the use of imprisonment as a means of incapacitation may also have career modification effects by altering offender behavior through inmate rehabilitation programs, the "incapacitative effect" refers only to crimes prevented in the community by interrupting criminal careers during periods of incarceration. This incapacitative effect depends fundamentally on the magnitude of individual crime rates, λ. Two types of incapacitation are often distinguished: collective incapacitation and selective incapacitation. Collective incapacitation refers to the effects of aggregate policies involving changes in the average sentences applied to average offenders. Collective strategies, such as a percentage increase in all prison sentences, were the subject of the previous Panel on Research on Deterrent and Incapacitative Effects (Blumstein, Cohen, and Nagin, 1978). Selective incapacitation refers to policies that target increased incapacitation more narrowly on selected offenders. One such policy prescribes longer prison terms for the few offenders who commit serious offenses at especially high rates. As part of its work, this panel commissioned a reanalysis of recent Rand Corporation data on variations in reported λ among inmates and on the selective incapacitative effects of using longer sentences for the high-rate offenders among those inmates.

STRATEGIES TO PREVENT PARTICIPATION

Research has identified demographic and nondemographic indicators of a high risk of eventual participation in crime. On the basis of the widely measured demographic variables of age, sex, race, and place of residence, young black males in large urban locations appear to be at particularly high risk of arrest: approximately 30 percent have been arrested by age 18 for an FBI index offense (see Blumstein and Graddy, 1982:Table 1). And while the peak age for the first arrest is 15, there is significant risk at even earlier ages: about one-third of the black males arrested by age 18 had been arrested by age 13. As noted in Chapter 2, family characteristics associated with the onset of delinquency at any age include earlier parental delinquency and criminality, poor child supervision, and marital conflict in two-parent households. Early, intense, and diverse antisocial behavior by a child, poor school performance, and low measured IQ are other indications of a high risk for participation in crime. Full-time employment at a young age when school attendance is expected may also be associated with participation in crime.

Several problems limit the potential of these factors in focusing preventive interventions. Most important, considerable ambiguity surrounds the interpretation of many indicators, especially the demographic variables, which often function as stand-ins for other unmeasured social and economic factors. In addition, the causal relationship between measured variables and criminal participation is often imprecise and may vary with circumstances.

Many children present some or all of the high-risk characteristics and antecedent behaviors but do not become offenders, and any classification rule invoking the indicators will produce many false positives (Loeber and Dishion, 1983).[1] Although the ability to predict future participation in crime increases during the late teenage and adult years, effective options for preventive intervention may well decrease as the high-risk youth becomes older and less amenable to change. However, some of the relationships observed at ages 8–10—the earliest at which any of the childhood characteristics have been studied in relation to adult offending— might also be observable at younger ages. Thus, an important research issue is determining the optimal age for intervention: if the intervention is early, the identification of high-risk children is likely to produce many errors; if the intervention is late, there will be less chance of success.

Experimental Evaluations of Preventive Interventions

Early identification of children or teenagers at relatively high risk of becoming offenders raises the possibility of intervention strategies to prevent members of high-risk groups from becoming offenders. During the 1960s and 1970s, federal funding was provided for many juvenile programs, some of which had crime prevention as one of their objectives. There is a large body of research evaluating these programs, which has been extensively reviewed (e.g., Lundman, McFarlane, and Scarpitti, 1976; Wright and Dixon, 1977; Farrington, Ohlin, and Wilson, 1986). In general, this research has been characterized by small sample sizes and designs that were either nonexperimental or did not have adequate controls. Also, the follow-up periods have usually been 2 years or less: although these periods are probably adequate to assess the short-term effectiveness of the interventions in correcting antisocial behaviors, they are not long enough to show effectiveness in preventing later criminal activity. However, the panel did identify some promising experimental studies of interventions oriented specifically toward the precursor problems of bad family management, low school performance, and early antisocial behavior. In these few studies, the findings were sufficiently strong to suggest that further replications might establish their effectiveness in inhibiting participation in offending.

Interventions with the Family

There are a few evaluations of efforts to train parents in identifying problem behaviors as they emerge and using such modes of discipline as rewards and time-out periods to change them. Loeber (1984) reviewed three studies of experimental interventions with families of problem—but not criminal—children aged 3–14, based on this orientation (Walters and Gilmore, 1973; Karoly and Rosenthal, 1977; Bernal, Klinnert, and Schultz, 1980). Two of the studies demonstrated temporary effectiveness in correcting the overt antisocial behavior: reductions of about 60 percent in the frequency of the targeted behaviors, ob-

---

[1]There have been several attempts to develop formal classification rules that could be used to identify predelinquent children. One of the oldest, the Glueck Social Prediction Table, included five family-related factors that differentiated 500 delinquents from a matched set of 500 nondelinquents (Glueck and Glueck, 1950). A number of methodological problems in this work have been identified (see Zeisel, 1968; Hirschi and Selvin, 1973), and in a validation of the scale—which targeted first-grade males in high-delinquency areas in New York City and followed them for 7 years—75 percent of the predictions of delinquency were inaccurate (see Lundman, 1984).

served up to 1 month after completion of the program. However, the only study with a follow-up period long enough to discover long-term behavioral changes— 2 years—failed to detect a decrease (Bernal, Klinnert, and Schultz, 1980). Longer follow-ups and searches of juvenile court records would be needed to learn whether the interventions succeeded in inhibiting participation in criminal behavior.

One particular intervention with families—family social learning—is based on the theory that early antisocial behavior is first learned through imitation of other family members and interaction with them, that ineffective parenting fails to inhibit minor antisocial behaviors from escalating in seriousness, and that these behaviors may lead children into trouble with school authorities or with the juvenile justice system (see Patterson, Chamberlain, and Reid, 1982). The goal of this type of intervention is to eliminate parental behaviors that serve as a model for aggressive antisocial behavior by the child and to suppress the child's antisocial behavior when it occurs. Theoretically, parental training could begin at any time before the child reaches high school age. While these preventive approaches have been advocated (Pulkkinen, 1983; Loeber, 1984) and tried, the follow-up periods in the few experimental studies of such interventions have been too short to permit evaluations of their effectiveness in inhibiting participation in offending.

Preschool Programs

The Perry Preschool Project, carried out in Michigan, was primarily directed at improving the school performance of disadvantaged black children through a Head Start program providing intellectual stimulation and enrichment (Schweinhart and Weikart, 1980). This Head Start program was unique because it also examined the impact of a preschool program in reducing later criminal activity. Results from a long-term evaluation suggest that the program had generally beneficial effects. The experimental group of 58 children receiving the enrichment showed gains in measured IQ at age 5, although this gain, in comparison with a control group, dissipated entirely by age 14. But at the latter age, the experimental subjects displayed higher school achievement, better self-reported classroom behavior, and less self-reported participation in offending than the control subjects (Berrueta-Clement et al., 1984). The findings with respect to school achievement were replicated in 10 similar experiments conducted at about the same time, but these experiments did not collect official records of participation in crime or delinquency (Consortium for Longitudinal Studies, 1983).

Comparisons of officially recorded criminal participation also suggest lower rates among the 58 preschool participants than among the control group of 65: 40 percent of the controls but only 25 percent of the participants were charged or arrested as adults.[2] While these differences are statistically significant and encouraging, an intervention based on a sample of this size needs further testing. Replication of the analysis of criminal participation for the other 10 Head Start experiments would be an important next step in further assessment of the program's potential for reducing criminal participation.

_____

[2] A somewhat smaller difference between preschool participants and controls was reported with respect to the percent arrested as juveniles (Berrueta-Clement et al., 1984). However, because some arrested juveniles were not included in the analysis, that difference is not discussed here.

Other Interventions

Various school- and community-based preventive interventions have been experimentally evaluated with respect to their effectiveness in correcting undesirable behavior in children identified as at risk (e.g., "aggressive," "antisocial," "vulnerable to delinquency") by parents, teachers, or professional observers. The interventions that have been studied include special school programs to improve self-concept or cognitive skills (e.g., Reckless and Dinitz, 1972; Garrison and Stolberg, 1983; Kettlewell and Kausch, 1983), behavior management techniques such as contracting and token economies (Stuart, Jayaratne, and Tripodi, 1976), individual counseling (McCord, 1978; Shore and Massimo, 1979), work-experience programs (Ahlstrom and Havighurst, 1971; Hackler and Hagan, 1975; Wodarski et al., 1979), buddy programs (O'Donnell, Lydgate, and Fo, 1979), and social learning programs (Wodarski and Pedi, 1978; Johnson and Breckenridge, 1982). The sample sizes in these studies ranged from 32 to 1,000, and follow-up periods ranged from none beyond the life of the program up to 30 years. Of these experimental studies, several interventions seem encouraging, but further study is needed.

One 2-year intervention (Bry and George, 1979, 1980; Bry, 1982) involved points awarded weekly by teachers for good behavior, discussions in group meetings, and extra school trips, and reports on behavior were made to parents. A group of 66 seventh-grade students selected on the basis of school or family problems was assigned randomly to receive the intervention or not. The experimental subjects did not experience the subsequent deterioration in school attendance and academic achievement that occurred in the 33 controls who did not receive the treatment. In a follow-up interview 1 year after the program, members of the experimental group reported a participation rate of 33 percent for vandalism, auto theft, grand theft, or robbery, compared with a rate of 55 percent among the control group. In another follow-up 5 years after the intervention ended, a search of county juvenile probation records showed that the participation rate in serious or chronic offending was 9 percent and 27 percent for experimental and control subjects, respectively. As with the Perry preschool programs, these results are encouraging, but replications in other sites with larger samples are necessary.

Summary: Preventive Interventions

The major reviews of experimental evidence on the effectiveness of preventive interventions suggest some encouraging possibilities, but they do not establish that any approach tested to date effectively reduces subsequent criminal participation. Head Start programs appear to improve school performance, and there is evidence suggesting that one such program reduced later participation in offending, but analysis of data on criminal participation from other Head Start sites is needed to establish the finding more definitively. Social learning programs for families of antisocial preadolescents have sometimes shown short-term effectiveness in ameliorating the early antisocial behavior that frequently precedes delinquency, but these programs have not yet been evaluated as effective in preventing delinquency itself. Future experiments of this type of intervention need to use longer follow-up periods, include searches of juvenile justice system records, and compare results across alternative family arrangements, such as single- versus two-parent households. The theoretical underpinnings and program operations of the interventions also need to be made explicit in this research so that results can be adequately evaluated and promising interventions tested in other settings.

Some of the findings of no difference between treatment and control or comparison groups may be attributable to reactive effects of the experiment. In preventive interventions designed to improve conduct at school, for example, children may resent being stigmatized or feel angry at being separated from their classmates. Moreover, since teachers usually know the identities of the treatment subjects but not of the control group subjects, inflated expectations or hostility related to the program could lead to differential subjective performance standards. If either a child's or a teacher's behavior is influenced by the structural characteristics of the experiment, then the program components may not achieve the desired effect. Future experiments of this type of intervention should be aware of these reactive effects. One alternative may be school-based programs that are designed to supplement basic education and are directed at all enrolled children rather than some selected "high-risk" group (see Greenwood and Zimring, 1985).

The design of some interventions may also reflect an incomplete or inaccurate theoretical orientation, which may account for findings of negative effects. Preventive interventions (or career modification strategies) grounded in social learning theory and behavior modification may ignore the possibility that correction of the targeted behavioral problems in one setting (say, the home) may not modify them in another setting (such as the school). And, as discussed by Loeber (1982), children with conduct disorders often display different problem behaviors in different settings. The typical behavioral intervention, however, focuses on modifying behavior in one set-

ting, with little or no transfer of program components—such as behavioral contracts, reinforcements, or punishments—into other settings. Correction of a problem behavior in the home would be ineffective in inhibiting participation in crime if it were replaced by disruptive behavior in the classroom. In this case, postintervention evaluations, especially long-term follow-up studies that examine police or court records, would be unlikely to show an effect of the narrowly targeted behavioral intervention.

In short, most of the evaluative research on preventive interventions is nondefinitive because of design problems, small sample sizes, inadequate follow-up periods, and inadequate randomization. Moreover, because of the difficulty and cost of large-scale, fully randomized experiments, research and evaluation in this area might advance more quickly under a two-stage process. In the first stage, quasi experiments and experiments with small samples could explore the effectiveness of many types of programs; in the second stage, the programs that had emerged as most promising could be replicated on a larger scale with a more rigorous research design. Head Start and social learning programs have shown promise in small-scale demonstrations, and they appear to be ready for larger-scale studies. For other types of interventions, more attention needs to be placed on design quality and on full reporting of the initial experimental results.

CAREER MODIFICATION STRATEGIES

In contrast to strategies intended to prevent nonoffenders from becoming offenders, career modification strategies are directed at identified offenders and are intended to reduce the frequency, seriousness, or duration of their criminal careers.[3] Interventions intended to modify criminal careers are most frequently evaluated in terms of the fraction of offenders rearrested or reconvicted within a specified follow-up period—the recidivism rate. While providing a gross measure of reductions in criminal activity, the recidivism rate does not adequately distinguish which aspects of careers are affected by an intervention. If follow-up periods are short relative to the average interval between arrests, for example, it is often difficult to distinguish arrest-free intervals during a still-active career from career termination. Moreover, unless recidivism is defined by crime-specific criteria, it would fail to detect reductions in offense seriousness—a desirable career modification. Few studies, however, have used measures that adequately tap the different dimensions of criminal careers.

A broad array of modification strategies was examined by Lipton, Martinson, and Wilks (1975) and by the earlier Panel on Research on Rehabilitative Techniques (Sechrest, White, and Brown, 1979). While that panel found no treatment strategies that were widely effective in reducing recidivism, they concluded that some treatments may be effective for certain groups of offenders and recommended more rigorous and imaginative research on offender rehabilitation. Among the interventions that the panel considered especially worthy of further considerations were alternative sentencing and confinement arrangements, extensive family interventions, employment and vocational programs, and increased support after an inmate's release from prison. In assessing the crime control potential of such career modification strategies, this panel did not

replicate the previous comprehensive reviews. However, adopting a career perspective, it did consider the implications of large-scale experiments involving alternatives to standard criminal and juvenile sanctions as well as evaluations of family interventions, employment programs, and postrelease support programs not explicitly incorporated in the earlier reviews. In addition, in view of the demonstrated relationship between the intensity of substance abuse and the frequency of offending, the panel also reviewed several recent large-scale studies of the effectiveness of treatment of substance abuse in modifying criminal careers. Among the selected studies, some show sufficient general promise to warrant further exploration; they are discussed in the remainder of this section.

Career Modification: Community-Based and Family Treatment Programs

Juveniles

Individually oriented treatment programs for juvenile offenders are typically introduced as alternatives to regular juvenile court processing (either incarceration or probation). The programs most often include community-based treatment such as counseling, group therapy, or vocational programs; treatment of the entire family; or in some cases, diversion from the juvenile court altogether (see reviews by Clarke, 1974a, b; Farrington, 1982; Farrington, Ohlin, and Wilson, 1986). Studies of the programs permit comparisons of subsequent recidivism rates for those processed in the regular juvenile court system (including residential treatment and probation) with those assigned to community-based treatment, diversion programs (including family treatment and no treatment), and intensive supervised probation. In nearly all the studied pro-

---

[3]Other strategies can affect behavior through broader environmental or social influences, such as changes in sanction or economic policy. These policies, while not directed at individual offenders, can modify criminal career dimensions.

grams, samples of persons arrested or referred at about the same time and age were randomly assigned to an experimental or control group. Such randomization minimizes problems involving selection bias and lends confidence that postintervention comparisons between experimental and control groups are a valid measurement of the differential effect of the experimental intervention on offending frequency, or at least on recidivism rates.

The majority of follow-up studies on alternative treatments concluded that juvenile delinquents treated with group therapy, usually supplemented by home visits or intensive parole with additional supervision, had recidivism rates that were no higher than delinquents released from training schools.[4] Other studies that reported lower recidivism rates for alternative treatments had methodological problems that affected the validity of the results. For example, in the Provo experiment (Empey and Erickson, 1972), treatment subjects had lower recidivism rates than the training school controls, but the randomization features of the experiment broke down because the judge was reluctant to institutionalize some offenders. During a 2-year follow-up period of the California Community Treatment Program (Palmer, 1974), youths randomly as-

signed to the alternative parole program had lower recidivism rates, based on parole revocations, than those sent to an institution. But a later review of these results (Lerman, 1975) pointed out that rearrest rates of the two groups did not differ. Apparently, parole revocations following arrest were used more frequently for those who had been institutionalized.

Recent experimental studies of alternative diversion programs also report recidivism rates that are no different from those associated with standard juvenile justice system processing.[5] In one such study at the Oregon Social Learning Center (see Reid, 1983), 70 chronic juvenile offenders (average age, 13) were randomly assigned either to a privately operated, family-oriented behavioral treatment program or a regular counseling program run by the juvenile court, and a third group of 38 similar juveniles was selected as an additional control group. The family intervention techniques included training parents to identify and record antisocial behaviors, emphasizing family negotiation strategies for better parent-child interactions, and behavioral contracts for both the child and parents. Follow-up data from juvenile court rec-

---

[4]Examples of the studies include Pond (1970), Empey and Lubeck (1971), Palmer (1971, 1974), Jesness et al. (1972), and Lerman (1975). Institutional programs for juveniles and adults were extensively reviewed by Sechrest, White, and Brown (1979), and a recent update (Farrington, Ohlin, and Wilson, 1986) reports that group counseling in juvenile institutions has little effect on recidivism. See also Coates, Miller, and Ohlin (1978) for a discussion of the experience in Massachusetts, which closed virtually all its juvenile correctional institutions in the 1970s. In their place, the state developed a network of community-based facilities (residential and nonresidential); this change has had no substantial effect on juvenile recidivism rates (see also Lundman, 1984).

[5]See Venezia (1972), Baron, Feeney, Thornton (1973), Quay and Love (1977, 1979), Berg et al. (1978), Berg, Hullin, McGuire (1979), Byles and Maurice (1979), Mrad (1979), and Severy and Whitaker (1982). In addition, one large evaluation of diversion programs as alternatives to either release without treatment or further penetration of the juvenile justice system reported that the recidivism rates associated with the three groups—diversion, release, and regular processing—were virtually identical in follow-ups conducted after 6 months and 1 year (Dunford, 1981). This study involved over 2,500 juveniles in four states who were referred for offenses other than personal crimes or status offenses, and who were randomly assigned to one of the three comparison groups. Slightly under half had a previous record of arrest and most were male. Diverted juveniles received individual and family counseling along with some employment, educational, and recreational services.

ords for the three groups revealed that, by 1 year after intake, the juveniles in the experimental treatment group had experienced a more rapid decrease in the average number of officially recorded offenses than juveniles in the other two groups. However, after 3 years, the differences between the groups had disappeared.

Inconsistent results from other studies that compare personal counseling, family crisis counseling, and specific forms of behavioral family therapy with regular processing suggest the need for further attention to the nature of the intervention. Individual and group counseling, whether in institutions or in the community, appear to have little effect in modifying the criminal behavior of serious juvenile offenders. The more recent behaviorally oriented programs, however, appear more promising, at least in the short term. In one diversion experiment that was based on behavioral reinforcement principles, juveniles referred by the police engaged in specialized family programs designed to affect family communication, coping skills, and negative environmental situations. The experimental group had lower rearrest rates in the follow-up year than those observed in a no-treatment control group in one of two sites (Binder, Monahan, and Newkirk, 1976; Binder, n.d.). The total study involved 1,104 juveniles, but the control groups had fewer than 100 youth at each site. Similar experiments carried out by Davidson et al. (1977) and Alexander and Parsons (1973) also reported some differences between experimental and control groups, but the sample sizes in those studies were small. These encouraging short-term results suggest that behavioral approaches to treatment may warrant experimental replication with more serious juvenile offenders, evaluation in other sites, longer follow-up periods, and larger control groups.

Adults

Experimental research on adults has generally found no benefit from various community-based interventions (e.g., Lamb and Goertzel, 1974; Folkard, Smith, and Smith, 1976; Lichtman and Smock, 1981), which were not considered by the earlier Panel on Research on Rehabilitative Techniques. A new type of sentencing alternative, intensive community surveillance, is presently being considered in several states as an option for adult felons currently sentenced to prison or regular probation (see Petersilia et al., 1985). Such programs would usually combine multiple weekly contacts with a probation officer with mandatory employment, community service, possible restrictions on movement (e.g., evening curfews), and restitution. This type of intermediate sentence could be imposed in place of incarceration on offenders who are identified as needing more supervision and control than is usually provided by regular probation, but less than represented by incarceration. Several evaluations of these programs are currently in progress.

Summary: Community-Based and Family Treatment Programs

Experimental research suggests that for juvenile offenders, community-based treatment does no worse than routine juvenile justice system processing—including use of probation and training schools—in affecting recidivism. These programs may be preferable because of their lower cost and reduced restrictiveness, but they may not be acceptable in all communities. If incarceration is replaced by these programs, juveniles generally may view the risk of serious punishment as small, and victims may feel that justice is not being served. Perhaps most important, few experiments are available that might provide information about the effects of community-based interventions on the offense frequency and seriousness of adult offenders, although some recent intensive surveillance programs (for a review, see Petersilia et al., 1985) warrant careful evaluation.

Some therapeutic and behavioral interventions appear successful in reducing antisocial and criminal behavior for juveniles when evaluated in small-scale experiments, but no specific intervention emerges as being consistently effective. Many other interventions exist (for example, outdoor education programs, physically oriented approaches like Outward Bound, and restitution programs for juveniles), but few of these alternative treatments have yet been experimentally tested (see Greenwood and Zimring, 1985).

As discussed in the above section on preventive interventions, the general absence of definitive results within a vast evaluation literature suggests a need to focus evaluation resources on careful, well-designed replications of small-scale programs that are especially encouraging, either because of some positive empirical results or promising theoretical perspective. At present, the results of studies on career modification strategies may appear discouraging partly because of the lack of continuity and cumulation that results from an approach to evaluation that views each study as a separate entity rather than as part of an ongoing investigation. Furthermore, many studies that show no effects suffer from poor research designs (i.e., small samples, lack of randomization, short follow-up periods); the lack of effect is not necessarily because of ineffective interventions. Careful inspection of these no-effect findings can be useful in designing subsequent follow-up experiments in a sustained series of cumulative research.

However, even promising experimental findings must be tested in practice because interventions that appear successful in a small short-term experiment may fail to have an effect once the program is implemented on a larger scale or in the context of the criminal justice system. Most career modification strategies (as well as preventive interventions) are pilot studies with limited samples, run by a small committed staff. It is possible that any positive results are the result of the commitment of the innovators, therapists, counselors, and other staff to their specific intervention. Several researchers have cautioned that because the level of staff commitment may decrease when a pilot effort is expanded to a large program or transferred to another jurisdiction, the success of the pilot program may not be replicated in the new setting (see Reid, 1983; Greenwood and Zimring, 1985).

Career Modification: Substance Abuse Treatment

Recent empirical research on drug use and criminal involvement indicates that, at the individual level, intensity of drug use is strongly correlated with frequency of criminal activity. In some studies, increases or decreases in daily narcotics use were associated with parallel changes in individual offending frequencies (Wish and Johnson, Volume II; McGlothlin, Anglin, and Wilson, 1978; Ball et al., 1981; Ball, Shaffer, and Nurco, 1983). There are also limited data that suggest that decreased use of alcohol may be associated with reductions in violent, assaultive criminal events (see Collins, Volume II; Chaiken and Chaiken, 1982a, 1984). In light of these findings, the rate of commission of some types of crime by drug-using offenders might be reduced through effective drug abuse treatment programs.

A considerable literature exists on the effectiveness of drug abuse treatment programs in reducing individual criminal behavior in drug-using criminals.[6] Most research is directed at the treatment of narcotic addiction, especially heroin, although research on treatment for other drugs, such as PCP and cocaine, is increasing. Several studies, such as those of the California Civil Addict Program, have shown that court-ordered drug-free outpatient treatment accompanied by supervision, including urine testing, and weekly visits to a parole officer is associated with reduced criminal activity and higher rates of employment (e.g., McGlothlin, Anglin, and Wilson, 1977; Collins and Allison, 1983; Anglin and McGlothlin, 1984). Other studies have also found that legal pressure is positively related to retention in treatment programs. This research is important because time in treatment is a significant factor in the reduction of criminal behavior after treatment (see Collins et al., 1984; Hubbard et al., 1984).

The evidence regarding the effects on illegal behavior of methadone treatment for heroin addicts (which is rarely court ordered) is less consistent. Some studies show modest reductions in nondrug criminal behavior, but only methadone clients in treatment for 2 to 3 years have substantially fewer arrests (e.g., Lukoff, 1974, 1976; Sechrest, 1979; McGlothlin and Anglin, 1981). In the Drug Abuse Reporting Program (DARP), several types of treatment have been examined, and methadone programs also appeared to lower arrests, but the largest reductions in criminal behavior occurred during treatment (see Sells et al., 1976; Simpson et al., 1978).

The Treatment Outcomes Prospective Study (TOPS), however, reports more favorable results. TOPS is following clients voluntarily admitted into a drug treatment program of their choice to assess the effectiveness of different treatment services, although it does not include a nontreatment comparison group (see Hubbard et al., 1983). A recent report indicates that voluntary clients in methadone maintenance treatment programs self-reported significantly lower levels of "predatory" criminal behavior 12 months after treatment ended, especially if they remained in treatment for at least 3 months (Hubbard et al., 1984). Similar effects were found for clients in voluntary outpatient drug-free programs. Because the TOPS clients chose to seek treatment and the outcome measure was self-reported criminal activity, their motivation to succeed may be an important factor in the results such that they cannot be attributed solely to the effects of the treatment programs. In addition to the criminal activity and drug results in the TOPS study, full-time employment after treatment increased for outpatient drug-free clients, but it declined somewhat for methadone clients (Hubbard et al., 1984).

Less is known about the effect of residential treatment programs on criminal behavior for heroin or other drug users, but most of the available research concludes that residential treatment appears to reduce criminal behavior (see Coombs, 1981; DeLeon, 1984; Hubbard et al., 1984). These types of programs are most likely to accept clients with the worst recent criminal histories and the most extensive patterns of drug use, but they are also more likely to be resisted by drug users, and some of the methods used (e.g., strict punishments, group pressure) have been controversial. Many of these programs are privately operated and usually do not publish statistics on the criminal behavior of clients after treatment.

A federal criminal justice initiative known as TASC (Treatment Alternatives

---

[6] Some of this literature is reviewed in Wish and Johnson (Volume II); see also Sells (1979), Gandossy et al. (1980), Collins et al. (1982a, b), Cooper et al. (1983), and Kaplan (1983:208–235).

to Street Crime) is directed at diverting drug users—including heroin users and addicts, as well as those abusing alcohol, barbiturates, PCP, and other drugs—into treatment instead of imprisoning them (U.S. Department of Justice, 1979). The programs often divert those for whom prison is seen as too severe, such as occasional marijuana users charged with possession. Although TASC is no longer federally funded, it continues in areas where it has local support. One recent evaluation of TASC programs for 1979–1980 compared treatment outcomes for TASC referrals, other types of criminal justice referrals, and clients not involved in the criminal justice system (Collins et al., 1984). The comparison of pre- and posttreatment behavior showed criminal participation was reduced in the year after treatment (either outpatient drug-free or residential programs) for clients from all referral sources. This reduction was stronger when the indicator of illegal behavior was arrests rather than self-reported behavior and when the clients were under some pressure from the criminal justice system. Moreover, legal pressure (e.g., periodic urine testing, threat of probation or parole revocation) significantly increased retention in treatment, which, in turn, led to lower participation in criminal behavior in the year after treatment ended as measured by both arrests and self-reports. However, no treatment-free control group was included in the study, and the total follow-up period was only 1 year.

In assessing the effectiveness of all types of drug abuse treatment programs, methodological difficulties often confound the evaluations of program effects. The most serious problems concern the lack of random assignment to different programs, inadequate follow-up periods, failure to follow up all clients (including program dropouts), limited use of control groups, and lack of proper controls for other related factors (Lukoff, 1974; Nash, 1976; Gerstein, 1981). Any comparison across types of treatment programs (i.e., methadone maintenance, residential treatment, drug-free outpatient programs) is especially problematic because of substantial differences in research designs and client populations (Gandossy et al., 1980). More careful experimental studies are thus desirable, especially to evaluate whether drug abuse treatment has primarily an incapacitative effect (through surveillance or residential programs) or a rehabilitative impact on drug-using offenders.

Career Modification: Interventions to Improve Employment Status

The empirical association observed between chronic unemployment and frequent criminal activity suggests that interventions that improve offenders' employment status might also modify their criminal careers. Of the approaches that have been tested as methods of reducing offenders' unemployment, the panel considered two that have been evaluated in terms of their effect on offending: occupational skills training and postrelease employment assistance to offenders.

Occupational Skills Training: Job Corps

Job Corps is a comprehensive program that provides occupational skills training, basic and remedial education, and other services to disadvantaged youths in a residential program that averages about 6 months. Enrollees in Job Corps are primarily minority males between the ages of 16 and 21, and they generally possess characteristics associated with a high risk of participation in crime, such as low school achievement and erratic employment histories. Of youths in Job Corps during the summer of 1977, at least 38 percent had been previously arrested and 19 percent had been convicted (Mallar et al., 1982:14). Although Job Corps enrollment is officially voluntary, it is widely believed that a defendant's promise to enroll in Job Corps is frequently obtained by a judge in lieu of standard criminal or juvenile justice proceedings.

In its comprehensive assessment of evaluations of federally funded youth employment programs, the National Research Council's Committee on Youth Employment Programs (Betsey, Hollister, and Papageorgiou, 1985) cited Job Corps "as a program for which there is strong evidence concerning program effectiveness [in achieving gains in employment and earnings.] The quality of the evaluation reviewed [(Mallar et al., 1982)] . . . lends confidence to these conclusions." That evaluation covered criminal activity and found different program effects on the criminal career during the residential stay and the postresidential period. The evaluation reports an estimated reduction in the annual arrest rate per participant during the period of program participation, but the estimation methodology, which includes both offenders and nonoffenders in computing rates, does not permit separation of participation in criminal activity from frequency effects. The authors attribute the reduction to the incapacitative effect of restricted activity and monitored behavior in the residential setting and to the reduced incentive to commit crimes because participants' material needs are met in the program. In a 4-year postprogram follow-up, crime-reduction effects were more ambiguous and crime-specific: arrest rates for the crimes of murder, robbery, and larceny or motor vehicle theft were lower for participants than for a matched sample of nonparticipants in Job Corps; rates were higher for burglary, drug violations, and some categories of personal crimes.

Postprison Assistance

The MacArthur Foundation (Farrington, Ohlin, and Wilson, 1986) recently reviewed four experiments involving postrelease assistance to expedite the adjustment of prisoners in the community. In one Danish experiment, 250 prisoners were randomly assigned just before release either to a treatment group that was given special help (finding work and accommodations, financial assistance, help with family relations, and negotiations with creditors) or to a control group that was not offered the help. Significantly fewer of those receiving the help were reconvicted during a follow-up period of at least 6 years after release from prison, and the difference was greatest among those with the highest expected rates of recidivism (Berntsen and Christiansen, 1965). The results were essentially replicated in a British study with a 2-year follow-up period (Shaw, 1974), but the intervention failed in another replication with a 1-year follow-up period (Fowles, 1978). In addition to the shorter follow-up period, the experiment that failed was targeted at short-term prisoners, and they may not have needed the postrelease assistance as much as the subjects in the successful experiment, who had served relatively long prison sentences.

Two major American experiments have tested the theory that unemployment counseling and benefits, by reducing the financial and employment difficulties of released prisoners, would also reduce recidivism rates. In a Baltimore pilot experiment (Living Insurance for Ex-Prisoners, or LIFE), over 400 released prisoners who were considered high risk were randomly assigned to a control group that received no benefits or to a treatment group that received unemployment benefits (of about $60 a week for up to 13 weeks) and job placement assistance

(Rossi, Berk, and Lenihan, 1980). The benefits were reduced by 50 percent of all earnings above $40 per week and were interrupted during any period of incarceration. Within a 1-year follow-up period, the releasees who received the financial assistance experienced a 22 percent rearrest rate for theft compared with a 31 percent rate for the control group while rates for violent crimes were virtually identical in the two groups. The nonfinancial placement assistance showed virtually no effect on the rearrest rate.

These findings were encouraging and so led to a more ambitious follow-up program, the Transitional Aid Research Project for Ex-Offenders (TARP). In TARP, representative samples of about 975 releasees each from Texas and Georgia prisons were randomly assigned to experimental and control groups and monitored through interviews and administrative records. The groups received no assistance, placement assistance only, or unemployment benefits according to one of three schedules that varied in terms of duration and the rate at which benefits were reduced to offset earnings. The overall finding showed no difference in rearrest rates between the groups that received assistance and those that did not during a 1-year follow-up after release (Berk, Lenihan, and Rossi, 1980:777; Zeisel, 1982a:378).

Berk, Lenihan, and Rossi interpreted this result in terms of two offsetting effects of the financial assistance: (1) a direct reduction in the incentive to engage in criminal activity, which would reduce rearrest rates; and (2) a reduction in time worked, which would increase spare time, leading indirectly to an increase in rearrest rates. They then argued that with a payment plan stripped of the work disincentive effects, "modest amounts of financial aid can reduce recidivism among ex-felons" (1980:784). Their result is consistent with the hypothesis of a null effect

of financial assistance on offending behavior, as later argued by Zeisel (1982a). Zeisel also pointed out that even under the countervailing-effect interpretation of Berk and his colleagues, it was not clear that such a payment plan without work disincentives could be devised; both Rossi, Berk, and Lenihan (1982:393) and Zeisel (1982b:396) stated that additional controlled experiments were the only reliable means of determining whether such a plan could be devised.

INCAPACITATION STRATEGIES

Knowledge of criminal careers is central in trying to estimate the number of crimes avoided by removing an offender from society, that is, the incapacitative effects of criminal justice policies. Incapacitation theory is based on the recognition that an offender cannot commit crimes in the general community while he is incarcerated. However, he may commit crimes in prison or his street crimes may be carried out by someone else (drug sales, for example), and these effects diminish the incapacitative effect. Incapacitative effects are achieved primarily by incarceration; criminal justice system policies on bail, sentencing, and parole release affect the probability or duration of incarceration. As described at the beginning of this chapter, there are two kinds of incapacitative effects: selective and collective.

Incapacitative effects can be increased through collective incapacitation policies only by increasing the total level of incarceration; with selective incapacitation policies, the incapacitative effects might be increased by reallocating current capacity primarily to offenders who represent the greatest risk of offending. Collective incapacitation policies are consistent with the equal treatment concerns of a just-deserts retributive sentencing policy, while selective incapacitation policies focus as much on the offender as the offense. Of course, the degree to which selective incapacitation policies could be effective depends critically on the ability to distinguish low-risk from high-risk offenders, i.e., offenders who are predicted to represent the greatest risk of future crime in terms of frequency, seriousness, or career duration. Furthermore, the opportunity to pursue selective incapacitation policies will always be circumscribed by the legal and ethical concerns that punishments for comparable offenses not be grossly dissimilar from one another nor grossly disproportionate with the seriousness of the offense.

Research on incapacitative effects, considering only collective incapacitation policies, was reviewed by a previous panel (Blumstein, Cohen, and Nagin, 1978). A brief update of some subsequent results on collective incapacitative effects is provided here, but the major focus is recent explorations of selective incapacitation. The technical details of various aspects of estimating incapacitative effects are in the technical note at the end of this chapter.

Collective Incapacitation

Estimates of collective incapacitative effects focus on average consequences for crime reduction associated with incarceration. Reviewing various analyses of collective incapacitative effects, Cohen (1978:201–210; 1983:12–21) estimates that, under incarceration policies prevailing in the early 1970s, crime reduction achieved through collective incapacitation was less than 20 percent. Achieving further reductions in crime from 1970 levels through increases in collective incapacitation were likely to be similarly modest and would have required major increases in prison populations.

Specifically, Cohen (1978:226, 240–241) estimated that, with an average λ of 5

index crimes per year per offender and expected time served per index crime of .02 year (a number exceeding the value found in many states), a 10 percent reduction from 1970 levels of index crimes would have required that the expected time served per index crime, and thus the prison populations, be more than doubled. For higher values of λ, the required prison population increases from 1970 levels are proportionately reduced: if λ were doubled to 10, for example, a prison population increase of about 50 percent would have yielded the same 10 percent reduction of crimes; alternatively, with λ of 10, a doubling of prison populations would have resulted in about a 20 percent reduction of crime.

Even these estimates of incapacitative effects are optimistic. Crimes committed by groups of offenders might not be disrupted by incarcerating a single offender: for example, an auto theft ring may replace the contributions of the incarcerated member. Moreover, the estimated incapacitative effect that results from an increase in average time served per crime is overstated because the estimates assume that if free in the community, offenders would continue committing crimes at rate λ, while in fact the criminal careers of some incarcerated offenders would terminate naturally during their incarceration. All of these factors lower the crime reduction achieved through collective incapacitation. (The potential deterrent, rehabilitative, or criminogenic effects of additional incarceration are not considered here.)

The estimates of collective incapacitative effects just cited were developed on the basis of U.S. incarceration experiences during the 1960s and early 1970s. Since that time, prison populations have increased substantially in the United States; between 1973 and 1982, for example, the number of inmates in state and federal institutions almost doubled, from

TABLE 5-1 Estimates of Crime Reduction from Collective Incapacitation Associated with Almost Doubling State and Federal Prison Populations Between 1973 and 1982

	Robbery			Burglary		
	1973	1982	Increase	1973	1982	Increase
Observed crime rate (UCR reported crimes per 100,000 population)	183.1	235.9	+28.8%	1,222.5	1,484.5	+21.4%
	$\lambda = 14.3$			$\lambda = 36.7$		
Upper-Bound:						
Prevented crime rate (UCR reported crimes by inmates per 100,000 population)	92.0	174.2	+89.3%	422.5	790.5	+87.1%
Incapacitative effect[a]	33.4%	42.5%	+27.2%	25.7%	34.7%	+35.0%
	$\lambda = 5.0$			$\lambda = 15.0$		
Lower-Bound:						
Prevented crime rate (UCR reported crimes by inmates per 100,000 population)	32.2	60.9	+89.1%	172.7	323.1	+87.1%
Incapacitative effect[a]	14.9%	20.5%	+37.6%	12.4%	17.9%	+44.4%

[a]Incapacitative effect = Prevented crimes/prevented and observed crimes.

SOURCE: Data from Cohen (1985b).

204,211 to 396,072. This 94 percent increase in imprisonment provides a natural setting for assessing the gains in crime reduction achieved from increased collective incapacitation.

Using a model described below, Cohen (1985a,b) examines the collective incapacitative effects of increases in incarceration nationally during the 1970s. The estimates of incapacitative effects in Table 5-1 compare the crime rates actually reported by the FBI in the annual Uniform Crime Reports (UCR) to comparable estimates of the *prevented* crime rates attributable to inmates, i.e., the increment to the reported crime rate that would have occurred had the incarcerated inmates been free in the community.[7]

---

[7]To develop a "prevented crime rate" for inmates that is comparable with the reported crime rate, the "prevented crime rate" includes only those "prevented crimes" for inmates that would have been reported in the UCR. In particular, multiple counting of the same crime committed by several offenders and crimes that are not reported to the police are removed from total "prevented crimes" for inmates.

A range of values of λ for inmates is examined. Nationally, for robbery, when λ is large, the incapacitative effect is estimated to have prevented 33.4 percent of the robberies that would have been committed in 1973 and 42.5 percent of those in 1982, a gain in the incapacitative effect of 27.2 percent. The number of crimes prevented through incapacitation is estimated to have increased by 89.3 percent (from 92.0 crimes per 100,000 prevented in 1973 to 174.2 in 1982) because of the 94 percent increase in incarceration. The percentage of crimes averted through incapacitation does not increase comparably, however, because the reported crime rate itself increased by 28.8 percent between 1973 and 1982, perhaps reflecting increases in the number of active offenders or in their frequency, or increases in the rate of reporting crimes to the police. The magnitude of crime reduction is comparable but somewhat lower for burglary: 25.7 percent in 1973 and 34.7 percent in 1982, for a 35.0 percent gain in the incapacitative effect. When lower values of λ are used, the incapacitative effects for robbery and burglary are estimated to be only in the range of 12 to 20 percent, with gains in the incapacitative effects of 37.6 percent for robbery and 44.4 percent for burglary (see Table 5-1).[8]

The procedure used to estimate the incapacitative effect (i.e., crimes that would have been committed by inmates had they been free in the community) highlights some important considerations in estimating incapacitative effects. The procedure relies fundamentally on the product of the number of inmates who would be active if not in prison times an estimate of their individual crime rate, λ. The value of λ for inmates is likely to be higher than that for street offenders, since prisoners are disproportionately drawn from the population of high-rate offenders with their greater exposure to arrest.[9] The overrepresentation of the population of high-rate offenders among inmates will be even greater if there is any selectivity in criminal justice system processing that increases the incarceration risk per arrest for high-rate offenders. Thus, estimates of the crimes that incarcerated inmates would otherwise be committing should rely on estimates of λ that are representative of inmates.

The two available estimates of λ based on self-reports by inmates diverge considerably. Estimates of λ for incoming prisoners, for example, range from an annual average of 15 burglaries per offender (Peterson and Braiker, 1980:Table 12) to 204 burglaries per offender (Chaiken and Chaiken, 1982a:Table A.3). Because of the sensitivity of estimates of incapacitative effects to the value of λ used, our analysis was done for a range of λ values. With appropriate adjustments, especially for the sensitivity of mean annual rates to a few people with very high rates, the inmate surveys provide the basis for reasonable bounds on λ for inmates (see Chapter 3 and Cohen, Appendix B). The first survey provides a lower-bound estimate of λ of 5 for robbery and 15 for burglary (Peterson and Braiker, 1980:Table 12). The upper-bound values of λ were derived from the panel's reanalysis of the data in the second inmate survey (Visher, Volume II). To avoid sensitivity to the extremely high rates reported by a few offenders, the mean λ was estimated by assigning the 90th percentile value of λ to all offenders with individual rates above that value: this 90th percentile value was 196 burglaries per year and 71 robberies per year. The resulting mean values of λ are 14.3 for robbery and 36.7 for burglary (Cohen, Appendix B:Table 16).

In estimating incapacitative effects, the number of inmates multiplied by λ must be adjusted by a number of factors that reduce the number of crimes prevented by incarceration: (1) only some inmates participate in any particular type of

---

[8]These estimates are comparable to the earlier projections of 10 to 20 percent further reductions in crime if prison populations were doubled from 1970 levels. Starting from a base level of 10 percent of crimes averted in 1970, a further 10 percent reduction from the 90 percent of crimes actually committed would yield an additional 9 percent of crimes prevented, for a total incapacitative effect of 19 percent. Likewise, from a base incapacitative effect of 20 percent in 1970, a further 19 percent reduction from the 80 percent of crimes actually committed would add 16 percent to crimes prevented, for an incapacitative effect of 36 percent. The expected total incapacitative effects from increased incarceration in the range of 19 to 36 percent are comparable with the 18 to 20 percent estimated for low values of λ in 1982 and the 35 to 43 percent estimated for large values of λ (see Table 5-1).

[9]In view of many chance factors involved in making an arrest, it is reasonable to anticipate that the arrest risk per crime is not likely to be very different across offenders except for a few highly skilled offenders. Thus, with a common arrest risk per crime for all offenders of 10 percent, the greater vulnerability to arrest for high-rate offenders is illustrated with a simple example: an offender who commits only one offense per year will be arrested on average only once every 10 years, but an offender who commits 10 crimes each year will be arrested on average once every year.

crime; (2) some criminal careers terminate during periods of incarceration; (3) some offenses are committed by groups of offenders; and (4) not all crimes are reported to the police or recorded in the Uniform Crime Reports. These adjustments are explained below.

Only a portion of all inmates would actively commit the crime type being examined if they were free in the community. In responses to the Rand inmate survey, just over 35 percent of prison inmates report committing robberies and 45 percent report committing burglaries (Chaiken and Chaiken, 1982a).[10] Naturally, as the crime type examined is broadened, a larger percentage of inmates would be active in that offense type. For the broad category of all index offenses, it is likely that only a small portion of inmates would not qualify as active offenders.[11]

Natural termination of criminal careers while incarcerated also reduces the number of inmates currently active in an offense type. Such career termination is of less concern when residual careers are much longer than average time served. On the basis of analyses of career length for robbery and burglary in Michigan,

Cohen (1985a, b) uses estimates of an average of 10 years remaining in either robbery or burglary careers. With an average time served of 2 years for robbery, 83 percent of inmates who would commit robbery are estimated to remain active in robbery careers during periods of incarceration; for time served averaging 1 year for burglary, 91 percent of inmates who would commit burglary are estimated to remain active in burglary careers during periods of incarceration.

Another adjustment relates to the individual crime rate, λ. Direct use of λ yields all crimes committed by each individual offender. Some offenses, however, are committed by groups of offenders, and the estimated number of offenders per crime must be used to eliminate multiple counting of the same crime. Data from national victimization surveys lead to estimates of 2.3 offenders per robbery and 1.6 per burglary (derived from Reiss, 1980b:Table 2); this adjustment reduces prevented crimes by 57 and 37 percent, for robbery and burglary, respectively.

Finally, compared with reported crimes published in the FBI's UCR, prevented crimes should be discounted for crimes that would not be reported to the police. With typical reporting rates from victim surveys of about 50 percent for robbery and burglary, this adjustment represents another reduction by one-half to the estimate of prevented crimes (Bureau of Justice Statistics, 1983).

Combining the various adjustments, the estimate of crimes prevented for inmates is given by:

$$
\begin{array}{l}
\text{UCR Crimes} \\
\text{Prevented} \\
\text{for Inmates}
\end{array}
=
\begin{array}{l}
\text{Number of} \\
\text{Inmates}
\end{array}
\times
\begin{array}{l}
\text{Percent Who} \\
\text{Participate} \\
\text{in Offense}
\end{array}
$$

$$
\times
\begin{array}{l}
\text{Percent not} \\
\text{Terminating} \\
\text{Careers While} \\
\text{Incarcerated}
\end{array}
\times
\begin{array}{l}
\text{Adjusted} \\
\text{Individual} \\
\text{Crime Rate} \\
(\lambda^*)
\end{array}
$$

where

---

[10]Inmates from three states—California, Michigan, and Texas—were surveyed. The responses varied across the states, with responses in Michigan falling between those in California and Texas. Inmates in California appear to include a higher proportion of offenders who are active in serious crimes (49 percent for robberies and 54 percent for burglaries) and who report committing these offenses at high rates. Texas inmates, by contrast, include a higher proportion of less serious offenders. The responses for the three states combined were used to represent inmates nationwide.

[11]Inmates not active in index offenses might include, for example, specialists in drug offenses or in white collar offenses like fraud, forgery, and embezzlement—offenses that together comprised 11.4 percent of current conviction offenses for U.S. inmates in 1979 (Bureau of Justice Statistics, 1982b).

$$\lambda^* = \frac{\text{Individual}}{\text{Crime Rate}} \times \frac{\text{Percent}}{\text{Crimes}} \div \frac{\text{Number of}}{\text{Multiple}}$$
$$\qquad (\lambda) \qquad \text{Reported} \qquad \text{Offenders}$$
$$\qquad\qquad \text{to Police} \qquad \text{Per Crime.}$$

The combined adjustments are considerable, reducing the number of prevented crimes obtained from the simple product of inmates times λ by about 16-fold for robbery and 8-fold for burglary; this calculation yields estimates of prevented crimes that are comparable to UCR reported crimes. The final estimates for a range of values of λ are presented in Table 5-1 (above). Failure to make the adjustments to prevented crimes would grossly overstate the incapacitative effect associated with changes in inmate populations.[12]

The increases in inmate populations experienced during the 1970s may have changed the incarceration rates per crime since the 1970 estimates provided by Cohen (1978). These changes would alter the estimates of the incapacitative effects that can be expected from further increases in incarceration. The technical note at the end of this chapter updates the estimates of potential incapacitative effects to reflect both 1981 incarceration levels and the effect of career termination.

Despite the large increases in inmate populations nationally, the expected time served per index crime remains relatively low because of similar increases in the number of reported crimes. In 28 of 31

states examined, the expected time served per index crime was under .025 year in 1981: prison population increases of at least 100 to 200 percent would still be required to reduce reported index crimes by 10 percent from 1981 levels (see Table 5-6 in the technical note). In nine of those jurisdictions, where the expected time served per index crime was under .01 year, prison population increases well in excess of 200 percent would be required to reduce reported index crimes by 10 percent. The large increases in prison populations required in order to reduce crime reflect the fact that only a small fraction of active index offenders are in prison at any time. Even a small decrease in the number of offenders free in the community represents a large increment to the incarcerated population. The lower the current incarceration risk per crime, the greater the increase in prison population required to attain a given percentage reduction in crime.

Incorporating career length, and the associated possibility that some criminal careers end during periods of incarceration, reduces estimates of the incapacitative effect and increases estimates of the prison population that would be required to achieve a 1 percent reduction from 1981 crime levels. This effect of career termination increases as time served by those incarcerated gets longer and as the fraction of offenders who have terminated their careers while incarcerated increases. For states where time served by those incarcerated is 1 year or less, incorporating the effect of career termination increases the estimated growth in prison population by 20 percent; where time served is 1.5 to 2 years, the estimated growth increases by 40 percent (see Table 5-8 in the technical note).

In summary, recent studies have examined the crime reduction effects of collective incapacitation from the substantial

---

[12]The estimates of crime reduction from incapacitation presented here for a recent 94 percent increase in inmate populations nationally are similar in magnitude to alternative estimates of crime reduction for a smaller 50 percent increase in the California inmate population presented by Greenwood (1985). The estimated crime reduction from each percent increase in prison population was thus higher in Greenwood's estimates for California, but his preliminary estimates of crime reduction were likely to be somewhat inflated because he did not take account of all the adjustments noted here.

increases in inmate populations in the United States during the 1970s. After adjustments to λ and to the proportion of active offenders among inmates, the near doubling of the inmate population between 1973 and 1982 is estimated to have raised the aggregate incapacitative effect of prison for burglary from 25.7 percent in 1973 to 34.7 in 1982, a growth of 35 percent when λ is large. The improvements in incapacitative effects for other cases shown in Table 5-1 are of similar magnitude.

It is estimated that further reductions in reported index crimes from 1981 levels would require at least 10 to 20 percent increases in inmate populations for each 1 percent reduction in crime. Despite large increases in inmate populations since 1970, the incarceration risk per index crime remained low in 1981, less than .02 year per crime in 24 of 31 states examined (see Table 5-6, below.) As was found in the earlier analysis of 1970 data (Cohen, 1978), when the prevailing incarceration risk per crime is low, even very large increases in inmate populations lead to only modest percentage reductions in crime through collective incapacitation.

Selective Incapacitation

The recent large increases in inmate populations continue to place pressure on available prison and jail resources and to highlight the desirability of targeting incarceration more narrowly to achieve greater crime reduction from the available limited capacity. Increasing interest in a strategy of selective incapacitation has been further sparked by observations that individual offending frequencies differ widely among offenders, with a small number of offenders committing crimes at very high rates (Peterson and Braiker, 1981; Chaiken and Chaiken, 1982a, b). Such a skewed distribution suggests the possibility of increasing the crime reduc-

tion benefits from incapacitation by selectively targeting incarceration on the small number of high-rate offenders.

This objective is one justification for habitual offender statutes, which existed in 47 states as of 1981 (Cooper, Kelley, and Larson, 1982). Habitual offenders are generally defined by the length and seriousness of their prior conviction records, and sometimes by the nature of the current offense. While the statutory provisions vary widely from state to state, convicted offenders who are designated "habitual" typically face an extra 10–20 years in addition to the regular sentence, or the possibility of a life term. Such enhancement of punishment could be consistent with a desire for increased retribution against those who persistently violate. The incapacitative efficiency of these laws, however, depends on the residual length of these offenders' criminal careers compared to their total time served. If the total time remaining in the career is less than the total time served, the time served after the career would have terminated represents a waste of prison space from an incapacitative perspective. Almost certainly, life sentences represent such a waste. Criminal careers longer than 20 years are also very unlikely, but research is needed on the residual career length of those meeting habitual offender criteria.

Because they attempt to identify a high-risk subset of convicted offenders for enhanced sentences, habitual offender statutes are an example of an attempt to achieve selective incapacitation. The potential usefulness of selective incapacitation rests on the ability to classify individual offenders in terms of their projected criminal activity. Such policies also raise important ethical concerns. Some of those concerns relate to the quality of the classification rules, especially in terms of erroneous classifications, and others relate to constraints on which classification variables may be used; these issues are addressed in Chapter 6. The discussion here focuses on the ethical concerns in justifying differential sentences.

Ethical Concerns

Under selective incapacitation policies, long prison terms would be reserved primarily for offenders identified as most likely to continue committing serious crimes at high rates. Offenders not so classified would be released from prison after short terms or would be subject to nonincarcerative sanctions. Selective incapacitation thus permits, and indeed encourages, different sentences for the same offense to accommodate the differences in crime potential among offenders. From a crime control perspective, such policies are attractive because of the promise they hold of preventing more crime for a given amount of prison space.

Fundamentally, ethical concerns about the use of offender classifications to structure criminal justice decisions for purposes of selective incapacitation are rooted in the challenge to the legitimacy of basing punishment of an individual on the possibility of future crimes rather than only on the crime already committed. In the extreme, a pure just-deserts model of criminal justice would preclude all considerations other than the seriousness of the instant offense and the offender's culpability in having committed it. That model is thus concerned primarily with the offenses committed rather than with offenders' criminal careers and it implies uniformity in sanctions for like offenses and proportionality among sanctions for different offenses. However, protection of the community is also widely accepted, both philosophically and operationally, as a legitimate objective of criminal justice decision making (*Harvard Law Review* Student Note, 1982). In this model, criminal justice decisions, including imposition of prison sentences, are intended not only to punish offenders for past committed crimes, but also to protect the community from future crimes that the offenders might commit if they were set free. Distinguishing between the justification for punishment in general and its precise allocation, this broader view of sanctions encompasses both retributive and utilitarian concerns (Hart, 1968), and it allows a limited degree of variation in the sanctions imposed for similar crimes on the basis of differences among offenders.

Recent work has moved the just-deserts and public protection positions closer to a mutually acceptable accommodation. In particular, public protection is posed not in opposition to just deserts; rather, the two positions are offered as matters of joint concern (J. Monahan, 1982; Morris and Miller, 1985; von Hirsch, 1985). In these formulations, just deserts serves as a limiting principle in which the criteria of blameworthiness and the seriousness of the instant offense establish a range of acceptable penalties. The choice of a sentence within that range that enhances public protection is posed as a reasonable subsidiary principle.

In selective incapacitation policies, differences in anticipated future crimes for different offenders convicted of the same offense would be used to choose their respective sentences, but only within the constraints on the range of acceptable differences in sentences for high- and low-risk offenders. The desired range of differences in sentences varies from minimal (von Hirsch and Gottfredson, 1984), to a reasonably narrow range reflecting the imprecision in measuring the appropriate "desert" (J. Monahan, 1982; Morris and Miller, 1985), to largely unconstrained ranges like those reflected in typically broad statutory limits (e.g., Greenwood, 1982). The degree of variation recommended for sentences may be influenced in part by developing knowledge about the criminal career, particularly by the accuracy of predictions about subsequent careers. J. Monahan (1981) suggests that the greater the accuracy of predictions, the greater the variation in sanctions that might be tolerated.

Another consideration in evaluating the acceptability of a selective incapacitation policy is the tradeoff between the additional crime control advantage and the level of disparity resulting from differential sentences. For example, would a potential 10 percent reduction in crime be sufficient to justify sentences as disparate as 10 years for high-risk offenders and 1 year for all other offenders? Would 20 percent—or 50 percent—crime reductions be enough? Alternatively, would a 10 percent reduction in crime justify a more limited sanction differential, for example, of 2 to 1?

Ethical questions cannot be resolved on empirical grounds, but empirical results exploring the differential outcomes associated with alternative policies can be valuable in providing a factual base for consideration. While the ethical constraints are absolute for some, others argue that improvements in identifying the most serious offenders warrant some expansion of a permissible sentencing range.

Sentences Based on Offender Characteristics: The Rand Inmate Survey Scale

Interest in exploring selective incapacitation policies was one stimulus for the second Rand inmate survey, in which 2,190 incarcerated offenders from three states were asked for the information needed to estimate their individual crime rates for robbery and burglary. When analysis of the survey data confirmed very high values of λ for a small number of offenders (Chaiken and Chaiken, 1982a), further interest was stimulated in developing statistical instruments that were capable of distinguishing among offenders in terms of λ. Using bivariate correlations, Greenwood (1982) developed a seven-factor scale reflecting prior criminal record, drug use, and employment to distinguish low-, medium-, and high-rate offenders among the inmate sample. For California inmates, mean individual crime rates were reported to vary sharply and in the expected direction, with λ for inmates classified as high rate by the scale being 12 to 14 times higher than the mean for those classified as low-rate inmates. The difference in mean rates was less dramatic for Texas and Michigan inmates: the mean λ for high-rate offenders was 6 to 9 times higher than that for low-rate offenders in Texas and less than 3 times higher in Michigan (Greenwood, 1982:Table ES.1).[13]

Greenwood (1982) estimated incapacitative effects on crime volume and prison population for alternative incarceration policies that targeted the predicted high-rate inmates for long prison terms while limiting sentences for other inmates. These estimates relied on mean crime rates for inmates identified as low-, medium-, and high-rate offenders by the scale, λ_i, together with statistics from other sources on incarceration risk for offenders, I_i^*. To estimate I_i^*, other data—the number of crimes reported, the fraction of all crimes that are reported to police, the number of offenders per crime incident, the number of arrests—were used to estimate the conditional probability of arrest, conviction, and incarceration after an offense, J, which was assumed to be invariant across the three offender groups. Also S_i, the average time served for an incarceration ·sentence, was esti-

---

[13]The derivation and predictive accuracy of the Rand scale are discussed in Chapter 6.

mated separately for each offender group i, using the expected terms reported by the Rand respondents. Both J and S_i entered the estimate of I_i^*. The total number of active adult offenders—both incarcerated and not—in each group, N_i, was then estimated from the number of inmates, R_i^*, and the varying risks of incarceration for each offender group, I_i^*, with N_i equal to R_i^*/I_i^* (see technical note for details).[14]

With these parameter estimates, Greenwood analyzed the effects of a selective incapacitation policy on crime rates and on prison population in California (using Equations 5-1', 5-2', 5-9, and 5-10 of the technical note). The total number of crimes and inmates associated with the prevailing sentencing practices serve as a benchmark for comparing the outcomes of alternative selective incapacitation policies. Although Greenwood analyzed six alternative policies separately for robbers and burglars, one of the analyses—his most selective "Policy 6" for robbers—has attracted particular attention, probably because it emerged from his analysis as the most effective and because robbery is the more serious crime. Therefore, the remainder of this discussion is focused on that analysis.

In the analysis of Policy 6, Greenwood suggested that a selective incapacitation policy of increasing the time served in prison for incarcerated robbers classified as high-rate offenders, while limiting the jail terms of other incarcerated robbers to 1 year, would produce a more advantageous tradeoff between crime control and prison population effects than could be achieved by collective incapacitation policies. Greenwood (1982:xix, 79) reports selective incapacitative effects for a range of increases in prison terms: a 20 percent

reduction in robberies by adults is associated with no change in the number of robbery inmates; with a smaller increase in prison terms for high-rate robbers, it would be possible to achieve a 15 percent reduction in robberies by adults with a 5 percent reduction in robbery inmates.

Greenwood's methods and results have been closely scrutinized by Cohen (1983, 1984b), by Spelman (1984), and by von Hirsch and Gottfredson (1984). These other analyses of the same data suggest that the original estimates overstate the effects of the proposed selective incapacitation strategy. Because their work and related work by Chaiken and Chaiken (1982a) raised questions about the validity of Greenwood's results, the panel commissioned a reanalysis of the original survey data and recomputation of the incapacitative effects estimated by Greenwood. The reanalysis (Visher, Volume II) reproduced fairly closely the Chaiken and Chaiken estimates of the λ distribution from the survey instrument and the power of the scale developed by Greenwood to distinguish among convicted robbers in the California inmate sample in terms of offending rates (Visher, Volume II:Tables 9, 17). However, it raised important questions about the ability of the scale to discriminate among offenders in the subsamples of burglars and robbers from other states (see Chapter 6).

Some differences also emerged in the estimated magnitude of the effects that might be expected from pursuing selective incapacitation strategies (see Table 5-2). While Greenwood does not specify the exact prison terms for the alternative estimates of selective incapacitative effects, the sentencing changes are reported to involve no more than doubling the length of prison terms for high-rate robbers (Greenwood, 1982:79). In reanalyses of the original data, however, a policy of doubling time served to about 8

---

[14]Greenwood (1982:113–116) uses a complex procedure to estimate the numbers of inmates in prison and jail in each offender group, R_i^*.

TABLE 5-2 Alternative Estimates of Crime Reduction and Prison Populations Projected for Highly Selective Incapacitation Policy Applied to California Robbery Inmates

Source	Percent Reduction in Adult Robberies	Percent Change in Robbery Inmates
No Career Termination		
Greenwood (1982:xiv, 79)	20	0
Greenwood (1982:xix, 85)	15	−5
Cohen (1983:Figure 2; Visher, Volume II:Figure 3)	13	−8
Visher (Volume II:Figure 3)	13	+1
With Career Termination		
Technical Note		
$T_R = \infty$[a]	14	−1
$T_R = 15$ years	10	+17
$T_R = 10$ years	9	+23
$T_R = 5$ years	6	+38

NOTE: Alternative outcomes reported in Greenwood (1982) are for selective policies of increased prison terms for high-rate robbery inmates and 1-year jail terms for all other robbery inmates; the effect varies with the length of prison terms for high-rate robbery inmates. All other estimates in this table are based on a policy of sending high-rate robbers to prison for just over 8 years, while all other robbery inmates are sent to jail for 1 year.

[a]Assuming that residual career length is infinite is analogous to ignoring the effect of career termination. Slight differences in the methods used to calculate the crime reduction and prison population effects explain the differences in these results compared with those reported by Visher (Volume II:Figure 3).

years by inmates classified as high-rate offenders, while reducing time served for all other inmates to 1 year, was estimated to reduce crime by 13 percent for California robbers, with an 8 percent decrease in the number of robbery inmates (Cohen, 1983:Figure 2; Visher, Volume II:Figure 3). Thus, with the assumptions and parameter values employed by Greenwood, the 15 and 20 percent reductions in robberies that he reports cannot be achieved without making sentences even more disparate than a ratio of 8 to 1.

The estimated incapacitative effects are potentially sensitive to the parameter values substituted into the equations defining the model (see the technical note at the end of the chapter). The distribution of λ computed in the Visher reanalysis (Volume II:Table 9) reflected both a lower mean value of λ and somewhat less skewness. In the incapacitation model,

however, lower values of λ imply higher projected numbers of active offenders and similar reductions in crime. Substituting her revised parameters into the incapacitation model used by Greenwood, Visher estimates that under Policy 6, doubling prison terms for inmates classified as high-rate robbers would result in a 13–14 percent reduction in adult robberies, with the number of robbery inmates essentially unchanged (Volume II:Figure 3). Visher reports that achieving a 20 percent reduction in robberies in California would require tripling the time served in prison by robbers classified as high-rate offenders by the scale, which would lead to an estimated 5 percent increase in robbery inmates.

To assess the robustness of the estimates of incapacitative effects, an analysis of the same classification scale and a similar sentencing policy was done for the

Michigan inmates. However, the inmates sampled from Michigan prison and jails apparently were very different from those in the California sample. In her reanalysis of the inmate data, Visher (Volume II) reports that Michigan inmates had lower scores than California inmates on the seven-point classification scale, largely because fewer Michigan inmates reported serious drug use or juvenile incarcerations. Therefore, while 48 percent of the California inmates convicted of robbery were classified as high-rate offenders by the scale, only 15 percent of robbery inmates in Michigan were so classified. According to several accuracy measures, the scale was much less accurate in distinguishing high-rate inmates from other inmates in Michigan than in California (see Visher, Volume II:Table 17). Finally, the sentencing policies for convicted robbers in Michigan and California are apparently quite different: Michigan nearly always incarcerates convicted robbers for prison terms averaging 5 years, while California sentences 50 percent of these offenders to jail for terms of no more than 1 year (Greenwood, 1982:Table B.2).

These differences between California's and Michigan's inmate characteristics and existing sentencing policies are likely to substantially affect estimated incapacitative effects. Visher (Volume II) showed that using the selective sentencing policy defined earlier (doubling prison terms for inmates classified as high-rate offenders and giving 1-year jail terms to all others) would *increase* robberies by adults in Michigan by an estimated 30 percent while the number of robbery inmates would decline by almost 50 percent. The substantial increase in crime in Michigan would be due to the large reduction in sentences for the many predicted medium- and low-rate offenders; they would serve only 1 year in jail under the policy rather than the average of 4 or 5 years in prison under current

policy. In addition, few inmates in Michigan would be classified as high-rate offenders—and thus subject to long prison terms—using the same classification scale. The analysis of Michigan inmates illustrates that incapacitative effects of any policy are likely to vary dramatically across jurisdictions because of variations in the predictive accuracy of the classification scale and in existing sentencing policies.

Recently, Cohen (1984a) pointed out that the projections by Greenwood and Visher (based on Equations 5-1′, 5-2′, 5-9, and 5-10 in the technical note) assume career length to be much longer than time served. The long incarceration times of 8 years or more analyzed in Greenwood's policies make that approximation particularly inappropriate and warrant including career length in the analysis to reflect termination of some careers during these long periods of incarceration. Using Equations 5-1, 5-2, 5-3, and 5-5 of the technical note with Visher's parameter values, Cohen reestimated the effects on crime and prison population, assuming that residual careers average 5, 10, and 15 years (see Table 5-2). Properly accounting for career termination during periods of incarceration decreases the estimate of crime reduction through incapacitation because only a portion of total time served by inmates reduces time free for active offenders; some portion of incarceration time is served after careers have terminated. The magnitude of the decrease is larger when time served is long or residual career lengths are short, because either increases the likelihood that careers terminate while offenders are incarcerated (see Table 5-3).

In the illustrative policy considered here, time served in prison would be doubled to just over 8 years for high-rate robbers. If residual careers for robbers averaged 15 years, then 35 percent of

TABLE 5-3 Percent of Prison Inmates Who Terminate Careers While Incarcerated

Mean Time Served, S (years)	Residual Career Length, T_R (years)		
	5	10	15
1	16.7	9.1	6.3
2	28.6	16.7	11.8
5	50.0	33.3	25.0
8	61.5	44.4	34.8

NOTE: The likelihood that careers terminate during incarceration is given by $S/(S + T_R)$. (See Equation 5-8 in the technical note at the end of this chapter.)

inmates serving average 8-year terms would be expected to end their careers before their release. This would lower the estimated crime reduction effect for such a policy to 10 percent. When remaining careers are assumed to be even shorter, the reduction in incapacitative effect is even more substantial—down to a 6 percent reduction in robberies for residual careers that average 5 years (see Table 5-2, above).

Accounting for career termination in Greenwood's incapacitation model has an opposite effect on the estimates of inmate populations under alternative incarceration policies. An underlying assumption of this steady-state model is an active offender population of constant size N, which can be determined from knowledge of λ and the total crime rate, C. A shorter career length implies that a larger fraction of offenders end their careers each year; these ex-offenders are assumed to be replaced by new offenders to maintain the value of N. The new offenders, in turn, become vulnerable to incarceration under the new policy and eventually add to prison population and serve a larger share of this incarceration time after their careers have terminated. Accounting for these termination and replacement processes results in estimates of the inmate population that are larger

than those that fail to adjust for these processes.

If the remaining careers of California robbers average 15 years, the impact of doubling time served by high-rate robbers, accounting for termination and replacement, results in an estimated 17 percent increase in robbery inmates (Table 5-2, above). If remaining careers are only 5 years, the impact of accounting for termination and replacement is even more substantial, resulting in a 38 percent increase in the prison population of robbers (see the technical note at the end of this chapter). These prison population estimates would represent 4 and 10 percent increases, respectively, in the *total* inmate population (for all offenses) in California.[15]

Table 5-2 summarizes the various estimates of the effects in California of a highly selective incapacitation policy of doubling prison terms to 8 years for inmates classified as high-rate robbers while imposing 1-year jail terms on all other robbery inmates. Depending on assumptions about career length, the policy is estimated to reduce the number of robberies by adults by 6 to 14 percent, with effects on robbery inmates ranging from essentially no change to a 38 percent increase. These alternative crime-reduction estimates are all smaller than the 15 to 20 percent decreases in adult robberies estimated by Greenwood.

The impact of career length on the estimates is substantial. Therefore, further research estimating the length of criminal careers, and especially the way residual career length varies during crim-

---

[15]Convicted robbers represented approximately one-quarter of the total prison population in California in 1980 (California Department of Corrections, 1980). A 17 percent increase in robbery inmates would thus represent a 4.25 percent increase in total prison population. Likewise, a 38 percent increase in robbery inmates would increase total population by 9.5 percent.

inal careers, is very important for evaluating alternative incapacitation sentencing policies. While long incarceration terms may be desirable for deterrent or retributive reasons, they make less efficient use of prison resources from an incapacitative standpoint. For any sentencing policy, the tradeoffs between the benefits of incapacitative crime reduction and the costs of prison population are most favorable when time served is short and residual career length is long.

Based on the estimates in Table 5-2, modest crime reduction is possible from a selective incapacitation policy applied to California robbers. These estimates, however, are themselves optimistic; in actual use, several factors would diminish the crime reduction achieved:

• The incapacitative effect will be less if the offenses of incarcerated inmates persist in the community, perhaps because the inmate is replaced by a new recruit or because incarceration of some members of offending groups does not disrupt the groups' crimes.

• The predictive power of the scale used to distinguish offenders may diminish as the scale developed on inmates is applied to a broader and potentially different population of all convicted offenders, especially in a different jurisdiction with different existing criminal justice decision practices.

• Self-reports of predictor variables will probably not be usable and will probably be distorted if they are used, and official records of those variables may have less predictive power because of record inaccuracies or gaps.

• The offending rates of low-rate offenders may increase in response to the shorter sentences imposed on those individuals under a selective policy because of a decreased deterrent effect.

• Finally, experience with efforts to reduce criminal justice system discretion

suggests that the system may adapt to prediction-based decision rules in ways that reduce the considerable sentence disparity of 8 years for predicted high-rate robbers and 1-year terms for all others.

Because the magnitudes of these effects could be measured only following implementation of the policies, they are unknown at present and can be expected to vary by crime type. However, because the effects would all operate to reduce incapacitive effectiveness, the preceding estimates of the effects on crime and on prison population should be treated as best-case estimates.

Parole Release Based on Offender Characteristics: The Salient Factor Score

Perhaps the most common use of differential treatment for purposes of selective incapacitation is found at parole, when community protection is a major consideration in early-release decisions. In the federal parole system, this consideration has involved the use of an explicit prediction scale known as the Salient Factor Score as an aid in assessing the risk of future crimes of candidates for parole release. Relying on factors reflecting an inmate's age, prior criminal record, and history of drug use, an individual's Salient Factor Score is computed; on the basis of that score, parole candidates are assigned to a recidivism risk category.[16] These risk levels vary from a 49 percent chance of recidivism—a return to prison or outstanding warrant in the first 2 years after release—for poor-risk inmates to a 12 percent chance of recidivism for very-good-risk inmates (Hoffman, 1983). When a broader recidivism criterion of rearrest in the first 3 years after release is used,

---

[16]The scale factors and predictive accuracy of the federal Salient Factor Score are discussed in Chapter 6.

the risk levels are a 66 percent chance of recidivism for poor risks and 22 percent for very good risks (Janus, 1985).

While considerable attention has been given to evaluating the predictive adequacy of the Salient Factor Score in distinguishing among different recidivism risk levels for federal inmates (see Chapter 6), the selective incapacitation effects from using the scale have been assessed only recently. Janus (1985) examined a 50 percent sample of releasees from federal institutions during the first half of 1978. To control for the impact of offense severity on time served, only inmates who scored "very high" in the "severity of offense behavior scale" were used.[17] Table 5-4 summarizes the differences in time served and the impact of these differences on arrests prevented for the different recidivism risk levels. The data show that the time served does vary with differences in the risk of future crimes: poor-risk offenders serve 10 months more than the average term for offenders, and very-good-risk offenders serve 3 months less than the average. These differences in time served need not arise solely from differences in parole release decisions; they might also reflect differences in the length of sentences imposed in court. The different risk levels also display different arrest rates during the follow-up period. The monthly arrest rate of poor-risk offenders (.035) is 3.5 times that of very-good-risk offenders (.010). Janus (1985:122) notes that even this difference across risk levels is probably understated because of likely differences in exposure during the follow-up for the different risk levels; poor-risk offenders—with their higher number of arrests—are more likely

to be reincarcerated and thus to be on the street for less time during the 3-year follow-up period. An adjustment for differential exposure time would therefore further increase the monthly arrest rate of the high-risk group compared with that of other risk levels.

The monthly arrest rates can be used to assess the increment to arrests prevented as a result of the differences in the time served by inmates in the different risk levels (Table 5-4). Janus reports that, compared with the average time served for the 620 inmates examined, the 10 months' longer time served by poor-risk offenders prevents 20.03 arrests. Also, because poor-risk inmates serve longer than the average term of 26.9 months and very good risks serve less than the average term, a total of 19.63 arrests are prevented for the 620 inmates examined. Thus, the differential terms result in a net 7 percent increase in the number of arrests prevented with no change in prison population.

One could also consider the maximum possible increment in crime reduction by using a different baseline for time served. The time served by the very good risks might be regarded as the lower end of the acceptable range of sentences for inmates convicted of very-high-severity offenses. The longer time served by each of the higher-risk groups would have selective incapacitative effects. Because offenders in higher-risk categories serve longer than those characterized as very good risks (Table 5-4), an additional 52.17 arrests are prevented, but there is also a 13 percent increase in the time served. Thus, an increment of 37.1 inmate-months in prison is required for each additional arrest prevented.

Janus's data also permit examining the degree to which the Salient Factor Score distinguishes among offenders in terms of individual arrest rates for active offenders or in terms of the continued participation by active offenders observed during the

---

[17]This offense category includes robbery; breaking and entering or burglary of armory, residence, or involving hostile confrontation with victim; counterfeiting currency; drug sales; extortion; explosives; and property offenses involving more than $100,000 but not more than $500,000 (U.S. Parole Commission, 1981).

TABLE 5-4 Selective Incapacitative Effects of Federal Parole Release Decisions Using the Salient Factor Score for "Very High Severity" Offenders

| Variable | Salient Factor Score by Risk Level | | | | |
	Poor 0–3	Fair 4–5	Good 6–7	Very Good 8–10	Total or Average, All Risk Levels
Number of Inmates (N)	59	102	136	323	620
Current Time Served					
Average time served at 1978 release, in months (S)	36.6	28.7	28.8	23.8	26.9
Arrests per inmate per month in a 3-year follow-up[a] (μ)	.035	.027	.018	.010	.026
Number of arrests prevented by current time served ($I = N \times S \times \mu$)	75.58	79.04	70.50	76.87	301.99
All Serve Average Time Served					
Number of arrests prevented if all served average time served of 26.9 months ($I^* = N \times 26.9 \times \mu$)	55.55	74.08	65.85	86.89	282.37
Increment (decrement) to arrests prevented by current time served versus average time served ($I - I^*$)	20.03	4.96	4.65	(10.01)	19.63
Percent change in arrests prevented by current time served versus average time served $[(I - I^*)/I^*]$	36	7	7	(11)	7
Increment (decrement) to time served from current time served versus average time served $[P^* = (S - 26.9) \times N]$	572.3	183.6	258.4	(1,014.3)	0.0
Percent change in time served from current time served versus average time served $[(P^* - 26.9 \times N)/26.9 \times N]$	36	7	7	(11)	0
All Serve "Very Good Risk" Time Served					
Number of arrests prevented if all served "very good risk" time of 23.8 months ($I' = N \times 23.8 \times \mu$)	49.15	65.54	58.26	76.87	249.82
Increment to arrests prevented by current time served versus "very good risk" time served ($I - I'$)	26.43	13.50	12.24	0.0	52.17
Percent change in arrests prevented by current time served versus "very good risk" time served $[(I - I')/I']$	54	21	21	0.0	21
Increment to time served from current time served versus "very good risk" time served $[P' = (S - 23.8) \times N]$	755.2	499.8	680.0	0.0	1,935.0
Percent change in time served from current time served versus "very good risk" time served $[(P' - 23.8 \times N)/23.8 \times N]$	54	21	21	0.0	13

NOTE: Offense types in the "very high severity" category include robbery; breaking and entering or burglary of armory, residence, or involving hostile confrontation with victim; counterfeiting currency; drug sales; extortion; explosives; and property offenses involving more than $100,000 but not more than $500,000 (U.S. Parole Commission, 1981).

[a]Assumes that all inmates were free in the community and still active in criminal careers for the entire 36-month follow-up. Time served as a result of subsequent commitments or career termination will increase the average monthly arrest rate reported here.

SOURCE: Derived from data presented in Janus (1985:Tables 1 and 3).

follow-up. Table 5-5 compares the entire sample in terms of various aspects of individual criminal careers for the different risk-level groups identified by the Salient Factor Score. The aggregate monthly arrest rate estimates provided by Janus combine offenders who are not rearrested after release and those who are

TABLE 5-5 Variations in Criminal Careers for Different Risk Levels Identified by the Salient Factor Score

Variable	Salient Factor Score by Risk Level				
	Poor 0–3	Fair 4–5	Good 6–7	Very Good 8–10	Total or Average, All Risk Levels
Number of released inmates	493	495	476	722	2,186
Total arrests in 3-year follow-up	757	638	377	285	2,057
Average arrests per month per offender (aggregate rates)	.043	.036	.022	.011	.026
Percent of offenders with at least one arrest in 3-year follow-up	65.5	57.4	41.4	22.0	44.1
Average time to first arrest for those arrested (months)	12.62	13.66	14.79	16.49	14.01
Average arrests per month free for active offenders with at least one arrest in 3-year follow-up[a]	.079	.073	.068	.061	.071
Average arrests per month free for all active offenders (corrected rate)[b]	.073	.066	.060	.051	.064
Percent of all active offenders expected to have at least one arrest in 3-year follow-up[c]	93	91	88	84	90
Percent of offenders who remain active during 3-year follow-up[d]	70.4	63.1	47.0	26.2	49.0

[a]This arrest rate is estimated from the reciprocal of the time to the first arrest for offenders who are arrested during the follow-up (see text).

[b]The corrected rate is estimated by adjusting downward the rate for active offenders who are arrested in the follow-up; see Chapter 3 and Cohen (Appendix B) for the estimation procedure used.

[c]For a follow-up t months long and individual arrest rate, μ, the probability that an individual who remains active during the follow-up will be arrested is estimated as $1 - e^{-\mu t}$.

[d]The total fraction of active offenders among releasees is estimated by dividing the percent of offenders with at least one arrest in the follow-up period by the percent of all active offenders expected to be arrested in that period.

SOURCE: Derived from data presented in Janus (1985:Tables 1 and 3).

rearrested in the 3-year follow-up. These aggregate rates vary substantially across risk levels, from a high of .043 arrest per month for poor-risk offenders to a low of .011 for very-good-risk offenders. The difference in these rates, however, is largely due to differences in arrest participation during the follow-up period: poor risks are much more likely to be rearrested (66 percent) than are very good risks (22 percent).

The average time to the first arrest in the follow-up period (for those ever arrested) provides a basis for estimating the individual arrest rate for the demonstrably active offenders. Since releasees are on the street until their first arrest after release, the rate calculated by using those intervals provides an estimate of the arrest rate while free for offenders who remain active. However, this estimate is biased upward somewhat by the loss of observations of arrests for offenders who remain active but whose first rearrest would occur after 3 years. The rate estimated only for the demonstrably active offenders is thus conditional on having at least one arrest during the follow-up period. The rate corrected for this bias reported in Table 5-5 ranges from .073 arrest per month free for poor risks to .051 arrest per month free for very good risks.[18]

___

[18]For μ^*, the biased frequency rate, the corrected frequency, μ, is estimated from the relationship: $\mu^* = \mu/(1 - e^{-\mu t})$; see Chapter 3 and Cohen, Appendix B, for the details of this adjustment.

This estimate of average arrest rates while free for all active offenders provides a basis for estimating the total size of the active offender population during the follow-up, including active offenders who are not yet arrested. For individual arrest rate, μ, the probability that an individual who remains active during a follow-up period of length t will be arrested can be estimated as $1 - e^{-\mu t}$; see Table 5-5. During a follow-up as long as 3 years, very few active offenders will fail to be arrested. Even among the very good risks, who have the lowest individual arrest rate, 84 percent of all active offenders can be expected to be arrested at least once in a 3-year follow-up period. Applying this 84 percent estimate to the 22 percent of offenders who are rearrested, total active offenders are 26.2 percent of the very good risks. Similarly, 70.4 percent of poor risks are estimated to remain active throughout the 3 years. The percentage of poor risks who are arrested in the 3-year follow-up period (65.5) is 198 percent higher than for very good risks (22.0 percent), and there are an estimated 169 percent more total active offenders in the poor-risk group. In contrast, the corrected individual monthly arrest rate (μ) for active offenders is only 43 percent higher. The Salient Factor Score is thus more effective at distinguishing subsequent participation as measured by arrests than at distinguishing arrest frequency.

Charge-Based Sentencing Policies

Partly in response to the ethical concerns associated with some forms of selective incapacitation, Cohen (1983, 1984a, b) has explored the degree of crime control that could be achieved by targeting incapacitation on offenders defined solely in terms of their convicted offenses, and perhaps prior record. This type of policy could avoid the use of more ethically controversial variables to distinguish among offenders convicted of the same offense type. A charge-based incapacitation policy would augment current sentencing practices by assigning minimum sentences uniformly to all offenders convicted of the same charge who have similar prior records (Cohen, 1984b). Under such a policy, the sentences of all offenders convicted of the targeted charge would receive at least the same minimum term of incarceration, while sentences already above that minimum would remain unchanged. The minimum sentence imposed would be selected from within the range of acceptable penalties for the targeted offense type; whether the sentence is at the high or low end of that range would depend on the predicted subsequent criminal activity associated with that offense type. While the offender-based selective incapacitation policies examined above have focused on differences among offenders, charge-based incapacitation policies extend incarceration uniformly to all offenders convicted of the same offense and focus on differences between offenses.

The basis for this approach to incapacitation is recent evidence from several different studies that important differences may exist in individual frequencies of offending for offenders charged with different offense types. Chaiken and Chaiken (1982a, 1984), for example, found that "violent predators"—inmates who reported committing the combination of robbery, aggravated assault, and drug dealing—committed not only those offenses but also burglary at the highest rates of all survey respondents.

Cohen (1984b) has estimated the potential incapacitative effects that could be achieved by targeting increased incarceration on offenders convicted of specific offenses. Her data show that charge-based incapacitation policies directed at different offense types would differentially reduce crime levels and increase prison populations. For example, in Washington, D.C., in 1973, the index crime and sentence offering the best tradeoff between crime reduction and prison impact was minimum 2-year prison terms for defendants convicted of robbery: robberies committed by adults would have decreased by 8 percent and adult "safety crimes" by 5 percent, while increasing the total prison population by 17 percent.[19] The same 2-year minimum prison term imposed on all burglary convictions would have reduced burglaries committed by adults by 6 percent and adult safety crimes by 3 percent, while increasing the total prison population by 25 percent.

A likely judicial response to this type of charge-based sentencing policy might be to impose the mandatory minimum 2-year prison terms only on offenders with previous convictions for the targeted offense. Restricting prison terms to repeat convictions, however, would seriously reduce the expected crime reduction. Even extremely long sentences for persons previously convicted of robbery or burglary would have reduced those offenses by only 1 and 4 percent, respectively. The reason for this low incapacitative effect is that only about 25 percent of convicted robbers and burglars have previous convictions for those offenses. Many defendants were never previously arrested for the target offense, and among those who were, robbery and burglary charges were often reduced or dropped during plea bargaining.

The effects of charge-based policies are estimated from individual arrest histories. Those estimates are most accurate for the portion of arrests that might have been averted through alternative sentencing policies imposed at previous convictions. Extrapolating from arrests to crimes de-

pends on assumptions of arrest probabilities across different offender subpopulations: those arrested in a sampling year are assumed to have the same arrest risk per crime as those not arrested that year; and among arrestees, those with arrests averted are assumed to have the same arrest risk per crime as those without arrests averted. Violations of these assumptions will lead to biases in the estimates of crime reduction from charge-based policies: if offenders with prior records are more likely to be arrested for their future crimes (perhaps because they are better known to the police), then the crime reduction from charge-based incapacitation is overestimated; the opposite will occur if prior records lead to greater adeptness in avoiding arrest. Adequately addressing these potential sources of bias requires empirical research into the variations in arrest risk per crime during individual criminal careers.

In addition to empirical concerns about the accuracy of the estimates, charge-based incapacitation policies raise their own ethical concerns. The basic strategy of ignoring differences among offenders convicted of the same offense is intended to avoid some of the ethical problems raised by differential sentences based on individual attributes. But charge-based sentencing policies impose a minimum sentence on all offenders convicted of the same offense and ignore variations in the blameworthiness of criminal conduct falling within the same convicted offense type. While sentences above the minimum prison terms are possible to accommodate aggravating circumstances, the mandatory minimum sentence represents a floor on the length of prison terms. Mitigations both in the harm done and in the culpability of the offender that are not adequately captured by variations in the convicted offense type will not be possible under a uniform mandatory minimum sentence policy.

---

[19]"Safety crimes" are murder, rape, robbery, and burglary (Avi-Itzhak and Shinnar, 1973).

Operational Issues in Assessing Alternative Selective Incapacitation Policies

Analysis of alternative selective incapacitation policies raises several operational issues. One of these relates to the choice of the policy variable that is used in the assessment. Throughout the discussion so far, the costs and benefits of selective incapacitation have been assessed by seeking the largest crime reduction while minimizing the increase in prison population. Operationally, however, one must consider such constraints as prison capacity and limits on the length of time to be served for any particular offense emerging from just-deserts concerns.

The effects associated with such constraints can be illustrated with data from Cohen (1984b) assessing the effects of various charge-based incapacitation policies applied to arrestees in Michigan. If the increase in the total prison population is constrained to a maximum of 20 percent, the alternative policies of targeting charge-based incapacitation on robbery, burglary, or auto theft convictions all emerge as best and are indistinguishable in their effects. Targeting any one of these offense types for mandatory minimum terms is estimated to result in a 12 to 13 percent reduction in the selected target offense and a 20 percent increase in the total prison population. These effects, however, result from different sentences for each target offense: 5-year minimum terms for either robbery or auto theft and 2-year terms for burglary.

A different best policy emerges when the prison population constraint is dropped and a constraint on sentence length is considered. If the mandatory minimum terms are constrained to be no more than 2 years, for example, targeting charge-based incapacitation on robbery convictions emerges as best, requiring the smallest increase in total prison population (2 percent) to achieve the largest reduction in the targeted offense, an 8 percent reduction in robberies committed by adults. In comparing alternative constraints on the minimum sentence, Cohen also notes that shorter prison terms are generally more attractive options because they involve the lowest marginal costs in terms of prison population increases for each estimated 1 percent reduction in crime.

Offenders are often diverse in their offending, engaging in several different offense types during their criminal careers. Thus, another consideration in choosing among alternative selective incapacitation policies might be the impact of a policy in preventing crimes other than the offense targeted for minimum prison terms. With a 20 percent constraint on increases in total prison population and considering reductions in safety crimes by adults, targeting charge-based incapacitation on burglary emerges as the best policy: a 20 percent increase in total prison population from 2-year minimum terms for burglary convictions results in an 11 percent reduction in adult safety crimes. In comparison, 5-year minimum prison terms for robbery convictions result in only a 6 percent reduction in total safety crimes by adults with the same 20 percent increase in total prison population.

The strategy of targeting particular offense types for longer prison terms also raises other operational considerations. In the analysis of charge-based incapacitation policies, the impact of alternative policies varied across jurisdictions. This makes it especially important that any policy analysis not be applied indiscriminantly to other sites. In Washington, D.C., robbery emerged as a clearly dominant policy target because it offers the most favorable tradeoff between large crime reduction and small prison popula-

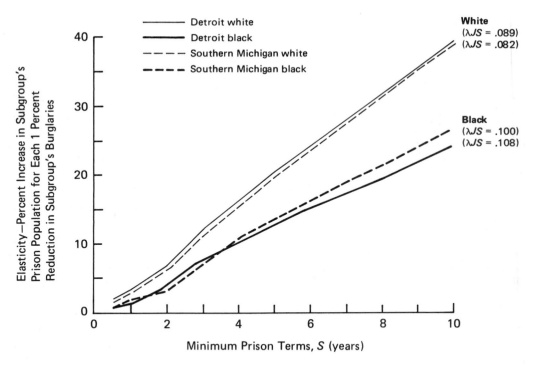

FIGURE 5-1 Variations in incapacitative effects for different population subgroups from uniform minimum prison terms imposed for burglary in Michigan. Source: Derived from data provided in Cohen (1984b).

tion increases in that jurisdiction. There was more ambiguity in the results for Michigan: if the increase in total prison population is constrained to 20 percent, burglary offers the largest reduction in safety crimes committed by adults; if sentence length is constrained to 2-year minimum prison terms, robbery is a better target offense. These variations in different settings and with different policy constraints make it essential that jurisdiction-specific analyses be conducted when considering alternative selective incapacitation policies.

Charge-based incapacitation policies are consciously designed to avoid the use of extra-legal predictor variables, but they may have a larger impact on some groups than on others. In particular, any group that is disproportionately involved in the target crime would be so affected. For example, Figure 5-1 shows Cohen's

(1984b) estimate of the percentage increase in prison population for each 1 percent reduction in adult burglaries for different race subgroups and jurisdictions in Michigan; the largest prison population increases occur among white offenders. These differences in impact reflect differences in individual frequency rates, λ, and in the prevailing levels of expected time served per crime, JS, for different subgroups: in general, the higher λJS is for any group under prevailing policy, the lower will be the increases in prison population resulting from alternative selective incapacitation policies.

Summary: Incapacitation Strategies

While incarceration leads to some reduction in crime through incapacitation, none of the various incapacitation strategies examined provide dramatic reductions. Even interventions that have only modest impacts on crime can involve sizable costs, especially when they are applied broadly to large target populations. In the case of collective incapacitation, for example, general increases in prison use to achieve a 10 percent reduction in crime may require more than doubling existing inmate populations, and even those estimates depend on the crimes of incarcerated offenders not being replaced or continued by other offenders still in the community.

The estimates also must be viewed as preliminary. They involve estimates of λ that may not be applicable to the particular population that would constitute the new prisoners. The estimates also ignore any effects that incarceration might have on the future criminal careers of the incarcerated offenders; it is possible that it might lengthen or shorten those careers. Improving the estimates of incapacitative effects requires continued research characterizing individual criminal careers, particularly efforts to identify variations in those careers and in their interaction with the criminal justice system. Further efforts should also be directed at assessing the influence of those variations on estimated incapacitative effects.

Because of the wide variations in offending rates, with only a small number of offenders committing serious crimes at high rates and having extended careers, the potential exists to achieve similar reductions in crime by focusing interventions more narrowly on smaller high-risk populations, i.e., by selective incapacitation strategies. This cost advantage was illustrated in the analyses of selective incapacitation. For example, it is estimated that selective incapacitation policies could achieve 5 to 10 percent reductions in robbery with 10 to 20 percent increases in the population of robbers in prison, while much larger increases in prison populations are associated with collective incapacitation policies. To

achieve even these small reductions in crime, however, targeted interventions require effective classifications to identify those offenders at highest risk of continued serious offending. The current status and future prospects of classification in criminal justice decisions are the subjects of the next chapter.

TECHNICAL NOTE

This note explores some technical details in estimating incapacitative effects. The first section presents the details of the general incapacitation model. The next section applies the model to estimate the crime reduction and prison population effects of a collective incapacitation policy of general increases in the use of incarceration from 1981 levels. The final section applies the model to estimate the effects associated with a selective incapacitation policy of differential sentences applied to inmates convicted of robbery in California.

A Model of Incapacitation

The crime control and prison population effects estimated by Greenwood (1982) and others arise from a model of individual criminal careers derived by Avi-Itzhak and Shinnar (1973) and Shinnar and Shinnar (1975), and summarized by Cohen (1978, 1983). In the steady-state model, all crimes are assumed to be committed by a fixed population of N individual offenders who, if left free, would commit crimes at an average rate λ per year throughout the time they remain active in their criminal careers, i.e., their mean residual career length, T_R.[20] The effects of the criminal justice system are described in terms of J, the probability that an of-

---

[20]The population of active offenders remains stable in size as offenders who end their criminal careers are replaced by new offenders with identical criminal career attributes.

fense will be followed by arrest, conviction, and incarceration, and S, the average time served by those incarcerated. Under these conditions, active offenders are incapacitated during a fraction of their criminal careers, I, while during a fraction $(1 - I)$, active offenders are free to commit crimes on the street. It can be shown (Avi-Itzhak and Shinnar, 1973:Appendix; Shinnar and Shinnar, 1975:Appendix) that the incapacitated fraction of careers, I, is given by

$$I = \frac{\lambda JS\left(\dfrac{T_R}{T_R + S}\right)}{1 + \lambda JS\left(\dfrac{T_R}{T_R + S}\right)}. \qquad (5\text{-}1)$$

The fraction of careers that active offenders are not incapacitated, i.e., when they are free on the street, is given by

$$1 - I = \frac{1}{1 + \lambda JS\left(\dfrac{T_R}{T_R + S}\right)}. \qquad (5\text{-}2)$$

In both Equations 5-1 and 5-2, the fraction $T_R/(T_R + S)$, which takes account of the reduction in crimes avoided because of spontaneous career termination during incarceration periods, S, reflects the likelihood that an offender is still active in a career after serving a sentence; the remaining fraction, $S/(T_R + S)$, is the likelihood that a career terminates while a sentence is being served. [21]

_____

[21]The expression for the likelihood that a career terminates while a sentence is being served depends on how career lengths and sentence lengths are distributed among offenders. The result reported here applies when career length is distributed exponentially with mean residual length T_R and when sentence length is also distributed exponentially with mean length S. Such distributions are generally compatible with observed patterns of career termination and with the distribution of time served by offenders.

Equations 5-1 and 5-2 can be used to estimate the annual numbers of crimes committed by active offenders who are free and of crimes averted for active offenders who are incarcerated. Crimes committed, C, are calculated as

$$C = N \times \lambda \times (1 - I), \qquad (5\text{-}3)$$

while crimes avoided through incapacitation, C_A, are calculated as

$$C_A = N \times \lambda \times I. \qquad (5\text{-}4)$$

Combining Equations 5-3 and 5-4 yields the total number of potential crimes. The reduction in crimes through incapacitation, $C_A/(C + C_A)$ is equal to I in equation 5-1.

Likewise, Equations 5-1 and 5-2 can be used to estimate the size of the annual inmate population, R. The average daily inmate population in a year (reflected in person-years in prison)[22] is given by

$$R = N \times \lambda \times (1 - I) \times JS. \qquad (5\text{-}5)$$

Some careers terminate during prison terms, and so not all inmates reflected in R are active offenders. When focusing on a single offender, the expected time during that offender's residual career that he spends incarcerated is given by

$$r_A = T_R \times I. \qquad (5\text{-}6)$$

Similarly, in any year, the number of active offenders found in an annual inmate population is given by

$$R_A = N \times I. \qquad (5\text{-}7)$$

When Equations 5-5 and 5-7 are combined, the fraction of total inmates (R) who would be active if free (R_A) is given by

_____

[22]Each unit of R is equivalent to one inmate incarcerated for a full year. Use of average daily population allows for population turnover during a year as some inmates are released and new commitments take their place in the inmate population.

$$R_A/R = \frac{N \times I}{N \times \lambda \times (1 - I) \times JS} = \frac{T_R}{T_R + S}.$$

$$(5\text{-}8)$$

While the total number of inmates (R) is easily observed, the total number of active offenders (N) both in and out of prison cannot be observed directly. The size of the active offender population, however, can be estimated from the inmate population. First, by applying the fraction in Equation 5-8 to the total number of inmates in a year, the number of active offenders among inmates (R_A) can be estimated. Then, with an estimate of I in Equation 5-7, the total number of active offenders, N, can be estimated.

When T_R is much larger than S, spontaneous career terminations are less likely, and the portion of a sentence during which an offender would be inactive becomes negligibly small. For reasons of analytical convenience and because reliable estimates of T_R have only recently become available, researchers have ignored career termination among inmates. With this approximation, the fractions of careers spent incapacitated and free are given by the simpler formulas:

$$I^* = \frac{\lambda JS}{1 + \lambda JS} \geq I \qquad (5\text{-}1')$$

and

$$1 - I^* = \frac{1}{1 + \lambda JS} \leq 1 - I. \qquad (5\text{-}2')$$

Ignoring career termination, the annual count of crimes committed is given by the product of the offender population, the individual offending rate, and the portion of a year offenders are free to commit crimes:

$$C^* = N \times \lambda \times (1 - I^*). \qquad (5\text{-}9)$$

This value of C^*, which is less than or equal to C and which fails to take account of spontaneous career terminations during incarceration, understates the number of crimes that are committed and so overstates the number of crimes that are avoided by incapacitation. Because of spontaneous career termination during incarcerations, only a portion of the total time served during a career can be counted as reducing crimes through incapacitation; the time spent incarcerated after a career ends has no incapacitative effect. Failure to exclude the time served after career termination thus overstates the portion of a career that an offender spends incarcerated ($I^* \geq I$), and understates both the time he is free on the street $[(1 - I^*) \leq (1 - I)]$ and the estimate of the number of crimes he commits ($C^* \leq C$). When time served (S) is longer relative to residual career length (T_R), the underestimate of crimes committed is also larger.

If there were no career terminations, the average daily incarcerated population would be the product of the number of crimes committed annually (C^*) times the expected time served per crime (JS):

$$R^* = C^* \times JS = N \times \lambda \times (1 - I^*) \times JS. \quad (5\text{-}10)$$

The underestimate of crimes committed when career termination is ignored leads to a similar underestimate of the size of the inmate population, and the value of $R^* \leq R$. While the fraction of a career during which an active offender is incarcerated is overestimated ($I^* \geq I$), the total time spent incarcerated is underestimated. This underestimation occurs because as an offender commits more crimes during a career ($C \geq C^*$), his vulnerability to incarceration also increases, but increasing portions of the incarceration time are served after his career terminates. As time served (S) increases relative to residual career length (T_R), the time spent incarcerated after the end of a career also increases, and the underestimate of the average daily incarcerated population gets larger ($R^* \le R$).

When career termination is ignored, all inmates are assumed to remain active in their criminal careers, and $R_A^* = R^*$. In this case, the total number of active offenders, N, is estimated from Equation 5-10, which reduces to

$$R^* = R_A^* = N \times I^*. \qquad (5\text{-}10')$$

Applying the Model to Estimate the Effects of a Collective Incapacitation Policy

Equations 5-3 and 5-5 can be used to estimate the responsiveness of crime levels to changes in incarceration levels from incapacitation alone. The elasticity of crime (E), or the percentage change in crime accompanying a 1 percent change in the expected prison stay per crime (JS), is given by

$$E_{C,JS} = \frac{dC}{d(JS)} \times \frac{JS}{C}$$

$$= \frac{-\lambda^2 N T_R^2/(T_R + S)^2}{[1 + \lambda JS T_R/(T_R + S)]^2}$$

$$\times \frac{JS}{\dfrac{\lambda N}{1 + \lambda JS T_R/(T_R + S)}}$$

$$= \frac{\lambda JS T_R^2/(T_R + S)^2}{1 + \lambda JS T_R/(T_R + S)}. \qquad (5\text{-}11)$$

The expression in Equation 5-11 also gives the elasticity of crime with respect to changes in J or S alone, since it can be shown that

$$E_{C,JS} = E_{C,J} = E_{C,S}.$$

The elasticity of the total annual inmate population with respect to a 1 percent change in the expected prison stay per crime is given by

$$E_{R,JS} = \frac{dR}{d(JS)} \times \frac{JS}{R}$$

$$= \frac{\lambda N[1 + \lambda JS^2 T_R/(T_R + S)^2]}{[1 + \lambda JST_R/(T_R + S)]^2}$$

$$\times \frac{JS}{\dfrac{\lambda NJS}{1 + \lambda JST_R/(T_R + S)}}$$

$$= \frac{1 + \lambda JS^2 T_R/(T_R + S)^2}{1 + \lambda JST_R/(T_R + S)}. \qquad (5\text{-}12)$$

Likewise, the elasticity of the annual inmate population to changes in J or S alone is given by the same expression, since

$$E_{R,JS} = E_{R,J} = E_{R,S}.$$

The elasticities in Equations 5-11 and 5-12 can be combined to form a cost/benefit ratio reflecting the percentage change in the annual inmate population required to achieve a 1 percent change in the volume of crimes. This cost/benefit ratio is given by

$$\frac{E_{R,JS}}{E_{C,JS}} = \frac{1 + \lambda JS^2 T_R/(T_R + S)^2}{-\lambda JST_R^2/(T_R + S)^2}. \qquad (5\text{-}13)$$

The expressions in Equations 5-11 to 5-13 differ significantly from those derived by Cohen (1978:Appendix B), which ignored the role of career length. The importance of taking career length into account is examined here by updating the Cohen (1978:Appendix C) estimates of the relationship between inmate populations and crime reduction with new estimates that rely on more recent data from 1981 and that include the effect of career length. The updated estimates rely on data on all new commitments from court to state prisons in 1981, median time served by first-time releasees from state prisons in 1981, and the number of index offenses known to the police in 1981.

In estimating the cost/benefit ratio in Equation 5-13, residual career length, T_R, is set at 10 years remaining in a career. An adjusted value of five crimes per offender per year is used for the individual crime rate, λ. This corresponds to a value of λ of about 20 crimes per year. However, since the same crime may involve more than one offender, the rate for individuals must be discounted by the average number of offenders per crime. On the basis of data from the national victimization surveys, it is estimated that there are an average of two offenders per crime (Reiss, 1980b); this adjustment reduces λ by half. Also, since crime reduction is measured in terms of crimes known to police, the rate at which victims report crimes to the police (also estimated from national victimization surveys) is used to reduce the value of λ by half again to reflect only the reduction in crimes that are known to police (Bureau of Justice Statistics, 1983).

The updated data and estimates are presented in Table 5-6 and Figure 5-2. As was previously found (Cohen, 1978), the updated cost/benefit ratios displayed in Figure 5-2 depend strongly on the value of expected time served per crime, *JS*. If sanction levels are already high (say, *JS* above .05 for $\lambda = 5$ and $T_R = 10$), the additional costs in terms of the percentage increase in prison population required to achieve a 1 percent reduction in crime are not unreasonable. Below *JS* = .05, however, the increases in prison population associated with a 1 percent decrease in crime are much larger.

On the basis of 1981 data, only one jurisdiction, Washington, D.C., has a sanction level above *JS* = .05. The estimated prison increase to achieve a 1 per-

cent reduction in index crimes known to the police in Washington is 3.7 percent when career length is ignored and 6.8 percent when career length is included. In contrast, several states (Hawaii, Massachusetts, Montana, New Hampshire, New Jersey, New Mexico, North Dakota, Rhode Island, and Utah) have values of *JS* less than .01, and they require increases in prison population of more than 20 percent to achieve only a 1 percent reduction in crime. The prison population increases will be larger if λ and T_R are smaller than assumed here and smaller for larger values of λ and T_R.

Several large changes in *JS* between 1970 and 1981 are also noteworthy. *JS* decreased by at least 40 percent between 1970 and 1981 in seven states (Georgia, Maine, Mississippi, Montana, New Hampshire, New Mexico, and North Dakota) and increased by a similar amount in two states (Hawaii and New York). The cost/benefit ratio increased between 1970 and 1981 in states where *JS* declined and decreased in the states where *JS* increased.

The differences in cost/benefit effects for different states are due to the considerable differences in the base levels of crime and prison populations for different values of *JS*. At high values of *JS*, the system is operating effectively and presumably already has a sizable proportion of offenders in prison and a fairly low crime rate. Any increase in *JS* will only marginally increase the initially large prison population, while making a large fractional dent in an already low crime rate. At low values of *JS*, with a high crime rate and relatively small prison population, the changes that result from increasing *JS* will have a greater proportional impact on an initially small prison population.

If one includes finite career length and the associated possibility that offenders

TABLE 5-6 Crime Rates and Prison Use by State in 1981: An Update of Collective Incapacitative Effects Including the Effect of Career Length

State	Index Crimes Known to Police[a]	New Commitments to State Prisons from Courts (all offenses)[b]	Estimated Probability of Prison/ Crime (J)[b]	Median Time Served in Years (S)[c]	Estimated Time Served per Crime in Years (JS)[d]	Cost/Benefit Ratio from Incapacitation		
						Percent Increase in Prison Population to Achieve 1% Reduction in Crime ($\lambda = 5$, without T_R)[e,f]	Percent Increase in Prison Population to Achieve 1% Reduction in Crime ($\lambda = 5$, $T_R = 10$)[f,g]	Change in Prison Increase When T_R Is Included
Alabama	191,834	4,006	.0209	.833	.0174	11.50	13.58	(+18%)
California	1,833,787	13,932	.0076	1.500	.0114	17.55	23.36	(+33%)
Delaware	40,002	563	.0141	.917	.0129	15.50	18.56	(+20%)
Georgia	313,453	6,770	.0216	1.000	.0216	9.26	11.30	(+22%)
Hawaii	64,060	199	.0031	2.750	.0085	23.41	38.33	(+64%)
Iowa	136,638	1,225	.0090	1.500	.0135	14.87	19.82	(+33%)
Kentucky	129,289	2,453	.0190	.833	.0158	12.65	14.93	(+18%)
Louisiana	226,773	2,732	.0120	1.750	.0210	9.49	13.27	(+40%)
Maine	48,034	404	.0084	1.750	.0147	13.59	18.94	(+39%)
Massachusetts	336,701	1,496	.0044	1.833	.0081	24.56	34.57	(+41%)
Mississippi	89,495	2,170	.0242	1.000	.0242	8.25	10.08	(+22%)
Missouri	264,250	2,880	.0109	1.250	.0136	14.68	18.71	(+27%)
Montana	39,750	409	.0103	.917	.0094	21.20	25.35	(+20%)
Nebraska	65,838	786	.0119	1.250	.0149	13.40	17.09	(+28%)
Nevada	72,602	956	.0132	1.250	.0165	12.15	15.50	(+28%)
New Hampshire	40,409	245	.0061	.917	.0056	35.97	42.96	(+19%)
New Jersey	457,367	3,467	.0076	.917	.0070	28.77	34.38	(+19%)
New Mexico	82,282	388	.0047	2.000	.0094	21.21	30.74	(+45%)

New York	1,214,935	9,035	.0074	1.833	14.67	.0136	20.73	(+41%)
North Carolina	268,998	7,628	.0284	1.167	6.04	.0331	7.65	(+27%)
North Dakota	19,681	180	.0091	.833	26.25	.0076	30.89	(+18%)
Ohio	587,007	8,426	.0144	1.333	10.45	.0192	13.56	(+30%)
Pennsylvania	436,967	3,394	.0078	1.500	17.17	.0117	22.85	(+33%)
Rhode Island	55,709	260	.0047	1.500	28.57	.0071	37.93	(+33%)
South Dakota	20,640	348	.0169	1.167	10.16	.0197	12.79	(+26%)
Tennessee	198,756	3,814	.0192	1.500	6.95	.0197	9.34	(+34%)
Texas	892,723	13,858	.0155	1.417	9.90	.0288	11.99	(+32%)
Utah	87,170	518	.0059	1.500	22.44	.0220	29.82	(+33%)
Washington, D.C.	69,540	1,141	.0164	3.333	3.66	.0089	6.83	(+87%)
West Virginia	51,091	756	.0148	1.333	10.14	.0547	13.16	(+30%)
Wisconsin	225,901	1,884	.0083	1.667	14.39	.0138	19.75	(+37%)

a Data from Federal Bureau of Investigation (1982:Table 3).

b The probability of prison for a crime (J) is estimated from the ratio of court commitments admitted to state prisons in 1981 for all offenses (Bureau of Justice Statistics, 1984c:Table 9) divided by index offenses known to police in 1981. Since index offenses comprised 71 percent of all admissions in reporting states in 1981 (Bureau of Justice Statistics, 1984c:Table 3), this overstates somewhat the risk of prison for index offenses known to the police.

c Time served is estimated from the median time served reported for all first-time releases from state prisons in 1981 (Bureau of Justice Statistics, 1984c:Table 5). Since releases for all offenses are included, this understates time served for index offenses somewhat. Also, only the median time served is reported for individual states, rather than the mean. A separate analysis comparing the mean and median times served by crime type for selected states, however, reports that "nearly always, the median of time served is a few months less than the mean, and that the median and means exhibit similar variations from offense to offense and from state to state" (Bureau of Justice Statistics, 1984e:3).

d The expected time served per crime is estimated from the product of the probability of prison for a crime (J) and the average time served per crime (S). While J is somewhat overestimated and S is somewhat underestimated for index offenses, the product JS is likely to be more reliably estimated because of the offsetting effect of these errors.

e Estimate does not account for career length (T_R) with cost/benefit ratio = $1/JS$ (Cohen, 1978:221 and Appendix B).

f An adjusted value of five index crimes per year per offender is used; see text.

g Estimate does account for career length (T_R) using Equation 5-13 in this note.

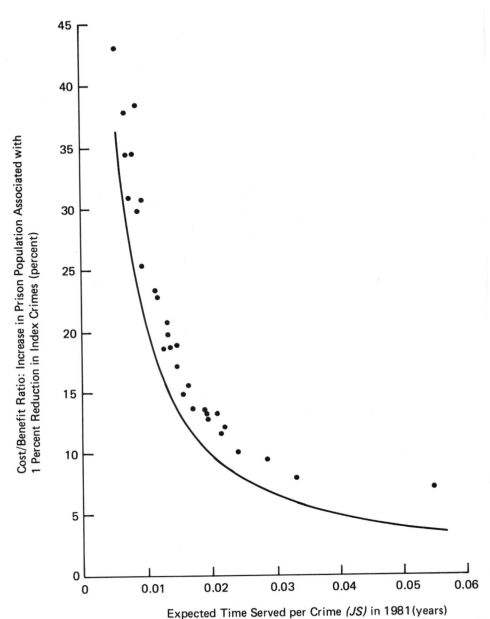

FIGURE 5-2 Cost/benefit ratio with career length for selected states as a function of imprisonment sanction levels, *JS*, prevailing in 1981. Note: Cost/benefit ratio with career length is derived using Equation 5-13 with $\lambda = 5$ and $T_R = 10$.

end their criminal careers while incarcerated, the estimates of prison population increases for each 1 percent reduction in crime will always be larger (see Table 5-6). The magnitude of this increase in the cost/benefit ratio varies with the

length of time served. As indicated in Table 5-7, the longer the time served relative to residual careers of 10 years, the greater is the impact of including career length in the analysis. As found in nine states, for time served of 1 year or less, the

TABLE 5-7   Effect of Including Career Length in Cost/Benefit Ratio ($\lambda = 5$, $T_R = 10$)

	Median Time Served (years)			
	≤ 1.0	> 1.0 and ≤ 1.5	> 1.5 and ≤ 2.0	> 2.75
Mean percent increase in cost/benefit ratio	19.6	30.5	40.5	75.5
Standard deviation of percent increase in cost/benefit ratio	1.6	2.8	2.7	16.3
Number of states in 1981	9	14	6	2

cost/benefit ratio increases an average of 20 percent; for time served in six states of between 1.5 and 2.0 years, the cost/benefit ratio increases an average of 40 percent. The impact of including career length is largest in two jurisdictions with very long time served: the cost/benefit ratio increases 87 percent in Washington, D.C., and 64 percent in Hawaii, where time served was 3.3 years and 2.75 years, respectively.

Applying the Model to Estimate the Effects of a Selective Incapacitation Policy

The model of a criminal career presented in this section was also used to generate alternative estimates of the effects of a selective incapacitation policy applied to predicted high-rate robbers found among California inmates. The analysis used the basic approach developed by Greenwood (1982), but with results derived from the reanalysis of the original inmate survey data done for the panel by Visher (Volume II).

California inmates convicted of robbery are partitioned into three groups— low-, medium-, and high-rate offenders— based on their scores on a seven-factor scale developed by Greenwood (1982).

(See Chapter 6 and Visher [Volume II] for discussions of the scale itself.) On the basis of reanalysis of the survey data, Visher (Volume II) estimated lower values for the mean individual crime rates in the three offender groups. Several other values of parameters for the incapacitation model shifted slightly when she reestimated the incapacitative effects in California (see Visher, Volume II:n. 23; Appendix A, Table 4).

The Visher inmate distribution for the three offense-rate groups is presented in the top row of Table 5-8. These estimates do not account for the effect of career termination on the inmate population. In particular, as careers get shorter, the inmate population will include increasing numbers of inmates who have ended their criminal careers while incarcerated; if they were released, these inactive inmates would no longer commit crimes. The total inmate population (R) can be partitioned into active inmates (R_A) and inactive inmates (R_I) using the relationships developed in Equations 5-5 and 5-8. Estimates of the numbers of active inmates found in the total inmate population are presented in the three bottom rows of Table 5-8 for residual robbery careers of 15 and 5 years, using the current average time served found in each offender group (see Table 5-9, below). As time served increases from low- to medium- to high-rate offenders, the proportion of active offenders in the total inmate population for that offender group decreases: for residual careers of 5 years, the proportion of active offenders is 79 percent among low-rate inmates, but it is only 67 percent among high-rate inmates.

The numbers of active inmates in Table 5-8 provide the basis for estimating the total number of active offenders in each offender group, whether incarcerated or free in the community. Using the fraction of careers that offenders spend incarcerated (I) from Equation 5-1, the number of active offenders (N) is esti-

TABLE 5-8 Distribution of California Inmates Convicted of Robbery by Predicted Robbery Frequencies

	Low Rate		Medium Rate		High Rate		Total	
	Number	Percent Active	Number	Percent Active	Number	Percent Active	Number	Percent Active
Total Inmates[a]	2,865		4,942		5,942		13,749	
Active Inmates[b]								
$T_R = \infty$	2,865	100	4,942	100	5,942	100	13,749	100
$T_R = 15$ years	2,629	92	4,361	88	5,118	86	12,108	88
$T_R = 5$ years	2,257	79	3,532	71	4,007	67	9,796	71

[a]Data from Visher (Volume II:Note 23).

[b]The number of active inmates (i.e., inmates who do not end their criminal careers while incarcerated) is estimated from Equations 5-5 and 5-8, where $S_{Low} = 1.347$, $S_{Med} = 1.997$, and $S_{High} = 2.415$ years (Table 5-9, below). When there is no career termination ($T_R = \infty$), the number of inactive offenders is negligibly small, and so all inmates are considered active.

mated from $N = R_A/I$. This procedure is used to estimate the size of the offender population under current incarceration policies; see Table 5-9.

Section A of Table 5-9 presents the estimates of the current values of the various sanction risks faced by robbers in California. In the absence of any reasonable empirical basis for distinguishing sanction risks, the same probabilities of arrest, conviction, and incarceration for a crime are used for all three offender groups. The basis for these estimates is described in Greenwood (1982). Average time served is estimated separately for each group on the basis of the inmates' reports of their expected release dates.

Using the relationships developed in Equations 5-3, 5-5, 5-9, and 5-10, Table 5-9 provides estimates of the number of robbery inmates and the number of robberies committed by adults in California under both the current policy and an alternative, more selective incarceration policy. The estimates are developed separately for each offender group and then combined to yield estimates of total inmates and total crimes. The more selective policy reduces time served to 1-year jail terms for all predicted low- and medium-rate offenders, while increasing time served for all predicted high-rate robbers to twice the current prison term

found among high-rate robbers. Alternative estimates are provided for the cases when there is no career termination (Table 5-9, Sections A and B) and when the residual robbery careers are 15 years (Sections C and D) and 5 years (Sections E and F).

Within any offender group (e.g., high-rate offenders), failure to account for career termination leads to the same percentage errors for the expected number of crimes and for the expected inmate population under any incarceration policy. For example, if the crimes committed under some policy are underestimated by 10 percent, the number of inmates under that policy is also underestimated by 10 percent. If an incarceration policy varies across offender groups, however, the magnitude of the estimation errors will vary across the groups and depend on the relationship between S and T_R in each group.

This variation across offender groups contributes to the much larger impact of career termination on the estimates of prison population than on crime reduction. In Greenwood's illustrative policy, high-rate offenders are assigned the longest time served. Failing to account for their career termination under the proposed policy leads to large underestimates of crimes committed and of inmate

TABLE 5-9 Estimates of Effects on Crime and Inmates of a Highly Selective Incapacitation Policy for California Inmates Convicted of Robbery

Parameters of the Model	Values of Parameters for Offenders			
	Predicted Low Rate	Predicted Medium Rate	Predicted High Rate	Total
Current Policy—No Career Termination[a]				
Average annual robbery frequency (λ)	0.9	8.1	20.8	—
Probability of arrest and conviction	.03	.03	.03	—
Probability of incarceration, given conviction	.86	.86	.86	—
Probability of incarceration, given a crime (J)	.0258	.0258	.0258	—
Probability of prison, given incarceration (p)	.12	.27	.46	—
Average jail term in years (s)	1.0	1.0	1.0	—
Average prison term in years (S)	3.892	4.692	4.075	—
Average time served in years $[\overline{S} = (1 - p)s + pS]$	1.347	1.997	2.415	—
Fraction of time free ($1 - I^*$)	.96967	.70555	.43554	—
Number of inmates ($R^* = R_A{}^*$)	2,865	4,942	5,942	13,749
Number of offenders ($N = R_A{}^*/I^*$)	94,461	16,784	10,527	121,772
Number of crimes $[C^* = N \times \lambda \times (1 - I^*)]$	82,437	95,920	95,367	273,724
Selective Policy—No Career Termination[b]				
Average time served in years ($\overline{S}$)	1.0	1.0	8.15	—
Fraction of time free ($1 - I^*$)	.97731	.82714	.18609	—
Number of inmates $[R^* = N \times \lambda \times (1 - I^*) \times (J\overline{S})]$	2,144	2,901	8,568	13,613 (−1%)[c]
Number of crimes $[C^* = N \times \lambda \times (1 - I^*)]$	83,086	112,450	40,748	236,284 (−14%)[c]
Current Policy—$T_R = 15$ Years[d]				
Fraction of time free ($1 - I$)	.97210	.73083	.47253	—
Total inmates ($R = R_A + R_I$)	2,865	4,942	5,942	13,749
Number of active inmates $[R_A = T_R/(T_R + \overline{S}) \times R]$	2,629	4,361	5,118	12,108
Number of inactive inmates $[R_I = \overline{S}/(T_R + \overline{S}) \times R]$	236	581	824	1,641
Number of offenders ($N = R_A/I$)	94,229	16,202	9,703	120,134
Number of crimes $[C = N \times \lambda \times (1 - I)]$	82,440	95,912	95,367	273,719
Selective Policy—$T_R = 15$ Years[d]				
Average time served in years ($\overline{S}$)	1.0	1.0	8.15	—
Fraction of time free ($1 - I$)	.97870	.83618	.26083	—
Total inmates $[R = N \times \lambda \times (1 - I) \times J\overline{S})]$	2,141	2,831	11,069	16,041 (+17%)
Number of active inmates $[R_A = T_R/(T_R + \overline{S}) \times R]$	2,008	2,654	7,172	11,834
Number of inactive inmates $[R_I = \overline{S}/(T_R + \overline{S}) \times R]$	133	177	3,897	4,207
Number of crimes $[C = N \times \lambda \times (1 - I)]$	82,999	109,737	52,642	245,378 (−10%)

TABLE 5-9 Continued

| | Values of Parameters for Offenders | | | |
	Predicted Low Rate	Predicted Medium Rate	Predicted High Rate	Total
Parameters of the Model				
Current Policy—T_R = 5 Years[e]				
Fraction of time free $(1 - I)$	.97595	.77028	.53365	—
Total inmates $(R = R_A + R_I)$	2,865	4,942	5,942	13,749
Number of active inmates				
$[R_A = T_R/(T_R + \overline{S}) \times R]$	2,257	3,532	4,007	9,796
Number of inactive inmates				
$[R_I = \overline{S}/(T_R + \overline{S}) \times R]$	608	1,410	1,935	3,953
Number of offenders				
$(N = R_A/I)$	93,846	15,375	8,592	117,813
Number of crimes				
$[C = N \times \lambda \times (1 - I)]$	82,430	95,929	95,370	273,729
Selective Policy—T_R = 5 Years[e]				
Average time served in years $(\overline{S})$	1.0	1.0	8.15	—
Fraction of time free $(1 - I)$	.98102	.85168	.37552	—
Total inmates				
$[R = N \times \lambda \times (1 - I) \times J\overline{S}]$	2,138	2,736	14,111	18,985 (+38%)
Number of active inmates				
$[R_A = T_R/(T_R + \overline{S}) \times R]$	1,781	2,280	5,366	9,427
Number of inactive inmates				
$[R_I = \overline{S}/(T_R + \overline{S}) \times R]$	357	456	8,745	9,558
Number of crimes				
$[C = N \times \lambda \times (1 - I)]$	82,858	106,066	67,111	256,035 (−6%)

[a]The variable values are based on a reanalysis of the original survey data available in Visher (Volume II). No adjustments for career termination are made.

[b]The selective policy involves 1-year jail terms for all inmates convicted of robbery and predicted to commit robbery at low or medium rates, and doubling the length of prison terms from 4.075 years under current policy to 8.15 years for all inmates convicted of robbery and predicted to commit robbery at a high rate. No adjustments for career termination are made.

[c]The difference between a decrease of 1 percent in the inmate population compared to a 1 percent increase estimated by Visher and the difference between a reduction of 14 percent in robbery and a 13 percent reduction estimated by Visher (Volume II) arises from differences in rounding the outcomes of various intermediate calculations.

[d]Remaining robbery careers (T_R) are estimated to last 15 years.

[e]Remaining careers (T_R) are estimated to last 5 years.

population for high-rate offenders. With their higher values of λ and greater incarceration risk per crime, however, high-rate offenders also contribute a much larger proportion to the inmate total than they do to the crime total for the three offender groups. As shown in Part F of Table 5-9, when remaining careers are 5 years long, high-rate robbers (both active and inactive) under the Greenwood policy contribute 75 percent to total robbery inmates, but only 26 percent to total rob-

beries by adults. Because of the greater representation of high-rate robbers among inmates, their larger underestimates have more influence on the results for all inmates. The differences in the size of errors found across offender groups combine with differences in the contribution of different offender groups to total crimes and total inmates to result in finite careers having a larger effect on estimates of inmate populations than on crime reduction.

6

Use of Criminal Career Information in Criminal Justice Decision Making

INTRODUCTION

All stages of decision making within the criminal justice system may use information regarding an individual's criminal career: a police officer in deciding whether or not to arrest a suspect, a prosecutor in deciding whether to pursue a case, a magistrate in setting pretrial release conditions, a sentencing judge in weighing community safety when deciding on a punishment, and a parole board in making a release decision. In all of these decisions, there are multiple, often competing, objectives, of which one reflects a concern for public safety: that concern involves at least an implicit attempt to assess an individual's criminal career. The dimensions of criminal careers cannot be measured directly, but decision makers often attempt to draw inferences about them from observable characteristics such as prior record, age, employment status, or drug dependency. The resulting characterization of an offender reflects a decision maker's own experience with offenders in the context of her or his personal background and

theories of behavior. Thus, these constructed portraits of offenders are likely to be based on varying information and to differ considerably across decision makers.

At each decision stage, the characteristics used to assess a suspect are constrained in part by the type of information at hand and by the time available to gather additional information. Additional time may permit successive decision makers to assemble a more complete picture. However, decision makers are rarely able to generate detailed information about the most operationally relevant criminal career dimensions: the frequency of offending and the time remaining in the career. Rather, they use the available information to roughly categorize individuals on the basis of a presumed likelihood of future criminal activity by converting an individual's observable attributes into some general risk classification, such as high, low, or medium risk. This process may be explicit, as in the formal scoring methods used by parole boards for release decisions and by prosecutors for case assignments to criminal career units, or implicit, and perhaps only as a secondary objective, in a judge's sentencing decisions.

For most decisions, a risk classification contributes to the selection of one of the available choices—low bond or high bond; a sentence to prison, jail, or probation; release on parole or denial—but it is almost never the only consideration. The complexity of these other considerations, such as retribution in sentences or strength of the evidence in prosecutorial decisions, makes it particularly difficult to isolate the role of criminal career information in the decision. In addition, in all these decisions, ethical considerations limit the ways in which a risk classification can be used in a decision. The nature of those limits varies considerably across the different stages of the criminal justice system; for example, the use of risk classifications at parole has long been accepted and is widely practiced, while such classifications at sentencing are more controversial.

There is also considerable debate about the kinds of variables that should legitimately enter any formal risk classification. The most legally relevant variable—the current offense—is an important consideration, as is information about prior adult convictions. Other defendant characteristics that might have predictive power, but that are more controversial, include variables like prior arrests (especially if not followed by convictions), or socioeconomic factors such as employment status. The most controversial variables are so-called ascribed characteristics, such as sex or race, over which the offender has no control.

Previous chapters summarized the state of knowledge about criminal careers and the means by which the criminal justice system might try to intervene to modify those careers. In this chapter we

examine ways in which criminal career information is used, both formally and informally, in decision making and the means by which better information might be provided to facilitate those uses. We first examine the various ways in which criminal career information is combined with other considerations in decisions at each stage of criminal processing. Such information is most relevant in decisions about whether to hold a person in confinement.

We next examine methodological approaches for the development of prediction scales. In some jurisdictions for some stages of the criminal justice system, the use of risk classifications invokes explicit prediction methods in which predictor variables are selected, weighted, and combined to generate a prediction score. This score is used to form a classification rule: individuals with prediction scores above a specified cut point are designated "high risk" and those with scores below that cut point are designated "low risk." Any such classification rule inevitably results in some errors among predicted high risks who are not (false positives) and predicted low risks who are not (false negatives). Use of prediction in criminal justice decision making raises some ethical questions: the weight to give to predicted future offending, "unacceptable" predictor variables, and the selection of the cut point, which dictates the mix of false positive and false negative errors. Although the choices of weights, variables, and cut points must be made locally, we attempt to identify the critical issues to be considered in making those choices.

Finally, since all prediction scales are dependent on the quality and completeness of the data available, we examine some issues in the use of individual records, and particularly juvenile records, which might contribute appreciably to improved classification.

CRIMINAL CAREER PERSPECTIVES IN CRIMINAL JUSTICE DECISION MAKING

A substantial body of research, summarized in a paper prepared for the panel (Gottfredson and Gottfredson, Volume II), has been directed at establishing the determinants of each major criminal justice decision: arrest, prosecution, pretrial release, sentencing, and parole.[1] The discussion in this section examines the degree to which those decisions selectively target individuals with serious criminal careers, i.e., those with the highest average values of offending frequency (λ), especially for serious crimes, and the longest residual careers. Chapters 2, 3, and 4 highlight the relevance of the instant offense, records of the prior adult and juvenile criminal activity, drug use, and employment history as indicators of more serious criminal careers; this chapter emphasizes the role of those factors in criminal justice decision making.[2]

---

[1]With respect to research on decisions on arrest, see, for example, Piliavin and Briar (1964), LaFave (1965), Black and Reiss (1970), Reiss (1971), and Smith and Visher (1981); on prosecution choices, see Forst and Brosi (1977), Forst, Lucianovic, and Cox (1977), Jacoby, Mellon, and Smith (1982), Feeney (1983); on pretrial release see Ebbeson and Konecni (1975), Bynum (1976), Bock and Frazier (1977), Roth and Wice (1978), Goldkamp (1979), Goldkamp and Gottfredson (1984); on sentencing, see major reviews by Blumstein et al. (1983), Hagan and Bumiller (1983), Garber, Klepper, and Nagin (1983), and Klepper, Nagin, and Tierney (1983); on parole, see major reviews by Schuessler (1954), Mannheim and Wilkins (1955), and D.M. Gottfredson, Wilkins, and Hoffman (1978).

[2]The literature contains research on many other factors, ranging from psychological tests to defendant demeanor in the courtroom, that we did not review and are not covered in this discussion.

Police Decisions

Faced with the decision to arrest a suspect, police officers must weigh the evidence of "probable cause" (LaFave, 1965) along with considerations of maintaining public order and protecting other people. Information about the criminal careers of suspects is most useful in advancing the latter objective. Except when an arrest occurs at the end of an investigation, such information has typically not been available at the time of the arrest decision. However, this situation is changing as telecommunications equipment and advanced record retrieval systems allow officers on the scene to check a suspect's wanted or warrant status.

Studies of police officers' arrest decisions report that the dominant variable accounting for a police decision to arrest is the seriousness of the alleged offense (see, e.g., Black, 1971; Sherman, 1980; Smith, 1982). Other factors that increase the probability of arrest are hostile behavior by the suspect, victims' preferences for arrest, a stranger-to-stranger relationship between the victim and the suspect, the officer's prior knowledge of the parties involved, and low socioeconomic neighborhood (see, e.g., Piliavin and Briar, 1964; Friedrich, 1977; Smith, 1986). Some evidence suggests that in encounters involving interpersonal disputes, suspects who appear to be under the influence of alcohol are more likely to be arrested (Smith and Klein, 1984); however, the effect of suspects' drug use on arrest decisions has not been examined.

Programs have been established to structure police decision making in order to focus additional resources on offenders with serious criminal careers. This can be accomplished by targeting prearrest in-

vestigation on such offenders, by postarrest investigation to assist in prosecuting
them, and by placing high priority on
serving warrants on them (Gay and Bowers, 1985). Of the three approaches, only
prearrest targeting leaves the choice of
targets to the police; postarrest priorities
are generally established by statute or by
prosecutors.

As one example, prearrest targeting
was a major theme of the Repeat Offender
Project (ROP) of the Washington, D.C.,
Metropolitan Police Department. A special ROP unit was established in 1982 to
target and apprehend offenders believed
to be committing five or more FBI index
offenses per week (an annual frequency
of at least 260) or to be trafficking in stolen
property. Initially, a committee of senior
officers selected ROP targets—without
any explicit rule—on the basis of information developed through informants and
investigations, as well as available police
records; other offenders became ROP targets because of outstanding warrants or
arrest opportunities that arose during investigations of other targets. This selection process led to the targeting of offenders who were older than average and
had longer-than-average records of previous adult index arrests. Subsequently, the
ROP unit adopted an explicit rule that
gave greatest weight to verified informants' information, but also incorporated
variables related to serious criminal careers, such as "criminal history" (not defined further), narcotics addiction, pending cases, and status as a parolee,
probationer, or unemployed person (Martin, 1984). This approach exemplifies a
philosophy expressed in other locations
using prearrest targeting, that official-
record indicators of the career should be
supplemented by additional information
on the current level of activity, which
may be obtained through informants or
other investigative methods (Gay and
Bowers, 1985).

Prosecution

The extent to which prosecution practices successfully target offenders with
serious criminal careers is related to how
much prosecution efforts are focused on
such offenders and whether such efforts
result in higher conviction rates or longer
sentences. Information on this issue derives largely from experience from career
criminal units (CCUs), many of which
were established with federal funding to
give special attention to "career criminals," but with each local prosecutor's
office defining its target populations.
However, other evidence is available
from statistical analyses of variables associated with measures of prosecution effort.

Decision Making in the Absence of Career Criminal Units

Since obtaining a conviction is a primary prosecution goal, it is not surprising
that the availability of evidence has been
found to be the principal determinant of
prosecution effort (see review in Rhodes,
1984). Other determinants are the seriousness of the current charge and the
relationship between the defendant and
victim. The degree to which prosecution
is focused on defendants with serious
criminal histories is far less clear. Several
studies have found evidence that charge
reductions or other indicators of plea bargaining occur less frequently in cases
involving defendants with extensive arrest histories (Bernstein et al., 1977;
McDonald, 1978; Jacoby, Mellon, and
Smith, 1982). Empirical results on allocation of effort vary, depending on the measure of prosecution effort being analyzed
(e.g., time from arrest to disposition, plea
bargaining indicators, attorney hours).[3]

---

[3]In an econometric analysis of 5,717 felony cases,
Forst and Brosi (1977) found no relationship be-

The influence of a juvenile arrest or adjudication record on adult prosecution decisions is largely unexplored. The bifurcation of juvenile and adult records certainly inhibits prosecutors from obtaining and using juvenile records at early decision points. Greenwood, Petersilia, and Zimring (1980) report that in a national survey, 60 percent of prosecutors responded that juvenile police records were "rarely or never" available at the time of filing, while a majority (74 percent) reported that adult records are "always or usually" available. Boland and Wilson (1978) hypothesized that because of the lack of information about juvenile activity, the adult criminal justice system makes no distinction between the first adult arrest of a chronic juvenile offender and the arrest of a true first offender. A test of the Boland-Wilson hypothesis requires a comparison between a jurisdiction with integrated juvenile and adult records and a comparable jurisdiction with more limited sharing of information. No adequate test has yet been carried out. One effort in this direction was undertaken by Greenwood, Abrahamse, and Zimring (1984) in comparing prosecutors'

decisions in Seattle, which has an integrated record system, with those in Los Angeles and Las Vegas, which do not; however, there were not enough relevant cases in Seattle for satisfactory analysis. In that study, Greenwood, Abrahamse, and Zimring (1984) argue that the availability of the juvenile record does not guarantee that its severity will influence case disposition.

There have been few studies of the influences on prosecution efforts of other variables related to serious criminal careers, such as drug use and employment status, and the evidence is not consistent.[4]

Career Criminal Unit Evaluations

Career Criminal Units were established in more than 100 prosecutors' offices during the 1970s. Their caseloads were generally restricted by case selection criteria that were left to the discretion of the local jurisdictions. One evaluation found that CCU cases received more attention: CCU convictions were found to consume between five and seven times as many attorney hours as other convictions; smaller but still sizable differentials in attorney hours were also observed for pleas and dismissals (Rhodes, 1980). Two CCU evaluations (Springer and Phillips, n.d.; Chelimsky and Dahmann, 1981) provide information on whether CCUs selected cases involving defendants with the most serious criminal careers and on whether the extra resources led to higher conviction rates or

---

tween prior record and time from arrest to disposition, which was the authors' proxy for effort. In part, this lack of relationship is appropriate because arrest history is included as a factor in their strength-of-evidence measure, which was found to positively influence prosecutor efforts. On the basis of an experimental study of 855 prosecutors, Jacoby, Mellon, and Smith (1982) report that defendants' criminality (as measured by prior convictions, arrests, and parole or wanted status) was related to the priority assigned to a case, once it had been accepted for prosecution. Hausner, Mullin, and Moorer (1982), analyzing a large sample of cases presented to U.S. attorneys, found that cases involving repeat offenders were more likely to be accepted than cases involving first offenders. But the analysis did not control for strength of evidence, and the acceptance decision patterns may not apply outside the federal system because the declined cases were also eligible for prosecution in state courts.

[4]One analysis of prosecution decision making in 1,196 burglary cases found the probability of case acceptance to be positively related to the existence of a prior record, but for defendants with prior records, a prior drug-related charge made prosecution *less* likely in the instant case. However, because the cases arose from a special burglary program, these conclusions may not generalize to other settings (see Rhodes, 1984).

longer sentences for the targeted defendants.

The four CCUs evaluated by Chelimsky and Dahmann showed marked variation in formal selection criteria. Definitions of "career criminals" differed in terms of current charge thresholds (e.g., robberies only, felonies only, or any charge); attention to prior arrests and convictions; and "status indicators," such as pretrial or parole release following an earlier case. While the evaluators claimed that it was impossible to say "with any certainty how closely the group of individuals prosecuted by these programs represented the ideal career criminal group" (1981:72), the selection criteria used by the four CCUs were in fact generally consistent with indicators of serious criminal careers, although the selection might have been improved by also considering drug involvement.

Evaluating the impact of CCUs on case processing is more problematic. On the basis of their reviews of 15 evaluations, Springer and Phillips (n.d.) conclude that prosecution by CCUs was more successful than routine prosecution in terms of pretrial detention rates, conviction rates, dismissal rates, and incarceration rates. In contrast, Chelimsky and Dahmann (1981) found no effect of CCUs on these rates, but concurred with the Springer and Phillips finding that the units had increased the seriousness of the charges for which convictions were obtained. The differences in conclusions may have arisen because only one of the four units evaluated by Chelimsky and Dahmann was in a large urban office. Had they evaluated other jurisdictions whose regular units were under a greater press of caseloads, Chelimsky and Dahmann might have found more substantial effects of CCUs on case outcomes.

Results of CCU evaluations should be treated carefully because of two common methodological problems in the research to date. First, pretest and posttest periods were typically of only 1 year, so that evaluations were based on only the earliest cases processed by the units, which may not have been representative of later performance. Second, the comparison group designs used in CCU evaluations cannot completely control for bias in case selection. In maintaining CCU caseloads at desired levels, the formal selection rules were frequently tightened or relaxed through unwritten informal revisions. These shifts may have invoked strength of evidence, perhaps by choosing important but weak marginal cases for which extra prosecutorial attention was likely to affect case outcome (thereby biasing evaluation results against the unit) or by skimming the best cases to improve the unit's success rate. In either case, informal practices could have distorted the evaluations of CCU effectiveness. Thus, the evidence is still ambiguous on the question of whether resource allocation has a measurable effect on case outcome rates: CCUs do appear to target high-rate serious offenders, but their effect on case outcomes is still unproven.

Pretrial Release

While the primary consideration in pretrial release decisions is ensuring appearance for trial, community safety during the period until trial is also often an important concern. Indeed, "preventive detention" statutes in some jurisdictions permit a judge to focus explicitly on the risk to the community in detaining a suspect prior to trial. No assessments are available of the effects of preventive detention laws in routine use. (See, however, Bases and MacDonald, 1972, for an early evaluation, and Gottlieb, 1985, for a preliminary report of an evaluation in progress.) Even in the absence of preventive detention laws, however, judges can and do consider current criminal justice status, prior record, and other factors related to criminal careers in their pretrial decisions.

Analyses of the pretrial release decision have generally considered the role of seriousness of the current charge, indicators of ties to the community, and evidentiary strength. Charge seriousness dominates the decision, measured in terms of either release of the defendant on personal recognizance or the amount of financial bond demanded (Gottfredson and Gottfredson, Volume II; Rhodes, 1984). The influence of charge seriousness reflects joint concern over the incentive for nonappearance at a trial that might result in a serious sentence as well as concern about harm to the community in the event of repetition of the crime during the pretrial period. Community-ties indicators (e.g., local residence of family) are intended to predict appearance at trial; however, they have not been consistently found to influence the decision to release a defendant on personal recognizance, and they seem not to affect the amount of bail or conditions of release in serious cases when the defendant is not released on recognizance (Goldkamp and Gottfredson, 1981a,b).

Adult criminal history emerges as comparable in importance to seriousness of the current charge in determining pretrial release decisions (M.R. Gottfredson, 1974; Bynum, 1976; Roth and Wice, 1978; Goldkamp, 1979; Goldkamp and Gottfredson, 1981a, b; Nagel, 1983; Stryker, Nagel, and Hagan, 1983). Two related measures have been found significant: indicators of the overall adult record (measured in such terms as total prior arrests or number of felony convictions in the preceding 5 years) and indicators of current criminal justice status (e.g., pending cases at the time of arrest).

Two other variables related to serious criminal careers—drug use and employment status—have been studied. For felony cases in urban courts, indicators of drug use have been found not to influence either the decision to release on recognizance or the bond amount set for defendants not released immediately (Roth and Wice, 1978; Goldkamp and Gottfredson, 1984). The most recent study of the federal system also found no evidence that drug use influences pretrial release decisions (Rhodes, 1985). In at least two jurisdictions, urinalysis tests for current drug involvement are made at the time of arrest. However, analyses are not yet available of the relationship of the test results to pretrial release decisions and to defendants' pretrial conduct. Employment status, however, has been consistently found to influence decisions on pretrial release on recognizance. Employed defendants are more likely than unemployed defendants to be released on personal recognizance, controlling for charge seriousness and prior record (see, e.g., Roth and Wice, 1978; Goldkamp and Gottfredson, 1981a). This finding may reflect both a recognition of their community ties as well as a reluctance to impose an extralegal penalty (namely, loss of job and income) before trial.

Sentencing

Determinants of sentencing were recently reviewed by a panel of the National Research Council, which concluded that "using a variety of indicators, offense seriousness and offender's prior record have emerged as the key determinants of sentences" (Blumstein et al., 1983:83). Despite measurement problems that tend to cause underestimates of its effect, prior record consistently emerges as one of the strongest effects on sentence, second only to the current charge (Blumstein et al., 1983:83–87; Gottfredson and Gottfredson, Volume II).

A review prepared for this panel (Rhodes, 1984) identified three studies, conducted in support of sentencing guidelines development, that have also found drug use to be an aggravating factor at sentencing for certain charges: sex crimes, fraud, weapons charges, and forgery. These offenses are neither so serious that incarceration is nearly automatic nor so minor that it would be inappropriate. With such intermediate offenses, there is more room for the influence of factors such as drug use that are not related to the current charge and prior record.

Sentencing is the decision point at which the potential effect of juvenile record availability receives the greatest attention, and analyses have provided some fragmentary evidence suggesting that routine availability of juvenile records might increase the sentences of young adult offenders with extensive juvenile records. Greenwood, Abrahamse, and Zimring (1984) compared sentencing practices for young adults in three jurisdictions: Las Vegas, with no disclosure of juvenile records before the presentence investigation; Los Angeles, with frequent pretrial information sharing between the two systems; and Seattle, with one of the few integrated repositories containing both juvenile and adult records. While their study was limited, the researchers found that, among young adult defendants, those with more extensive juvenile records were more likely than others to be sent to a state prison in all three sites (1984:53). They attribute the finding in part to informal record sharing, and they also point out that even in the absence of information, a sentencing judge may presume the existence of a median juvenile record, in which case presentation of a minimal record would be treated as a mitigating factor.

Uncertainty concerning the influence of juvenile records on sentencing in the adult system makes clear the need for more careful comparisons of individual case decisions in a "two-track" system (in which juvenile records are shielded from adult authorities) with decisions in a similar "one-track" system with shared information. The most comprehensive analysis of decision making in a one-track system was based on data from London, where juvenile court information is shared with adult authorities. That study concluded that the number of juvenile convictions does influence sentence severity at the first adult conviction (Langan and Farrington, 1983). While the relationship between expected incarceration time and age is confounded by the different institutional options available at different ages, the probability that a conviction leads to incarceration increases monotonically with the number of prior convictions over the entire age range of 10 to 24. Replication and comparison of this analysis in comparable American settings—for example, Seattle and another jurisdiction in the state of Washington with separate juvenile and adult repositories—would be an important step in ascertaining the effect of a single repository for both juvenile and adult records in informing the sentencing decision.

Parole Release

In their release decisions, parole authorities consider retributive concerns, support for maintaining institutional discipline, and facilitating inmate reentry into society. The parole decision also invokes prediction of future offenses, frequently by means of formal guidelines (Hoffman and Beck, 1974; Hoffman, 1983).

Analyses of parole decisions have generally measured the decision outcome either in terms of time served in prison or a binary release/no release outcome at the time of first eligibility for parole. Neither of these measures is entirely satisfactory. "Time served in prison" confounds the parole decision with the sentence, especially the minimum sentence; the binary indicator fails to reflect the severity of punishment imposed. Furthermore, neither indicator captures aspects like the term and special conditions of parole.

Despite the difficulty of analyzing parole decisions, two variables emerge as dominant influences: the charge that led to the incarceration and the adult criminal history (Scott, 1974; D.M. Gottfredson et al., 1978; Elion and Megargee, 1979). Not surprisingly, these variables are also the primary bases of parole guidelines used to structure decisions in the federal system and in many states.

Other indicators of serious criminal careers also play a role in parole decision making. Surveys of board members (Parker, 1972) and analyses of cases (Elion and Megargee, 1979) suggest that knowledge of juvenile offenses and other life events incorporated in presentence reports play an influential although not decisive role. Alcohol use has been consistently found to be a predictor, although a weak one, of parole denials (see Gottfredson and Gottfredson, Volume II). A history of drug abuse is considered a negative indicator at parole hearings, according to both a survey of parole board members (Parker, 1972) and a content analysis of parole board hearings (Carroll and Payne, 1977a, b), but it rarely emerges as a dominant influence on the decision to release (e.g., Scott, 1974; D.M. Gottfredson et al., 1978).

Misconduct during incarceration—information not available at sentencing—emerges as a strong factor affecting parole decisions (see Gottfredson and Gottfredson, Volume II). Its influence on parole decisions presumably reflects its value in predicting recidivism as well as its motivational value in maintaining institutional discipline (Glueck and Glueck, 1930; Mannheim and Wilkins, 1955; Carlson, 1973; Gottfredson and Adams, 1980).

Conclusions

Criminal justice decisions—arrest, pretrial release, prosecution, sentencing, and parole—are made with different ranges of discretion, different objectives, and different information available at the time of the decision. Despite the differences in objectives, each decision includes some assessment of whether the subject is pursuing a serious criminal career and hence is a candidate for confinement. A key question is whether these assessments do in fact lead to more severe sanctions for offenders whose careers involve the most frequent and serious offending over the longest durations.

A review of relevant research shows that seriousness of the current charge and prior adult record—two factors closely related to serious criminal careers—dominate the decision-making process. Employment status only influences decisions regarding pretrial release. The impact of a juvenile criminal history on decision making has been thoroughly explored only in sentencing; even though items in the juvenile history are related to adult criminal behavior, legal restrictions and the inaccessibility of juvenile history information have minimized its use in most criminal justice decisions. Drug use, especially concurrent use of narcotics and other drugs, which is strongly associated with frequent and serious criminal activity, has not been found to be an important determinant of criminal justice decisions.

ISSUES IN PREDICTION-BASED CLASSIFICATION

Introduction

While a variety of considerations are weighed at each stage of criminal justice decision making, the prediction of future offending is a consideration common to all stages. Most often these predictions are "clinical," i.e., based solely on the decision maker's judgment and previous experience. For more than 60 years, efforts have been made to improve the quality of these predictions and to systematize their use by means of statistically derived, prediction-based classification rules. Such empirically based rules require development of scales that relate prediction variables to estimates of future offending and transform every offender's scale score into a risk classification level, such as high risk or low risk. The risk classification of each offender is then considered as one factor in making individual decisions. Prediction-based classification rules have been developed for use in pretrial release (Goldkamp and Gottfredson, 1981a), in assignment to a career criminal unit for prosecution (Rhodes et al., 1982), at sentencing (Greenwood, 1982), for institutional classification (D.M. Gottfredson and Bonds, 1961), and for parole release (Hart, 1923; Mannheim and Wilkins, 1955; Hoffman and Beck, 1974).

General arguments for the use of such rules have included enhancing the visibility of the decision process, improving the equity of decisions, and providing routine feedback on the outcomes of decisions. But perhaps most important, it has been argued that using such rules informs decision makers of systematic patterns occurring beyond their own experience and so can improve the accuracy of their predictions. Interest in prediction-based rules has recently been increased by attention to selective incapacitation policies, especially by claims that selective incapacitation can reduce crime, prison populations, or both.

Increased public concern about crime, coupled with the pressure of growing prison populations, has intensified the search for more efficient ways to use limited criminal justice resources. New limitations on the discretion of parole boards

have encouraged the consideration of future risk at earlier decision points, especially at sentencing. Finally, newly developed prediction scales have attracted attention as candidates for incorporation in prediction-based classification rules.

In order to address the technical and ethical issues in prediction-based classification rules, it is important to first outline the process by which they are developed. Three basic steps are involved in deriving a scale that assesses the likely future course of an individual's criminal career: first, assessing the ethical limitations on the role of prediction in decision making and on the choice of the predictors; second, combining appropriate risk factors to form a prediction scale and using that scale to define a classification rule; and third, validating the performance of the rule in terms of its classification errors.

Many jurisdictions may not have the necessary data or are otherwise unable to develop their own prediction scale and accompanying classification rule, and so have considered the transfer of an existing prediction-based classification rule for their own jurisdiction. However, transferring such a rule outside the jurisdiction in which it was developed creates accuracy problems that must be considered carefully. These problems in the transfer of classification rules are discussed at the end of this section.

Ethical Issues

Opinions differ on the proper role in criminal justice decision making of predictions of future criminality. In one view, because a convicted offender is already vulnerable to state intervention within statutory limits, use of predictive criteria following conviction, especially in deciding whether to release on parole, is widely accepted by many people. From another view, because of the symbolic import and strong just-deserts component of sentences, many people find the use of prediction at sentencing to be acceptable only within narrow limits, if at all. Some people would permit the use of prediction only in certain preconviction decisions, such as selection for pretrial release on personal recognizance or, possibly, for intensive prosecution.

Predictive considerations have long played an implicit though informal role in criminal justice decision making. Explicit prediction-based classification rules have been widely used for several decades as a basis for structuring decisions framed in terms of reducing punishment, such as parole release and pretrial release; few ethical objections have been raised against those uses. More recently, explicit rules have been advocated and used as a basis for imposing punishment and increasing the risk of punishment: at sentencing (Greenwood, 1982), in selection for intensive prosecution (Forst et al., 1982), and in targeting for proactive police investigation (see Martin, 1984; Moore et al., 1984, for discussions).

In addition to their presumed advantage in effectively targeting crime control resources on worst-risk offenders, explicit rules can make the exercise of discretion more precise and fair. By formalizing the decision criteria, rule-bound decisions articulate the bases for discretionary decisions and make those decisions more predictable. At the same time, when rules serve only as guidelines, the discretion to diverge from them is retained, but usually carries some burden for providing reasons for the divergence.

Several ethical considerations are involved in using prediction-based classification rules in decision making. One consideration is the relative importance given to the predicted incremental danger to the public compared with the cost to the defendant of the contemplated additional sanction. Inaccurately classifying

offenders as high risk is acknowledged as a greater concern as the sanction becomes more severe and as the predicted criminal behavior becomes less serious (J. Monahan, 1981; Morris and Miller, 1985). For example, imposing life sentences under the predictive presumption of habitual offender laws is generally less acceptable than briefly detaining the writers of threatening letters to the White House during a presidential public appearance.

For any classification rule, the ratio of false-positive to false-negative error rates can be adjusted by setting more or less stringent threshold scores for classifying a subject as high risk. But the ability to simultaneously reduce both rates requires improved knowledge about correlates of the criminal career. Informing policy makers of the estimated error rates is one essential step in enabling them to decide what role prediction-based classifications should play. The choice may well be different for different crimes and sanctions, for different stages of the criminal justice process, and in different jurisdictions.

Ethical Considerations in Selecting Candidate Risk Factors

Ethical considerations limit the choice of variables that can be used in prediction-based classification rules. Seriousness of the instant charge appears to have nearly universal acceptance on ethical grounds and is also most useful from a crime control perspective. Charge seriousness occupies a central ethical place in the just-deserts theory of punishment (von Hirsch, 1985:10), and its power to enhance incapacitative effects has been demonstrated empirically, using data from several jurisdictions (see Chapter 5; Cohen, 1984a). Except for charge seriousness, virtually all other variables having predictive content have been the subject of ethical objections to their use in classification rules. The main concerns are addressed in terms of three general considerations: relationship to blameworthiness; logical and empirical relationship to the criterion variable; and congruence with fundamental social values.

Blameworthiness. As noted by Moore (Volume II), among defendant characteristics having predictive power, those that are more blameworthy are more widely accepted as ethical bases for increasing sanctions. In assessing blameworthiness, it is useful to distinguish between harm and culpability. Harm is measured in terms of specific consequences to the victim. The offender's culpability is diminished to the extent that the harm occurred through chance, negligence, diminished mental capacity, or ignorance, rather than through specific intent, or that the crime was motivated by victim provocation, duress, or a matter of conscience (von Hirsch, 1985:64–74). In terms of blameworthiness, these circumstances of the instant crime moderate the charge itself as a basis for decisions (1985:74–76). Other individual characteristics that are statistically associated with criminal careers differ in terms of ethical acceptability, in part because they involve different levels of blameworthiness. Since children are considered less responsible than adults, for example, a given juvenile record is widely considered less blameworthy than a similar adult record. Evidence of prior illegal drug use may be considered less appropriate than evidence of previous violent or property crimes because drug use itself imposes no harm on others. Objections to the use of prior unemployment have invoked both the lack of harm and the offender's imperfect control over employment status. On grounds of their lack of blameworthiness, unalterable characteristics such as race and sex are considered inadmissible as predictors, and would be even if they were found to be correlated with the frequency of serious offending.

Relationship to the Criterion Variable. In gauging the admissibility of various defendant characteristics as bases for decisions, the classification variable should have theoretical and empirical relationships to the criterion variable. Moore (Volume II) emphasizes the need for theoretical linkages. Historically, a strong theoretical linkage to a particular criterion variable has sometimes been substituted for empirical evidence in justifying a particular variable as a basis for decisions: for example, the theoretical connection between indicators of community ties and appearance at trial led to their use in pretrial release guidelines long before empirical evidence concerning the relationship was developed (Ares, Rankin, and Sturz, 1963).

Measures of an offender's prior criminal career are widely considered appropriate predictors of future behavior on theoretical and empirical grounds. Among available measures, an arrest record samples a larger fraction of incidents in a criminal career than does a conviction record; hence, it is preferable on grounds of empirical standing, but is less preferable in terms of the value of its proven certainty. Both drug use and employment status have multiple theoretical relationships to frequency of offending, but there is stronger empirical evidence of a connection to drug use than to employment.

Concern for Equal Protection. It is widely agreed that classification rules should not affront basic social values, such as concern for equal protection of all citizens under the law. Historically, equal protection concerns have been especially acute with respect to personal characteristics such as race or religion. There is no empirical evidence that these variables have important predictive power with respect to criterion variables of concern to criminal justice decision makers. But even if predictive power were shown, these variables would be widely viewed as totally inappropriate bases for offender classifications.

While disapproval of such variables is virtually universal, there are responsible differences of opinion with respect to the legitimacy of their correlates. Moore et al. (1984:73) argue that "interest in justice counsels restraint in the use of . . . variables associated with class and ethnic background, including wealth, religion, race, and national origin." In contrast, while Morris and Miller (1985:47) admonish against use of "race or any superficial substitute" in making predictions, they would permit incorporation of "facially neutral factors such as education, housing, and employment which reflect racial inequalities." However, even though the races differ appreciably on these factors in the general population, it is not clear that these race differences prevail among active offenders.

In sum, assessing any particular classification variable requires careful balancing of all three values discussed above, along with the variable's contribution to crime control. The choices of admissible predictor variables may thus be different across jurisdictions using prediction-based classification rules. However, with respect to race and ethnicity, it is worth reiterating their general inappropriateness as predictor variables because they have no relationship to blameworthiness, there is no demonstrated theoretical or empirical basis for linking them to pertinent criterion variables, and their use affronts concern for equal protection.

Developing Classification Rules

Defining the Criterion Variable

Predictions in criminal justice decisions are usually concerned with avoiding some undesired behavior, such as crimes, parole violations, or failures to appear at trial. The criterion variable is the specific measure of undesired behavior, and may include, for example, crimes of all types, only violent crimes, or only crimes of specific types such as robbery or burglary.

Research on prediction has traditionally relied on dichotomous criterion variables measuring recidivism—i.e., rearrest, reconviction, or parole revocation within some follow-up period. The follow-up periods are sometimes uniform in length (usually between 1 and 5 years) for all sample members and sometimes vary among the individuals being followed (e.g., the length of each individual's pretrial or parole period). Comparisons across subsamples are based on the fraction of each group that recidivates before the end of the observation period.

For scale development, there are three important shortcomings of dichotomous recidivism indicators: they are not sufficiently sensitive to variations in the underlying continuous variable, λ; they fail to distinguish adequately between offenders whose careers have terminated and those who remain active but avoid arrest; and they measure individual crime rate as observed through an official filter, such as arrest or parole revocation, and so incorporate factors that may be associated with the official decision rather than with the offender's behavior.

Because of the insensitivity of dichotomous recidivism indicators, preliminary conclusions about recidivism probabilities based on short follow-up periods have sometimes been substantially revised in light of experience during a longer follow-up period. Maltz (1984:73) presents an example of a recidivism rate differential between two subsamples that was large and statistically significant at 6 months, had nearly disappeared by 24 months, and appeared likely to be reversed by 36 months. Such an outcome would occur if one sample contained offenders with a higher average λ but a shorter average residual criminal career length than the other: a relatively high proportion of active offenders in the first sample would be rearrested shortly after release, but a higher proportion would also drop out of offending before ever being rearrested.

These differences between samples would be more adequately reflected by the use of continuous criterion variables that more reliably capture criminal activity over time. For samples of released offenders, one such continuous variable is elapsed time (t) between release and the first recidivism event as measured in official records. In any given sample of released offenders followed for some observation period, some will continue criminal activity (and may eventually be rearrested) while others will cease criminal activity during the observation period. In measuring recidivism and developing predictive scales for classifying offenders, it is important to distinguish the two groups of released offenders. The criminal justice system is primarily concerned with offenders who remain active at high offending frequencies. Various failure-rate models have been developed that use the statistical distribution of t to estimate both μ, the annual arrest rate for active offenders, and δ, the dropout rate, reflected in the fraction of the sample whose criminal careers terminate before the end of the observation period (e.g., Maltz and McCleary, 1977; Harris and Moitra, 1978; Bloom, 1979).

The earliest failure-rate models assumed that all released offenders remained active in their criminal careers and estimated their assumed constant arrest rate, μ (Stollmack and Harris, 1974). By ignoring the termination of some criminal careers, this assumption thus led to underestimates of the true value of μ for those who did remain active. Later refinements to the basic model permitted joint estimation of the values of δ and μ (Maltz and McCleary, 1977) and of different values of δ and μ for different subsets of a sample (Carr-Hill and Carr-Hill, 1972; Greenberg, 1978; Harris, Kaylan, and

Maltz, 1981). By permitting heterogeneity in μ and δ, these models could partition observed changes in estimates of μ during the follow-up period into effects due to early attrition of high-rate offenders (who are quickly rearrested and removed from the samples at risk soon after release) and dilution effects due to offenders whose careers have terminated, who constitute an increasing fraction of the remaining sample over time.

Another approach to defining the criterion variable, used by the Rand Corporation with inmate samples (Chaiken and Chaiken, 1982a), invokes self-reported values of λ rather than the recidivism measures more commonly used. This approach has the advantage of accounting for all the crimes by active offenders rather than only those filtered through the arrest or other criminal justice decisions leading to designation of a recidivist event. This reliance on crimes committed reflects differential rates of actual offending and thus avoids distortions associated with differences in vulnerability to capture by the criminal justice system. Since offenders' self-reports are retrospective, however, the measure cannot capture postrelease differences in career termination patterns, which can be reflected in failure-rate analyses.

Selecting and Weighting Variables

The process of selecting and weighting variables to form a prediction scale involves a series of steps. The initial task is to select some set of candidate predictors—variables on which data are available and for which a connection to criminal careers might be expected on the basis of theory or empirical research. Among all the candidate predictors that could be used in the scale, some will be rejected because of the poor quality of available data or their redundancy with other candidate variables. From the remaining variables, others may be eliminated through exploratory statistical analyses that reveal them to have little predictive power. Once a set of candidate predictors has been selected, weights are assigned. This section describes the major features of techniques that have been used to develop weights. Copas and Tarling (Volume II) and Farrington and Tarling (1985) contain more complete discussions.

Burgess Scores. The Burgess score method was one of the first classification techniques applied in criminal justice (Burgess, 1928; Ohlin, 1951). To use it, the predictor variables must all be coded dichotomously (e.g., present = 1, absent = 0) and defined so that presence of a factor is statistically associated with the high-risk category. Thus, this technique may discard useful information that cannot be captured in a simple yes/no variable (e.g., frequency of drug use). The analyst incorporates as predictors those variables that most effectively discriminate between high-risk and low-risk members of the sample. An individual's Burgess score, which is the number of predictors present, is used to classify the individual. Burgess scores place equal weight on each predictor variable in the constructed scale, a feature that is appropriate only if each predictor conveys the same amount of information about the criterion variable and if all the predictors are mutually independent (Copas and Tarling, Volume II). In early applications, the Burgess score was used to predict a dichotomous criterion variable, parole violation. One can also apply the technique to classify offenders on the basis of a continuous criterion variable, such as λ, that has been recoded categorically, high-, medium-, or low-λ, as illustrated in Greenwood (1982).

The Burgess technique was originally justified more for its simplicity than for its statistical properties. The subsequent emergence of more sophisticated approaches to weighting the predictor variables, such as multiple regression and discriminant analysis, led to dismissal of the Burgess scale and its variants as "inadequate" (Wilkins and McNaughton-Smith, 1964). Nevertheless, Burgess scores continue to be used in classification, primarily because their accuracy in repeated samples has usually been found comparable with that of scales derived using methods of multivariate statistical analysis (Ohlin and Duncan, 1949; D.M. Gottfredson and Ballard, 1965; Ward, 1968; Simon, 1971; Van Alstyne and Gottfredson, 1978).

Least-Squares Methods. The 1950s saw the first application of least-squares estimation of a linear predictor function to criminal justice classification (Kirby, 1954; Mannheim and Wilkins, 1955). In contrast to Burgess scales, least-squares estimates place more weight on predictor variables that provide more information about the criterion variable, and they do not require that information be thrown away by dichotomizing continuous criterion or predictor variables. When linear prediction was recognized as inappropriate for analyzing the dichotomous criterion variables then common in criminal justice prediction research (Palmer and Carlson, 1976), attention shifted to alternative multivariate methods such as discriminant analysis, probit analysis, and logistic regression analysis. A scale estimated by using least-squares weights describes the construction sample more accurately (under a minimum-squared-error criterion) than does a Burgess scale or any other weighted sum of the same predictor variables. However, even in construction samples, the improvements over the Burgess scales are small in actual practice (see discussion in Farrington and Tarling, 1985; see also D. M. Gottfredson and

Ballard, 1965; Ward, 1968; Challinger, 1974; Gottfredson and Gottfredson, 1980; Nuffield, 1982).

One problem with least-squares weights is their sensitivity to outliers in a construction sample. Because outliers are unlikely to recur in repeated samples, the accuracy of least-squares scales estimated on a construction sample containing outliers deteriorates, or shrinks, by a greater proportion than the accuracy of Burgess scales when both are applied to other samples from the same population. The magnitude of shrinkage is proportionally greater for techniques that rely more heavily on the data and less heavily on the analyst's prior specification.[5] Ongoing work with "bounded-influence" regression (Krasker and Welsch, 1982; Ruppert, 1985)—which uses a weighting function to bound the influence of outliers on the regression estimates—and with "pre-shrunk" regression estimators (Copas, 1983) shows promise for reducing the shrinkage of predictive accuracy due to outliers.

Special problems emerge when the correctly specified prediction equation gives a significant weight to one or more variables that have been rejected as ethically inadmissible for decision making (see Fisher and Kadane, 1983). Suppose, for example, that employment status (coded as 1 for unemployed and 0 for employed offenders) is deemed inadmissible but is found to be correlated with λ. Suppose also that unemployment is more common among offenders having long arrest records. Then estimation of a least-squares equation that includes arrest record but omits employment status would fail to produce a prediction scale that is neutral with respect to the inadmissible employment status variable. Rather, the effect of unemployment will be reflected in the least-squares weights estimated for admissible correlated predictors. In this example, a long arrest record would lead, on average, to an overprediction of the effect of record length alone on λ because the weight on record length would also reflect influences of its omitted correlate, employment status. To develop an employment-neutral prediction scale, one would have to include employment status in the estimation equation, estimate least-squares weights for all predictors, and then omit the inadmissible employment-status variable by setting its weight to zero in computing values of the scale for individuals.

Failure-Rate Analysis. The primary use of failure-rate analysis has been to evaluate the effectiveness of programs in reducing recidivism. But recently it has also been used to assess the validity of classifications based on a predictive scale. Schmidt and Witte (1980) and Maltz (1984) used failure-rate analysis to estimate the influence of covariates of t, the time to failure, that could serve as predictors. In principle, by partitioning a sample into categories defined in terms of candidate predictors and comparing the recidivism experiences of the subsamples, the techniques could be used to select the most powerful predictor variables (Maltz, 1984:131).

However, a more direct approach is to

---

[5]The formulas for expected shrinkage that are reported by Copas and Tarling (Volume II) imply that statistical shrinkage increases with the number of parameters estimated in the construction sample: e.g., the number of coefficients in a multiple regression equation and the number of subgroup means in an interactive analysis such as Automated Interaction Detection (AID) (Sonquist, Baker, and Morgan, 1973). Moreover, when a "search" strategy is used to incorporate only the parameter estimates that are significantly different from zero, shrinkage is proportional to the number of parameters computed rather than to the number incorporated.

use failure-rate models, such as the proportional hazards model of Cox (1972), that make even less restrictive assumptions about the arrest frequency rate, μ. Barton and Turnbull (1981) have applied a model developed by Kaplan and Meier (1958) to investigate age and education effects on elapsed time to rearrest. Failure-rate models have been applied only rarely to criminal justice prediction problems (Barton, 1978; Barton and Turnbull, 1979, 1981), and so their properties and the extra statistical power they can provide in separately predicting frequency rates for active offenders and dropout rates are not yet widely understood and appreciated.

Defining the Classification Rule

After a prediction scale has been developed, it can be used to compute a scale score for every offender. This score is related to a prediction about the criterion variable for that offender. Commonly, scales are defined so that higher scores are associated with higher risk in terms of the criterion variable. In a typical application a cut point score k is chosen, and a classification rule is defined that takes the form: Classify the offender as "high risk" if his scale score is equal to or greater than k, and classify the offender as "low risk" otherwise. Offenders classified as high risk are recommended for incarceration or other intensive treatment, and offenders classified as low risk are recommended for release or other less intensive treatment.

Because no prediction system can be perfect, two types of classification errors occur. A false-positive error occurs when an offender classified as high risk would be a low-risk offender if given the opportunity. Ethical opposition to prediction-based classification rules has tended to focus on these errors, which lead to rec-

ommendations for "unnecessary" incarceration or other more intensive treatment. A false-negative error occurs when an offender classified as low risk is actually a high-risk offender. False-negative errors impose a cost on society in the form of decreased community safety. Decisions that are based on predictions reflect explicit or implicit assumptions about the relative costs of the two types of errors.

The numbers of each type of error depend on both the predictive power of the scale and the choice of the cut point. For any given scale, the number of false-positive errors can be reduced by making the cut point higher, but only at the cost of more false-negative errors. Conversely, lowering the cut point will increase the number of false-positive errors and decrease the number of false-negative errors. Simultaneously reducing errors of both types requires development of a new scale with greater predictive accuracy.

The relationship between choice of cut point and classification errors is illustrated in Table 6-1, which displays offender counts, error rates, and accuracy measures associated with each possible cut point of the seven-factor scale developed by Greenwood (1982) for classifying incarcerated robbers and burglars. The rule specified by Greenwood classified all inmates with scores of 4 or more as high risk, and thus candidates for extended sentences. Under that rule, 27.2 percent of all offenders in the construction sample would be classified as high risk, a *selection ratio* of 27.2 percent. Under that rule, 54.7 percent of the inmates classified as high risk were truly low risk (i.e., low and medium λ in Greenwood's terms), a false-positive rate of 54.7 percent. The false-negative rate associated with that rule was 16.9 percent. A more restrictive classification rule, with the cut point raised to 6, for

TABLE 6-1 Classification Performance of Rand Scale, by Cut Point Value, for Convicted Robbers and Burglars (three states)

Cut Point (k) (Class = High if Score ≥ k)	Number of Offenders		Selection Ratio for High Rate (percent)	False-Positive Rate (percent)	False-Negative Rate (percent)	Number of Errors			Relative Improvement Over Chance (RIOC)[a]
	High-Rate	Low-Rate				False Positives	False Negatives	Total	
0	4	67	100.0	75.4	0.0	668	0	668	Indeterminate
1	17	167	91.9	73.7	5.6	601	4	605	0.750
2	33	180	71.2	68.8	8.2	434	21	455	0.661
3	55	122	47.2	60.8	11.5	254	54	308	0.532
4	48	77	27.2	54.7	16.9	132	109	241	0.312
5	41	36	13.1	47.4	20.4	55	157	212	0.371
6	11	18	4.4	48.7	23.4	19	198	217	0.356
7	9	1	1.1	10.0	31.3	1	209	210	0.867
Total	218	668	—	—	—	—	—	—	—

[a]See text for discussion of RIOC.

SOURCE: Data from Visher (Volume II).

example, would lead to a lower false-positive rate, only 48.7 percent, but a higher false-negative rate, 23.4 percent.[6]

Regardless of the predictive power of the scale, the minimum number of errors is constrained by the relationship between the selection ratio and the *base rate,* the fraction of offenders who are truly high risk in terms of the criterion variable. If the selection ratio exceeds the base rate, the number of offenders classified as high risk will exceed the number who are actually high risk, and so some false-positive errors must occur. Similarly, if the base rate exceeds the selection ratio, some false-negative errors must occur. The actual error rates observed will depend on the predictive accuracy of

the scale, but they can never be smaller than the minimum number of errors that result from the relationship between the base rate and the selection ratio. Only when a cut point is chosen so that the selection ratio is equal to the base rate is it possible for both error rates to be zero.

The choice of cut point, however, depends on actual classification accuracy and on the relative concern for the different kinds of errors. The error rate most commonly considered is the false-positive rate, the ratio of false-positive errors to the number of positive (high-risk) classifications, but it fails to reflect the social cost of false-negative errors. Conversely, the false-negative rate, the ratio of false-negative errors to the number of negative predictions, ignores the social cost of false-positive errors. Moreover, because these measures are rates rather than counts, they fail to convey the full impact of changes in cut points on classifications. Returning to Table 6-1 as an example, a shift of the cut point from 4 to 6 produces only a moderate decrease in the rate of false-positive errors (from 54.7 percent to 48.7 percent) and a moderate increase in the rate of false-negative errors (from 16.9

---

[6]In reporting classification accuracy, Greenwood (1982:59, Table 4.8) invokes a slightly different definition of high-λ offenders than the one used elsewhere in his report. Under the redefinition of high λ, the base rate is 28 rather than 25 percent. Values in Table 6-1 are derived from computations by Visher (Volume II), and because Visher retained the base rate of 25 percent and computed λ using a different procedure from that of Greenwood, values in Table 6-1 for a cut point of 4 imply slightly different values of accuracy measures from those implied by Greenwood (1982:Table 4.8).

percent to 23.4 percent). But because the shift greatly reduces the selection ratio for high-rate offenders, it affects the error counts far more dramatically than the error rates: the number of false-positive errors drops from 132 to only 19, and the number of false-negative errors increases from 109 to 198.

An accuracy measure that reflects both types of errors but assigns them equal cost is the total error rate, the fraction of all classifications that are either false positives or false negatives. A shift in the cut point that increases the selection ratio will increase false-positive errors and decrease false-negative errors, but its effect on the total error rate cannot in general be anticipated in advance. Since the total error rate is simply the sum of the two kinds of errors, its use implies that they have equal social costs. Assignment of equal costs, however, is not appropriate in most situations. The costs depend on the severity of the intervention to be imposed on offenders classified as high risk and the gravity of the harm one is trying to prevent. For example, the U.S. Secret Service uses risk-prediction profiles to identify potential presidential assassins, who are followed and perhaps detained for a few hours' questioning during a local presidential appearance. False-positive errors are of far less concern in this application than they are in a selective incapacitation policy like the one analyzed by Greenwood (1982), where convicted burglars classified as high risk were to be incarcerated for 8 years compared with 1 year for other convicted burglars.

Another problem with all three accuracy measures is that they fail to provide an appropriate reference base. Ideally, one would like to compare the accuracy of the classification rule with the accuracy achieved by decision makers in actual practice. The latter is generally unknown because decision makers do not articulate

their classifications, so it is necessary to define other reference points. Accuracy achieved by any rule is sometimes measured as improvement over random accuracy, the accuracy that would be achieved if classifications were made randomly using the same selection ratio as in the rule (Duncan et al., 1953). Because random accuracy is influenced by the difference between the selection ratio and the base rate, it is also desirable to measure accuracy achieved by the rule relative to the maximum accuracy that could be achieved under the given base rate and selection ratio.

Loeber and Dishion (1983) have defined a measure called relative improvement over chance (RIOC), which relates the accuracy achieved to maximum accuracy and random accuracy. Their measure is defined by

$$\text{RIOC} = \frac{\text{Achieved accuracy} - \text{random accuracy}}{\text{Maximum accuracy} - \text{random accuracy}}.$$

Formulas are provided by Copas and Tarling (Volume II) for computing maximum accuracy and random accuracy. The value of RIOC is zero for a classification rule that fails to improve on random accuracy and unity for a rule that achieves maximum accuracy given the current selection ratio and base rate.

While RIOC does provide one more measure for assessing classification accuracy, it, like the total error rate, gives equal weight to false-positive and false-negative errors. Moreover, for any prediction rule, its value is quite sensitive to the difference between the selection ratio and the base rate. As illustrated in Table 6-1, RIOC is highest at the extreme cut points of 1 and 7, and lowest at the cut point of 4, where the selection ratio is most nearly equal to the base rate. Therefore, RIOC is not a helpful measure for setting cut points. Furthermore, in using

RIOC to choose among alternative scales for a particular application, care must be exercised to ensure that the values of RIOC reported for the alternatives are under similar base rates and selection ratios. Finally, like other accuracy measures, it provides no comparison between accuracy using the rule and accuracy under existing practice.

A measure of the predictive accuracy of the underlying scale that is independent of the particular classification rule is the mean cost rating (MCR): the average change in accuracy achieved at each successively higher scale score over the entire range of scores—0 to 7 for the Rand scale illustrated in Table 6-1, for example.[7] The value of MCR is increased by true-positive classifications and decreased by false-negative classifications over the entire range of the scale. Therefore, while a high value of MCR will identify a prediction scale with generally high accuracy over a range of classification rules, it may not identify the prediction scale that leads to the highest classification accuracy under any particular base rate and selection ratio.

In short, no classification accuracy measure or set of measures provides sufficient basis for defining the best classification rule associated with a given prediction scale that reflects all relevant concerns. Rather, alternative scales and cut points have to be evaluated on the basis of social consensus concerning the relative importance of false-positive and false-negative errors. This consensus will depend in

---

[7]The formula for MCR is given as follows. Let

$$\text{Mean Cost} = \frac{1}{2} \sum_{k=1}^{K} (C_k + C_{k-1})(U_k - U_{k-1}),$$

where C_k is the proportion of negatives incorrectly rejected at score k, and U_k is the proportion of positives correctly predicted at score k. Then MCR $= 1 - 2 \times$ (mean cost), a transformation to obtain an index in the interval [0,1], with higher values corresponding to improved performance.

part on the severity of sanctions to be imposed on high-risk offenders and the gravity of the risk one is trying to prevent. A decision-theoretic approach to the choice of a classification rule, in which the relative cost of false-positive and false-negative errors is expressed as a "civil-libertarian ratio," is illustrated in Blumstein, Farrington, and Moitra (1985).

Validating the Predictive Relationship

Before implementing a prediction scale that has been developed by using data from one construction sample, it is essential to validate the scale's accuracy in predicting the criterion variable for other samples. A careful validation should include four elements:

• a previously developed prediction scale and classification rule and measures of classification accuracy in the construction sample at alternative cut points;

• a validation sample that represents the population to which the rule will be applied, and that contains no observations that were included in the construction sample;

• a criterion variable that adequately captures the behavior of interest; and

• a follow-up period that is sufficiently long to observe variations in the criterion variable and to assess the accuracy of the classification rule.

The following discussion illustrates the importance of these aspects of the validation process by describing some typical violations and the problems that can result from inadequate validation of the prediction scale.

A common problem in validating a prediction-based classification rule is that the validation sample is selected to represent the same population as the construction sample, rather than the population to which the rule will be applied. In one approach, called "sample fractionation," members of a single available sample are randomly assigned to construction and validation subsamples. With this approach, accuracy is expected to decrease only slightly in the validation sample. This shrinkage effect is due solely to sampling variation; the expected magnitude of shrinkage can be computed using formulas reported by Copas and Tarling (Volume II).

Unfortunately, measures of shrinkage obtained in this way provide no information about further deterioration in accuracy that would be expected when the prediction scale is applied to other populations whose characteristics may be different from those in the construction sample. A frequent cause of this difference is selection bias in obtaining the construction and validation samples. Although all scales are intended for application to offenders at some decision point (such as sentencing), scale development is almost always based on selected samples for which only one of the possible decisions has been made. For example, in studies of the use of prediction-based classification rules at sentencing, with recidivism as the criterion variable, analyses of official records have used samples of released offenders because only they are free to be rearrested. An analysis based on offender self-reports involved only incarcerated offenders because they were accessible for interviews (Greenwood, 1982). Because the factors that influence incarceration and release decisions are also related to the behavior being predicted, this selective sampling creates the potential for selection bias, which must be addressed in the development of prediction-based classification rules.

Because of selection bias, both the predictor weights and the classification accuracy measures developed in a construction sample made up entirely of releasees or entirely of incarcerated inmates will be inappropriate for samples of convicted offenders awaiting sentence. For example, incarcerated samples will overrepresent offenders who have committed especially serious crimes and those with especially long arrest records. The few inmates with short arrest records are likely to have committed more serious crimes. In such a sample, an analysis that failed to take adequate account of selection bias could produce a scale for predicting serious offending that mistakenly assigns a negative weight to the length of an arrest record.

The best way to avoid distortions arising from selection bias is to use samples that adequately represent the population to which a scale will be applied. In the case of prediction scales for use at sentencing, for example, an appropriate sample would include all those who are sentenced—both incarcerated and unincarcerated offenders. The absence of easily accessible and uniform data on all sentenced offenders—which are now scattered among local courts, probation offices, jails, state correction facilities, and parole offices—has greatly inhibited analysis of appropriate samples.

If selected samples must be used, a variety of statistical techniques are available to estimate and reduce the impact of selection bias. If data exist to permit analysis of both the release decision and the subsequent behavior of a sample of releasees, including all variables relevant to both outcomes, an "endogenous selection" model (Heckman, 1979) can be used to correct for selection bias in developing predictor weights. The estimated weights then provide unbiased predictions of the behavior of offenders about whom the release decision is to be made, rather than only of released offenders. Heckman's technique has been applied in conjunction with logistic regression analysis to find predictors of the pretrial release decision and the probability of pretrial rearrest (Rhodes, 1985). Even though the Rhodes analysis incorporated more than 40 candidate predictors of the release decision and of pretrial rearrest, it is still possible that selection bias arising from unobserved factors (e.g., subjective decisions based on judges' prior experience or unusual family circumstances of a defendant) might persist.

Because Burgess scales are less dependent on the construction data than scales developed with more sophisticated methods, the accuracy of classification scales based on Burgess methods is relatively unaffected by selection bias. Consequently, even though the more sophisticated approaches outperform Burgess scales in construction samples, Burgess scales incorporating variables with widely acknowledged predictive validity continue to be developed and to perform reasonably well in a variety of samples. As more is learned about characteristics that differentiate convictees who are released from those who are incarcerated, data on those characteristics can be collected and included in the analysis. The application of models such as Heckman's to data incorporating those characteristics will lead to improved predictive scales developed from selected samples.

Even a correctly developed classification rule can be expected to change over time. Introduction of a scale may change behavior patterns. For example, offenders may avoid seeking drug treatment to prevent creation of a record of drug abuse that would increase their scale score, or prosecutors aware of the weight on prior convictions may insist on retaining multiple charges in plea bargaining. Such changes will cause deterioration of predictive accuracy. In addition, the behaviors of offenders and criminal justice authorities may change over time for reasons independent of the scale, for example, as the age composition of offenders varies or the resource constraints of criminal justice agencies are altered.

For both reasons, periodic validation and recalibration of the prediction-based rule are integral parts of the implementation process. In validation, the accuracy of an existing prediction-based classification rule is measured in an entirely new sample. The deterioration of accuracy may become sufficiently large to warrant *recalibration*—reestimation of predictor variable weights and reconsideration of the choice of cut point. The accuracy of the recalibrated rule should then be verified by using another independent sample. The distinction between these two steps is not always maintained. For example, early "validations" of the 1980 Iowa Risk Assessment System involved recalibration through the incorporation of new "special risk factors" found to have predictive power in the validation sample. Then, the combined construction and validation samples were used to compute accuracy measures (Statistical Analysis Center, 1984). Because of this nonindependent approach, the reported accuracy measures from the validation were overstated.

Issues in Transferring Classification Rules

The cost and difficulty of developing a prediction-based classification rule have led many jurisdictions to consider instead transfer of an existing rule. However, there are a number of reasons for proceeding very cautiously with such transfers and for expecting the classification accuracy of a rule to deteriorate significantly when it is applied in a new jurisdiction. Even if offenders with similar characteristics have similar criminal careers in different jurisdictions, differences in criminal justice system behavior—as measured by the decisions of police, prosecutors, and judges—may lead to cross-jurisdictional differences in the behavior of offenders at any given stage in the process. For example, as discussed above, selection bias within a single jurisdiction will lead to differences between samples of released and incarcerated offenders. And because of cross-jurisdictional differences in the decision processes that lead to different types of offenders reaching different stages of the criminal justice process, samples of incarcerated offenders may differ across jurisdictions even if offenders on the street do not.

The impact of cross-jurisdictional effects on estimated relationships involving predictor variables and criminal behavior was documented in Visher's (Volume II) reanalysis of the second Rand inmate survey, which sampled the same offender types—incarcerated robbers and burglars—in California, Michigan, and Texas. All inmate responses from the three states were combined in the construction of Greenwood's seven-factor scale for selective incapacitation. But as reported by Visher (Volume II), the mean offending frequency (λ) for predicted high-rate offenders in the Texas sample was only about one-third that of the California and Michigan samples. It is possible that this difference arose because Texas offenders behave differently from those in the other states. But it is more likely that Texas criminal justice policies lead to incarceration of a larger share of less serious offenders because of differential selection effects. These differences lead one to expect cross-state variation in the observed predictive relationships, and indeed Visher (Volume II:Table 15) reports differences across states in the factors that show significant predictive power and in the overall goodness-of-fit between scale items and values of λ.

In a comparison of felony case processing in six large urban jurisdictions, case attrition rates (through nonacceptance at screening, nolle prosequi, or dismissal) ranged from 40 to 76 percent (Brosi,

1979:14). Such variations limit the transfer ability of classification scales across jurisdictions and mandate at least local validation and recalibration of any such scale on a sample selected from the new jurisdiction.

A further potential impediment to successful transfer of a predictive scale arises from cross-jurisdictional variations in the meaning, completeness, and quality of data on both the predictor and criterion variables. Such variations can arise from definitional differences (e.g., a purse snatcher may be charged with robbery or larceny); from differences in the accuracy with which predictor variables are verified (for example, employment status as determined during a presentence investigation is likely to be more accurate than employment status determined immediately after arrest); or from cross-jurisdictional differences in definitions of predictor variables (such as the characterization of previous charges and dispositions as felonies or misdemeanors).

In considering the transfer of a predictive scale, it is important to recognize that the accuracy of a scale developed to predict one type of behavior tends to deteriorate when it is used to predict some other behavior. Although this tendency is clear in principle, it is frequently overlooked in practice. For example, Fischer's (1984) accuracy comparison of several scales on a common data base ranks them in order of their ability to predict the criterion variable for the Iowa Risk Assessment System instrument—a seriousness-weighted index of a broad range of crime types. While the ranking presented there reflects accuracy in predicting the Iowa criterion variable, it should not be assumed to apply with respect to other criterion variables, such as likelihood of parole violation or rearrest for a specific crime. The principle would apply, for example, to jurisdictions attempting to implement Greenwood's (1982) seven-factor scale to predict rearrest for any of a broad range of crimes, despite the fact that it was developed to predict individual crime rates for robbery and burglary for incarcerated offenders.

For all these reasons, comparative analysis of differences in case attrition and in variable definition should precede transfer of a statistical prediction device across jurisdictions. Evidence of substantial cross-jurisdictional variation warrants caution in transferring any predictive device, even if the jurisdictions are otherwise similar.

EXPLICIT CLASSIFICATION SCALES

Recognition of empirical relationships between frequency, duration, and seriousness of offending, on one hand, and observable offender characteristics, on the other, has led to development of explicit classification scales based on these relationships for use in criminal justice decisions. This section reviews four classification scales receiving extensive current attention:

- the seven-factor scale developed by Greenwood using data from the Rand Corporation inmate survey, and described in a report that popularized the term "selective incapacitation" (Greenwood, 1982);
- the Salient Factor Score used in federal parole guidelines, perhaps the longest-lived system in current use (Hoffman and Beck, 1974; Hoffman, 1983);
- a risk assessment device for parole release in Iowa, which has claimed dramatic improvements in predictive accuracy over other approaches (Fischer, 1983, 1984); and
- a scale developed by INSLAW, Inc., for use by U.S. attorneys in assigning federal cases for special attention in career criminal units (Rhodes et al., 1982).

All these scales share a common concern for distinguishing offenders in terms of criminal career attributes, and the scales are empirically derived from observed statistical relationships between readily obtainable offender attributes and criminal career dimensions. In each case, the scale is intended for use in identifying offenders who, on the basis of their criminal careers, pose the greatest risk for continued serious offending. This review of the scales focuses primarily on their classification accuracy and on the adequacy of the variables used in each scale. We do not address the process by which the variables were selected and weighted, primarily because that process is not well documented in the available literature.

Rand Inmate Survey Scale

Growing interest in pursuing selective incapacitation as a sentencing policy prompted Greenwood (1982) to devise a method for distinguishing which offenders commit offenses at high rates. The scale is unique in its use of offending frequency (λ) as the criterion variable, rather than officially recorded events, such as arrest, which enter the more common recidivism measure. Thus it introduced two important changes: (1) a focus on crimes rather than arrests and (2) a concern for differences in frequency of offending—a continuous variable—rather than a simple binary recidivism measure. However, in contrast to a recidivism measure that combines the effects of frequency and career termination, the Rand scale focuses only on frequency. Using the scale as intended—for determining the length of incarceration—implies an assumption that there is no career termination, that offending at the estimated frequency will continue indefinitely.

Using data from a self-report study of 2,190 incarcerated offenders in California, Michigan, and Texas, Greenwood selected seven variables that individually classified inmates reasonably well into high, medium, and low rates of offending for robbery and burglary and that he deemed appropriate for sentencing purposes. The variables, shown in Table 6-2, were each scored either 0 or 1 to form an additive Burgess-type scale that results in a prediction score between 0 and 7 for each inmate. Inmates were then classified as committing crimes at a low rate (scoring 0 or 1), medium rate (scoring 2 or 3), or high rate (scoring 4 or more). Empirical, ethical, and operational concerns regarding the Rand Inmate Survey Scale are reviewed extensively elsewhere (Visher, Volume II; see also Cohen, 1983, 1984b; Spelman, 1984; von Hirsch and Gottfredson, 1984). Some of the results of these reanalyses and critiques of the Rand data are highlighted here, especially the work of Visher, which was commissioned by the panel.

The principal utility of the scale for achieving future crime reduction depends on the accuracy of the scale in prospectively identifying offenders who will commit crimes at high rates in the future. The existing research, as Greenwood states, is limited to retrospective data on past offending and no validation of the instrument on future offending was carried out. Without explicit prospective validation, the scale's utility for prospectively identifying future high-rate offenders depends on the retrospective accuracy of the scale and on the extent to which past high-rate offending continues into the future.

The analysis shows that the retrospective accuracy of the seven-variable classification rules is no better than other similar instruments (see Cohen, 1983; Visher, Volume II:Table 19). Specifically, even within the sample used to construct the scale, 55 percent of the classified high-rate group (27 percent of the total sample) were false positives who did not commit crimes at high rates. Similar 50 to 60 percent false-positive errors (typically measured by no new arrests,

TABLE 6-2 Variables Used in Rand Scale to Distinguish Inmates by Individual Crime Rates

Variable[a]	Source
1. Prior conviction for same charge (robbery or burglary)	Official criminal records[b]
2. Incarcerated more than 50 percent of 2 years	Self-report
3. Convicted before age 16	Self-report
4. Served time in state juvenile facility	Self-report
5. Drug use in preceding 2 years	Self-report
6. Drug use as a juvenile	Self-report
7. Employed less than 50 percent of preceding 2 years	Self-report

[a]All variables are scored as 0 or 1 depending on the presence or absence of the attribute.

[b]Data available only for prison, not jail, inmates.

parole violations, or revocations during a designated follow-up period) have been found in the predicted worst-risk groups for various statistically based prediction devices intended to assess the risk of recidivism for use in parole release decisions.[8]

Further examination of the scale's ac-

---

[8]For example, in a 1976 validation of the Federal Parole Commission's Salient Factor Score, 44 percent of the "poor risks" (20.3 percent of the sample) were rearrested or had a parole violation warrant issued in a 1-year follow-up after release on parole (Hoffman and Beck, 1980). In a validation of a slightly revised Salient Factor Score (Hoffman, 1983), 49 percent of the predicted poor risks (23.9 percent of the sample) recidivated during a 2-year follow-up (i.e., were recommitted to prison, had outstanding parole violation warrant issued, or were killed while committing a crime). J. Monahan (1981:103) reports that a similar risk-assessment device developed by the Michigan Department of Corrections found a 40 percent recidivism rate (i.e., arrest for a new violent crime while on parole) in their "very-high-risk" group (4.7 percent of the sample). M.R. Gottfredson, Mitchell-Herzfeld, and Flanagan (1982) report a 49.6 percent readmission rate to state correctional institutions in a 5-year follow-up for their high-risk group (16.3 percent of their sample of 1972 releasees from correctional institutions in a northeastern state).

curacy revealed important cross-state variation in its predictive power. False-positive rates for high-rate robbers were 60 percent in California and Michigan and 48 percent in Texas. Focusing on high-rate offenders, especially robbers, these false-positive rates reflect a 57 percent relative improvement over chance (as measured by RIOC) in California, but only 21 percent and 38 percent in Michigan and Texas, respectively (Visher, Volume II:Table 19).

The Rand scale has not yet been validated on samples other than the one used to construct the scale. Because of random variations in attributes across samples drawn from the same population, statistical shrinkage will slightly reduce the accuracy observed in the construction sample. Even larger reductions in accuracy can be expected if the scale is applied to different populations. In comparison with a population of all convicted offenders, the more selected subpopulation of inmates used to develop the scale may differ in important ways in their attributes and in the relationship of those attributes to high-rate offending. If so, the application of a scale developed on inmates to a broader population would reduce classification accuracy still further. Also, because the scale captures only frequency and not termination of careers, its prospective accuracy will deteriorate further as careers end. Thus, even the modest classification accuracy of the scale, reflected in a 55 percent false-positive rate for high-rate robbers in the construction sample, is likely to overstate the accuracy that would be obtained in actual implementation of the scale.

Some ethical concerns also exist about the variables that make up the scale. The variables (indicated in Table 6-2) invoked are consistent with previous empirical research, and few people question the use of prior adult criminal record. But measures of the juvenile record, drug use, and recent employment may be questioned on grounds of blameworthiness. The controversy surrounding these variables may lead to their exclusion in implementing the classification scale. Such exclusion of statistically useful variables may further diminish the accuracy of the amended classification scale, thereby diminishing the crime-reduction effects of implementing the scale. In anticipation of such possible amendments, it is advisable—as was done in Greenwood's analysis of the inmate scale—to examine the accuracy of alternative versions of the scale under various exclusion conditions. While Greenwood (1982:61–66) compares different scale versions in terms of differences in mean crime rates for scale-identified offender groups, no data on individual error rates are reported.

These error rates were subsequently derived in the panel's analysis of the Rand inmate data and are reported in Table 6-3. Elimination of potentially controversial variables relating to drug use, employment, and juvenile criminal record does not substantially affect the false-positive rate among predicted high-rate inmates, nor does it reduce the overall predictive accuracy of the scale. Adult criminal record variables alone perform nearly as well on these measures as did the full seven-factor scale. Elimination of variables from the scale, however, does significantly reduce the accuracy of the scale in identifying high-rate offenders; the percent of true high-rate offenders who are missed by the scale increases from 50 to 87 percent when the scale is limited to only adult criminal record variables (Modified Scale A).

The accuracy of the scale also varies with the cut point that is used to designate high-rate offenders (see Table 6-1). In Greenwood (1982), all inmates with scores of 4 or more are designated as high-rate offenders. As shown earlier, this choice of a cut point comes closest to matching the scale's selection ratio (27.2 percent predicted to be high rate) to the

TABLE 6-3 Changes in the Error Rates of Rand Inmate Scale as Predictor Variables Are Eliminated

Scale	Error Rates for High-Rate Offenders		
	False Positives Among Predicted High-Rate Offenders (percent)	False Negatives: Actual High-Rate Offenders not Correctly Identified (percent)	Total Inmates Predicted Correctly (percent)
Original scale—7 factors	55	50	46
Modified scale B[a]	60	81	41
Modified scale A[b]	60	87	45

NOTE: Accuracy is assessed on the sample of inmates convicted of robbery or burglary in the three states surveyed, the same sample used to construct the scale.

[a] Only variables relating to prior criminal record are included; drug use and employment variables are excluded (see Table 6-2).

[b] Only the variables relating to adult criminal record are included; juvenile record, drug use, and employment variables are excluded (see Table 6-2).

defined base rate of 25 percent high-rate offenders. At this cut point, 50 percent of high-rate offenders are correctly identified by the scale and there are 55 percent false positives among predicted high-rate offenders.

As is found when prediction variables are eliminated from the scale (Table 6-3), altering the cut point for designating high-rate offenders substantially changes the accuracy with which high-rate offenders are identified. When a score of 6 or more is required, only 9.2 percent (20 of 218) of all high-rate offenders are correctly identified (Table 6-1). This accuracy in identifying high-rate offenders increases to 75.2 percent (164 of 218) when the cut point is lowered to 3. The false-positive rate, by contrast, is far less sensitive to changes in the cut point over much of its range (see Table 6-1). As the cut point is lowered, more inmates are designated as high-rate offenders on the basis of their scale score. For example, the false-positive rate increases from 48.7 percent at a cut point of 6 to 60.8 percent at a cut point of 3 or more.

There are also questions about the availability of the scale variables for operational use. In Greenwood's analysis,

all of the variables, except past convictions for the same charge, are based on self-reports by inmates. Implementation of the scale at sentencing would have to depend on official records rather than self-reports as the source of data for scale variables. For some of the scale variables, especially those relating to juvenile record, drug use, and employment, this requirement may be more than records systems can routinely deliver.

Salient Factor Score

Most scales for classifying prisoners for parole release have focused on recidivism as the criterion variable. Parole guidelines were first put into use in the federal system in 1972 (for a review, see Gottfredson and Gottfredson, Volume II). The current guidelines (last revised in 1981) have two components that are provided to parole commissioners as aids for their decisions: the seriousness of the commitment offense and an empirically derived assessment of future recidivism risk, based on six offender characteristics. The latter is known as the Salient Factor Score (SFS 81 since 1981) and is reproduced as Table 6-4. The higher the score,

TABLE 6-4   Salient Factor Score (SFS 81)

A. PRIOR CONVICTIONS/ADJUDICATIONS (ADULT OR JUVENILE) .... _____
        None............... = 3
        One .... = 2
        Two or three .... = 1
        Four or more .... = 0
B. PRIOR COMMITMENTS OF MORE THAN THIRTY DAYS (ADULT OR JUVENILE) _____
        None............... = 2
        One or two .... = 1
        Three or more ...... = 0
C. AGE AT CURRENT OFFENSE/PRIOR COMMITMENTS .... _____
        Age at commencement of the current offense:
        26 years of age or more... = 2***
        20–25 years of age .... = 1***
        19 years of age or less... = 0
        ***EXCEPTION: If five or more prior commitments of more than thirty days (adult or
        juvenile), place an "x" here _____ and score this item........................... = 0.
D. RECENT COMMITMENT FREE PERIOD (THREE YEARS) .... _____
        No prior commitment of more than thirty days (adult or juvenile),
        or released to the community from last such commitment at least
        three years prior to the commencement of the current offense .... = 1
        Otherwise.. = 0
E. PROBATION/PAROLE/CONFINEMENT/ESCAPE STATUS VIOLATOR THIS TIME . _____
        Neither on probation, parole, confinement, or escape status at the time of the current offense;
        nor committed as a probation, parole, confinement, or escape status violator this time .... = 1
        Otherwise.. = 0
F. HEROIN/OPIATE DEPENDENCE .... _____
        No history of heroin or opiate dependence .... = 1
        Otherwise.. = 0
TOTAL SCORE .... _____

SOURCE: Hoffman (1983:Appendix A). Reprinted with permission from *Journal of Criminal Justice*, Volume 11, Hoffman, Peter B., Screening for risk: a revised salient factor score (SFS 81), © 1983, Pergamon Press, Ltd.

the higher is the likelihood of no recommitment (see Hoffman, 1983; Janus, 1985).

Since initial implementation of federal parole guidelines, the Salient Factor Score has been revised and validated prospectively on several new samples (see Hoffman, 1983; Hoffman and Beck, 1976, 1980; Hoffman, Stone-Meierhoefer, and Beck, 1978). Two measures of predictive power—point-biserial correlation, mean cost rating—show that for all versions, the score and the four risk categories are at the high end of the accuracy range reported in other parole recidivism studies (Gottfredson and Gottfredson, 1980). In addition, these accuracy measures have been very stable over several validation samples. Hoffman (1983) reports that for construction and validation samples, respectively, 46 and 49 percent of parolees classified as poor risks by SFS 81 were considered failures (primarily because of reincarceration) at the end of a 2-year follow-up period. This accuracy is typical of statistical classification scales that assess offending risk, 50 to 55 percent of those classified as poor risks appearing as false positives. It is noteworthy that the SFS shows little evidence of deterioration from the construction sample of 1970–1972 prison releasees to the validation sample of 1978 releasees. Indeed, the false-positive rate among poor risks declines from 54 percent in the construction sample to 51 percent in the validation sample and the false-negative rate remains unchanged at 24 percent. Contrasting offenders classified as poor risks to the combination of all other offenders, the relative improvement in accuracy over that obtained by chance (RIOC) also increases slightly from 24 percent in the construction sample to 28 percent in the validation sample.

In another validation study of SFS 81, using a broader criterion of rearrest in a 3-year follow-up period for the same validation sample, the scale performed better: 66 percent of the poor-risk offenders incurred an arrest, compared with 22 percent of the very good risks, for a 34 percent false-positive rate (Janus, 1985; see also Hoffman, Stone-Meierhoefer, and Beck, 1978). In moving from Hoffman's (1983) recidivism criterion of reincarceration in a 2-year follow-up to the broader criterion of rearrest used by Janus (1985), the recidivism base rate increased from 30 to 44 percent, and so some reduction in the false-positive rate would be expected. Similarly, the RIOC in identifying the poor risks (compared with all others) also improved somewhat, increasing from 28 percent to 38 percent in the validation sample. The increase in the base rate is undoubtedly responsible for some of the improvement in predictive accuracy, but there may also be some gain in predictive accuracy because the scale is applied to rearrest rather than reincarceration.

In addition, the study reports that the SFS appears to distinguish among releasees in the four predicted risk groups according to their arrest frequency rates, μ: those classified as fair or poor risks were rearrested sooner and at higher average rates than releasees classified as very good or good risks. As was demonstrated in Chapter 5 (Table 5-5), however, the differences in μ across different risk groups are much smaller when only the frequencies for active offenders (i.e., those with at least one arrest in the fol-

low-up period) are compared. The different risk groups also displayed little difference in offense seriousness (Janus, 1985:122–123). The SFS thus appears to discriminate most effectively between persisters and those who do not incur another arrest within 3 years (which includes mainly offenders who have terminated their criminal careers) and is less effective in distinguishing frequency rates for active offenders. This finding still leaves a challenge to find adequate predictors of differential frequency rates among those who do persist in their criminal careers after release.

The SFS appears to be a simple, stable, and fairly reliable prediction-based classification scheme, which is also reasonably accurate using rearrest in a 3-year follow-up as the criterion variable. The latest version, SFS 81, emphasizes criminal history items; it reflects concerns about difficulties in recording some variables and omits measures of employment stability, family ties, and high school education, which were included in earlier versions. Heroin or opiate dependence and age at current offense are the only remaining items that might be challenged on ethical grounds. Comparisons of alternative versions of the SFS on the same sample (Table 6-5) show no detectable deterioration in accuracy associated with these changes in scale variables (Hoffman, 1983). The percentage of favorable outcomes for different risk levels, the mean cost rating, and the RIOC change hardly at all for the more restricted versions of the scale.

Iowa Risk Assessment Instrument

Another classification instrument for assessing parole recidivism risk has recently been developed in Iowa (Chi, 1983; Fischer, 1983, 1984). All of the information about this instrument appears in unpublished reports and re-

TABLE 6-5 Changes in the Accuracy of the Salient Factor Score as Predictor Variables Are Eliminated[a]

Risk Category	Percent Favorable Outcome[b]	
	SFS 81[c]	SFS 76[d]
Very good	88 (N = 735)[e]	89 (N = 642)
Good	75 (N = 502)	73 (N = 662)
Fair	61 (N = 542)	64 (N = 497)
Poor	51 (N = 560)	50 (N = 538)
All cases	70 (N = 2,339)	70 (N = 2,339)
Mean Cost Rating (MCR)	.41	.40
Relative Improvement Over Chance (RIOC)[f]	.28	.29

[a]Accuracy is assessed on an independent validation sample of inmates released from federal institutions in 1978.

[b]Favorable outcomes are defined as no commitment of 60 days or more for a new offense, no return to prison as a violator, no parole violation warrant outstanding, and not killed while committing a criminal act.

[c]Predictor variables reflect prior criminal record, offender's age, and drug use (see Table 6-4).

[d]In addition to variables reflecting prior criminal record, age, and drug use, the earlier scale included an employment stability measure.

[e]The number of cases in each risk level is reported in parentheses.

[f]The RIOC measure was computed from data reported by Hoffman (1983) using a selection rule that treats "poor risks" as high-risk and aggregates all other risk-levels.

SOURCE: Data from Hoffman (1983:Tables 1 and 2).

search documents. Moreover, the existing documentation concerning the construction of the scale, validation attempts, and accuracy leaves many questions unanswered. Early reports claimed that the Iowa classification system was more than 80 percent accurate in identifying poor parole risks. In response to those dramatic reports, considerable momentum has developed for disseminating and replicating the scale widely. Because of the widespread interest in the Iowa scale and concerns about its development and val-

idation, the panel asked that the Iowa risk assessment instrument be included in the review of the accuracy of classification scales it commissioned (see Gottfredson and Gottfredson, Volume II).

The approach used to develop the initial scale presented by Iowa is not publicly documented. Personal communications with the developers revealed that they used interactive methods (using logic similar to Automatic Interaction Detection (AID); see Sonquist, Baker, and Morgan, 1973) to develop the scale. Statistically, such methods use up large numbers of degrees of freedom in fitting the model very closely to the construction sample data. Furthermore, the "validation" results presented were actually based on a contaminated validation sample that combined cases from the original construction sample with a much smaller subsequent sample. As a result of these and other criticisms, Iowa developed a revised scale, shown in Table 6-6. This latest version of the Iowa offender risk assessment instrument (Fischer, 1984; hereafter referred to as the 1984 version) primarily includes criminal history items: current offense type; disposition if current offense involves escape, jailbreak, or flight; total "street time" (time not incarcerated for a felony) since age 14; prior arrest history for violent offenses; and prior juvenile and adult convictions and incarcerations. The prior record variables are weighted by offense seriousness and time since a prior event. A detailed substance abuse score also figures into the classification. According to this information, each offender is assigned to risk categories for two separate risk assessments: general/safety risk and violence risk. The revised scale is conceptually very similar to the Salient Factor Score, although with an appreciably larger number of variables to be scored.

The scale has been validated prospectively using follow-up recidivism data. The contamination of the validation samples with construction sample data that

TABLE 6-6   The Iowa Offender Risk Assessment Scale: 1984 Version

	General Risk	Violence Risk
A. CURRENT OFFENSE SCORE		
Robbery, Larceny from Person, Aggravated Burglary, Arson	2	3
Murder, Manslaughter, Kidnapping, Rape, Sodomy	1	3
Burglary, Selling Narcotics, Motor Vehicle Theft, Forgery, Bad Checks, Fraud	2	1
Aggravated Assault, Extortion, Armed with Intent, Conspiracy to Commit Violent Felony, Larceny, Stolen Property	1	1
Vandalism, Weapons, Conspiracy to Commit Nonviolent Felony	1	0
None of Above	0	0
B. PRIOR VIOLENCE SCORE		
Sum of prior violent felony charges weighted by seriousness and time back to arrest:		
91+		
11–90	4	5
0–10	2	3
	0	0
C. STREET TIME SCORE		
Total time free on street (i.e., not incarcerated for a felony) since age 14:		
0–6 years		
6–11 years	3	3
11–14 years	2	2
14+ years	1	1
	0	0
D. CRIMINAL HISTORY SCORE		
Sum of prior felonies resulting in conviction or incarceration weighted by seriousness, time back to arrest, and total street time:		
140+		
41–139	6	6
16–40	3	5
0–15	1	1
	0	0
E. CURRENT ESCAPE SCORE		
If current incident for prison escape, jailbreak, or flight:		
Convicted		
Arrested/Charged Only	3	4
Not Above	1	2
	0	0
F. SUBSTANCE ABUSE SCORE		
History of PCP Use, Non-Opiate Injections, Sniffing Volatile Substances	7	5
History of Opiate Addiction		
History of Heavy Hallucinogen Use	4	4
History of Drug Problem	3	4
History of Opiate or Hallucinogen Use, or Alcohol Problem	2	1
No History of Above	1	1
	0	0

G. SERIOUS OFFENDER CLASSIFICATION
(Used with Violence Risk Score)

Current Conviction for Violent Felony, or Escape/Jailbreak/Flight; Prior Conviction for Felony Against Person in last 5 years of Street Time; Prior Violence Score 35+; Substance Abuse Score 7   _____Yes

None of Above Factors   _____No

TOTAL SCORE
  X-Score = A + B + C
  Y-Score = D + E + F

SOURCE: Fischer (1984).

distorted the validation of earlier versions of the Iowa scale does not appear to be a problem in the 1984 validation (Statistical Analysis Center, 1984). Fischer (1984:23) reports that of 1,000 cases of 1978–79 releasees available for development of the 1984 version, 186 were reserved for use as a validation sample and that separate outcome measures are reported for these construction and validation samples. A further problem of inadequate controls for varying times at risk, found in the evaluation of the earlier scales, also appears to have been remedied by use of a 4-year follow-up period for all members of the validation sample of the 1984 scale.

As noted above, early versions of the scale reported by the Iowa Statistical Analysis Center claimed accuracy levels greater than any other known criminal risk assessment scale, but the reanalysis of the outcome data by Gottfredson and Gottfredson (Volume II) concluded that the accuracy claims for the early scales were highly inflated.[9] The evaluation of the 1984 version is much more careful. On the basis of follow-up data on rearrest and reincarceration reported in Fischer (1984:24–25), the RIOC contrasting the combined poor and very poor risks to all others is calculated to be 54.1 percent in the construction sample and 58.8 percent in the validation sample. These improvements in accuracy are associated with 29 and 38 percent false-positive rates in the two samples, respectively. In comparison, as mentioned earlier, the RIOC for predicted high-rate offenders, using Greenwood's seven-factor scale, averaged 31 percent for the total sample and varied widely among states and crime

types: 57 percent for high-rate California robbers but only 19 percent for Michigan burglars. These comparisons among different prediction instruments suggest that the latest Iowa classification system may be somewhat more accurate than other prediction devices. Gottfredson and Gottfredson (Volume II) attribute this improved accuracy to the general strategy of relying on reasonably homogeneous subsamples in developing intermediate classification devices that are then combined into a final scale.

The 1984 Iowa scale differs in substantial ways from the earlier versions. In particular, several variables that might be ethically objectionable have been eliminated from the scale. Among the excluded variables are marital status, employment status, job skill level, and age at first arrest; and a previous heavy emphasis on juvenile record (rather than adult criminal record) was also eliminated. The 1984 scale relies heavily on current offense, recent criminal record, and substance abuse. Removing the controversial variables apparently led to no reduction in scale accuracy (see Gottfredson and Gottfredson, Volume II).

Proposed INSLAW Scale

At the prosecution stage, formal selection rules are widely used for assignment of cases to career criminal units for special attention. One such rule developed at INSLAW for CCUs in U.S. attorney's offices has strong empirical underpinnings (Rhodes et al., 1982); see Table 6-7. Based on a follow-up of 1,708 offenders after their release from federal custody, a nine-factor scale was developed that classified offenders on federal probation or parole in terms of the time to first rearrest within a 60-month period. Because the scale was developed on a sample of released offenders rather than on an arrestee sample and was neither validated

---

[9]After a careful study of the empirical underpinnings of the mean cost rating measure used in the Iowa validation, Gottfredson and Gottfredson (Volume II) concluded that the MCR as calculated by the Iowa researchers is inflated compared with standard MCR measures reported for other scales and is "essentially meaningless."

TABLE 6-7 Proposed INSLAW Scale for Selecting "Career Criminals" for Special Prosecution

Variable Points	
Heavy Use of Alcohol	+5
Heroin Use	+10
Age at Time of Instant Arrest	
Less than 22	+21
23–27	+14
28–32	+7
33–37	0
38–42	−7
43+	−14
Length of Criminal Career	
0–5 years	0
6–10	+1
11–15	+2
16–20	+3
21+	+4
Arrests During Last Five Years	
Crimes of Violence	+4 per arrest
Crimes Against Property	+3 per arrest
Sale of Drugs	+4 per arrest
Other Offenses	+2 per arrest
Longest Time Served, Single Term	
1–5 months	+4
6–12	+9
13–24	+18
25–36	+27
37–48	+36
49+	+45
Number Probation Sentences	+1.5 per sentence
Instant Offense Was Crime of Violence*	+7
Instant Offense Was Crime Labeled "Other"**	−18
Critical Value to Label an Offender As a "Career Criminal": +47 points	

*Violent crimes include homicide, assault, robbery, sexual assault, and kidnapping. **Other crimes include military violations, probation and parole violations, weapons and all others *except* arson, burglary, larceny, auto theft, fraud, forgery, drug sales or possession, and violent crimes.

SOURCE: Rhodes et al. (1982:Table V.1).

on an independent sample nor implemented in practice, no assessment can be made about its accuracy beyond the construction sample.

Relying on time to rearrest as the dependent variable, the INSLAW scale is intended to distinguish among offenders in terms of their frequency rates—which are reciprocally related to the time to rearrest. On the basis of a statistical model that fit time to rearrest to offender attributes, including prior record, 200 "career criminals" were identified. Again, by

relying on predicted time to rearrest as a basis for estimating individual arrest rates, combined with estimates of a homogeneous risk of arrest per crime by offense type, sharp differences in estimated individual offense rates, λ, were calculated. Individuals identified by the scale as career criminals were each estimated to commit an average of 38 nondrug crimes per year, compared with estimated rates of only 4 nondrug crimes per year for other offenders.

There are no published results on the

accuracy of these estimates of λ that are based on actual rearrest experiences observed in the two offender risk groups. The only measures of accuracy reported, based on arrests observed during the follow-up period, are error rates. The false-positive rate was 15 percent among scale-identified career criminals and the false-negative rate was 36 percent among all other offenders; the RIOC is 74 percent, and the scale appears quite accurate in distinguishing among offenders in the construction sample in terms of their risk of future arrests. Some deterioration in this accuracy can be expected as the scale is applied to independent validation samples, especially if the scale, which was developed using released offenders on probation and parole, is applied to the intended target population of arrestees.

The INSLAW scale presented in Table 6-7 invokes a number of offender characteristics in ways consistent with what is known about the relationship of those characteristics to the frequency, seriousness, and duration of offending. Drug and heavy alcohol use are treated as aggravating factors, as is early age at onset (in the form of elapsed career length). Age is presented as an aggravating factor until age 32 and as a mitigating factor after age 38, but over the entire age range, the older the suspect, the better the score. Both frequency and seriousness of prior arrests are aggravating factors. Because of its consistency with available knowledge of criminal careers, the INSLAW scale shows promise; it should be validated on other samples, perhaps leading to experimental implementation. Because some scale variables may be controversial—e.g., substance abuse and reliance on past arrests rather than convictions—such analyses should include assessments of changes in accuracy under alternative scale formulations; in light of experience with other scales examined here, large

reductions in accuracy are not anticipated.

Summary

Some recent classification scales relying on similar predictor variables—reflecting primarily prior criminal record and drug use—have displayed greater accuracy in identifying worst-risk offenders than earlier scales. When criteria of rearrest in follow-up periods of at least 3 years are used, false-positive rates among offenders classified as worst-risks are under 30 percent in construction samples and under 40 percent in validation samples (see especially Rhodes et al., 1982; Fischer, 1984; and Janus, 1985 in Table 6-8). This difference from the 50 to 60 percent false-positive rates that have traditionally characterized statistical classifications of poor-risk offenders is due in part to reliance on broader criterion variables, particularly recidivism measures based on arrests rather than recommitment to prison, and measures using longer follow-up periods that increase the likelihood of detecting recidivism. The resulting higher base rates contribute to greater classification accuracy, especially in relation to low selection ratios. For example, the INSLAW scale, with its high base rate and low selection ratio, results in a low false-positive rate (15 percent) but a high false-negative rate (36 percent). However, to the extent that the gains in accuracy are beyond those expected merely from the increased base rates, the broader criterion variables may yield a more sensitive measure of releasees' offending behavior.

The Rand scale displays the least improvement from earlier 50–60 percent false-positive rates. As the only scale based on self-reports, it is unique in attempting to predict actual crimes committed rather than arrests. There may be more measurement error in individual

TABLE 6-8 Accuracy of Several Explicit Classification Scales Assessing Offending Risk

Scale Attribute	Salient Factor Score 81		Iowa Assessment Scale	INSLAW Scale	Rand Inmate Scale
	Hoffman (1983)	Janus (1985)	Fisher (1984)	Rhodes et al. (1982)	Greenwood (1982)
Construction sample	Federal prisoners released in 1971–72 (N = 3,955)		Iowa state prisoners released in 1976–80 (N = 814)	Federal probationers and parolees released from custody in 1970–71 (N = 1,708)	Prison and jail inmates in California, Michigan, and Texas in 1978 (N = 886)
Validation sample	Federal prisoners released in first half of 1978 (N = 2,339)	(N = 2,186)	Iowa state prisoners released in 1976–80 (N = 186)	None	None
Recidivism criterion	Reincarceration	Rearrest	Rearrest or reincarceration for serious crime	Time to rearrest for serious crime	Individual frequency rates for robbery and burglary[a]
Length of follow-up (years)	2	3	4	5	None (1- to 2-year retrospective observation period)
Base rate (%)[b]					
Construction sample	31	N.R.	37	42	25
Validation sample	30	44	26	N.V.	N.V.
Selection ratio (%)[c]					
Construction sample	34	N.R.	33	12	27
Validation sample	24	23	30	N.V.	N.V.
False-positive rate (%)					
Construction sample	54 (3–69)[d]	N.R.	29 (0–64)	15 (0–58)	55 (3–75)
Validation sample	51 (0–70)	34 (0–56)	38 (4–74)	N.V.	N.V.
False-negative rate (%)					
Construction sample	24 (0–31)	N.R.	20 (4–37)	36 (30–42)	17 (0–25)
Validation sample	24 (6–30)	38 (21–44)	11 (0–26)	N.V.	N.V.
Relative Improvement Over Chance (RIOC)[e]					
Construction sample	.24	N.R.	.54	.74	.31
Validation sample	.28	.38	.59	N.V.	N.V.

NOTE: N.R. = not reported; N.V. = not validated.

[a]The criterion variable in the Rand Inmate Scale is individual frequency rates of committing crimes, and not a traditional binary recidivism variable (e.g., rearrested or not during a follow-up period).

[b]Percent unfavorable outcomes found in the total sample.

[c]Percent predicted to be high risks in the total sample.

[d]The minimum and maximum possible values of the false-positive (FP) and false-negative (FN) rates appear in parentheses. These are determined from the selection ratio (SR) and base rate (BR) as follows: FP $\leq$ 1 − BR; FN $\leq$ BR; FP $\geq$ SR − BR when SR $\geq$ BR, = 0 otherwise; FN $\geq$ BR − SR when BR $\geq$ SR, = 0 otherwise.

[e]The Relative Improvement Over Chance (RIOC) compares actual classification accuracy to the maximum accuracy possible and the random accuracy associated with the selection ratio and base rates in sample (see text):

$$RIOC = \frac{[(1 - FP)\, SR + (1 - FN)\,(1 - SR)] - [(SR)\,(BR) + (1 - SR)\,(1 - BR)]}{[MIN(SR, BR) + MIN(1 - SR, 1 - BR)] - [(SR)(BR) + (1 - SR)\,(1 - BR)]}.$$

crime rates estimated from self-reports than in criterion measures based on officially recorded arrests, and this increased error in the dependent variable would reduce the accuracy of predictions. The Rand scale is also only a preliminary attempt at calibrating a classification scale: simple bivariate relationships are used to identify potential predictor variables, and Burgess weights (scored either 0 or 1) are assigned to the selected variables. This approach contrasts with the extensive multivariate analysis, which involves more flexible characterization of the contributions by individual predictor variables. These analyses are reflected in the more complex weighting schemes found in other scales.

The recent classification scales are also noteworthy because when independent validation samples representing similar populations have been used, as with the federal parole system's Salient Factor Score and the 1984 Iowa risk assessment scale, there is little evidence of substantial statistical shrinkage in their accuracy. This result is due in part to the use of reasonably large samples in scale development—more than 800 individuals—which reduces the impact of statistical shrinkage due to sampling variation. Also, validation studies indicate that offender populations appear to be reasonably stable over time: there was no detectable reduction in accuracy between applications of the Salient Factor Score to a sample of federal prisoners released during 1970–1972 and another sample released in 1978.

The various classification scales also show no evidence of important reductions in scale accuracy when various controversial variables like employment status are removed from them. It thus appears that accommodating just-deserts concerns by avoiding ethically objectionable classification variables will not seriously impair classification accuracy.

ADULT, JUVENILE, AND NON-JUSTICE SYSTEM RECORDS AND THEIR INTEGRATION

Attention to certain offender characteristics—whether achieved through formal rules or informal practice—can, to some extent, improve the accuracy of offender classification in terms of criminal career dimensions. Incorporating these classifications into decisions requires that decision makers receive timely and accurate information about predictor variables, and doing so will require improvements in criminal justice and other record-keeping systems. We focus here on adult criminal histories, the record of prior adult arrests and dispositions; juvenile records, the records of police contacts and juvenile court adjudications; and other records maintained outside the justice system on such matters as drug use, employment history, school performance, and social history. These record categories differ in terms of how accessible they are to criminal justice decision makers.

Adult Records

In most jurisdictions, the arrest and fingerprinting of an individual normally initiates both an update of the local arrest record and retrieval of the record for use by the prosecutor at screening and for use by the judge at the initial court appearance shortly after arrest, when charges are filed and pretrial release conditions are set. In some jurisdictions, local authorities do not receive the entire history of arrests in other jurisdictions for several weeks, when arrest records are received from repositories in state identification bureaus and the FBI. These delays can lead to the use of incomplete prior record information at the important stages of initial screening by the prosecutor, charging, and pretrial release decisions. However, many states have established statewide computerized criminal history files, and many metropolitan areas have established regional systems combining arrest histories from participating jurisdictions. From these networks, records of prior arrests by participating jurisdictions can be retrieved quickly and linked to the proper individual using demographic identifiers and fingerprint classification.

An arrest is the result of a law enforcement action based on the evidentiary standard of "probable cause"; it is not "guilt beyond a reasonable doubt." Therefore, it is argued that, under the latter standard, only prior convictions should be used as an indicator of previous criminal activity and that records of arrests not followed by a record of a conviction should not be used. Advocates of this position point to potential biases in decisions to make and record arrests and to the possibility that use of arrest records in decision making may encourage more filing of charges or filing on multiple counts on the basis of weaker evidence, at least for offenders who are considered especially persistent. Furthermore, advocates of the position argue that police arrest records receive no independent scrutiny and are therefore more likely to contain undetected inaccuracies than are court conviction records, which are open to the public.

In contrast, advocates of current practice argue that exclusion of arrest data until disposition data become routinely available would, in some jurisdictions, preclude access to useful information for years. Moreover, some advocates consider an arrest record to be a more sensitive and valid measure of a criminal career than a conviction record because the former more fully reflects variations in the rate of activity, because a failure to convict is not necessarily indicative of factual innocence, and because plea bargaining can distort the meaning of convic-

tion records. Conviction records are also vulnerable to distortions when their influence on decisions is altered: for example, when the number of prior convictions became an explicit basis for sentencing under guidelines introduced in Minnesota, prosecutors seemed less willing to dismiss charges than they previously had been (Minnesota Sentencing Guidelines Commission, 1984:81).

It is generally acknowledged that disposition records are less readily available than arrest records. Those who advocate a requirement for disposition data argue that the requirement would encourage police, prosecutors, and courts to undertake the costly cooperative effort needed to improve the availability of those data. They argue that information on prior case dispositions and sentences is useful because it describes an offender's previous sanctioning experience, which permits adjustment for incarceration time in estimating the frequency of previous arrests while free, a measure that has been found to predict future arrest frequency (Barnett and Lofaso, 1985). However, while conviction information can always be retrieved through a search of written court records, only in a few jurisdictions—where courts, prosecutors, and police operate an integrated criminal justice information system—is it routinely available in time for screening, charging, and pretrial release decisions. Data on actual time served in jail or prison following arrest or conviction are even less generally available, since corrections records on individuals are linked to police and court records in only a few states. And data on dispositions other than convictions are not systematically recorded.

Because knowledge of previous case dispositions and sanctions can contribute to a current decision, court disposition and corrections data should be integrated with arrest records. Even before full integration is accomplished, several steps should be taken to enhance the validity of arrest records, which would benefit both decision makers and those who study criminal careers. These steps include promoting standards for the completeness of arrest records; encouraging cross-jurisdictional standardization of nomenclature that describes aggravating or mitigating attributes of the alleged offense as well as its legal category; and quickly noting arrests that are unfounded, either by police officials or by the screening prosecutor.

Regardless of the quality of arrest records, opinions will continue to differ about their appropriate use in decision making. However, decisions about their use should be influenced by attention both to the ethical issues discussed earlier in this chapter and to the value of arrest-history information in predicting the future course of a criminal career.

Juvenile Records

In considering the use of juvenile records as decision aids for adult defendants, it is useful to distinguish between police records of contacts with juveniles and juvenile court records of referrals and dispositions. According to a recent report prepared for the Bureau of Justice Statistics (SEARCH Group, Inc., 1982:29–34), police agencies have broad legal discretion in recording contacts with juveniles. But other criminal justice agencies encounter great difficulty in obtaining this information about individuals prior to their conviction in adult court. Routine exchange is hindered by laws restricting the fingerprinting of juveniles, a restriction that complicates subsequent record retrieval and unambiguous matching. Generally, fingerprints of juveniles may be taken only following contact concerning a serious offense, must be stored separately from adults' fingerprints, and must eventually be sealed or purged under various conditions. In most jurisdictions,

these restrictions mean that the arrest histories available for formal adult proceedings usually do not include records of juvenile contacts with police and, usually, court dispositions that occurred before the defendant reached legal adulthood. Police information is sometimes shared informally with prosecutors (for whom it may affect charging decisions), but in a national survey, 60 percent of responding prosecutors reported that police records of juveniles were "rarely or never" provided at the time charges were filed (Greenwood, Petersilia, and Zimring, 1980).

Juvenile court records may legally be used in adult courts in most states for postadjudication decisions, such as disposition and classification. In many states they may be used for predisposition decisions such as pretrial detention. However, the sharing of juvenile court records with adult authorities is operationally hindered by statutory prohibitions against storing juvenile court records in the same repositories as adult records. Such records are routinely retrieved during presentence investigations, which occur long after arrest. They can usually be obtained, although with some difficulty, by police agencies for investigative prearrest use; but time constraints and the absence of positive fingerprint identification generally prevent access to them in time for early postarrest decisions. Under these circumstances the disposition information in juvenile court records is even less likely to be available for use shortly after an arrest than is the record of local police.

The completeness of juvenile record repositories themselves is affected by the sealing and purging of the records. Many states have adopted statutes that specify conditions under which juvenile records must be sealed (i.e., restricted from disclosure outside the repository except pursuant to a court order) or purged (i.e., destroyed). Motivated by concern over stigmatization of adults for their delinquent activities as juveniles, these statutes generally authorize record sealing within a few years after a person reaches adult age and purging several years later if the subject is not arrested as an adult and petitions the court requesting these actions (SEARCH Group, Inc., 1982:49–51). In addition to legal requirements for sealing and purging individual records, some repositories have begun more general purging as a means of reducing the cost of storing juvenile records.

In combination, the prohibitions against merged juvenile and adult records, the failure to routinely include juvenile court data in police record systems, and the sealing and purging of juvenile records create a situation in most jurisdictions in which criminal justice authorities frequently make their decisions with no information about police contacts with juveniles. Even when police contact information is available, it is usually not accompanied by information about the disposition following the contact. These conditions, particularly the purging of juvenile records, have also hampered the efforts of researchers to study criminal careers over the ages of transition from juvenile status to adulthood.

Restrictions on the storage and dissemination of juvenile records resulted from the orientation of juvenile courts toward rehabilitation rather than punishment and from the belief that juveniles are less responsible than adults for acts that would be labeled criminal by the adult justice system. Some people believe that the fingerprinting of juveniles, a key to accurate identification, may create a "criminal self-image" that may weaken self-imposed restraints against future crime. It is also argued that dissemination of records outside the juvenile court system stigmatizes a juvenile with the designation "delinquent," which may lessen

opportunities for legitimate employment, thereby increasing the likelihood of subsequent offending. The prospect of having juvenile records purged after an arrest-free period is advocated as an incentive for juveniles to terminate criminal careers before adulthood. Others have argued that the ambiguity of notation that is characteristic of juvenile court records makes them very difficult to interpret and summarize (e.g., Greenwood, Abrahamse, and Zimring, 1984). Finally, in pursuing their objective of rehabilitation, juvenile courts collect "social data" on such episodes as misconduct in school, mental health status, family history, and other topics that are not only especially sensitive to an individual but may also involve other parties whose privacy would be compromised by dissemination. It is argued that routine sharing of these records could disrupt continued cooperation by the agencies that now provide such background information to the juvenile court.

For those who advocate the use of juvenile records, the challenge is to respond to these concerns by designing systems and procedures that inform adult justice system decision makers more fully about juvenile delinquent careers without undermining the rehabilitative goal of juvenile courts. Maintaining accessible fingerprint records of juveniles arrested for serious crimes—crimes that would be felonies if committed by an adult—may be warranted as a means of eliminating cases of mistaken identity. Using fingerprints to identify persons uniquely, systems could be developed for the routine transfer of juvenile disposition data to police records. Augmenting police records with data on juvenile dispositions could both improve the fairness with which those records are subsequently used and eliminate the need for access to the juvenile court files with their sensitive social data. Juvenile arrest and disposition histories could be maintained in a separate repository, with no disclosure permitted for uses outside the criminal justice system. Adult justice system agencies would gain access to the juvenile record at the time of a person's first serious criminal involvement as an adult. In defining criteria for access, different jurisdictions might choose different thresholds of crime seriousness and different stages of criminal justice processing (e.g., arrest, indictment, or conviction). Requiring a high level of seriousness would reflect a desire to avoid opening a juvenile record in connection with only a minor offense. Precluding access until after conviction would reflect a belief in the principle that a juvenile record should not influence decisions in the adult system that are made before guilt is established with legal certainty. Alternatively, permitting prosecutors and judges to see a juvenile record when making charging, pretrial release, and plea bargaining decisions would allow them to become more fully informed of the public safety risks associated with their decisions. Different jurisdictions will weigh these concerns differently and so may choose different thresholds and stages. One choice that seems reasonable would be the first adult arrest for a felony. A juvenile record would be appended to an adult record only if the adult arrest leads to a conviction. The juvenile record, with appropriate safeguards against dissemination, would be retained in the juvenile repository at least as long as it retains value for decision making in the adult criminal justice system.

When juvenile records are no longer operationally useful, they should be preserved in an otherwise inaccessible way for research purposes. Research on a number of important questions has been hindered by the bifurcation of juvenile and adult record systems. As highlighted in Chapter 3, particular problems have

been the misleading conclusion of desistance—"false desistance"—from offending that is implied by the truncation of juvenile court records when individuals "graduate" to adult jurisdiction and the inability to include the record before age 18 in career-length estimates for adult samples. The bifurcation has hampered research on such key questions as the effect of juvenile justice interventions on adult criminal careers and the influence of information about juvenile careers on the processing of cases involving young adults. There would be considerable research value in linked records of juvenile and adult arrests and dispositions. Record purging precludes such research. Therefore, while access to juvenile records should be carefully controlled to protect individuals' identities, those records should be stored as a basis for research.

Other Records

Some information that is useful in predicting the course of criminal careers is not available in either the adult or juvenile justice system records. For example, Chaiken and Chaiken (1984:211) found that official-record information was not sufficient to distinguish the offenders they designated as "violent predators" from other offenders. Despite violent predators' self-reports of frequent, violent delinquency as juveniles, their juvenile records either did not exist or were found to be indistinguishable from those of other offenders. Greenwood (1982) pointed to two specific characteristics that distinguish high-rate offenders—a history of drug use and significant periods of unemployment. Data on these characteristics are not routinely included in arrest histories or court disposition files, although they sometimes appear with other social data in juvenile court records or adult presentence investigation.

Presentence investigations will undoubtedly continue to be the primary vehicle for the collection of information on drug use, employment status, and family and social history. Although maintaining such data in permanent criminal justice records might improve the quality of preconviction decisions, that benefit might be at least partly offset by other consequences. For example, routine disclosure of drug treatment agency records to justice agencies for predictive use might discourage users from seeking treatment or disrupt the therapeutic relationship between users and counselors. Urinalysis at the time of arrest is an alternative means of determining drug use, and test results could be appended to the arrest record for use following subsequent arrests. This procedure would assist efforts to provide police and prosecutors with information about an arrestee's history of drug use and would avoid problems associated with information sharing between treatment agencies and justice agencies.

In addition to data on employment history, substance abuse, and other social history, presentence reports in most jurisdictions also include the investigators' sentencing recommendation. To the extent that these recommendations have influence, it is important that their underlying predictive assumptions be based on facts. Presentence investigators should be informed of base rates of characteristics (such as substance abuse or truancy) that are often used to distinguish among offenders. They should also be informed of correlations between those characteristics and the frequency of serious offending.

CONCLUSIONS

Criminal justice decision makers use knowledge about criminal careers both in making specific decisions affecting individual offenders and in establishing policies for those decisions. They do so more often on the basis of their own knowledge and experience than on the basis of statistical analysis of information about representative offenders. Because of the growing body of data and research on offenders, there are considerable opportunities for expanding and improving the bases for decision making in terms of predictors of specific offenders' careers.

Exploiting such opportunities does not preclude the pursuit of other criminal justice objectives, such as assuring appearance at trial or imposing deserved punishment. Decision makers can combine prediction-based classifications with additional information—ties to the community, victims' preferences, seriousness of the crime, or amenability to various forms of correctional treatment—that is pertinent to those other objectives. In concert with these other objectives, attempts to reduce crime through incapacitation of offenders could be improved by familiarity with the accumulating knowledge about offenders' criminal careers. That knowledge would inform decision makers of typical criminal careers and of the indicators of high- and low-risk offenders. It is likely that the research knowledge will confirm some of their current beliefs and practices. But it is also likely that some factors they believe to be important as predictors of offending will be found not to be so, while other factors they may not view as salient will be shown to be important.

Because decision makers' predictions about offenders' criminal careers are not routinely recorded, it is impossible to measure directly the improvement that could be achieved by giving decision makers statistical predictions about the offenders who come before them. Indirect evidence suggests that with available statistical scales, gains in crime control efficiency through selective incapacitation would be modest at best—a 5–10 percent reduction in robberies by adults, for example, with an increase of 10–20 percent in the number of convicted robbers who are incarcerated. Similar crime control through general increases in incarceration would require substantially higher increases in prison populations. The gains from selective incapacitation are limited in part because decision makers already invoke many of the offender characteristics that figure prominently in the scales. As criminal career research progresses and the quality of available data improves, the crime-control efficiency of selective incapacitation can be expected to improve somewhat.

As progress continues and new prediction scales emerge, there will be a tendency to take scales developed in one jurisdiction and use them in another, to use scales developed for one stage of the criminal justice process at another stage, and to take scales developed at one time and use them at a later time. It is important to recognize that such transfer must be done with great caution and with validation and recalibration in each new setting. The characteristics of convicted offenders at the sentencing stage in one state may be considerably different from those in another state. Hence, the factors that distinguish high-risk offenders in one state may well be different from those in the other state. Similarly, the factors that distinguish high-risk prisoners who have already been filtered through multiple stages of the criminal justice system (probably through several occurrences of recidivism) are likely to be different from those that distinguish high-risk arrestees being considered for pretrial release. Furthermore, since there may be changes over time in both the environment associated with offending and the selection processes within the criminal justice system, predictors even within a particular jurisdiction must be periodically recalibrated.

Since prediction scales are potentially vulnerable to variation by jurisdiction, by stage of the criminal justice system, and over time, successful validation in several jurisdictions can increase confidence in scale transferability by identifying key variables that seem to have consistently high predictive value, by helping to refine data collection forms and variable definitions, and by developing initial candidate scales that can be adapted in any new setting. It is crucial, however, that every scale be tested, validated, and recalibrated at each decision stage and jurisdiction in which it is to be used.

In choosing offender characteristics to be incorporated in prediction scales, it is important to consider the ethical appropriateness of any candidate variable. In general, the seriousness of the instant offense is the most acceptable predictor, followed closely by a record of prior convictions. Any other characteristics that are considered for use should have theoretical import and validity, reflect blameworthiness, bear a strong predictive relationship to a criminal career, and should take account of other social concerns such as equal protection. Other ethical issues involve concern about errors, especially when prediction is used to increase individual punishment, but also when it is used to decrease some individuals' punishment. In all such prediction, ethical questions must be addressed carefully and must be resolved locally.

In the use of prediction scales, the validity of data on the predictor variables is a crucial concern. Records available to the criminal justice system raise many questions involving the use of such data. First, some variables used as predictors—such as drug use or juvenile convictions—may be poorly or ambiguously recorded in the information sources available. If such data are to be used, information systems will have to improve the accuracy of their records, avoiding errors both of omission and of commission. In considering the variables and records to be used as predictors, it is also important to anticipate reactions as a consequence of such uses. If information about drug involvement is used as a predictor of offending—as current information suggests it should—one must consider whether such use would inhibit individuals from participating in drug treatment programs. Addressing these concerns may require continuing to restrict the source of information about certain variables: for example, to obtain certain information only from criminal justice sources rather than from therapeutic agencies.

Juvenile records are of particular concern because of the bifurcation between the adult and the juvenile criminal justice systems. Records of juvenile adjudications are typically unavailable to the adult criminal justice system, presumably to avoid lifetime stigmatization as a result of some minor juvenile escapades. While that principle is certainly reasonable for individuals whose juvenile involvement is indeed minor and especially for those who do not persist into an adult criminal career, the bifurcation does not seem reasonable for juveniles whose delinquency careers are serious and who persist into serious adult offending. Thus, while juvenile records should continue to be protected from general public access, the adult criminal justice system should have access to juvenile records of at least those offenders arrested as adults on a felony charge.

There is a clear capability in the current state of the art to develop predictors that are better than chance, but it is still unclear how much better than current practice statistically assisted prediction can be. One can expect currently available scales to produce only limited improvements to existing decision practices in terms of crime control. It is reasonable to expect, however, that future research will improve criminal justice decisions, at a minimum by highlighting additional salient predictor variables and by pointing to variables that are often used but are indeed weak.

7

An Agenda for Future Research

BACKGROUND

As the previous chapters of this report indicate, the past decade has witnessed considerable progress in efforts to measure the basic dimensions of criminal careers and the factors associated with them. Much of that progress is attributable to a growing interest in the criminal career paradigm as an appropriate and effective way to study the people processed by the criminal justice system, their patterns of offending, the factors that influence their offending, and the potential influence of public policies—both within the criminal justice system and outside it—on individual criminal careers.

The earlier chapters have also shown that the state of knowledge regarding criminal careers is increasing rapidly. Some basic estimates of the mean values of career dimensions among different subpopulations have begun to be developed, and some estimates have been found to be consistent in independent studies with different modes of measurement, lending greater confidence to the results. Estimates of the individual of-fending rate, λ, have been particularly informative because they highlight the considerable diversity among offenders.

The emerging picture of career diversity has motivated efforts to develop predictors of those career dimensions. Such attempts have been stimulating and provocative for both researchers and decision makers, and have also encouraged critical attention to the role that prediction in its current state of development should have in criminal justice decision making. That attention has reinforced the necessity for developing better information on the strength and validity of various candidate predictors and has led to a focus on the underlying technical issues involved in classification and prediction. In addition, attention to the ethical questions that are involved has resulted in some convergence of the different viewpoints.

The policy value of current and future research on criminal careers is already substantial. This value derives partly from a recognition that an individual of-fender—the unit underlying the criminal career paradigm—is the primary subject of decision making within the criminal justice system. For example, identifying life events or individual characteristics that influence the onset of criminal activity and determining the effect of preventive interventions in reducing the likelihood of future criminal behavior are important priorities for research with major policy implications. In a similar vein, the available research indicates that many youths who have some contact with the juvenile justice system do not persist in criminal activity as adults, but further research is needed on the factors that influence the termination of a criminal career. Basic research on the nature and measurement of criminal careers, and policy research on the effect of various intervention strategies at different stages of a criminal career, will contribute to the development of better policy options.

The criminal career paradigm highlights the need for longitudinal research on both offenders and nonoffenders. And the potential for results from research is enhanced considerably by the opportunity to capitalize on methodological developments in other fields that are examining the longitudinal progression of "careers" in such areas as substance abuse, mental health, and employment.

Building on developments over the past decade, our research agenda first presents a major new research initiative that is now warranted as the next step—a prospective longitudinal research project. Such an effort would provide a basis for tracking individual criminal careers over time and for linking the characteristics of an individual's career to other life events and experiences, especially to interactions with the criminal justice system. A longitudinal study could now build from the collection of measurements of the key dimensions of the criminal career to link them to factors that can more properly be viewed as causal.

Following a discussion of some of the

elements of this high-priority project, we turn to some important specific research questions that should be pursued; many of them could be addressed within the context of the proposed longitudinal study, but they need not be. In all cases, they derive from concerns that have been raised in earlier chapters of this report about important issues that need more careful measurement or validation or that are not known at all. These research questions are organized into three major categories: (1) exploration of promising intervention strategies; (2) continuation of basic research on criminal career dimensions and their correlates; and (3) new directions in measurement and modeling of criminal careers. The final section addresses some organizational arrangements for carrying out the proposed research agenda as well as for facilitating effective and responsible implementation as well-founded research results emerge.

A LONGITUDINAL STUDY OF CRIMINAL CAREERS

Many issues about criminal careers cannot be adequately addressed in cross-sectional research: the influence of various life events on an individual's criminal career; the effects of interventions on career development; and distinguishing between developmental sequences and heterogeneity across individuals in explaining apparent career evolution. Answering these and related questions requires a prospective longitudinal study of individuals of different ages.

Recognition of the inherently longitudinal and dynamic characteristics of criminal careers has led over the past several years to a number of studies that involved longitudinal data collections. While each of these studies has been valuable in its own way, they have been limited, primarily because of the small samples of serious offending that are involved. They have provided important theoretical insights into the development of criminal careers and methodological insights into measurement of the phenomena; hence, they have prepared the way for undertaking a major longitudinal study of offending.

Even though the fundamental criminal career phenomenon of interest is inherently longitudinal, studying it longitudinally rather than in a sequence of cross-sectional samples is a matter of design choice, for both economic and scientific reasons. First, drawing and following a single longitudinal sample may well be less expensive than assembling the necessary records on a comparable sequence of multiple cross-sectional panels. Also, a single longitudinal panel avoids the variation across individuals in either a single cross-sectional sample or in a sequence of cross-sectional waves. Thus, a longitudinal design is probably more efficient in terms of cost per unit reduction of error.

Second, the recovery of life history events for an individual is subject both to considerable memory decay and to errors in the sequencing of events in time. To describe and understand criminal careers, it is essential to recover as many offenses and other life events as possible and to order them precisely in time. In repeated cross-sections with different individuals, information would have to be collected for a very long time on any individual to attain the necessary level of accuracy. Repeated cross-sections involving the *same* individuals are needed to achieve that level of accuracy. Furthermore, organizing information about individuals' group involvements requires reconstruction of their social networks, and a prospective longitudinal design will more readily permit the recovery of information on those relationships.

Thus, the panel concludes that future research on criminal careers should include, as a major component, a prospective longitudinal study with several cohorts. Such a study would offer an arena within which to pursue a broad range of issues related to criminal careers, such as the developmental experiences engendering compliant behavior, the behavioral precursors of subsequent delinquency and criminality, the influence on subsequent behavior of interactions with the juvenile and criminal justice systems, and the factors associated with career termination. Generally, the project would seek to make detailed measurement of the initiation and termination of individual criminal careers, including a focus on the distinction in those patterns among different kinds of crime, especially between the more and the less serious. With those criminal career observations, as well as information on important life events (e.g., family conflict, divorce, school failure or dropout, drug initiation, processing by the criminal justice system, employment, marriage, etc.), the sequential ordering of events will begin to suggest directions of respective influence. This research would properly be augmented by ethnographic studies to develop information about group and community influences that might not be elicited in the individual reports. Longitudinal projects similar to what is proposed here have had quite impressive results.

The panel believes that a significant effort should be invested now in the design of a longitudinal study and that the federal government should take the lead in initiating what promises to be a national resource for researchers as well as for criminal justice policy makers. The initial design effort should include (1) defining the sampling frames and specifying the appropriate sample sizes in various strata; (2) developing the sampling strategy, including making the selection between representative populations and high-risk populations offering more instances of serious offending and choosing between drawing local samples for convenience, efficiency, and record completeness, and national samples for breadth of representation; (3) developing reinterview schedules that are frequent enough to capture event sequences accurately yet not frequent enough to influence behavior; (4) formulating and testing appropriate instruments; and (5) identifying and planning experimental interventions with randomly drawn subsamples.

Any such longitudinal project should have a breadth of perspective that represents the diversity of disciplinary and theoretical orientations that are relevant to research on criminal careers. In addition to the disciplines concerned directly with criminal careers, those perspectives include related individual careers in education, substance abuse, mental health, and employment. All the perspectives should contribute to the design of the initial sampling plan and of the basic data collection instruments. It is also important that the data that emerge from such a project be shared widely with the research community—especially those involved in the project design. Data collected from such a project should be fed into some public-use data facility quickly so that all participants and the research community would generally have access to it.

One way to carry out the proposed longitudinal study would involve the creation of a consortium of investigators to design the project and to be responsible for contracting with and overseeing an appropriate organization to collect the data. The instruments and procedures to be used would be negotiated within the consortium, and the results would be made available to the consortium and the research community generally for common use and analysis, with appropriate safeguards to protect the subjects. This is the kind of approach followed by the Bureau of Labor Statistics in its National Longitudinal Study of Labor Force Participation, by the U.S. Department of Education's High School and Beyond study of 1972 and 1980 high school graduates, and by the University of Michigan's Survey of Income Dynamics. A consortium could also solicit other investigators to suggest data that should be collected or questions that should be addressed, which would be incorporated to the extent feasible and appropriate. This aspect is similar in concept to the use of a space shuttle to carry a diversity of experiments for individual investigators. The design and execution of the basic data collection instruments are analogous to the large overhead associated with creating and flying the space shuttle, which can generally have capacity for augmenting its "payload" to satisfy a broad constituency of potential users.

A very different way to carry out the study would be to identify an individual investigator skilled and knowledgeable in the relevant research issues and award that investigator a grant to organize whatever staff, consultants, and advisers are necessary for the project. Such an approach would undoubtedly attract a skillful investigator, but any single researcher is likely to be limited to a particular theoretical perspective and consequently to fail to adequately address contributions from other perspectives. Any individual principal investigator is likely also to want to monopolize the data collected until all the results are assembled.

A variant to this approach would be to involve multiple principal investigators at their own institutions, with a steering committee of the principal investigators and other researchers who would bring additional theoretical perspectives and methodological skills. With this approach, each study would presumably be of smaller scale than the single one, and each investigator would be free to pursue his or her design strategy, but the aggregation of investigators would represent a broad range of theoretical perspectives. Such a program represents a compromise between the total commitment to a single investigator with its limited perspective and the coordination problems associated with a consortium.

The panel has not tried to decide which approach to the design and implementation of a major longitudinal study on criminal careers would be best—a consortium of investigators in institutional setting, a single major project, or an aggregation of individual projects connected by a broad steering committee—but it does believe strongly that whatever approach is chosen should be structured so that a range of disciplinary perspectives can be reflected in the research program and that the data that are collected are shared with a broad range of researchers. The specific choice of organizational form should be decided by researchers and probable funding sources, such as the National Institute of Justice, the Bureau of Justice Statistics, the Office of Juvenile Justice and Delinquency Prevention, the National Institute of Mental Health, the National Institute for Drug and Alcohol Abuse, and private foundations.

SPECIFIC RESEARCH QUESTIONS

Research on Intervention Strategies

Much of the research on criminal careers that the panel has considered is immediately applicable to the realm of policy choices, and a number of research efforts related to intervention strategies are warranted: one class of efforts relates to programs for successful prevention; another involves other interventions that may encourage career modification, interruption, or termination.

As research identifies determinants of participation in criminal careers or deter-minants of termination of criminal careers, possible policy choices will be suggested. The question of whether policy manipulation of a statistically identified determinant will result in a change in the criminal behavior must then be explored through well-designed experiments. An important issue in this effort is the timing of an intervention and the tradeoffs in intervention effectiveness associated with earlier or later action: errors associated with misidentifying high-risk populations diminish with older ages, but later interventions may be less effective because the offending pattern is more difficult to change.

Preventive Interventions

The most attractive possibilities in preventive interventions appear to be parenting education, social learning and behavior modification programs, and educational enrichment. Replications of an evaluation of a Head Start educational program in Michigan are clearly warranted. Follow-up data on other Head Start experiments should be collected to compare the later criminal behavior of treatment and control groups. If those results appear encouraging, some new pilot experiments could be undertaken, leading eventually to larger-scale experiments.

Analysis of the results from promising interventions requires careful attention to intermediate and long-term follow-up data to evaluate their effectiveness. Many preventive interventions appear to reduce the frequency of conduct disorders or school problems in the short term (1 to 2 years) but are not successful in preventing delinquency. The multitude of one-shot, nondefinitive research projects in this area suggests that another approach is warranted. The search for effective interventions requires systematic, cumulative research with longer-term randomized experiments that are grounded in promising theoretical orientations.

Career Modification Strategies

Other interventions are more appropriate after criminal activity has begun. Career modification strategies would benefit from research on late teenage or early adult offenders who spontaneously desist from offending and the identification of offenders who are most likely to respond to the intervention. Certain life events, such as employment, may encourage career termination, and this relationship could be translated into a program of job counseling for high-risk youth. Research on career-modifying interventions for younger adolescents has found behavioral modification strategies and programs designed to enhance one's sense of responsibility to be tentatively encouraging. The effectiveness of interventions directed at modifying the criminal career either through termination or reduction in seriousness or frequency is easily tested through experiments. Such research efforts would benefit from a 3- to 5-year follow-up, possibly in conjunction with the major longitudinal effort recommended earlier. Last, postprison adjustment interventions that have not been entirely successful might be made more effective with a slight change in the program design to alleviate the work disincentive effect that financial assistance may induce during the transition back to the community: for example, programs might require some community service in exchange for the assistance.

Selective Incapacitation

Decisions in the criminal justice system are currently based in part on an explicit intervention strategy of incapacitation. Many criminal justice practitioners already use fragmentary information about criminal careers to make decisions about incarceration, which temporarily interrupts a criminal career. Some decision makers may also make erroneous decisions by invoking wrong predictors that they mistakenly believe to be valid. It is particularly important, therefore, to measure the effectiveness of incapacitation associated with current decisions that do try to identify offenders with higher individual crime rates and more serious offending patterns. This effect might be estimated from current self-report data by measuring to what extent higher-rate offenders are already receiving longer sentences. The greater the selection of high-rate offenders in current practice, the less the benefit one can anticipate from developing improved predictors.

One can obtain some degree of selective incapacitation in a number of ways without necessarily invoking any explicit predictor variables. If some particular crime types are associated with high-rate offending, then incapacitation strategies might be more effective by increasing the likelihood that offenders convicted of that crime type receive a sentence. This type of incapacitation policy invokes information that uniformly is accepted as appropriate—the crime type of conviction. Research should focus on the benefit to be attained by such a policy. If only a small increment of predictability is provided by using other more controversial predictors (such as employment status), then one can avoid the ethical problems posed by the use of those variables.

There is a need for further validation of the assumptions that underlie available estimates of the crime control and prison population effects of selective incapacitation policies and for analysis of the sensitivity of the estimates to violations of those assumptions. Information is especially weak about crime spurts that occur just before arrest or just after release from jail or prison, about possible interactions between the frequency of offending (λ) and the probability of arrest following a given offense (q), about trends in q as offenders age, about the degree to which the crimes removed by incarcerating an offender are replaced by other offenders still in the community, and about the influence of selective incapacitation strategies on general deterrence effects. With such information incorporated into more complete models, better estimates can be developed of the incapacitation effects of alternative policies on pretrial release, assigning priorities for court processing, sentencing, and parole release.

Individual Deterrent Effects

Another important set of interventions are the sanctioning actions of the criminal justice system. In particular, it is still uncertain whether time spent in prison has an individual deterrent effect on some offenders, in terms of reducing their postincarceration criminal activity, or a criminogenic effect, in terms of increasing individual crime rates and lengthening criminal careers. Alternatively, both effects may occur, but on identifiably different groups of offenders; if so, we need to learn how to distinguish the two groups.

Measurement of Criminal Career Dimensions and Their Correlates

It is clear that improved measures of criminal career dimensions are needed—especially career length, participation in serious crimes, and the individual frequency of criminal activity—for the general population and for high-risk subsets of the population. But perhaps more important is the identification of particular behaviors, life events (such as marriage or first employment), or previous career characteristics (such as juvenile criminal

activity) that can be linked to the course of individual criminal careers. Such identification may require frequent longitudinal observations during key periods. Establishing such linkages is particularly useful in view of the considerable diversity among offenders in their individual crime rates and their career length. If the individuals with the highest values of λ and T_R become candidates for selective interventions, then it is essential to develop information that will indicate the feasibility of such decisions, and how best to identify offenders who have the highest values.

An important task in the study of criminal careers is linking empirical relationships to theoretical frameworks in order to avoid accumulating diverse independent correlations among fragmented sets of variables. The nature of the criminal career paradigm invites the application of dynamic theories to account for the developmental aspects of careers. Different theories might well be needed to explain the initiation of delinquent behavior, the persistence of criminal activity into adulthood, and the eventual termination of offending. It is likely that theoretical perspectives from diverse disciplines can make important contributions to this effort.

Individual Crime Rates

One of the most interesting and important issues in criminal career research has been the recent attention to developing estimates of individual crime rates, λ, and the accumulation of reasonably consistent, independent estimates of those rates through both self-reports and official records. If results continue to be consistent, researchers will be encourged to undertake further measurements in both modes. Certainly further measurement and analysis are needed, especially for the serious crime types. In studying λ, particular attention should be given to its longitudinal variation during an individual's career. In what ways is the simplified model of a stable individual crime rate in error, either in terms of age trends in the value of λ while active or in shifts between high-rate and low-rate periods? Some researchers have identified the latter scenario as particularly common among heavy narcotics users. Are there other life events that lead to a switch into or out of a high-rate period, and does the occurrence of high-rate periods follow identifiable patterns?

The importance of individual crime rates is emphasized by the considerable skewness of the λ distribution demonstrated in the Rand self-report inmate survey, which also highlights the need for attention on the correlates of λ as a high research priority. Among the strong candidates as determinants are characteristics of the juvenile career, particularly information about the age of first juvenile offense and specific offense types committed, and this research will require continuity of data in the juvenile and adult periods. There are some indications that the careers of adults in their mid-20s are likely to be more serious if the juvenile careers of those offenders started very early. Moreover, certain types or combinations of juvenile criminal behavior or its frequency may be important indicators of probable serious adult offending. These issues need further development and testing, and they probably could best be addressed in a longitudinal context.

The influence of drug use on criminal careers, particularly individual crime rates, is a particularly complex issue. Serious drug use as a juvenile or as an adult is indicative of a high rate of offending for those who engage in predatory crimes, such as robbery and burglary. If an effective drug treatment program were available to deal with the offender's dependency and if that dependency could then be reduced along with the rate of offending, then drug-related criminal behavior could be modified by addressing the offender's drug problem. This type of intervention strategy requires identifying other indicators that will suggest which drug users are likely to be amenable to treatment. But the drug-crime relationship may also be closely tied to broader environmental factors, such as historical changes in the U.S drug trade, which may have contributed to the rise in aggregate crime rates in the 1970s. Thus, both the predictive features and the manipulable features of the drug-crime relationship warrant considerably more exploration, particularly in the context of available drug treatments and their effectiveness and the impact of environmental influences.

It is also important to study whether the information contained in an individual's history of *arrests*—the number, the mix of types, their rate of accumulation—has more predictive power than the information in conviction records alone. Research on this question could contribute to the debate over using complete arrest histories rather than only conviction records. A part of this question should include a comparison of adult only and combined adult and juvenile records to estimate the incremental value of information about juvenile careers in identifying serious adult careers. During the early stages of an adult career, full and ready access to the juvenile record is important; at present, there is often sharp discontinuity in records at the age of transition (18 years in most jurisdictions). Further research on the impact of this bifurcated court system on young adult offenders is needed.

Group Offending

Exploring the effect of group influences on criminal behavior might benefit from the perspective of the criminal career paradigm. It would be desirable to identify groups of offenders whose criminal careers are linked through joint participation in some of the same offenses. Studies of their respective career patterns should indicate whether certain group patterns, such as a diversity of partners, are associated with high- or low-rate offending. It would be particularly important to determine to what extent some identifiable individual offenders serve as recruiters to offending and to what extent behavior can be explained as compliant responsiveness to recruitment efforts. The importance of group influences at initiation, the transition from group to solo offending, and the role of groups in later adult careers are other research issues related to group influences on criminal careers.

Career Length

Initial research on career length has yielded some valuable insights regarding its relationship to age: termination rates during the 30s tend to be the lowest, a reflection of the fact that offenders who are still active in their 30s, especially those who started before age 20, are among the most committed to a criminal career. The use of existing data on the correlates of recidivism to explore patterns across follow-up periods of different lengths would help isolate other correlates of career length. Nonrecidivism can be a reflection of a combination of termination and diminished λ, and those two effects should be distinguished. The longer the follow-up period, the more likely it is that nonrecidivism reflects career termination. Long-range studies of career length will require individual arrest histories or self-report records for years after many careers have terminated.

Two variables often associated with nonrecidivism are steady employment and marriage: they may well be associated with career termination, and they warrant closer study. The further question of whether explicit intervention through facilitating these transitions (e.g., through special counseling efforts) also has an effect should also be pursued. It may be that selection differences associated with these transitions by offenders result in diminished criminality, but that interventions oriented at achieving those ends do not. This possibility can be tested in appropriately structured experiments. Last, ethnographic studies that focus in detail on individual life histories can be expected to provide a richness of detail about factors contributing to termination of criminal careers that would not be available in even the most careful survey study.

Participation

Future research on participation is likely to benefit less from further measurement and more from attention to important correlates of initiation of criminal careers and the different correlates of minor and serious criminal involvement. In particular, more research is needed on life events that may be linked to criminal behavior in offender populations but that have not been adequately studied in a longitudinal context. Examples of these include abusive family situations, parental alcohol or drug abuse, divorce or death of a parent, or other traumatic life events, particularly if they occur in the preschool or elementary school years.

This type of research is particularly valuable for indicating which individuals are most likely to initiate delinquent careers, which individuals are likely to commit only minor offenses and then terminate their delinquent activity, and which individuals are likely to move on to more serious delinquency. If such indicators could be developed, the potentially effective intervention strategies discussed earlier might be more effectively targeted.

New Directions in Measurement and Modeling

Much too often the two approaches to measuring criminal career dimensions—self-reports and official records—have been presented as mutually competitive. They are much more appropriately viewed as complementary modes of observation of a common underlying process, and specific effort should be directed at deriving estimates, especially of λ and its distribution, that use information from both data sources. The strengths of each approach will help to illuminate, and ultimately to correct, the sources of error in the other.

Specifically, it is important to learn more about some key linkages, particularly that between the arrest process that official records depict and the underlying crime process that is of primary concern. A key element in this linkage is the sampling probability from crimes to arrests—the probability of an arrest conditional upon a crime—and any bias it contains or correlations it might display with the underlying individual crime rate. Self-reports, in conjunction with official records for the same individuals, provide an opportunity for exploring this linkage. Such exploration is an issue of high priority, largely because improved insight into the error structure of the two approaches of measurement, the connection between their error structures, and the link between arrests and the underlying crime process would increase the usefulness of the large numbers of official-record data sources that are available as primary records for studying criminal careers.

Most research on trends in crime seriousness over a criminal career has revealed individual diversity, albeit with some greater tendency for offenders to repeat the previous offense type or to stay within the group of property or violent offenses. Most of those results, however, derive from observations of the arrest process, and inferences about patterns in the underlying crime process have proven to be rather difficult. This area is of considerable interest and importance for developing knowledge about the structure of criminal careers. It also has import for policy because of the significant influence that crime-mix patterns could have on incapacitative effects. One important stumbling block has been the fact that most of the data on crime-mix patterns have reflected the arrest process, and arrest patterns are not necessarily reflective of the underlying crime process because of the great variability in arrest probability (q) across different crime types. The arrest process has been dominant because the sequence of arrests is well recorded in official arrest histories, and the sequence of crimes is rarely asked for in self-reports.

These issues could be pursued more directly for serious offenses in self-report questionnaires that probe into sequences of participation by first asking respondents if they have *ever* done a particular offense and then asking them when they *first* did it and when they *last* did it. The issue of changes in crime mix may possibly be more effectively addressed by focusing on changes in crime-type participation patterns rather than the micro-analysis of the sequence of crime types that is easily available from arrest records.

Further research on estimates of incapacitative effects is also needed. Estimation of the incapacitative effects of imprisonment are most commonly computed using a formula derived from a model first introduced in 1973. This model uses standard assumptions for tractability: homogeneous offenders, a Poisson stream of crimes, exponential career lengths, parameters that are constant over time, and prison sentences that are short compared with career lengths and independent of prior record. The panel's analyses have shown that the incapacitation effects estimated by Greenwood (1982) are very sensitive to the effects of finite career lengths. Further exploration is needed on the sensitivity of the results to model assumptions, and changes in the model are needed to reflect the consequences of the considerable heterogeneity in values of λ. Also, the model should take account of the fact that sentences often do reflect predictive considerations and the possibility that sentences could be related to a judge's estimate of an individual's offending frequency.

Recent developments in research on stochastic processes associated with hierarchical distributions offer promise for further development of the incapacitation model (Lehoczky, Volume II). Any such model development should be tied closely to knowledge about the structure of criminal careers and to the potential incapacitative effects associated with those criminal career histories. Also, models should be extended to reflect various theoretical perspectives on the factors that influence criminal career dimensions. One such model, reflecting a labor-market viewpoint, was developed by Flinn (Volume II); other theoretical approaches should be pursued.

In exploring various selective incapacitation polices, it would be desirable to measure the selective incapacitation effects associated with several classification instruments. Any such attempt should engage in simulated experiments using individual arrest data. It is important in the simulated experiments that the data set on which the experiments are run be different from the one that gave rise to the classification rule in order to avoid shrinkage problems (see Chapter 6).

Seemingly powerful predictors that emerge in the first stage can then be tested experimentally for their potential usefulness in actual applications.

SUPPORTIVE ORGANIZATIONAL ARRANGEMENTS

In this final section we identify two organizational arrangements that could facilitate the further development of a cohesive research community and the expansion of knowledge about criminal careers: continuation of the current Crime Control Theory Program at the National Institute of Justice (NIJ) and development of a criminal career research data repository.

Continuation and Expansion of the Crime Control Theory Program

Much of the research on criminal careers reviewed by this panel has been supported by the Crime Control Theory Program at NIJ, which also supported the work of the panel. Over a period of 6 years, with a limited budget of less than $1 million per year, this program has made some important contributions to knowledge about criminal careers and their policy usefulness. We believe that much of the success of this program has been a direct consequence of its research management strategy. The program managers provide general guidance on the policy objectives; give heavy emphasis to peer review for research proposals; display a strong commitment to the continuity of the research stream, to the development of a research community, and to interchange of information through annual meetings at which research results are critically examined by peers and colleagues; and look to the scientific review process for filtering valid from invalid results. This strategy, which the panel endorses, has long been associated with effective progress in medical research and in the physical sciences. The panel hopes that this effort will not only be continued, but that additional resources will be provided to permit the program to support some of the research questions discussed in this chapter.

Criminal Career Data Repository

A major need common to all research on criminal careers is access to a rich set of data on individuals. Ideally, such data would record detailed information on how the sample was drawn; on crime and arrest sequences; on each individual's early childhood experiences; on his parents, siblings, and peers; on school experiences and work experiences; on deviant behavior of various sorts; and on interaction with the criminal justice system. No single data source yet collected contains so rich a set of information on an appropriately broad sample. In some cases, data are available only for juvenile years; in other cases, only adult arrest events are available; and in only a few cases are individual background data available. Together, however, the wide variety of information that has already been collected and used in individual criminal career research projects represents a rich collection on which considerable secondary analysis is warranted and should be pursued.

In order to facilitate such secondary analysis, it would be appropriate to organize and code those data sets so that they can be made accessible to a large community of potential users for comparative research and cross-validation. The community working with the data would be in a strong position to test prediction models developed in one setting or from one sampling frame against data collected in another and to cross-validate various studies. Even within a single study, the data from the initial construction sample from which a particular predictive model was developed could be tested against a validation sample, which would develop measures of shrinkage as part of validation.

The initial data sets to be maintained in a criminal career data repository should include, at a minimum, the Rand inmate surveys, the National Youth Survey of Elliott et al., the official-record arrest data collected and analyzed by Blumstein and Cohen, the data on two Philadelphia cohorts collected by Wolfgang et al., the various cohort data of Shannon, Robins, McCord, and the London longitudinal data of West and Farrington. The location of such a repository would have to be explored, but one possibility is the already-established Criminal Justice Archive and Information Network (CJAIN) at the University of Michigan, the current repository for all data collected with NIJ support; the data maintained in the CJAIN are available to any user.

The field of criminal career research is beginning to yield valuable information on the dimensions of criminal careers—participation, frequency, seriousness, and career length—and the factors associated with each dimension. Advances in measurement and modeling have been instrumental in the accumulation of knowledge about individual careers. Additional research that addresses the questions posed in this chapter will contribute to more effective strategies to prevent, modify, interrupt, or terminate criminal careers. Progress can be expected from secondary analysis of available data, from well-designed experiments, and, most importantly, from a major program of longitudinal study.

Participation in
Criminal Careers

Christy A. Visher and Jeffrey A. Roth

INTRODUCTION

This appendix is concerned with those who participate in criminal careers. More specifically, it reviews estimates of the fraction of the population that commits at least one crime during some observation period. This fraction, called the *participation level*, is of interest as an indicator of the pervasiveness of delinquents and criminals in society, and many find the estimates—some exceeding 60 percent over the lifetime of urban males—surprisingly high. But more important from the perspectives of testing theory and developing policy is an understanding of how participation varies across subpopulations, and of what factors are associated with greater risk of future participation.

The authors wish to thank Alfred Blumstein for stimulating the development of this appendix. We are grateful for helpful comments by many participants in the Workshop on Criminal Career Research, especially David Farrington and Robert Gordon. Delbert Elliott, Lyle Shannon, Paul Tracy, Neil Weiner, and Marvin Wolfgang helped us by providing special tabulations and interpretations of their data. We also appreciate the skillful editing by Jean Shirhall. We are responsible for any remaining errors in the appendix.

Obstacles to the Understanding and Measurement of Pervasiveness

Given the importance of measuring participation, it is unfortunate that, as noted by Gordon (1976), substantial confusion and ambiguity exist in the literature concerning appropriate measures of pervasiveness and their definitions. The student of participation is thus confronted with such terms as "arrest probability" (Christensen, 1967); "offender rate" or " 'real' rate of onset" (Wolfgang, Figlio, and Sellin, 1972:133); "probability of committing at least one offense" (Wolfgang, Figlio, and Sellin:281); "prevalence," used in somewhat different senses by Gordon (1976), Blumstein and Graddy (1982), and Elliott et al. (1983); "incidence," used in two senses by T. Monahan (1960) and in other senses by Gordon (1976), Elliott et al. (1983), and Farrington (1983a); "static prevalence" (Little, 1965); "delinquency rate" (Hindelang, Hirschi, and Weis, 1981); "hazard rate" (Gordon and Gleser, 1974); "age-specific risk" and "age-specific rate," defined differently but used interchangeably (Ball, Ross, and Simpson, 1964); and "criminality" (Hutchings and Mednick, 1975).

While each of these terms reflects some

aspect of pervasiveness, standardization is lacking across authors with respect to the base (e.g., a cohort, a population, surviving cohort members, surviving cohort members not already offenders) and the observation period (e.g., lifetime, lifetime through a stated age, preceding year, time between record updates, time not incarcerated between record updates). Even when the measures are standardized with respect to these variables, their values depend on the *domain* of "crime" in which participation occurs (e.g., all offenses, index crimes, felonies, specific crime types) and on the participation *threshold* (self-reported commission, self-reported police contact, recorded police contact, court referral, conviction). Therefore, comparison of estimated values across studies is not at all straightforward.

As explained by Gordon (1976), the root of some of the confusion is imprecise adaptation of the epidemiological concepts of "prevalence" and "incidence." As he explains, prevalence is generally intended to refer to the fraction of a group currently experiencing a condition, such as heart disease. Incidence describes the group's experience over an interval of time, and the incidence of heart disease during a year is the number of contractions of heart disease divided by the size of the population. Thus, "prevalence" is a concept counting persons, "incidence" is a concept counting occurrences, and both concepts use the population as a base.

Following Gordon (1976:209), "choosing a verbal label for the kind of rate that is of main interest here is a matter of discretion." However, choosing a consistent set of labels that permits comparisons across studies is important for understanding. To avoid misunderstandings, we refer to the concept as *participation*.

The study of participation would be straightforward if individuals maintained and made available accurate diaries of their legal and illegal activities, including precise dates. By using the diaries, it would be easy to measure the fraction participating in robbery, or the larger fraction participating in a broader category of crime, such as "FBI index offenses," or the still larger fraction

that has ever committed a nontraffic offense. At the aggregate level, the participation fraction could be tabulated across subpopulations of interest. At the individual level, a binary indicator of participation-nonparticipation could be analyzed using sophisticated statistical techniques to identify factors associated with a higher probability of participation.

Unfortunately, accurate diaries for representative samples of individuals do not exist. In their place two imperfect devices are commonly used to measure participation—criminal justice agency records of arrests, court referrals, or convictions and the self-reports of survey respondents. Official records cover only offenders whose participation comes to police or court attention at least once. Presumably, therefore, those offenders commit more serious crimes than other offenders, and they may be unrepresentative in other ways as well (e.g., less adept at avoiding detection, more often under the influence of drugs or alcohol, more often from neighborhoods under intensive police patrol). Also, because official records are maintained for operational rather than research purposes, special efforts are needed to augment them with other pertinent information beyond the demographic data used in police identification. Self-reports of participation, on the other hand, may be sought from more representative samples and may easily be augmented with information on other variables that are hypothesized to be risk factors. But the results from the sample that actually responds to the survey may be biased (e.g., if serious offenders are less likely than nonoffenders to cooperate with interviewers). Also, the self-reports may be distorted by the respondents' failure to recall events accurately, by their misunderstanding of instructions, and by their intentional deception.

These and other problems with official-record and self-report participation measures are discussed by Weis (Volume II). As explained in this appendix, however, many findings obtained by using one of the approaches can be reconciled with findings obtained by using the other. Before reporting findings, we first discuss the importance of understanding participation and then specify a conceptual framework for analyzing it.

Importance of Participation

Studies of participation have long been recognized as valuable for both intellectual understanding and policy development (T. Monahan, 1960; Ball, Ross, and Simpson, 1964). Intellectually, as noted by Blumstein and Graddy (1982), specific attention to offender participation is a first step in improving the understanding of the "causes of crime." Many studies of the causes of crime have analyzed aggregate crime rates. However, the aggregate crime rate may mask variation in participation levels, in individual offending frequencies, or in the average duration of criminal careers.

There is no a priori reason to assume that a common set of causes influences individuals' offending participation, frequency, and duration. Thus, disaggregating crime rates into those dimensions is an essential preliminary step if multiple causal structures are to be discovered or confirmed empirically. For example, only by partitioning the aggregate crime rate into its multiple dimensions can one design studies that allow for the possibility that one set of factors (e.g., peer influences, family stress, and school problems) is associated with participation, a second (e.g., economic needs, situational stress, opportunity) with the frequency of serious offending, and a third (e.g., effects of aging, the assumption of legitimate adult activities) with termination of the criminal career. While the separation of these dimensions by no means rules out the possibility that some factors influence all three dimensions, the analytical separation facilitates testing the hypothesis that different forces are operative at the three career stages.

If different sets of individual characteristics are associated with the respective career dimensions or stages, identifying them could improve the efficiency and equity of resource allocations within the criminal justice system and elsewhere. For example, subject to ethical constraints, knowledge of

patterns in participation could suggest strategies for designing community-based preventive programs that reduce criminal participation and for giving high-risk groups of children special priority in admissions to the programs. Similarly, if factors that distinguish offenders from nonoffenders, such as demographic characteristics, were found not to distinguish among offenders in terms of their frequency of serious offending, the effectiveness of criminal justice decisions about arrested offenders could be improved.

Consideration of policies aimed at specific criminal career dimensions rather than broad-based "crime control" may have differential implications for the acceptability of various policy alternatives. It has been suggested that correlates of frequency and duration are more neutral in terms of race or socioeconomic status than correlates of participation (Blumstein and Graddy, 1982). In that event, strategies based on career modification or the incapacitation of high-rate serious offenders may become more widely accepted than early preventive intervention strategies. Thus, greater understanding of the pervasiveness of offenders, their desistance patterns, and their individual offending frequencies as separate components of "the crime problem" is important from both intellectual and policy standpoints.

A Conceptual Framework for Offender Participation

This discussion draws on the conceptual framework of Gordon and Gleser (1974) and defines terms that are used throughout the rest of this appendix. For simplicity, the terminology is introduced with respect to a single birth cohort.

Suppose that a cohort of N individuals was born in a single year, and that I_t of the cohort members initiate criminal careers by committing their first crimes at age t. Although I_t could theoretically be computed for any age between birth and the age by which all cohort members have died, only a negligible number of criminal careers begin before age 6 or after age 45. One approach to computing cumulative participation involves the distribution of the *age-specific initiation rate*, a_t, which is defined by

$$a_t = I_t/N \qquad (1)$$

for each age.[1] Thus, a_t is simply the proportion of the cohort that initiates a criminal career by committing a first offense at age t. Adding up the initiation rates from zero to any age of interest t^* (18, for example), one can calculate the *cumulative participation rate*, D_{t^*}, defined by

$$D_{t^*} = \sum_{t=0}^{t^*-1} a_t. \qquad (2)$$

Perhaps the most common participation measure in the literature reviewed here is D_{18}, cumulative participation by age 18. Another common measure is cumulative lifetime participation, obtained by setting t^* to about 45, since few individuals commit their first crime after that age.

While a_t is useful in calculating cumulative participation, it does not present a clear picture of the relationship between initiation of offending and age. The reason is that a cohort member who began offending by age 15 is no longer at risk of *becoming* an offender at age 16. Thus, a falling-off of initiation rates at later ages reflects both

behavioral patterns of interest to the researcher and artifacts of the declining population at risk of becoming a first offender.

To isolate the behavioral relationship, it is common to compute and analyze the *age-specific hazard rate*, h_t, the conditional probability of becoming an offender given that one has not already done so. For age t, h_t is defined by

$$h_t = \frac{I_t}{N - Z_t} = \frac{a_t}{1 - \sum_{s=0}^{t-1} a_s}, \qquad (3)$$

where Z is the number of cohort members who became offenders before some age, and s and t are indices of age. The term "hazard rate" is borrowed from reliability analysis in operations research, in which, for example, one wants to ignore already-burnt-out light bulbs in computing the probability that a bulb will fail in the next hour of a test. The hazard rate is identical to the "offender rate" or "real rate of onset" reported by Wolfgang, Figlio, and Sellin (1972:132–133, 282). Because the concept isolates behavioral patterns from mathematical artifacts (also see the discussion in Gordon and Gleser, 1974), its use in analyses of criminal career initiation is becoming increasingly common.

Age-specific participation may be computed from hazard rates, according to the following formula:[2]

$$D_t = \sum_{s=0}^{t-1} a_s = \sum_{s=0}^{t-1} h_s \sum_{r=0}^{s-1} (1 - h_r), \qquad (4)$$

where r is an index of age.

Equations 1 through 4 are operational only if the age at the first offense is known—

---

[1] As defined in Equation 1, a_t is the fraction of the original cohort that commits a first offense at age t. Because some of the original cohort members will have died before age t, a_t understates the probability that a surviving cohort member will initiate a criminal career at age t. That probability is given by:

$$\hat{a}_t = \frac{I_t}{N - X_t},$$

where X_t is the number of cohort members who have died before age t. Over the age range of interest in most studies, say, 16 to 30, X_t is negligibly small, and so no mortality adjustment is made.

Of potentially greater importance is sample attrition because of cohort members who refuse to be interviewed or who leave the jurisdiction. Until the cohort reaches middle age, attrition from these causes reduces the denominator more than does mortality. But because those who refuse or leave may commit crimes of which the researcher is unaware, the numerator is also erroneously reduced, leaving the net effect on a_t uncertain.

[2] Gordon and Gleser (1974) first corrected an error made by T. Monahan (1960) in simply summing hazard rates to compute prevalence rates. However, the "correct" equation (9) of Gordon and Gleser itself contains a typographical error. The Monahan error was repeated by Wolfgang, Figlio, and Sellin (1972) in summing their first-index-offense probabilities (p. 282) to calculate age-specific index-offense probabilities (p. 126), but the magnitude of the error is negligible.

an unusual circumstance. More commonly, D_t is measured through the self-reports of t-year-old respondents when asked if they have ever committed a crime. If arrest rather than commission is used as the participation threshold, however, the equations can be applied to official arrest records recorded by date. To distinguish between the two thresholds, participation measures based on committing crimes ("*doing*" crime) are denoted D; measures based on arrests ("*busts*") are denoted B. For many purposes, attention is focused on the fraction of a cohort or other sample that is currently participating in crime, i.e., that commits at least one crime during an observation period. This fraction, the *current participation* level, is denoted d.

Current participation is related to crimes per capita, C, through the parameter, λ, the individual offending frequency (i.e., crimes committed per year). The relationship is given by:

$$C = d\lambda. \qquad (5)$$

An important implication of Equation 5 is that variations in aggregate crime measures can be due to variations in either current participation, d, or offending frequency, λ. Research on λ is reviewed by Cohen (Appendix B).

The remainder of this appendix is divided into three sections. The next section draws on a variety of studies to develop ranges of estimates for cumulative participation by age 18, cumulative lifetime participation, and current participation. Then, based on other analyses in the same body of literature, the second section reviews findings concerning factors associated with participation. The final section presents conclusions and suggestions for further research.

ESTIMATES OF CRIMINAL PARTICIPATION

This section draws on previous research to provide estimates of participation in offending, according to the measures just defined. The review is organized by type of participation estimate: participation in offending by age 18 (D_{18} and B_{18}), lifetime participation (B_L), participation by high school age (D_{HS} and B_{HS}), and crime-specific current participation (d).[3] We report the values associated with each study as they were reported in published results or, in some cases, as they were derived from data presented. Before summarizing the empirical estimates, we briefly review the history of attention to participation in offending. We also discuss the scope of our research review and present an overview of the types of studies and data sources that are commonly used in estimating participation in offending.

Background

Scholarly attention to participation in offending (or "prevalence") became prominent in the 1940s and 1950s with the first self-report studies of criminal behavior, which used small local samples (e.g., Porterfield, 1946; Wallerstein and Wyle, 1947; Nye, 1958). As reported by T. Monahan (1960:67), in the late 1950s, the Senate Committee on Juvenile Delinquency stated that "probably up to 20 percent of the male population coming of age could easily be expected to have a juvenile court record if the 1955 rate remains constant" and a member of the committee (Thomas C. Hennings) noted that additional delinquents would have avoided court contact. As Monahan also noted (1960:67), the estimation procedure that the Senate committee used was very approximate and tenuous, resting on unverified assumptions about the fraction of adjudicated delinquents who were repeaters. After the Senate report was released, Monahan attempted to calculate precisely the estimate in which the Senate was interested, denoted here as B_{18}. An employee of the Municipal Court of Philadelphia,

---

[3] An arrest-based measure of current participation, b, could be defined analogously to d, and crime-based measures for participation by age 18 (D_{18}) and lifetime participation (D_L) are also possible. However, values for D_{18}, D_L, and b do not generally appear in the published literature.

Monahan used 1957 data on the age distribution of first offenders referred to Philadelphia Juvenile Court, to estimate that about 27 percent of all Philadelphia boys and 8 percent of the girls would appear in juvenile court in Philadelphia on a delinquency charge before reaching age 18. Unfortunately, his method was slightly in error (see Gordon and Gleser, 1974), but nonetheless his calculations established the feasibility of estimating cumulative participation from a single year's data.

A few years later, a clear appreciation for the participation (or "prevalence") statistic, also related to officially recorded delinquency, appeared in Ball, Ross, and Simpson (1964:90):

Accurate delineation of the incidence and prevalence of juvenile delinquency is an indispensable prerequisite to analysis of adolescent behavior; it is important to know whether 2 percent, 20 percent, or 40 percent of the American adolescents appear in court before adulthood.

This important paper included a formal discussion of the methods, definitions, and equations for calculating cumulative participation from annual statistics, and it also reported estimates based on first court appearances in Lexington, Kentucky.

Shortly thereafter, Little (1965) responded to the work of Ball, Ross, and Simpson, noting that their techniques of estimating "prevalence" could result in misleading estimates. In particular, in any single year, persons of different ages represent different birth cohorts. Thus, trends in participation across successive cohorts (i.e., "cohort effects") will cause participation estimates based on a single year's data to misrepresent offender participation among any single cohort. However, in relatively stable periods, these estimates are sufficiently close approximations to be useful for many purposes. This analytic issue is discussed more fully later in this appendix.

In the 1970s, attention to the concept and to the estimation of participation in offending was revived by Gordon (1973, 1976; Gordon and Gleser, 1974). In the only review of its kind to date, Gordon (1976) assembled the results of 10 "prevalence"

studies and assessed their consistency across different samples and communities. Only studies that were based on official records of juvenile delinquency (by age 18) were included. Gordon adjusted the estimates in different samples for variation in race composition "in order to enhance formal comparability" (1976:203). For example, for samples that were dominated by white males, Gordon used data from other samples on black and female participation to arrive at an estimate for *all* males and females. Gordon concluded that for some purposes a useful criterion of delinquency is the juvenile court record, and, using this definition, he estimated B_{18} at about 17 percent for white urban males (1976:270–272).

Scope of Literature Review

In selecting studies for this review of criminal participation estimates, we used several criteria. First, the study had to report participation rates occurring in populations of interest or to provide the data needed to calculate them. This restriction eliminated studies designed to achieve particular rates, by selecting institutionalized populations (for which participation is 100 percent), matched offender and nonoffender samples (for which participation is designed to be 50 percent), or samples with other predetermined rates (e.g., Glueck and Glueck, 1934, 1940, 1950; Empey and Erickson, 1966; Erickson, 1973; Morash, 1984).

Second, measures of criminal involvement that reflect both participation and individual frequency confuse two separate and distinct elements of a criminal career and were therefore not useful for the panel's purposes. For this reason, studies using aggregate data, such as UCR arrest or crime rates (e.g., Bordua, 1958; Clark and Wenninger, 1962; Chilton, 1964) are not included in this review. This consideration also eliminated studies that reported mean frequencies for specific crimes without separately tabulating the "zero" or "none" category (e.g., Arnold, 1965; Clark and Harvek, 1966; Williams and Gold, 1972; Elliott and

Voss, 1974; Gold and Reimer, 1975; Krohn et al., 1980; Ensminger et al., 1983) and reports of other indices of criminal involvement that combined participation with frequency (e.g., "commission of burglary two or more times"; Havighurst et al., 1962; Hathaway and Monachesi, 1963; Berger and Simon, 1974).

Third, following the emphasis in the panel's report, we focused primarily on studies of participation in specific serious crimes, such as robbery, burglary, and aggravated assault, or in official-record categories that included those crimes, such as "arrests for nontraffic offenses," "juvenile court referrals," and "convictions for indictable offenses." This focus further restricted the scope of our literature review and eliminated self-report studies that tapped only participation in status offenses or minor delinquency, such as underage drinking, vandalism, and theft under $2 (e.g., Slocum and Stone, 1963; Akers, 1964; Gould, 1969; Hindelang, 1971; Waldo and Chiricos, 1972), or that combined serious and minor offenses into one scale (e.g., Nye, 1958; Dentler and Monroe, 1961; Winslow, 1967; Hirschi, 1969; Gold, 1970; Walberg, Yeh, and Patton, 1975; Wilkinson, 1980).

The fourth restriction was that the study be published in the English language, either as a book, journal article, or report to a research sponsor. Papers presented at professional meetings, unpublished data, or working papers were not included in this review.

Types of Studies and Data Sources

Participation estimates are available from four types of studies:

- life-table calculations,
- prospective longitudinal studies,
- retrospective official-record searches, and
- self-reports of cross-section samples.

The first type of study uses *life-table techniques* to derive participation estimates from annual statistics that describe court or police activity in a single jurisdiction. These studies reflect the participation behavior of multiple birth cohorts as of a point in time, and the method is similar to that used to estimate mortality or morbidity at successive ages. Although many police departments and courts could compile life-table participation statistics, only a few such studies have appeared in the research literature (i.e., T. Monahan, 1960; Ball, Ross, and Simpson, 1964; Little, 1965; Farrington, 1981).

If an agency maintains separate age statistics for first offenses (whether defined by arrests, referrals, or convictions), it is possible to compute cumulative participation by a given age. This life-table method of computing B is useful because it produces a current "snapshot" of participation patterns among the birth cohorts at risk at the time of the analysis. If the age-specific first-offense rates remain constant across those cohorts, the results are identical to those from a longitudinal study of one cohort (Gordon and Gleser, 1974), and they provide reasonable approximations of a cohort's behavior if trends across cohorts are not unduly severe. Perhaps because the approach does not permit analysis of the relationship between participation and variables other than the demographic attributes (age, sex, and race) recorded at arrest, it is not widely used to analyze B.

Life-table estimates of age-specific current participation, b, in a given year can also be easily computed by combining justice agency data on the age distribution of arrestees or court referrals during the year with data for the same year on the age distribution of the general population. At any age, b is simply the ratio of offenders to the total population. Published studies using life-table approaches have generally reported cumulative estimates only; annualized estimates rarely appear in the literature.

A second type of study is the *prospective longitudinal study*. Stimulated in part by interest in the relationships between participation and a broad array of characteristics, researchers have used longitudinal studies to track one or more cohorts of individuals over substantial follow-up periods. The studies are called "prospective" because they involve samples of persons not known in advance to be criminals—their criminality is expected to emerge in the future, if at all. If the cohort is representative of all cohorts at risk of offending during the observation period, the longitudinal approach does not produce participation estimates markedly different from those that would be obtained in a life-table study.

The special strength of the longitudinal study lies in its relating participation to an array of variables. Prospective longitudinal studies enable researchers to relate criminal career initiation and participation not only to age, sex, and race but also to characteristics of individuals (e.g., poor school achievement, early antisocial behavior), characteristics of their families (e.g., low socioeconomic status, antisocial behavior in parents), and life events (e.g., parental discord and breakup, onset of substance abuse).

A prospective longitudinal study involves a sample of individuals selected at a point in time. Initially, information concerning the correlates of interest is gathered from the subjects, from their parents or teachers, or from records of school performance or teacher ratings. The subjects are then tracked over time, and their records are periodically updated. The updates may consist of indicators of criminal activity gathered from official records or self-reports and information on the correlates of interest or life events that might trigger criminal career initiation. Tracking and record updates begin shortly after the sample is selected but events occurring before sample selection may also be recorded. In practice, the samples are sometimes selected (and their records located) retrospectively (e.g., a 1945 birth cohort selected in 1964), but on some basis other than known criminal activity. As long as the sample is still representative of the cohort (despite mortality, mobility, and other influences), the resulting data may be analyzed as if the sample had been selected at the beginning of the observation period, with the advantage that results become available sooner.

Because of the effort involved in tracking subjects and updating their records, only a few prospective longitudinal studies have been carried out with large samples. We report criminal participation estimates from 10 major prospective longitudinal studies conducted in the United States, Great Britain, or Denmark. Analyses are typically performed and interim results published between successive waves of data collection. Because estimates in interim reports frequently change as additional data are gathered or errors corrected, we tried to obtain the latest comprehensive reports in preparing this review. Thus, estimates reported here may differ from published interim estimates based on the same data set.

One type of prospective longitudinal study is the two-wave prospective study, which has been used to test the power of some indicator (e.g., teacher ratings of behavior), measured at one point in time, to predict future participation by some subsequent age. While a large number of such studies have attempted to ascertain predictive power with respect to various measures of "delinquency" (see Loeber and Dishion, 1983), this review is limited to those yielding estimates of participation as previously defined.

The third and fourth types of study involve single-wave, cross-section samples, for which participation is estimated from either *retrospective official records* or *self-reports*. Officially recorded participation, B_a, is the proportion of age-a members of the sample who have an official criminal record (police arrest, court referral, or conviction) at the time of sample selection. The samples are usually selected to achieve a particular distribution of one or more hypothesized correlates of participation. However, many of the samples also provide a basis for estimating participation in a subpopulation of interest.

Surveys of cross-section samples can also provide estimates of self-reported offending. By their nature, studies in this category are well suited to estimation of crime-specific participation. Depending on how questions are worded, studies in this category can yield estimates of either the fraction of persons who have participated in specific offense types at any time before the age at time of interview (cumulative participation, D_a), or only during the year (or some other interval) preceding the interview (current participation, d). Single-wave survey studies focusing exclusively on minor offenses have been excluded from this review, and participation estimates in the reviewed studies are reported only for the more serious crime types. The samples in some of the cross-section studies reviewed here reflect an age range, such as "high school age," and the resulting cumulative participation estimates are denoted D_{HS}.

Estimates of Criminal Participation by Age 18

Criminal participation by age 18 is perhaps the most frequently reported measure of participation in crime. The measure reflects involvement in deviant or criminal behavior as a juvenile since, in most U.S. jurisdictions, the authority of the juvenile court ends at a person's 18th birthday. Moreover, this measure is easily compared across multiple samples because of its precise definition. We located 22 U.S. or foreign studies that reported participation by age 18 for large birth cohorts representing an entire urban area, for samples representing some subpopulation of interest, or for smaller "high-risk" samples (see Table 1). In all these studies, estimates were based on official records of criminal activity—recorded police contact, arrest, juvenile court referral, or conviction—and thus we report B_{18}. Self-report estimates of participation are usually obtained by sampling high school students of different ages, and so the number of 18-year-olds in any single study is too small to support estimates of participation precisely by age 18.

In the following pages, estimates of B_{18} are drawn from longitudinal studies of two Philadelphia cohorts, other U.S. longitudinal studies, life-table analyses, analyses of multiple data bases, and British studies.

The Philadelphia Cohorts

In 1964, Wolfgang and his colleagues began assembling records from the Juve-

nile Aid Division of the Philadelphia Police Department on officially recorded police contacts with a cohort of 9,945 boys born in 1945 who resided in Philadelphia when they were between the ages of 10 and 18 and were therefore at risk of police contacts in Philadelphia throughout that entire age range. As reported by Wolfgang, Figlio, and Sellin (1972) and shown in Table 1, B_{18}, as measured by police contacts for nontraffic offenses (but including status and liquor violations), reached 34.9 percent for the entire sample, with levels of 28.7 for whites and 50.2 for blacks.[4]

As expected, participation estimates based on the FBI's Uniform Crime Report (UCR) index offenses (homicide, rape, robbery, aggravated assault, burglary, larceny, and auto theft) were lower than estimates based on all crimes, especially for whites (13.6 percent for all males, 8.2 for whites, and 26.8 for blacks). For non-index offenses, B_{18} was only slightly lower than that for all nontraffic offenses, which indicates that very few offenders participated in index crimes only. Participation in crimes involving injury or theft was much lower than the other participation rates because of the narrower definition of criminal behavior—only about 7 percent for an offense causing injury and 10 percent for an offense involving theft.

Wolfgang and his colleagues later selected a second birth cohort for study, 28,338 males and females born in Philadelphia in 1958 and residing there through age 17. Based on Tracy, Wolfgang, and Figlio (1985), comparisons are presented in Table 1 between cohorts I and II. With the identical domain of "all nontraffic offenses" for the two studies, the overall value of B_{18}, based on recorded police contacts for males, declined slightly, from 34.9 in cohort I to 32.8 in cohort II. However, this small decrease represents the net effect of larger decreases for each race separately (about 20 percent) and an increase in the proportion

---

[4]Some of the studies reviewed in this paper use the race designation "black," while others use "nonwhite." Because blacks comprise nearly all the nonwhite samples studied here, we have used the designation "black" throughout.

TABLE A-1   Estimates of Criminal Participation by Age 18

Reference	Nature of Sample	Correlates Examined	Source (official records, self-reports)	Definition of Crime, Concept Reported or Inferred	Participation Estimates[a] (percent)		
					T	W	B
I. U.S. Studies							
Wolfgang, Figlio, and Sellin (1972)	Philadelphia cohort I: 1945 birth cohort of 9,945 male residents	Socioeconomic status, race, school achievement	Recorded police contacts	All nontraffic offenses including status[b]	34.9	28.7	50.2
				S-W injury[c]	6.7	3.3	15.0
				S-W theft	10.1	6.5	19.0
Tracy, Wolfgang, and Figlio (1985)	Philadelphia cohort II: 1958 birth cohort of 28,338 residents	Socioeconomic status, race, school achievement	Recorded police contacts	All nontraffic offenses including status	M: 32.8 F: 14.1	22.7 9.2	41.8 18.5
				S-W injury	6.7	3.1	9.9
				S-W theft	11.0	5.0	16.3
				UCR index offenses by cohort			
				I	13.6	8.2	26.8
				II (males)	17.9	8.9	26.0
				II (females)	4.0	1.8	6.0
				UCR non-index offenses by cohort			
				I	31.8	26.3	45.1
				II (males)	27.9	19.9	35.1
				II (females)	12.1	8.3	15.7
Wolfgang (1977)	974 randomly selected males from Philadelphia cohort I	Delinquency/crime	Recorded police contacts	All nontraffic offenses including status	35.1		
Shannon (1982a)	Racine, Wis., cohort I: 1942 birth cohort of 1,352 residents followed up to 1974	Youth participation as correlate of adult participation	Police records	Contact for nontraffic offenses including status[d]	M: 41.0 F: 8.7		
	Racine, Wis., cohort II: 1949 birth cohort of 2,099 residents followed up to 1974	Youth participation as correlate of adult participation	Police records	Contact for nontraffic offenses including status[d]	M: 47.3 F: 15.1		
	Racine, Wis., cohort III: 1955 birth cohort of 2,676 residents followed up to 1977	Youth participation as correlate of adult participation	Police records	Contact for nontraffic offenses including status[d]	M: 44.1 F: 22.2		

Study	Sample	Variables	Data source	Delinquency measure	Rates
Robins and Wish (1977)	223 black males, born during the 1930s in St. Louis	Juvenile behaviors: marijuana use, school problems, leaving home	Police and court records	Arrests for any offenses or juvenile court referrals	38.1
Robins, West, and Herjanic (1975)	145 offspring of black male sample (above), age 18+ by 1974	Parental crime and delinquency, anti-social grandparents, delinquent siblings	Police and juvenile court records	Juvenile court referrals or arrests for non-traffic offenses	M: 31.4 F: 13.6
McCord and McCord (1959); McCord (1978)	506 males born in 1925-1934	Adolescent treatment, attitudes, age of onset	Official records through ages 41-50, from 1939 to 1978	Juvenile court convictions for nontraffic offenses	26.1 27.5[e]
Palmore and Hammond (1964)	319 ADC clients[f] (in 1950) born 1942-1944	School performance, family instability, neighborhood crime	Police and juvenile court records	"Known to police or juvenile court"	M: 56.0 52.0 63.5 F: 15.4 8.4 32.0
Polk et al. (1981)	1,227 Marion County, Ore., male high school sophomores in 1964	Social class, peer delinquency, education, marital status,	Police and juvenile court records	Juvenile court referrals for any offenses	25.0
T. Monahan (1960); reanalyzed by Gordon and Gleser (1974)	Philadelphia juveniles, 1941, 1949-1954; age distribution at first juvenile court appearance / Age distribution of population	None	Philadelphia Juvenile Court / Philadelphia Board of Education Annual Report	Court referrals after arrests or complaints; traffic offenses negligible	1941: M: 17.1 13.1 37.8 F: 3.9 2.6 11.5 / 1949-1954: M: 22.3 16.5 40.8 (25.8 17.9 50.9)[g] F: 6.0 3.3 14.8 (6.4 3.4 15.8)[g]
Ball, Ross, and Simpson (1964); reanalyzed by Gordon (1976)	Fayette County, Ky., juveniles, 1960; age/sex distribution of first juvenile court appearance; age/sex distribution of population	None	Fayette County Juvenile Court; U.S. Census Bureau, 1960 / Age-specific initiation rates, cumulated to age 18[b]	Juvenile court referrals, including only "serious or unusual" traffic offenses	M: 20.7 (16.8 43.1)[h] F: 5.2 (4.2 10.8)[h]
Christensen (1967)	Philadelphia County Court statistics on first juvenile referral U.S. data on total arrests and mortality	Rural, urban, and suburban	Philadelphia County Court Annual Report, 1965 Uniform Crime Reports; 1966 Statistical Abstract	Arrest for nontraffic offenses[b,i]	M: 25.1 F: 6.5

TABLE A-1 Continued

Reference	Nature of Sample	Correlates Examined	Source (official records, self-reports)	Definition of Crime, Concept Reported or Inferred	Participation Estimates[a] (percent)		
					T	W	B
Belkin, Blumstein, and Glass (1973)	Statistics on age-specific first-arrest rates	None	Philadelphia cohort I (ages 1–30); Christensen (1967) (ages 31+)	Arrests for nontraffic offenses	M: 34.0 F: 8.0		
Blumstein and Graddy (1982)	Statistics on age-specific first-arrest rates Age/sex/race population distribution	None	Philadelphia cohort I (ages 1–30) Random sample of 4,811 Washington, D.C., arrest histories of active offenders (age 31+); U.S. Census Bureau	Arrests for FBI index offense (males only)[b]	12.3[i]	8.2	26.9
II. British Studies							
Little (1965)	1942 London birth cohort; age distribution at first arrest Age distribution of general population	None	London Commissioners of Police 1951 Census	Arrests for indictable[k] offenses. Actual cohort compared with projected estimates for 1952 and 1962	Cohort: 7.8 1952: 6.8 1962: 9.6		
Little (1965)	Juveniles, Great Britain, 1962; age distribution at first offense	None	Home Office criminal statistics	Convictions for indictable offenses[b]	M: 12.3 F: 1.9		
Farrington (1981)	Random sample of 9,000 convicted persons, 1979; age distribution of first conviction and general population	None	Home Office	Convictions for indictable offenses[b,l]	M: 15.0 F: 3.0		

Study	Sample	Predictors	Source	Offense measure	Participation estimate[a]
London Home Office (1985)	Random sample of persons born in Great Britain in 1953, 1958, and 1963; age distribution at first conviction	None	Home Office Statistical Department	Convictions for standard list offenses[m]	1953: M: 16.6 F: 2.6 1958: M: 17.0 F: 2.9 1963: M: 15.9 F: 3.1
Douglas, Ross, and Simpson (1968); Wadsworth (1979)	1946 birth cohort of 5,011 males and females residing in Britain at age 8	Social class, family structure, school behavior	Police and juvenile court records	Convictions or police cautions for indictable offenses[n]	M: 14.6 F: 2.0
Farrington (1983a)	1953-1954 London birth cohort, 411 males	Family income, class, and size, criminality, I.Q., achievement, personality, truancy, delinquent peers, antisocial behavior	London Criminal Records Office	Convictions for indictable offenses	25.7
Ouston (1984)	1959-1960 London inner city birth cohort, 2,352 residents followed up to 1978	Social class, school behavior, IQ	Police and juvenile court records	Convictions or police cautions for any offense	M: 29.0 F: 6.0
Miller et al. (1974)	Newcastle, England, 1947 birth cohort, 763 youths followed up to 1965	Family structure, school behavior, individual characteristics	Juvenile court records	Court appearances for range of offenses, including traffic	M: 28.0 F: 5.6

[a] Participation estimates refer to all sample members (T) and, when possible, are broken down by race (W, white; B, black), and sex (M, male; F, female).
[b] Other ages available in published data.
[c] The Sellin-Wolfgang (S-W) measures are described in Sellin and Wolfgang (1964).
[d] Adjusted to remove contacts for suspicious behavior, for investigation, or for information (L. W. Shannon, 1985, personal communication).
[e] Discrepancy among published values, probably as a result of record updates.
[f] ADC clients are children born to mothers in welfare programs. (ADC = Aid to Dependent Children).
[g] Corrected values by Gordon and Gleser (1974).
[h] Adjusted values by Gordon (1976), which assumes white/black population ratio and offending incidence identical for first and subsequent offenses.
[i] The exact age was 17.5 years.
[j] Interpolated using race composition for lifetime participation.
[k] Approximately equivalent to U.S. felonies, misdemeanors, and serious motor vehicle offenses.
[l] Interpolated from other age break-points.
[m] Includes indictable offenses and some other nontraffic offenses.
[n] The exact follow-up age was 17.

of blacks, among whom participation is greater. Similarly, when only UCR index offenses were considered, B_{18} remained virtually the same among whites (8.2 to 8.9) and among blacks (26.8 to 26.0), but this resulted in an increase in B_{18} for such crimes for all males (13.6 to 17.9) because of the changes in the racial composition of Philadelphia. Across the two cohorts, B_{18} for *non-index* offenses declined for both races separately and for the male population as a whole, which suggests greater police attention to the more serious index offenses.

The data for females in the 1958 Philadelphia cohort are based on a sample of 14,000, which is by far the largest group of U.S females for which data on individual criminal behavior are available. For the females in the 1958 cohort, B_{18} was about 14 percent for a nontraffic offense. The participation data for females were also differentiated by race: B_{18} was twice as high among black (18.5) as among white females (9.2). When data on UCR index and non-index offenses for all females were used, B_{18} for index offenses (4.0) was about one-third of that for all offenses, and B_{18} for non-index offenses (12.1) was slightly below the level for nontraffic offenses.

Because the records of police contact are limited to contacts occurring in Philadelphia, the reported estimates should be considered as reasonable lower bounds. The empirical significance of arrests elsewhere is probably fairly small at age 18, but doubtless increases as a cohort ages, moves, and travels in connection with military service.

Other U.S. Longitudinal Studies

In a series of longitudinal studies, Shannon (1982a) and colleagues followed cohorts of males and females born in Racine, Wisconsin, in 1942, 1949, and 1955 through ages 32, 25, and 21, respectively. In all three cohorts, B_{18} among males, based on recorded police contacts, was high (41.0 percent in cohort I, 47.3 percent in cohort II, and 44.1 percent in cohort III) compared with other similar studies. These high levels (see Table 1) are probably due to the fact that considerable emphasis was placed on

recording police contacts for very minor infractions of the law, including status offenses (Shannon, 1985, personal communication).

In a multigenerational study, Robins and colleagues analyzed the arrest histories of 223 black males born between 1930 and 1934, who were selected from St. Louis elementary school records, and 145 of their offspring who had attained age 18 by 1974 (Robins, West, and Herjanic, 1975; Robins and Wish, 1977). On the basis of arrests for any crime, B_{18} was 38.1 in the original sample of males and 31.4 and 13.6 for males and females, respectively, among their offspring. Criminal participation among both male samples and the female sample was slightly lower than the estimates among black males and females in the Philadelphia cohorts, despite the narrower focus in Robins's study on juvenile court referrals.

Another group tracked in a prospective longitudinal study is a group of 506 males born between 1925 and 1934 in Massachusetts and identified by school, church, or other agency as either "difficult" or "average" (McCord and McCord, 1959; McCord, 1978). Half the sample members were randomly assigned to the Cambridge-Somerville youth study, which provided counseling on a fairly regular basis to these youths between the ages of 5 and 13. The other half of the group was not counseled as part of the program. The primary intent of the longitudinal follow-up was to establish whether the counseling had reduced criminal behavior, other deviance, and other problems as the sample aged. Records of the group were updated when they were in their 30s and again around 1978, when the subjects were between 41 and 50 years old. This study differs from other U.S. longitudinal studies in that it relied on convictions rather than arrests as the indicator of participation. The similarity of the conviction-based Cambridge-Somerville estimates (26.1 percent for juvenile offenses) to other arrest-based estimates in Table 1 indicates the high-risk nature of the Cambridge-Somerville sample.

Palmore and Hammond (1964) analyzed police and juvenile court records through

1963 for a sample of 319 males and females born during 1942–1944 and whose mothers received Aid for Dependent Children during 1950 in New Haven, Connecticut. Using a criterion of "known to police or juvenile court," they computed estimates of B_{18} for this high-risk sample, 56.0 for males and 15.4 for females. The value for males substantially exceeds all other estimates, including those of Shannon, which are based on a broad criterion measure. The black-white differential for males is far less pronounced in Palmore and Hammond's high-risk sample than in more representative urban samples, such as the Philadelphia cohorts, but the race differentials for females are actually greater than those in Philadelphia cohort II.

In 1964, the same year that Wolfgang and his colleagues began their research, Polk and colleagues (Polk, Frease, and Richmond, 1974; Polk et al., 1981) began tracking a cohort of 1,227 male high school sophomores in Marion County, Oregon, the county that includes Salem. Because the county's population is nearly all white, it is reasonable to compare their estimate of B_{18} in Marion County, 25.0, with the estimate among whites in Wolfgang and colleagues' cohort I, 28.7, and cohort II, 22.7. Gordon (1976:249) described the consistency of these numbers as "a further indication that the rate structure for white populations remains practically invariant over a wide range of the urban-rural continuum—and consequently over a wide range of types of places." The Marion County sample apparently excludes youths who dropped out of high school before the sophomore year. While such dropouts are fairly rare, their participation in criminal activity would be expected to be relatively high. For this reason, and because some sample members may not be recognized as offenders because their crimes occurred in other jurisdictions, the figures of Polk and colleagues are best treated as a lower bound.

U.S. Life-Table Analyses

In addition to the 1957 participation estimates he developed (discussed earlier), T.

Monahan (1960) estimated B_{18} for other years as well, using the life-table approach. On the basis of published Philadelphia Juvenile Court statistics, Monahan computed distributions of age at the first juvenile court appearance for any offense (including a negligible proportion of traffic offenses) for the year 1941 and for the entire period 1949–1954. By cumulating these distributions of initiation rates, he computed B_{18} for those years. (Data on other ages are available in the original source.) As shown in Table 1, Monahan's estimates are quite stable considering the span of time covered by his research. For males, B_{18} was computed to be 17.1 in 1941 and 22.3 in the period 1949–1954. These estimates are about four times the participation rates for females, 3.9 in 1941 and 6.0 in 1949–1954. Monahan also reported substantial participation differentials by race: B_{18} among black males exceeded B_{18} among white males by a ratio of about 3 to 1 in 1941 and by about 2.5 to 1 in 1949–1954. Among females, black participation exceeded white participation by a ratio of about 4 to 1 in 1941 and 5 to 1 in 1949–1954.

It was later discovered by Gordon and Gleser (1974) that because of an error in his computational formula, Monahan's results were underestimates of B_{18}. Monahan had correctly computed the initiation rate at each age, but in computing B_{18} he had treated the initiation rates as if they were conditional hazard rates. Gordon and Gleser's results, correcting for this error, also appear in Table 1. Only among black males does the correction change the results by more than one percentage point, raising B_{18} from 40.8 percent to 50.9 percent.

Gordon (1976:215) has noted that for blacks, Wolfgang's arrest-based participation measure for the 1945 birth cohort is nearly identical to Monahan's measure (corrected) for 1949–1954, based on a narrower criterion of court referrals—about 50 percent. For whites, however, the corrected court-based measure (17.9 percent) is only about 60 percent of the arrest-based measure. If the referral- and arrest-based statistics for blacks actually referred to the same population and incidents, they would be expected to follow the pattern observed for whites, since not all arrests lead to court referrals. Three possible explanations have been suggested by Gordon (1976:237–240, 276). First, court referrals can be made by parents, schools, and other parties in addition to police, and referrals from these sources may occur more frequently for blacks than for whites. Second, Wolfgang's data include only boys born in 1945 who resided in Philadelphia throughout the period 1955–1962, at a time when whites were overrepresented among out-migrants and blacks were overrepresented among in-migrants. Gordon suggested that if participation rates were lower for out-migrating whites than for nonmigrating whites, and higher for in-migrating blacks than for nonmigrating blacks, then the apparent inconsistency between the analyses of Monahan and Wolfgang would be diminished; however, he acknowledged a lack of supporting evidence for these conjectures. A third possibility is that a higher percentage of black arrests may lead to court referral, either because black arrestees' alleged crimes are more serious or because arresting officers are more likely to refer blacks than whites regardless of the alleged offense (Gordon, 1976:239). Additional data would be needed to test these hypotheses.

Ball, Ross, and Simpson (1964), using juvenile court referral data from Fayette County, Kentucky, computed age-specific criminal participation for the year 1960, using the life-table approach. The data include referrals for a broad range of crimes, but only "serious or unusual" traffic offenses. Age-specific initiation rates were cumulated to measure B_{12}, B_{16}, and B_{18} for males and females. As shown in Table 1, their results for B_{18}, 20.7 for males and 5.2 for females, are slightly lower than Monahan's corrected estimates. Later, Gordon (1976) used other data reported by Ball and colleagues to compute B_{18} separately for white males (16.8), black males (43.1), white females (4.2), and black females (10.8). Gordon's estimates are only approximate since they rely on assumptions that racial composition is identical among first offenders and recidivists.

Analyses of Multiple Data Bases

Three U.S. studies computed estimates of B_{18} in the course of projecting national arrest volumes (Christensen, 1967; Belkin, Blumstein, and Glass, 1973; Blumstein and Graddy, 1982). Because no single data base includes age-specific initiation rates for the entire age range spanning both juvenile and adult offenders, each of these studies involves the merging of data from multiple sources.

Christensen combined Washington, D.C., and Philadelphia County Court statistics to compute both age-specific and lifetime participation estimates. As shown in Table 1, his estimate of participation by age 17½ was 25.1 for males and 6.5 for females, based on UCR Part I (index) and Part II (non-index) offenses.

Six years later, Belkin, Blumstein, and Glass (1973) revised the Christensen estimates by replacing his Philadelphia County Court statistics on age-specific initiation rates up to age 18 with the newly available data from Wolfgang's Philadelphia cohort I, discussed earlier. As shown in Table 1, the new data led to higher B_{18} estimates for both males (34.0 instead of 25.1) and females (8.0 instead of 6.5) relative to the Christensen estimates.

Later, Blumstein and Graddy (1982) combined the Philadelphia cohort I data on juveniles with age-specific first-arrest rates for adult male offenders active in the District of Columbia in 1973. With the combined data set, age-specific participation rates were computed separately for white and black males. Because they focused on only arrests for index offenses, their estimates of B_{18} are smaller than those for males in the U.S. studies previously discussed: 8.2 for white males and 26.9 for black males.

British Studies

In a British study, Little (1965) was apparently the first to note that life-table participation estimates differ analytically from age-specific estimates for any single cohort and that the empirical differences will be large if criminal participation is steadily increasing or decreasing in successive cohorts. Using longitudinal data on a 1942 London birth cohort, Little reported participation based on arrest for an "indictable offense" (roughly equivalent to U.S. felonies, misdemeanors, and serious traffic offenses) of 7.8 percent by age 18, the age attained by the cohort in 1960. This estimate exceeds his 1952 life-table estimate of 6.8 percent, but is exceeded by the 1962 life-table estimate of 9.6 percent (see Table 1) because crime was increasing throughout Britain generally during the 1952–1962 period.

Although Little did not report separate participation estimates for males and females, he noted that approximately 90 percent of persons arrested during the period were male. Applying the life-table approach to 1962 data, he reported B_{18} separately for males and females convicted of an indictable offense (12.3 and 1.9, respectively). Using the same method, Farrington (1981) reported a further increase in participation 17 years later, as measured by conviction for an indictable offense in 1979. Farrington estimated B_{18} at about 15.0 for males and 3.0 for females.

On the basis of retrospective searches of court records, the London Home Office (1985) Statistical Department reported the findings from a series of cohort studies of the convictions of persons born during four selected weeks of 1953, 1958, and 1963. Participation estimates for persons convicted of "standard list" offenses (slightly broader than indictable offenses) are consistent with Farrington's projections using the life-table method. Over the 10-year period, B_{18} for males was 16.6, 17.0, and 15.9, respectively, for the three cohorts—a slight decline in the 1963 cohort. For females, estimates increased slightly across the three cohorts: 2.6, 2.9, and 3.1.

Several British longitudinal studies have provided estimates of participation. The first (Douglas, Ross, and Simpson, 1968; see also Wadsworth, 1979), known as the National Survey, reported that 14.6 percent of males and 2.0 percent of females were convicted or cautioned by the police for at least one indictable offense by age 17. The sam-

ple is a 1946 cohort of 5,011 persons born in England, Wales, or Scotland. The cohort was 16 years old in 1962, the reference year for the Little (1965) estimate. The National Survey estimate for males is quite consistent with Little's life-table estimate (12.3), as well as with Farrington's (1981) life-table estimate for 1979 (15.0).

A high-risk sample of 411 London males born in 1953–1954 and residing in a working-class area of London was the subject of the Cambridge Study in Delinquent Development. Data collection for this study began in 1961–1962; results are found in at least five major publications (see West, 1969, 1982; West and Farrington, 1973, 1977; Farrington, 1983a), as well as numerous others. For the Cambridge study the domain of crime was limited to convictions for "criminal offenses," defined as indictable offenses more serious than traffic, drunkenness, and common assault. Despite this more restrictive definition, which apparently excludes police cautions, the higher estimate of participation relative to the National Survey, 25.7 by age 18, reflects the high-risk nature of this group.

Another high-risk sample (Ouston, 1984) from London was born in 1959–1960, 6 years later than Farrington's sample and 14 years later than the National Survey's 1946 birth cohort. As part of a comparative study of 12 inner-London schools, data on teacher ratings of behavior, school performance, and criminal behavior were collected on 2,352 males and females. Criminal records were searched in 1978, when the sample was 17 years old, for information on all official police cautions or juvenile court convictions. As shown in Table 1, criminal participation among males in this sample (29.0) was slightly higher than in the Cambridge study data (Farrington, 1983a).

Finally, in another longitudinal British study (Miller et al., 1974), 763 children born in Newcastle in 1947 were followed from birth to age 22, and criminal records of court appearances for a broad range of offenses were collected up to age 18.5. Data were also gathered on family structure, school performance, and individual characteristics. Estimates of participation (28.0 for males, and 5.6 for females) are consistent with the findings of the British longitudinal studies by Farrington and Ouston, but considerably higher than those of the National Survey (whose cohort was born only 1 year later) and the Home Office estimates for the 1953, 1958, and 1963 cohorts. The broader definition of criminal involvement in the Miller et al. study, that study's urban sample, and the wider geographical coverage of both the National Survey (England, Scotland, and Wales) and the London Home Office estimates probably account for the differences.

In all these British studies, the ratio of male-to-female participation estimates appears greater than that in U.S. studies. The average ratio for the eight male/female comparisons in Table 1 is about 6:1. The variation in U.S. and British male/female ratios is discussed in a later section on male and female differences in participation.

Criminal Participation by Older Ages, Including Lifetime

Cumulative participation has also been estimated for ages beyond 18 years. When the cutoff age exceeds 45 years, the estimate is often referred to as a cumulative "lifetime" participation, B_L, estimate, since first arrests (and even first convictions) are rare after age 45 (see Blumstein and Graddy, 1982). A review of the literature revealed 16 studies from which estimates of participation beyond age 18 could be calculated, including 7 studies that provide estimates of B_L (see Table 2).

U.S. Arrest Projections

Estimating cumulative participation through ages greater than 18 requires records of both juvenile and adult arrests. In the United States, assembling the necessary records is complicated by the fact that juvenile and adult arrest histories are usually stored in separate repositories. For several prospective longitudinal follow-ups of selected samples, the necessary data were compiled after the researchers obtained permission from the appropriate juvenile and criminal justice agencies. But researchers using life-table approaches have had to compute their estimates by merging juvenile arrest data from one sample with adult arrest data from another. These procedures, in turn, have necessitated various adjustments as part of the estimation process.

Christensen (1967) projected B_L, based on arrests for nontraffic offenses, at 50.0 for all U.S. males and 12.0 for all U.S. females. These figures reflect (1) direct estimates for city areas, based on the Philadelphia Juvenile Court data and District of Columbia data on age-specific first-arrest rates, and (2) projections for suburban and rural areas, based on aggregate arrest and age-sex-race data. Lifetime participation by race was reported separately by Christensen for the three geographic areas (urban, suburban, rural). In calculating an overall U.S. rate, we used a lower urban estimate for black males (80.0) than that reported by Christensen (p. 224) to account for some of the problems he raised with regard to the validity of his estimate. Christensen reported higher overall estimates of B_L for black males (68.3) and females (19.7) than for white males (46.9) and females (10.9). According to the Christensen estimates reported in Tables 1 and 2, about half the lifetime risk of offending is experienced by age 18 for males, and two-thirds for females. However, the black/white ratios from his data are much smaller than those estimated earlier by Monahan (1960) and Gordon (1976).

Christensen's estimates of B_L were computed with some adjustments for sex and race survival differentials, but they were based on fairly sparse first-arrest data at higher ages. Also, Christensen's statistics on rates of first-arrest beyond age 18 were based on a special study of convicted felons, rather than all arrestees, in the District of Columbia (see Christensen, 1967). Christensen noted that convicted felons as a group are likely to have first arrests at younger ages than arrestees generally, which would tend to bias his estimates upward in the early adult age range. Nevertheless, Christensen's approximations are credible, and the effect of this bias should be negligible at older ages, when first arrests are unlikely to occur.

Revised national estimates of B_L were developed by Belkin, Blumstein, and Glass (1973). They generally followed Christensen's approach, but obtained data on age-specific first-arrest rates from Philadelphia cohort I to substitute for the Philadelphia Juvenile Court data. As shown in Table 2, this change increased the estimated B_L—based on nontraffic arrests—for both males (from 50.0 to 60.0 percent) and females (12.0 to 16.0 percent) relative to the Christensen estimates.

The most recent national estimates of B_L focus on only serious offenses and use more reliable data at older ages. With arrests for index offenses as the criterion, Blumstein and Graddy's (1982) estimates of B_L are 14.6 for white males, 52.0 for black males, and 22.8 for all males. Consistent with Christensen and Belkin and colleagues, about half the risk of arrest—even for serious offenses—is incurred by age 18 for both races. All three studies relied on similar data up to age 18, but Blumstein and Graddy's data covering arrests after age 30 omit arrests before age 18. Therefore, as they note, the estimates beyond age 30 would be biased upward because of persons who were arrested as juveniles but not arrested again until some age beyond 30. Because the number of such individuals is likely to be small, this bias is not thought to be large.

U.S. Longitudinal Studies

One of the oldest groups of subjects of a prospective longitudinal study is a group of 473 male and female children treated at a child guidance clinic between 1924 and 1929 (Robins, 1966). Police arrest records were searched through age 43 in all locations where subjects were found to have resided. For the subjects who were interviewed, officially recorded criminal activity was studied in relation to their childhood antisocial behavior, family conditions, and antisocial behavior among their family members.[5] Discussion of those relationships is deferred to a later section. As a by-product, however, this study produced estimates of B_L based on official arrest data. As shown in Table 2, B_L among former male patients (60.0) is much higher than the other estimates even though juvenile arrests are excluded. For "major" crimes (apparently the FBI's index offenses), participation was 36.0 among males and 5.0 among females, which is higher than B_{18} for index offenses among white males and females in the Philadelphia cohort data. The high-risk nature of this sample accounts for much of this variation; Robins's definition of arrest was also slightly broader than that of many others.

The Cambridge-Somerville youth study (McCord, 1979) generated estimates of B_L for treatment and control groups. Records for the entire sample were updated in 1978, when the subjects were between 41 and 50 years old. This study differs from the other studies of B_L in the United States because it relied on records of convictions rather than records of arrests. For the entire sample, McCord (1981) estimated B_L at 30.2 percent, based on convictions as adults for serious offenses. Because McCord's sample was predominantly white, the Blumstein and Graddy estimate of B_L among white males, based on index offenses (14.6), is the most comparable, and McCord's estimate is twice that, which indicates the high-risk nature of her sample.

In a separate publication, McCord (1979) reported more complete data on B_L, including juvenile convictions, but for only 201 males from the treatment sample. This estimate of B_L is only slightly higher (35.3); separate estimates of B_L for property offenses (26.4) and personal offenses (16.9) were also reported.

Shannon's study of three birth cohorts in Racine, Wisconsin (see Table 1 and related discussion), generated estimates of participation by ages 20 to 30. The proportion of

---

[5]In the update interview of the child guidance patients, Robins and Lewis (1966) obtained the names of 67 sons of sample subjects who had attained age 18 by 1960. Their police records were used to estimate B_{18}, which was reported as 24.5 for the patients' sons—comparable to the estimate for white males reported in Philadelphia cohorts I and II.

TABLE A-2 Estimates of Criminal Participation by Older Ages, Including Lifetime Participation

Reference	Nature of Data	Correlates Examined	Source (official records, self-reports)	Definition of Crime, Concept Reported or Inferred	Participation Estimates[a] (percent)		
					T	W	B
I. U.S. Studies							
Christensen (1967)	Philadelphia County Court statistics on first juvenile referral; U.S. data on total arrests and mortality	Rural, urban, suburban differences	Philadelphia County Court Annual Report, 1965 Uniform Crime Reports; 1966 Statistical Abstract	Arrests for nontraffic offenses, B_L	M: 50.0 F: 12.0	46.9 10.9	68.3 19.7
Belkin, Blumstein and Glass (1973)	Statistics on age-specific first-arrest rates	None	Philadelphia cohort I (see Table 1) (ages 1-18); Christensen (1967) (age 19+)	Arrests for nontraffic offenses, B_L	M: 60.0 F: 16.0		
Blumstein and Graddy (1982)	Statistics on age-specific first-arrest rates for males	None	Philadelphia cohort I (see Table 1) (ages 1-30) Random sample of 4,811 D.C. arrest histories of of active offenders (age 31+)	Arrests for FBI index offenses, B_L	22.8	14.6	52.0
Robins (1966)	473 St. Louis child guidance patients treated 1924-1929	Childhood behavior, family conditions, antisocial family members, psychiatric diagnosis	Police records through age 43[b]	Arrests for any offense by age 43[c] Arrests for FBI Part I offenses by age 43[c]	M: 60.0 F: 30.0 M: 36.0 F: 5.0		
McCord (1981)	506 males born in 1925-1934; follow-ups in 1939, at age 30, and at 41-50 years	Family influences, treatment variables	Official records from 1939-1978[b]	Convictions for serious offenses, B by ages 41-50	30.2[d]		

McCord (1979)	253 males born in 1925-1934 and treated in Cambridge youth study; follow-up (N = 201) at age 41-50	Family influences, social class, treatment variables	Official records from 1939-1978	Adult and juvenile court convictions, $\underline{B}$ by ages 41-50	
				Serious offenses	35.3
				Property offenses	26.4
				Personal offenses	16.9
Shannon (1982a)	Racine, Wis., cohort I: 1942 birth cohort of 1,352 residents followed up to 1974	Delinquency, type of neighborhood	Police records	Recorded police contact,$\underline{e}$ $\underline{B}$ by age 33 (males and females)	68.0
				Contact for nontraffic offenses, $\underline{B}$ by age 33	M: 59.3 F: 17.7
				Contact for felonies against persons, $\underline{B}$ by age 33	M: 5.1 F: 1.8
	Racine, Wis., cohort II: 1949 birth cohort of 2,099 residents followed up to 1974	Delinquency, type of neighborhood	Police records	Recorded police contact,$\underline{e}$ $\underline{B}$ by age 26 (males and females)	69.0
				Contact for nontraffic offenses, $\underline{B}$ by age 25	M: 56.9 F: 25.1
				Contact for felonies against persons, $\underline{B}$ by age 26	M: 5.7 F: 2.9
	Racine, Wis., cohort III: 1955 birth cohort of 2,676 residents followed up to 1977	Delinquency, type of neighborhood	Police records	Recorded police contact,$\underline{e}$ $\underline{B}$ by age 22 (males and females)	59.1
				Contact for nontraffic offenses, $\underline{B}$ by age 22	M: 53.1 F: 28.9
				Contact for felonies against persons, $\underline{B}$ by age 22	M: 12.7 F: 4.6
Wolfgang (1977)	974 randomly selected males from Philadelphia cohort I: 1945 birth cohort of 9,945 male residents	Delinquency/crime	Recorded police contacts	All nontraffic offenses including status, $\underline{B}$ by age 30	47.3

TABLE A-2 Continued

Reference	Nature of Data	Correlates Examined	Source (official records, self-reports)	Definition of Crime, Concept Reported or Inferred	Participation Estimates (percent)
II. Foreign Studies					
Farrington (1981)	Random sample of 9,000 convicted persons, 1979; age distribution at first conviction; age distribution of general population, 1977	None	Home Office criminal statistics	Convictions for indictable offenses[f], B_L	M: 43.6 F: 14.7
Wadsworth (1979)	1949 birth cohort of 5,011 alive and in Britain at time of study and who were residents at age 8	Social class, family structure, family life, school behavior, personality assessments	Official court and police records through 1966	Convictions or police cautions for indictable offenses, B by age 21[g]	M: 17.9 F: 2.5
London Home Office (1985)	Random sample of persons born in Great Britain in 1953 and 1958. Age distribution at first conviction	None	Home Office Statistical Department	Convictions for standard list offenses[h] B by age 25 (1953) B by age 21 (1953) B by age 21 (1958)	M̲ — F̲ 28.3 — 5.3 23.3 — 3.9 24.2 — 4.7
Farrington (1983a)	411 London males born in 1953-1954	Antisocial behavior, family influence, social class	London Criminal Records Office	Convictions for indictable offenses B by age 21 B by age 25	31.9 33.9
Mitchell and Rosa (1981)	642 British male youths aged 5-15 in 1961	Parent and teacher reports of behavior	Juvenile and adult court conviction records through 1976	Convictions for specific offenses, B by age 25 Theft Violence All crimes	11.2 2.3 14.3

			Criminal convictions,[e] $\underline{B}$ by ages 30-44		15.9

Criminal convictions, minor convictions,[i] $\underline{B}$ by ages 30-44

	Criminal	Minor
Adoptees	16.2	34.4
Controls	8.8	28.1
Adoptive fathers	12.9	19.7
Biological fathers	36.4	15.9
Controls' fathers	11.4	19.0

Criminal convictions,[k] approximate $\underline{B}_L$

	M	F
Adoptees	15.9	2.8
Adoptive fathers/mothers	6.2	1.9
Biological fathers/mothers	28.6	8.9
All	15.9	4.7

Hutchings and Mednick (1975) — 662 male adoptees born in Copenhagen, 1/1/27-12/31/41; 1,145 male adoptees and 1,145 controls; 1,119 adoptive and 971 biological fathers of adoptees — Criminality in adoptive and biological parents — Official records of court convictions before 1971

Mednick, Gabrielli, and Hutchings (1984) — 14,427 adoptees in 1927-1947, their biological and adoptive parents[j] (N = 64,283) — Criminality in adoptive and biological parents — Official records

NOTE: $\underline{B}_L$ = lifetime participation; $\underline{B}$ = measures based on arrests (busts).

[a] Participation estimates refer to all sample members and are broken down by sex (M, male; F, female) and, in the studies by Christensen (1967) and Blumstein and Graddy (1982), by race (W, white; B, black).

[b] Excludes juvenile offenses.

[c] Excludes first arrests after average age 43.

[d] Interpreted from bar graphs.

[e] Includes contact for suspicious behavior, for investigation or information, and for traffic offenses.

[f] Approximately equivalent to U.S. felonies, misdemeanors, and serious traffic offenses.

[g] Precisely age 20 years, 10 months.

[h] Includes indictable offenses and some other nontraffic offenses.

[i] "Summary" offenses, minor offenses such as vagrancy, disorderly conduct, but not traffic offenses.

[j] Presumably Danish, though not stated.

[k] Neither domain of "crime" nor cutoff of age/date for record search was reported.

subjects with recorded police contacts for nontraffic offenses was fairly stable across the cohorts: from 53 to 59 percent of the male subjects had at least one nontraffic police contact. Shannon's estimates of participation levels, based on felony arrests by the age at data collection cutoff, rose substantially over time, from 5.1 percent for males in cohort I by age 33 to 5.7 for males in cohort II by age 26, and to l2.7 for males in cohort III at only 22. Shannon (1982a:23) noted that this change may reflect policy changes on the part of the Racine police, especially for juveniles, as the department focused more closely on serious offenses.

In 1977, Wolfgang published estimates of criminal participation for all nontraffic offenses through age 30, based on follow-up of a 10 percent random sample of Philadelphia cohort I. The analysis of the follow-up data indicates that, by age 30, participation among all males had reached 47.3 percent.

Foreign Studies

Four of the British studies that generated estimates of B_{18} (see Table 1) also provided estimates of participation by older ages, including one projection of B_L in England. As shown in Table 2, Farrington (1981), using the life-table method for estimating participation, reported B_L at 43.6 for males and 14.7 for females, based on convictions for indictable offenses. Because a high percentage of all arrests in England end in conviction, Farrington's projections are comparable to the arrest-based estimates of Belkin, Blumstein, and Glass (1973) (60.0 for males and 16.0 for females) and are quite similar.

Two other studies (Wadsworth, 1979; London Home Office, 1985) reported participation estimates by age 21, based on longitudinal studies of individuals. In cohorts of individuals born in 1946 (Wadsworth, 1979), 1953, and 1958 (London Home Office, 1985), estimates of B_{21} for males were 14.6, 23.3, and 24.2, respectively. Not surprisingly, in the 12-year time span, participation among males increased by about one-third. The estimates of B_{21} among fe-

males—2.0, 3.9, and 4.7 in the same time period—showed a more dramatic increase of over 50 percent from 1946 to 1958. However, this percentage increase is somewhat misleading because of the low rates of participation by females.

Farrington (1983a) reported B_{21} for the Cambridge study—an urban working-class sample of 411 males (born between 1953 and 1954)—to be 31.9 percent. Despite his slightly narrower definition of conviction (indictable offenses only), this level of participation is considerably higher than the 1953 cohort estimate (23.3) published by the London Home Office Statistical Department. However, the three cohorts studied by the Home Office included children born throughout England, Scotland, and Wales, whereas the Cambridge study's urban sample should be considered relatively high risk. By age 25, participation in the Cambridge sample had increased to 33.9, which is about 20 percent higher than the national estimate for the 1953 cohort (28.3).

In another English study, Mitchell and Rosa (1981) computed crime-specific participation rates for 642 British boys selected in 1961 and followed for 15 years, to an average age of 25. Based on convictions for all offenses, B_{25} was 14.3, which is less than half that reported by Farrington for his London sample at the same age. The discrepancy no doubt reflects the high-risk nature of Farrington's working-class sample.

Several longitudinal studies of adopted Danish children have yielded participation estimates as a by-product of investigations of genetic causes of criminality. The first of these (Hutchings and Mednick, 1975) reported participation estimates based on convictions for criminal offenses (*statsadvokatsager*) among 662 male children born in Copenhagen between 1927 and 1941 and adopted shortly after birth. Among the adopted children, B_L was reported to be only 15.9. All members of the sample were at least 30 years old when the record search and tabulation were completed. Although the domain of criminal convictions in Denmark is said to be equivalent to the domain of convictions for indictable offenses in Great Britain, B_L for this cohort is lower than B_{21} estimated from the National Survey in Britain.

Hutchings and Mednick also reported B_L based on both criminal offenses and minor offenses (*politisager*) for 1,145 adopted males, 1,145 nonadopted controls (matched on age, father's occupation, and residence), the adoptive and biological fathers of the adopted children, and the fathers of the controls. As shown in Table 2, the estimate of 16.2 for the adopted children was about double the estimate for the nonadopted control sample (8.8). More than one-third of the biological fathers of adoptees had records of serious criminal conviction, a figure that becomes even more startling when one notices that of all five groups in the sample the biological fathers had the lowest participation rate for minor convictions (15.9). Considering all the studies reviewed here, only this group—biological fathers of the adopted youths—seems to break the general rule that criminal participation for less serious crimes usually exceeds that for more serious crimes.

Mednick, Gabrielli, and Hutchings (1984) recently reported new criminal participation statistics based on the entire data base of 14,427 adoptees between 1927 and 1947, together with their biological and adoptive parents. Thus, the analysis is based on 64,283 subjects, the largest sample of any study reviewed here. However, neither the domain of "crime" nor the cutoff age or date for the search of official court records was reported. As in the smaller sample, biological fathers of male adoptees had a high rate of participation based on criminal convictions (28.6); for the adoptees themselves, B_L was 15.9, and for their adoptive fathers, B_L was 6.2. The same relative findings are reported for female adoptees and their biological and adoptive parents, but at lower absolute values. Combining parents and children, B_L was reported as 15.9 for males and 4.7 for females.

Criminal Participation by High School Age

Another category of participation estimates arises in studies of self-reported (D)

and officially recorded (B) offending in cross-section samples of high-school-age youths. Eleven studies report estimates of crime-specific D_{HS} and six studies provide estimates of B_{HS}, the latter based on either self-reported police contacts or searches of official records. These studies differ from prospective longitudinal studies in that criminal activity is observed retrospectively at the time of sample selection. Most of these studies also include a variety of ages within the sample. The latter characteristic makes it impossible to derive age-specific participation estimates. The studies are important, however, because of the crime-specific estimates they provide for persons of roughly high school age, although not necessarily for representative population subgroups. Results from the studies are summarized in Table 3.

Self-Report Studies

Short and Nye (1958; Nye, 1958) were some of the first researchers to use the self-report method to estimate participation rates. They reported D_{HS} for two samples, designated sample I (2,350 Washington high school students) and sample II (515 rural midwestern high school students). In both samples D_{HS} among males was higher for assault (13.9, 15.7) and auto theft (14.8, 11.2) than for grand theft (theft of items worth more than $50—5.0, 3.5). Robbery participation was self-reported by 6.3 percent of the rural sample. For these four serious crime types, females were much more likely to be involved in auto theft or assault (about 5 percent) than robbery or grand theft (1–2 percent).[6] For both males

---

[6]Estimates of self-reported participation in offending for specific crime types are highly contingent on how questions are worded. In reviewing studies that report participation estimates based on self-reports, we included only those estimates for serious crime types—principally assault, auto theft, burglary, robbery, and grand theft (at least $50). We tried to separate "joyriding" from auto theft and "fighting" from assault, but often the authors did not provide enough information (e.g., the exact wording) to be able to distinguish participation estimates for serious crimes from those for minor crimes. For

and females, D_{HS} was not markedly different across the two samples, which may reflect a relatively low degree of urbanization among the Washington sample.

After the work of Short and Nye was published, self-report studies of criminal activity among youths flooded the research literature. Most of them were excluded from this review because participation estimates were not derivable from the published reports. Five studies, however, reported participation estimates for serious crimes, which appear in Table 3.

In a reanalysis of data from a large study carried out in California by Hirschi (1969), Jensen and Eve (1976) calculated crime-specific estimates of D_{HS}, which were not reported by Hirschi. This study is one of only two studies that include self-reported estimates of D for whites and blacks (the other is Hindelang, Hirschi, and Weis, 1981). For grand theft, D_{HS} in the Jensen and Eve reanalysis differs markedly between white males (6.0) and black males (12.0), but the estimates for auto theft do not differ by race (11.0, 13.0). The same pattern exists for females, although the low rates of participation for grand theft among females of both races may make such comparisons unreliable. About 4 percent of the females admitted to ever committing an auto theft, but less than 2 percent admitted to theft of items worth at least $50.

Three similar studies also reported crime-specific estimates of D_{HS} for males and females (Kratcoski and Kratcoski, 1975; Cernkovich and Giordano, 1979; Figueira-McDonough, Barton, and Sarri, 1981). For grand theft, the three estimates vary widely, despite consistent definitions of this offense across the studies. Even if participation estimates for the two large theft categories

($50–$500 and $500+) are combined in the study by Figueira-McDonough and her associates (which is likely an overestimate because most offenders committing large thefts have probably also committed smaller ones), the estimates for males (16.0, 12.7, 9.4) are not easily reconciled. Differences in samples may account for some of this variation. The location of the Figueira-McDonough study was less urban than that of Cernkovich and Giordano. The highest estimate (16 percent) is from the oldest study (Kratcoski and Kratcoski, 1975), but the least is known about the nature of that sample; possibly their "theft 50+" category captured participation in auto theft. The estimates of participation in grand theft for females show less variation (3.0, 4.6, 1.4). Participation among males in auto theft (5.5, 10.7) and robbery (17.0, 5.0) also varied considerably across studies; differences in question wording and respondent interpretation are likely explanations.

Self-reported participation by males in burglary was much more consistent in all three studies (20.0, 16.5, 21.2). Also, self-reported involvement in assault is identical in Cernkovich and Giordano and Figueira-McDonough and colleagues (11.6) despite the differences in samples. Among females, participation estimates for burglary (3.0, 3.7, 4.5) are more consistent than those for assault (6.6, 3.9).

For a major study of the effect of alternative survey techniques on self-reported offending, Hindelang, Hirschi, and Weis (1981) interviewed 1,610 male and female Seattle high school students during the school year 1977–1978 and calculated crime-specific estimates of D_{HS}. In comparison with the Short and Nye results obtained more than 20 years earlier, only involvement in theft exceeding $50 showed a substantial increase among males, perhaps an artifact of inflation; the rate of auto theft among high school males appears to have declined. In comparison with the three studies just discussed, estimates of participation reported by Hindelang and colleagues are higher for grand theft, similar for auto theft, lower for robbery, slightly lower for burglary, and similar for assault.

example, in the Short and Nye (1958) study, the offense description of "used force to get money from another person" was serious enough to be categorized as robbery in Table 3, and "beat up on kids who hadn't done anything to you" is referred to as assault. It is also common for youths to exaggerate their deviant behavior, which may inflate self-reported estimates of participation (see Hindelang, Hirschi, and Weis, 1979; Elliott and Huizinga, 1983).

TABLE A-3 Cumulative Criminal Participation Rates in Cross-Section Samples of High-School-Age Youths

Reference	Nature of Sample	Correlates Examined	Source (official records, self-reports)	Definition of Crime, Concept Reported or Inferred	Participant Estimates (percent) Male		Female	
I. Self-Reports								
Short and Nye (1958)	Sample I: 2,350 Washington male and female high school students	Social class, family structure, parental behavior	Self-reports for specific crimes	D by high school age	I	II	I	II
				Theft $50+	5.0	3.5	1.3	2.0
				Robbery[a]	--	6.3	--	1.3
	Sample II: 250 male and 265 female rural midwestern high school students			Auto theft	14.8	11.2	4.5	5.4
				Assault	13.9	15.7	3.1	5.7
Jensen and Eve (1976)	Reanalysis of data from Richmond Youth Project	None reported	Self-reports for specific crimes	D by ages 13-18	W	B	W	B
				Theft $50+	6.0	12.0	1.0	2.0
				Auto theft	11.0	13.0	4.0	4.0
Kratcoski and Kratcoski (1975)	104 males and 144 females from three high schools, 11th and 12th grades	Social class	Self-reports for specific crimes	D by ages 16-18				
				Theft $50+	16.0		3.0	
				Burglary	20.0		3.0	
				Robbery	17.0		5.0	
Cernkovich and Giordano (1979)	822 high school students in two urban, midwestern schools	None reported	Self-reports for specific crimes	D by ages 15-18				
				Auto theft	5.5		1.1	
				Robbery	5.0		0.9	
				Theft $50+	12.7		4.6	
				Burglary	16.5		3.7	
				Aggravated assault	11.6		6.6	
Figueria-McDonough, Barton, and Sarri (1981)	1,735 male and female high school students, aged 15; from four areas in midwestern county, 1980	None reported	Self-reports for specific crimes	D by age 15				
				Burglary	21.2		4.5	
				Auto theft	10.7		2.8	
				Theft $50-500	6.0		1.0	
				Theft $500+	3.4		0.4	
				Aggravated assault	11.6		3.9	

TABLE A-3 Continued

Reference	Nature of Sample	Correlates Examined	Source (official records, self-reports)	Definition of Crime, Concept Reported or Inferred	Male W	Male B	Female W	Female B
Hindelang, Hirschi, and Weis (1981)	1,610 male and female Seattle high school students, 1977-1978	Social class, IQ, school performance	Self-reports for specific crimes	D by high school age				
				Theft $50+[b]	16.5	17.3	1.7	6.5
				Auto theft	9.7	7.3	0.8	1.7
				Burglary	16.8	12.9	4.9	4.3
				Aggravated assault	10.2	15.4	3.1	8.9
				Robbery	4.1	7.9	0.7	5.3
Porterfield (1946)	200 male and female Texas students entering college	None	Self-reports for specific crime types	Aggravated assault	3.0		1.0	
				Burglary	8.0		0.0	
Elliott and Huizinga (1984)	Five-wave panel of 1,725, national youth sample, 1976-1980	Drug use, peer groups, school progress, social class	Self-reports for specific crimes	D by age 17[c] (males and females)				
				Felony theft		28.6		
				Robbery		15.3		

II. Official Records

Reference	Nature of Sample	Correlates Examined	Source (official records, self-reports)	Definition of Crime, Concept Reported or Inferred	Male W	Male B	Female W	Female B
Reiss and Rhodes (1961)	9,238 white Tennessee school enrollees during 1957, ages 12-18 urban/suburban	IQ, father's occupation, school, social status	Juvenile court records, adjudicated delinquency	B by males, ages 12-18				
				All crimes[d]	5.1			
				Serious crimes	2.1			
Gold (1966)	522 male and female urban Michigan youths, including school dropouts	Social class	Juvenile court records, unspecified crimes	B by males, ages 13-16	11.0			
			Self-reports of police contact (unspecified crimes)	B by males, ages 13-16	16.5			
Hirschi (1969)	Richmond Youth Project: 3,605 7-12th graders in California, 1964	Social class, family structure, school attitudes	Police records; unspecified crimes, but broad definition	B by males, ages 13-18	26.0	53.0		
			Self-reports of police contacts	B by males, ages 13-18	34.0	42.0		

Study	Sample	Variable	Records/Measure	Measure type	Values
Williams and Gold (1972)	847 13-16-year-olds, national sample drawn in 1967	Social class	Police records; unspecified crimes	B by ages 13-16	6.0 ... 2.0
				(black males and females)	5.0
				(white males and females)	4.0
			Court records; unspecified crimes	B by ages 13-16 (males and females)	2.0
			Self-reports of police contact; unspecified crimes	B by ages 13-16	
				(black males and females)	21.0
				(white males and females)	22.0

					W	B	W	B
Hindelang, Hirschi, and Weis (1981)	(see above)	(see above)	Official police records	B by high school age	26.7	46.5	9.3	23.7
			Self-report of probation by juvenile court		8.7	18.8	2.1	9.3
			Self-report of police contact		16.8	21.2	5.4	9.8

Study	Sample	Variable	Records/Measure	Measure type	Values
Feldhusen, Thurston, and Benning (1973)	1,150 Wisconsin 3rd, 6th, and 9th graders selected in 1961	Teacher ratings of behavior	Police records, excluding traffic, through 1969	B by ages 17-23 (males and females)	42.5
			Juvenile court conviction records through 1969	B by ages 17-23 (males and females)	16.0 ... 14.3 ... 5.0

NOTE: D = participation measures based on committing crimes (doing crime); B = measures based on arrests (busts).

aData for robbery not reported for Sample 1.
bFigures reported by authors on p. 39 do not correspond with data in their Appendix B.
cBased on a constructed cohort from the original panel data; see Elliott and Huizinga (1984:Table 7).
dExcludes traffic incidents and truancy.

For many specific crime types, self-reported participation rates among males are nearly the same for blacks and whites, or slightly higher for whites. In Hindelang, Hirschi, and Weis, the rates for white and black males were approximately equal for theft exceeding $50 and shoplifting exceeding $50; this similarity is contrary to the findings of Jensen and Eve for a sample studied 15 years earlier. White males exceeded black males with respect to auto theft (again contrary to Jensen and Eve) and burglary, while blacks exceeded whites with respect to assault causing injury and robbery. For all crimes, participation among females of both races was lower than among males of either race.

In a cross-section survey of 200 male Texas students entering college, average age of 18, Porterfield (1946) reported D_{HS} of 3.0 for aggravated assault and 8.0 for burglary. These estimates are substantially lower than others reported in Table 3, probably because freshmen entering college are not representative of 18-year-olds generally.

Finally, Elliott and Huizinga (1984) reported data that permit computation of crime-specific cumulative participation, although annual current participation rates were originally collected from a five-wave panel design in the National Youth Survey (see Elliott et al., 1983). The participation estimates for robbery and felony theft are based on the experiences of males *and* females combined. The sample includes three birth cohorts (1965, 1962, 1959) whose overlapping age ranges during the 5-year study period cover ages 11–21. Cumulative participation by age 17 is reported here for comparison with other studies in Table 3. The theft measure is composed of four offenses—auto theft, grand theft (over $50), breaking into a building or vehicle, and buying stolen property. Therefore, not unexpectedly, Elliott and Huizinga's constructed estimate of D_{HS} for theft (28.6) is much higher than the other estimates, which are based only on grand theft. However, D_{HS} for robbery (15.3) is lower than the estimate from Kratcoski and Kratcoski (17.0).

Official-Record Studies

In one of the first published studies to estimate criminal participation from official records, Reiss and Rhodes (1961) computed participation on the basis of juvenile court adjudication at age 12 or later for a sample of 9,238 white male Tennessee school enrollees selected during 1957. The sample ranged in age from 12 to 18 years and contained a mix of urban and suburban children in the area surrounding Nashville, Tennessee. Participation estimates were reported to be 2.1 for serious crimes and 5.1 for all nontraffic offenses other than truancy. The participation measure used by Reiss and Rhodes—adjudicated delinquent after age 12—is narrower than that used in other studies in Table 3. Gordon (1976), using untested but not unreasonable assumptions, demonstrated that the Reiss and Rhodes estimates could be reconciled with the estimates obtained in other studies using broader measures of participation.

Four studies are unusual because they present both official-record and self-reports of B_{HS} (Gold, 1966; Hirschi, 1969; Williams and Gold, 1972; Hindelang, Hirschi, and Weis, 1981). For a sample of 522 Flint, Michigan, youths, Gold (1966) estimated B_{HS} at 11.0 for males according to juvenile court records, and 16.5 according to self-reports of being caught. The self-report estimate is consistent with the official estimates from Philadelphia, since the sample was youths aged 13–16, and the estimate of 16.5 lies midway between the estimates for age 12 (6.3) and age 16 (27.0) in Philadelphia cohort I.

In a study of 3,605 junior high and high school youths in California during the mid-1960s, Hirschi (1969) reported B_{HS} based on police records and self-reports of police contacts. The average age in this sample was about 14 years. However, the official-record estimates of B_{HS} for white (26.0) and black males (53.0) are about the same as similar estimates among 18-year-old Philadelphia white and black males (28.7, 50.2). Self-reports of B_{HS} for white males (34.0) exceeded the official-record estimate, but the reverse was true for black males (42.0). If the official records are assumed to be accurate, these findings suggest that the white males exaggerated their contacts with police, but the black males underreported their contacts. Alternatively, the police may have been more likely to record contacts with blacks than with whites, either because the alleged crimes of blacks were more serious than those of whites or for some other reason.

Using a 1967 national sample of males and females aged 13–16, Williams and Gold (1972) also estimated B_{HS} based on both self-reports and official records. Unlike the results of Gold (1966) and Hirschi (1969) from single jurisdictions, B_{HS} among both white and black males, based on self-reported police contacts (22.0, 21.0), substantially exceeded B_{HS} based on recorded police contacts (4.0, 5.0). Moreover, the official-record B_{HS} estimates lie well below both the Gold (1966) and Hirschi (1969) estimates and the range of 6.3 to 27.0 percent in Philadelphia cohort I for males in this age group. These facts together suggest the possibility that officially recorded arrests may be underreported in the Williams and Gold national sample because of the difficulty of obtaining complete records from multiple jurisdictions.

Hindelang, Hirschi, and Weis (1981) also reported B_{HS} estimates based on official police records and self-reports of police contact and court-ordered probation. Almost half of the black male subgroup (46.5) had an official police record, compared with 26.7 percent of white males. Unlike the other estimates of self-reported B_{HS} (Gold, 1966; Hirschi, 1969), all demographic subgroups of this Seattle sample reported *lower* rates than their official records indicated. Underreporting rates ranged from over 50 percent for black males and females to 37 percent for white males. Court-ordered probation was also rather common among this sample—8.7 percent of white males and 18.8 percent of black males. Interestingly, more black females admitted court-ordered probation (9.3) than white males; only 2.1 percent of white females admitted such involvement with the juvenile court. Official-

record estimates were not reported for juvenile court probation.

Finally, in a two-wave study (Feldhusen, Thurston, and Benning, 1973), a sample of schoolchildren aged 9–15 were identified by teachers as either "aggressive-disruptive" or "social." After 8 years, criminal records were obtained for the sample to ascertain whether the observations of early deviant behavior predicted subsequent delinquent behavior. Because delinquency before the first observation (at an average age of 12) was ignored, this study does not yield a precise estimate of cumulative participation by the average follow-up age of 20. Using arrest records for nontraffic offenses as an indicator of criminal activity, Feldhusen and colleagues reported B_{17-23} for males and females to be 42.5 percent. The separate participation rates based on juvenile court referrals for males and females are 16.0 and 5.0, respectively, for a combined rate of 14.3. These estimates are consistent with B_{18} in comparable samples (e.g., T. Monahan, 1960), which suggests that the increment to B between ages 18 and 20 in this sample is about equal to B before the first observation of the sample at age 12.

Current Participation Rates

The fourth type of participation estimate reviewed here is the current participation rate, d—the percentage of a population committing an offense within some observation interval. Estimates of d are usually based on self-reports of criminal activity within the past year. In Table 4, data are presented from four studies that report d for serious offenses (Weis, 1976; Bachman, O'Malley, and Johnston, 1978; Tittle, 1980; Elliott et al., 1983). In studies in which observation periods longer than 1 year were used (Bachman, O'Malley, and Johnston; Tittle; Weis), we annualized the rates to permit comparisons among them. These annualized rates should be interpreted cautiously, however, since they assume that offenses were evenly distributed over the observation interval. It is likely that our

TABLE A-4 Current Participation Rates (annualized by various ages)

Crime Type	Reference	Nature of Sample	Correlates Examined	Source (official records, self-reports)	Age	Participation Estimates[a] (percent)				
						T	M	F	B	W
Theft $50+	Elliott et al. (1983)	1,725 national youth aged 11-17 in 1976, 15-21 in 1980	Social class, family structure	Self-reports for specific crimes in last year	11-17	2.2	3.7	0.5	3.1	2.1
					15-21	3.1	4.9	1.1	3.1	3.0
	Tittle (1980)	1,984 adults in Oregon, Florida, and Iowa interviewed in 1976	Social class, size of city, religion	Self-reports for specific crimes in preceding 5 years (annualized)	15-24	3.2	(2.0	0.8	3.0	1.0)[b]
					25-44	1.4				
					45-64	0.6				
					65+	0.4				
	Bachman, O'Malley, and Johnston (1978)	2,213 10th grade males from national sample chosen in 1966 and followed until 1974	Grade completed, unemployment, marital status, drug use	Self-reports for specific crimes (annualized)[c]	13-15		3.3			
					16-17		6.0			
					18		9.0			
					19		11.0			
					23		7.0			
	Weis (1976)	301 11th graders and 254 8th graders in middle-class area (about 1970)	None	Self-reports for specific crimes in preceding 3 years (annualized)	12-14		2.1	1.2		
					15-17		2.9	--		
Burglary (breaking and entering)	Elliott et al. (1983)	(see above)	(see above)	(see above)	11-17	4.1	6.2	1.6	4.6	4.0
					15-21	2.4	3.4	1.3	2.2	2.4
	Weis (1976)	(see above)	(see above)	(see above)	12-14		6.5	2.7		
					15-17		6.9	0.7		
Robbery	Elliott et al. (1983)	(see above)	(see above)	(see above)	11-17		8.0	2.0	9.0	4.0
					15-21		3.0	1.0	3.0	2.0
	Bachman, O'Malley, and Johnston (1978)	(see above)	(see above)	(see above)	13-15		2.0			
					16-17		2.7			
					18		4.0			
					19		7.0			
					23		1.0			

Crime	Source				Age					
Assault (with weapon or injury)	Elliott et al. (1983)	(see above)	(see above)	(see above)	11-17	6.1	8.7	3.1	9.3	5.7
					15-21	4.6	6.4	2.5	4.4	4.5
	Tittle (1980)	(see above)	(see above)	(see above)	15-24	5.2	(3.0	1.6	2.6	2.0)[b]
					25-44	2.0				
					45-64	0.8				
					65+	0.2				
	Bachman, O'Malley, and Johnston (1978)	(see above)	(see above)	(see above)	13-15		9.0			
					16-17		12.7			
					18		16.0			
					19		20.0			
					23		11.0			
	Weis (1976)	(see above)	(see above)	(see above)	12-14		2.6	0.9		
					15-17		1.3	0.2		
Auto Theft	Elliott et al. (1983)	(see above)	(see above)	(see above)	11-17	0.9	1.3	0.5	1.9	0.7
					15-21	1.3	1.9	0.6	0.4	1.4
	Bachman, O'Malley, and Johnston (1978)	(see above)	(see above)	(see above)	13-15		3.0			
					16-17		4.0			
					18		5.0			
					19		6.0			
					23		3.0			

[a]Participation estimates refer to all sample members (T) and, when possible, are broken down by race (W, white; B, black), and sex (M, male; F, female).

[b]Participation rates for all ages.

[c]Observation intervals were not equal among the five time periods.

annualized estimates of d for the three studies underestimate the true annual participation rate because some offenders in the sample presumably participated during more than one of the years in the observation period.

National Youth Survey

In 1977, Elliott and his colleagues began tracking 1,725 males and females aged 11–17 in a representative national household sample. Self-reports of criminal behavior were obtained annually through 1981. Based on these reports, annual current participation rates were reported in Elliott et al. (1983). Although the authors did not present any statistics on crime-specific cumulative participation by a given age (except for the rates for the "synthetic cohort" in Table 3), they did present extensive breakdowns of *current* participation for specific crime types—the first available for a series of years for the same sample.

As shown in Table 4, d for aggravated assault and robbery for both age groups was higher for males and blacks than for females and whites, and lower for groups aged 15–21 than for groups aged 11–17.[7] For breaking and entering, the black-white differential was much smaller but the declining trend as the cohort aged remained. Active auto thieves were shown to be extremely rare among all groups—only 1–2 percent of youths were involved in auto theft in any given year. Participation in grand theft was especially high among males and blacks, and increased slightly with age. More precise age-specific data are presented below during a discussion of the relationship between age and participation.

---

[7]This drop in participation rates at older ages occurs for most offenses studied by Elliott et al. (1983). However, Farrington, Ohlin, and Wilson (1986:Chap. 8) suggest that this decline might reflect changes in sample composition over the 5 years because sample dropouts tended to be black, lower class, and urban groups, which often have high participation rates. Alternatively, the decline might reflect the fact that respondents become less cooperative and admit to fewer offenses over time.

Youth-in-Transition Project

Another national longitudinal study of high school youths, male sophomores selected in 1966, was conducted by Bachman and his associates, and results were presented in several studies (see, e.g., Bachman et al., 1967; Bachman, 1970; Bachman, Green, and Wirtanen, 1971; Bachman, O'Malley, and Johnston, 1978). On the basis of subjects' self-reports gathered between 1966 and 1974, Bachman, O'Malley, and Johnston (1978) reported d for five age categories and four crime types—robbery, assault, auto theft, and grand theft (over $50). The initial observation period covered the 3-year period when the subjects were aged 13–15, the second observation period was 18 months, and the three other observation periods were each 12 months. When annualized, these current participation rates for all four crime types peaked at age 19. Also, at all ages, assault was the most common crime type, followed by grand theft; robbery and auto theft were relatively rare crimes.

In comparison with these results, Elliott and colleagues' National Youth Survey showed d to be slightly higher among males for robbery, somewhat lower for auto theft, and slightly lower for grand theft. The more restrictive assault definition (aggravated assault only) accounts for the NYS estimates of d for males being lower than those from the Youth-in-Transition study. Other differences between the two longitudinal national studies may well be attributable to the 10-year gap in the initiation of the two studies.

Self-Reports by Cross-Section Samples

Two studies report d based on single interviews with respondents. Tittle (1980) presented estimates of d based on the self-reports of a sample of 1,984 adults in three states. The age variation within the sample enabled Tittle to present estimates of d for a much wider set of age ranges than is presented in reports based on longitudinal studies. For both grand theft and assault, d was highest within the age range 15–24 and then declined for successively older groups. These results are perhaps the only crime-specific estimates of d available at these older age ranges.

Weis (1976) sampled males and females in both the 8th grade (aged 12–14) and 11th grade (aged 15–17) for a study of delinquency among middle-class youths. Questionnaires were used to obtain information primarily about status offenses and minor criminal activity in the preceding 3 years. Only 3 offenses of the 34 deviant behaviors studied could be classified as serious—grand theft (over $50), individual weapon fight, and illegal entry. Among males aged 16–17, d for grand theft (2.9) and assault (1.3) was much lower than the estimate for the same age group in Bachman and colleagues' study (6.0, 12.7).

Summary of Participation Estimates

In view of the overrepresentation of males among offenders, in this section we use the previous discussion as the basis for establishing participation rates for all males and for white and black subgroups. Our estimates of participation in offending among males are summarized in Tables 5 and 6. We report two measures because of their relatively wide availability, participation by age 18, B_{18}, and lifetime participation, B_L.

Participation by Age 18

For a broad domain of "crime" (but excluding nonoffense contacts), information in Table 5 suggests range estimates for B_{18} of 13.1–28.7 for white males, 31.4–50.9 for black males, and 17.1–34.9 for all males. These ranges exclude the two outlier studies—Palmore and Hammond (1964), and Shannon (1982a)—which used a broader definition of police contact (see earlier discussion). Calculating arithmetic averages for these ranges, average B_{18} (based on nontraffic offenses, but excluding Shannon's estimates) is 19.8 for white males, 41.9 for black males, and 26.7 for all males.

Variation within the range for white males seems largely explainable by differ-

ences in level of criminal justice contact: for example, recorded police contact in the Philadelphia cohort studies (28.7, 22.7) and court referral in T. Monahan's (1960) data (13.1). Thus, the average police contact rate of 25.7 and the referral rate of 15.9 for white males suggest that 62 percent of all police contacts led to court referral.

The range for black males is somewhat more difficult to interpret. As indicated previously, the estimates of Monahan, as corrected by Gordon and Gleser (50.9), and Philadelphia cohort I (50.2) appear inconsistent, but several possible explanations have been offered. The estimate from Philadelphia cohort II (41.8) is not comparable to any other estimate because it is based on a much more recent sample. Both estimates by Wolfgang and colleagues are higher than the estimates by Robins, West, and Herjanic (31.4) and Robins and Wish (38.1) for their high-risk St. Louis samples, but their "court referral" is a more stringent criterion than arrest. The estimate of B_{18} for the St. Louis sample born in the 1930s (38.1) is consistent with T. Monahan's data from the Philadelphia Juvenile Court in 1941 (37.8).

When considering all males, the range of 17.1–34.9 (observed when Shannon's Racine cohorts and the Palmore and Hammond study are excluded) is fairly straightforward to interpret. At the low end, the estimates of Ball, Ross, and Simpson (20.7) and Polk et al. (25.0), both based on police records, likely reflect the less urbanized setting of their samples. As Gordon (1976) has noted, Polk et al.'s sample was almost entirely white; thus, the position of the Polk estimate midway between the two estimates of Wolfgang and colleagues for white males demonstrates consistency. The lowest estimate (17.1—T. Monahan) is based on data from the Philadelphia Juvenile Court in 1941. Monahan also estimated a rate of 25.8 for court referrals during 1949–1954 in urban Philadelphia, which is consistent with the estimates by Wolfgang and his colleagues, based on police contacts (31.2, 34.9), if court referral rates are on the order of 75 percent. Christensen's estimate of 25.1 was derived directly from Monahan's. McCord (1978) reported B_{18} for convicted

TABLE A-5 Official-Record Data on Male Participation Rates by
Age 18 ($\underline{B}_{18}$) (in percent)

Crime Type and Level of Involvement	White	Black	All Males
U.S. studies			
Known to police or juvenile court	52.0	63.5	56.0
Nontraffic arrest or police contact	22.7, 28.7	41.8, 50.2	25.1, 32.8, 34.0, 34.9, 41.0, 44.1, 47.3
Juvenile arrest and/or court referral	13.1, 16.8, 17.9	31.4, 37.8, 38.1, 43.1, 50.9	17.1, 20.7, 25.0, 25.8
Juvenile court conviction	--	--	26.1, 27.5
Arrest for index offense	8.2, 8.2, 8.9	26.0, 26.8, 26.9	12.3, 13.6, 17.9
British studies			
Conviction <u>or</u> police caution, indictable offenses	--	--	14.6, 28.0, 29.0
Conviction for indictable offense	--	--	12.3, 15.0, 15.9, 16.6, 17.0, 25.7

NOTE: See Table A-1 and related discussion for sources and further
description of specific estimates.

males of 26.1–27.5, not surprisingly high in view of the high-risk nature of her sample.

When a more serious definition of criminal activity is used—arrest for an index offense—the estimates of B_{18} for white males (8.2–8.9) and black males (26.0–26.9) separately are consistent and much lower than the estimates based on nontraffic offenses. Differences in racial composition produce a wider range of estimates for all males combined (12.3–17.9). The index arrest estimates are based on the two Phila-

delphia cohorts and the most recent national arrest projection (Blumstein and Graddy, 1982); however, the latter projection was derived, in part, from the Philadelphia data.

Participation by age 18 in index offenses, observed in Philadelphia cohorts I and II, suggests an interesting pattern over time. For both black and white males, B_{18} in cohort II (26.0, 8.9) was approximately the same as that in cohort I (26.8, 8.2). However, participation for *all males* increased (cohort

I—13.6, cohort II—17.9) because cohort II included a greater proportion of blacks than cohort I, among whom B_{18} based on index property offenses was higher.

The estimates from British studies, shown in the bottom portion of Table 5, were also discussed earlier. In general, the variation among the nine estimates results from differences in the nature of the samples. The average of these estimates (19.3) is lower than the U.S. range (26.1–27.5), which is based on juvenile court convictions for a broader range of offenses than in the British studies. But it is higher than the estimates based on FBI index arrests, which cover a more narrow domain than British "indictable offenses."

Thus, the only estimates of B_{18} for males that need interpretation are those for the three Racine cohorts, 41.0, 47.3, and 44.1 based on police records of nontraffic offenses (Shannon, 1982a), and the Palmore and Hammond estimates (52.0, 63.5, 56.0). The domain of "crime" represented by the

Shannon estimates is fairly broad; as we mentioned earlier, it includes status offenses as well as many minor behaviors, truancy, and running away. Such a broad domain could explain the high values of the estimates. The Palmore and Hammond study was based on a high-risk sample—children born to welfare clients—and they only had to be "known to the police or juvenile court" to be classified as delinquent. Presumably, this definition would include incidents such as truancy, running away, and other status offenses.

Lifetime Participation

In Table 6, the separate estimates of B_L for any offense for white (46.9) and black (68.3) males are those derived by Christensen (1967) from multiple data bases. Surprisingly, no subsequent refinements of his estimates have been attempted for this broad domain of criminal activity despite (or perhaps because of) his cautions about

TABLE A-6 Official-Record Data on Male Lifetime Participation Rates ($\underline{B_L}$) (in percent)

Crime Type and Level of Involvement	White	Black	All Males
Nontraffic arrest	46.9	68.3	50.0, 60.0, 60.0
Arrest for index offense	14.6	52.0	22.8, 36.0
Conviction for serious offenses (unspecified)	--	--	6.0,[a] 29.0, 30.2, 35.3, 43.6
Conviction for index property offense	--	--	26.4
Conviction for index violent offense	--	--	16.9

NOTE: See Table A-2 and related discussion for sources and further description of specific estimates.

[a]This anomalous 6 percent applies to the adoptive fathers in Mednick, Gabrielli, and Hutchings (1984), who were presumably screened for absence of criminal records before being permitted to adopt.

the estimation difficulties raised at higher ages by black-white survival differentials and the sparseness of initiation-rate data.

For all males, Christensen's national estimate of B_L is 50.0 for nontraffic arrests. Replacing Christensen's distribution of early age-specific initiation rates with those of Wolfgang, Figlio, and Sellin's Philadelphia cohort I, Belkin, Blumstein, and Glass estimated B_L at 60.0, which seems to be the best available national estimate of B_L among all males. That figure is reasonably comparable to estimates obtained from three U.S. longitudinal studies that followed male cohorts to the oldest ages. Robins's estimate of 60.0 for her sample of youths treated at a child guidance clinic appears consistent, but most of that sample was born before 1920. According to Wolfgang's (1977) follow-up to age 30 of a 10 percent sample of Philadelphia cohort I, 47.3 percent had been arrested for a nontraffic offense, but this estimate excluded first arrests occurring after age 30. McCord estimated B_L through age 40–51 at 35.3 for *conviction*, a more stringent criterion, but one based on a high-risk sample.

Estimates of B_L for index offenses by males are taken from Blumstein and Graddy. In turn, B_{18} in that study was computed from the 10 percent follow-up of Philadelphia cohort I; beyond age 18, their estimates were computed using a sample of 1973 District of Columbia arrestees. Thus, the estimates are clearly most appropriate for urban populations. Narrowing the domain of criminal behavior from all nontraffic offenses to only index offenses reduces B_L substantially among white males (14.6) and all males (22.8), but B_L for black males (52.0) remains at a high level.

Disaggregating still further, Table 6 shows B_L separately for the FBI's index property and violent offenses, but only from McCord's study. For property offenses, 26.4 percent of McCord's male sample had a conviction record by age 41–50, whereas only 16.9 percent had a conviction record for violent offenses.

In summary, using arrest or recorded police contact as the criterion, the literature suggests that B_{18} among urban males is about *one in three* for all crimes more serious than traffic offenses, and *one in five* for all index crimes. The corresponding estimates for B_L are about 60 percent for all nontraffic crimes and *one in four* for all index crimes, which suggests that 60 to 80 percent of all criminal careers—as measured by official records—are initiated by age 18.

Self-Report Estimates

Participation estimates based on self-reports of involvement in specific crime types are difficult to summarize. Participation estimates for burglary appear reasonably consistent (12.9–21.2), but more variation exists in the range of male participation estimates for auto theft (5.5–14.8), grand theft (3.5–17.3), and robbery (4.1–17.0). Some of this variation can be explained by differences in when and where the study was carried out. Other factors, such as question wording and respondents' age or race, may also account for some of the inconsistencies, but this information was often not reported.

Among females, D_{HS} is fairly consistently about one-quarter that of males—2 to 4 percent reported involvement in any specific crime type. Because these estimates are based on self-reported participation (D) rather than only participation that attracted official attention (B), it is not surprising that they seem high relative to estimates of B_{18} based on broader categories, such as nontraffic offenses.

The more interesting comparison is between police contacts as reported by respondents and as recorded by police. These are compared in only four studies (see Table 3 and related text). Unfortunately, those studies reached different conclusions—the self-report measure was higher than the official-record measure in two samples (Gold, 1966; Williams and Gold, 1972) and among blacks in Hirschi's (1969) sample. But the official-record measure was higher among whites in Hirschi's sample and among both whites and blacks in Hindelang, Hirschi, and Weis (1981). Differences among these studies in sample composition, location, and year of study—in addition to unknown differences in question wording—make it difficult to reconcile these disparate findings. Thus, these comparisons between self-report and official-record measures of arrest participation are best described as inconclusive.

FACTORS ASSOCIATED WITH PARTICIPATION

The participation rates reported in the preceding section suggest that demographic variables, such as sex, race, and age, are at least correlated with participation in offending. These relationships are summarized and discussed below (Tables 7–9). Studies linking the demographic attributes of age, sex, and race with participation rates have been conducted primarily because the data for such research were readily available from police records or interviewer observation—scientific theory has not established a causal relationship between demographics and criminal participation.

Several of the studies already discussed include analyses of theoretically more interesting correlates of participation, such as family influences, income and social class, and early antisocial behavior. These relationships are the primary focus for the rest of this appendix (Tables 10–16). For the most part, the discussion of correlates is based on findings from research yielding the participation estimates presented in the earlier tables. The life-table studies based on agency statistics are, by their nature, not suited to providing results on correlates of participation, other than demographic correlates. For this reason, the studies that augmented individual data from official records and self-reports with data on relevant attributes are the basis for discussion here. In nearly all instances, the reported correlations are consistent with several alternative theories of crime. Therefore, strong correlations merely suggest fruitful areas for research using more sophisticated designs to test competing theories; in themselves, they do not generally confirm or disconfirm theories.

Two other types of analysis that have yielded insights on factors that may be associated with participation are also excluded from this discussion. Studies that compare hypothesized correlates for samples of known criminals and matched samples of presumed noncriminals have produced some interesting results. However, because known criminals were deliberately selected at a predetermined rate (e.g., 50 percent of sample), those studies cannot produce participation estimates and are therefore outside the scope of this review. An additional problem with such studies is that the criminal subjects are usually incarcerated inmates, since they are relatively easy to locate and measure in terms of the attributes of interest. Incarcerated subjects are not representative of offenders generally, however, since the imprisonment decision is influenced by dimensions of the criminal career, such as its seriousness, intensity, and duration. Therefore it is not possible to isolate the relationship of the attributes to participation.

The problem of isolating the specific relationship of attributes to participation also led to a decision to exclude many analyses in the studies reviewed that relate potential correlates to indices or scales of "criminality." As mentioned earlier, such indices are usually intended to capture multiple career dimensions in a single number and, occasionally even the dispositions of arrests for criminal incidents. In analyses in which scale values of zero clearly indicated the absence of known criminal activity, it was sometimes possible to isolate results on correlates of participation in which case the results are summarized here. With these limitations in mind, correlates of participation are discussed in the following subsections.

Sex and Participation

In considering Tables 1–4, perhaps the most striking impression is the consistency with which male participation in offending exceeds female participation in offending, regardless of data source, definition of "offender," culture, or measure of participation. Drawing on the summaries in Tables 1

TABLE A-7 Summary of Male/Female Ratios of Participation, by Type of Estimate

Type of Study (number of studies/samples)	Range of Male/Female Ratios
BROAD CRIME DEFINITION (official records)	
Participation by age 18-25 ($\underline{B}_{18-25}$)	
U.S. studies	
Aggregate statistics (5)[a]	3.9-4.4
Longitudinal studies (6)[b]	1.8-3.6
Single-wave (5)[c]	2.5-8.0
British studies (12)[d]	4.8-7.3
Lifetime participation ($\underline{B}_L$)	
U.S. studies (3)[e]	2.0-4.2
Danish studies (3)[f]	3.0-5.3
SPECIFIC CRIMES (self-reports)[g]	
Aggravated assault (10)	1.8-4.5
Robbery (5)	3.0-5.6
Theft over $50 (9)	1.8-6.7
Auto theft (4)	2.1-3.8
Burglary (5)	3.0-6.7

NOTE: It is implicit in each ratio that the rate for females is 1.

[a]T. Monahan (1960) (2); Ball, Ross, and Simpson (1964); Christensen (1967); Belkin, Blumstein, and Glass (1973).
[b]Palmore and Hammond (1964); Feldhusen, Thurston, and Benning (1973); Robins, West, and Herjanic (1975); Shannon (1982a) (3); Tracy, Wolfgang, and Figlio (1985).
[c]All are based on high school samples: Gold (1966); Williams and Gold (1972); Hindelang, Hirschi, and Weis (1981) (3).
[d]Little (1965); Miller et al. (1974); Wadsworth (1979) (2); Farrington (1981, 1983a); Ouston (1984); London Home Office (1985) (6).
[e]Robins (1966); Christensen (1967); Belkin, Blumstein, and Glass (1973).
[f]Hutchings and Mednick (1975) (3).
[g]Includes D_{HS} (participation by high school age) and $\underline{d}$ (current participation); Porterfield (1946); Short and Nye (1958); Tittle (1980); Kratcoski and Kratcoski (1975); Weis (1976); Cernkovich and Giordano (1979); Figueria-McDonough, Barton, and Sarri (1981); Hindelang, Hirschi, and Weis (1981); Elliott et al. (1983).

through 4 that report separate but comparable male and female participation rates, Table 7 reports the range of male/female participation ratios for various groups of studies.

Except for the prospective longitudinal studies, the U.S. participation estimates in Table 7 that are based on official records generally estimate male participation rates at 3 to 5 times female rates, which is consistent with other research (Gordon, 1976:212; Hindelang, Hirschi, and Weis, 1979). In fact, only 3 of the 13 U.S. life-table and cross-section estimates of participation based on official records lie outside this range (Hindelang, Hirschi, and Weis, 1981; Robins, 1966). Of the six ratio estimates from longitudinal studies, the relatively low ratio of 2.3:1 reported by Robins, West, and Herjanic (1975) for offspring of black males is consistent with a suggestion (discussed below) that male/female participation ratios may be lower among blacks than whites. (Note that in all the ratios presented below it is implicit that the female rate is 1.) But no comparable explanation exists for the low male/female ratios observed by Tracy, Wolfgang, and Figlio (1985) in Philadelphia cohort II for both blacks and whites. It is interesting to note that for all nontraffic offenses, the three consecutive Racine cohorts studied by Shannon (1982a) show successively lower male/female ratios for B_{18} (4.7, 3.1, 2.0), a result of increasing participation over time by females and relatively stable participation among males. Moreover, that pattern appears when the analysis is restricted to index offenses (data not shown; Shannon, 1985, personal communication).

The Danish estimates of B_L also produce male/female ratios in the range of 3 to 5. However, the seven British studies, which generated 12 estimates, show a higher range, with male participation (based on conviction) at levels 5 to 7 times those for females. Because the Danish studies showing ratios similar to the U.S. ones are also based on convictions, the higher British ratios likely reflect cross-national differences in behavior rather than the narrower definition of participation.

Table 7 also reports ranges of the male/female ratio of crime-specific participation rates based on self-reports. The crime-specific participation rates for females are quite small, so these male/female ratios should be interpreted cautiously. The range of ratios is also relatively wide. Nonetheless, few of the 32 available crime-specific ratios exceed the ratio of 5 to 1 observed for the broader categories of crime.

Eight of the participation studies reviewed provide comparable male/female participation ratios separately for blacks and whites. For 17 of the 20 estimates, the male/female ratio is lower among blacks than among whites, which reflects much greater racial differentials in female participation than in male participation (the exceptions are from self-report studies). Thus, Palmore and Hammond (1964), using a very broad definition of crime, reported a male/female participation ratio of 6.2 for whites but only 2.0 for blacks. Based on juvenile court referrals, T. Monahan's (1960) data reveal male/female participation ratios of 5.3 for whites and 3.2 for blacks. Christensen's (1967) data are also consistent—4.3 for whites and 3.5 for blacks. Using self-report data, Hindelang, Hirschi, and Weis (1981) reported similar male/female ratio patterns by high school age for robbery (5.8 for whites and 3.0 for blacks), theft exceeding $50 (9.7 and 2.7), auto theft (12.1 and 4.3), burglary (3.4 and 3.0), and assault (3.2 and 1.7).

A few studies report essentially no difference in male/female ratios for blacks and whites. In Philadelphia cohort II (Tracy, Wolfgang, and Figlio, 1985), the ratios were only slightly lower for blacks (2.2) than for whites (2.5) for nontraffic offenses, and similar patterns emerged for UCR index (4.3, 4.9) and non-index (2.2, 2.4) offenses. (See also Ball, Ross, and Simpson, 1964; Elliott et al., 1985). But as a rough approximation, it appears that, in the United States, offenders are 3 to 5 times more prevalent among males than among females, and that the ratio is toward the high end for whites and toward the low end for blacks.

Race and Participation

Drawing on results in Tables 1 through 4 that report separate participation estimates for black and white males in a common sample, Table 8 reports black/white ratios of participation estimates. For example, for a broad definition of crime, the black/white ratio for B_{18} is approximately 1.75:1 in the Philadelphia cohorts. In the high-risk sample studied by Palmore and Hammond, the ratio for B_{18} is only 1.2. The two ratios derived from life-table estimates are higher and consistent with each other (2.6, 2.8), but an especially low ratio is reported by Christensen (1.5) for B_{L}.

When attention is restricted to only the more serious crimes, the ratio for B_{18} is much higher: 3.3 and 2.9 in Philadelphia cohorts I and II, respectively, for all FBI index offenses. Blumstein and Graddy report ratios of 3.3 and 3.6 for B_{18} and B_{L}, respectively.

While the ratios for crime-type groups are all derived from official records, ratios for five specific crime types have been estimated from studies based on self-reports (Jensen and Eve, 1976; Hindelang, Hirschi, and Weis, 1981; Elliott et al., 1983). Black/white ratios from those studies (see Tables 3 and 4) are consistently lower than the ratios for broader crime types based on official records. In contrast to the broader crime-type groups, the black/white participation ratios for auto theft, burglary, and grand theft are generally around 1:1, and

TABLE A-8 Black/White Participation Ratios for Males in Official-Record Studies

Source	By Age 18	Lifetime
Broad Crime Definition		
T. Monahan (1960)	2.8	
Ball, Ross, and Simpson (1964)	2.6	
Palmore and Hammond (1964)	1.2	
Christensen (1967)	--	1.5
Hirschi (1969)[a]	2.0	
Wolfgang, Figlio, and Sellin (1972)	1.7	
Hindelang, Hirschi, and Weis (1981)[a]	1.7	
Tracy, Wolfgang, and Figlio (1985)	1.8	
Average Ratio[b]	1.8	1.5
All Index Offenses		
Wolfgang, Figlio, and Sellin (1972)	3.3	
Blumstein and Graddy (1982)	3.3	3.6
Tracy, Wolfgang, and Figlio (1985)	2.9	
Average Ratio[b]	3.2	3.6

NOTE: It is implicit in each ratio that the rate for white males is 1.

[a]Based on participation by high school age.
[b]Calculated from the sum of all estimates of participation for blacks and the sum of all estimates for whites in Tables 5 and 6.

some ratios are less than 1. Only for robbery and assault do black/white ratios based on self-report data approach those based on official records in Table 8. However, these variations across data sources (self-reports and official records) may be due to the different age groups represented and the generally lower participation estimates for specific crimes. The comparability of official-record and self-report results concerning race differentials is considered by Weis (Volume II).

Age and Participation

Several of the studies summarized in Tables 1 through 4 provide year-by-year data that can be used to study the relationship between age and participation. It is important here to distinguish between two alternative ways of defining that relationship: as the probability of *initiating* a criminal career at a given age (summarized in Table 9) and the probability of *committing* an offense at a given age (see Figure 1).

It is useful to recall the distinction between two alternative notions of the probability of initiating a criminal career. The "age-*a* initiation rate" is the probability that a member of a sample becomes an offender at age *a*. Many of the participation rates by age 18 that are reported in Table 1 were computed, for example, by summing initiation rates from ages 6 (about the earliest that persons are ever arrested) through 17. But in trying to understand the relationship between age and initiation probabilities, the initiation rate can be misleading, because at successively later ages, more of the offenders in the sample have already begun offending and are therefore not still at risk of becoming offenders for the first time. That is, a sample member who *became* a first offender by age 16 has zero probability of *becoming* an offender at age 17. Thus, it is helpful to estimate the probability of becoming an offender at age 17 among only the 16-year-olds who are not already offenders. These conditional probabilities, or *hazard rates*, are reported in Table 9 for four studies in which either the rates or the data for computing the rates were pub-

lished. For each study, the peak values of the hazard rate are underscored.

Hazard rates for initiating criminal careers are highest in the age range 15–18 for all seven distributions in Table 9. They decline quite rapidly during the late teens, and are well below half their peak values by age 21. Even for the broad domains of crime examined in the studies by Wolfgang and colleagues and in the British studies, the peak hazard rate at any age is less than .1. Two of the patterns reported in Table 9 are somewhat surprising. First, while hazard rates for the first index offense are higher for blacks than for whites at all ages, the black rate does not peak until age 18, 3 years after the peak for whites, according to Blumstein and Graddy. Second, in Philadelphia cohort I, the peak age for the first FBI index offense is 15, 1 year earlier than the peak age for all offenses. The latter finding raises questions about the extent to which delinquent careers progress from less serious to more serious offense types. Evidence concerning such progressions is considered systematically by Cohen (Appendix B) and in Chapter 3.

The relationship between age and the probability of *committing* an offense is best examined with age-specific current participation rates, *d*. Four studies reported this participation measure for specific crime types (see Table 4 and earlier discussion). However, in three of the studies (Weis, 1976; Bachman, O'Malley, and Johnston, 1978; Tittle, 1980), estimates of *d* were not reported for consecutive ages. Nevertheless, some age trends are apparent in those studies.

In a five-wave longitudinal study, Bachman, O'Malley, and Johnston (1978) found a consistent increase in *d* through the mid-teens to a peak at age 19 (the fourth wave) for four crime types, and then a sharp decline at age 23 (the last wave). Weis (1976) reported that *d* was higher among those aged 15–17 years than those aged 12–14 years for burglary and grand theft; however, for assault, *d* was higher among the younger group. Using broader age categories, Tittle (1980) found that *d* decreased markedly in the mid-20s. For example, among those

TABLE A-9 Age Distribution of Hazard Rates for Males

Age	Blumstein and Graddy (1982)[a]		Philadelphia Cohort I, Wolfgang, Figlio, and Sellin (1972)			Farrington (1983a)[c]	Ouston (1984)[d]
	Whites	Blacks	All Offenses	Index	All Offenses[b]		
6	.000	.001	--	--	--	--	--
7	.000	.001	.002	.001	.000	--	--
8	.002	.004	.006	.003	.001	--	--
9	.003	.010	.013	.007	.002	--	--
10	.003	.012	.018	.008	.005	.015	--
11	.008	.026	.024	.011	.014	.015	.008
12	.007	.030	.032	.015	.028	.021	.018
13	.007	.041	.046	.014	.031	.039	.040
14	.010	.042	.056	.018	.044	.052	.050
15	.020	.052	.073	.021	.068	.049	.068
16	.018	.047	.095	.018	.080	.039	.077
17	.014	.042	.051	.012	.100	.060	.067
18	.005	.059	--	--	.045	.027	.006
19	.011	.052	--	--	.027	.028	--
20	.003	.039	--	--	.029	.032	--
21	.003	.017	--	--	.025	.007	--
25	.002	.013	--	--	.012	--	--
30	.001	.007	--	--	--	--	--

NOTE: Underscoring denotes highest rate in column.

a Index offenses.
b Estimates from a 10 percent follow-up sample of original cohort.
c British study; convictions for indictable offenses.
d British study; official police caution or juvenile conviction, but records were not searched through the 18th year.

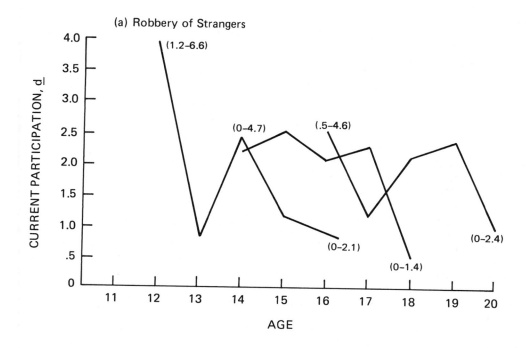

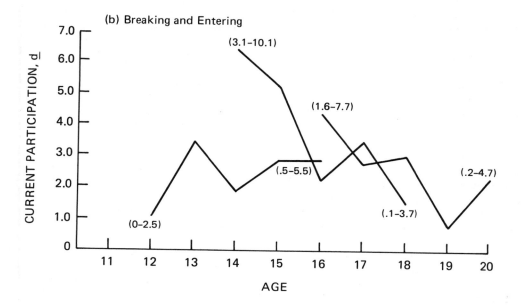

FIGURE A-1 Age and current participation rates for specific crime types for three cohorts. Source: Derived from data in Elliott et al. (1983).

aged 15–24 years, d was 3.2 percent, but it dropped to only 1.4 percent among respondents aged 25–44 years.

Despite some consistent patterns, the results from these studies are not based on annual age-specific estimates of d. The estimates of d for all three studies had to be annualized because observation periods exceeded 1 year and two studies used cross-section samples with multiple ages, which may confound age and cohort effects. To our knowledge, the only longitudinal study to report d annually for successive years is the National Youth Survey (Elliott et al., 1983).

Figure 1 plots d over the 5 years of data collection for three birth cohorts in the National Youth Survey, using breaking and entering and robbery of strangers as representative crime types. The 1,725 males and females in the national sample were 11–17 years old in 1976 and 15–21 years old in 1980. We selected the 1960, 1962, and 1964 birth cohorts (aged 12, 14, and 16 years, respectively, in 1976) from the seven cohorts in the study. Confidence intervals (with $p = .05$) reported by Elliott et al. (1983) appear in parentheses for the first and fifth years.

Looking first at the age-specific ds for breaking and entering—a typical teenage offense—the pattern for each cohort shows a general decline over the 5 years of data collection. However, this decline occurs in both the 1960 birth cohort (aged 12–16 during the study) and the 1964 birth cohort (aged 16–20 during the study) despite the age differences. In addition, the peaks in d occur for *consecutive* ages (ages 13, 14, 16, respectively) for each of the three cohorts, rather than for the same age, as would be expected if crime-specific d generally peaked at a specific age. A similar pattern exists for robbery. Thus, these patterns do not appear consistent with a general increase in d through the mid-teens and a decline during the late teens and early 20s. Moreover, the confidence intervals shown in Figure 1 reveal large overlaps in the first and fifth estimates for each cohort, which support the view that these year-to-year changes in d are not statistically significant. For example, to interpret the apparently

sharp decline in d for robbery from age 12 (3.9 percent) to age 16 (0.9 percent) as an age effect is misleading, since the confidence interval around the upper estimate (1.2–6.6) overlaps that of the lower estimate (0–2.1). Given these two confidence intervals, the hypothesis that d at ages 12 and 16 is similar in this sample is not untenable. The confidence intervals also overlap for the five other pairs of d estimates. A tabulation not reported here, in which all cohorts were combined, also did not suggest systematic interaction between d and age over the range 11–20.

Other Factors Associated with Participation

Only a few of the studies discussed above had estimation of participation levels as a sole objective. Rather, most of them were intended to relate participation to characteristics of individuals, their families, or other environmental factors. In the literature reviewed here, the usual approach to studying such relationships was to compare participation across subsamples defined in terms of the characteristics of interest. A few of the studies reported bivariate statistics or used multivariate techniques to examine the relationship between participation and a set of several characteristics simultaneously. Throughout this discussion, the reader should bear in mind that even the strongest and most consistently replicated statistical associations would not support many predictive uses of these factors, because predictions based on them would lead to unacceptably high error rates.

Tables 10 through 16 summarize the comparative and multivariate (MVA) results of studies that relate participation to the following sets of characteristics: socioeconomic status (SES), family structure and disruptions, family influences (including parental behavior), family members' criminal behavior, school performance and intelligence, early antisocial behavior, and other characteristics. We have limited this review to published reports from which estimates of overall participation can be derived (either based on official records or self-reports) and have omitted other types of studies (e.g., matched samples) for the reasons previously explained. Also, we omitted much of the literature oriented primarily toward delinquency prediction (for reviews, see Loeber and Dishion, 1983; Loeber and Stouthamer-Loeber, 1986). Because of these omissions, and because the designs of the reviewed studies were guided by a variety of theoretical orientations and objectives, the following discussion should not be regarded as a complete treatment of factors associated with participation. Nevertheless, it does summarize the implications of one important body of literature for the understanding of participation in offending.

Socioeconomic Status

The debate over the relationship between social class and criminal behavior is one of the oldest in criminology, and much of it has been carried on in literature other than that reviewed here (e.g., Merton, 1938; Kvaraceus, 1944; A. Cohen, 1955; Nye, Short, and Olson, 1958; Akers, 1964; Hirschi, 1972). (For other reviews, see Tittle, Villemez, and Smith, 1978; Hindelang, Hirschi, and Weis, 1979; Clelland and Carter, 1980.) Nevertheless, the literature summarized in Table 10—focusing only on studies that report *participation rates*—constitutes an important part of the debate.

Although disagreement exists over the nature of the relationship between social class and criminal participation, recent studies support the view that social class is generally *not* related to *self-reported* criminal behavior because this method of data collection primarily taps nonserious offenses, including vandalism, fighting, school infractions, and small thefts (e.g., Hindelang, Hirschi, and Weis, 1979; Clelland and Carter, 1980). However, a strong relationship usually appears when participation is measured by official police or court records—presumably because of a higher level of seriousness in those data. As noted by Hindelang, Hirschi, and Weis (1981: 181), a finding of no relationship in analyses of self-reports but of an inverse association

in official-record studies dates back to Short and Nye (1957) and can be supported by early statements on conflict theory (Bonger, 1916; Sellin, 1958). The findings presented in Table 10, however, suggest a more complicated relationship.

Results are presented in Table 10 for three official-record studies published in the 1960s and early 1970s—Reiss and Rhodes (1961), Gold (1966), and Philadelphia cohort I, as analyzed by Wolfgang, Figlio, and Sellin (1972) and reanalyzed by Jensen (1976). In various ways, all appear consistent with the hypothesis that delinquent or criminal behavior is more prevalent among members of lower socioeconomic classes. Within occupational categories, Gold (1966) reported a similar pattern that is also consistent with higher participation rates among lower socioeconomic groups.

Reiss and Rhodes (1961) analyzed participation rates for serious delinquency (i.e., having a court record of conviction for aggravated assault, armed robbery, grand larceny, auto theft, or burglary), by white-collar/blue-collar status of the subject's father and by IQ. For all IQ levels, participation in offending among sons of blue-collar fathers exceeded participation among sons of white-collar fathers; however, the differential increased with IQ level, both relatively and absolutely.

Data on socioeconomic status, race, and participation published by Wolfgang, Figlio, and Sellin (1972:55) were the subject of a later reanalysis by Jensen (1976). The data clearly show an inverse relationship between socioeconomic status and participation, both overall and for each race separately. They also show a substantial racial effect within each socioeconomic status, and Jensen differed from Wolfgang, Figlio, and Sellin only in his view of the appropriate relative emphasis on the two attributes.

On closer examination, however, the findings from these studies are probably not reliable indicators of the class-crime relationship, especially for urban areas in the 1980s. Wolfgang, Figlio, and Sellin used an ecological measure of social class, mean

TABLE A-10 Socioeconomic Status and Criminal Participation

Reference	Method/Variable	Results (percent)	Relationship to Participation
Wolfgang, Figlio, and Sellin (1972:55); Jensen (1976:Table 1)	Compare B_{18} (arrest); mean census tract income	SES / T / B / W $<\$5,783$ — 44.8 / 52.9 / 35.6 $>\$5,783$ — 26.5 / 36.0 / 25.6 Age / $<\$5,783$ / $>\$5,783$ 12 — 10.0 / 3.0 16 — 34.0 / 16.0 18 — 45.0 / 27.0	(+) Race/SES interaction suggested by data; earlier age at onset for low SES
Polk, Frease, and Richmond (1974)	Compare B_{15} (juvenile court); father's occupation	White collar (WC) 24.1 Blue collar (BC) 26.6	(0)
McCord (1979)	B_L (conviction); neighborhood SES, father's occupation	Property Crime 0 Personal Crime 0	Neither measure significant in bivariate correlations or in MVA
Robins, Gyman, and O'Neal (1962)	Compare B_{18}; father's occupation	Patients / Controls BC 65.4 / 16.3 WC 56.9 / 8.6	

Study	Description	Data	Finding
Reiss and Rhodes (1961:723)	B_{HS} (adjudication--serious crime); white/blue collar, IQ	IQ WC BC Low 3.6 4.5 Middle 1.2 2.2 High .4 1.7	(+) Independent of IQ
Gold (1966:38)	Compare B_{HS} (juvenile court); father's occupation	Prof. or manager 2.9 Skilled worker 8.6 Operator 13.9 Laborer 15.0	(+); attributed in part to police referral judgment
Williams and Gold (1972:Figure 7)	Compare B_{HS} (self-reported contacts); father's occupational status (white males only)	Highest 19.0 Second 13.0 Third 9.0 Lowest 11.0	"Negligible" relationship for white males (Q = 0.07); "no reliable" relationship for white females (Q = -0.11)
Elliott et al. (1983)	Compare $\underline{d}$ (self-reports); socioeconomic class	Ages Ages 11-17 15-21 Breaking & Entering Middle 4.0 1.0 Working 4.0 2.0 Lower 4.0 3.0	Mixed

TABLE A-10 Continued

Reference	Method/Variable	Results (percent)			Relationship to Participation
			Ages 11-17	Ages 15-21	
Elliott et al. (1983) (continued)		**Aggravated Assault**			(+)
		Middle	3.0	3.0	
		Working	6.0	4.0	
		Lower	8.0	6.0	
		Theft Over $50			Mixed
		Middle	1.0	2.0	
		Working	3.0	3.0	
		Lower	3.0	4.0	
		Robbery			(+) for younger ages only
		Middle	3.0	1.0	
		Working	5.0	3.0	
		Lower	7.0	1.0	
		All Index Offenses			(+)
		Middle	15.0	9.0	
		Working	18.0	12.0	
		Lower	24.0	14.0	

Study	Comparison	Category		Age 8 / Ages 8–10	Age 14
Wadsworth (1979)	Compare B_{15} (conviction); father's occupation	Prof. or salaried		7.0	
		Other nonmanual		16.0	
		Unskilled manual		23.0	
		Agriculture		15.0	
				(+)	
Farrington (1983a)	Compare B_{25} (conviction); family income			Age 8	Age 14
		Low		48.0	38.0
		Other		29.4	30.9
				(+)	N.S.
					MVA^{a} (21–24)+
	Compare B_{25} (conviction); family housing			Ages 8–10	Age 14
		Poor		45.0	44.0
		Other		27.4	31.6
				(+)	N.S.
				MVA (10–13)+	
	Compare B_{25} (conviction); family social class			Ages 8–10	Age 14
		Low		39.2	43.1
		Other		32.6	32.5
				N.S.	N.S.
					MVA (17–20)+

NOTE: SES = socioeconomic status; T = all sample members; B = black; W = white; B is percent of population ever arrested: B_{15} by age 15, B_{18} by age 18, B_{25} by age 25; B_L, lifetime; B_{HS}, by high school age; d = percent of population committing a crime within a year.

[a] Many of the variables examined by Farrington (1983a) in this and subsequent tables were included in his various multivariate analyses (MVA), and the results are reported here *if the* variable was significant in those analyses.

census tract income, which may have little relation to individual socioeconomic status (see Tittle, Villemez, and Smith, 1978; Hindelang, Hirschi, and Weis, 1981). The study by Gold (1966) was based on a high school sample from Flint, Michigan, and only 28 youths had juvenile court records. Thus, Gold's data by social class in Table 10 are based on very few individuals. Finally, the Reiss and Rhodes study is based on a large sample but some of the offenses recorded in their juvenile data occurred as early as 1950.

As shown in Table 10 also, three studies from approximately the same time period and based on official records show small or negligible relationships between socioeconomic status and participation (Robins, Gyman, and O'Neal, 1962; Polk, Frease, and Richmond, 1974; McCord, 1979).

Robins, Gyman, and O'Neal reported a small class relationship among their patient sample and a slightly larger association in the control group. But only 11 of the controls were classified as delinquents on the basis of police arrest records. McCord first computed measures of partial correlation between alternative indicators of socioeconomic status and participation by average age of 43, then estimated a regression equation including only the explanatory variables with strong partial correlations. Even though McCord's two measures of socioeconomic status tapped different dimensions, father's occupation and neighborhood quality, neither showed even a strong partial correlation. The lack of a relationship may reflect a small effect of childhood social class on adult criminal behavior or homogeneity in socioeconomic status within the sample. Nearly 60 percent of the respondents' fathers in McCord's study were classified as unskilled workers, over 90 percent were classified as either unskilled workers or skilled tradesmen, and all neighborhoods were "congested urban." Similarly, homogeneity may have masked relationships in the study by Polk, Frease, and Richmond, and the one by Robins, Gyman, and O'Neal. In the former, the location of the study, Marion County, Oregon, does not include any large cities and the measure of socio-

economic status was simply a dichotomous indicator of the father's occupational status. In Robins and colleagues' sample of children seen at a guidance clinic, more youths were from lower-class families.

Finally, in a study of juvenile delinquency, Hindelang, Hirschi, and Weis (1981) examined the class/participation relationship based on a broad range of offenses in official records. Unfortunately, participation rates by status group were not presented. However, the authors reported gammas of only −.17 (based on median income of census tract) and −.05 (based on father's occupation) and concluded that "by neither measure of social class and by no measure of delinquency is there even a moderate relation between the two" (p. 196). These conclusions are consistent with the data in Table 10.

Thus, the relationship between social class and participation, as measured by official records, is not as clear-cut as previous literature has suggested. When participation is restricted to serious offenses in official records (e.g., Reiss and Rhodes, 1961; Gold, 1966), the relationship appears stronger. Recent evidence, however, is limited in part because of the difficulty of linking official records and individual interviews for a common sample. Some existing data sets presumably contain the necessary data, but the analyses have not been reported in the literature (e.g., McCord, 1979; Hindelang, Hirschi, and Weis, 1981; Shannon, 1982a; Thornberry and Farnworth, 1982).

Results of the few self-report studies summarized in Table 10 are somewhat ambiguous. Elliott et al. (1983) reported crime-specific current participation rates by a three-category socioeconomic classification. Only for aggravated assault and all index offenses was current participation consistently greatest among the lowest socioeconomic group. For breaking and entering, theft exceeding $50, and robbery, the group with the highest participation rates varied by age between the lowest and middle socioeconomic group. Auto thieves were so rare in all classes that no pattern can be ascertained. In other analyses of these data

(Elliott and Huizinga, 1983), social class differences emerged when criminal participation was restricted to serious offenses (felony assault scale, all index offenses, and robbery), and this association persisted after controlling for race.

Williams and Gold (1972:Figure 7) reported a relationship between social class and participation (based on self-reports of police contacts) that appears inverse to the relationship observed by others using official records. Reported participation among white males decreases from 19 percent in the highest category of father's occupational status to 9 percent in the third-highest category and rises to 11 percent in the lowest category.[8] But based on gamma statistics, they characterize this relationship as "negligible," report that inclusion of blacks further "diminishes" the relationship, and report "no reliable relationship between social status and police contacts among girls" (1972:221). Noting the difference between these results and the results of studies based on official records, Williams and Gold speculated that among youths who come to police attention, blacks, who are almost exclusively of lower status, are more likely than whites to be referred to courts and "become more officially delinquent during the judicial process" (1972:227). However, they provide no direct tests for racial or socioeconomic correlates of the decisions to refer and to record, and only 53 black males were in their sample.

Hindelang, Hirschi, and Weis (1981:196) also collected data on social class and self-reported participation, although participation *rates* were not reported. Using father's occupation as the measure of social class and a constructed index of involvement in *serious* offenses, they reported gamma between social class and participation for white males of only −.08, which is inconsistent with the results from Elliott et al.'s study.

Finally, two British studies show strong relationships between social class and participation. In examining participation based on conviction for an indictable offense by age 25, Farrington (1983a) reported significantly higher participation among members of the lower status group, as measured by family income at age 8 and quality of housing at ages 8–10, but not by parent's occupation at either ages 8–10 or age 14. However, using multivariate techniques to identify correlates of participation within specific age intervals, he reported that the occupation-based measure at age 14 was related to conviction at ages 17–20. In addition, family income at age 14 was significantly related to participation at ages 21–24 and family housing at ages 8–10 was related to conviction at ages 10–13. In other analyses of the same data, not reported in Table 10, Farrington (1979b) reported that low social class at age 8, but not at age 14, was related to self-reported delinquency.

For a national British cohort, Wadsworth (1979) reported participation estimates based on convictions by age 15 at 6.8 among children of professional-salaried workers, 15.5 among children of other nonmanual workers, 22.9 among children of unskilled workers, and 15.3 among children of agricultural workers. For the industrial occupations, similar findings (not shown) were reported by Ouston (1984) for a sample of London youths.

In summarizing the U.S. literature reviewed here, it appears that socioeconomic status is weakly correlated with participation in offending based on official records. However, few of the U.S. studies were based on large, recently selected samples that display substantial variation in social class. In contrast, British studies generally show a strong correlation between participation and various measures of social class. The two U.S. studies that found a relationship between social class and participation for serious crime types controlled for two of the characteristics that are related to socioeconomic status, race and measured IQ. When participation is measured by self-reports of serious offenses, similar relationships emerge, but the relevant data are

---

[8]Williams and Gold (1972:225) also reported that the association between social class and participation, based on official police records, is negligible among white boys, but "statistically reliable" among white girls.

limited. Divergence in results between some self-report studies and the official-record studies may reflect socioeconomic correlates of criminal justice system behavior and record-keeping practices, especially with respect to less serious offenses, socioeconomic differentials in respondent cooperativeness or recall during interviews, the broader spectrum of delinquent acts included in most self-report data, or some combination of these effects. Some findings of a relationship between "crime" and social class in other literature may confound effects of social class on participation and on individual frequency. Measures of criminal activity that incorporate both of these dimensions of the criminal career (e.g., mean scores of scales with values 0, 1, 2, 3+) may account for some of the inconsistent results in the research on social class and crime.

Family Structure and Disruptions

Table 11 summarizes results relating participation in offending to family size, structure, and disruptions. According to West (1969:73), "investigators all agree ... that families with a large number of children contribute a disproportionately large number of juvenile delinquents." This statement is consistent with findings from studies summarized in Table 11. On the basis of family size at subject's age 15, Wadsworth (1979) reported that participation among children with one or two siblings only slightly exceeded participation among children with no siblings (9.1 and 10.0, respectively) but that participation among offspring in families of four or more increased substantially to 24.3. Similarly, Farrington (1983a) reported participation rates nearly twice as high among sons of "large" families as among sons of "other" families.[9]

Explanations for the correlation between

participation and family size have included overcrowding and the low standard of living associated with large low-income families (see, e.g., Rutter and Giller, 1984:186). Wadsworth (1979:42) suggests that inherited characteristics associated with criminal behavior (e.g., low intelligence, low birth weight) may be more common in large families. Nye (1958) suggests that direct control of children is more difficult in large families, a situation that may hamper parental supervision and could delay learning to inhibit antisocial behavior.

It could also be argued that even if participation were otherwise independent of family size, a child in a large family faces greater risk of having a delinquent sibling. Through some mechanism, such as learning, peer association, adverse labeling of the family, or family stress created by one sibling's delinquency, participation in offending among the other children might be indirectly increased. One study summarized in Table 13 is consistent with this hypothesis, though the analysis is based on a very small sample (Robins, West, and Herjanic, 1975). Among male children with no delinquent siblings, participation was virtually identical for boys with one or two siblings (21 percent) and boys with three or four siblings (20 percent). Among boys with one or more delinquent siblings, participation was about three times as high, regardless of whether the total number of siblings was one or two (69.2) or three or four (57.1). Similarly, the data for females show participation rates to be relatively independent of family size but adversely affected by the presence of a delinquent sibling. However, further research with larger and more representative samples is needed to partition the effects on participation of family size from those of delinquent siblings.

As shown in Table 11, Wadsworth (1979) reported that participation by age 21 (based on convictions) increased with further family growth after the subject's birth, and that the effect was aggravated by later or longer periods of growth. In a related analysis, Wadsworth reported that participation declined steadily as the length of time as an only child increased. He also reported that

---

[9]"Large" family size and "other" were not explicitly defined in this study. Few U.S. studies have examined the relationship between family size and participation in offending. Those that have (e.g., Nye, 1958; Hirschi, 1969) used composite indices of criminal activity that were dominated by trivial offenses.

TABLE A-11 Relationship of Participation to Family Structure and Family Disruptions

Reference	Method/Variable	Results (percent)			Relationship to Participation
			Ages 11-17	Ages 15-21	
Elliott et al. (1983)	Compare $\underline{d}$ (robbery); broken family	Unbroken Broken	5.0 6.0	1.0 4.0	(+) at older ages only
	Compare $\underline{d}$ (index offenses); broken family	Unbroken Broken	18.0 28.0	10.0 17.0	(+)
Wadsworth (1979)	Compare B_{15} (conviction); broken family	Not broken Father's death Mother's death Marital breakup	14.2 14.4 19.6 26.6		(+)
	Compare B_{15} (conviction); age at family breakup	No breakup 0-4 years 4-8 years 8-11 years 11-15 years	14.2 30.7 21.5 20.5 9.9		(+)

TABLE A-11 Continued

Reference	Method/Variable	Results (percent)			Relationship to Participation
Farrington (1983a)	Compare B_{25} (conviction); broken family		Separation (Age 10)	Broken Home (Age 15)	(+)
		Broken	51.1	54.2	
		Intact	28.9	31.2	
Rankin (1983)[a]	Compare D_{HS}; broken family		B/E Assault	Auto Theft	Small (+) relationship
		Broken	31.2 25.2	5.5	
		Intact	29.5 24.3	4.2	
McCord (1979)	Compare B_L (conviction); father absent	Property Crime	0		MVA, controlling for SES and parental behavior
		Personal Crime	+		
Wadsworth (1979)	Compare B_{21} (conviction); family size at age 15	1 sibling	9.1		(+)
		2-3 siblings	10.1		
		4+ siblings	24.3		
Farrington (1983a)	Compare B_{25} (conviction); family size at age 15	Large	50.6		(+)
		Other	29.1		

Wadsworth (1979)	Compare $\underline{B}_{21}$ (conviction);$\underline{b}$ family growth after first birth (in years)	Only child 0-4 only 0-6 only 6-15 only 0-15	7.0 8.9 10.5 13.6 16.8	(+)
	Compare $\underline{B}_{21}$ (conviction);$\underline{b}$ maternal marriage age	<20 years >30 years All	13.2 10.5 8.2	(+); no known illegitimate births in sample
	Compare $\underline{B}_{21}$ (conviction);$\underline{b}$ marriage-birth interval	1 year or less 1-3 years 4+ years	14.6 8.6 4.5	(+); no difference at 9-month cutoff
	Compare $\underline{B}_{21}$ (conviction);$\underline{b}$ years as only child	To age 11 To age 6 To age 4 To age 2 Never	5.5 5.7 8.1 10.4 12.7	(+); relationship is not as strong with minor offenses

$\underline{a}$A reanalysis of the National Survey of Youth (conducted in 1967 and 1972) originally conducted by Gold (see Williams and Gold (1972); Gold and Reimer (1975)); crime-specific participation rates controlling for family disruption are reported for breaking and entering (B/E), assault, and auto theft.

$\underline{b}$Indictable offenses only.

children of mothers who were married before age 20 or after age 30, or who were married less than 1 year when the child was born, had higher participation rates than other children.

The consistent effects of measures of family structure (e.g., family size, birth order, birth spacing) on participation suggest that these relationships have a common origin. It is likely that these family-structure variables are closely associated with low socioeconomic status and other adverse family conditions associated with poor housing. In one multivariate analysis of factors related to delinquency in older children and preteens (Farrington, 1983a), family size did not significantly affect participation, but low family income and poor housing were important predictors (see also Rutter and Giller, 1984).

Four studies reviewed in Table 11 provide some evidence that family breaks, especially parental separation and divorce, increase participation in offending (Wadsworth, 1979; Elliott et al., 1983; Farrington, 1983a; Rankin, 1983). For the two age groups in Table 11, Elliott et al. found a higher self-reported current participation rate for robbery and for index offenses among children living with one natural parent than among children living with both. When the definition of participation was broadened to status offenses or a general delinquency index, the relationship persisted but was slightly weaker (data not shown).

Rankin (1983) reanalyzed the self-report data gathered by the National Survey of Youth (Williams and Gold, 1972; Gold and Reimer, 1975) and found very small effects of family disruption on three serious offenses—breaking and entering, assault, and auto theft. However, contrary to Elliott et al. (1983), family disruption had a much larger effect on three types of minor delinquency—running away, truancy, and fighting. Moreover, parental death and marital breakup had similar effects on running away, although less than 10 percent of the sample had experienced the death of a parent.

McCord (1979) looked at the relationship

between family disruption and lifetime participation in her longitudinal study. In a series of bivariate regressions, father's absence was unrelated to convictions for property crimes, but was weakly related ($p = .07$) to convictions for personal crimes. In other analyses, however, McCord (1982) showed that the operative factor was actually family conflict and not a broken home. Men raised in broken homes had *lower* rates of participation in serious crimes than men from intact homes with conflict. Other studies have also found significant effects of family conflict on participation (see Farrington, 1979a; Rutter, 1981).

Two British studies, using convictions as the criterion, show strong relationships between family disruption and participation. Wadsworth (1979) reported that the effect of a marital breakup on participation is more important than the death of a parent: compared with a participation rate of 14.2 among children of unbroken homes, death of the father had no effect, and death of the mother only a small one (to 19.6). Divorce or separation nearly doubled participation by age 25, to 26.6, in his sample. Farrington (1983a) found that two types of family break—separation from a parent by age 10 or a broken home by age 15—each raised participation based on convictions above 50 percent, compared with participation of about 30 percent among children of unbroken homes. In another analysis of these data, Farrington (1979b) found family disruption at age 10 related to self-reported delinquency at age 14, but not at age 18. The Wadsworth data also show clearly that family breaks before age 11 increase participation in offending, but that the magnitude of the effect declines with age at the breakup. Participation was actually lower among children who experienced the break between ages 11 and 15 (9.9) than among children of unbroken homes (14.2).[10]

_____

[10]See Gibson (1969) for another examination of age and family disruption, using early data from the Cambridge study. He found that age (before or after 5 years) is not important, but that controlling for other family influences affects the broken home/delinquency relationship. Broken homes have *less*

Thus, the participation literature shows some support for the view that family breaks increase participation in crime and delinquency, but there are subtleties in the data. Divorce or separation appears to have a stronger adverse effect than death of a parent, but this is an especially difficult area to research because of the large samples needed for a reasonable sample of both delinquent youths and youths who have lost a parent. Whether family disruption affects both participation in serious offenses and "acting-out" behaviors, such as running away or truancy, cannot be answered fully with the data presented in Table 11. Moreover, several studies that were not included in this review suggest that family disruption may have different effects depending on the sex, race, and age of the youth (Datesman and Scarpitti, 1975; Austin, 1978; Wilkinson, 1980). Future research should pay close attention to these potentially confounding demographic factors. Finally, some researchers have argued that the relationship between "broken homes" and official delinquency is spurious, reflecting differential treatment in the juvenile justice system (e.g., Rankin, 1983). However, Farrington (1979b) reported that family disruption was related to both self-reported delinquency and official records of conviction. Other researchers with the appropriate data should examine associations between various types of family disruptions and the self-report and official-record measures of delinquency (e.g., Elliott et al., 1983; Rankin, 1983).

Other Family Influences

Several of the studies reviewed here report strong empirical associations between participation and various aspects of behavior by family members that affects the sampled individuals, including parental behavior, parent-child relationships, and antisocial behavior by parents and grandpar-

ents. However, rarely was a specific parental characteristic associated with participation much above 50 percent. The analyses are summarized in Table 12.

Farrington (1983a) contrasted participation based on convictions by age 25 between subjects whose parents fell into the "most adverse" quartile and other subjects, according to interviewers' ratings of various parental behaviors. As shown in Table 12, the strongest contrasts were found with respect to ratings of supervision and an overall index of parental behavior when the child was 8. In multivariate analyses, the parental behavior index was also significantly correlated with participation between ages 10 and 13, controlling for IQ, poor housing, and other family and subject characteristics. The weakest correlates investigated by Farrington, nervousness in the father and attitude, still differentiated the two groups, but were not statistically significant. Farrington also reported a strong relationship between participation and the rated quality of the subject's relationship with his parents: participation was higher among those with poor parental relations (46.5) than among others (30.2).

Farrington also looked at the effect of parental employment on official delinquency. Youths whose fathers had erratic employment were much more likely to have an official record of conviction by age 25 (53.2) than other youths (30.3). However, youths whose mothers worked full time were no more likely to be convicted than youths whose mothers did not work or only worked part time. The effect of father's employment probably reflects its correlation with low social class, low family income, and poor housing.

Wadsworth (1979) reported that participation by age 15 declines dramatically as teacher ratings of parental interest in school progress increase. Similarly, McCord (1979) found that such parental attributes as quality of supervision, mother's affection and self-confidence, father's deviance and absence, and parental conflict and aggression all correlated with lifetime participation in property and/or personal crime.

Other recent studies and reviews of the

---

effect on socially disadvantaged families than on families without social disadvantages (e.g., poor housing, large family, low income).

TABLE A-12 Family Influences (Parental Behavior) and Estimates of Participation

Reference	Method/Variable	Results (percent)			Relationship to Participation
		Attribute (age)[a]	Most Adverse	Others	
Farrington (1983a)	Compare B25 (conviction); parental behavior (most adverse quartile and all others)	Behavior (8)[a]	47.3	28.5	(+); MVA (10-13) +
		Supervision (8)	52.9	28.4	(+)
		Nervous mother (10)	41.8	28.6	(+)
		Nervous father (10)	37.2	32.4	(N.S.)
		Attitude (14)	40.2	30.7	(N.S.)
			Property Crime	Personal Crime	
McCord (1979)	Compare BL (conviction); home background	Supervision	+	+	Bivariate correlations with BL
		Mother's self-confidence	+	+	
		Mother's affection	+	0	
		Father's deviance	+	0	
		Father's absence	0	+	
		Parent conflict	0	+	
		Parent aggression	0	+	
Farrington (1983a)	Compare B25 (conviction); relationship with parents (age 18)	Poor	46.5		(+)
		Other	30.2		

		Parental Interest			
Wadsworth (1979)	Compare B$_{15}$ (conviction);$\underline{b}$ interest in school progress (teacher rating, ages 10-11)	1 (low)	18.3		(+)
		2	9.8		
		3	6.4		
		4 (high)	5.3		
Farrington (1983a)	Compare B$_{25}$ (conviction); father's employment (at ages 8-10)	Erratic	53.2		(+)
		Other	30.3		
			Ages 8-10	Age 14	
	Compare B$_{25}$ (conviction); mother's job	Full-time	28.2	32.0	(N.S.)
		Other	34.8	33.1	(0)
Robins and Lewis (1966)	Compare B$_{18}$ (arrest); antisocial behavior$\underline{c}$ by parents (P) or by grandparents (GP)	By any P or GP	28.6		(+); contrasts slightly greater for paternal relatives than maternal relatives and GPs than Ps; based on 67 cases
		None by P or GP	4.0		
		By either GP	33.3		
		None by GP	3.2		
		By either P	28.5		
		By neither P	12.8		

TABLE A-12 Continued

Reference	Method/Variable	Results (percent)			Relationship to Participation
Robins and Lewis (1966) (continued)		By mother	23.5		
		None by mother	18.0		
		By father	32.0		
		None by father	11.9		
		By grandmother	28.6		
		None by grandmother	17.0		
		By grandfather	31.2		
		None by grandfather	8.6		
Robins, West, and Herjanic (1975)	Compare B_{18} (arrest); antisocial behavior by P and GP		M	F	(+); based on 145 cases
		Either grandparent	39.1	15.6	
		Neither grandparent	22.5	11.1	
		Either parent	42.8	22.8	
		Neither parent	0.0	0.0	

NOTE: B is percent of population ever arrested: B_{15} by age 15, B_{18} by age 18, B_{25} by age 25; B_L lifetime.

[a] Includes parental conflict, disciplinary patterns, and attitude toward children.
[b] Indictable offenses only.
[c] Includes arrests, excessive drinking, poor work record, neglect of family, persistent gambling, illicit sexual behavior.

effects of family influences (other than family criminality) on conduct disturbances and minor delinquency in young children and later criminal behavior have also pointed to the strong adverse effects of poor supervision, passive attitudes, and ineffective discipline (Patterson, 1982; Hirschi, 1983; Rutter and Giller, 1984:180–188). Thus, the findings in Table 12 relating the behavior of parents to participation in offending by their offspring appear consistent with the larger literature relating parental behavior to other measures of criminality among children. (For a review of studies relating nondelinquent disturbances of conduct to family functioning, see Rutter, 1977; Hinde, 1980; Patterson, 1980; Loeber, 1985.)

The other studies included in Table 12 examined the relationship between participation and antisocial behavior by both parents and grandparents. Robins and Lewis (1966) studied participation among the 67 offspring of subjects of the earlier follow-up of patients of a child guidance clinic. The offsprings' participation, as measured by arrest, was correlated with reports of both their parents' and grandparents' antisocial or deviant behavior (e.g., arrests, excessive drinking, poor work record, desertion, neglect, cruelty, gambling, and extramarital relations). As expected, antisocial behavior in earlier generations had a strong positive association with participation. More surprising is that the magnitude of the effect appeared greater for antisocial behavior by the subject's grandparents than by the parents. Unfortunately, the small sample size prevented Robins and Lewis from testing the grandparents' influence while controlling for antisocial behavior by aunts and uncles. Thus, it is possible that the influence was indirect, through antisocial behavior and perhaps marriage to an antisocial partner by the grandparents' offspring.

A similar three-generation study (Robins, West, and Herjanic, 1975) examined participation among the offspring of 223 black males followed in an earlier study (Robins and Wish, 1977). The sample is probably atypical, however, because no male or female subject without an antisocial parent was arrested by age 18. However, as shown in Table 12, the results were more as expected, in the sense that parental and grandparental antisocial behavior showed similar association with participation.

Family Members' Criminal Behavior

Six studies reviewed here present data on participation among offspring of criminal and noncriminal parents (Robins and Lewis, 1966; Robins, West, and Herjanic, 1975; Farrington, 1983a; Hutchings and Mednick, 1975; McCord, 1977; and Mednick, Gabrielli, and Hutchings, 1984). These are summarized in Table 13.

With one exception, the six studies consistently show a positive association between criminal participation by parents and by their offspring. The lone exception appears in Robins and Lewis (1966:504), who found lower participation by age 18 among sons of delinquent patients of a child guidance clinic (17.1) than among sons of nondelinquent patients (21.9), but the difference is probably not statistically significant. In another sample, Robins, West, and Herjanic (1975) found the expected relationship between parents' and children's participation; the effect was greatest in families in which the mother (or both parents) was arrested, and slightly lower when only the father was arrested. The association with the children's participation was found to hold for both parental delinquency and criminality as adults.

Similarly, Farrington (1983a) reported that conviction of at least one parent before age 10 dramatically increased the probability of subsequent conviction of the son. In addition, in the same study, a convicted sibling before age 10 had an equally strong effect on participation as measured by a conviction before age 25. These two measures of family members' criminal behavior were also significantly related to conviction at two earlier ages in multivariate analyses that controlled for earlier delinquent behavior and other personal characteristics. These findings support the previous results of Robins, West, and Herjanic (1975), who found that participation was higher for individuals with delinquent siblings.

McCord (1977) also had data on fathers'

TABLE A-13 Family Members' Criminal Behavior and Participation

Reference	Method/Variable	Results (percent)				Relationship to Participation
Farrington (1983a)	Compare B_{25} (conviction); convicted parent (age 10)	Yes	55.3			(+); MVA (14-16)+ (17-20)+
		No	26.5			
	Compare B_{25} (conviction); convicted sibling (age 10)	Yes	57.8			(+); MVA (14-16)+ (17-20)+
		No	30.9			
Robins and Lewis (1966)	Compare B_{18} (arrest); males only; parents' arrest as juvenile	Yes (35)	17.1			(-); small $\underline{N}$
		No (32)	21.9			
Robins, West, and Herjanic (1975)	Compare B_{18} (arrest); parents' arrest			$\underline{M}$	$\underline{F}$	(+); $\underline{N}$ = 145
		Father arrested		44.2	24.2	
		Not arrested		11.8	0.0	
		Father delinquent		46.1	14.3	
		Not delinquent		25.0	13.3	
		Mother arrested		48.4	26.7	
		Not arrested		21.8	9.1	
		Mother delinquent		63.6	44.4	
		Not delinquent		28.8	9.1	
		Both arrested		57.1	30.8	
		Neither arrested		0.0	0.0	

Compare B_{18} (arrest); older sibling delinquency and family size	1+ delinquent		(+); small N, especially for large families
	1-2 siblings (24) 69.2	18.2	
	3-4 siblings (11) 57.1	25.0	
	0 delinquent		
	1-2 siblings (62) 21.0	8.3	
	3-4 siblings (9) 20.0	0.0	

McCord (1977) Compare B_L (conviction); father's conviction	Larceny/assault +	Bivariate correlations
	Disorder +	
	Traffic 0	

Hutchings and Mednick (1975; computed from Tables 3a-3c) Compare B_L; convictions of biological parents (B) and adoptive parents (A)	Parent/Status	Minor	Criminal	Relative to non-adopted male with noncriminal father, adoption and a criminal father each raises B_L from 0.08 to 0.16 for criminal offenses. Among adoptees, criminality in biological father raises B_L from 0.14 to 0.23; in adoptive father, from 0.14 to 0.27
	Adoptive fathers			
	Criminal	38.0	27.0	
	Noncriminal	34.0	14.0	
	Biological fathers			
	Criminal	36.0	23.0	
	Noncriminal	34.0	14.0	
	Nonadoptees' fathers			
	Criminal	31.0	16.0	
	Noncriminal	28.0	8.0	

TABLE A-13 Continued

Reference	Method/Variable	Results (percent)	Relationship to Participation
	"Cross-fostering" comparison of B_L	Parent/Status Neither B nor A criminal: 10.0 A criminal, B not: 12.0 B criminal, A not: 21.0 A and B criminal: 36.0 All: 16.0	Consistent with additive biological and familial effects
Mednick, Gabrielli, and Hutchings (1984)	Compare B_L (conviction); convictions of biological and adoptive parents	M F Adoptees 16.0 3.0 Adoptive parents 6.0 2.0 Biological parents 29.0 9.0	(+)
	Compare B_L (conviction); (read from graph)	Parental Property Violent Convictions Crimes Crimes None 10.0 4.0 1 12.0 4.0 2 15.0 5.0 3+ 22.0 6.0	(+)

criminal behavior for her sample of men who had participated in the Cambridge-Somerville youth study. Although participation rates cannot be computed from the published data, McCord reported that fathers who were convicted of either assault or larceny were significantly more likely than other fathers to have sons who were convicted of those crimes. A similar relationship existed for drunkenness and other minor, nontraffic crimes.

Hutchings and Mednick (1975) presented several sets of statistics on participation among samples of adoptees and their biological and adoptive parents. The data were intended to isolate participation influences that are interpreted as genetic (e.g., criminality in the biological parents) from relationships that are primarily environmental (e.g., criminality in the adoptive parents). Their statistics were based on the criminal records as of 1971 for 1,145 males born in Copenhagen, Denmark, between 1927 and 1941 and subsequently adopted. Comparative statistics were also presented for 1,120 nonadopted controls, matched for sex, age, father's occupation, and place of residence.

From the data reported by Hutchings and Mednick, it is possible to contrast three pairs of participation rates: for adopted sons conditional on criminal activity of their biological and adopted fathers and for nonadopted controls conditional on their natural fathers' criminality. These contrasts are reported in Table 13. With respect to minor crimes, participation among adopted sons was only marginally associated with criminality in the parent generation in all three contrasts. With respect to serious crimes, participation was 8 percent for nonadopted sons with noncriminal fathers and 16 percent for those with criminal fathers. For adopted sons, participation was 14 percent if the adoptive father was noncriminal but 27 percent if he was criminal. A smaller participation differential was related to criminality of the adoptees' biological fathers: 14 percent if the biological father was noncriminal, but 27 percent if he was criminal. The association with the biological father's criminality was interpreted by the authors as evidence of a partially genetic influence on participation.

In the same study, Hutchings and Mednick reported results of a "cross-fostering" analysis of participation, controlling simultaneously for criminality of the adoptive and biological father. As shown in Table 13, the statistics, which were based on 662 adoptees selected in an unspecified way from the original 1,145, show an increase in participation from 10 percent when both the adoptive and biological fathers were noncriminal, to 12 percent when only the adoptive father was criminal, to 21 percent when only the biological father was criminal, and to 36 percent when both were criminal.

In assessing the results, the authors noted that because of adoption agency policy, the social classes of the biological and adoptive fathers were correlated. Therefore, as noted by Robins (1975), adoption studies do not completely separate genetic and environmental influences on participation. However, in a later analysis of an expanded Danish adoptee cohort, Van Dusen et al. (1983) found a correlation of only .14 between the social classes of the biological and adoptive parents as defined by occupation; they also found that participation was related independently to the social classes of both sets of parents, with higher participation among children of lower class parents.

Two characteristics of the Hutchings and Mednick work may have affected its validity as a test of genetic influences on participation. First, while only a negligible fraction of the adoptive fathers could not be located, about 15 percent of the biological fathers could not be found. If criminal participation levels differ between the biological fathers who were and were not located, the relationship between their participation and that of their sons would be overstated or understated, depending on the direction of the difference. Second, the data base did not include any information on the criminality of either the biological or adoptive mothers, and so the description of intergenerational transmission of criminality is incomplete.

In a later study, Mednick, Gabrielli, and Hutchings (1984) presented participation results based on 14,427 adoptions, apparently all that occurred in Denmark between 1927 and 1947. As shown in Table 13, among all parties involved in the adoptions, participation was highest among the biological parents, followed by the adoptees. Participation was lowest among the adoptive parents, who were presumably screened to prevent known offenders from adopting children. The following "cross-fostering" results were also reported:

If neither the biological nor the adoptive parents are convicted, 13.5 percent of the sons are convicted. If the adoptive parents are convicted and the biological parents are not, this figure rises only to 14.7 percent. However, if the adoptive parents are not convicted and the biological parents are, 20.0 percent of the sons are convicted. If the adoptive parents as well as the biological parents are convicted, 24.5 percent of the sons are convicted (p. 224).

It is not clear whether conviction of one set of parents is intended to refer to at least one member of the set or to both members, and no data were presented to support a later assertion that participation among the offspring was associated more closely with the mother's conviction than the father's.

The study also included a graph relating conviction participation among adopted sons to the number of convictions of the biological parent. The numbers, as read from the graph, suggest a strong tendency for participation in property crimes to rise with the number of parental convictions (Table 13). A slight tendency in the same direction is apparent for violent crimes, although parental age was not controlled. However, because of the time required to accumulate multiple convictions, the parents with three or more convictions may have been older than the parents with none or one conviction. Because participation increases with age, age-controlled statistics are necessary to isolate genetic influences.

The qualifications expressed above concerning the earlier cross-fostering analysis are also applicable here. In particular, 36 percent of the biological fathers and 17 percent of the biological mothers could not

be located. No information or even speculation was offered concerning characteristics of those parents; the authors said only that the "sons of parents not fully identified have levels of criminal law convictions and rearing social status that are approximately the same as for the sons of those parents [who were] fully identified" (p. 893).

The authors also reported a statistically significant association between participation among male adoptees and time in the orphanage awaiting adoption (51 percent were placed in the first year and 89 percent were placed before age 2). They suggest that this association may be explained by institutionalization effects or a bias toward later adoption of less desirable boys, who are eventually convicted at above-average rates. If the duration of institutionalization was longer for the sons of criminals than for other children, the association would lead to an overstatement of the relationship between participation levels in the two generations. But the study did not test this association.

The observed association between the biological fathers' and sons' participation could potentially be explained by nongenetic relationships between the two generations that involve correlates of participation. For example, Mednick, Gabrielli, and Hutchings (1984) reported that the children's participation was related to the duration of institutionalization prior to adoption. If the duration was also related to the father's criminality (e.g., because criminals' children are systematically rejected as less desirable than other children), that relationship would contribute to the association between participation indicators in the two generations. Similarly, Kamin (1985) suggested that in attempting to place children in adoptive homes that resembled their natural homes, adoption workers may have unknowingly invoked criminogenic family characteristics that did not appear in the permanent records available to Mednick and associates. Moses (1985) noted that a monotonic increasing or decreasing trend in participation over successive cohorts of fathers and sons could cause the observed association. However, Mednick, Gabrielli, and Hutchings (1985) replied that Kamin's "criminogenic placement" effect was unlikely under adoption agency procedures as of the relevant period. They also argued that the reported associations occurred even when separate analyses were performed for subcohorts, each of which involved a time span too short to reflect long-term participation trends.

To summarize, studies of family influences show clearly that, in unbroken families, participation among offspring is increased if the parents or siblings have official criminal records. Thus, the literature reviewed here is consistent with a major recent review of the correlates of delinquency (Rutter and Giller, 1984:182), which stated that "of the parental characteristics associated with delinquency, criminality is the most striking and consistent." Moreover, this association exists even when the children are separated from their biological parents because of adoption. This pattern is consistent with theories of participation that invoke inherited characteristics; however, further research is needed to eliminate rival explanations and to assess the consistency of the pattern in locations outside Denmark.

Early Antisocial Behavior

Of the participation studies reviewed for this paper, eight present analyses of the relationship between early antisocial behavior and participation in offending. Those studies are actually a small part of the vast literature relating childhood behavioral problems to later deviant behavior (see Loeber, 1982; Loeber and Dishion, 1983; Rutter and Giller, 1984:Chapter 2). Most of the larger literature, however, does not focus on participation in *serious* delinquency or criminal activity as the criterion. Nevertheless, the data presented in Table 14 are consistent with this larger literature and clearly show that indicators of early antisocial behavior are related to later criminal activity, as measured by official records. These results are summarized in Table 14.

In Table 14, the results from Feldhusen, Thurston, and Benning (1973) show that relative to children rated "social" by their teachers, participation based on police records was twice as high among children earlier rated "aggressive/disruptive," and participation based on court convictions was eight times as high. Prospective discriminatory power of other teacher ratings ("good" versus "potentially delinquent") is also shown by Reckless, Dinitz, and Kay (1957). The average age of their subjects when the study began was 12 years.

Two British studies also tested the predictive power of teacher ratings of childhood antisocial behavior on officially recorded participation by early adulthood. In both samples, the subjects were about 10 years old. Mitchell and Rosa (1981) used the more restrictive participation measure (convictions), and the teacher's index was most strongly associated with theft offenses. Compared with others in the sample, more than twice as many children who were rated in the most adverse group had a conviction by age 25 for theft. Violent offenses were less well predicted by the teacher ratings. Ouston (1984) reported participation rates by age 18 for youth earlier classified as "neurotic," "anti-social," "mixed," or "average." Both male and female children with the antisocial ratings had the highest participation rates. However, the "average" male children had higher rates than the children rated "mixed." For females, the average group did have the lowest participation rates.

Robins (1966) combined the samples of St. Louis child guidance patients with a control group and assessed the relationship between referral and lifetime participation. On the basis of all nontraffic arrests, the referred males were three times more likely to have an arrest than those not referred; the relationship was even stronger for females. When only index offenses are considered, none of the nonreferred males or females had adult arrests; in contrast, 30 percent of referred males and 5 percent of referred females had index arrests as adults. However, this finding should be interpreted cautiously because the sample of nonreferred children was small and index arrests are relatively rare among general samples.

To explore developmental sequences

TABLE A-14 Early Antisocial Behavior and Participation

Reference	Method/Variable	Results (percent)	Relationship to Participation
Reckless, Dinitz, and Kay (1957)	Compare B (police/court records); teacher rating	"Good" 8.0 "Potentially delinquent" 23.0	
Feldhusen, Thurston, and Benning (1973)	Compare B_{17-23} (police or court record); teacher ratings		(+)
			Police	Court	
		"Aggressive/disruptive"	48.0	24.0	
		"Social"	22.0	3.0	
Ouston (1984)	Compare B_{18} (police/court); teacher ratings at age 10		M	F	(+)
		Neurotic	28.6	9.7	
		Antisocial	38.9	21.1	
		Mixed	12.5	16.7	
		Average	24.0	3.8	
Mitchell and Rosa (1981)	Compare B_{25} (convictions); index of early deviant behavior; teacher rating		Theft	Vandal	Violence	(+)
		Most adverse	15.6	5.0	3.4	
		Other	6.9	1.6	1.6	
Robins (1966)	Compare B_L (adult arrests); referral to child guidance clinic		Non-traffic	Index	(+)
		Males			
		Referred (350)	60.0	30.0	
		Not referred (69)	22.0	0.0	
		Females			
		Referred (123)	36.0	5.0	
		Not referred (29)	3.0	0.0	

Robins and Wish (1977)	Robins and Taibleson's (1972) actuarial method controlling for sequence and time at risk, B_{18} (police or court record); early deviant behaviors	Marijuana use	+
		Elementary school absence	+
		Elementary school failure	0
		School dropout by age 15	+
		Alcohol use by age 15	0
		Sex by age 15	0
		Leaving home by age 18	0
	McNemar's test for matched pairs	Marijuana use	+
		Elementary school absence	+
		School dropout by age 15	0

Farrington (1983a)	Compare B_{25} (conviction) ratings of early development (most adverse quartile and all others)	Attribute (Age)	Most Adverse	Others	
		Neurotic extraversion (10)	33.9	33.1	(0)
		Neurotic extraversion (14)	34.4	33.3	(0)
		Neurotic extraversion (16)	45.2	29.7	(+); MVA (17-20)+
		Troublesome (8-10)	61.8	26.0	(+); MVA (10-13)+
		Daring (8-10)	53.3	25.9	(+); MVA (14-16)+
		Dishonesty (10)	49.4	27.8	(+); MVA (14-16)+
		Popularity (8-10)	39.8	30.0	(0)
		Nervousness (8)	24.2	36.1	(+)
		Nervousness (14)	37.7	32.4	(0)
		Aggression (12-14)	54.2	24.1	(+); MVA (17-20)+
		Truancy (12-14)	63.0	27.4	(+); MVA (17-20)+
		Hostile to police (14)	54.5	27.7	(+); MVA (21-24)+
		Money saved (18)	46.5	25.6	(+)
		Proaggression (18)	45.4	30.0	(+)
		Prodrugs (18)	41.9	30.3	(+)
		Anti-establishment (18)	51.0	28.1	(+); MVA (21-24)+

culminating in delinquency, Robins and Wish (1977) employed an actuarial technique developed by Robins and Taibleson (1972). Designed explicitly to exploit the power of longitudinal data bases on individuals, the technique searches for chains of hypothesized causal links, restricting the search to causes occurring before their hypothesized effects, and adjusting for the longer exposure period that follows "causes" that occur at earlier ages. Using this technique, they found no empirical link between B_{18} and alcohol use or sexual activity by age 15, failure in elementary school, or leaving home before age 18. In separate analyses, they found participation increased with marijuana use, excessive elementary school absences, and school dropout by age 15. However, the effect of school dropout disappeared when the other behaviors were controlled simultaneously.

Using ratings of various characteristics, Farrington (1983a) compared cumulative participation by age 25 between the "most adverse quartile" of the Cambridge sample and the rest of the sample. Of the characteristics tested, the following showed the greatest discriminatory power with respect to participation: "troublesomeness" at ages 8–10, daring at ages 8–10, truancy at ages 12–14, aggressiveness at ages 12–14, hostile attitudes toward police at age 14, and antiestablishment attitudes at age 18. Of sample members ranking in the most adverse quartile on each of these attributes separately, more than half were convicted of an indictable offense by age 25. In similar comparisons, proaggression and prodrug attitudes at age 18 showed less discriminatory power, and "neurotic extraversion" at ages 10 and 14 showed virtually none. Nervousness showed an inconsistent relationship: conviction by age 25 was actually less prevalent among the most nervous quartile of 8-year-olds than among other 8-year-olds. However, the relationship was reversed when measurements of nervousness at age 14 were used.

Wadsworth (1979:95–97) presents a summary discussion relating early antisocial behavior to participation among male youths. He reported no consistent relationships between participation and parental reports of aggressiveness, bed-wetting, or referral to a child guidance clinic. He did report a relationship to the Pintner and Maudsley personality tests, symptoms such as stammering and tics at age 15, and truancy. He found cheating on schoolwork a correlate of participation in minor crimes, and he reported greater participation in sex offenses among boys experiencing late puberty.

In summary, the studies reviewed here show that later participation increases with the emergence of early antisocial behavior as observed by parents, teachers, and peers. However, even among the highest risk groups identified in these studies, participation in subsequent offending does not exceed 65 percent. Thus, this literature leaves unanswered the question of why the antisocial behavior patterns of many children and adolescents terminate short of officially recorded delinquency and adult arrest.

School Performance and Intelligence

Nine of the studies reviewed report that poor school performance and low intelligence are associated with higher participation. The results of these studies are summarized in Table 15, except those of Reiss and Rhodes (1961), which are summarized in Table 10.

Wolfgang, Figlio, and Sellin (1972:63) found a nearly monotonic, increasing relationship between participation and a school-achievement scale, for both blacks and whites in Philadelphia cohort I. Among the two lowest achievement categories, participation among black males exceeded 50 percent, and the black-white differential was large. The race differential nearly disappeared among the highest category of achievers.

In an early study, Polk, Frease, and Richmond (1974) reported that for sons of both blue-collar and white-collar families, a better high school grade-point average was related to lower participation, based on juvenile court records. Also, Palmore and Hammond (1964) report lower officially recorded participation for both black and white high school students with averages of

TABLE A-15 School Performance, Intelligence, and Participation

Reference	Method/Variable	Results (percent)				Relationship to Participation
Wolfgang, Figlio, and Sellin (1972: 63); Jensen (1976: Table 2)	Compare B_{18} (arrest); school achievement test results	Achievement Level	B	W	T	(+); interaction with race found using Goodman's techniques (Jensen)
		Very low	56.1	45.9	53.2	
		Low	58.0	41.6	49.7	
		Average	48.3	32.3	36.4	
		High	36.5	16.3	18.1	
		Very high	14.3	13.2	13.3	
Polk, Frease, and Richmond (1974)	Compare B_{HS} (juvenile court); grade-point average in high school	High 8.9				(+); independent of social class
		Medium 22.5				
		Low 42.2				
Robins, Glyman, and O'Neal (1962: Table 12)a	Compare B_{18} (juvenile court); school achievement	Grammar school		74.2		(+); but strongly correlated with measured IQ
		Some high school		47.5		
		Graduated high school		9.1		
Palmore and Hammond (1964)	Compare B_{19} (arrest/court referral); school grades at ages 8-10		B	W		(+); school achievement, independent of race
		< "C" average	58.7	44.8		
		$\geq$ "C" average	30.8	12.5		

TABLE A-15 Continued

Reference	Method/Variable	Results (percent)			Relationship to Participation
Ouston (1984)	Compare B_{18} (police/court); reading scores and IQ at age 10	Reading Test	M	F	(+); slightly stronger relationship at age 14 (not shown)
		< 90	31.6	7.7	
		91–100	22.5	3.8	
		> 100	12.5	3.8	
		Nonverbal IQ			
		< 90	29.4	8.4	
		91–100	23.7	2.8	
		> 100	7.7	3.3	
Wadsworth (1979)	Compare B_{15} (convictions); teacher ratings at age 10	Hard worker	5.3		(+)
		Average worker	9.5		
		Poor/lazy worker	16.1		
Farrington (1983a)	Compare B_{25} (conviction); intelligence and achievement (most adverse quartile and all others)	Attribute	Most Adverse	Others	
		IQ (8-10)	48.0	29.1	(+); MVA (10-13)
		IQ (14)	47.0	28.1	(+)
		Vocabulary (10)	45.1	28.4	(+)
		Vocabulary (14)	47.3	29.5	(+)
		Attainment (10)	51.1	28.2	(+)
		School leaving age	45.1	26.4	(+)

Hindelang, Hirschi, and Weis (1981)		B_{HS}	D_{HS}	
Gammas relating trichotomized school grades to B_{HS} (arrests) and D_{HS}	White males	-0.34	-0.41	(+) for all but black males; authors doubt validity of grade and self-report data for this group
	Black males	-0.05	-0.12	
	White females	-0.41	-0.35	
	Black females	-0.24	-0.35	
		B_{HS}	D_{HS}	
Gammas relating knowledge scale to B_{HS} and D_{HS} (only serious offenses)	White males	-0.22	-0.20	(+) for all but black males; authors doubt validity of self-report data for this group.
	Black males	-0.26	0.07	
	White females	-0.15	-0.18	
	Black females	-0.10	-0.21	

aAdditional analyses of a study of children referred to a psychiatric clinic (Robins, 1966).

C or better compared with students with lower averages. Similar to the Philadelphia results, black youths in the lower achievement category had participation rates above 50 percent.

In the study of a high-risk sample of children referred to a guidance clinic, Robins, Gyman, and O'Neal (1962) found that having at least one juvenile court appearance by age 18 was much lower for youths who graduated from high school (9.1 percent) than for youths who left school before grade nine (74.2 percent). (For further evidence that school failure may be a precursor of delinquency, see Havighurst et al., 1962.) In a larger study, Reiss and Rhodes (1961) reported an inverse relationship between measured IQ and officially recorded participation among children of white-collar and blue-collar parents (see Table 10), but they did not control for school achievement.

Three British studies examine the relationship between school performance/intelligence and participation, also based on official records. Wadsworth (1979) reported that higher teacher ratings of pupil diligence at age 10 were associated with a lower rate of conviction for an indictable offense by age 15. In a series of comparisons, Farrington (1983a) found participation by age 25 adversely affected by low IQ, limited vocabulary, and leaving school at an early age. Moreover, in his multivariate analysis of factors predicting at least one conviction between the ages of 10 and 13, IQ at ages 8–10 had a significant effect independently of antisocial behavior and parental characteristics. Ouston's (1984) study of another London sample found that standardized reading and IQ scores at age 10 were clearly related to participation rates, based on police and court records. As would be expected, in a similar analysis with test scores taken at age 14, these same measures were slightly more predictive of later delinquency.

Last, Hindelang, Hirschi, and Weis (1981) examined the association between officially recorded and self-reported participation and grouped values of school grades and general-knowledge test scores. For white males and females of both races, they

reported gamma statistics demonstrating the expected relationship. For black males, the associations were statistically insignificant and, for the general-knowledge measure, in the "wrong" direction. However, the authors expressed strong doubt concerning the validity of the grades and self-report data for this group.

Taken as a body, the participation literature indicates that regardless of race and social class, higher school achievement is associated with a lower participation level. (See also discussions in Gordon, 1976; Hirschi and Hindelang, 1977; Rutter and Giller, 1984.) However, school achievement and low intelligence appear to be closely intertwined and further research is needed to sort out their relationship to participation.

Miscellaneous Attributes

Researchers have also examined the relationship of participation in offending to various other characteristics, such as legitimate activities, psychiatric diagnosis, physical attributes, and peer involvement. Because these relationships have been studied using a variety of methodologies, the studies summarized in Table 16 should be considered only a small, possibly unrepresentative, portion of the relevant research.

As shown in Table 16, Elliott et al. (1983) found that in the early years of their study, youths employed full-time reported higher levels of current participation than nonemployed respondents. However, in later years, the participation difference between full-time employed and nonemployed respondents essentially disappeared. Because the respondents were aged 11–17 at the time the study began, the data may reflect a maturation process, as employment is transformed from a source of freedom from parental controls to an adult activity tying the individual to society. Both Farrington (1983a) and Viscusi (1983) reported a strong positive relationship between participation and an unstable job record or low job status in early adulthood (ages 18–19), which is consistent with the trend in Elliott et al.'s data. Viscusi studied over 2,000 young black men from Philadelphia, Boston, and Chicago and found that for a variety of criminal behaviors, currently unemployed men reported higher participation rates than employed men. This relationship persisted even when controls were introduced for drug use and criminal history variables. Farrington's unemployment measure was also a significant predictor of conviction between ages 21–24, even controlling for convictions at earlier ages and low family income during childhood.

Farrington (1983a) also examined the association between conviction by age 25 and involvement with delinquent peers and drug use. Not surprisingly, Farrington reported greater participation among those who reported involvement with negative peers (not further defined) around age 14 (59.2 percent) than among other youths (25.3 percent). Drug use was also a significant factor influencing participation by young adults in this London sample and in the study by Viscusi (1983).

Robins (1966) reported extremely high participation rates among adults diagnosed as sociopaths. However, this finding does not necessarily indicate a causal relationship because arrest was 1 of 19 factors used in making the diagnosis and was the third most common in this sample.

The results of Farrington (1983a) that bear on the relationship between participation and physical attributes are also summarized in Table 16. The vast majority of studies of physical correlates of criminal activity have been conducted by comparing samples of incarcerated criminals with samples of presumed noncriminals in terms of the attributes of interest. Because such studies confound relationships involving both participation and frequency (λ), they were not reviewed here. The reader is referred to Mednick et al. (1982) and to Wilson and Herrnstein (1985) for more comprehensive reviews of that literature.

Farrington (1983a) reported higher participation among boys who were rated clumsiest, shortest, and lightest in weight at ages 8–10. However, the participation differentials were slight with respect to size measurements taken at that age, and were non-existent with respect to remeasurements at ages 14 and 18. Wadsworth (1979:99) reported similar body-size effects, but observed that they were eliminated when social class and birth-order effects were statistically controlled. (Tabular data were not reported.)

One physical attribute, low pulse rate, is considered a measurable indicator of an undersensitive autonomic nervous system, which has been hypothesized to be associated with higher rates of participation (see Wadsworth, 1976). As shown in Table 16, Farrington reported a weak relationship between low pulse rates at age 18 and convictions by age 25. Wadsworth (1976:249) observed no difference in pulse rate at age 8 in a mildly threatening situation among members of his sample who were and were not eventually convicted. However, those convicted of violent or sexual offenses exhibited significantly lower pulse rates, an observation consistent with the theory.

CONCLUSION

Perhaps the most striking finding about criminal participation is the pervasiveness of involvement in serious crimes. The best available estimates suggest that 25–35 percent of urban males will be arrested for at least one index offense in their lives, and 15 percent will be arrested before reaching age 18. There are systematic demographic patterns of participation in serious crime: males are more widely involved than females, and blacks more than whites; also, the majority of criminals begin their careers before reaching their early 20s. But demographic participation patterns offer little policy guidance, because they are too broad to offer a basis for decision making, because their interpretations are ambiguous, and because basic social values would be affronted by decision rules that invoked demographic characteristics.

Other family and individual characteristics related to participation are of more interest to scholars and policy makers. The family influences most consistently found to be associated with higher levels of participation in serious crime include:

TABLE A-16 Miscellaneous Attributes and Participation

Reference	Method/Variable	Results (percent)							Relationship to Participation
			1976	1977	1978	1979	1980		
Elliott et al. (1983)	Compare d (robbery); employment status	Unemployed	5.0	3.0	4.0	3.0	2.0		Positive association in earlier years, but appears to flatten as cohort ages; may reverse by age 25
		Part-time	5.0	4.0	4.0	2.0	1.0		
		Full-time	9.0	7.0	4.0	4.0	2.0		
	Compare d (index offenses); employment status	Unemployed	18.0	15.0	12.0	13.0	14.0		
		Part-time	21.0	16.0	14.0	12.0	10.0		
		Full-time	32.0	26.0	20.0	20.0	15.0		
Farrington (1983a)	Compare B_{25} (conviction); delinquent friends (age 14)	High	59.2						(+); MVA (17-20)+
		Other	25.3						
	Compare B_{25} (conviction); drug use (age 18)	Drug use	49.6						(+)
		No drug use	26.6						
Viscusi (1983)	Compare d; life-style variables (age 19)	Unemployed	(+)						MVA, controlled for recent probation or jail sentence
		Used drugs	(+)						
		In school	(-)						
		Gang member	(+)						

Farrington (1983a) Compare B_{25} (conviction); employment record at age 18

Unstable	60.0
Other	25.0

(+); MVA (21-24)+

Robins (1966) Compare B_L (arrest); psychiatric diagnosis as adult

Diagnosis	Nontraffic	Other
Sociopath (94)	94.0	69.0
Other (255)	48.0	18.0
Well (87)	34.0	12.0
Control (90)	17.0	2.0

(+); arrest is 1 of 19 symptoms for diagnosis; third most common among sociopaths

---

Farrington (1983a) Compare B_{25} (conviction); physical attributes (most adverse quartile and all others)

	Most Adverse	Others	
Clumsiness (8-10)	44.1	30.4	(+)
Height (8-10)	43.7	31.7	(0)
Weight (8-10)	38.4	33.0	(0)
Height (14)	37.1	32.3	(0)
Weight (14)	33.0	33.3	(0)
Height (18)	36.1	33.0	(0)
Weight (18)	30.8	34.8	(0)
Pulse rate (18)	39.2	32.3	(0)

- inadequate parenting, in the form of inconsistent or sporadically violent discipline, poor parent-child communication, and poor supervision;
- parental delinquency and criminality;
- parental discord and family breakups; and
- some indicators of low socioeconomic family status, such as low income and poor housing.

High rates of delinquency participation have been found consistently for children exhibiting the following behaviors at an early age:

- antisocial behaviors, such as aggressiveness, fighting, and lying; and
- poor school performance.

Some studies suggest that certain factors measured in the mid-teen years are empirically related to participation, although they do not necessarily precede initiation of the criminal career. These include:

- association with delinquent peers;
- abuse of hard drugs;
- employment status, which may have different effects for juveniles and adults; and
- large family size.

These family and individual characteristics will be familiar to many readers as "causes of crime" that have been discovered and supported in large bodies of empirical research. However, much of that research has measured crime in ways that reduce distinct career dimensions—participation, offending frequency, diversity and seriousness in crime types, and duration—to a single number. By limiting attention to research in which the various career dimensions can be partitioned, this review and that of Cohen (Appendix B) attempt to isolate the separate relationships between individual and family characteristics and the respective career dimensions.

Even though the associations just listed emerge consistently in the participation literature, two limitations should be noted. First, while the empirical relationships reported here provide prospective indicators of increased participation risk, predictions based on them will produce substantial error rates because, generally, at least 40 percent of the individuals presenting any risk factor do not become offenders, as measured by arrest before age 18. Some gains in accuracy could probably be achieved using scales that combine multiple characteristics associated with participation risk. But the magnitude of those gains may be disappointing because the risk factors do not occur independently of one another. One relatively unexplored approach to improving predictive accuracy is the search for specific stressful events associated with the *initiation* of criminal careers, such as school failure or a family death. These events may alter base participation rates from the levels that would have been expected on the basis of demographic characteristics and other risk factors.

Second, caution is essential in assuming that relationships observed in one time and place are applicable to others. Associations involving B_{18} in Philadelphia cohort I, for example, describe behavior occurring by 1963 at the latest; major changes in demography, social norms, and social programs since that time may well have made those associations inapplicable today. Similarly, differences between Britain and the United States suggest caution in assuming that relationships observed in one of the countries would apply in the other. Consequently, there is a clear need to develop new U.S. data bases that describe individuals' career initiation and participation behavior as well as their pertinent characteristics and experiences, as of the present time.

New data bases would be especially helpful in resolving unanswered questions about criminal participation if they were designed to facilitate synthesis of official records and self-reports of illegal activity and contacts with the criminal justice system. To maintain both the chronological accuracy and richness of detail needed to merge information on event sequences, such data bases should be developed longitudinally. A longitudinal design would include periodic reinterviews of subjects to gather incident reports concerning their illegal activity and police contacts, as well as other relevant information. It would also include recurrent searches for official records of the subjects' criminal and juvenile justice system contacts. With carefully designed samples, such data bases would be useful in resolving some contradictions between the official-record and self-report participation literatures (especially those concerning the roles of race and social class), in facilitating more crime-specific participation research, in clarifying patterns of current participation, and in understanding the influences of specific events and interventions on participation.

Research on Criminal Careers: Individual Frequency Rates and Offense Seriousness

Jacqueline Cohen

INTRODUCTION

The level of crime experienced in a society varies with both the participation by individuals (b or d) in that society and the frequency of offending by active offenders (λ). Increases in crime may be due to increases in either the participation rate or the frequency of offending. Distinguishing among the different dimensions of criminal careers has implications both for our understanding of the factors contributing to crime and for efforts to control crime.

The characterization of criminal careers invoked here assumes that offending is not pervasive throughout a population, but rather is generally restricted to a subset of individuals who are actively committing crimes during some period of time. It is also assumed that the constituents of the subset of active offenders vary with time as some individuals become criminally active (onset of careers) and others terminate their criminal activity. Under this characterization,

the defining attribute of offenders is commission of at least one crime.

Participation, the subject of Appendix A, refers to the size of the criminally active offender subset during some observation period. This subset of active offenders includes both new offenders (first offense occurs during the observation period) and persisting offenders (criminal activity began in an earlier period and continues into the current observation period). Participation rates during any observation period will thus depend on the number of individuals who become offenders and how long they remain criminally active. The longer criminal careers are, the greater will be the contribution of persisters to participation in any observation period.

The subset of active offenders in any observation period is distinguished by having a positive frequency of committing crimes (e.g., five crimes per year per active offender). Beyond the requirement of at least one offense for active offenders, frequency rates may vary substantially across active offenders, with some offenders having very high rates and others low rates of offending. Frequencies may also vary over time for an individual. Individual offenders who have the highest frequencies will contribute most to total crimes.

The author would like to thank Arnold Barnett, Alfred Blumstein, David Farrington, and Jeffrey Roth for their helpful comments on an earlier version of this paper.

Many different offense types may contribute to an individual's frequency. Individual offenders, for example, may vary in the scope of their offending, from "specialists" (who engage predominantly in only one type of offense or one group of closely related offenses) to "generalists" (who engage in a wide variety of offense types). The degree of specialization may also vary across offense types; some offense types may be committed exclusively by specialists, while others are routinely committed as part of an offender's varied mixture of offense types. The mix of offenses committed by any offender may also vary as offending continues—individual offenders may become either more or less specialized, or increase or decrease the seriousness of their offending. If there are consistent patterns of change in the mix of offenses, then commission of serious offenses may be characteristic of certain periods during criminal careers (e.g., later careers may be periods of more serious criminal activity).

The various aspects of individual criminality—participation, career length, frequency, and crime mix—will affect the contribution of individual offenders to the total volume of crime experienced at any time. Offending may be widespread, with many offenders each committing crimes at relatively low rates; in this event, individual offenders contribute very little to the total volume of crime. Alternatively, individual frequencies may be high and participation low; individual offenders would then be responsible for a larger portion of total crimes.

Career lengths may be short or long. If careers are characteristically short, then there is likely to be a large turnover of active offenders as individuals quickly terminate careers and new individuals become criminally active. In this event, new offenders would be major contributors to crime. Also, with short careers, current participation levels may be relatively low, while cumulative participation (all individuals who were *ever* criminally active) is more widespread in the population. If criminal careers are characteristically long, the same individuals commit crimes over longer periods of time, and these persisters are major contributors to total crime.

This appendix provides a critical review of the emerging body of research that empirically characterizes various dimensions of individual offending. Because of its scope and volume, the full range of the literature is beyond the reach of a single paper. Narrowing the focus of this review builds on a natural partition of the various dimensions of criminal careers. Participation delimits the subset of active offenders in a population; this dimension of criminal careers is addressed in Appendix A. This appendix focuses on the progress, or course, of individual offending during criminal careers, as measured by frequency rates and offense seriousness.

Frequency rates are addressed first, followed by offense seriousness. In reviewing the research findings, special attention is given to their validity in light of various methodological concerns. In many instances, frequencies or offense seriousness are not addressed directly in the reported results, and whenever possible, available data have been reanalyzed in order to present results on frequency rates and offense seriousness in comparable terms.

INDIVIDUAL OFFENDING FREQUENCIES FOR ACTIVE OFFENDERS

Individual offending frequencies, λ, are a fundamental feature of individual criminal careers. Despite the importance of λ in estimating the magnitude of offending during criminal careers, research that statistically characterizes the intensity of offending for large numbers of ordinary offenders is relatively recent. Much of the early research on individual criminal careers consisted of biographical or autobiographical studies.[1] While such case studies provided interesting and often insightful reports on the individuals studied, there was little in-

---

[1] Some of the classics among these studies are Booth (1929), Shaw (1930, 1931), Sutherland (1937), and Martin (1952).

dication that the individuals were representative of a larger group of offenders. Indeed, the subjects were more likely chosen for their fascinating uniqueness than for their representativeness.

More recently, a large body of research has examined the attributes of large samples of offenders. This research includes both studies of self-reported delinquency and studies using official records, such as arrest histories.[2] Because this research has been largely motivated by interest in the causes and prevention of crime, it has focused on identifying the correlates—social, economic, psychological, and otherwise—of offending. This research has typically developed estimates of participation (i.e., the prevalence of offenders) or of continued offending in different population subgroups. Estimates of the intensity of offending by identified offenders, λ, are rarely provided. A related body of literature attempts to develop typologies of offenders with similar social or psychological attributes.[3]

---

[2]The self-report literature is extensive and includes over 100 studies. A partial bibliography is available in the review of the National Council on Crime and Delinquency (1970). A critical review of much of this research is found in Reiss (1973) and Hindelang, Hirschi, and Weis (1979). The following represent only a small sample of the available research in this area: Reiss and Rhodes (1959), Hirschi (1969), Gold (1970), Waldo and Chiricos (1972), Williams and Gold (1972), Elliott and Voss (1974), Elliott and Ageton (1980), Hindelang, Hirschi, and Weis (1981), Elliott et al. (1983). A recent review of participation measures, including those based on self-reports, is available in Visher and Roth (Appendix A).

Analyses of official records typically involve longitudinal analysis of large samples of criminal records. Among such studies are Glueck and Glueck (1937, 1940), McCord and McCord (1959), Robins (1966), Wolfgang, Figlio, and Sellin (1972), West and Farrington (1973, 1977), Robins, West, and Herjanic (1975), Robins and Wish (1977), McCord (1978), Farrington and West (1981), Hindelang, Hirschi, and Weis (1981), Farrington (1983b, 1984).

[3]See Warren (1971) and Gibbons (1975) for reviews of the typology literature. Examples of typology research are found in Kinch (1962), Gibbons (1965), Hurwitz (1965), Roebuck and Quinney (1967), and Davies (1969).

Recent interest in the crime control effects of incapacitation has underscored the importance of developing estimates of λ. Recognizing the impact of variability in λ on estimates of incapacitative effects, the National Research Council Panel on Deterrent and Incapacitative Effects (Blumstein, Cohen, and Nagin, 1978:80) made the following recommendation:

Empirical investigation should also be directed at estimating the parameters measuring the level of individual criminal activity, especially the individual crime rates . . . and career lengths. . . . Furthermore since estimates of the incapacitative effect are sensitive to variations in these parameters, these estimates should not be restricted to highly aggregated population averages. They should be disaggregated by crime type and demographic group and should reflect the statistical distribution of the parameters.

Recent studies in two research programs—one at the Rand Corporation and the other at Carnegie-Mellon University—have begun to provide explicit, disaggregated estimates of λ. That research is reviewed in this section, in particular the very different approaches used and the resulting estimates of λ. A number of other studies provide estimates of participation rates and aggregate incidence rates for a study population. These data provide a basis for developing estimates of λ for the studied populations. The results of these new analyses are also reported below.

Throughout this review of estimates of λ, various methodological issues in the measurement of λ are discussed and suggestions are made for further research in this area. The section begins with a discussion of the distinction between λ, the main interest here, and more commonly available estimates of aggregate incidence rates.

Distinguishing Individual Frequency Rates from Aggregate Incidence Rates

Individual frequency rates, λ, apply only to active offenders. This restriction distinguishes λ from the more commonly available measure of *aggregate* incidence rates, which reflect the frequency of offenses, or arrests, in the general population. Aggregate incidence rates are exemplified by the annual crime rates and arrest rates reported by the Federal Bureau of Investigation. The key feature distinguishing λ from aggregate incidence rates is the population base on which the estimates are calculated.

In calculating λ, only individuals with at least one offense, or arrest, are included in the population base. Estimates of λ thus reflect the average frequency of offending for individuals who are actively committing crimes. Aggregate incidence rates, by contrast, apply to a total population. The population at risk includes offenders and nonoffenders alike.

Aggregate incidence rates reflect the combined contribution of participation rates for offenders in a population, d or b, and individual frequency rates, λ or μ, for active offenders. Consider, for example, estimates of aggregate arrest rates for some population i:

$$\begin{array}{l}\text{Aggregate} \\ \text{arrest} \\ \text{rate for} \\ \text{population } i\end{array} = \dfrac{\begin{array}{c}\text{Number of arrests} \\ \text{of persons} \\ \text{in population } i\end{array}}{\begin{array}{c}\text{Number of persons} \\ \text{in population } i\end{array}}$$

This aggregate measure can be partitioned between the participation rate for offenders (b) and the frequency rate for those offenders (μ):

$$\begin{array}{l}\text{Aggregate} \\ \text{arrest} \\ \text{rate for} \\ \text{population } i\end{array} = \dfrac{\begin{array}{c}\text{Number of persons} \\ \text{arrested in population } i\end{array}}{\begin{array}{c}\text{Number of persons in} \\ \text{population } i\end{array}}$$

$$\times \dfrac{\begin{array}{c}\text{Number of arrests of} \\ \text{persons in population } i\end{array}}{\begin{array}{c}\text{Number of persons} \\ \text{arrested in population } i\end{array}} \quad (1)$$

$$= \text{Participation rate}_i \\ \times \text{Frequency rate}_i$$

The conceptual distinction between participation rates and individual frequency rates has important implications for the evaluation of incapacitative effects. The crime control potential of incapacitation hinges on the magnitude of an individual's offending frequency, λ. This is the expected number of crimes averted by incapacitating an offender. Aggregate incidence rates include rates of zero for nonoffenders, who are not vulnerable to incarceration, except in the rare cases of wrongful conviction. Aggregate incidence rates, therefore, would seriously underestimate the crime reduction achieved by incapacitation. Likewise, the impact of incapacitation policies on prison populations depends on the participation rates of offenders in a population. The more widespread that offenders are in a population, the greater will be the potential increases in prison populations as a result of incapacitation strategies. To the extent that λ exceeds one offense per offender, aggregate incidence rates will overstate the prevalence of offenders. In this event, use of aggregate incidence rates in place of participation rates would lead to overestimates of the potential impact of increased incapacitation on prison populations. Accurate estimates of the tradeoffs between increases in prison population and reductions in crime through alternative incapacitation policies depend critically on having separate estimates of participation and frequency rates.

The partition of aggregate incidence rates into participation rates, on the one hand, and individual frequency rates for active offenders, on the other, may also be useful in evaluating the effectiveness of other crime control policies. To date, evaluations of deterrent and rehabilitative effects have relied almost exclusively on aggregate outcome measures.[4] To the extent that partici-

---

[4]Recidivism rates are a special variant of aggregate incidence rates. While restricted to a population of identified offenders, the prospective performance of this population is the combined result of the level of continued participation by active offenders and the magnitude of individual frequency rates for those who remain criminally active. In particular, failure to recidivate during a follow-up period may occur because some offenders end their criminal careers altogether, or because some offenders who do remain criminally active do so at low frequency rates. In the latter case, extending the length of the follow-up period increases the likelihood of observing eventual recidivism; in the former case, recidivism will never occur no matter how long the follow-up period.

pation rates and frequency rates are differentially affected by deterrence or rehabilitation policies, important effects on these component parts may be obscured in the aggregate measures. Analyses of effects on the partitioned measures may provide valuable insights for improving the crime control effectiveness of deterrence and rehabilitation policies. It may be, for example, that different strategies will be more effective if they are targeted on selected population subgroups.

Review of Estimates of Individual Frequency Rates

The main interest in this subsection is empirically based estimates of λ. Relatively few studies provide explicit estimates of λ, and they are limited to samples of serious adult offenders. Three such studies are reviewed in this section. Indirect estimates of λ, derived expressly for the panel from other published data on current participation rates and aggregate incidence rates, are also reviewed. The indirect estimates have been developed for a wider variety of study populations.

The studies that provide explicit estimates of λ are summarized in Table 1. Separate rates are generally estimated for individual offense types, and total rates are presented for larger offense classes. Offense-specific frequencies reflect the average number of offenses committed when that offender is active in that offense type. Active offenders are distinguished by having at least one offense (or one arrest) for a crime type. Individuals with no offenses of a particular type during the observation period are excluded in the computation of rates for that offense type.

By this criterion, the earliest self-report survey, the Rand survey of 49 prison inmates (Petersilia, Greenwood, and Lavin, 1977), is properly excluded from consideration. The offending rates reported in that study apply to the total sample of 49 offenders; rates of zero for inmates who reported *no offenses* of a given type are included in the reported rates. As the direct precursor of the two later Rand inmate

surveys, however, the study is included here.

All of the studies summarized in Table 1 are based on samples of adult offenders. The samples are also generally restricted to more serious, or more criminally active, subsets of adult offenders. The three self-report surveys, all by the Rand Corporation, are based on surveys of inmates serving sentences in state prisons and, in one study, inmates in local jails. These inmate samples are thus restricted to offenders whose current offense or prior criminal record was serious enough to have warranted a sentence of incarceration.

The two studies using official arrest records are based on samples of adult arrestees. While potentially including a broader range of offenders, these studies also focus on offending by a more serious subset of offenders. To enter the sample, an offender must have had at least one arrest for a serious index offense (murder, rape, robbery, aggravated assault, burglary, or auto theft) during the sampling period. This criterion excluded offenders who engaged exclusively in minor offenses or who were never arrested for a serious index offense.

By focusing on subsets of offenders who are active in serious offense types, studies of frequency rates can develop estimates of λ in those serious offense types. Because they are generally quite rare, these more serious offense types have often been excluded from surveys of general population samples. The studies that provide estimates of λ for serious offenders are in direct contrast to the much larger body of research on participation in offending, which is typically based on self- or official reports of offending and deviance for juveniles sampled from a general population, and which is therefore dominated by the more common minor offenses, such as vandalism or simple assault. This difference in design reflects the different focus of the studies, in the first instance, the intensity of serious offending by more continuously active offenders, and in the second, the scope of deviance found in a broad population.

In addition to focusing on active offenders, the studies in Table 1 also restrict the

TABLE B-1 Summary of Empirical Research on Individual Frequency Rates for Offending

Sampling Frame	Observation Period	Controls for Time Active	Reliability Checks Used	Offending Frequency Rates	Reported Correlates

Petersilia, Greenwood, and Lavin (1977)

Self-Reports/Adults

Sampling Frame	Observation Period	Controls for Time Active	Reliability Checks Used	Offending Frequency Rates	Reported Correlates
Cross-section Random sample of 60 inmates from resident male population in one California prison in 1975 confined on conviction for armed robbery and with at least one prior prison term. Usable interviews were obtained for 49 inmates.	Retrospective Self-reported data on offenses, arrests, convictions, and incarcerations during three contiguous periods: a. First reported juvenile offense to first incarceration as a juvenile (or age 18 if not incarcerated) (mean length 2.8 years) b. Release from first juvenile incarceration (or age 18) to first adult incarceration (mean length 7.8 years) c. Release from first adult incarceration to start of current confinement (mean length 11.1 years)	Time incarcerated was excluded from time at risk for offending to yield street time during each observation period: Period / Mean Street Time (years) 1 / 2.8 2 / 5.2 3 / 3.9 Only the time from the first offense to the current incarceration is considered.	Rap sheets containing officially recorded arrests and convictions were compared with self-reports of arrests and convictions. Excluding the juvenile period, which is under-reported in official records, offenders reported only about one-half of officially recorded arrests and convictions. The more serious offenses of rape and robbery were most accurately reported (robbery 63%, rape 100%); the least serious offenses of grand larceny, aggravated assault, and auto theft were least accurately reported.	Based on open-ended question asking how many times respondent committed each of 9 offenses during observation periods; monthly rates are provided for four aggregate classes of offenses. The rates are aggregate incidence rates computed by dividing total reported offenses by total street months for the entire sample. Frequency rates for active offenders within the sample are not reported. Offending was often intermittent. Half to two-thirds of offenders experienced crime-free intervals whose duration ranged from 10 to 30% of total time free.	Age Aggregate incidence rates are reported to decline over time for all offense classes except violent offenses. Employment o As adults two-thirds or more of respondents reported working during 75% or more of street time. o While working as adults, three-fourths of respondents reported being employed full time. o About one-half of respondents reported that a job was their usual source of income. Drugs and Alcohol o 43% classified by Department of Corrections as addicted or users of drugs. o 40% reported being under the influence of drugs or alcohol at time of crimes as juveniles; for adult crimes, this rose to 60%. o 30% reported that obtaining money for drugs or alcohol was the main reason for adult crimes.

TABLE B-1 Continued

Sampling Frame	Observation Period	Controls for Time Active	Reliability Checks Used	Offending Frequency Rates	Reported Correlates
Peterson and Braiker (1980)					
Cross-section Twenty percent random sample of resident male population of inmates at five California prisons in 1976 (original N = 1,323). Eighteen percent of the sample were unavailable because they were no longer residents at the institution or because they were in secure custody (available N = 1,085). A total of 624 inmates (47%) provided usable survey responses (81 of these did not report committing any of the crimes in the survey). No significant differences in terms of convicted offense, age, or race/ethnicity were found when comparing final sample to total resident population of California prisons. However, individuals with more extensive prior incarceration records and inmates serving long terms were overrepresented in the sample. Using reported offense rates, probability of arrest and incarceration after an offense, and the expected time served in prison, the sample was	**Retrospective** Three-year period immediately prior to start of current term of incarceration. At the time of the survey, half the respondents had served less than 2 years; three-fourths had served 3 years or less.	Time incarcerated or hospitalized was excluded from time at risk for offending to yield street time during 3-year observation period. Thirty respondents provided meaningless data on time served; they were arbitrarily assigned the median street time of all other respondents (28 months). All offenders were criminally active at start of current incarceration. Respondents reporting an offense type any time during 3-year observation period were assumed criminally active for the entire period.	Surveys were anonymous, so no reliability checks with officially recorded data were possible. Six percent of respondents denied committing all offense types, including the one for which they were incarcerated. For all offenses except rape, the number of respondents reporting that they committed an offense was at least 2-3 times larger than the number reporting it as their current convicted offense. An internal reliability check was available in the form of another question on frequency of burglaries in a typical month. Categorizing offenders as 0-rate, below median, or above median on each measure, the correlation between the two estimates is .790. (The two measures, however, vary substantially on the actual frequency of offenses committed.)	Frequency of offending was obtained from responses to fixed categories: 0, 1-2, 3-5, 6-10, and more than 10. The midpoint of a category was used in estimating rates. If more than 10, respondents were asked to indicate the total number in an open-ended question. Offense-specific λs per year of street time are provided. Separate estimates are provided for the resident inmate sample, for a sample of incoming prisoners, and for a sample of street offenders. Individuals varied in the offense types they committed—49% of respondents reporting any crime reported committing 4 or more of 11 offense types. Categorizing offenders as 0-rate, below median, or above median--most offenders reported committing no offense or one offense, and a small number reported very high rates.	**Age** Decrease in criminal activity with age is primarily associated with a decrease in number of different offense types offenders engaged in. **Race** White respondents reported committing more offense types and at somewhat higher λs than black respondents. **Prior Record** Offenders with more extensive prior criminal records committed more offenses. **Drugs** Drug users reported substantially more property crimes than other offenders. **Juvenile Crime** Offenders who began committing crimes at younger ages and who committed more serious crimes as juveniles reported more crimes as adults.

reweighted to estimate the distribution of λ for offenders committed to prison and for a sample of street offenders (i.e., active offenders who have a nonzero chance of incarceration per crime committed).

Chaiken and Chaiken (1982a)

Cross-section
Sample of male inmates sentenced from selected counties and incarcerated in California prisons (N = 357) and jails (N = 437), Michigan prisons (N = 422) and jails (N = 373), and Texas prisons (N = 601).

The resident population at the institution was weighted to yield a sample simulating a cohort of incoming prisoners. No further adjustments to a sample of street offenders are provided.

Retrospective
Surveys were administered between October 1978 and January 1979. The observation period ranged from 13 to 24 months during the 2 calendar years preceding the arrest leading to the current incarceration.

Time incarcerated or hospitalized was excluded from time at risk to yield street time during the 2-year observation period. (Street time could range from 1 to 24 months.)

All offenders were criminally active at start of current incarceration. Respondents reporting an offense type any time during the observation period were assumed to be criminally active in that offense type for the entire observation period.

o Retest on 250 respondents.
o Internal quality based on consistency checks of responses to redundant items.
o External reliability based on consistency checks of self-reported arrests and convictions with official-record data.

To test sensitivity of offending frequency rates to poor reliability or internal quality, frequency rates were calculated after excluding 42% of sample with "bad data." Frequency rates never vary by more than a factor of 2.

For frequencies of 10 or less, respondents were asked to indicate the exact number of offenses in an open-ended question. For frequencies greater than 10, respondents first chose a category that best described the smallest unit of time in which offenses were committed (e.g., monthly, weekly, daily) and then indicated the number of offenses committed in that unit of time.

Offense-specific offending frequencies per year of street time are provided for offenders active in an offense type (i.e., those who reported committing the offense during the observation period).

Individual offending frequencies are highly skewed: most offenders committed no or very few offenses and a small number of offenders committed offenses at very high rates.

Offending frequencies for inmates vary substantially across states—highest in California, lowest in Texas.

"violent predators," who are active in the combination of robbery, assault, and drug dealing, committed these and other offenses at very high rates.

o Official-record information on these 3 offense types does very poorly in identifying violent predators.

o Violent predators are distinguished from other offenders by their:
- youth
- extensive self-reported juvenile criminal activity and drug use
- irregular employment
- use of multiple drugs as an adult
- lack of family obligations.

High-rate offenders in less serious property offenses (fraud, forgery, credit card crimes) are distinguished by their:
- education
- being married
- recent unemployment (as opposed to irregular employment).

TABLE B-1 Continued

Sampling Frame	Observation Period	Controls for Time Active	Reliability Checks Used	Offending Frequency Rates	Reported Correlates

Chaiken and Chaiken (1982a) (Continued)

| | | | | | Low-rate offenders can be predicted with high accuracy using prediction models. The models perform uniformly poorly in predicting high-rate offenders (10 or more offenses per year): well over half are in fact low-rate offenders. |

Official Records/Adults[a]

Blumstein and Cohen (1979)

| Cross-section/cohorts Sample of all adults (18 or older) arrested in Washington, D.C., during 1973 for murder, rape, robbery, aggravated assault, burglary, or auto theft (N = 5,338). Analysis focuses on cohort subsamples who turned 18 between 1963 and 1966 and whose first arrest as adults was between ages 18 and 20 (N = 80 to 200 active offenders for individual offense types). | Retrospective Adult arrest histories from age 21 through December 31, 1972, were used. The period including the first adult arrest and the sampling period, 1973, were excluded from the analysis   The observation period ranged from 4 to 7 years for the four cohort subsamples examined. | Time incarcerated was excluded from the time at risk during the observation period.   By virtue of a first adult arrest before age 21 and the sampled arrest in 1973, all offenders were presumed to be criminally active throughout the entire observation period.   Offenders who were ever arrested for an offense type were assumed to be criminally active in that offense type for the entire observation period. | Offending frequencies based on arrest histories and estimates of the probability of arrest per crime were found to be strikingly similar to independently derived estimates of λ based on self-reports by inmates. | Offense-specific arrest frequencies and offending frequencies are provided for offenders active in an offense type (i.e., those with at least one arrest for the offense type at some time during their arrest histories). | Age Offense-specific arrest frequencies within cohorts were generally trendless over age for young adults.   Cohorts Offense-specific arrest frequencies were higher for more recent offender cohorts (those born later).   Prior Arrests Offense-specific arrest frequencies within cohorts were generally stable as prior arrests increase.   (Frequency rates by cohort and by prior arrests are based on reduced sample sizes for individual offense types.) |

Cross-section/cohorts
Sample of all adults (age 18 and older) arrested in the Detroit SMSA between 1974 and 1977 for murder, rape, robbery, aggravated assault, burglary, or auto theft (N = 18,635).

Analysis focuses on cohort subsamples who turned 18 between 1964 and 1967 and whose first arrest as adults was between ages 18 and 20 (N = 100 to 300 active offenders for individual offense types).

Retrospective
Adult arrest histories from age 21 to the start of the sampling period were used. The period including the first adult arrest and the sampling period, 1974-1977, were excluded from the analysis.

Observation period ranged from 4 to 7 years for the four cohort subsamples examined.

Time incarcerated was excluded from the time at risk during the observation period.

By virtue of a first arrest before age 21 and the sampled arrest in 1974 to 1977, all offenders were presumed to be criminally active throughout the entire observation period.

Offenders who were arrested for an offense type between age 18 and the start of the sampling period were assumed to be criminally active in that offense type for the entire observation period.

Offending frequencies based on arrest histories and estimates of the probability of arrest per crime were found to be similar to independently derived estimtes of λ based on self-reports by inmates.

Offense-specific arrest frequencies and offending frequencies are provided for offenders active in an offense type (i.e., those with at least one arrest for the offense type between age 18 and the start of the sampling period).

Race
Offense-specific arrest frequencies within cohorts were generally similar in magnitude for active offenders among whites and blacks.

Age
Offense-specific arrest frequencies within cohorts were generally trendless over age for young adults.

(Frequency rates by race and by cohort are based on reduced sample sizes for individual offense types.)

---

[a] Average arrest frequencies, μ, were divided by offense-specific estimates of the probability of arrest for a crime to yield estimates of average offending frequencies, λ.

calculation of frequency rates to periods when the offenders were at risk of committing offenses in the community. Time when the offender was incapacitated through incarceration or long-term hospitalization (e.g., more than a 1-month stay) was excluded from the time at risk. The resulting frequencies reflect the intensity of offending while an offender is criminally active in the community, λ, the rate of offending that would be expected if the offender were never incarcerated. The estimates of λ are to be distinguished from the *effective* rates for offenders, λ^*. In estimating the reduction in crime associated with different periods of incarceration, the appropriate quantity is the individual's active offending frequency. This is the rate at which crimes would be committed if the offender were not incarcerated. Any time spent incarcerated will reduce the annual active rate to yield the effective rate for offenders. For example, an offender may commit crimes at a rate of 10 per year while he is free in the community. If this offender is incarcerated for 6 months, however, he can only commit crimes at rate 10 for the 6 months he is free. His active rate is 10 offenses per year, but his effective rate during the entire year is only 5, since he was only actively committing crimes in the community for half of the year.

The effective offending rate reflects the reduction in the potential level of crime as a result of current incapacitation policies. Because effective rates are already discounted by current incapacitation levels, using the effective rate instead of the active rate would lead to underestimates of the total crime reduction associated with increases in incapacitation. When the effective annual offending rate is used, incarceration during all of the following year would be incorrectly estimated to avert only five offenses. This fails to include the additional five offenses that would have occurred had the offender not been incarcerated for one-half year. On the basis of the offender's offending frequency while free, incarceration for a full year can be expected to avert 10 offenses.

Estimating λ from Self-Reports: The Rand Inmate Surveys

Survey of Habitual Offenders. The study of 49 habitual offenders by Petersilia, Greenwood, and Lavin (1977) laid the groundwork for later Rand surveys of larger samples of inmates. The original 49 inmates were chosen as exemplars of serious, recidivistic offenders. To be included in the sample, an inmate had to be currently serving a sentence for at least one armed robbery conviction and have at least one prior sentence of incarceration. Through personal interviews, the inmates were asked about their frequency of offending and prior criminal record (arrests, convictions, and incarcerations) for nine offense types, as juveniles, as young adults (before their first incarceration as adults), and prior to the start of the current sentence. In addition, they were asked about other aspects of their personal histories, including family circumstances, school and employment experiences, drug and alcohol use, personal motivations for crime, and styles of committing crimes (e.g., the amount of planning and preparation, use of accomplices).

The findings on average levels of offending over time for the 49 offenders, including offenders who were active in an offense and those who were not, are summarized in Table 2. As one reads down the table, the offense classes become more inclusive; the total rate includes offending in any of the nine offense types surveyed. Except for violent offenses, the reported monthly rates declined markedly as offenders got older. The anomalous slight increase in monthly rates with age for violent offenses is attributed by the authors to the sampling criterion that required an armed robbery prior to the current incarceration, which marks the end of the adult period (Petersilia, Greenwood, and Lavin:27).

As indicated above, all 49 offenders are included in a rate, whether or not they were active in that offense type. The opposite trends across age observed for violent offenses and all other offense types illustrate

TABLE B-2 Aggregate Offense Rates per Month of Street Time for 49
Habitual Offenders

Offense Class	Juvenile Period	Young Adult Period	Adult Period	Total
Violent[a]	0.10	0.16	0.20	0.15
Safety[b]	1.15	0.43	0.24	0.49
Nondrug[c]	2.37	0.92	0.38	0.99
Total[d]	3.28	1.52	0.64	1.51
Mean number of offense types reported	2.50	2.50	1.85	4.00

NOTE: The reported rates are aggregate incidence rates for the
sample and not frequency rates for active offenders only. Rates were
obtained by dividing all offenses reported by the total number of
months at risk for the entire sample, whether active in an offense or
not.

[a]Violent offenses include robbery, aggravated assault, and rape.
[b]Safety offenses include burglary in addition to the violent
offenses.
[c]Nondrug offenses include auto theft, purse snatching, theft over
$50, and forgery in addition to safety offenses.
[d]Total offenses include drug sales in addition to nondrug
offenses listed above.

SOURCE: Petersilia, Greenwood, and Lavin (1977).

the important contribution of participation
in aggregate incidence rates. As more offense types are included in successive rows
of the table, the aggregate rates decline
more markedly with age. As indicated by
the last line of Table 2, the decline with age
is influenced by the decline in the number
of offense types reported by the offenders.
By contrast, because of the sampling criterion used, aggregate rates increase for the
class of violent offenses as the number of
offenders active in robbery increases in successive age periods.

The 49 habitual offenders surveyed were
serious habitual offenders. Together, they
averaged 21 years of criminal activity from
the time of their first reported offense to the
current incarceration. Almost 50 percent of
that time was spent incarcerated. Despite
their strong commitment to crime, these
chronic offenders averaged only 18 offenses
per year of street time. Because these rates
fail to exclude offenders who were not criminally active in an age period, however, the
reported rates underestimate individual offending frequencies for active offenders.

One of the more interesting findings of
this study is the offenders' extensive involvement in employment. Two-thirds of
the offenders reported that after age 18 they
were working at least 75 percent of the time
they were not incarcerated. Three-quarters
of the respondents indicated that while employed, as adults, they were working full

time. This high participation in legitimate employment by chronic offenders—about 56 percent, on average, were employed full time in any month free (.75 × .75 = .56)—matches that found in nationwide surveys of prison inmates, in which about 60 percent of all inmates in 1974 and in 1979 were employed full time in the month prior to their arrest (Bureau of Justice Statistics, 1979b:73, 1981c:283). While employment was widespread among the 49 offenders, the jobs held tended to be economically marginal. Only half of the respondents reported that a job was their usual source of income as an adult.

First Inmate Survey. Peterson and Braiker (1980) reported the results of the first large-scale survey of self-reported offending by prison inmates. The original sample was drawn randomly from the inmate population at five California prisons in 1976. Usable survey responses were obtained from 624 inmates (47 percent of the original sample). The low response rate raises some concern about possible response biases in the final estimates.

A comparison of the respondent sample with the total inmate population revealed no significant differences in terms of convicted offense type, age, or race-ethnicity. Inmates with more extensive prior records, however, were overrepresented among respondents. The inmate respondents might thus be expected to have higher individual offense rates than inmates generally. In addition, by relying on a sample drawn from the resident population, with their longer prison terms, the offense rates of the inmate sample will not apply directly to either a cohort of incoming prisoners or the more general population of active offenders who are not incarcerated.

The survey asked respondents to indicate the total number of times they had committed each of 11 offense types while not incarcerated during the 3 years preceding the start of the current incarceration. The frequency of offending was obtained from responses to fixed categories: 0, 1–2, 3–5, 6–10, and more than 10 offenses. If the frequency was more than 10, respondents

were asked to indicate the total number of offenses they committed. For frequencies of 10 or less, researchers used the midpoint of a category to estimate rates. Respondent reports of time incarcerated or hospitalized were used to estimate street time during the 3-year observation period. Offense-specific individual frequency rates—reflecting the number of offenses committed per year of street time—were computed only for offenders who reported that they were active in an offense type. Using estimates of the probability of arrest and incarceration for a crime, and the expected time served in prison, the researchers adjusted the estimates of λ for the inmate sample to reflect the rates expected for a sample of incoming prisoners and for a sample of "street offenders" (i.e., active offenders who are at some risk of incarceration after an offense).

Estimates of d and λ for the three groups of offenders are shown in Table 3. As was expected, the λs reported by the resident inmate sample are higher than those estimated for a sample of street offenders. The difference reflects the greater risk of longer terms in prison faced by high-rate offenders. Even if high-rate offenders are no more vulnerable to incarceration for any single offense than are other offenders, their higher λs increase the chance that they will be incarcerated during some observation period. Except for drug sales, street offenders averaged under five offenses per year free for several serious offense types.

A number of factors raise concerns about the reliability of the estimates in Table 3. First is the imprecision of the frequency categories used in the survey. As designed, the frequency categories provide the greatest resolution for low frequencies; they are far less precise for larger numbers. Aside from the error resulting from using the midpoint of a frequency category to estimate λ, the uneven treatment of categories may have implicitly suggested to respondents that low frequencies were more sensible responses. This has been found in other contexts to bias responses downward (Locander and Burton, 1976; Bradburn and Sudman, 1979).

Second, further unreliability is likely to

TABLE B-3 Participation ($\underline{d}$) and Individual Offending Frequencies (λ) of Active Offenders, Estimated from Self-Reported Offenses in First Rand Inmate Survey of California Prisoners

Offense Type	Resident Prisoners		Incoming Prisoners[a]		Street Offenders[a]	
	Current Participation[b]	Individual Offending Frequency[c]	Current Participation[b]	Individual Offending Frequency[c]	Current Participation[b]	Individual Offending Frequency[c]
Rape	6	2.89	8	1.35	7	0.97
Armed robbery	34	5.16	37	4.61	32	1.97
Aggravated assault	20 Shot/cut	2.04	59	4.47	59	2.38
	36 Threat	3.19				
	35 Beating	2.81				
Drug sales	39	115.00	48	155.00	44	136.00
Burglary	46	14.15	58	15.29	48	7.23
Auto theft	27	3.90	32	5.25	26	3.48
Forgery	32	4.87	40	5.56	38	4.35
Cons	56	11.44	63	9.45	54	7.56
Homicide/attempted murder	18	1.60	9	0.27	10	0.16

[a]The sample of resident prisoners (N = 624) was weighted using estimates of the probability of arrest and incarceration for a crime and the expected time spent in prison in order to develop estimates of current participation and individual offending frequencies during the observation period for a sample of incoming prisoners and a sample of street offenders.

[b]Percentage active in offense (i.e., at least one offense during 3-year observation period).

[c]Average number of crimes committed per year of street time among offenders who commit that offense at least once in 3-year observation period.

SOURCE: Peterson and Braiker (1980:Tables 9, 10a, 11, and 12).

have been introduced by the use of a 3-year observation period. Except for highly salient events or regularly repeated events, the recall problems inherent in reporting total frequencies for a period as long as 3 years are likely to be substantial. The recall problem is exacerbated by the delay introduced by the length of time served between the end of the observation period and the date of the survey. Peterson and Braiker (1980:16) note that, "in most cases, the respondent did not have to reconstruct events occurring long ago." As evidence for this claim, they indicate that half the respondents had served less than 2 years at the time of survey, and three-quarters had served 3 years or less. This means, however, that half the respondents were being asked to report on the frequency of their criminal activities that occurred 5 years or more before the survey. The frequency estimates are thus vulnerable to large reporting errors.

Third, if respondents reported committing an offense, they were assumed to be active in that offense throughout the 3-year observation period. Ignoring possible initiation or termination of careers in that offense type sometime during the 3-year observation period would understate offending frequencies during truly active periods within those 3 years. In a later section on estimating λs from participation rates and aggregate incidence rates, however, it will be demonstrated that this bias is less serious when λs are large.

Fourth, the survey was anonymous and so provided only limited opportunities for internal checks on the quality of responses. On the basis of checks that were made, there is reason to suspect that the λs were underestimated. As many as 6 percent of the respondents denied committing any type of offense, including the one for which they were incarcerated. Those respondents were either all falsely convicted or, what is more likely, many of them underreported their offenses.

Another internal reliability check was available in the form of a question that asked the frequency with which burglaries were committed in a "typical month."

Based on responses for a typical month, the median frequency was four burglaries per month active; based on the total number of burglaries committed during reported street months in the 3-year observation period, the median monthly frequency rate while active was only .24. This 16-fold difference in reported rates led the authors to express uncertainty about the accuracy of the absolute magnitude of rates reported by offenders (1980:26). The difference may reflect the fact that while estimates of λ based on reports for the total observation period may be underestimated, estimates based on reports for a "typical month" are vulnerable to overestimates arising from erroneously applying short-term spurts in criminal activity during that month to the entire observation period. When the two frequency estimates are compared, there is much better agreement (correlation of .79) on relative magnitudes using categories of none, low (for those below the median), and high (for those above the median). Thus, the analysis of correlates later in this appendix is based on these grosser characterizations of offense rates; absolute rates are presented only to illustrate significant differences that are found.

Estimates of λ for the entire observation period reveal certain general features of individual offending. First, individual frequency rates are highly skewed; most of the offenders reported that they committed zero or only one crime within each offense type, but a few offenders reported very high offending frequencies (Table 4). This same general distribution of frequencies was observed for burglary when either total number of offenses reported for the observation period or the rates based on a typical month were used.

Second, individuals also indicated considerable variability in their types of offending. Very few offenders (18 percent) reported committing only one type of offense exclusively; 49 percent reported committing four or more types of offenses during the observation period.[5]

---

[5]Peterson and Braiker (1980:Table 17). These percentages are based on the 543 respondents who

TABLE B-4 Distribution of Number of Offenses Reported, First Rand Inmate Survey (N = 624)

| Offense Type | Percentage of Respondents Reporting Each Number of Offenses in 3-Year Observation Period | | | | |
	0	1-2	3-5	6-10	10+
Armed robbery	66	19	7	5	4
Burglary	54	16	11	8	11
Car theft	73	17	5	3	3
Aggravated assault					
Beating	65	25	6	3	1
Cut/shot	80	15	4	1	1
Threat	64	22	7	4	3
Forgery	68	15	8	5	4
Rape	94	4	0.6	0.3	0.3
Attempted murder/ murder	82	13	4	1	0.3
Cons	44	18	12	16	10
Drug sales[a]	61	15	5	7	11

[a]For drug sales, the frequency categories are 0, 1-10, 10-50, 50-100, and more than 100.

SOURCE: Peterson and Braiker (1980:Table 7).

Third, variability in the number of offense types in which an offender was involved was a major factor in the decline in total offense rates observed for older offenders. As seen in Table 5, average total offense scores were lower for older offenders. These scores, however, reflect the combination of participation in an offense type and offending frequencies by those active in that offense. There is considerable stability across age when considering only average intensity scores for active offenders (the middle column of Table 5). The decrease in total offense scores arises primarily from a decrease in the number of offense types reported by older offenders (last column of

Table 5). The offending frequencies for active offenders reveal little evidence of systematic trends with age for most offense types (Table 6). Only the rates for aggravated assault (and drug sales after age 21) declined significantly with the age of the offender. (Because of the small number of offenders and the very low rates, the decline for homicide with age is not statistically significant.)

The results for age do not necessarily represent aging effects for individual offenders because they are based on rates observed in an age cross-section (age in the 3-year observation period). The same offenders were not compared over different ages. Thus, the age differences reflect a combination of aging effects for individuals and cohort effects across offenders. Separating the aging effects from the cohort effects would require longitudinal data on frequencies for several cohorts and assumptions

TABLE B-5 Variations in Individual Offending Frequencies (λ) by Age,
First Rand Inmate Survey

Age[a]	Total Offense Score[b]	Intensity Scale Score[c]	Number of Active Offense Types[d]
Under 21	0.64	1.44	4.61
21-25	0.57	1.42	4.09
26-30	0.49	1.44	3.29
Over 30	0.35	1.33	2.70

[a]Age was taken at the midpoint of the 3-year observation period.

[b]For each of the 11 offense types studied, respondents were assigned a score that reflected their level of activity in that offense. If the respondent reported that he never committed the offense, he was assigned a score of 0 for that offense. Respondents committing the offense at a rate below the median were assigned a score of 1; if their rate was above the median, they were assigned a score of 2. Scores were averaged over the 11 offense types in the study to yield a respondent's "total offense score." Individual scores were then averaged across respondents.

[c]For each offense type studied, respondents who reported committing that offense were assigned a score indicating whether their offense rate for that offense type was below the median (score = 1) or above the median (score = 2). Scores were averaged over all offenses in which the respondent was active, to yield his "intensity scale score." These scores were then averaged across respondents.

[d]Mean number of separate offense types respondents reported committing out of 11 offenses studied.

SOURCE: Peterson and Braiker (1980:Tables 27-29).

about the nature of the relationships among age, cohort, and period effects.

Fourth, λs varied systematically with other attributes of the offenders. As indicated in Table 7, both the intensity score for active offenders and the number of active offense types were lower for blacks than whites. Offenders with more extensive prior records reported being active in more offense types and had a higher average intensity score within active offense types than other offenders. Likewise, self-reported drug users reported higher numbers of active offense types and a greater intensity of offending within active offense types than nondrug users.

Finally, offenders reporting extensive juvenile crime reported active involvement in more offense types and a greater intensity of offending in active types than other offenders. These attributes generally maintained significant independent contributions in multivariate analyses to distinguish high-rate offenders. Drug use, however, was significant for property crimes but not violent crimes in multivariate analyses.

Second Inmate Survey. Rand's second survey of inmates, described in Marquis (1981), Chaiken and Chaiken (1982a), and Peterson et al. (1982), is the most comprehensive of the Rand surveys; it includes inmates from prisons and jails in three states (California, Michigan, and Texas). Use of multiple jurisdictions and inclusion of the presumably less serious category of offenders—jail inmates—provided the opportunity to assess the variability in λ among different inmate samples.

As in the first Rand inmate survey, response rates in the second survey were generally low, averaging from 49 to 71.5 percent among jail and prison inmates in California and Michigan (Table 8). Response rates were lowest for inmates at state prisons. The notable exception was the 82 percent response rate among Texas prison inmates. There was also considerable variability in response rates across institutions. (The Texas jail inmates were dropped from the analysis because they were found to include many offenders awaiting transfer to state prison and hence were much like prison inmates.)

Because of the low and varying response rates, important differences in offender attributes were found between the originally designated sample and the initial respondent sample in all three states. Respondent representativeness was improved in Texas by weighting respondents by the response rates found in different institutions. In California and Michigan, responses by replacement respondents (who were selected at the same time the original sample was drawn) were included. This improved respondent representativeness on most characteristics. Nevertheless, younger inmates (under age 25) were overrepresented in the final sample and inmates with low reading levels were underrepresented among respondents in both states. In California, Hispanics were also underrepresented among respondents.

Building on the experience gained from the first inmate survey, the researchers included some design changes in the second survey. First, rather than draw an equal probability sample of the resident population of state prisons, they drew a sample of prison inmates to simulate a cohort of incoming prisoners. This was done to facilitate analysis of the implications of sentencing policies. A cohort of incoming prisoners is closer in characteristics to offenders convicted and sentenced to incarceration than is the resident population, which includes many more individuals sentenced to long terms than does an incoming cohort. The sample of prison inmates was drawn by

TABLE B-6 Variations in Individual Offending Frequencies (λ) with Age for "Street Offenders," Based on Self-Reported Offenses in First Rand Inmate Survey

Offense Type	Age of Inmate in 3-Year Observation Period			
	Under 21	21–25	26–30	Over 30
Armed robbery	1.9	2.1	2.5	1.0
Burglary	3.9	13.9	8.3	5.3
Auto theft	4.3	2.3	1.3	5.2
Aggravated assault	3.1	2.8	2.6	1.4
Forgery	1.2	3.3	7.5	2.6
Rape	0.9	0.9	1.9	0.8
Homicide	0.3	0.2	0.1	0.05
Cons	5.1	8.4	8.1	9.6
Drug sales	62.0	237.0	112.0	91.0

SOURCE: Peterson and Braiker (1980:Table 30).

TABLE B-7 Variations in Individual Offending Frequencies (λ) by
Attributes of Offenders, First Rand Inmate Survey

Attribute	Total Offense Score[a]	Intensity Scale Score[b]	Number of Active Offense Types[c]
Race	***	*	**
White	0.64	1.50	4.22
Black	0.48	1.39	3.56
Hispanic	0.56	1.38	3.90
Prior criminal record	***	***	***
No felonies	0.36	1.28	2.92
Prior felonies	0.54	1.42	3.91
Prior prison	0.64	1.52	4.19
Drug use	***	***	***
Drug user	0.69	1.54	4.56
Not drug user	0.46	1.37	3.39
Juvenile crime	***	***	***
None	0.30	1.29	2.32
Not serious	0.50	1.40	3.63
Infrequent, serious	0.65	1.48	4.31
Frequent, serious	0.81	1.64	5.15

[a]For each of the 11 offense types studied, respondents were
assigned a score reflecting their level of activity in that offense.
If the respondent reported that he never committed the offense, he was
assigned a score of 0 for that offense. Respondents committing the
offense at a rate below the median were assigned a score of 1; if their
rate was above the median, they were assigned a score of 2. Scores
were averaged over the 11 offense types in the study to yield a
respondent's "total offense score." Individual scores were then
averaged across respondents.

[b]For each offense type studied, respondents who reported
committing that offense were assigned a score indicating whether their
offense rate for that offense type was below the median (score = 1) or
above the median (score = 2). Scores were averaged over all offenses a
respondent was active in to yield his "intensity scale score." These
scores were then averaged across respondents.

[c]Mean number of separate offense types respondents reported
committing out of 11 offenses studied.

*Significant at the .05 level.
**Significant at the .01 level.
***Significant at the .001 level.

SOURCE: Peterson and Braiker (1980:Tables 27-29, 34, 82, and 84).

TABLE B-8 Response Rates to Second Rand Inmate Survey

Sample	Percent of Original Sample Responding[a]	Final Sample Size
California		
Prisons	49.4 (N = 307)	357
Jails	66.4 (N = 437)	437
Michigan		
Prisons	49.0 (N = 335)	422
Jails	71.5 (N = 373)	373
Texas		
Prisons	82.2 (N = 601)	601

[a]Figures do not include an even lower response rate of 34-35 percent for replacement respondents in California and Michigan prisons.

SOURCE: Peterson et al. (1982:Tables 2, 10, and 11).

selecting offenders with probabilities inversely proportional to the total time to be served on their sentence. Because of the generally shorter terms served in local jails and, thus, lesser bias toward long terms in the resident population, the sample of jail inmates was drawn randomly from, or included all, convicted inmates residing in the selected jails on the sampling date.

In comparisons of the attributes of the originally designated sample with those of an incoming cohort and resident inmates, the sample's characteristics were found to be generally closer to those of the incoming cohort than to those of the resident inmates in Texas and Michigan. This was not so in California, where only imprecise estimates of the total time to be served were available for prison inmates (Peterson et al., 1982:56–60).

There were some noteworthy differences between the simulated incoming cohort sample and an actual incoming cohort in all three states. Younger offenders were underrepresented in all three scheduled samples. Overrepresentation of young inmates among actual respondents in California and Michigan, as noted above, decreased the differences in age between the actual respondents and an incoming cohort. Inmates with no prior prison terms were slightly overrepresented in the actual samples in California (67 percent vs. 63 percent in an incoming cohort) and Michigan (63 percent vs. 60 percent in an incoming cohort). Inmates convicted of robbery were overrepresented in the actual sample in California (38 percent vs. 30 percent in an incoming cohort), as were inmates convicted of assault in the Michigan sample (15 percent vs. 10 percent in an incoming cohort). Time served was apparently underestimated for these offense types, which increased their representation in the sample.[6]

---

[6]This imprecision in time-served estimates, and especially the underestimate of time served by robbery inmates, for California inmates might have implications for the crime-reduction benefits estimated for selective incapacitation policies applied to robbery inmates (Greenwood, 1982). Use of these underestimates of time served for policies would understate the crime reduction already achieved and overstate the reduction possible from increases

Because of these differences, the results for the inmate samples may not apply precisely to a cohort of incoming prisoners. Also, unlike in the first inmate sample, no attempt was made to adjust the results from the sample to estimate λ for a sample of street offenders. Given the greater risk of imprisonment for high-rate offenders, the rates in the inmate sample will be higher than the rates that would be expected in a more representative sample of street offenders.

A second and major change in the second survey was in the design of survey items eliciting frequency of offending. Instead of a uniform 3-year observation period, respondents were asked about 2 calendar years preceding their current incarceration. The arrest leading to the current incarceration identified the second calendar year and marked the end of the observation period, which varied from 13 months (for inmates arrested in January of the second calendar year) to 24 months (for inmates arrested in December of the second calendar year). Inmates were given a calendar on which to identify the exact months of the observation period. As in the first survey, months spent incarcerated or hospitalized during the observation period were reported by the inmate and subtracted to yield time at risk, or street months, during the observation period.

The question eliciting counts of crimes committed was also much more sensitive to high rates of offending. For total counts of 10 or less, the respondent was asked to indicate the exact number of offenses committed during his street months. For counts greater than 10, respondents were asked first to choose a category that best described the smallest unit of time in which offenses were committed (e.g., monthly, weekly, daily) and then to indicate the exact number of offenses committed in that unit of time. They were also asked to indicate the num-

ber of months during the observation period in which they committed offenses at that rate.

While potentially enhancing the resolution of rate estimates, the increased complexity of the frequency items greatly increased respondent problems in answering those items. The computation of individual rates, in turn, depended on the respondents' reports of street months, number of crimes committed, and number of months in which crimes were committed. The extent of respondent confusion is reflected in the number of respondents who gave ambiguous answers to at least one of the three components. On the basis of a reanalysis of the data from the second inmate survey, Visher (Volume II:Table 11) indicates that 35 to 40 percent of the responses by inmates active in robbery or burglary were ambiguous. This widespread ambiguity in responses was likely one of the reasons why minimum and maximum rates were computed for each respondent in the original analysis.

Finally, a number of internal and external reliability checks were used in the second survey to assess the quality of the self-reports. Internal quality was judged by the consistency of responses to redundant items in the survey. External reliability was assessed only for prison inmates by comparing self-reported arrests and convictions with official-record data. Eleven percent of the respondents erred on more than 20 percent of the possible 27 internal-quality indicators. Almost 60 percent erred on more than 20 percent of the 14 external-reliability indicators (Chaiken and Chaiken, 1982a: Tables B.3 and B.7).

The indicators of internal and external quality were compared with various other self-reported attributes of the respondents (Chaiken and Chaiken, 1982a:225–226), and most attributes were found to be unrelated to response quality. There were three notable exceptions, however:

• Prisoners convicted of burglary and those with a self-image of being a "family man," "working man," or "straight" had good reliability.

---

in time served. However, this is apparently not a problem; the selective incapacitation analysis appears to be based on the respondents' self-reports of their expected total time served and not on aggregate, imprecise averages available from the Department of Corrections.

• The responses of older respondents were of better quality than those of younger respondents, but older respondents tended to leave more questions blank.

• For the most part, there were no differences in response quality by race; black respondents, however, had substantially worse internal quality, especially on indicators of confusion and inconsistency.

To assure that none of the results was driven by poor-quality responses, the researchers estimated frequency rates for both the total sample and a sample that excluded the 42 percent of respondents with poor-quality responses.[7] There were no systematic patterns in the resulting frequency rates, which usually varied well within a factor of two in the two estimates.

Estimates of d and λ for active offenders in the prison and jail inmate samples are shown in Table 9. As found in the first inmate survey, the λs are highly skewed; most offenders reported committing no or only a few offenses and a small number reported very high frequencies—considerably higher than those reported in the first inmate survey. In the first survey, the 90th percentile rate for armed robbery was under 20 offenses per year of street time for active offenders. This contrasts with a 90th percentile rate for robbery among California prisoners of 155 offenses per year in the second survey. The mean λs in the second survey are seven and eight times larger than those reported in the first survey. These much higher λs, based on offenses reported for smaller units of time (months, weeks, or even days in some cases), were foreshadowed by the results in the first survey, which yielded much higher λs when estimates were based on the number of crimes committed in a "typical month."

It is also noteworthy that λ varied between prison and jail inmates and across states. For serious offenses, λ and d were generally higher for prison inmates than for

jail inmates. This suggests that judges were effectively distinguishing between high- and low-rate offenders in their sentencing decisions. Those decisions, however, are strongly influenced by an offender's criminal record; according to official records, first offenders are more likely to be sentenced to jail than to prison (Blumstein et al., 1983). To the extent that these first offenders in official records are actually just beginning their offending careers, their retrospective reports in the survey will not reveal many offenses. If followed into the future, however, they may reveal much higher rates of offending. Their retrospective rates, based on the survey, may be deflated partly by their being considered criminally active for the entire observation period. A prospective study of offending frequencies is required both to assess the stability over time of frequencies that have been estimated retrospectively and to assess the degree to which current sentencing patterns distinguish among future high- and low-rate offenders.

The differences in λ across states parallel the differences in reported index crime rates (crime per 100,000 population) in the three states, which were highest in California and lowest in Texas (Table 10). These differences across states may reflect differences in offending behavior across states. They may also reflect differences in the thresholds for incarceration in the different states, with incarceration being applied broadly in Michigan and Texas and restricted more narrowly to serious offenders in California. This latter interpretation is consistent with the differences in incarceration rates across the states (Table 10). Incarceration, especially in state prisons, was far less frequent in California than in either Michigan or New York. The negative relationship between incarceration rates and λs is also consistent with deterrent effects, i.e., individuals commit crimes at lower rates where sanction rates are higher. Distinguishing between these competing hypotheses requires data on the relative participation rates of high-rate offenders among inmate and street-offender populations in each state and on the offense-specific incar-

---

[7]The cutoff for poor-quality responses was set such that about 20 percent of the respondents were excluded on the internal-quality indicators and 20 percent excluded on the external-quality indicators.

TABLE B-9 Participation (d) and Individual Offending Frequencies (λ), Second Rand Inmate Survey

Offense Type	Measure	California		Michigan		Texas
		Prison	Jail	Prison	Jail	Weighted Prison[a]
Burglary	d[b]	54.2	42.9	45.4	34.0	46.8
	λ:	(N = 193)	(N = 187)	(N = 191)	(N = 127)	(N = 281)
	Median	9.8	6.3	6.2	4.9	3.6
	90th Percentile	384.0	189.0	400.0	213.0	112.0
	Mean	116-204	63-97	84-122	89-144	44-58
Robbery (business and person)	d	48.6	22.9	37.6	19.9	25.3
	λ:	(N = 174)	(N = 100)	(N = 159)	(N = 74)	(N = 152)
	Median	8.0	5.5	5.7	4.8	3.2
	90th Percentile	155.0	118.0	155.0	97.0	22.0
	Mean	49-74	31-51	75-108	17-37	10-16
Assault	d	46.6	27.4	33.6	22.6	25.6
	λ:	(N = 166)	(N = 120)	(N = 142)	(N = 84)	(N = 154)
	Median	3.6	2.8	2.8	1.9	1.5
	90th Percentile	18.0	12.0	12.0	16.0	7.6
	Mean	7.1-7.6	6.0-6.9	4.8-5.3	4.7-5.7	3.2-3.4

Theft (other than auto)					
d̄	41.6	41.8	39.7	30.6	36.4
	(N = 149)	(N = 183)	(N = 167)	(N = 114)	(N = 219)
λ:					
Median	16.0	9.0	7.0	6.0	5.7
90th Percentile	724.0	583.0	296.0	384.0	387.0
Mean	185–326	173–236	97–125	87–203	122–150
Auto theft					
d̄	24.3	20.6	23.2	15.8	18.8
	(N = 87)	(N = 90)	(N = 98)	(N = 59)	(N = 113)
λ:					
Median	6.0	3.1	4.8	4.9	2.0
90th Percentile	99.0	56.0	413.0	43.0	10.0
Mean	38–102	49–56	214–248	82–86	7–10
Fraud					
d̄	19.3	15.9	16.1	11.3	14.2
	(N = 69)	(N = 69)	(N = 68)	(N = 42)	(N = 85)
λ:					
Median	6.9	5.3	4.6	5.3	4.5
90th Percentile	268.0	327.0	263.0	367.0	180.0
Mean	156–202	207–268	115–137	183–1064	34–120
Forgery and credit cards					
d̄	28.4	25.1	14.1	15.7	21.5
	(N = 101)	(N = 110)	(N = 59)	(N = 59)	(N = 129)
λ:					
Median	4.8	4.5	4.5	3.3	4.3
90th Percentile	197.0	269.0	344.0	77.0	110.0
Mean	62–94	90–132	84–106	66–152	29–49
Drug dealing					
d̄	54.5	45.0	41.4	35.6	34.6
	(N = 195)	(N = 197)	(N = 175)	(N = 133)	(N = 208)
λ:					
Median	166	103	122	92	36
90th Percentile	4,013	3,251	3,612	3,054	2,508
Mean	927–1,681	1,081–1,487	994–1,287	714–1,275	664–810

TABLE B-9 Continued

Offense Type	Measure	California		Michigan		Texas
		Prison	Jail	Prison	Jail	Weighted Prison[a]
Total (excluding (drug dealing)	d	84.8	74.9	78.0	66.5	74.4
		(N = 302)	(N = 327)	(N = 329)	(N = 248)	(N = 447)
	λ:					
	Median	42	17	17	9	9
	90th Percentile	989	735	645	438	338
	Mean	258-455	221-288	222-302	147-242	107-141
Total	d	89.8	81.6	83.8	73.8	79.9
		(N = 321)	(N = 356)	(N = 354)	(N = 275)	(N = 480)
	λ:					
	Median	135	72	104	24	15
	90th Percentile	3,004	2,305	2,005	2,200	1,288
	Mean	794-1,390	794-1,121	257-683	479-948	385-489

NOTES: The number of offenders active in each offense type is given in parentheses. This number was estimated by applying the proportion active to the total size of each sample, as reported in Table 8.

The range for mean λs reflects the high and low estimates available for each respondent. All other rates in the table are based on the average or low value for a respondent.

[a]The respondent sample of prison inmates in Texas is weighted to reflect the very different response rates at different institutions.

[b]Participation is measured by the percentage of respondents who report committing the offense type. The number reported here is the average of two variables measuring activity for the respondents. These two measures vary substantially for some samples in burglary, theft, and auto theft.

SOURCE: Chaiken and Chaiken (1982a:Tables A.3-A.14).

TABLE B-10 Variations in Levels of Crime and Sanctions Across Survey States

Indicator	California	Michigan	Texas
Median individual offending frequencies[a]			
Robbery			
Prison	8.0	5.7	3.2
Jail	5.5	4.8	N.A.
Burglary			
Prison	9.8	6.2	3.6
Jail	6.3	4.9	N.A.
Reported index crime rate in 1976 (crimes per 100,000 population)[b]	7,204	6,478	5,407
1978 incarceration rate (sentenced inmates per 100,000 population)			
Prison[c]	88	162	189
Jail[d]	58	28	10

[a]Chaiken and Chaiken (1982a:Tables A.3 and A.6).
[b]Federal Bureau of Investigation (1977).
[c]Bureau of Justice Statistics (1980b).
[d]The total population and sentenced population in jails in each state are available in Bureau of Justice Statistics (1981a). The proportion sentenced was applied to the total rate of jail inmates per 100,000 population provided in Bureau of Justice Statistics (1979a).

ceration risk per conviction or per arrest in each state.

In identifying the correlates of λ, the Rand researchers first characterized offenders by the cluster of different offense types that they reported committing in the observation period. Excluding the 13 percent of respondents who reported that they did not commit any of the eight offense types studied, almost 90 percent of the remaining respondents fell within 10 clusters (Table 11). These clusters ("criminal varieties"), based only on the types of offenses committed, tend also to distinguish offenders by their offending frequencies. The more versatile offenders, who committed multiple offense types, also committed those offenses and others at very high rates. As

reported in Table 11, violent predators—who were distinguished by their reports of committing robbery, assault, and drug deals in the observation period—not only committed those offenses at higher rates than other offenders, but also reported committing the most burglaries and had high rates for thefts.

Official-record data of arrests or convictions for robbery, assault, and drug deals did little to distinguish the violent predators from other offenders. Offenders who reported committing those offenses often had no official record for one or more of the offense types. On the basis of their self-reports, the violent predators were distinguished from other offenders by their

TABLE B-11 Variations in High-Rate Offending by Offender Types, Second
Rand Inmate Survey

Offender Type	Percent of Respondents in Offender Type (N = 1,777)	Annual λ, 90th Percentile			
		Robbery	Burglary	Assault	Theft
Violent predators (robbery, assault, drug dealing)	15.0	135	516	18	517
Robber-assaulters	7.8	65	315	14	726
Robber-dealers	9.2	41	377	--	407
Low-level robbers	11.8	10	206	--	189
Mere assaulters	5.1	--	--	3.5	--
Burglar-dealers	9.8	--	113	6	406
Low-level burglars	8.4	--	105	--	97
Property and drug offenders	6.3	--	--	9	663
Low-level property offenders	8.2	--	--	--	560
Drug dealers	5.5	--	--	--	--
Total	87.1				

NOTE: The 13 percent of offenders who did not report committing
any of the offense types studied are excluded from the total number of
respondents reported here.

SOURCE: Chaiken and Chaiken (1982a:Tables 2.5 and 2.20).

- youthfulness,
- extensive self-reported juvenile criminal activity and drug use,
- irregular employment,
- use of multiple drugs as adults, and
- lack of family obligations.

In contrast to the violent predators, high-rate offenders among the less serious property offenders (fraud, forgery, credit card crimes) were distinguished by their

- higher education levels,
- being married, and
- being recently unemployed.

To assess the accuracy of prediction models, the inmate sample was split, and one-half of it was used to estimate the model. The estimated model was then applied to the remaining half of the sample. On the basis of the results for the validation sample, low-rate offenders can be predicted with high accuracy by using prediction models. The models did uniformly poorly, however, in predicting high-rate offenders. Well over half of those predicted to be high-rate offenders were in fact low-rate offenders, and a substantial portion reported *no crimes* at all of the predicted offense type (Chaiken and Chaiken, 1982a: Table 3.7). Such high error rates are common when attempting to predict such rare events as high-rate offending. (This is often referred to as the problem of low base rates.)

Some caution is also needed in generalizing results of predictive factors based on inmate samples to broader groups of offenders. As noted above, the distinguishing features of the violent predators included extensive involvement in drug use and serious crimes as juveniles and youthfulness (compared with other inmates in the sample). The seriousness of juvenile involvement in crime and drugs for these young adult offenders may well be a distinguishing attribute of violent predators *in prison*, but be less decisive in identifying violent predators in a convicted sample. For youthful violent predators found among inmates, it is likely that their serious juvenile history was a key factor in the decision to incarcerate them (see, for example, Greenwood, Abrahamse, and Zimring, 1984).[8] Other young violent predators who do not have a serious juvenile history might be less likely to be incarcerated and, therefore, might be found in a convicted sample but less so in an inmate sample. This would reduce the role of a serious juvenile history as a distinguishing factor for violent predators in a convicted sample. In general, to the extent that variables found to distinguish among inmates also influence the selection process that generates inmates, those variables may be less reliable as predictors of high-rate offending in non-inmate samples.

As indicated earlier, because of ambiguous responses, the Rand researchers estimated a minimum and a maximum λ for each offender. In the prediction analysis, the minimum and maximum estimates were averaged to yield a single estimate for the respondent. When the responses were unambiguous, the minimum and maximum estimates were identical. The reanalysis of the inmate survey data by Visher (Volume II) indicates that these minimum and maximum estimates represent extreme upper and lower bounds on λ. For example, if an offender indicated he committed between 1 and 10 offenses in his calendar period, but failed to indicate the exact number of offenses, he was assigned 1 as the minimum λ and 10 as the maximum. If he failed to indicate the number of months in which he committed a crime, he was assigned 1 as the minimum and his reported number of street months was used as the maximum. In calculating the minimum offense rate, the minimum number of crimes committed was divided by the maximum number of street months. For the maximum offense rates, the maximum number of crimes committed was divided by the minimum number of street months. These estimating strategies tend to move the estimates to the most extreme possible values, rather than to provide a reasonable estimate for the individual. Just as the mean of all offenders is sensitive to the presence of a few individuals with very high rates, so the average of the minimum and maximum for a single individual is sensitive to very high maximum rates. Taking the average of these extreme rates is likely to overstate the true rate for an individual.

Visher (Volume II) used an alternative strategy for dealing with the ambiguous responses. Rather than develop the extreme values possible for the estimate, she developed a "best estimate" for each individual. For example, individuals who indicated 1 to 10 offenses but did not report the exact number committed were assigned a value from 1 to 10 based on the distribution of those values for unambiguous respondents. The particular value assigned to an offender could often be further pinpointed within the range 1 to 10 by the respondent's answer to a later categorical question that asked whether the inmate committed 0, 1–2, 3–5, 6–10, or more than 10 offenses in the observation period. On the basis of this response, the ambiguous respondent was assigned an exact value within the selected category according to the distribution in that category found among unambiguous respondents.

---

[8]It is also noteworthy that the analysis of sentencing patterns for young adults in Greenwood, Abrahamse, and Zimring (1984) did not find evidence that young adults are treated more leniently than older offenders who are convicted of the same offense and have similar records. This result contradicts the widely held belief that young adults with serious juvenile records are treated with unwarranted leniency because juvenile criminal histories are not considered at sentencing.

Using the minimum-maximum strategy, the Rand estimate yields an average of 5.5 crimes committed [(1 + 10)/2] for all ambiguous respondents in the 1–10 category. This frequency of 5.5 is one-third to two-thirds higher than the average number reported by unambiguous respondents. When the distribution-matching strategy is used, the average number of crimes committed for ambiguous respondents matches the lower average that is found among unambiguous respondents (Visher, Volume II:Table 8).

Similar estimating strategies were used for other ambiguous responses. The original Rand estimates and the estimates resulting from Visher's reanalysis for burglary and robbery are presented in Table 12. Visher's estimates are always much closer to the minimum estimate. In a highly skewed distribution like that found for λ, any individual with an unknown rate is much more likely to have a rate that is lower, rather than higher, than the mean. Relative to the distribution for unambiguous responses, averaging the minimum and maximum estimates for each ambiguous individual overweights the higher rate and underweights the more likely lower rate for the individual. Visher's "best estimate" approach is likely to provide a more reasonable estimate of λ for ambiguous respondents.

Also shown in Table 12 are the offense rates found by Visher when only unambiguous respondents are included in the analysis. The distribution is still highly skewed, with most active offenders reporting relatively low annual λs. The distributions of

TABLE B-12 Alternative Estimates of Individual Offending Frequencies (λ) from Second Rand Inmate Survey

	Rand Survey		Visher Reanalysis	
	Minimum λ	Maximum λ	All Cases, λ	Unambiguous Cases, λ
Robbery				
25th percentile	1.8	2.3	1.5	1.1
50th percentile	3.6	6.0	3.8	2.8
75th percentile	12.0	21.5	12.4	6.9
90th percentile	68.0	100.5	71.6	43.2
Mean	40.6	62.2	43.4	36.5
			(N = 594)	(N = 294)
Burglary				
25th percentile	2.4	2.8	2.0	1.8
50th percentile	4.8	6.0	4.7	4.3
75th percentile	23.3	35.0	23.4	17.5
90th percentile	196.0	265.0	195.9	158.4
Mean	75.8	118.6	79.0	55.7
			(N = 824)	(N = 451)

NOTE: Frequencies are for active offenders in California, Michigan, and Texas combined.

SOURCE: Visher (Volume II:Tables 9 and 11).

TABLE B-13 Alternative Estimates of Individual Offending Frequencies
(λ) from Two Surveys of Inmates in California Prisons

	First Inmate Survey (1976) Incoming Cohort[a]	Second Inmate Survey (1978-1979)[b]	Reanalysis of Second Inmate Survey[c]
Robbery			
Median	(2.0)[d]	8.0	5.1
Mean	7.0[e]	49-74[f]	42.4
Burglary			
Median	(3.0)[d]	9.8	6.0
Mean	15.3	116-204	98.8

[a]Three-year observation period (Peterson and Braiker, 1980:Tables 2 and 10a).

[b]Less than 2-year observation period (Chaiken and Chaiken, 1982a:Tables A.3 and A.6).

[c]Derived from Visher (Volume II) reanalysis of original Rand data. These rates include both prison and jail inmates and so they are not directly comparable to the other rates for prison inmates only reported in this table.

[d]Medians are not reported for incoming prisoners in the original report. The medians are estimated here using the ratio of the mean to the median reported for the actual respondent sample in Peterson and Braiker (1980:Table 10a).

[e]The robbery rate reported in the first survey is for armed robbery only (mean of 4.61). Applying the proportion of armed robberies found among all reported robberies reported in national statistics--65.8 percent--(Federal Bureau of Investigation, 1974), the total robbery rate is estimated as 7.0.

[f]The range for the mean reflects the minimum and maximum estimates for each respondent. The median is based on the average of the minimum and maximum estimates for each respondent.

rates at or below the median are quite similar. The rates for high-rate offenders and the mean of all offenders, however, are lower among the unambiguous respondents. This reflects the greater complexity, and thus greater risk of confusion or errors, in providing responses for frequencies greater than 10. Since ambiguous responses are more likely to occur for high-rate offenders, excluding ambiguous responses entirely would underestimate λs.

The various estimates of λ are compared in Table 13 for California prison inmates in the two Rand surveys who were active in robbery and burglary. The rates for the second survey, based on minimum-maximum estimates, are an order of magnitude higher than the rates in the first survey. Even using Visher's "best estimate" approach, the mean rates from the second survey are five to seven times higher than the mean rates reported only 2 years earlier by prison inmates in California.

Several factors may account for the siz-

TABLE B-14 Distribution of Responses in Frequency Categories by California Prisoners in the Two Rand Inmate Surveys

Offense Type	Survey Sample	Percentage of Respondents in Frequency Category				
		0	1-2	3-5	6-10	10+
Burglary	I	54	16	11	8	11
	II	46	15	13	7	19
Car theft	I	73	17	5	3	3
	II	75	11	6	5	3
Cons	I	44	18	12	16	11
	II	44	17	11	6	21
Drug sales	I	61	15	6	7	11
	II	49	10	10	6	26
Forgery	I	68	15	8	5	4
	II	73	10	8	2	7

SOURCE: Chaiken and Rolph (1983:Table 5).

able difference in the magnitude of the estimates from the two inmate surveys. First, the original inmate survey used a 3-year observation period (versus 13 to 24 months in the second survey). Providing an accurate count of total frequencies over such a long period was no doubt difficult for respondents, and many of the more distant offenses undoubtedly went unreported in the first survey. Second, recall problems were aggravated by the length of time inmates had served between the observation period and administration of the first survey.[9]

In addition to its more complex frequency items, the second survey also used the original categorical response set of the first survey. The responses to these replicated items provide one indication of the underreporting problem in the first survey. Despite the fact that the observation period in the first survey (median of 28 months of street time) was twice the length of the observation period in the second survey (median of 14 months of street time), the distributions over the frequency categories for the two surveys were strikingly close (Table 14). Reported offending increased markedly for only burglary and drug sales. The correlation between the distributions for the two surveys is .96. For most offense types, offenders reported the same relative frequencies, regardless of the length of the observation period. To the extent that these reported frequencies reflect only offenders' most recent experiences, more offenses will go unreported and frequency rates based on the entire observation period will be underestimated as the length of the observation period increases.

Differences in the length of the observation periods also contribute to differences in the computed rates in another way. Rates

[9]Recall that half of the respondents had served at least 2 years at the time of the first survey. More than half of the respondents in the second survey had served less than 1 year at the time of the survey.

for active offenders were based on the reported frequency of offenses by offenders who reported committing at least one offense in the observation period. In the computations the offender was assumed to be active in a reported offense type over the entire observation period. This fails to account for initiation and termination of activity in an offense that may occur any time during the observation period. Failure to exclude these periods of inactivity will bias the rates for active offenders downward. This bias toward underestimates becomes more severe as the observation period gets longer. Rates based on the longer 3-year observation period in the first survey are thus more likely to be underestimated than are rates in the second survey, which had a shorter observation period.

All the above factors would lead to underestimates of offense rates in the first survey. Correspondingly, there are reasons to expect that the offense rates from the second survey are overestimated. As already discussed, using a minimum-maximum strategy to estimate individual rates is likely to lead to inflated estimates. Even the lower rates obtained by the "best estimate" approach of Visher (Volume II), however, are vulnerable to overestimation. One factor potentially leading to overestimates in the second inmate survey is the shorter observation period combined with the requirement that inmates had to report committing at least one crime of a given offense type to be considered active in that offense category. The estimated frequencies for active offenders were thus conditional on at least one reported offense; their unconditional rates while active would be lower.

The overestimates in λ arising from the required one offense become larger as the length of the observation period gets shorter. A minimum of one offense in a 3-year observation period contributes a minimum of .333 to the estimated annual rate. In a 1-year observation period, the estimated annual rate has a minimum annual frequency of 1. Restricting the required offense for active offenders to available street time, one required offense in only 1 available month of street time yields

a minimum annual frequency of 12. This overestimate, however, becomes less serious as the number of crimes committed increases and, thus, is less likely to have a serious effect on the mean frequency rate. An estimated rate of 1.5 offenses in a 1-year observation period is clearly more vulnerable to overestimation than is an estimated rate of 10 offenses in the same 1-year observation period.

Certain design features in the items eliciting frequencies on the second survey are more important contributors to overestimates of λ. The second survey used frequency reports for smaller units of time for high-rate offenders to provide much greater resolution among rates at the high end of the frequency continuum. Reliance on smaller time intervals, however, may well lead to overestimates of rates when offending is irregular over the entire observation period, i.e., spurts of high levels of activity are interspersed with periods of low levels of activity. Evidence of such spurts in offending behavior was found in self-reports to the National Youth Survey; for example, an annualized rate of 130 shoplifting offenses, based on a rate of 2 to 3 offenses per week, was found to represent only 20 shoplifting offenses, all committed during 2 months in the summer (Elliott et al., 1983:117). The higher rates in the second inmate survey were also foreshadowed in the first survey: the responses for burglaries committed in a "typical month" yielded a median frequency rate of 4 burglaries per month active whereas the responses for total burglaries during all reported street months within the 3-year observation period yielded a median rate of only .24 burglaries per month active (Peterson and Braiker, 1980:26).

To the extent that the frequency responses for short time intervals represent rates in periods of peak activity and not an average of high- and low-rate periods, extrapolating from peak rates in short periods may seriously overestimate annual rates. The magnitude of the bias will depend on the difference between high and low rates and on the relative proportion of total time free devoted to peak-rate activities. The

TABLE B-15 Adjusting Offending Frequencies (λ) from the Second Rand
Inmate Survey for Spurts in Activity

Offense Type	Adjusted Mean Offending Frequency[a]	Change from Original Frequency Estimate[b]			
		Minimum		Maximum	
		Mean Frequency	Percent Change	Mean Frequency	Percent Change
Robbery	39	49	-20.6	74	-47.4
Assault	7.5	7.1	+5.6	7.6	-1.3
Burglary	115	116	-1.2	204	-43.8
Theft (other than vehicle)	160	185	-13.7	326	-51.0
Motor vehicle theft	29	38	-24.5	102	-71.9
Forgery	53	62	-15.3	94	-44.1
Fraud	48	156	-69.2	202	-76.2
Drug deals	850	927	-8.3	1,681	-49.4

[a]The mean rates are adjusted downward to reflect the offender's
frequency over spurts in activity and quiescent periods (Chaiken and Rolph,
1985:Appendix).

[b]Minimum and maximum frequencies were estimated for each active offender
in a sample reflecting a cohort of incoming inmates to California prisons
(Chaiken and Chaiken, 1982a:Tables A.3-A.14).

larger the difference between high and low rates and the smaller the fraction of peak periods in total time free, the larger will be the overestimate.

Chaiken and Rolph (1985:Chapter 2) examined the effect of offending spurts on λ in the second survey and found that much of the criminal activity reported by the respondents occurred near the time of their current incarceration. Moreover, the duration of the periods of criminal activity and the counts of crimes reported did not increase as the duration of street time available to respondents increased. Frequency rates for offenders with very short street times were thus especially vulnerable to overestimation because of spurts in activity during those shorter observation periods and the absence of corresponding data for quiescent periods. To account for these spurts of activity, Chaiken and Rolph adjusted the estimated rates downward to reflect an estimate of λ averaged over active and quiescent periods. As indicated in Table 15, the adjustments resulted in about a 15 to 25 percent reduction in the original minimum

frequency estimates for most offense types and a 40 to 80 percent reduction in the original maximum frequency estimates. Mean λs for California prison inmates, for example, decreased from a maximum of 204 burglaries per year free to a mean annual rate of 115 burglaries; mean annual robbery rates decreased from a maximum of 74 to 39 after adjusting for offending spurts. Only the mean λs for assault were unaffected by the adjustment for short-term spurts in activity.

Even with the adjustment for spurts, a few individuals were estimated to commit crimes at very high rates—an average of one or more crimes a day. The mean λ is very sensitive to these few very high-rate offenders and is thus vulnerable to serious overestimation arising from errors in the estimated rates for these individuals. To reduce the impact of these high-rate offenders, mean λs can be reestimated by identifying an upper threshold value for individual frequencies and assigning that value to all offenders whose estimated rates exceed it. The frequency estimates from the

Visher (Volume II) reanalysis of the original inmate survey data can be used to illustrate the change in the mean λ when different thresholds are used (Table 16). When the 90th percentile is used as a threshold for robbery, for example, the upper threshold value is 107.1 robberies per year for California inmates. The 10 percent of active robbers with λs above that threshold each committed an estimated average of 300.4 robberies per year. When the 90th percentile value of 107.1 is assigned to these high-rate robbers, the mean λ decreases from 42.4 to 21.8. When the 90th percentile is used for burglary in California, the mean λ is similarly reduced by half, from 98.8 to 44.6 burglaries annually.

Although various features of the estimation procedures used in the two surveys contribute to underestimates of frequency rates for the first survey and overestimates for the second, it is also possible that the relative differences in rates between the two surveys reflect real differences in the population bases used in the two estimates. In the first survey, participation is based on reporting at least one offense in a 3-year observation period. This contrasts with at least one offense in half the time in the second survey. The longer time window of the first survey increases the likelihood that low-rate offenders were included among active offenders in an offense type. Low-rate offenders were less likely to be detected as active during the shorter observation period of the second survey. The different lengths of the observation period thus may have affected sample composition for active offenders in the two surveys. A greater representation of low-rate offenders in the first survey would lower the mean offense rate from that survey compared with the mean obtained from the second survey.

Estimating Individual Frequency Rates from Arrest Histories

In addition to self-reports of crimes, official arrest histories have also been used to estimate offending frequencies. Two such estimates are reviewed here. One is based on the longitudinal arrest histories of all adults arrested for murder, rape, robbery, aggravated assault, burglary, or auto theft in Washington, D.C., during 1973 (Blumstein and Cohen, 1979); the other, on adult arrestees in the Detroit Standard Metropolitan Statistical Area (SMSA) during 1974–1977 (Cohen, 1981, 1983). (Data for both studies were drawn from computerized criminal history files maintained by the Federal Bureau of Investigation.) In Table 17 the demographic attributes of arrestees in the two study sites are compared with those of persons arrested for index offenses (excluding larceny) in other U.S. cities. The two arrestee populations differ markedly with respect to race. The Washington, D.C., arrestees, who mirror the unique racial composition of that city in the early 1970s,[10] are not representative of arrestees in other cities, but the arrestees in the Detroit SMSA match more closely the racial composition of urban arrestees found nationally. Because the study populations are restricted to adult arrestees in each jurisdiction, juveniles (under age 18) are underrepresented in the two arrestee populations. Among adults only, the arrestees are closer in age to arrestees in other U.S. cities, although those aged 18–24 are somewhat underrepresented.[11] With respect to sex, the arrestees are almost exclusively males. The differences between the two jurisdictions provide a basis for assessing the degree to which individual arrest and offending frequencies vary across jurisdictions.

The original populations in both study

---

[10]In the 1970 census, the population of Washington, D.C., was 71.1 percent black, compared with 12.3 percent black for the total urban population of the United States (Bureau of the Census, 1981:Tables 15 and 24).

[11]This difference for age is not accounted for by similar differences in the general population. In the 1970 census, for example, about 20 percent of the adult population (age 18 or over) in Washington, D.C., and in all urban areas of the United States were 18–24 years old. Analysis of the arrestee data, however, indicates that multiple arrests in a year are more common for young adults than older adults. This would inflate the representation of young adults in the count of *arrests* in the national data for cities.

TABLE B-16 Mean Frequency Rates (λ) from Second Rand Inmate Survey, Adjusted by Imposing Upper Threshold Values for High-Rate Offenders (prison and jail inmates combined)

	Burglary				Robbery			
	Three States (N = 829)	California (N = 325)	Michigan (N = 261)	Texas (N = 243)	Three States (N = 596)	California (N = 253)	Michigan (N = 206)	Texas (N = 137)
Adjusted Mean λ								
All Active Inmates	79.0	98.8	96.2	34.1	43.4	42.4	64.8	13.1
99th Percentile	70.9	90.7	85.2	31.7	33.3	37.5	42.0	13.1
95th Percentile	53.9	72.7	67.4	24.8	23.2	30.4	25.0	7.0
90th Percentile	36.7	44.6	50.3	14.9	14.3	21.8	15.8	4.8
85th Percentile	26.3	38.8	30.8	9.7	9.2	15.9	9.3	4.3
80th Percentile	15.1	28.1	16.0	6.9	7.1	11.0	7.0	3.6
75th Percentile	9.8	17.9	9.6	6.0	5.7	8.6	5.8	3.4
Threshold Value of λ								
99th Percentile	1,092.2	1,301.8	1,186.8	490.2	685.9	527.7	936.4	246.8
95th Percentile	437.7	575.5	530.6	212.4	193.0	227.7	212.5	48.9
90th Percentile	195.9	200.0	295.1	76.1	71.3	107.1	86.2	15.2
85th Percentile	113.4	154.8	135.8	30.1	30.4	57.9	31.5	11.2
80th Percentile	47.5	94.7	52.9	14.0	18.2	29.8	18.4	7.4
75th Percentile	23.4	48.6	24.0	10.0	12.2	19.9	13.1	6.1
Mean λ in Upper Percentile								
99th Percentile	1,610.6	1,826.0	1,759.6	634.7	1,357.9	837.5	2,107.5	247.3
95th Percentile	889.5	1,046.1	1,031.6	386.9	558.2	443.7	894.9	152.9
90th Percentile	599.2	702.6	723.1	263.3	346.3	300.4	544.2	91.0
85th Percentile	454.5	522.3	552.1	190.5	249.3	225.5	388.5	66.0
80th Percentile	361.2	437.3	440.3	149.0	192.8	182.7	295.0	52.3
75th Percentile	295.2	357.9	361.2	121.9	156.1	151.3	242.1	40.2

NOTE: Derived from data in the Visher (Volume II) reanalysis of the original Rand inmate survey data.

TABLE B-17 Comparison of Attributes of Arrestees Nationwide with Arrestees in Washington, D.C., and Detroit, 1973-1977

Attribute	1973 UCR Index Arrests for Cities (excluding larceny)[a]		1973 Washington, D.C., Adult Arrestees[b] (N = 5,338) (percent)	1974-1977 Detroit SMSA Adult Arrestees[b] (N = 18,635) (percent)
	Total (percent)	Persons > 18 (percent)		
Race				
White	55.3		8.1	56.8
Nonwhite	44.7		91.8	43.2
Sex				
Male	92.5		89.7	95.5
Female	7.5		10.3	4.5
Age				
<18	42.1		0.1	21.0[c]
18-20	17.2	29.7	18.6	23.6
21-24	14.9	25.7	24.4	23.1
25-29	9.9	17.1	19.9	15.1
30-34	5.7	9.8	12.3	7.3
35-39	3.5	6.0	8.4	3.8
40-44	2.5	4.3	5.0	2.3
45-49	1.7	2.9	4.6	1.7
≥50	2.5	4.3	6.7	2.1

[a]National data for cities are based on arrests and not arrestees. Persons with more than one arrest in a year are counted more than once in the arrest data (Federal Bureau of Investigation, 1974).

[b]Blumstein and Cohen (1979:Table 1) and Cohen (1981).

[c]Age in 1974 is reported here. The large number of arrestees under age 18 includes many persons who enter the data because of later arrests as adults during the period 1975-1977.

sites numbered several thousand—5,338 in Washington, D.C., and 18,635 in the Detroit SMSA. The analyses of offending frequencies, however, focus on selected cohorts within these cross-sections of arrestees. Cohort subsamples were used so that changes in frequency rates could be analyzed over time for the *same arrestees* rather than a changing mix of arrestees in the cross-sections.[12] Cohorts were defined to include individuals from the original study populations who reached age 18 in the same year and whose first arrest as adults occurred at ages 18–20. These criteria ensured that cohort members were the same age and that they were active in criminal careers as adults before age 21. The resulting frequency rate estimates were thus based on the arrest experiences of offenders who had

[12]Comparisons over age, using the cross-section of arrestees, for example, include different subsets of arrestees at different ages. Frequency rates at age 18 are based on the histories of both young and old arrestees in the sampling year, while frequency rates at age 30 are restricted to older arrestees in the sampling year; arrestees under age 30 in the sampling year will not enter frequency rate estimates for age 30.

TABLE B-18   Sample Sizes for Cohorts of Arrestees Used to Estimate
Frequency Rates from Official Arrest Histories

Offense Type	Washington, D.C., Adult Arrestees, 1973	Detroit SMSA Adult Arrestees, 1974-1977	
		Whites	Blacks
Robbery	181	44	120
Aggravated assault	172	75	65
Burglary	153	126	133
Larceny	167	123	146
Auto theft	100	64	64
Weapons	80	48	67
Drugs	110	69	78
All others	303	258	233

NOTE: Four separate cohorts were identified in each study site:
those aged 18 in each of the years 1963-1966 among Washington, D.C.,
arrestees, and those 18 in 1964-1967 among Detroit SMSA arrestees. The
numbers reported in this table are for the four cohorts combined; the
numbers in each cohort are smaller.

SOURCE: Blumstein and Cohen (1979:Table 7) for Washington, D.C.;
sample sizes for the Detroit SMSA are available from the private files
of the author.

at least two arrests, one in the sampling year
and one at ages 18, 19, or 20. This restriction, combined with the further requirement that the arrest in the sampling year be
for an index offense other than larceny,
limits the analysis to frequency rates for
reasonably serious adult arrestees. As is
evident in Table 18, the focus on cohorts
within an original annual cross-section of
arrestees considerably reduces the sample
size available for analysis. When cohorts are
combined, offenders active in individual
offense types (i.e., at least one arrest for that
offense during their arrest histories) number under 200. Sample sizes are even
smaller for individual cohorts.

Estimates of μ. Individual arrest frequencies, μ (mean arrests per offender annually), were estimated for the cohorts in
Washington, D.C., and in the Detroit
SMSA. Only the period from age 21 (after

the first arrest as an adult) to before the
sampling year was used in the analysis. The
requirement of an arrest prior to and then
another arrest after the estimation period
was intended to ensure—with reasonable
certainty—that arrestees were criminally
active throughout the estimation period.
The required arrests at either end of the
estimation period were excluded from the
analysis, and time spent incarcerated was
excluded from the time at risk of arrest in
the estimation period.

The mean μs estimated for adult arrestees
in their 20s between 1966 and 1973 are
reported for the two jurisdictions in Table
19. Arrest frequencies were lowest for auto
theft and aggravated assault; offenders who
were active in those offenses averaged
about one arrest every 5–7 years of street
time. The highest arrest frequencies were
found for drug offenses and the residual
category of "all others"; while free in the

TABLE B-19   Mean Individual Arrest Frequencies (μ) from Official
Arrest Histories

Offense Type	Washington, D.C., Adults	Detroit SMSA Adults		Black to White Ratio[a]
		Whites	Blacks	
Robbery	0.23	0.13	0.23	1.74
Aggravated assault	0.19	0.18	0.18	0.97
Burglary	0.26	0.18	0.22	1.19
Larceny	0.27	0.13	0.29	2.13
Auto theft	0.14	0.13	0.15	1.15
Weapons	0.22	0.22	0.19	0.89
Drugs	0.32	0.31	0.24	0.77
All others	0.40	0.38	0.38	0.79
Any index	0.59[b]	0.25	0.39	1.54
Index (excluding larceny)	0.46[b]	0.24	0.30	1.24
Total (excluding traffic)	1.09[c]	0.55	0.56	1.01

NOTE: Arrest rates, arrests per offender per year free, were
estimated by offense type for only those offenders with at least one
arrest for that offense some time during their arrest histories.   Only
arrests prior to the sampling years and after the first arrest as an
adult were considered.   When computing μs for cohorts among 1973
arrestees in Washington, D.C., only the most serious charge was
considered (Blumstein and Cohen, 1979); for cohorts among 1974-1977
arrestees in the Detroit SMSA, all charges recorded for an arrest were
counted (Cohen, 1981).   This will inflate the rates for Detroit
arrestees somewhat compared with those for Washington, D.C.,
arrestees.   However, since only 10 percent of Detroit arrests involve
more than one charge, the rates are reasonably comparable.

[a]The ratios were computed before μs were rounded to the two
significant figures reported in this table.

[b]Arrests for murder and rape are excluded from index rates in
Washington, D.C.   The resulting underestimates of index frequencies are
likely to be small since in 1973 murder and rape constituted only 7.3
percent of all adult arrests for index offenses.   Also, reported index
rates in Washington, D.C., are simple averages of index rates found for
the five offender types in this table who have at least one index
arrest (i.e., robbers, aggravated assaulters, burglars, larcenists, and
auto thieves).   For index rates excluding larceny, both arrests for
larceny and larcenists are excluded from the simple average.

[c]Reported "total" rates for Washington, D.C., are simple averages
of the "total" rates found for each of the eight offender types
identified in the table.

community, these active offenders averaged one arrest every 2.5 to 3.5 years. Offenders active in robbery and burglary averaged one arrest every 4 years; white offenders in the Detroit SMSA had somewhat lower frequencies for these offense types.

There are striking similarities in offense-specific μs, both between races in the same jurisdiction and across jurisdictions. The largest differences are between whites and blacks, but even these are small. The ratio of black to white frequencies in the Detroit SMSA is very close to 1 for most offense types. The largest differences, of about 2:1, are found for robbery and larceny. Also, frequency rates for Washington, D.C., arrestees—who were predominantly black—are very similar to the arrest frequencies of black offenders in the Detroit SMSA. These racial differences in arrest frequencies, however, do not come close to the ratios of 10:1 or even 5:1 observed for robbery and other violent offenses in aggregate incidence rates of arrests per capita (see Table 1–2, this volume). The substantial racial differences found in aggregate incidence rates appear to reflect primarily the differences between the races in participation in crime. Among active offenders, frequency rates are more similar for black and white offenders.

Mean arrest frequencies were also analyzed for variations with the offender's age, number of prior arrests, and cohort membership. Individual arrest histories were broken down into separate observation years, each characterized by the attributes of offenders at the start of that year. Mean arrest frequencies were then estimated by aggregating all observation years with the same attributes. Multivariate regression analysis on the resulting mean μs did not generally reveal significant trends in offense-specific rates, either as offenders got older or as they accumulated additional arrests. There was, however, some indication of a cohort effect among Washington, D.C., arrestees, i.e., μ was higher for more recent cohorts, but a similar cohort effect was not found in the Detroit SMSA data.

The general stability over time within cohorts contrasts with other observations of strong effects in the full cross-section of arrestees: arrest frequencies systematically declined with age and increased as arrests accumulated for adult offenders. These opposite results suggest that the variability in frequency rates observed in a cross-section arises predominantly from heterogeneity in rates for the different mixes of offenders compared within a cross-section. Arrest frequencies appear to be more stable over time within the same cohort. The results within cohorts, however, must be regarded as preliminary because of the small samples of arrestees on which they are based and because of the limited number of years—extending only through the 20s for adult offenders—that were examined.

An important factor potentially affecting the accuracy of estimates of μ is incomplete arrest history data. Failure to record large numbers of arrests in centrally maintained criminal history repositories, for example, could lead to serious biases in estimates of arrest frequencies. This possibility was highlighted by the findings of recent audits of criminal history files. In checking samples of arrest records maintained by various local police departments and courts in Michigan, the Michigan State Police (1983a, b) found that 21 to 47 percent of felony arrests were not recorded in the central criminal history files. A similar audit by researchers at the Police Foundation (Sherman and Glick, 1984) found both under- and overcounts in arrest histories for arrests appearing in local records.

Nonrecording rates during the sampled years in the Detroit SMSA and Washington, D.C., studies varied substantially (Table 20). In the Detroit SMSA, under half of the arrests reported in local police statistics were recorded in the central arrest history data, but in Washington, D.C., recording in arrest histories was almost complete. The low recording rate in the Detroit SMSA was due mainly to a police policy of forwarding to the central repository only arrest reports with known dispositions. Other factors that may affect police reporting to central repositories are the extent to which local departments are linked routinely to the central repository. Lack of geographic proximity,

TABLE B-20 Extent of Incomplete Arrest History Data: Ratio of Arrests in Arrest Histories to Arrests in Police Reports

Offense Type	Washington, D.C., Adults in 1973	Detroit SMSA Adults in 1974-1977[a]
Robbery	.97	.43
Aggravated assault	.91	.40
Burglary	.94	.47
Auto theft	.99	.44

NOTE: The complete census of arrests for adults available in the FBI's computerized arrest history data for Washington, D.C., and the Detroit SMSA for the sampling years was compared with local police reports of arrests in the same jurisdictions and years in State of Michigan 1975 Uniform Crime Report and State of Michigan 1977 Uniform Crime Report for the Detroit SMSA, and in the Annual Report of 1973 and Annual Report of 1974 of the Metropolitan Police Department in Washington, D.C.

[a]The numbers of adult (aged 17 or older) arrests for the Detroit SMSA are estimated separately by crime type by applying the adult proportion of arrests reported statewide to local statistics.

absence of administrative ties, and heavy reliance on locally maintained records could all contribute to reduced reporting to a central repository.

Incomplete arrest history data can lead to complex biases in estimates of μ. When substantial numbers of arrests are not recorded in arrest histories, the number of arrestees found in the arrest history data for a sampling year will be understated, as will the total number of arrests that year. Some individuals with only one arrest in the sampling year will be missing from the arrest history data, as will some individuals who had several arrests that year. Since failure to record *arrestees* is more likely for offenders with only one arrest, low-rate arrestees, with their smaller expected number of arrests, are also more likely to be missing from samples based on incomplete arrest history data. This would lead to *over*estimates of μ. But incomplete recording also understates the number of arrests for arrestees who are sampled, which contributes to *underesti*-mates of μ. The ratios in Table 20 reflect both nonrecording of arrests and under-counting of arrestees in the arrest history data. The accuracy of arrest-frequency estimates will therefore depend on the relative strengths of these two opposing potential sources of bias.

Aside from the potential errors arising from incomplete arrest history data, arrests—even when fully recorded—are only a sample of all crimes committed by offenders, and so arrest frequencies will include only a portion of total offending frequencies. Nevertheless, estimates of μ, like those in Table 19, can be used to generate estimates of λ. If the probability of arrest for a crime, q, is independent of λ, then the mean μ is just the product of the mean individual crime rate and the risk of arrest per crime, $\mu = \lambda q$. Using this relationship with estimates of the probability of arrest per crime, μ can be transformed into λ.

Assuming a single arrest risk for all offenders in an offense type, Blumstein and Cohen (1979) and Cohen (1981) used aggregate data on the number of reported arrests, A_i, divided by the number of reported crimes for offense type i, C_i, to develop offense-specific estimates of the probability of arrest for a crime. This simple ratio was then adjusted by the offense-specific rate at which victims report crimes to the police, r_i, to account for unreported crimes among crimes committed. Another offense-specific adjustment was made to account for arrests of multiple offenders for the same crime incident, O_i, that are included among reported arrests. The final estimate of the probability of arrest per crime for offense type i is

$$q_i = (A_i/O_i)/(C_i/r_i).$$

Reported arrests and crimes, A_i and C_i, are generally available in local police reports. Victim reporting rates, r_i, are sometimes available for specific jurisdictions; if not, national data are available annually (e.g., Bureau of Justice Statistics, 1982a). Estimates of the average number of offenders per crime incident, O_i, are available from national criminal victimization data in Reiss (1980b).[13]

Estimates of the arrest risk per crime for different offenses in Washington, D.C., and in the Detroit SMSA are reported in Table 21. The probability of arrest per crime is highest for aggravated assault, which probably reflects the direct confrontation between offender and victim in this offense and the high proportion of offenders who are known to victims—36.5 percent in 1980

(Bureau of Justice Statistics, 1982a:Table 51). Arrest risks per crime for other offense types are generally under 5 percent. These estimates of q by offense type, which are based on aggregate data, are similar in magnitude to estimates developed from self-reports of arrests and crimes by prison inmates (Table 3-2; Peterson and Braiker, 1980:Table 2; and Petersilia, 1983:Table 4.4).

Estimates of λ. The estimates of q in Table 21 were combined with the estimates of μ in Table 19 to obtain estimates of λ (Table 22). Within any single offense type and jurisdiction, the same arrest risk, q, was applied uniformly to all active offenders. As indicated in Table 22, mean λs for adult arrestees in Washington, D.C., and the Detroit SMSA were generally similar in magnitude for most offense types. Frequencies were lowest for offenses involving actual or threatened violence; offenders active in aggravated assault were estimated to commit an average of two to three of these crimes annually, and offenders active in robbery were estimated to commit three to five robberies per year free. Individual frequencies for property crimes were generally higher—at five or more crimes per year free. The largest difference in λs was found for auto theft; λ, on average, was three auto thefts per year free in Washington, D.C., compared with nine in the Detroit SMSA.[14]

---

[13]The bias due to including multiple offenders per crime in reported arrests was first pointed out in Shinnar and Shinnar (1975). The average number of offenders per crime incident, O_i, is derived from crime incidents in which the number of offenders is known and is reported by victims in the victimization surveys. The adjustment used here thus involves the assumption that the number of offenders per crime incident is not substantially different for crime incidents in which the number of offenders is *not* known. The adjustment will overstate O_i and understate q_i if the number of offenders is more likely to be known in crime incidents involving multiple offenders.

[14]This suggests an interesting hypothesis about the potential influence of different criminal opportunities—reflected by differences between jurisdictions in the availability of targets—on λ. Like the differences in individual auto theft frequencies for active offenders, reported auto thefts per 100,000 population were also lower in Washington, D.C., than in the Detroit SMSA. While the reported index crime rate in Washington, D.C., for 1973 (6,949 index crimes per 100,000 population) was 94 percent of the corresponding index crime rate in the Detroit SMSA for the years 1974–1977 (7,411 index crimes per 100,000 population), the reported auto theft rate in Washington, D.C. (642), was only 63 percent of the rate in the Detroit SMSA (1,014). Exploring this hypothesis further would require, at a minimum, data on the numbers of registered and newly manufactured vehicles in each jurisdiction.

TABLE B-21   Estimates of the Arrest Risk per Crime (q) by Offense Type

Offense Type	Washington, D.C.[a]	Detroit SMSA[b]
Robbery	.069	.043
Aggravated assault	.111	.062
Burglary	.049	.038
Larceny	.026	.030
Auto theft	.047	.015
Weapons[c]	(.056)	(.051)
Drugs[c]	(.040)	(.068)
All other[c]	(.038)	(.028)

[a]Blumstein and Cohen (1979).

[b]Cohen (1981).

[c]The probability of arrest per crime, q, is only roughly approximated for the predominantly victimless offenses of "weapons," "drugs," and "all other" for which the number of reported crimes, C_i, is very close to the number of reported arrests, A_i. Commission of these crimes typically goes unreported unless they are discovered by the police, and when discovered by the police, they usually result in arrest. The rate of reporting these offenses to the police, r_i, is arbitrarily set at one-quarter of the average reporting rate for all offense types in the victimization surveys, and the average number of offenders per crime incident for all offenses in the victimization surveys is used for O_i.

When various offense types are combined, active offenders are estimated to commit 9 to 13 index offenses and 15 to 26 total offenses annually. The λs for individual offense types are similar in the two jurisdictions, but total frequencies are higher in Washington, D.C., than in the Detroit SMSA. This reflects official records that include more diverse offending in the former than in the latter. When 12 major offense categories are considered, arrestees in Washington, D.C., averaged 2.7 crime types in their arrest histories, compared with 2.1 crime types for both black and white arrestees in the Detroit SMSA.[15]

Several factors can affect the accuracy of λ when it is estimated from arrest history data.

In addition to the problems of incomplete arrest data, discussed above, biases may arise from potential errors in the offense-specific estimates of the arrest risk per crime, q_i. Reported crimes, C_i, and reported arrests, A_i, are subject to nonrecording errors. Likewise, both the reporting rate by victims, r_i, and the multiple-offender rate for crime incidents, O_i, are subject to recall and other response errors by respondents to victimization surveys. The multiple-offender ratio is also vulnerable to errors if the number of offenders varies systematically between crime incidents for which the victim knows (and reports on victimization surveys) the number of offenders and those for which the number of offenders is not known or not reported.

In view of the various potential sources of errors in estimates of q developed from aggregate data, it is advisable to explore the sensitivity of estimates of λ to reasonable

[15]The 12 offense categories are murder, rape, robbery, aggravated assault, burglary, larceny, auto theft, weapons, drugs, stolen property, fraud, and a residual category for all other offense types.

TABLE B-22 Mean Individual Offending Frequencies (λ) Derived from
Official Arrest Histories

Offense Type	Washington, D.C., Adults[a]	Detroit SMSA Adults[b]
Robbery	3.4	4.7
Aggravated assault	1.7	2.9
Burglary	5.7	5.3
Larceny	10.9	7.3
Auto theft	3.0	9.3
Any index	13.2[c]	8.7[d]
Index (excluding larceny)	7.4[c]	6.7[d]
Total (excluding traffic)	25.9[c]	14.6[d]

[a]Blumstein and Cohen (1979:Table 19).

[b]Derived from data in Cohen (1983:Table 16).

[c]In Washington, D.C., rates for index offenses do not include
murder and rape. Also, the "index" rates reported here are simple
averages of the "index" frequencies found in Blumstein and Cohen
(1979:Table 19) for the five offender types with at least one index
arrest (i.e., robbers, burglars, aggravated assaulters, larcenists, and
auto thieves). Similarly, total frequencies are a simple average of
"total" rates found for all offender types examined in the same table.

[d]Murder and rape are included in index frequencies for the
Detroit SMSA. In computing λ for "index" and "total" offense types,
the arrest probabilities for individual offense types are weighted by
the distribution of offense types found in the aggregate.

variations in q. First, a generous range on the possible values of the various components that enter the estimates of q must be established (Table 23). Using a typical arrest frequency value, $\mu = 0.2$, the variations in estimates of q and in the associated estimates of λ can then be explored. Invoking logical and empirical constraints on the various component values, the ranges explored are .1 to .3 for the ratio of A to C, .25 to .75 for r, and 1.25 to 2.5 for O.

The resulting range in the estimates of q is large, .010 to .180 (a low of 1 arrest for every 100 crimes and a high of 1 arrest for every 5.6 crimes). The q estimates vary sixfold as O and r are varied across the columns of Table 23, and threefold as the ratio $A:C$ is varied across the rows. The impact of these variations in q on estimates

of λ can be substantial. At the highest value of q, λ is just over 1 crime committed annually; at the lowest value of q, by contrast, λ averages 20 crimes committed annually. For the most typical value of q available in current estimates, .05, the range of λ is narrower—from 1.7 crimes annually at the maximum value of q to 10 crimes per year at the minimum value of q. The actual value of λ is likely to be found in an even narrower range between these worst-case extremes. Thus, the variation in estimates of λ as a result of errors in estimating q is likely to be within a reasonable range.

Another factor potentially distorting the estimates of λ derived from μs is the reliance in existing estimates on a single offense-specific q_i for all offenders in that offense. In these estimates, all arrestees for

TABLE B-23 Sensitivity of Offending Frequencies (λ) to Errors in Estimating the Arrest Risk per Crime (q)

Typical Range for Ratio of Reported Arrests to Reported Crimes (A:C)	Current q Estimates (O = 2.0, r = .5)		Minimum q Estimates (O = 2.5, r = .25)		Maximum q Estimates (O = 1.25, r = .75)	
	q[a]	λ[b]	q	λ	q	λ
.1	.025	8.0	.010	20.0	.060	3.3
.2	.050	4.0	.020	10.0	.120	1.7
.3	.075	2.7	.030	6.7	.180	1.1

[a]Probability of arrest per crime is estimated as $q = (A/O)/(C/r)$.

[b]Mean offending frequency is estimated as $\lambda = \mu/q$ for a typical value of μ = 0.2.

an offense type are assumed to be equally vulnerable to arrest for their crimes. To the extent that offenders actually differ in their arrest risk per crime, applying the same offense-specific q_i uniformly to all offenders not only distorts the variations in λ_i estimated for different offender subgroups, but also introduces errors into the mean value of λ_i estimated for the entire population.

Variations in q for any offense type may result from differential enforcement practices that increase arrest vulnerability for some offenders compared with others. Such differential treatment for the same offense type is especially worrisome when examining differences in λ across demographic subgroups; concerns have been raised, for example, about the possibility that police exercise greater discretion in arresting females, juveniles, and whites. A lower q_i for these subgroups would lead to their underrepresentation among arrestees and to a corresponding underestimate of their λ_i if the same q was applied uniformly to the μs of all subgroups in offense-specific analyses. Some preliminary evidence suggests, however, that biases resulting from differences in q may not be a serious problem for demographic subgroups. In particular, reasonably close consistency has been found between the attributes of arrestees (especially sex, age, and race) for an offense type

and those of offenders in the same offense type described by victims in victimization surveys (Hindelang, 1978a, 1980; Hindelang, Hirschi, and Weis, 1979).[16]

Another potential source of variation in offense-specific qs is variation in enforcement practices that are associated with offending behavior. On the one hand, high-rate offenders in an offense type may be especially skillful at avoiding detection and arrest, which would result in a negative relationship between λ and q in that offense. On the other hand, their high rate of activity may increase their vulnerability to arrest per crime as they become known to the police and are targeted as suspects, which would contribute to a positive relationship between λ and q in that offense.

Failure to address subgroup differences in q that vary systematically with differences in λ can lead to biases in the estimates of λ derived from μ, even in offense-specific

---

[16]In relying on victim reports, the results for offender attributes are limited to crime incidents in which victims can describe the offender, either because of direct observation of the offender or because of a subsequent arrest. The results will apply to offenders generally if the subset of crime incidents for which offender attributes are known is adequately representative of crime incidents generally.

TABLE B-24   Example of Biases in Estimates of Individual Offending Frequencies (λ) Arising from Use of a Single Probability of Arrest per Crime (q) for an Offense Type

	Offender Subpopulations				Weighted Total Population Mean
	1	2	3	4	
Proportion of offenders in each subpopulation	.75	.15	.09	.01	1.0
Individual annual offending frequency (λ)	1.0	5.0	10.0	100.0	3.4
Case 1: Negative relationship between λ and q					
Probability of arrest per crime (q)	.06	.05	.04	.03	.056
Individual annual arrest frequency (μ)	.06	.25	.40	3.00	.149
Individual annual offending frequency (λ) estimated using population average $q = 0.056$	1.1	4.5	7.1	53.6	2.7
Case 2: Positive relationship between λ and q					
Probability of arrest per crime (q)	.03	.04	.05	.06	.034
Individual annual arrest frequency (μ)	.03	.20	.50	6.00	.158
Individual annual offending frequency (λ) estimated using population average $q = 0.034$	.9	5.9	14.7	176.5	4.6

analyses. Hypothetical data can be used to explore the biases in λ that arise when q and λ vary systematically with one another for an offense type. Say there are four offender subgroups (see Table 24) and that, consistent with the observations of highly skewed distributions of λ, most offenders commit crimes at rates below the mean frequency of 3.4 set for the entire offender population, and a small fraction (1 percent in this exam-

ple) commit crimes at very high rates. Case 1 (see table) explores the biases that arise when λ and q are negatively related, that is, q is lower for offenders with higher λs. In this case, applying the population average value of q uniformly to all offender subgroups leads to an underestimate of λ for that population. Conversely, if λ and q are positively related, as in Case 2 in Table 24, use of the population average for q in all subgroups leads to an overestimate of λ for the population. The potential for biases in λ from use of a single value of q for all offenders in an offense type highlights the importance of empirically investigating the nature of any further variations in q after controlling for differences among offense types.

Some preliminary evidence is available on the relationship between λ and q. Analysis of experiences in 2 early years of a 5-year survey of offending by a sample of U.S. youths revealed a tendency for the arrest risk *per offender* to increase with increases in the number of self-reported offenses (Dunford and Elliott, 1984:Table 7). Less than 1 percent of the offenders who reported committing only 1 or 2 offenses in 2 years were arrested during those years, but 19 percent of those who reported committing more than 200 offenses during that period were arrested. These data on offenders and arrests provide a basis for calculating the arrest risk *per crime*, q, for different offender subgroups.[17] The results, reported in Table 25, are rather striking: the estimated values of q are reasonably close over wide ranges of λ. Nevertheless, there is a downward trend in q as λ increases, especially at lower values of λ. Beyond 20 crimes in 2 years, the arrest probability q does not vary substantially with further increases in the number of crimes committed.

The research available to date generally fails to find systematic or substantial variations in q. With the exception of higher arrest risks for low-rate offenders, there is little variation in q with differences in λ or in the demographic attributes of offenders. While still only preliminary, these results suggest that the errors may be small when a single q is used to derive λ from μ.

---

[17]These estimates of q were provided by Blumstein (1985, personal communication) and are calculated as follows: if q is the probability of arrest per crime, and $p = 1 - q$ is the probability of not being arrested for a crime, then the probability of *no* arrests for persons committing n offenses is p^n and the probability of at least one arrest for these n offenses is $1 - p^n$.

Alternative Estimates of Individual Offending Frequencies

The explicit estimates of offending frequencies derived from the analyses of self-reports by inmates and arrest histories reviewed above are limited to serious adult offenders. A number of other studies provide estimates of participation rates by offenders, b, and aggregate incidence rates, A, for the same sampled population. Those studies provide an opportunity to develop frequency estimates for a wider array of offenders, particularly juvenile offenders.

Aggregate incidence rates reflect the number of offenses per sampled individual, including both active offenders and nonoffenders. When combined with b, however, A provides a basis for estimating μ. Relying on the relationship in Equation 1, the general strategy is to divide A by b to yield arrest frequency rates, μ, for the active subset within a sample.

If μ and b vary together systematically across offender subgroups, the resulting estimates of μ will be subject to the same biases illustrated in Table 24 (replacing q with b and λ with μ in the example). The estimate of μ derived in this manner is most accurate when μ and b vary independently across offenders. A more pervasive problem is that, taken directly, the estimates of raw μs are artificially inflated by the requirement that all active offenders must have at least one event to enter the participation measure and by the fact that raw frequencies can never be smaller than one. The rates can be adjusted, however, to eliminate the bias from the required event in the measurement period and to produce unconditional frequency rates for active offenders. The basic approach to adjusting raw frequencies is to restrict the estimate of frequency rates to the period *after* the required first event. Simply, the one required event is subtracted from the raw frequency rate and then the length of the measurement period is adjusted to also exclude the time to this first event. As a reasonable approximation, and assuming that the time between offenses is distributed exponentially with mean $1/\lambda$, the expected time to

TABLE B-25 Estimation of Probability of Arrest per Crime ($\underline{q}$) from Data on Offenders and Arrestees in National Youth Survey

Number of Self-Reported Offenses in 1976 and 1978	Midpoint Number of Offenses	Number of Offenders[a]	Fraction Arrested[a]	Probability of Arrest per Crime ($\underline{q}$)[b]	Standard Deviation of $\underline{q}$ Estimate[c]
1-2	1.5	149	.0067	.004479	.004467
3-5	4	151	.0199	.005004	.002871
6-10	8	181	.0110	.001388	.000978
11-20	15	207	.0290	.001959	.000793
21-50	35	233	.0300	.000871	.000327
51-100	75	131	.0382	.000519	.000230
101-200	150	109	.0734	.000508	.000176
201+	250	90	.1889	.000837	.000193

[a]Dunford and Elliott (1984:Table 7).
[b]If $\underline{q}$ is the probability of arrest per crime and $\underline{p} = 1 - \underline{q}$ is the probability of not being arrested for a crime, then the probability of no arrests for persons committing n crimes is $\underline{p}^n$ and the fraction ever arrested is just $1 - \underline{p}^n$. The midpoint value for the range of crimes committed is used for n to estimate $\underline{q}$. The results, however, are roughly comparable within the entire range. For the 11-20 group, for example, $\underline{q} = .002670$ for n = 11 and $\underline{q} = .001470$ for n = 20, compared with the midpoint value of $\underline{q} = .001959$ for $\overline{n}$ = 15.
[c]The standard deviation for the estimate of $\underline{q}$ is estimated from:

$$\underline{S} = \sqrt{[\underline{q}\ (1 - \underline{q})]/[(\text{number of persons})(\text{offending rate})]}.$$

In the 11-20 example, $\underline{S} = \sqrt{[(.001959)(.998041)]/[(207)(15)]} = .000793.$

the first offense—conditioned on the fact that there is at least one offense in a measurement period of length t—is given by

$$E(T_1|T_1 \le t) = \frac{\int_0^t x\lambda e^{-\lambda x}\,dx}{1 - e^{-\lambda t}}$$

$$= \frac{1}{\lambda} - \frac{te^{-\lambda t}}{1 - e^{-\lambda t}}. \qquad (2)$$

The requirement of at least one offense in t reduces the unconditional mean time between offenses, $1/\lambda$, by the quantity $te^{-\lambda t}/(1 - e^{-\lambda t})$.

If the raw frequency is given by N offenses in a measurement period of length t (where $N \ge 1$ for each offender), the adjusted unconditional frequency after the first offense can be approximated by

$$\lambda = \frac{N - 1}{t - \frac{1}{\lambda} + \frac{te^{-\lambda t}}{1 - e^{-\lambda t}}} = \frac{N}{t} - \frac{N}{t}e^{-\lambda t}$$

or

$$\frac{\lambda}{1 - e^{-\lambda t}} = \frac{N}{t}. \qquad (3)$$

Given the value of the raw frequency rate, N/t, and the length of the measurement period, t, it is possible to solve Equation 3 for the desired adjusted frequency, λ, using iterative numerical methods. Equation 3 indicates that for large values of λ or long t, the upward bias in N/t estimated directly from the data is small, and the adjustment is less important. In these cases N/t is very close in value to the desired unconditional λ.

The estimates of frequency rates obtained directly from inmate self-reports (Peterson and Braiker, 1980; Chaiken and Chaiken, 1982a) and from arrest histories (Blumstein and Cohen, 1979; Cohen, 1981, 1983) are vulnerable to a similar upward bias. In both types of estimates, frequency rates for an offense type are estimated only for offenders who have at least one offense (or one arrest) for that offense type. In the arrest histories, the required arrest can occur any time in a career; in the inmate self-reports, the required crime must occur during the observation period prior to the current incarceration. As indicated above, however, the upward bias in frequency rates is small when the length of time during which the required event may occur is long—as in the arrest histories, or when frequency rates are large—as in the inmate self-reports. For typical raw offending frequencies of five crimes or more per year found in the inmate self-reports for example, λ is overestimated by less than 1 percent. For an annual raw frequency of 5, the adjusted unconditional frequency is 4.97.

The reasonableness of the approximation in Equation 3 was assessed using data on the juvenile arrest experiences (as measured by police contacts) of a cohort of boys born in 1945 and residing in Philadelphia between the ages of 10 and 18. In an analysis done expressly for the panel, the authors of the original study (Wolfgang, Figlio, and Sellin, 1972) provided annual estimates of individual arrest rates for active offenders at each age from 13 to 17 and separately by the offender's age at first arrest. For each crime category examined, the number of active offenders in a year (i.e., juveniles with at least one arrest for that offense type in that year) was identified, along with the offenders' total arrests for the same offense type in that year, which yielded an annual raw arrest frequency.

Forty-four juveniles first arrested for a property index offense (burglary, larceny, or auto theft) at age 15, for example, were arrested again for a similar offense at age 16. These 44 active property offenders experienced a total of 50 property arrests at age 16. The resulting average annual μ of 1.14 property arrests is inflated by the requirement of one property arrest that year for these active property offenders. Using Equation 3, the adjusted unconditional μ for property offenders is reduced to .28 arrest annually.

To test the adequacy of the adjustment, a separate estimate was generated from the raw arrest history data for these juveniles. Using data on the dates of arrests for individuals, the one required arrest for each active offender was eliminated and the actual time to this required arrest was excluded from the time at risk of a property arrest during that year. The resulting empirically based μ for these 16-year-old active offenders was almost identical to the approximation. Considering only the actual arrest experiences for each individual after the required arrest at age 16, the average annual μ is also estimated to be .28 property arrest per year per active offender.

The adjusted estimates of μ based on Equation 3 are compared in Table 26 with the estimates derived directly from the arrest history data. Averaging across the individual ages, the adjusted μs in the various offense categories are strikingly similar to the estimates derived directly from the arrest history data. This same strong correspondence is also found within the separate estimates by age at current arrest and age at first arrest; the correlations between the two alternative estimates exceed .96 for each offense category. The adjustment in Equation 3 has the advantage that it relies on aggregate data on incidence rates and participation rates for a sample and does not require individual-level data on the actual timing of offenses or arrests. Nevertheless,

TABLE B-26 Assessment of Adequacy of Approximation of Arrest Frequencies (μ) (juvenile offenders in Philadelphia)

Offense Type and Offender Race	Raw Annual Arrest Frequency[a]	Adjusted Annual Arrest Frequency[b]	Arrest History Estimate of Annual Arrest Frequency[c]
All offenders			
Robbery	1.112	0.232	0.244
Violent index[d]	1.061	0.131	0.124
Property index[e]	1.210	0.410	0.401
Non-index[f]	1.331	0.611	0.639
Total	1.469	0.839	0.879
White offenders			
Robbery	1.133	0.273	0.295
Violent index	1.049	0.109	0.092
Property index	1.172	0.342	0.331
Non-index	1.239	0.459	0.479
Total	1.317	0.587	0.620
Nonwhite offenders			
Robbery	1.109	0.229	0.238
Violent index	1.064	0.144	0.131
Property index	1.239	0.459	0.453
Non-index	1.439	0.789	0.812
Total	1.632	1.082	1.133

NOTE: Annual arrest frequencies, μ, were estimated from the number of arrestees and their associated number of arrests each year for a cohort of boys born in 1945 and residing in Philadelphia from ages 10-18. The estimates were developed expressly for the Panel on Research on Criminal Careers by the authors of the original study (Wolfgang, Figlio, and Sellin, 1972).

[a]The raw frequency rate is calculated from the ratio of arrests to active arrestees in each year. When individuals must have at least one arrest in the measurement period to be counted among active offenders, the raw frequency rate is inflated by this required event.

[b]Relying on only the raw frequency rate and the length of the measurement period, the adjustment in equation (3) is used to remove the upward bias introduced by the required one event for active offenders.

[c]Relying on individual-level data on the actual timing of arrests for active offenders, the arrest history data provide direct estimates of arrest frequencies after the first arrest in each year.

the approximation appears to be quite adequate for providing estimates of μ that remove the upward bias introduced by the requirement that active offenders have at least one event in the measurement period. This approximation will be used below to derive frequency rates for active offenders from published data for various offender samples. Wherever possible, these estimates will be disaggregated to explore the variations in frequency rates with offender attributes. (See Table 27 for a description of the various data sets that are used.)

The adjusted μs reported in Table 26 for juvenile offenders in Philadelphia are strikingly consistent with the μs reported earlier for adult offenders (Table 19). Not only are offense-specific μs similar in magnitude for adult and juvenile offenders, similar patterns are also observed between racial groups. As for white and black adult arrestees in the Detroit SMSA, the differences are small between the adjusted μs for white and nonwhite juvenile offenders. The largest nonwhite-to-white ratio for juveniles is the value of 1.8 for total offenses.

Further confirmation of the adequacy of the adjusted estimates of μ is found in data from the arrest histories of adult (age 18 or older) men arrested and arraigned in Brooklyn, New York, during the summer of 1979. McGahey (1982) reports that during the 2 years preceding the sampled arrest, the average monthly arrest rate for this sample while free was .049. This rate, equivalent to 1.176 arrests while free in the full 2-year period, applies to the total sample, including sample members who had no arrests in the measurement period. Combining this aggregate incidence rate for the total sample with the participation rate of 44 percent ever arrested during the measurement period yields an average μ of 2.673 (1.176/.44) arrests in 2 years free for offenders who are active in the measurement period (i.e., those with at least one arrest). Adjusting this rate, using Equation 3 to eliminate the one required arrest, the annual μ is estimated to be 1.22. This estimate, an average of one arrest every 10 months, is similar in magnitude to the total μs found for active offenders among Philadelphia juveniles (.84 arrest per offender per year) and among Washington, D.C., adults (1.1 arrests per offender per year free).

The variation in μ by age at current arrest and age at first arrest for juvenile offenders in Philadelphia is shown in Table 28. Arrest frequencies for active juvenile offenders generally do not display the consistent sharp increases with age that are observed in aggregate population arrest rates (see, for example, Figure 1-2 in this volume). Except for robbery, which rises sharply at ages 15 and 16, arrest frequencies for active offenders do not display strong systematic increases with age. Indeed, μ decreases over age for property offenses.

The variation in μ as age at first arrest increases is also shown in Table 28. Once again, frequencies for property offenses tend to decline as age of initiation increases. An even stronger decline with age of initiation is evident for total offenses. The μs are more stable over different starting ages for robbery and violent index offenses.

In Table 28, age at current arrest and age at first arrest are treated separately. Because these variables vary together, i.e., older starters are only available for arrest at older current ages, these separate analyses could well mask opposite effects of these variables on μ. Multivariate regression analysis was used to explore this possibility (Table 29). To allow for the tendency of μ to peak at age 16, age at current arrest was partitioned at age 16 to permit different age trends up to age 16 and between ages 16 and 17. Separate regressions were run for each offense category. The dominant effect on μ was a consistently significant negative effect for age at first arrest in all offense categories: older starters had lower μs. This decline for older starters is not due to the reduction in time at risk of offending before age 18 for offenders first arrested at older ages. For each age at first arrest and age at current arrest, μ was estimated only for offenders who were active that year (as indicated by at least one arrest that year). All estimates were thus restricted to a common exposure time.

There were fewer significant trends in μ

TABLE B-27 Summary of Published Data Used to Derive Alternative Individual Frequency Rates

Study	Sample	Observations of Offending	Alternative Frequency Rate Estimates
Wolfgang, Figlio, and Sellin (1972)	1945 birth cohort of 9,945 boys from general population residing in Philadelphia from ages 10–18	Official records of 7,505 arrests (police contacts) for 2,698 arrestees between ages 13 in 1958 and 18 in 1963 (excluding traffic and juvenile status offenses)	Numbers of arrests and arrestees active at each age were used to estimate annual arrest frequencies, μ, by age, age of first arrest, and race (no adjustments for time served)
McGahey (1982)	Random sample of 607 adult males (18 or older) arrested for felonies or serious misdemeanors and held for arraignment in Brooklyn, N.Y., during summer of 1979	Official records of arrests in 2 years preceding the sampled arrest	Average monthly arrest rate while free for all arrestees (including those with no prior arrests) was used to estimate the annual arrest frequency, μ
Barnett and Lofaso (1985)	1945 birth cohort of 9,945 boys from general population residing in Philadelphia from ages 10–18	Official records of subsequent arrests as juveniles (police contacts) for 1,033 boys with at least three arrests before age 18	Numbers of subsequent arrests and arrestees were used to estimate annual arrest frequencies, μ, by number of prior arrests (time served was removed from time at risk)
Elliott et al. (1983)	National probability sample of U.S. youths aged 11–17 in 1976 (1,725 respondents in 1976 represent 73% of originally designated sample)	Self-reports of crimes committed in preceding year on each of five annual surveys: N = 1,719 in 1976 N = 1,655 in 1977 N = 1,626 in 1978 N = 1,543 in 1979 N = 1,494 in 1980	Aggregate annual incidence rates ($\underline{C}$, crimes per capita) for respondent sample and annual participation rates ($\underline{d}$, fraction of sample reporting at least one crime that year) were used to estimate annual offending frequency, λ

Sechrest (1979)	Two samples of addicts in methadone drug treatment programs: N = 473 patients entering treatment in 1969–1970 in Brooklyn, N.Y.; N = 271 patients entering treatment in 1970–1971 in Santa Clara, Calif.	Official records of arrests in 2 years preceding and 2 years following entry into treatment program	Annual aggregate incidence rates, $\underline{A}$ (arrests per capita), in the sample and annual arrest participation rates, $\underline{b}$, were used to estimate annual arrest frequencies, μ_s. These are combined with estimates of the probability of arrest per crime, $\underline{q}$, in each jurisdiction to yield average annual offending frequencies, λ
Johnson et al. (1983)	Sample of 201 active heroin users in Harlem section of New York City (1980–1982) interviewed weekly about daily drug use and crimes committed in past week	Self-reports of crimes committed during total reporting period; average of 57 days for each respondent	Aggregate annualized incidence rates, $\underline{C}$, and participation rates, $\underline{d}$, within 2-month reporting period were used to derive annual offending frequencies, λ, by offense type
Inciardi (1979)	Sample of 239 male and 117 female active heroin users in Miami, Fla., during 1978	Self-reports of crimes committed during year preceding interview	Total offenses and participation rates, $\underline{d}$, by offenders were used to derive offending frequencies, λ

TABLE B-28 Variation in Annual Arrest Frequency (μ) by Age at
Current Arrest and Age at First Arrest (juvenile offenders in
Philadelphia)

	Robbery	Violent Index[a]	Property Index[b]	Total[c]
Age at current arrest				
13	.12	N.A.[d]	.48	.63
14	.12	.08	.46	.72
15	.39	.12	.38	.87
16	.36	.19	.39	.94
17	.16	.08	.29	.83
Age at first arrest				
≤13	.19	.14	.51	1.07
14	.10	.20	.25	.69
15	.61	N.A.	.25	.74
16	.20	N.A.	.36	.57
17	N.A.	.19	.11	.36

NOTE: Annual arrest frequencies, μ, were estimated from the
number of arrestees and their associated number of arrests each year.
These estimates, developed expressly for the Panel on Research on
Criminal Careers by the authors of the original study (Wolfgang,
Figlio, and Sellin, 1972), were then adjusted using equation (3) to
eliminate the effect of the one required arrest each year.

[a]Violent index offenses include arrests for murder, rape, and
aggravated assault. Robbery, which is usually included among violent
offenses in the FBI's annual Uniform Crime Report, is treated as a
separate crime category here.
[b]Property index offenses include arrests for burglary, larceny,
and auto theft.
[c]Total offenses include all arrests for any type of offense
except traffic and juvenile status offenses (i.e., runaway, truancy,
and incorrigibility).
[d]In some age categories, the arrest data were insufficient to
provide reliable adjusted arrest frequency estimates.

TABLE B-29 Regression Results Exploring Effect of Age at First Arrest and Age at Current Arrest on Arrest Frequencies (μ) of Juvenile Offenders in Philadelphia (significant coefficient)

Offense Type	Age at First Arrest	Age at Current Arrest 13-16	Age at Current Arrest 16-17	R^2
SW injury[a]	-*	NS	NS	.37
SW theft[b]	-(+)	NS	NS	.37
Property index[c]	-(+)	NS	NS	.33
SW non-index[d]	-**	+***	NS	.71
Non-index[e]	-**	+**	NS	.71
Total offenses[f]	-**	+***	NS	.73

NOTE: Annual arrest frequencies, μ, were estimated by age at current arrest and age at first arrest from the number of arrestees and their associated number of arrests each year. These estimates, developed expressly for the Panel on Research on Criminal Careers by the authors of the original study (Wolfgang, Figlio, and Sellin, 1972), were then adjusted using equation (3) to eliminate the effect of the one required arrest each year.

[a]The Sellin-Wolfgang (SW) injury offenses include all offenses involving injury to victims.
[b]The Sellin-Wolfgang (SW) theft offenses include all offenses involving loss of property.
[c]Property index offenses include burglary, larceny, and auto theft.
[d]Sellin-Wolfgang (SW) non-index offenses include all offenses not involving injury to victims or loss or damage to property (excluding traffic and juvenile status offenses).
[e]Non-index offenses include all offenses (other than juvenile status offenses and traffic offenses) not included among the FBI's index offenses of murder, rape, robbery, aggravated assault, burglary, larceny, or auto theft.
[f]Total offenses include all offenses except traffic and juvenile status offenses (i.e., runaway, truancy, and incorrigibility).

NS = Coefficient not significant.
   +Significant at .10 level.
   *Significant at .05 level.
  **Significant at .01 level.
 ***Significant at .001 level or better.

TABLE B-30 Variation in Arrest Frequencies (μ) with Arrest Record (juvenile offenders in Philadelphia)

Number of Arrests So Far	Number of Offenders	Subsequent Mean Annual Arrest Rate While Free (all offenses)
3	1,033	1.15
4	708	1.43
5	534	1.52
6	386	1.79
7	303	1.92
8	224	2.08
9	175	2.25

SOURCE: Barnett and Lofaso (1985:Table II).

over age at current arrest. In the more aggregate categories of non-index offenses and total offenses, which include many distinct offense types, μ increased and reached a peak at age 16. This same increase was not observed in the less aggregate offense categories. These results suggest that the increases with age at current arrest may reflect the effect of varying numbers of active crime types within the aggregate offense categories. While μ may be relatively stable over age within any single offense type, older offenders may be active in more offense types, thus increasing their total μ in the aggregate offense categories.

Using a slightly different estimation technique on the arrest data for Philadelphia juveniles, Barnett and Lofaso (1985) assessed the relationship between past and future μs. Without exception, there was a clear upward trend: offenders who had more arrests were also subsequently arrested at higher rates (Table 30).

Barnett and Lofaso explored the possibility that the variation observed with prior

arrests was attributable to the fact that those with fewer prior arrests included many offenders who terminated their criminal activity while still juveniles. Failure to exclude this time after career termination from the time at risk of subsequent arrests would lead to underestimates of arrest frequencies for offenders who remain active. They found that for each arrest after the third, about 28 percent of offenders do not have another arrest as juveniles. Because the arrest data are truncated at age 18, however, it is possible that many of these apparently ended careers actually continue into adulthood. Assuming that no offenders actually terminated their careers during their juvenile years, and using the estimated μs for juvenile offenders, Barnett and Lofaso (1985) estimated the expected number of offenders who will have an arrest-free period to age 18, even though they remain active in criminal careers. This expected number was not significantly different from the observed number; thus, career termination does not appear to be a substantial factor in the variation in arrest frequencies observed for juvenile offenders.

The authors then explored the role of prior arrest frequencies in the observed relationship. Within the limited time available until age 18, offenders who accumulated large numbers of arrests must have done so at higher frequencies than those with only a few arrests. Thus, arrest record may be a reasonable proxy for prior arrest frequencies. Examining both the number of prior arrests and prior arrest frequencies together, they found arrest frequency in the past to be predictive of subsequent arrest frequencies for juveniles who remained active, but the relationship between the number of prior arrests and subsequent arrest frequencies disappeared.

The data for juveniles in Philadelphia provide estimates of μ based on official police and court records. Actual offending frequencies, λs, for juveniles—based on self-reports of crimes committed—were derived from published data from annual surveys of a national sample of U.S. youths. From 1976 to 1980, the same national sample of youths (males and females), aged 11–17 in 1976, were surveyed annually about the crimes they committed in the preceding year (Elliott et al., 1983). The number of respondents declined somewhat in subsequent years, but there was little loss from the original respondent sample of 1,725 adolescents in 1976.

Elliott et al. (1983:Part II) report extensive data on aggregate incidence rates (C, crimes per capita) for all sampled youths, and participation rates, d. These rates were reported separately for each survey year, by offense type, and by various attributes of the respondents. Dividing the incidence rates by the corresponding participation rates yields estimates of λ (see Equation 1). Equation 3 is then used to eliminate the upward bias introduced by the requirement that all active offenders in a year must have at least one offense during that year.

The final adjusted estimates of λ (averaged over the 5 survey years) are reported in Table 31. Overall, youthful offenders active in serious offenses reported committing an annual average of 8 robberies, 7

felony thefts, 4 felony assaults, and 7 index offenses. Combining all offense types, these active offenders are estimated to have committed 37 crimes annually. These frequencies are remarkably similar in magnitude to the average offending frequencies estimated from arrest histories of adult arrestees (Table 22). Despite differences in data sources, estimation techniques, and attributes of the offender samples (including, predominantly, urban black males among adult arrestees), a strong convergence is emerging in the estimates of λ. In part, this convergence reflects the generally small differences in λ observed for different offender attributes (Table 31). While λs for male offenders are always larger than those estimated for female offenders, the male-to-female ratios are generally under 2:1. This is substantially smaller than the differences usually observed for the sexes in aggregate incidence rates (e.g., Table 1-2, this volume). The differences in λ by race are similarly small compared with the large differences observed in aggregate incidence rates (e.g., Table 1-2, this volume). There is also a general absence of sharp increases with age among juveniles (e.g., Figure 1-2, this volume). The notable exception in Table 31 is the consistent increase in total λ with age.

A similar age pattern was observed among adult arrestees and adult inmates, as well as among juvenile arrestees in Philadelphia. In all instances, frequencies for any single offense type were relatively stable over age, while frequencies for aggregate offense categories, which include many different offense types, increased with age among juveniles and decreased with age among adults. This pattern suggests that the age effect observed in aggregate offense categories may be due to changes in the number of active offense types for offenders, i.e., offending first becomes more diverse during the juvenile years as new offense types are added and then becomes more specialized in the adult years as the number of active offense types declines.

Like the pattern observed for other demographic attributes, there was also very little

TABLE B-31 Variation in Annual Offending Frequency (λ) in National Youth Survey

Offender Attribute	Robbery	Felony Theft[a]	Felony Assault[b]	Index[c]	Total[d]
All offenders	7.5	6.5	3.9	6.8	36.6
Sex					
Male	8.4	7.1	4.4	7.6	42.2
Female	3.3	4.4	2.6	3.7	26.7
Race					
White	9.6	5.8	3.4	6.4	34.9
Black	4.6	7.4	3.9	6.3	39.6
Hispanic	3.1	18.4	4.3	7.3	42.2
Age					
13	6.3	3.6	4.0	6.0	21.4
14	5.4	6.5	3.4	5.6	25.0
15	15.3[e]	6.2	5.5	10.0[e]	28.4
16	6.7	4.5	3.3	5.2	31.8
17	6.5	8.7	3.4	7.1	47.9
18	5.6	6.3	3.7	5.3	45.0
19	5.2	8.8	6.6	7.9	57.3
Employment					
Unemployed	5.4	8.4	4.1	6.8	23.7
Part time	8.3	5.5	3.6	6.3	30.5
Full time	9.0	7.3	4.5	7.7	66.4

NOTE: Annual offending frequencies, λ, were estimated expressly for the Panel on Research on Criminal Careers from data available in Elliott et al. (1983:Part II) reporting aggregate incidence rates (C, crimes per capita in the sample) and annual participation rates (d, fraction of sample with at least one crime) for each offense type. The resulting raw frequency rates were large enough that no adjustment was needed for the required one crime per year. Annual frequencies, λ, are averaged over the 5 survey years.

[a]Felony theft includes self-reports that the respondent stole a motor vehicle, stole something worth more than $50, broke into a building or vehicle, or bought stolen goods.

[b]Felony assault includes self-reports that the respondent committed aggravated assault, sexual assault, or participated in gang fights.

[c]Index offenses include self-reports of offenses involving robbery, felony assault, or felony theft (excluding the purchase of stolen goods).

[d]In addition to robbery, felony assault, and felony theft, total offenses include minor assaults, minor thefts, drug sales, prostitution, carrying a weapon, and certain public order violations (panhandling and disorderly conduct).

[e]The frequency rates for 15-year-olds are inflated by a very high number of robberies reported by 15-year-olds in 1977. When this unusual rate is excluded from the average, the annual frequency estimates are reduced to 5.8 robberies and 5.4 index offenses.

TABLE B-32 Estimates of Annual Offending Frequencies (λ) Based on Arrest Histories for Addicts in Drug Treatment Programs

Offense Type	Individual Arrest Rates, μ		Probability of Arrest per Crime, q[a]		Individual Offending Rates, λ	
	Santa Clara	Brooklyn	Santa Clara	Brooklyn	Santa Clara	Brooklyn
Property	.91	.61	.043	.026	21.2 (N = 45)	23.3 (N = 41)
Robbery	.77	.36	.091	.059	8.4 (N = 5)	6.1 (N = 9)
Assault	.65	.42	.194	.133	3.3 (N = 22)	3.1 (N = 16)

NOTE: Derived from data on aggregate incidence rates, A, and annual participation rates, b, in Sechrest (1979:Tables 4 and 6). Rates reported are a simple average of annual rates estimated for active offenders in the 2 years before program entry and 2 years immediately after program entry for 277 addicts in 1970-1971 in Santa Clara, Calif., and 473 addicts in 1969-1970 in Brooklyn, N.Y. No adjustments were made for any time not at risk because of incarceration or hospital confinement. Average number of active offenders per year for the 4 years of data is in parentheses.

[a]The probability of arrest per reported crime, q, is based on the ratio of reported arrests to reported crimes in Santa Clara for 1970 (California Department of Justice, 1980) and in New York City for 1971 (Vera Institute of Justice, 1977). These raw ratios were adjusted for nonreporting by victims to the police using reporting rates found in victim surveys for 1974 in California (Bureau of Justice Statistics, 1981b) and in New York State (Bureau of Justice Statistics, 1980a). A second adjustment was made for the average number of offenders per crime incident, O. The same adjustment factor, based on national data (Reiss, 1980b), was applied in both states.

variation in λ with the employment status of these youths. Whether unemployed or working, offenders active in serious offense types committed those crimes at similar rates. Total offenses, by contrast, which include many less serious offense types, did vary with employment status. During the adolescent and young adult years surveyed—when youths are normally expected to be attending school—increased time that active offenders spent working was associated with *increased* λs. This increase in offending with increased work was due primarily to higher λs in less serious offense types. Once a youth was active in the more serious offense types, neither employment status nor other demographic attribute

strongly influenced λ in those offense types.

In contrast to the limited effects observed for employment and other demographic attributes, offending frequencies vary substantially with drug use by active offenders. Three studies provide data on aggregate incidence rates and participation rates in crime for drug users. These data have been used to derive estimates of offending frequencies for active offenders among drug users (Tables 32-34).

Table 32 reports annual arrest frequencies, μ, and offending frequencies, λ, for participants in two methadone drug treatment programs, one in Brooklyn, New York, and the other in Santa Clara, California. In

TABLE B-33 Estimates of Annual Offending Frequencies (λ) from Self-Reported Offenses in Weekly Interviews with Heroin Users

| Offense Type | Heroin Use[a] | | | Total |
	Irregular	Regular	Daily	
Any nondrug offense	133.3 (N = 53)	172.7 (N = 73)	215.2 (N = 60)	174.8 (N = 186)
Robbery	8.9 (N = 12)	16.7 (N = 18)	26.5 (N = 27)	20.4 (N = 57)
Burglary	12.8 (N = 19)	35.9 (N = 33)	60.5 (N = 35)	41.2 (N = 87)
Shoplifting (for resale)	67.8 (N = 31)	74.7 (N = 48)	105.7 (N = 42)	84.5 (N = 121)
Other larceny	14.8 (N = 22)	40.4 (N = 41)	32.4 (N = 37)	32.1 (N = 100)
Forgery	6.8 (N = 6)	11.4 (N = 7)	18.4 (N = 8)	13.4 (N = 21)
Con games	138.1 (N = 16)	125.2 (N = 21)	85.9 (N = 21)	113.8 (N = 58)

NOTE: Derived from data in Johnson et al. (1983:Tables VI.1 and VIII.2). Aggregate incidence rates ($\underline{C}$, crimes per capita in the sample) were computed for a 2-month period from annualized rates provided in Table VIII.2. These were divided by participation rates ($\underline{d}$, fraction of sample reporting at least one crime) for the 2-month reporting period in Table VI.1 to yield raw frequency rates for active offenders in the average 57-day reporting period available for each respondent. The raw frequencies for the reporting period were then adjusted to eliminate the one required offense in that reporting period using equation (3), and the annualized adjusted rates are reported here. The number of active offenders generating each frequency estimate is in parentheses.

[a]Irregular heroin users reported using heroin 0, 1, or 2 days per week. Regular users reported use on 3-5 days per week. Daily users reported use on 6-7 days per week.

both study sites, official arrest records were obtained for all program participants for the 2 years preceding and 2 years following entry into the program. The resulting annual incidence rates of arrests per capita, A, found in the sample and the arrest participation rates, b, are reported separately for each year by Sechrest (1979:Tables 4 and 6). These data were used to derive μ for the subsets of active offenders, using Equations 1 and 3. Averaging over the 4 years, active offenders among drug addicts averaged one

TABLE B-34 Estimates of Annual Offending Frequencies (λ) from Self-Reports by Heroin Users

Offense Type	Males	Females
Robbery	29.7	28.7
Assault	3.3	(2.7)[a]
Burglary	24.8	4.9
Vehicle theft	7.4	(2.2)[a]
Theft from vehicle	12.5	8.3
Shoplifting	68.2	63.1
Other theft	12.0	7.6
Forgery/counterfeiting	17.8	25.4
Con games	17.6	12.6
Drug sales	186.7	118.8

NOTE: No adjustments were made for any time not at risk due to incarceration or hospital confinement.

[a]Rate is based on fewer than 20 active offenders and thus is subject to more sampling variation than other rates in this table.

SOURCE: Derived from data on total offenses and participation rates in Inciardi (1979:Tables 4 and 5).

arrest every 1.5 to 3 years for serious crimes in Brooklyn, and one arrest every 1.1 to 1.5 years in Santa Clara. These arrest frequencies for drug addicts are at least twice as high as those found for comparable offense types among adult arrestees generally (Table 19).

Separate estimates of q were developed for Santa Clara and Brooklyn by use of aggregate data on A and C reported in local police statistics, reporting rates by victims, r, in California and in New York State, and national estimates of the number of offenders per crime incident, O. Even relying on local data for different jurisdictions, the resulting arrest probabilities for separate offense types (Table 32) are remarkably similar to the estimates for Washington, D.C., and for the Detroit SMSA reported earlier (Table 21). In each jurisdiction, q is highest for assault at .10 to .20, followed by robbery at rates of about .05 to .10 per crime, and then by property offenses at rates under .05.

Combining q with μ yielded almost identical estimates of λ for drug addicts in the two study sites (Table 32). The higher arrest frequencies in Santa Clara compared with Brooklyn appear to result from higher arrest probabilities per crime in Santa Clara. Active offenders among drug addicts in treatment programs are estimated to commit crimes at about twice the annual rate found for adult arrestees generally (Table 22).

The λs estimated from official arrest histories for active offenders in drug treatment programs are comparable in magnitude to the λs estimated from the self-reported crimes of irregular heroin users in another sample of drug users (Table 33). Using weekly self-reports of daily drug use and crimes, Johnson et al. (1983) characterized a sample of active heroin users in terms of their intensity of heroin use. Irregular users reported using drugs less than 3 days a week, regular users on 3 to 5 days a week, and daily users on 6 or 7 days a week. On the basis of self-reported crimes during an average 57-day reporting period for each respondent, Johnson et al. (1983) estimated d for the 2-month reporting period and annualized incidence rates, C. These rates were used to develop the estimates of λ reported in Table 33.

Offending frequencies generally increased as drug use increased. The λs for daily drug users in Table 33 are at least six times higher than the λs estimated for offenders generally (e.g., Tables 22 and 31). Similarly high λs were estimated from incidence and participation rates reported in Inciardi (1979) for active heroin users (Table 34). It is also noteworthy that among active offenders in this sample of heroin users, males and females reported committing crimes at very similar rates for most offense types.[18] The higher λs estimated for daily heroin users when compared with other offenders are consistent with the large differentials in λs that have been observed for drug users between periods of heavy drug use and periods of no drug use (McGlothlin, Anglin, and Wilson, 1978; Ball et al., 1981, 1983; Gropper, 1985).

Summary

Despite differences in observation techniques (self-reports or arrest records), in the samples used (inmate, arrestee, or general population samples), and in the jurisdictions examined (with their differences in population characteristics and criminal justice practices), considerable convergence is emerging in mean λ estimates for specific offense types. Frequency rates, however, do vary across offense types; mean λs within violent crimes are lower than within property crimes: While they are free in the community

- active violent offenders are estimated to commit an average of 2 to 4 serious assaults per year, and
- active property offenders are estimated to commit an annual average of 5 to 10 crimes for each of the property crimes they commit.

Mean frequencies for inmates are higher than those found among offenders in the community. On the basis of inmate self-reports in California and Michigan, when they are not incarcerated, these inmates are estimated to commit

- an annual average of 15 to 20 robberies per offender active in robbery, and
- an annual average of 45 to 50 burglaries per offender active in burglary.

These higher rates for inmates are to be expected because high-rate offenders are more likely to be found in a prison population, both because their high frequency of crimes increases their exposure to arrest, and because selectivity in criminal justice decision making increases their risk of incarceration if arrested. Frequencies estimated for Texas inmates, however, do not follow this pattern; they more closely resemble λs found for offenders in the community in other jurisdictions.

Individual frequencies vary considerably across offenders. The distribution of λ is highly skewed: the median offender in any offense type engages in under 10 crimes, but the 10 percent of offenders with the highest rates exceed 100 crimes each annually. Finding the factors that distinguish these highest-rate offenders is especially important in developing policies intended to reduce crime.

In contrast to patterns observed in aggregate population arrest rates and in participation rates, mean λs do not vary substantially with the demographic attributes of sex, age, or race. Differences in mean λs are observed, however, with age of onset of careers, drug use, employment, and prior criminal involvement. Active offenders who begin criminal activity at young ages, use drugs heavily, are unemployed for long periods of time as adults, and have extensive

---

[18]Burglary is a notable exception; male frequencies for burglary are about five times higher than female rates. This difference for burglary may be partially offset by a difference in λ of similar magnitude in the opposite direction for pickpocketing, which is not included in Table 34 because of the small numbers of offenders active in this offense type.

records of criminal activity generally commit crimes at higher rates than other offenders.

Methodological Issues in Estimating Individual Frequency Rates

A number of methodological problems are apparent in reviewing empirical estimates of individual frequency rates. These relate primarily to the representativeness of samples used to generate estimates and various problems in measuring rates within those samples. This section discusses the problems and various proposals for addressing them in future research.

Biases in Offender Samples: Differences in Sampling Probabilities

Problems of sample representativeness are common to estimates of individual frequency rates. The cross-section samples used to estimate offending frequencies are generally not representative of the population of offenders actually active in crime at any time. Offenders are distinguished from nonoffenders by their commission of at least one crime. In self-report samples, the active offenders are identified from their self-reports of offenses committed. In official-record samples, only active offenders identified by the criminal justice system through arrest, conviction, or incarceration enter the analysis.

The sampling bias is introduced by the requirement that sampled offenders must have at least one criminal event—e.g., a self-reported offense or an arrest—during some fixed sampling period. To the extent that λ, and the associated μ, varies in magnitude across offenders, all active offenders are not equally likely to enter the sample. In particular, offenders with a higher λ, or a higher individual μ in arrestee samples, will be more likely than other offenders to meet the sampling criterion of at least one criminal event in the sampling window. As a result, these higher rate offenders will be overrepresented in offender samples.

The nature of this sampling bias can be illustrated using a simple characterization of individual offending. For purposes of this example, each offender is assumed to have a constant λ. That rate, however, varies across individuals. As was found in the Rand surveys, the distribution is highly skewed: many offenders have a low rate, and a small number of offenders have very high rates. In this example the mean rate is five offenses and the median rate is less than one offense. The distribution of offenders in the total active population in this example is shown in Table 35. The probability that an offender will have at least one offense in a sampling period is also presented for several values of λ and for different sampling periods. Regardless of the length of the sampling period, high-rate offenders are always more likely to have at least one offense and thus to be included in a sample of active offenders. The bias against including low-rate offenders is most severe in very short sampling periods. In a 1-day sample, the highest rate offenders in the table are more than 200 times more likely to be sampled than the lowest rate offenders. In the 1-year sample, the disproportionality of sampling reduces to 10.5 between the highest and lowest rate offenders.

Despite the higher sampling probabilities for individual high-rate offenders, the contribution of those offenders to the offender sample will depend on their relative representation in the total offender population and on the length of the sampling period. The composition of the total offender population and of various offender samples for different-length sampling periods in this example is shown in Table 36. The overrepresentation of high-rate offenders in cross-section offender samples is greatest for the short sampling periods. In a 1-week sample, for example, only 1 percent of the total population have λs greater than 50, but those high-rate offenders represent 7.2 percent of the offender sample. As the length of the sampling period increases, the offender sample becomes more representative of the total offender population. For the parameter values used in this illustration, a sampling period of 3 years provides a reasonably representative sample of the total offender population.

TABLE B-35 Variations in Sampling Probabilities for Offenders with
Different Individual Offense Rates (λ): An Illustration

Annual Individual Offense Rate, λ	Proportion of Offender Population with Frequencies $\leq \lambda$ [a]	Probability of At Least One Event in Sampling Period [b]							
		1 Day	1 Week	1 Month	3 Months	6 Months	1 Year	3 Years	5 Years
0.1	.05	--	.002	.008	.025	.049	.095	.259	.393
0.5	.26	.001	.010	.041	.118	.221	.393	.777	.918
1	.52	.003	.019	.080	.221	.393	.632	.950	.993
3	.67	.008	.056	.221	.528	.778	.950	1.000	1.000
5	.74	.013	.092	.341	.713	.918	.993	1.000	1.000
10	.85	.027	.175	.565	.918	.993	1.000	1.000	1.000
20	.93	.053	.319	.811	.993	1.000	1.000	1.000	1.000
50	.99	.126	.617	.984	1.000	1.000	1.000	1.000	1.000
100	.9995	.237	.853	1.000	1.000	1.000	1.000	1.000	1.000

[a]Assumes λ is distributed according to a gamma distribution:

$$f(\lambda \mid \underline{a}, \underline{b}) = \frac{b^{\underline{a}}}{\Gamma(\underline{a})} \lambda^{\underline{a}-1} e^{-\underline{b}\lambda}$$

with shape parameter $\underline{a}$ = .25 and scale parameter $\underline{b}$ = .05 and $\Gamma(\underline{a})$ the gamma function. The expected value of λ is given by $\underline{a}/\underline{b}$ = 5 and the variance of λ is $\underline{a}/\underline{b}^2$ = 100.

[b]Assumes λ is constant for individual offenders. The probability of at least one event in an interval of length $\underline{t}$ is given by $1 - e^{-\lambda \underline{t}}$.

While oversampling high-rate offenders is a problem in both self-report and official-record studies, the bias toward high-rate offenders is especially severe in samples based on official contacts with the criminal justice system. This problem was dramatized in several studies that included both self-report and official-contact measures of offending for general population samples.

The Cambridge study (West and Farrington, 1973, 1977) prospectively followed a cohort of London boys. The primary measure of offending was convictions in court. At various intervals during the observation period, the youths were also asked to report the frequency with which they committed offenses. West and Farrington (1973:165) report that "official delinquents [with convictions] had committed more delinquent acts according to their own admission than

non-delinquents." This higher rate of self-reported delinquency for official delinquents is illustrated in Table 37.

The National Youth Survey (Elliott et al., 1983) prospectively followed a representative national sample of U.S. youths aged 11–17 in 1976. These youths were interviewed annually and asked about the frequency of their offending in the previous year. In addition, data on their recorded police contacts through 1980 were obtained from local police authorities, and data on arrest records through 1978 were analyzed. Based on their self-reported offenses in the 3 years 1976–1978, respondents were classified into offender categories that reflected the intensity and seriousness of their self-reported offending (Dunford and Elliott, 1984). "Career offenders," for example, include persons who reported committing 12 or more total offenses per year or 3 or more index offenses per year in 2 or more consecutive years. In a comparison of self-reported offending patterns for youths who were arrested with those not arrested by 1978, youths who were arrested were also more likely to report committing a greater number of offenses or more serious offenses (i.e., they were more likely to be "career offenders") than nonarrested youths (Table 38).

It is also noteworthy that only 6 percent of the surveyed youths had arrest records by 1978. This arrest participation rate is quite low compared with the rates of 35 and 33 percent found among juveniles in the two Philadelphia birth cohorts (see Appendix A), and the conviction participation rate of 20 percent found among boys in London

(West and Farrington, 1973). Several factors contribute to the lower arrest participation through 1978 in the National Youth Survey. First, many of the youths were still under age 15 by the 1978 cutoff date. The number of youths arrested can be expected to increase as arrests through 1980 are included. Also, females made up about one-half of the National Youth Survey sample, which lowers arrest participation compared with the all-male samples in Philadelphia and London. Finally, the National Youth Survey is based on a representative national sample and includes about 30 percent of youths from rural areas. This broader geographic representation can be expected to lower arrest participation compared with the samples from large urban areas in Philadelphia and London.

TABLE B-36 Variations in Distribution of Sampled Offenders for Different Sampling Periods: An Illustration

Annual Individual Offense Rate, λ	Proportion of Offender Population with Frequencies $\leq \lambda$ [a]	Proportion of Offenders with Frequencies $< \lambda$ in Sample of Active Offenders[b]							
		1 Day	1 Week	1 Month	3 Months	6 Months	1 Year	3 Years	5 Years
0.1	.05	--	.001	.001	.003	.004	.007	.014	.021
0.5	.26	.011	.020	.032	.056	.083	.121	.195	.224
1	.52	.050	.064	.106	.181	.256	.348	.469	.495
3	.67	.110	.139	.223	.352	.453	.545	.635	.653
5	.74	.156	.197	.308	.460	.562	.641	.713	.727
10	.85	.292	.369	.528	.678	.747	.793	.834	.843
20	.93	.506	.597	.757	.850	.882	.904	.923	.927
50	.99	.887	.928	.966	.979	.984	.987	.990	.990
100	.9995	.9999	.9999	.9999	.9999	.9999	.9999	.9999	.9999

[a]Assumes λ is distributed according to a gamma distribution:

$$\underline{f}(\lambda \mid \underline{a}, \underline{b}) = \frac{b^{\underline{a}}}{\Gamma(\underline{a})} \lambda^{\underline{a}-1} \underline{e}^{-\underline{b}\lambda}$$

with shape parameter $\underline{a}$ = .25 and scale parameter $\underline{b}$ = .05 and $\Gamma(\underline{a})$ the gamma function. The expected value of λ is given by $\underline{a}/\underline{b}$ = 5 and the variance of λ is $\underline{a}/\underline{b}^2$ = 100.

[b]Active offenders have at least one offense in the sampling period. The example assumes λ is constant for individual offenders. The distribution of offenders in a sample is obtained by applying the probability of at least one event in the sampling period for an offender from Table 35 to a discrete approximation (using only the values of λ in this table) of the continuous gamma distribution of the offender population and renormalizing the resulting distribution.

TABLE B-37 Relationship Between Official Delinquency (Conviction) and
Self-Reported Offenses in the Cambridge Study of London Boys

Official Record of Convictions	Number of Youths	Average Number of Delinquent Acts Admitted at Ages 14-15[a]
Convicted before ages 14-15	47	15.5
First convicted after ages 14-15	61	11.6
Not convicted	297	8.3

[a]The measure reported is the number of different offense types
admitted; it is only a rough approximation of variations in frequency
rates over different delinquency statuses.

SOURCE: West and Farrington (1973:165).

TABLE B-38 Comparison of Official Record of Arrests with Self-Reported
Offending for 1976-1978 in National Youth Survey

	Percentage in Each Self-Reported Offender Category			
Arrest Status	Nonoffenders[a]	Noncareer Offenders[b]	Career Offenders[c]	Total[d]
Individuals with arrests by 1978	13 (N = 9)	37 (N = 26)	50 (N = 35)	100 (N = 70)
Individuals without arrests by 1978	39 (N = 461)	44 (N = 516)	17 (N = 207)	100 (N = 1,184)
Total	N = 470	N = 542	N = 242	N = 1,254

[a]"Nonoffenders" report three or fewer delinquent acts per year and
report no index offenses.
[b]"Noncareer offenders" report any combination of annual rates except
those classifying nonoffenders or career offenders.
[c]"Career offenders" report 12 or more total offenses per year or 3 or
more index offenses per year in 2 or more consecutive years.
[d]Only subjects participating in all five annual surveys, consenting to a
police record search, and having that search completed through 1978 were
included, i.e., 73 percent of the 1,725 youth participating in the study and
53 percent of the 2,360 in the originally designated sample.

SOURCE: Dunford and Elliott (1984:Table 6).

TABLE B-39 Distribution of Self-Reported Offending Groups by
Official Contact

| Self-Reported Offender Categories | Percentage of Respondents in Each Self-Reported Offender Category: Community Sample | | | | | Institutionalized Sample (N = 245) |
	Total (N = 942)	Picked up by Police (N = 64)	Appeared in Juvenile Court (N = 73)	Placed on Probation (N = 35)	Institutionalized (N = 20)	
Nonoffender[a]	9	0	1	0	0	0
Low frequency, minor[b]	35	17	21	17	10	2
High frequency, minor[c]	24	25	25	17	15	7
Low frequency, major[d]	19	23	22	29	30	11
High frequency, major[e]	14	34	32	37	45	80
Total	100	100	100	100	100	100

[a]Nonoffender: no reported offenses in previous year.
[b]Low frequency, minor: fewer than 48 minor offenses (the median
reported) and no major offenses in the previous year.
[c]High frequency, minor: 48 or more minor offenses and no major offenses
in the previous year.
[d]Low frequency, major: fewer than five major offenses (the median
reported) in the previous year. Major offenses include motor vehicle theft,
grand theft, aggravated assault, selling hard drugs, rape, robbery, and
breaking and entering.
[e]High frequency, major: five or more major offenses in previous year.

SOURCE: Cernkovich, Giordano, and Pugh (1983:Tables II and III).

A similar pattern of more frequent high-rate offending for offenders with official records is reported in Cernkovich, Giordano, and Pugh (1983). These researchers compared self-reported offending with self-reports of official contacts in a stratified population sample of youths aged 12–19 residing in a north central U.S. city. Self-reported offending in this sample was also compared with reports in a sample of institutionalized juveniles. As indicated in Table 39, high-frequency, serious offenders were more likely to be found among respondents who reported official criminal justice contacts. Less than 15 percent of the total community sample were high-frequency major offenders, but 32 to 45 percent of respondents with official criminal justice contacts were high-frequency serious offenders. This increased representation may result partly from a greater willingness of some respondents to report offenses *and* official contacts. In another sample of institutionalized youths, however, in which knowledge of official contacts did not depend on self-reports, 80 percent were high-frequency, serious offenders, based on their self-reported offenses. The frequency of offending alone did not distinguish respondents with official contacts from other respondents. High-frequency, minor offenders were generally less prevalent among respondents with official contacts. Respondents with official contacts were distinguished primarily by their higher frequency of major offenses (Table 39). The

TABLE B-40 Percentage of Community Sample Reporting Criminal Justice
Sanctions in Previous Year

Self-Reported Sanctions	Self-Reported Offender Categories[a]				
	Nonoffender	Low Frequency, Minor	High Frequency, Minor	Low Frequency, Major	High Frequency, Major
Picked up by police	0.0	3.3	7.2	8.4	17.2
Appeared in juvenile court	1.2	4.5	8.1	9.0	18.0
Placed on probation	0.0	1.8	2.7	5.6	10.2
Institutionalized	0.0	0.6	1.4	3.4	7.0
Total	100	100	100	100	100

[a]See definitions of offender categories in Table 39.

SOURCE: Cernkovich, Giordano, and Pugh (1983:Table II).

greater likelihood of sanctions for these more serious offenders is reported in Table 40.

The various studies reviewed above indicate the overrepresentation of high-rate offenders, especially in more serious offense types, in samples based on official criminal justice contacts. The much greater overrepresentation in these samples, compared with samples of self-reported offenders, results from the generally lower rates for the criteria for entering a sample. A sample of arrestees, for example, includes individuals with at least one arrest in the sampling period. Similarly, active offenders in a general population sample include individuals who report committing at least one offense in the sampling period. While 32.5 percent of the community respondents reported committing at least one major offense in the previous year, only 7 percent reported being arrested and 2 percent reported being institutionalized (Table 39). As indicated in Table 35, the problem of oversampling high-rate offenders is more severe when rates for the criterion event are low. Looking at the column for a 1-year sampling period, for example, at low rates for λ of one

offense or fewer per year, which are commonly found for individual arrest frequencies, oversampling of offenders with μ equals 1 is considerable compared with offenders with lower rates. For offenders with rates of one, the probability of entering the sample is .632; for offenders with rates of .5 or lower, the probability is no more than .393. The differences in sampling probabilities are less severe for rates higher than one.

In general, estimates of frequency rates derived from cross-section official-record samples are not generalizable to all offenders. The estimated frequency rates are those of the more active and more serious offenders who come to the attention of the criminal justice system, and thus they constitute an inflated estimate of mean offending rates for all offenders. Nevertheless, the distribution of frequency rates found in these unrepresentative, more serious samples are often of greatest interest and value from the perspective of policy concerns, such as identifying effective means of crime control.

The illustration of sampling probabilities in Table 35 indicates that one way to reduce the severe overrepresentation of high-rate offenders in these official record samples is to increase the length of the sampling period. The length of the sampling period needed will depend on the anticipated rates for the sampling event. The lower the mean rate at which sampling events occur (e.g., one arrest or fewer per year per active offender), the longer the sampling period that is needed to improve the representation of offenders with low arrest rates. For q, the arrest risk per crime, an individual arrest rate, μ, corresponds to offense rate $\lambda = \mu/q$. Except when λ and q are highly negatively correlated, increasing the representation of low μ offenders in an official-record sample will also increase the representation of low λ offenders, and arrestees will become a more representative sample of all offenders.

Another strategy for increasing the representativeness of offender samples is to include only offenders whose first event occurs in the sampling period (e.g., first arrest or first reported offense). This sample of starting offenders mirrors the distribution of offending rates in the total offender population. Excluding the recidivists in the sampling period eliminates the overrepresentation of high-rate offenders. However, because of the overrepresentation of recidivists in offender samples, a larger sampling frame may be required to ensure an adequate sample for analysis when the sample is restricted to only first-time offenders in a sampling period. Also, the analysis of frequency rates for first-time offenders must be based on prospective data; the sampling criterion ensures that all offenders were inactive before the sampling period.

Biases in Offender Samples: The Problem of Low Response Rates to Self-Report Surveys

While official-record samples are biased by the overrepresentation of high-rate offenders, there is some evidence to suggest that high-rate offenders are underrepresented in self-report samples. This is because surveys of self-reported offending are generally characterized by reasonably high nonresponse rates. In a follow-up survey of a 10 percent random sample of the Philadelphia cohort (Wolfgang and Collins, 1978), for example, only 58 percent of the designated sample were actually interviewed. The Rand inmate surveys involved response rates of 47 to 72 percent among California and Michigan inmates (Peterson and Braiker, 1980:6; Peterson et al., 1982:Tables 10 and 11). In the National Youth Survey, 27 percent of the original sample did not participate (Elliott et al., 1983:116–117). Participation dropped further as informed consent was requested of sample members so that official-record information could be obtained.

Farrington (1984) noted that "the boys [in the Cambridge study] from the most uncooperative families were significantly more likely to be convicted than the remainder, and the convicted boys tended to be more uncooperative themselves to the research." This same problem was noted in the follow-up of the Philadelphia birth cohort. Official delinquents were less likely to be interviewed (51 percent) than nondelinquents (64 percent). Response rates also declined with increasing seriousness of offending: 63 percent one-time offenders were interviewed, compared with 53 percent for "recidivists" (two to four arrests), and only 38 percent for "chronics" (five or more arrests) (Wolfgang and Collins, 1978:32–33).

Nonresponse in self-report samples is more characteristic of more serious offenders. Exclusion of these more serious offenders from self-report data will contribute to underestimates of offense rates.

Obtaining Valid Frequency Estimates from Self-Reports

Assuming the problems of sample representativeness are resolved—either by improved sampling techniques to increase representativeness or by properly narrowing the scope of application of sample results—there are other measurement problems in developing rate estimates for the sample itself. In self-report surveys, these problems relate to obtaining accurate frequency estimates from individuals.

Obtaining accurate estimates of the frequency of offending is extremely problematic in retrospective self-report surveys. The earliest self-report studies, relying on gross categories like "never," "occasionally," and "often," provided only crude estimates of frequency. Such response categories are likely to be highly variable in their meaning, both for different offense types and for different respondents. As a result, they cannot be translated into numerical frequencies with any precision.

As interest in obtaining explicit frequency measures increased, the survey items also increased in numerical precision. Alternative strategies included use of numerical categories or reliance on open-ended questions the respondent completed by indicating an exact number of offenses. The most complex survey designs involve a mixture of categories and open-ended responses. The respondent is first guided through a series of categorical choices to pick the unit of time that best describes his rate (e.g., yearly, monthly, weekly, daily). The respondent then supplies—in an open-ended way—the typical number of offenses in that unit of time. Studies that have included alternative frequency items in the same survey instrument report very high variability in the λs derived from responses to different item types.

Individual offense rates in the first Rand survey of prison inmates (Peterson and Braiker, 1980:26), for example, were based primarily on respondent choices among several numerical categories that described the number of offenses committed in the 3 years prior to their current incarceration: 0, 1–2, 3–5, 6–10, or more than 10. As reported earlier, respondents who indicated more than 10 offenses were asked to supply an exact number in an open-ended question. In another part of the survey, an open-ended question asked respondents how many burglaries they committed in a typical month. The median rate of 4 burglaries reported for a typical month was substantially higher than the median monthly rate of only .24 derived from the total number of burglaries reported for the 3-year period. This extreme difference foreshadowed the

much higher estimates of λ obtained in the second inmate survey, in which smaller units of time were used to report frequencies over 10 in the 2-year observation period.

Similarly, the National Youth Survey (Elliott et al., 1983:15) asked an open-ended question on the number of offenses committed in the previous year. If the reported number of offenses was 10 or more, the respondents were also asked to indicate the frequency category (e.g., "once a month," "once a week," "2–3 times a day") that best described their offending. The midpoint of the category was used to generate alternative estimates of λ. While the two responses were in general agreement, Elliott et al. (1983:117) reported that, "At the upper end of the frequency continuum, estimates based on the midpoint of the category are substantially higher than the frequency responses given directly."

In sum, estimates of λ are extremely sensitive to the design of the survey item. Estimates for high-rate offenders are especially vulnerable to design effects. The accuracy of various estimates of λ thus hinges on the relative accuracy of alternative survey items.

There are a priori reasons for believing that λs based on smaller units of time may be overestimated, and that λs based on total offenses reported for a longer time period may be underestimated. Smaller, "typical" time units (e.g., monthly frequencies) are particularly vulnerable to overestimates when offending is intermittent, e.g., there are short periods of high offending. In this event, it is doubtful that respondents average across periods of high and low activity to give the typical frequency of offending. It is more likely that frequencies during the more salient high-rate periods are reported as "typical."

A subsequent analysis of responses to the second Rand inmate survey (Chaiken and Rolph, 1985) explored the intermittent character of offending. The inmates reported more criminal activity for the period just prior to the current incarceration, regardless of the length of the available observation period. In this event, short observation periods for some inmates would be especially vulnerable to overestimates of frequency rates because those observation periods are more likely to include periods of spurts in activity and to exclude quiescent periods. Adjusting for spurts in activity did reduce the frequency rate estimates (see Table 15).

Use of longer time periods has the potential advantage of smoothing out periods of high and low offending. As the observation periods get longer and more distant, however, underestimates associated with memory lapses are likely to become an increasing problem.

Empirical research assessing the relative accuracy of alternative self-report measurement strategies is essential. This research should examine existing strategies to provide a basis for calibrating existing estimates of λ and explore the efficacy of alternative techniques intended to improve the accuracy of estimates. A program of basic research that may produce results applicable to this problem is outlined in a report from the National Research Council on cognitive aspects of survey methodology (Jabine et al., 1984).

Efforts to obtain accurate self-reports of λ suffer from many of the same problems confronted in surveys of the frequency of crime victimizations. Considerable attention has been devoted to identifying and resolving measurement problems in victim surveys. The design of improved self-report instruments for offenders may benefit from the accumulating store of knowledge on the design of victim surveys (see Penick and Owens, 1976).

One potential solution to improved self-reported frequencies may lie in a strategy of repeated interviews of the same persons that ask about their experiences in recent and short time intervals, like "last week" or even "yesterday." A strategy of repeated short-term interviews (four interviews in about 1 month) was used in research on noninstitutionalized opiate users in neighborhoods of Harlem in New York City (Johnson et al., 1983:9). Annualizing frequencies from a short observation period, however, is vulnerable to biases arising from observations generated during spurts, or lulls, in individual activity. To avoid such

biases, the short-term interviews should be repeated at random intervals over a longer observation period, perhaps a year or more. Such a scheme might involve four or six interviews about the previous week's activities, spread randomly over an 18-month period. Repeating the interviews for randomly selected weeks increases the chances that the weeks surveyed are a representative mix of spurt and lull periods for an individual. Spacing these interviews over a longer total observation period (e.g., 18 months) also reduces the testing effects of the survey on the behavior itself.

The research on New York City drug users came close to this design through the use of subsequent 28-day interview cycles conducted 3 to 6 months after the first interview cycle. These later interview cycles, however, were only available for about one-third of the sample. Also, the results in this study may be limited by the small number of interview cycles per person and the relatively short total observation period of only 6 months. All respondents provided a minimum of four weekly interviews. A more representative picture of the frequency of offending and drug use might have been obtained by scattering these interviews over the full observation period, rather than bunching interviews into cycles of 4 consecutive weeks.

Despite their limitations, the data available for the small number of respondents interviewed in more than one cycle in the New York City study provide a basis for beginning to assess the merits of a repeated, short-term interview strategy. In particular, they provide a preliminary basis for examining the extent to which intermittent spurts and lulls in offending are really a problem in frequency estimation. If evidence of spurts is found, the data can be used to provide preliminary estimates of the magnitude of the differences in offense rates in high- and low-rate periods as well as estimates of the usual duration of the spurts and lulls.

From a practical point of view, use of a strategy of repeated interviews with the same persons is vulnerable to sample attrition problems. Also, reliance on multiple interviews will limit the size of the sample of offenders that can be interviewed. Suppose, for example, that resources are available for 1,000 interviews. Interviewing each person four times will reduce the potential sample size fourfold. Because of the smaller sample size, it then becomes especially important to select for interview individuals who are, in fact, more likely to be active offenders. Selection might be accomplished through a screening interview to identify offenders in a much larger general population sample. This screening interview might simply ask if the individual had ever committed any offenses, or whether he or she had committed any offenses in the past year or two. The "ever committed" option is more likely to yield a more representative sample of high- and low-rate offenders. The longer prior observation period of this option, however, increases the risk that individuals passing through the screen will no longer be active offenders at the time of the screening interview. The shorter and more recent screening period (1 to 2 years) of the second option is more likely to yield currently active offenders. There will, however, be some underrepresentation of low-rate offenders passing through the screen. As indicated in the illustration in Table 36, for example, offenders with λs of one or less represent about 35 percent of a 1-year sample compared with 52 percent of all active offenders.

The foregoing discussion focused principally on alternative sampling and interview strategies for estimating individual frequency rates from self-reports. The discussion, however, also raised a more general issue in the design of research on individual offending patterns. It is clear from the consideration of the pros and cons of alternative strategies that no one strategy is well suited to measuring all aspects of offending behavior.

Measures of participation require general population samples. Unless the samples are very large, however, they will not provide adequate numbers of active offenders for estimating frequency rates. The strategy of repeated interviews is certainly not feasible for very large population samples. A multistage sampling strategy that addresses only a limited set of questions at each sampling stage would seem to be the best strategy. Administering a relatively brief screening interview to large population samples should be adequate to estimate participation in crime. More extensive surveys of the details of offending could then be administered to the smaller sample of active offenders identified by the screening interview.

Obtaining Valid Frequency Estimates from Official Records

Reliance on arrest history data in developing estimates of frequency rates also involves measurement problems. These relate primarily to the reliability of arrest records and the adjustments used to estimate crimes committed from arrests recorded.

Obtaining accurate estimates of offense rates from arrest histories rests fundamentally on official arrest histories. Of principal concern are record completeness and accuracy. The analyses reviewed in this paper relied on centralized, computerized criminal history files maintained by the FBI. Similar computerized criminal history files are increasingly being developed by state agencies (Bureau of Justice Statistics, 1985).

With respect to estimating μ, the problem of record completeness refers principally to the extent to which all arrests occurring at the local level are in fact included in the centralized files. Failure to include arrests in individual histories could lead to biases in estimates of μ. Missing arrest reports are an especially severe problem for less serious offenses. Entries in the FBI history files, for example, are usually triggered by submission to the FBI of a fingerprint record associated with an arrest or admission to a detention or correctional facility. Many arrests for less serious offenses (e.g., for nuisance offenses like vagrancy, drunkenness, disorderly conduct, trespassing) generally fall below the threshold for submission of a fingerprint record and thus will not be recorded in the FBI's files.

For the very same reason, however, arrests for more serious charges, especially felonies, are likely to be far more reliably recorded in official-record data. Nevertheless, an audit of the central criminal history records in Michigan found nontrivial, nonrecording of arrests, even for serious offense types (Michigan State Police, 1983a, b). This nonrecording was attributed to increasing use of pretrial release for offenders arrested on serious charges and to charge reductions at early case screening by prosecutors, both factors that reduce the likelihood that fingerprints will be obtained and forwarded to centralized repositories.

Some portion of nonrecorded events can also be attributed to differences between local agencies and auditors in the classification of events, especially the classification of offense types. Such classification differences are most likely to occur when locally recorded criminal events, based on crime categories found in local statutes, must be converted to some other crime classification scheme. Ambiguities in this conversion will likely result in undercounts of some offense types and overcounts of others. Such differences in classification are likely to be reasonably uniform within a jurisdiction, i.e., the same "misclassification" will occur consistently. Inconsistencies in classifications, however, can introduce more serious distortions in comparisons across jurisdictions, since the same offense label may be applied to different criminal behaviors. Thus, a higher arrest frequency for some crime type in one jurisdiction might reflect a difference in classification rather than a difference in actual offending. Comparisons of offenders whose records are largely confined to a single jurisdiction are likely to be less vulnerable to classification differences.

Nonrecording of some events leads to complex biases in estimates of μ derived from officially recorded criminal histories. These errors include not only underestimates from missing arrests for arrestees who are included in the history data, but also overestimates from the failure to include some low-rate offenders whose one arrest in the sampling year is not recorded in the arrest history data. The accuracy of the esti-mates computed directly from arrest history data thus depends on the relative strengths of these two opposing biases. To adjust μ for arrestees on whom data are entered requires an estimate of the undercount of arrests for just those arrestees. Extrapolating these adjusted rates to all arrestees then requires a further assessment of the degree to which μ for arrestees who are missing entirely from the history data differs from that of included arrestees. Research empirically investigating the relative magnitudes of these two potential sources of bias is needed, especially in jurisdictions where nonrecording in the central criminal history repository is widespread.

Arrest history records are, of course, also subject to the variety of data transformation and data entry errors associated with creating computerized files. These include errors in identification of the individual and coding problems in converting local descriptions of events into a uniform coding scheme. If they are not systematic and large, such errors are part of the normal variability in measurement. They should not seriously bias estimates derived by aggregating sampled individuals. They pose a more serious threat, however, to estimates for particular individuals.

Another cause for concern in relying on officially recorded arrests to estimate μ is the possible confounding of enforcement practices with offending behavior. The arrest rate, μ, reflects the contributions of both λ and q, that is, $\mu_j = \lambda_j \times q_j$ for any offender j, and high values for μ may therefore be due to high values for λ or q. This confounding of enforcement practices with offending behavior is especially problematic when comparing μ across crime types or across jurisdictions, both situations in which enforcement patterns are likely to vary. It may also be a problem in comparisons among offender subgroups if q varies systematically with offender attributes.

One solution to the distortions introduced by the arrest process is to invoke explicit estimates of q in order to estimate underlying offense rates from available estimates of μ. This procedure has been used in a preliminary way, for example, by

Blumstein and Cohen (1979). To accommodate the main sources of variability, estimates of q are developed separately by crime type and for the specific jurisdictions being studied. Nevertheless, these results are potentially limited by applying a single arrest probability to all offenders within any crime type and jurisdiction. Such estimates fail to address systematic variability in q with offender attributes and will distort comparisons of λ across the groups. A relationship between individual offense rates, λ_i, and arrest probabilities, q_i, would be especially problematic.

The results available to date generally fail to find systematic variations in q, especially with demographic attributes. Such results are consistent with the practice of using a single estimate of q to derive λ from μ. While encouraging, further research empirically investigating the patterns of variation in q is needed, especially systematic variations with λ and with other offender attributes. These analyses will benefit from combining self-report data on crimes committed with data on arrests from self-reports and official records for the same individuals, as was done in the second Rand inmate survey (Peterson et al., 1982) and the National Youth Survey (Dunford and Elliott, 1984). Such data provide an opportunity for developing disaggregated estimates of q that will permit more refined adjustments to estimates of μ derived from arrest histories.

Measurement Problems in Developing Individual Frequency Estimates

Most estimates of frequency rates aggregate data over individuals to generate estimates of the mean or median rate for a sample. However, there are occasions when distinguishing among offenders who have different frequency rates is important, so that estimates for particular individuals are needed.

The data available for an individual represent the particular realization of an offense history that is observed for an individual and are distinct from the underlying rates that gave rise to that realization. For example, two offenders who are both observed to commit exactly three offenses in a year need not have the same underlying rates. When offending is probabilistic rather than deterministic, an offender with an annual frequency equal to three need not commit exactly three offenses each year. Instead, his observed number of offenses will vary from year to year, but in the long run if he is observed over a long enough period, it is expected that his observed mean annual rate will be three. Thus, because of the probabilistic nature of offending, there is some likelihood that offenders whose λ is 10 or 20, for example, will have a realization of only three offenses in a year, as will some offenders with λ of only 1.

Relying on only the observed realization of offenses (or arrests) for each individual to estimate his frequency is thus vulnerable to error. Instead, estimates for individuals should be developed using statistical estimation techniques like those proposed in Rolph, Chaiken, and Houchens (1981) and Lehoczky (Volume II). Those techniques better approximate the likely underlying frequency rate for an individual by using information on the distribution of offending in the total sample to adjust individual rates estimated from the observed number of offenses for each individual.

A Sampling Strategy for Detecting High-Rate Offenders

This review has highlighted some important difficulties in measuring offense rates for individuals. In addition to these direct measurement problems, other difficulties plague efforts to identify differences in λ using more readily available and directly measurable attributes of offenders (see, for example, the discussion of prediction and classification in Chapter 6 and in Gottfredson and Gottfredson, Volume II). Nevertheless, for important policy and research reasons, there is increasing interest in being able to identify high-rate offenders within the general offender population.

The earlier discussion of sampling biases highlighted the problems in obtaining representative samples of offenders. Precisely those features of sampling processes that contribute to sampling bias problems—particularly the requirement of an event during the sampling period—can be turned to advantage to identify high-rate offenders with reasonable accuracy. Capitalizing on the overrepresentation of high-rate offenders, samples drawn in short time periods, say a week or a month, will include disproportionately large numbers of high-rate offenders. The shorter the sampling period, the lower the false-positive errors of including low-rate offenders. In the illustration in Table 36, for example, only 25.3 percent of offenders in the 6-month sample have annual frequencies greater than 10; in the 1-week sample of the same population, those high-rate offenders increase to 63.1 percent.

A further refinement of the selection strategy might involve drawing a 1-week sample (e.g., those arrested in 1 week, or those admitting to crimes during the past week in a general population survey) and then looking at the offending in that sample in another week, say 1 or 2 months later. The persons identified as criminally active in both samples are very likely to be high-rate offenders. Such a strategy has the advantage that it relies on only observed offending or arrest experiences to identify high-rate offenders and does not invoke other potentially controversial variables, such as various personal attributes of offenders.

Explicit Behavioral Models of Offending

Various models of individual offending are implicit in virtually all estimates of frequency rates, regardless of the data source used. Because of the inherent difficulties in obtaining direct observations of crimes committed by individual offenders, estimates of frequencies rest on other observable data, like arrests and self-reported crimes, as indirect indicators of the underlying crime process of interest. The various estimation strategies that are applied to these indirect data rest fundamentally on models characterizing both individual offending and the processes that give rise to the observable data. The accuracy of the frequency estimates that emerge depends on the adequacy of these usually unstated assumptions.

Because the available observable data are only indirect indicators of actual crimes committed, improving the precision of techniques for measuring these observable data can only go so far in improving the accuracy of estimates for the underlying, but unobserved, crime process. Improved knowledge about unobserved crimes committed requires explicit behavioral models that link the unobserved crime process with the observed data. With explicit models, the adequacy of estimates can be measured against the adequacy of the model's assumptions.

Models of individual offending have moved from undifferentiated treatments of offending, like those underlying such traditional aggregate measures as per capita crime rates and recidivism rates, to differentiated characterizations that partition offending levels among the various aspects of a criminal career, especially participation, frequency, crime seriousness, and career length. In their early formulations, these differentiated models of criminal careers relied on a number of simplifying assumptions, principally that individual careers are stationary over time and often invariant across offenders. This simple characterization of careers underlies most currently available estimates of frequency rates.

More recent developments have begun to enrich the basic model to better accommodate the complexities of real criminal careers (Chaiken and Rolph, 1985; Flinn, Volume II; Lehoczky, Volume II). One issue of concern has been possible nonstationarities in λ during individual careers. Two forms of nonstationarity have been addressed: spurts in criminal activity as offenders move between active and quiescent periods, and changes in frequencies as offenders age. These more recent model developments represent considerable conceptual advances over the very simple model of criminal careers that underlies most available estimates of the various career dimensions. As the models of criminal careers continue to reflect more fully the underlying behavioral processes, there will be increased confidence in the credibility of empirical estimates derived from those models.

OFFENSE SERIOUSNESS DURING CRIMINAL CAREERS

The study of frequency rates reflects a concern for the intensity of individual offending—how often offenders commit crimes. The analysis of offense seriousness, in contrast, is concerned with the pattern of offense types that are committed. At a static level, the offense mix for different offenders might be compared to assess differences in the distribution of offense types. Identifying offenders who are more likely to engage in serious, predatory crimes is of particular policy interest. At a dynamic level, analyses of offense seriousness focus on the changes in offense types during criminal careers. Two issues of concern are the extent of "specialization" and the extent of "escalation" in offense types as careers progress. Specialization refers to the tendency of individual offenders to repeat the same offense type as offending continues. Escalation, by contrast, is a tendency to move to more serious offense types. The opposite pattern is also possible—successive offenses decrease in seriousness. In both instances, the emphasis is on changes in the mix of offense types committed, not on the frequency of offending in each offense type.

These alternative patterns are found in commonly held conceptions of criminality. Criminals are sometimes pictured as specialists who may try several different offense types until they find the particular offense that best suits their skills and opportunities, which they then adopt as their specialty. Probably the most commonly held view of criminality is one of escalation, i.e., individual offenders who remain criminally active become gradually more hardened and dangerous in their commitment to crime and move to increasingly more serious offense types. An alternative scenario is one of de-escalation, e.g., the serious youthful offender who continues offending moves to less serious offenses and becomes a chronic, nuisance offender as he gets older. Accurately identifying prevailing patterns of offense seriousness has obvious implications for crime control policies. Some crime control policies may be concerned primarily with reducing serious, predatory crime. Knowing more about patterns of individual offending may be useful in focusing these crime control efforts on offenders most likely to be engaging in those offenses. If there is specialization in those offense types, for example, then offenders who remain active and who have records in those offenses are prime candidates for committing future offenses of the same type. If offending escalates in seriousness for offenders who remain active, then crime control efforts are most useful later in an offender's career; if offending de-escalates in seriousness, they are most useful early in an offender's career.

A number of studies that have empirically investigated offense seriousness are reviewed in this section, in particular their research approaches and reported findings. Whenever possible, data from the various reported sources have been reanalyzed to address a common set of issues, using the same statistical techniques on each data set. Following that, some of the methodological issues in research on offense seriousness are discussed.

Review of Empirical Research

The study designs and reported results of the studies included in this review are summarized in Table 41. The studies all rely on official-record data. Some use the broad category of police contacts, which may include police stops for questioning that do not lead to arrest or any formal charges but which are recorded in police files. Others rely on arrests or convictions, which more directly link an individual to a particular charged offense. The only explicit criterion for including studies in this review was that they examine empirical data on offense types for some population of offenders. The studies included are not meant to be exhaustive. However, they do cover a variety of approaches to the topic.

Research into offense switching relies on official-record data because those represent the only reliable source of information on the *sequence* of different types of offenses in criminal careers. Data on actual offenses committed are usually obtained from self-reports by offenders. Short of having offenders keep daily journals of their criminal activities, or obtaining self-reports of offenses through frequent and regular interviews (e.g., daily or weekly), accurate chronicles of the sequence of all offenses committed by individual offenders are not available. The usual self-report interval of a year or more is too long to obtain reliable information on the sequence of offenses during the reporting period for individuals. Repeated surveys of the same sample, however, could provide self-report data on the mix of crime types in successive periods.[19]

It is important to stress that analyses that rely on official data reflect offense seriousness for only official contacts. The results are not likely to be representative of offenses actually committed. The distortion in offense types between actual offenses committed and official contacts arises from differences among offense types in the chance that an offense will result in an official contact. Offense types with a high arrest probability, like murder and aggravated assault, are more likely to appear in official-record data. Correspondingly, offense types with a low arrest probability, like larceny or drug law violations, will be underrepresented in official records. Differences across offense types in the time interval between a crime and an arrest for that crime may also distort the ordering of offense types. While commission of a robbery may precede a larceny, a shorter time to arrest, if one occurs at all, for larceny than for rob-

bery might result in a larceny arrest preceding a robbery arrest. Because of differences in the probability and timing of arrests for different offense types, the results of analyses of patterns of offense seriousness based on official contacts cannot be generalized to crimes committed.

Because the studies included in this review rely on official-record data of offense seriousness, they are necessarily based on samples of offenders known to the criminal justice system through some form of official contact. In some studies, the basis for entering the research sample was an official-record event during some sampling period of a year or more. Those studies involve cross-section samples of arrestees (studies 3 to 5 in Table 41), of juveniles processed or adjudicated in juvenile court (studies 7 and 8), or of inmates (studies 2 and 9). By virtue of the sampling event, all members of the cross-section sample are presumed to be criminally active during a common time period. Two studies—both of juveniles—rely on birth cohorts from the general population (studies 1 and 6). Analysis of offense seriousness in these studies focuses on the subsample of offenders within a cohort who have at least one police contact.

All the studies in Table 41 involve either retrospective or prospective longitudinal data on sequences of offense types for individual offenders. Such data are essential for analyzing switching patterns among offense types in successive events. Dynamic processes like "specialization" or "escalation" make no sense except in the context of longitudinal data on individuals' event histories. Even in studies in which samples of offenders were drawn from cross-sections of active offenders in some observation period, the analysis is based on *longitudinal* data for the cross-section samples of offenders.

Some studies not included in this review report only results on the offense mix for a sample of offenders. These one-time distributions over offense types provide some insight into the frequency of different offense types, highlighting which types are rare and which commonplace in a sample of offenders, but they provide no sequence

---

[19]The research on the criminal activities and drug use for a sample of New York City offenders (Johnson et al., 1985) is unique in its use of almost daily interviews. However, no analysis of the sequence of offenses is reported. The observation period (averaging only 2 months) and the sample size (just over 200) may be too small to yield a large enough sample of offenses for detailed analysis of sequences. The National Youth Survey (Elliott et al., 1983) used repeated annual surveys with the same sample, and these data could be analyzed for yearly changes in offense seriousness.

TABLE B-41 Summary of Empirical Research on Offense Seriousness

Study	Sampling Frame	Observation Period	Analysis of Offense Seriousness
		Juveniles and Adults	
Shannon (1981, 1982a)	Cohort Three birth cohorts of males and females born in Racine, Wis., in 1942 (N = 1,352), 1949 (N = 2,099), and 1955 (N = 2,676)	Prospective Police contacts of 4,079 individuals with "continuous residence"[a] in Racine followed from age 6 to age 32 for 1942 cohort (N = 633), to age 25 for 1949 cohort (N = 1,297), and to age 21 for 1955 cohort (N = 2,149) 15- to 26-year follow-up	Excluding contacts for traffic and suspicion, average seriousness scores are flat on successive contacts "Geometric scaling" for clusters of offense types (see Shannon, 1968, for description of method) found random combinations of unrelated offense types
		Adults	
Frum (1958)	Cross-section Random sample of 319 inmates with prior criminal records who were incarcerated in Indiana prisons Possible selection bias toward more serious offenses at end of record: offense leading to current incarceration was included in analysis	Retrospective 148 inmates with official record of arrest before age 18 were observed from first official contact before age 18 to contact leading to current imprisonment	Criminal profile of sequence of crime types reveals: o escalation in seriousness o record length negatively related to offense seriousness (offenders beginning with less serious offenses accumulated more total convictions

Peterson,
Pittman,
and O'Neal
(1962)

Cross-section
All males (N = 119)
40 and over arrested
in 1958 by St. Louis,
Mo., police depart-
ment; age 40 chosen
to allow criminal
patterns to stabil-
ize (one-half of
sample were 48 or
older when sampled)

Retrospective
Pre-1958
arrest histories:
   o Early record before
age 30
   o Late record age 30
or older
   Final sample N = 88
(eliminated 31 cases
with no record of
fingerprint check with
FBI)

Evidence of specializa-
tion found in mix of
prior crime types when
histories were char-
acterized as having
"assaultive," "non-
assaultive," "neither,"
or "both" types of
arrests

Moitra
(1981)

Cross-section
All adults (N = 5,338)
arrested for murder,
rape, robbery,
aggravated assault,
burglary, or auto
theft in Washington,
D.C., during 1973

Retrospective
Pre-1973 adult arrest
histories of 2,969
offenders with at
least two arrests
for any offense
types prior to 1973

Transitions among
offense types on suc-
cessive arrests show:
   o Evidence of special-
ization in all
offense types
   o Marked tendency for
transitions within
related groups of
property or violent
offense types
   o No evidence of escalation in seriousness
   Controlling for number
of arrests, average
seriousness scores
are stable on
successive arrests

Average seriousness is
lower when there are a
larger number of
arrests in a history

TABLE B-41 Continued

Study	Sampling Frame	Observation Period	Analysis of Offense Seriousness
Blumstein, Cohen, and Das (1985)	Cross-section All adults arrested for murder, rape, robbery, aggravated assault, burglary, or auto theft in Detroit SMSA (N = 18,635) or combination of seven other southern Michigan SMSAs (N = 13,562) during sampling period, 1974-1977	Retrospective Presampling period adult arrest histories of offenders with at least two arrests for any offense type prior to the sampled arrest in Detroit SMSA (N = 3,536) or southern Michigan (N = 2,218)	Findings are identical to those reported above for Moitra (1981) analysis
		Juveniles	
Wolfgang, Figlio, and Sellin (1972)	Cohort 9,945 boys born in 1945 and residing in Philadelphia from ages 10 to 18 (7,043 white; 2,902 nonwhite)	Prospective Police contacts observed during 1955-1963 (from ages 10-18)	Used offense types characterized by harm done, not legal offense categories (traffic offenses are excluded)

Wolfgang, Figlio, and Sellin (1972) (continued)	10,214 total delinquent contacts for 3,475 offenders: o 1,613, one contact only (1,110 white; 503 nonwhite) o 1,862, two or more contacts as juveniles (909 white with 3,348 contacts; 953 non-white with 5,253 contacts)	On transitions between successive police contacts, slight tendency to repeat same offense type; otherwise next offense type independent of prior offense type Small increments in seriousness of successive police contacts of same type
Bursik (1980)	Retrospective Official record through 17th birthday (years not specified) for youths with at least five contacts Cross-section Random sample of juveniles adjudicated delinquent in Cook County (Chicago), Ill., and age 17 by data collection; 134 white, 335 nonwhite, apparently includes males and females	Analysis of four offense types: o Personal injury o Personal property (robbery) o Impersonal property o Other Specialization in offense types indicated by significantly more repeating of same offense type on successive transitions No evidence of tendency toward increasing or decreasing seriousness

TABLE B-41 Continued

Study	Sampling Frame	Observation Period	Analysis of Offense Seriousness
Rojek and Erikson (1982)	Cross-section Random sample of 1,619 juveniles (male and female) processed by Juvenile Court in Pima County, Ariz., during 3 years o Excluded 439 juveniles with no prior arrests when sampled o Excluded subjects who did not reside in study area for 2 years or more Final sample, N = 1,180 Possible selection bias toward more serious offenses at end of record: offense leading to current court processing was included in analysis	Up to five arrests in official offense history Vast majority of subjects were "at risk" from ages 8-18	Analysis of five offense types: o Crimes against persons o Crimes against property o Miscellaneous felonies and misdemeanors (other crimes) o Runaway o Other status offenses Only property and run-away offenses exhibited significant specialization evident in repeating same offense type on successive transitions Offenders with more than one arrest were more often arrested for serious offense types (44% arrested for property offenses compared to 21% among one-time offenders)[b]

Smith and Smith (1984)	Cross-section	Retrospective	Used Wolfgang, Figlio, and Sellin (1972) offense categories based on harm done; offending characterized by diversity of offense types
	Sample of 767 male juveniles incarcerated in New Jersey correctional facilities between October 1977 and December 1978	Previous arrests in official court records; average of 11.7 juvenile arrests per offender, 70% for index crimes	Some evidence of specialization, especially among those first arrested for robbery
	Possible selection bias toward more serious offense types at end of record; arrest leading to current incarceration was included in analysis		Increased switching within related groups of violent or all other offense types
	This overrepresentation of serious offense types (robbery or injury) on the last arrest is found especially for offenders first arrested for robbery		No evidence of escalation in seriousness or successive arrests

a"Continuous residence" involved absence of no longer than 3 years from Racine, Wis., after age 6 during the follow-up period.

bIt is not clear how multiple offenders were characterized by offense type--whether by last arrest only, by most serious arrest, or by most frequent offense type. Use of the offense type of the last arrest (the one that led to sampling) is the most likely interpretation.

information. Some of these studies report offense mix at several different observation times. These multiple glimpses provide some insight into aggregate trends in offense mix (for example, increases or decreases in the representation of particular offense types over time), but they do not reflect the dynamics of change for individual offenders. Because they rely on aggregate data, they cannot separate changes in offense types over time for individuals from changes in the mix of offenders. An increase in the representation of serious offenses, for example, might result from movement toward increasingly more serious offenses by active offenders or from the attrition of offenders who engaged predominantly in less serious offense types. In the latter instance only the more serious offenders would remain in the sample and there would be little or no change in offense mix for those who are still criminally active. Data on offense mix alone without data on individual sequences cannot distinguish these different processes.

Early U.S. Studies

Not surprisingly, the two oldest studies reviewed are also the crudest methodologically (Frum, 1958; Peterson, Pittman, and O'Neal, 1962). Relying on small samples of offenders, the studies focused on uniquely characterizing the criminal history of each sample member. Concerned with escalation, Frum (1958) formed criminal profiles of each sample member that documented the exact time sequence of offense types in that individual's criminal history. These were then sorted to form subsets that exhibited the same general pattern. Peterson, Pittman, and O'Neal (1962) were interested in specialization. On the basis of the mix of offense types they found in individuals' complete criminal histories, they characterized the individuals as having "assaultive," "nonassaultive," "neither," or "both" types of arrests in their criminal histories. The relative frequency of the pure types, "assaultive" and "nonassaultive," among sample members was used as an indication of the extent of specialization.

On the basis of his analysis of criminal history profiles—tracking offense types from the first juvenile offense to the most recent offense leading to incarceration—Frum reported a general pattern of escalation in seriousness and concluded that the study "offers partial confirmation of the popular view that children who commit minor delinquencies and who persist in crime progress into areas of more and more serious crime" (1958:49). Notably, there were also a substantial number of offenders (53/148 = 36 percent) whose histories showed persistence in serious property felonies from the juvenile to the adult period.

Frum's conclusions about offense-switching patterns, however, are likely to be seriously biased by his use of a sample of prison inmates. Offenders sentenced to prison are more likely to have been convicted of more serious offenses and to have a larger number of convictions in their records. Thus there will be a bias toward more serious offense types at the end of the inmates' criminal histories. This selection bias could account for much of the escalation to, and specialization in, serious offense types observed by Frum. Offenders who do persist, but in less serious offense types, are less likely to be in prison and would not have entered his sample.

According to Peterson, Pittman, and O'Neal (1962), "stable deviance," or specialization, exists when a prior arrest history (i.e., excluding the arrest that led to sampling the offender) contains arrests for either assaultive offenses or nonassaultive offenses, but not both.[20] Under this definition, a single nonassaultive arrest in a long history of assaultive arrests, or vice versa, is

---

[20]In Peterson, Pittman, and O'Neal (1962:44), assaultive offenses are crimes of violence against persons, including criminal homicide, suspicion of homicide, aggravated and simple assault, and concealed weapons offenses. Nonassaultive offenses involve theft of property, including burglary, larceny, auto theft, forgery, embezzlement, and trading in stolen property. Rape and robbery were explicitly excluded because of their ambiguity with respect to violence—rape includes statutory rape and robbery involves both the threat or use of force against persons and theft of property.

enough to violate the criteria of specialization. Using this apparently restrictive definition, they report surprisingly high rates of stable deviance: 91 percent stable in the total sample of 88 men and 86 percent stable when offenders with "neither" offense type are excluded. Both figures, however, overstate stability, in one case by counting offenders with no prior assaultive or nonassaultive arrests among stable deviants, and in the other by excluding those offenders entirely. These residual offenders, whose histories may contain a wide range of offense types other than assaultive or nonassaultive, are more appropriately treated as unstable. If one requires at least one prior assaultive or nonassaultive arrest and applies the authors' criteria for offense specialization, 58 percent (51/88) of the offenders displayed stable deviance—20 percent with only property offenses and 38 percent with only offenses against persons in their arrest histories. Another 33 percent (29/88) of offenders had no prior assaultive or nonassaultive arrests, and 9 percent (8/88) had "mixed" histories, including both assaultive and nonassaultive offenses throughout their histories.

Even after adjustment for histories with no prior assaultive or nonassaultive arrests, the resulting specialization rate may still be inflated by offenders who have only one prior arrest in their histories. A single arrest of some type is not sufficient to indicate a tendency to repeated offending in the same type. Unfortunately, the distribution over prior arrests was not reported. While the median number of arrests per person in the full sample was reported to be 11, which suggests that multiple arrests per person were quite common, there also appear to be systematic differences in the number of prior arrests across different offender subgroups. The "mixed" offenders were reported to have very high numbers of prior arrests—a median of 52.3 arrests per person. It is thus possible that the specialists have fewer prior arrests and include a disproportionate share of offenders with only one prior arrest.

Perhaps the best indicator of the extent of specialization is the number of offenders who exhibited stable deviance in both the early adult period, before age 30, and the later adult period, at or after age 30. According to the numbers reported in Table 1 of the study, 28 percent (25/88) of the offenders were specialists, i.e., had prior arrests of only one type in both the early and late adult periods—18 percent in assaultive crimes and 10 percent in the nonassaultive, "theft" crimes. Thus specialization, which here required long-term activity restricted within two major offense classes, was reasonably common.

It must be noted that these results are based on a sample of *older* arrestees—men aged 40 or over who were arrested for criminal homicide or suspicion of homicide, aggravated assault, burglary, or larceny in St. Louis during 1958. Half of the sample was 48 or older in 1958. The minimum age of 40 was used "so that individuals would have had an opportunity to stabilize their criminal patterns" (p. 45). If such stabilization does in fact increase as offenders get older, then the level of specialization observed in this study is likely to be higher than would be found in a more representative sample of active, and younger, offenders. Certain age dependencies in specialization are suggested by comparing arrest activity in early (before age 30) and late adult periods. The later an offender's first arrest for assaultive or nonassaultive offenses, the more likely that offender will be a specialist in crimes against persons; there were 72 percent assaultive specialists among those first arrested at 30 or older, but only 40 percent among those first arrested before age 30. This suggests some tendency for older offenders to engage in violent offenses rather than property offenses.

In contrast to the small samples surveyed in earlier studies, Shannon (1981) used longitudinal data on 4,079 youths (male and female) in three birth cohorts (1942, 1949, and 1955) "residing continuously" in Racine, Wisconsin.[21] Police contacts of this

---

[21]"Continuous residence" is defined as having no more than 3 years' absence from Racine, Wisconsin, during the follow-up periods from age 6 to age 32 for the 1942 cohort, to age 25 for the 1949 cohort, and to age 21 for the 1955 cohort.

sample were examined for escalation in seriousness and for any clustering of contacts in related offense types. Several different approaches to the measurement of escalation were employed, including average seriousness scores on successive contacts and by age at contact, and the proportion of serious contacts or of persons with serious contacts by age at contact. Shannon reported that almost without exception no consistent trends in seriousness of offenses were observed across the various measures.

Average seriousness for all contacts does exhibit an interesting pattern over age at contact, however. For both the 1942 and 1949 cohorts, average seriousness was relatively stable through age 15. After age 15, average seriousness declined to a new, stable level of seriousness. For the 1955 cohort, average seriousness remained at a higher stable level through age 21. In these results, average seriousness was based on all contacts, including traffic offenses and police stops for investigation or suspicion. To the extent that these less serious offenses characteristically occurred only after age 15 and were more common in the earlier cohorts, including them in the analysis might explain the drop in seriousness after age 15 in the first two cohorts. In fact, Shannon (1981:95–100) reported that average seriousness was remarkably flat when contacts for suspicion, investigation, and traffic were excluded.

Clustering of police contacts in related offense types was assessed using a technique of "geometric scaling," introduced earlier by the author (Shannon, 1968). This technique scores an individual's offense history based on the types of offenses found; the sequence in which different types appear is ignored.[22] The technique involves finding the distribution of offend-

ers over observed combinations of offenses. The usefulness of the scale is assessed partially by the number of offense combinations needed to represent the great bulk of observed offense histories. The fewer the combinations, the more useful the scale is in characterizing a large number of offense histories. In both the original 1968 article reporting data from Madison, Wisconsin, and the more recent analysis of birth cohorts in Racine, Shannon (1981:48) noted that "the recorded contacts of most offenders are of a random nature and most combinations of contacts are not meaningful in that they do not involve related activities."

As Shannon pointed out, the attempts to identify meaningful clusters of related offense types are seriously hampered by the overwhelming predominance of single contacts and the high frequency of minor violations for vagrancy, disorderly conduct, and traffic offenses found in the data. These contacts swamp any potential relationships among more serious offenses in the data. Excluding single contacts and minor nuisance violations from the analysis might result in more conceptually useful clusters for the more serious recidivists among offenders.

Analyses Using Transition Matrices

The remaining studies in this review (Table 41, numbers 4 to 9) are the most comprehensive. The studies examine an array of issues concerning changes in offense seriousness based on large samples of offenders and their arrests (or police contacts) for a wide range of offense types. All of the studies analyze transition matrices that reflect the chance of a next arrest for type j after an arrest for type i. Both juveniles and adults are represented, but no one study includes continuous transitions from juvenile years into adulthood. Nevertheless, the separate analyses of juveniles and adults provide some tentative insights into similarities and differences in offense switching during these two periods. The large samples of offenders in these studies also permit examination of differences in switching among demographic groups.

---

[22]The details of the scoring procedure are not provided in Shannon (1968) or Shannon (1981). From the brief description of the technique that is available, it appears that individual histories are scored using a series of ones and zeroes to indicate either the presence or absence of each offense type. The most frequently appearing series are then identified.

The earliest of the studies, Wolfgang, Figlio, and Sellin (1972), analyzed offense switching for offenders found in a birth cohort. The study sample included all males born in 1945 and residing in Philadelphia from age 10 to age 18. The full cohort of 9,945 boys consisted of 7,043 whites and 2,902 nonwhites. Of these, 3,475 (2,017 whites and 1,458 nonwhites) were considered delinquent by virtue of at least one recorded contact with the Philadelphia police. The analysis of switching included all police contacts (other than traffic offenses) in Philadelphia before age 18.

The offense types used in the study were characterized by the nature of the harm done and not by standard criminal code categories. The offense categories used and the overall distribution of police contacts in each category are presented in Table 42. Offenses were distinguished primarily by whether they involved injury to a person, damage to property, or theft of property. Offenses that involved more than one of those elements (e.g., robbery) were included in the "combination" category. Offenses including none of those elements were classed as "non-index." The least serious non-index offenses were by far the most common offense type (63.2 percent). The most common serious offense type was theft (16 percent of all police contacts). Offenses involving violence, either against persons or property, accounted for 13.3 percent of all police contacts.

The three other studies focusing on juveniles (Bursik, 1980; Rojek and Erikson, 1982; Smith and Smith, 1984) relied on cross-section samples of juveniles processed, adjudicated delinquent by the juvenile court, or incarcerated during the sampling period. Since the juveniles in these samples had reached juvenile court at least once, they are likely to represent more serious subsamples of juvenile offenders than the juveniles studied by Wolfgang, Figlio, and Sellin (1972).

Bursik (1980) used a random sample of juveniles who were adjudicated delinquent in Cook County (Chicago), Illinois, and had reached age 17 by the time of data collection. The sampling years were not speci-

fied. The sample included 134 whites and 355 nonwhites and, although not indicated, apparently both males and females. Evidence of offense switching found in official records, including all police contacts and court appearances through their 17th birthday, was analyzed.[23] The sampled event was included in the analysis.

Offenses were grouped in this study on the basis of criminal code categories to form four offense categories: personal injury, personal property (e.g., robbery), impersonal property (e.g., theft), and all others. It is not clear whether less serious juvenile status offenses and traffic offenses were included in the analysis. The analysis was limited to the first four transitions for juveniles who had at least five contacts. This further restricts the results to offense seriousness for more active juvenile offenders. The more serious nature of the sample, compared with the Philadelphia cohort, is evident in the smaller representation of "other" offenses and the considerably higher representation of theft-type offenses included in the impersonal property category (see Table 42).

Rojek and Erikson (1982) analyzed data for a random sample of 1,180 juveniles (male and female) processed by the juvenile court in Pima County, Arizona, during a 3-year period. The analysis was restricted to juveniles who had at least one prior arrest when sampled and who resided in Pima County for at least 2 years. Official offense histories for the sampled juveniles were obtained from all police agencies operating in Pima County. The vast majority of the sample was described as "at risk" (of arrest) from age 8 to age 18. It appears that the analysis included all arrests in a history,

---

[23]It is not clear in Bursik (1980) whether police contacts and court appearances are treated as separate events in the analysis. When court appearances result from a police contact and thus relate to the same triggering offense, only one of the official contacts should be counted. Only when court appearances are not the result of a police contact, as sometimes happens for juvenile status offenses about which a parent or school authority files a complaint directly in juvenile court, should court appearances be treated as distinct events.

TABLE B-42 Distribution of Offense Types among Juvenile Offenders in Several Jurisdictions (All Offenders, All Contacts)

Study	Offense Type	Percentage of Official Contacts
Philadelphia birth cohort (Wolfgang, Figlio, and Sellin, 1972)[a]	Injury	8.4
	Theft	16.0
	Damage	4.9
	Combination (robbery)	7.4
	Non-index	63.2
Cook County, Ill., juvenile court sample (Bursik, 1980)[b]	Personal injury	11.6
	Personal property (robbery)	11.5
	Impersonal property	45.6
	Other	31.3
Pima County, Ariz., juvenile court sample (Rojek and Erikson, 1982)[c]	Persons	3.7
	Property	36.0
	Other crimes	11.0
	Runaway	29.0
	Other status	20.3
New Jersey juvenile correctional facilities sample (Smith and Smith, 1984)[d]	Injury	12.6
	Robbery	5.1
	Property	48.8
	Damage	4.1
	Non-index	29.3

[a]Derived from data provided in Wolfgang, Figlio, and Sellin (1972:Matrices 11.1-11.9 and Tables 11.2-11.6). Data include up to 9 police contacts for each individual, which represented 92 percent (9,384/10,214) of all police contacts (traffic offenses excluded).
[b]Derived from data provided in Bursik (1980:Tables 2a and 2b). Data include all contacts up to the fifth for those juveniles who have at least 5 contacts, for a total of 2,345 contacts. Distribution of offense types excludes first contacts that were not reported in the original study.
[c]Derived from data provided in Rojek and Erikson (1982:Table 2). The data include up to 5 contacts for each individual, for a total of 3,545 contacts.
[d]Derived from data on 9,000 arrests for 767 incarcerated juveniles, available in official court records (Smith and Smith, 1984:Table 1).

including the one that led to sampling the offender.

This sample is distinguished from the other studies reviewed here by its large representation of females, 37 percent of the sampled juveniles. The analysis also focused explicitly on juvenile status offenses (including runaway), 49.3 percent of all offenses (Table 42). Thirty-nine percent of all contacts for males were for runaway and other status offenses; for females, the two categories accounted for 72 percent of all contacts (55 percent for runaway alone).

Smith and Smith (1984) obtained data from official court records for all juveniles incarcerated in New Jersey state correctional facilities any time between October 1977 and December 1978. Because of their small number in the original sample, females were eliminated, and the analysis focused on the previous arrests, including the one leading to the current incarceration, of 767 males aged 13–18 when sampled. These incarcerated youths averaged 11.7 arrests each, 70 percent of which were arrests for FBI index crimes. Also, 25 percent of the sample had previously been incarcerated. The serious nature of this sample is reflected in the mix of offenses in their records (Table 42). Property crimes (just under 50 percent) and injury offenses (12.6 percent) represented major portions of all arrests in their records.

The remaining two studies reviewed here analyze offense-switching patterns for cross-section samples of adult arrestees from Washington, D.C. (Moitra, 1981), and from the Detroit SMSA and a collection of smaller SMSAs in southern Michigan (Blumstein, Cohen, and Das, 1985). Both studies examined the arrest histories of adults arrested for the serious index offenses of murder, rape, robbery, aggravated assault, burglary, and auto theft during the sampling period. For the Washington, D.C., sample of 5,338 offenders, the sampling period was a single year (1973). For the Detroit SMSA ($N = 18,635$) and southern Michigan ($N = 13,562$) samples, a 4-year sampling period (1974–1977) was used. The sampling criterion based on offense type narrows the analysis to a sample presumably arrested for more serious offenses—all had at least one arrest for one of the serious criterion offenses. In the analysis of changes in offense seriousness, however, virtually all previous offense types were considered.[24] The analysis stopped at the arrest prior to the sampled arrest, thus avoiding a bias of switching toward the more narrow subset of serious offenses found among sampled arrests.

Females were not explicitly excluded from the adult samples, but they were represented in very small numbers in all samples: 10.3 percent in Washington, D.C., 4.5 percent in Detroit, and 6.3 percent in southern Michigan. The samples were dominated by males, and separate analyses by sex were not provided. Arrestees in Washington, D.C., in 1973 were predominantly black (92 percent), as was the general population of that city (71 percent black in the 1970 census). The Michigan samples were more racially diverse—43 percent and 37 percent black in the Detroit SMSA and southern Michigan, respectively. Separate analyses of offense seriousness by race were provided for the Michigan samples.

Offense categories were defined in terms of criminal code classifications. Only arrestees who had at least two arrests prior to the sampled arrest were included in the analyses. Because of the larger sample sizes, the offense types were disaggregated more finely than in any of the juvenile studies (Table 43). For comparison with the juvenile samples, offense types were also aggregated to include violent offenses, property offenses, robbery, drug offenses, and all other offenses.

The more serious nature of these adult

---

[24]The analysis of Michigan arrestees by Blumstein, Cohen, and Das (1985) excluded the least serious offense types that make up the "public order" and "other" offense categories. This excluded nuisance offenses like drunkenness, vagrancy, disorderly conduct, trespassing, and obscene behavior, which accounted for 35.7 percent of all arrests in the Michigan jurisdictions. These same offense types represent 26.3 percent of total arrests in the Washington, D.C., sample and 29.8 percent of arrests prior to the sampling period.

TABLE B-43 Distribution of Offense Types in Adult Arrestee Samples (all offenders and all arrests)

	Percentage of Arrests for Each Offense Type					
	Washington, D.C.[a]		Detroit SMSA		Southern Michigan	
			Blacks	Whites	Blacks	Whites
Offense Type	(N = 19,205)	(N = 13,488)	(N = 9,026)	(N = 6,373)	(N = 5,929)	(N = 4,781)
Murder	1.4	(2.0)	1.1	0.8	1.3	0.6
Rape	1.4	(2.0)	1.3	1.3	1.9	1.2
Robbery	10.8	(15.4)	13.1	7.8	11.8	5.2
Aggravated assault	13.0	(18.5)	8.1	6.7	11.6	8.0
Drugs	6.5	(9.2)	8.5	17.1	8.6	10.9
Burglary	10.6	(15.1)	22.1	27.3	20.8	28.4
Larceny	14.8	(21.1)	25.4	19.6	25.1	22.6
Auto theft	4.5	(6.5)	8.2	7.4	5.7	8.7
Weapons	4.5	(6.4)	6.5	4.5	7.0	4.8
Fraud	2.7	(3.9)	5.6	7.5	6.2	9.6
Public order	7.9	--	--	--	--	--
Other	21.9	--	--	--	--	--

Collapsed Offense
  Types

Violent[b]	20.3	(28.9)	17.0	13.2	21.8	14.6
Property[c]	32.7	(46.5)	61.4	61.9	57.8	69.2
Robbery	10.8	(15.4)	13.1	7.8	11.8	5.2
Drugs	6.5	(9.2)	8.5	17.1	8.6	10.9
Other[d]	29.8	--	--	--	--	--

NOTE: The data include all arrests up to, but not including, the sampled arrest for arrestees who had at least two arrests prior to being sampled.

[a]The renormalized distribution, excluding public order and "other," appears in parentheses.

[b]Violent offenses include murder, rape, aggravated assault, and weapons violations.

[c]Property offenses include burglary, larceny, auto theft, and fraud.

[d]Other offenses combine public order offenses and "other" offenses.

SOURCE: Washington, D.C., data derived from Moitra (1981:Table 2.1d); Michigan data derived from Blumstein, Cohen, and Das (1985).

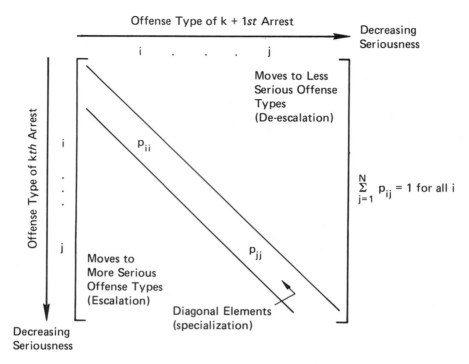

FIGURE B-1   Transition matrix for offense-type switches between successive arrests.

arrestee samples is evident in the higher representation of violent offenses, especially in Washington, D.C., for which the category of less serious "other" offenses is included. There are also important differences among the adult samples. Arrests for property offenses were especially prevalent in the Michigan samples due primarily to the higher representation of burglary and larceny arrests. Comparing whites and blacks in the two Michigan samples, robbery and larceny were more prevalent among black offenders, and burglary was more prevalent among white offenders. For robbery and larceny, this is consistent with differences in arrest frequencies reported for the same samples in Table 19.

Transition matrices are particularly well suited to analyses of changes in offense seriousness. They have the advantage of accommodating differences in the mix of offense types and the sequence in which offense types occur. The matrices are made up of individual transition probabilities, p_{ij},

which reflect the frequency with which an offense of type i is followed on the next arrest by an offense of type j. These probabilities are estimated from the number of arrest sequences (or police contacts for juveniles) from type i to type j (n_{ij}) observed among all arrest sequences that start with type i ($n_{i.} = \Sigma_{j=1}^{N} n_{ij}$ for N offense types) with $p_{ij} = n_{ij}/n_i$.

The structure of an offense transition matrix is illustrated in Figure 1. Offense types of the kth arrest in arrest sequences form the rows of the matrix, and offense types of the next arrest in a sequence form the columns. All switches from arrests of offense type i are distributed over the elements of row i. Thus, the transition probabilities of each row of the matrix sum to 1. Specialization in offense types is indicated by the size of the diagonal elements, p_{ii}, of a transition matrix (Figure 1). The diagonal indicates the relative propensity to repeat the same offense type on successive arrests. Escalation (or de-escalation), by contrast, is indicated by the relative size of nondiagonal elements. The offense types in Figure 1 are ordered from the most serious to least serious. In this case, the tendency to switch to more serious offense types on successive arrests is represented by the transition probabilities falling below the diagonal. Switches to less serious offense types on successive arrests are represented by the transition probabilities above the diagonal. If there is escalation, switches to more serious offense types will be more frequent than switches to less serious offense types, and the frequency of switches below the diagonal will be greater than above. The reverse will hold if there is de-escalation on successive arrests.

Clustering of related offense types would also be evident in the nondiagonal elements of the transition matrix. Clusters of offense types are formed when there is a greater tendency for switching among offense types within a cluster and a lower tendency to switch to offenses outside a cluster. In the context of offense-type switching, there is particular interest in determining whether violent offenses and property offenses form distinctive clusters. As was evident in Table 42, these aggregations of offense types are often used on the basis of a priori conceptual similarities in the offenses. It would be useful to know whether these clusters can also be observed empirically among offense types.

Typically, a separate matrix is estimated for each transition to permit examination of changes in offense-switching patterns on successive arrests. Transition processes that vary on successive transitions are nonstationary, and separate matrices for each transition should be preserved because they contain valuable information about offense-switching patterns. A particularly interesting form of nonstationarity is trends across transitions that indicate increases or decreases in specialization or in escalation. Nonstationarity might also arise from changes in the sample of offenders at successive transitions; while offenders with only a few arrests enter early transition matrices, the later matrices are limited to offenders who have a sufficiently large number of arrests. When there are no important differences across transition matrices, the transition process is stationary. In this event, the chance of moving from type i to type j is the same regardless of the transition number. Stationary transition processes can be represented by a single transition matrix estimated by combining all pairs of successive arrests.

In addition to varying across transitions, offense-switching patterns may also vary for different subgroups of offenders. The variation across groups can be partially tested by estimating separate transition matrices for different subgroups of the population. Population differences will be evident in differences in the estimates.

Transition matrices can also be assessed to determine whether offense-type switching between arrests is a Markov process. In a first-order Markov process, the offense type of the next arrest depends, at most, on the offense type of the immediately preceding arrest and is independent of all other prior offense types. To the extent that offense switching is indeed Markovian (or can be made Markovian by some modification of offense-type categories), the extensively developed theory of Markov chains can be brought to bear to explore the dynamic and equilibrium properties of offense-type switching between arrests, including such considerations as the expected number of times the same offense will be repeated, or the expected distribution of offense types on any particular arrest, or the likelihood of switching to some offense type permanently (see Cox and Miller, 1965; Kemeny, Snell, and Thompson, 1966; Karlin and Taylor, 1975). Note that offense switching need not be Markovian for analyses of changes in offense seriousness. The simple transition probabilities can be estimated for each arrest, whether Markovian or not. Also, the analyses of stationarity, homogeneity, specialization, and escalation do not invoke, or in any way depend on, Markov properties for the transition matrices.

A full treatment of offense switching using transition matrices includes consideration of stationarity, specialization, escala-

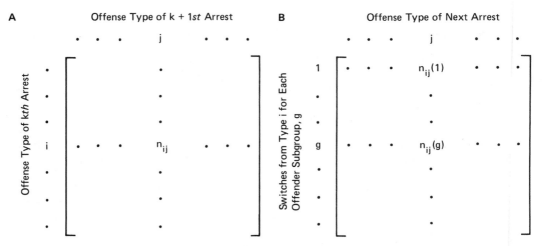

FIGURE B-2 Contingency table analysis of offense switching. **A:** Frequencies of offense switches between adjacent arrests. **B:** Frequencies of offense switches from type i for different offender subgroups.

tion, homogeneity across population subgroups, and the Markov property. These issues are examined to varying degrees in the studies reviewed here. Where not reported in the original study, sufficient data were often provided to permit supplementary analyses. The results of reanalysis or supplementary analysis of the data for this appendix are summarized below. Of particular interest are consistencies or differences in results across different samples, especially comparisons of results for juvenile and adult offenders.

The general method for analyzing transition matrices derives from the analysis of contingency tables introduced by Goodman (1962, 1968) and later extended by Haberman (1973, 1979). These techniques were applied in varying degrees to transition matrices for offense switching in Wolfgang, Figlio, and Sellin (1972), Bursik (1980), Rojek and Erikson (1982), and Smith and Smith (1984). Similar analyses were possible using the original data from Moitra (1981) and Blumstein, Cohen, and Das (1985). The basic approach is to transform matrices of transition probabilities,

$$p_{ij} = n_{ij} \Big/ \sum_{j=1}^{N} n_{ij},$$

back into the original contingency tables of n_{ij} reflecting the number of arrests of type i followed on the next arrest by offense type j. Standard χ^2 tests are then applied to various forms of these contingency tables, testing the observed frequency distribution against the null hypothesis of independence between the rows and columns of the table. Under independence, column entries do not depend on their location in any particular row.

Subgroup Differences. The contingency table method is illustrated here to examine differences in offense switching across subgroups of offenders. The general structure of the contingency table for offense switches from one arrest to the next is presented in Figure 2A. A separate table like this is available for each offender subgroup. To test for homogeneity across these subgroups, the individual tables of offense switching for each subgroup are recombined to form new tables, as in part **B** of Figure 2. By taking the corresponding rows for switches from a specific offense type i from all the separate subgroup tables, the rows of the new table represent switches from type i for each offender subgroup. A separate table like the one in Figure 2B is formed for each offense type i.

Homogeneity across subgroups is evaluated by using a standard χ^2 test on each of the newly formed tables (Goodman, 1962, 1968). Typically, offenders are distinguished by race-ethnicity, sex, or age, and the test assesses whether the frequency of switches from type i to type j is independent of these offender subgroups.[25] The results of tests for homogeneity in offense switching across racial/ethnic groups in various studies are summarized in Table 44. Significant differences between races were found in every sample examined except the study of juveniles in Pima County, Arizona.

The particular offense switches contributing to significant differences across subgroups can be assessed using a statistical test applied to individual entries in a frequency table. As discussed in Haberman (1973, 1979), a standardized normal deviate, called the adjusted standardized residual (ASR), can be formed from the deviation between observed and expected frequencies for each table entry.[26] Since the ASR is distributed as a standard normal variable, a simple test of the significance of departures from independence is available for individual observed frequencies in a table. Statistically significant values of the ASR indicate that individual offense switches are significantly more (or less) likely than would be expected if switching was independent of the row variable in a transition matrix.

A consistent pattern of significant ASRs is observed for the Detroit SMSA and Philadelphia samples. As illustrated in Tables 45 and 46, nonwhite offenders were generally more likely than white offenders to switch to serious offenses, especially those involving violence or robbery. For example, the likelihood of switching from violent offenses to robbery for black offenders in the Detroit SMSA was .16. This is more than twice the same likelihood found for white offenders (.07) and results in a significant ASR value of 5.6.[27] Nonwhites were less

---

[25]The same general method described for homogeneity was also used to assess stationarity in offense-switching patterns on successive arrests. All switches from a specific offense type i for successive transition matrices (i.e., the first to second arrest, the second to third arrest, and so on) were combined in the same frequency table, and a χ^2 test was performed to assess whether the frequency of switches from type i to type j was independent of the particular transition in which the switch occurred. By use of this test, switching was found to be stationary over successive transitions for juveniles in Wolfgang, Figlio, and Sellin (1972), Bursik (1980), and Rojek and Erikson (1982). On the basis of the χ^2 test described here, combined with analysis of probability plots for successive transitions (Forbes, 1971), general stationarity was also observed for adults in Washington, D.C. (Moitra, 1981), and in two Michigan jurisdictions (Blumstein, Cohen, and Das, 1985). In view of this widespread stationarity, the separate transition matrices for successive arrests are appropriately aggregated to form a single summary transition matrix for each offender subgroup, and these summary matrices are used in the various analyses reported here.

[26]The adjusted standardized residual (ASR) for switches between row i and column j in a complete frequency table is given by:

$$\text{ASR}_{ij} = e_{ij}/s_{ij},$$

where e_{ij} is the standardized residual;

$$e_{ij} = (n_{ij} - n_{i.} \times n_{.j}/n_{..}) / \sqrt{n_{i.} \times n_{.j}/n_{..}}$$

and s_{ij} is the estimate of the asymptotic standard deviation,

$$s_{ij} = [(1 - n_{i.}/n_{..})(1 - n_{.j}/n_{..})]^{1/2}.$$

Before adjustment by s_{ij}, the standardized residual is just the contribution of an individual table entry to a χ^2 statistic before squaring, where

n_{ij} is the observed frequency count in row i and column j;

$$n_{i.} \text{ is the row marginal} = \sum_{j=1}^{C} n_{ij}$$

for C total columns;

$$n_{.j} \text{ is the column marginal} = \sum_{i=1}^{R} n_{ij}$$

for R total rows; and

$$n_{..} \text{ is the table total} = \sum_{i=1}^{R} \sum_{j=1}^{C} n_{ij}$$

[27]With only two categories of offenders (white vs. black, or white vs. nonwhite), the ASRs for white offenders are just the negative of the ASR values reported for nonwhite or black offenders in Tables 45 and 46. So, for example, the ASR for transitions from violent offenses to robbery for black offenders in the Detroit SMSA is 5.6 (Table 46); for white offenders in the same sample, the corresponding ASR is −5.6. In this example, black offenders are significantly more likely, and white offenders significantly less likely, to switch from a violent offense to a robbery on the next arrest than would be expected if switching from violent offenses was independent of race.

TABLE B-44 Test of Homogeneity of Offense Switching Across
Racial-Ethnic Subgroups for Different Offender Samples

ADULT SAMPLES

Offense Type	Detroit SMSA[a] (without desistance) x^2 White/Black	Southern Michigan Counties[a] (without desistance) x^2 White/Black
Individual Offense Types[b]		
Murder	20.8[c]	3.8
Rape	8.6	13.6
Robbery	30.0*	22.5*
Aggravated assault	36.7*	15.9
Drugs	47.8*	33.6*
Burglary	58.3*	52.5*
Larceny	77.6*	47.0*
Auto theft	31.9*	40.8*
Weapons	39.0*	21.5*
Fraud	19.5*	37.8*
Total	370.2*	289.0*
	(90 d.f.)	(90 d.f.)
Collapsed Offense Types[d]		
Violent[e]	54.0*	21.6*
Property[f]	56.1*	92.2*
Robbery	6.0*	13.6*
Drugs	41.2*	22.2*
Total	157.3*	149.6*
	(12 d.f.)	(12 d.f.)

JUVENILE SAMPLES

Offense Type	Philadelphia[g] (with desistance) x^2 White/ Nonwhite (5 d.f.)	Offense Type	Cook County[h] (without desistance) x^2 White/ Nonwhite (3 d.f.)	Offense Type	Pima County[i] (with desistance) x^2 White/Black/ Hispanic (10 d.f.)
Non-index	182.9*	Personal injury	1.0	Persons	17.1
Injury	31.1*			Property	17.5
Theft	39.2*	Personal property	0.5	Other crimes	5.4
Damage	68.6*				
Combination (robbery)	15.8*	Impersonal property	13.4*	Runaway	6.7
Total	337.6*	Other	24.4*	Other status	14.6
	(25 d.f.)	Total	39.3*	Total	61.3
			(12 d.f.)		(50 d.f.)

TABLE B-44   Continued

---

[a]Derived from data on race-specific offense switching provided by the authors of Blumstein, Cohen, and Das (1985).

[b]For individual offense types, χ^2 was calculated with 9 degrees of freedom.

[c]The χ^2 value is unreliable. While the p-value for χ^2 is <0.05 or better, the contingency table contains a number of low expected values (n < 5). Those will tend to inflate the χ^2 value and introduce errors in the p-value.

[d]For collapsed offense types, χ^2 was calculated with 3 degrees of freedom.

[e]Includes murder, rape, aggravated assault, and weapons.

[f]Includes burglary, larceny, auto theft, and fraud.

[g]Derived from data on race-specific offense switching available in Wolfgang, Figlio, and Sellin (1972:Matrices 11.11 to 11.26 and Tables 11.27 and 11.28).

[h]Derived from data on race-specific offense switching available in Bursik (1980:Tables 2a and 2b).

[i]Derived from data on race/ethnic-specific offense switching available in Rojek and Erikson (1982:Table 7).

*χ^2 significant at the .05 level or better.

likely to switch to less serious drug offenses or to desist from offending. Rates of switching to offenses involving theft of property were similar across races.

In Cook County, nonwhite juveniles were more likely than white juveniles to move to the violent offenses of personal injury or personal property (e.g., robbery), and less likely to move to the least serious offenses in the catch-all "others" category. Black adult offenders in both the Detroit SMSA and southern Michigan were more likely than white adult offenders to move to robbery and larceny and less likely to move among the property offenses of burglary, larceny, auto theft, and fraud. Black offenders in Detroit were also less likely than white offenders to move to drugs from other offense types, and black offenders in southern Michigan were more likely than white offenders to move to the violent offenses of murder, rape, aggravated assault, and weapons. When the offense types are collapsed for the Michigan samples, the higher likelihood of violent offenses among black offenders is also observed in the Detroit sample.

The Pima County sample of juveniles is the only study in which there was no evidence of differences in offense switching between racial-ethnic subgroups. This sample is distinguished from the other samples by its much lower representation of blacks (6 percent of the sample), by its larger representation of females (37.5 percent of the sample), and by its explicit consideration of juvenile status offenses (59.3 percent of all official contacts in the sample). All these factors contribute to a greater representation of less serious offense types in the sample, and they may obscure racial-ethnic differences among more serious offense types.

The Pima County sample is the only one that includes enough females to test differences in offense switching by sex. As might be expected, offense switching is significantly different for male and female offenders in Pima County. Female offenders were much more likely than males to desist or to move to a runaway offense. Switches to these two categories together accounted for 73 percent of the switches by females, compared with only 36 percent by males. It is not possible with these published data to restrict the analysis of switching patterns of

TABLE B-45 Differences in Offense Switching by Race of Offender for
Adults in the Detroit SMSA: Transition Probabilities and Adjusted
Standardized Residuals (ASRs)

Offense Type on kth Arrest	Offense Type on k + 1st Arrest			
	Violent	Property	Robbery	Drugs
Violent				
Black	.39	.37	.16	.08
White	.34	.44	.07	.15
(ASR)	(1.8)	(-2.6)	(5.6)	(-4.8)
	+	**	***	***
Property				
Black	.12	.72	.10	.06
White	.10	.73	.06	.10
(ASR)	(1.8)		(4.8)	(-5.9)
	+		***	***
Robbery				
Black	.22	.39	.31	.07
White	.16	.40	.35	.08
(ASR)	(2.4)			
	*			
Drugs				
Black	.13	.44	.09	.34
White	.09	.37	.05	.50
(ASR)	(2.6)	(2.7)	(3.4)	(-5.9)
	**	**	***	***

NOTES: Derived from data on race-specific offense switching
provided by Blumstein, Cohen, and Das (1985). Only ASRs significant at
the .10 level or better (two-tailed test using standard normal
distribution) are reported in parentheses. ASRs for black offenders
are reported in the table. With only two categories of offenders
compared, the ASRs for white offenders are just the negative of those
reported for black offenders.

+Significant at the .10 level.
*Significant at the .05 level.
**Significant at the .01 level.
***Significant at the .001 level.

males and females to the more serious, nonstatus offenses.

Two studies examined differences in offense switching by age. Rojek and Erikson (1982) computed separate transition matrices for three age-of-onset categories (12–13, 14–15, 16–17 years old at first arrest). These three starting groups could have been compared directly to one another using contingency tables in which each row was drawn from a separate age-of-onset matrix. Rather than use this direct test for differences across different starting age groups, Rojek and Erikson compared the matrix for each starting age to the matrices for the first four transitions based on the entire sample. No significant χ^2 values were found in any of these comparisons, and the authors concluded that "none of the age-specific matrices differs from the transition probabilities [for the first four transitions]" (Rojek and Erikson, 1982:18). This information, however, is not very useful in assessing differences in offense switching across the different age-of-onset groups. Unfortunately, the transition matrices by age of onset were

TABLE B-46 Differences in Offense Switching by Race of Offender for Juveniles in Philadelphia Birth Cohort: Transition Probabilities and Adjusted Standardized Residuals (ASRs)

Offense Type on kth Contact	Offense Type on k + 1st Police Contact					
	Non-index	Injury	Theft	Damage	Combination	Desist
Non-index						
Nonwhite	.47	.09	.12	.03	.06	.24
White	.43	.04	.09	.01	.04	.39
(ASR)	(3.1)	(7.1)	(3.9)	(3.2)	(3.1)	(-12.0)
	**	***	***	**	**	***
Injury						
Nonwhite	.42	.10	.09	.03	.07	.29
White	.38	.07	.08	.003	.02	.46
(ASR)				(2.4)	(3.2)	(-4.4)
				*	**	***
Theft						
Nonwhite	.42	.06	.21	.03	.11	.17
White	.39	.04	.22	.02	.06	.28
(ASR)		(2.4)			(3.8)	(-5.0)
		*			***	***
Damage						
Nonwhite	.49	.11	.18	.04	.04	.13
White	.37	.04	.07	.09	.03	.39
(ASR)	(2.9)	(3.1)	(4.0)	(-2.2)		(-7.0)
	**	**	***	*		***
Combination (robbery)						
Nonwhite	.39	.09	.14	.02	.14	.22
White	.40	.02	.13	.01	.14	.30
(ASR)		(3.3)				(-2.3)
		***				*

NOTES: Derived from data on race-specific offense switching available in Wolfgang, Figlio, and Sellin (1972:Matrices 11.11 to 11.26 and Tables 11.27 and 11.28). Only ASRs significant at the .10 level or better (two-tailed test using standard normal distribution) are reported in parentheses. ASRs for nonwhite offenders are reported in the table. With only two categories of offenders compared, the ASRs for white offenders are just the negative of those reported for nonwhite offenders.

*Significant at the .05 level.
**Significant at the .01 level.
***Significant at the .001 level.

not published and so reanalysis of the data was not possible.

Wolfgang, Figlio, and Sellin (1972) examined offense switching over 16 periods (6 months each) from ages 10 to 18. Because of the fine disaggregation by age, the offense types were aggregated to form three categories: non-index, index, and no offense. In each age matrix, an offender was characterized by his state at the end of the age period. An offender with no police contacts during an age period was characterized by the "no offense" category for that period. Likewise, if the last contact during an age period was an index offense, the offender was characterized as having an index offense in that period. Separate transition matrices were estimated for all adjacent age periods.

Variations in offense switching over age were assessed by pair-wise comparisons of adjacent transition matrices. In general, the χ^2 tests of equality between pairs of adjacent matrices were not significant, which indicates stationarity in switching across age. This pattern was broken at three points. First, the transitions between matrices for ages 13–13.5 and ages 13.5–14.0 were significantly different; there was a reduction in the probability of remaining a nonoffender. There was another major reduction in the "no offense" category at ages 14.5–15 versus 15–15.5. Third, the new pattern continued to ages 16.5–17 versus 17–17.5 and 17–17.5 versus 17.5–18, when the likelihood of moving to the "no offense" category increased again.

The analysis by age accommodated absence of a police contact within any age period through the "no offense" category. This "no offense" category dominated the transitions in all age periods examined. Also, because of the small number of police contacts in any 6-month period, offense types were highly aggregated as index or non-index offenses. Thus, the dominance of the "no offense" category and the limited variability in offense types examined tend to obscure any patterns of offense switching over age that might be occurring.

An alternative strategy for examining age differences would have been to limit the analysis to recidivists who had at least two police contacts and to characterize each offense transition at successive police contacts by age of the offender at that transition. A separate matrix could then be estimated for each age at transition. This would focus the analysis of age differences on actual offense switching at successive police contacts. Other analyses of subgroup differences might examine how patterns of offense switching vary across offenders with different career lengths, or with variations in the length of time between successive arrests.

Summarizing, the same general difference in offense switching was observed across races in several jurisdictions and for both juveniles and adults. Nonwhite, or black, offenders were more likely than white offenders to move to violent offense types and less likely either to desist entirely or to move to less serious offense types.

Only one study (Rojek and Erikson, 1982) included a sufficient number of females for a comparison of offense switching by sex. As might be expected, after each official contact, female offenders were much more likely than male offenders to desist from offending or to move to the juvenile status offense of runaway. The limited analyses of differences in offense switching by age of the offender do not support any strong conclusions about age effects.

Specialization. Specialization is the tendency to repeat the same offense type on successive arrests. Specialization is indicated by the diagonal elements of a transition matrix, $p_{ii}(k)$, representing the probability of a next arrest of the same type. Several studies have noted some degree of specialization in offense types, as indicated by a tendency of these diagonal elements to be elevated in magnitude compared with the levels expected if switching was independent of prior offense type.

Wolfgang, Figlio, and Sellin (1972), for example, compared the magnitude of the diagonal element, p_{ii}, with the other entries in the same column (p_{mi}, $m \neq i$). Noting that the probability of repeating the same offense was moderately higher than the chances of moving to that offense from any other offense type (see Table 46), they concluded "that there is some tendency to repeat the same offense type [especially for theft offenses]" (p. 206). Specialization was also more evident among white than nonwhite offenders. Similar results were reported by Smith and Smith (1984) for incarcerated juveniles.

The analyses of adult offenders assessed the extent of specialization by comparing the diagonal entries of the transition matrix with the overall prevalence of an offense type (Moitra, 1981; Blumstein, Cohen, and Das, 1985). One approach would involve taking the ratio of the diagonal transition probability, $p_{jj}(k)$, to the corresponding column marginal probability, $p_j(k)$, with $z_j(k) = p_{jj}(k)/p_j(k)$.[28] A z-value of unity indicates that repeating the same offense type is just as likely as switching to that offense from any other offense type. Specialization would be reflected in z-values greater than 1, where repeating the same offense type is more likely than the level of switching to that offense generally.

The z-values found for Washington, D.C., and Michigan adult offenders are presented in Table 47. The z-values exceed 1, sometimes substantially, in virtually all cases. The z-values are lowest (less than 2) for "other" offenses in the Washington, D.C., sample and for burglary and larceny in all the Michigan samples. The z-values are highest for homicide and rape, followed by fraud, drugs, and auto theft. Burglary and larceny in Michigan and "other" offenses in Washington, D.C., have the greatest diagonal transition probabilities of all offense types; their lower z-values suggest that these high diagonal values are largely a result of a higher probability of switching to these offense types generally, and not a reflection of greater specialization.

The studies of juveniles in Philadelphia

and New Jersey, and of adults in Washington, D.C., and Michigan all found some elevation in the magnitude of diagonal transition probabilities. These assessments of specialization, however, were not very precise. While the diagonal elements may be greater than other switching probabilities, there is no basis for judging when a difference is substantively important as an indicator of specialization. Is a ratio of 2:1 sufficient to indicate specialization, or must the ratio be considerably larger?

The ratios alone are not sufficient for assessing specialization. The main problem is that the range of possible ratio values varies considerably with the magnitude of the column marginal probability. For a prevalent offense, like larceny, which had a column marginal of .148 in Washington, D.C., the maximum ratio can be no more than 6.75.[29] By contrast, the ratio can get very large for relatively rare offenses. For homicide, with a column marginal probability of .015, the maximum value of the ratio is 67 (1.0/.015). This dependence of prevalence means that ratios cannot be compared across offense types that vary substantially in prevalence. A ratio of 5 may be quite large for an offense type with a maximum ratio of only 6.75, but the same ratio value of 5 reflects less specialization when the maximum value is 67.

The variability in ratios observed in Table 47 corresponds to the variability in the column marginal probabilities. In particular, the ratio is smallest for the most prevalent offenses of burglary and larceny (with column marginals of .200 to .275 in Michigan), and largest for the rarest offenses of homicide and rape (with column marginals of .015 or less in all samples). What is needed is some common basis of comparison for assessing the significance of elevated values for diagonal probabilities. One such statistic is the ASR.

Separate ASRs are computed for every entry in a transition matrix, including the diagonals (see note 26). The ASR compares

---

[28]The column marginal probability is given by,

$$p_j(k) = \sum_{i=1}^{R} n_{ij}(k) / \sum_{i=1}^{R} \sum_{j=1}^{C} n_{ij}(k)$$

for R rows and C columns in a transition matrix.

---

[29]In a case of complete specialization, the diagonal transition probability is 1.0 and the maximum ratio is 1.0/.148 = 6.75.

TABLE B-47 Specialization Among Adult Offenders: Ratio of Diagonal Transition Probabilities to Prevalence of Offense Type

Ratio $z_j(\underline{k}) = p_{jj}/p_{.j}$

Offense Type	Diagonal Probability Washington, D.C., p_{jj}	Prevalence of Offense Type Washington, D.C., $p_{.j}$	Washington, D.C., Adults[a]	Detroit SMSA Adults[b]		Southern Michigan Adults[b]	
				Whites	Blacks	Whites	Blacks
Murder	.173	.015	11.82	16.67	11.50	29.33	9.14
Rape	.167	.013	12.52	11.46	14.16	15.00	10.05
Robbery	.292	.104	2.82	4.18	2.37	5.11	2.10
Aggravated assault	.306	.128	2.40	3.14	2.82	3.44	2.45
Drugs	.334	.069	4.86	2.94	3.75	4.40	4.02
Burglary	.289	.103	2.82	1.65	1.88	1.53	1.72
Larceny	.347	.148	2.34	1.67	1.66	1.70	1.58
Auto theft	.271	.042	6.45	3.57	4.15	3.45	3.94
Weapons	.175	.046	3.81	2.63	2.75	3.22	3.04
Fraud	.202	.026	7.71	4.84	5.25	4.28	4.48
Public order	.281	.079	3.56	--	--	--	--
Other	.356	.228	1.56	--	--	--	--

[a]Moitra (1981:Table 2.9). The reported ratio of diagonal probabilities to prevalence of offense types was calculated before rounding of the probabilities and prevalence reported in this table.

[b]Derived from data made available by Blumstein, Cohen, and Das (1985).

an observed frequency count of switches between offense types with the frequency that would be expected if offense switching was independent of previous offense type. This controls for differences in prevalence. Each residual difference between observed and expected frequencies is then adjusted to form a standardized deviate whose distribution is approximately normal. Relying on this common statistical distribution, ASRs can be compared with one another, and their individual statistical significance can be evaluated.

Specialization, reflected in a higher probability of repeating the *same* offense type, would violate the independence assumption. This special form of dependence on previous offense type is reflected in significant, positive ASRs for the diagonal elements of a transition matrix. Diagonal ASRs were used to assess offense specialization in Bursik (1980) and Rojek and Erikson (1982). The results of this test of specialization in these and other offender samples are reported in Table 48.

The strongest pattern to emerge in Table 48 is the difference in specialization between adults and juveniles. While some specialization is evident for juvenile offenders in the upper half of the table, specialization is found in all offense types for adult offenders. The much higher magnitude of the ASR values for adults also indicates that specialization by adult offenders is stronger than that found among juvenile offenders. This seems to suggest a somewhat more exploratory approach to crime by juvenile offenders and a stronger commitment to particular offense types by those who persist in crime as adults.

This difference between juvenile and adult offenders may reflect a developmental process in which more specialized offending patterns emerge gradually as offending continues over time. It might also reflect a selection process wherein juvenile samples include a mixture of casual offenders who desist from offending very quickly and a core of committed offenders who are more specialized in their offending. As the casual exploratory offenders leave offending in the juvenile years, adult samples would consist

more heavily of the committed, specialized offenders.

Sorting these rival hypotheses requires samples with data on both the juvenile and adult periods for the same individuals. The changes—or stability—in specialization over time could then be examined for the subset of offenders who begin as juveniles and persist into adulthood. Unfortunately, none of the available samples permits such an analysis.

While specialization is pervasive among adults, it is not uniformly strong in all offense types. The most specialized offense types in all adult samples were drugs and fraud. Auto theft was also highly specialized among black offenders in the Detroit SMSA and among Washington, D.C., offenders. Higher specialization in these offense types is consistent with the frequent role of these offenses as part of larger, organized illegal economic enterprises. The least specialized offenses among adult offenders were the violent, and often impulsive, offenses of murder and weapons violations in all samples (except blacks in southern Michigan) and rape in the Washington, D.C., sample. These results are different from those suggested by the high diagonal z-ratios in Table 47, where murder and rape had the highest ratios, but that difference reflects the much larger range of variability that is possible in the diagonal ratios for these very rare offenses. The ratio values are higher for these offenses, but not especially high relative to the maximum possible values of these ratios.

Specialization is more sporadic among juvenile offenders. The Pima County sample exhibited the least specialization; only property and runaway offenders showed a significantly greater tendency to repeat those offenses on successive arrests than would be found if switching was independent of prior offense types. This result was found for all three racial-ethnic groups. This lower level of specialization cannot be attributed to the larger representation of females in the Pima County sample. Specialization is in fact less frequent for female offenders; it occurs only for runaway offenses. But even among male offenders,

TABLE B-48 Test of Offense Specialization in Different Offender Samples Using Adjusted Standardized Residuals (ASRs) for Diagonal Transition Probabilities

Philadelphia Juveniles (with desistance)			Cook County Juveniles (without desistance)			Pima County Juveniles (with desistance)			
Offense Type	White	Nonwhite	Offense Type	White	Nonwhite	Offense Type	White	Black	Hispanic
Non-index	2.6[a](1.0)	3.2 (1.0)	Personal injury	1.0[b](1.5)	2.2[c](1.4)	Persons	1.6[b](2.9)	-1.3[b](0)	0.1[b](1.1)
Injury	2.2[c](1.6)	1.2[b](1.2)	Personal property	3.1[a](3.3)	4.5 (1.8)	Property	6.0 (1.4)	4.2 (1.7)	3.9 (1.4)
Theft	9.8 (2.0)	7.0 (1.5)	Impersonal property	3.9 (1.2)	6.3 (1.2)	Other crime	2.2[c](1.7)	0.6[b](1.4)	1.2[b](1.4)
Damage	8.6 (4.3)	1.3[b](1.4)	Other	5.6 (1.4)	4.4 (1.3)	Runaway	8.5 (1.7)	5.4 (2.2)	6.7 (1.9)
Combination (robbery)	6.7 (2.9)	5.3 (1.8)				Other status	-2.0[b](0.8)	2.2[c](1.8)	1.2[b](1.2)

	Detroit SMSA Adults (without desistance)		Southern Michigan Adults (without desistance)		Washington, D.C. Adults (without desistance)
Offense Type	White	Black	White	Black	All
Murder	6.9 (15.0)	9.2 (11.3)	9.2 (30.0)	6.5 (8.6)	18.6 (11.4)
Rape	10.4 (11.0)	14.0 (15.0)	10.8 (15.0)	11.1 (10.0)	19.3 (12.2)
Robbery	19.4 (4.2)	16.1 (2.4)	14.8 (5.1)	9.9 (2.1)	26.9 (2.8)
Aggravated assault	11.0 (3.2)	13.3 (2.8)	13.2 (3.4)	13.2 (2.4)	26.3 (2.4)
Drugs	27.0 (3.0)	21.8 (3.7)	24.6 (4.4)	20.5 (4.0)	34.6 (4.9)
Burglary	17.4 (1.7)	19.8 (1.9)	12.6 (1.5)	12.5 (1.7)	27.5 (2.8)
Larceny	11.3 (1.7)	19.9 (1.7)	12.1 (1.7)	13.9 (1.6)	30.9 (2.3)
Auto theft	14.9 (3.6)	22.2 (4.1)	14.1 (3.4)	12.2 (3.9)	32.6 (6.4)
Weapons	5.8 (2.7)	9.8 (2.8)	6.7 (3.2)	10.4 (3.0)	16.4 (3.8)
Fraud	23.5 (4.8)	21.8 (5.3)	22.6 (4.3)	17.0 (4.5)	30.7 (9.6)
Public order	--	--	--	--	28.3 (3.6)
Other	--	--	--	--	20.5 (1.6)

NOTES: Unless otherwise noted, the reported ASRs for diagonal transition probabilities are significant at the .001 level using a one-tailed test. The ratio of observed to expected frequencies is reported in parentheses.

[a]Significant at .01 level using a one-tailed test.
[b]Not significant.
[c]Significant at .05 level using a one-tailed test.

SOURCES: Data for Philadelphia juveniles were derived from analysis of data published in Wolfgang, Figlio, and Sellin (1972:Matrices 11.11 to 11.28); data for Cook County juveniles are from Bursik (1980:Table 3); data for Pima County juveniles were derived from analysis of data published in Rojek and Erikson (1982:Table 7); data for Detroit SMSA adults and for Southern Michigan adults were derived from analysis of data in Blumstein, Cohen, and Das (1985); data for Washington, D.C. adults were derived from analysis of data available in Moitra (1981:Tables 2.1a to 2.1d).

there is evidence of specialization only for property and runaway offenses (Rojek and Erikson, 1982:22).

In the Philadelphia samples, white offenders were more specialized than nonwhite offenders. Specialization was significant in all offense types among whites, but it was only significant for non-index, theft, and combination offenses for nonwhites. Interestingly, despite the greater tendency of nonwhites to switch to violent offense types from other offense types (see discussion of subgroup differences), nonwhites did not exhibit specialization in either injury or damage offenses. Thus, arrests for violent offenses were more pervasive generally for the nonwhite offenders. However, they were no more likely to follow previous arrests for violent offenses than to follow arrests for any other offense types.

The Cook County sample included serious juvenile offenders. All had been adjudicated delinquent in juvenile court, and all had at least five arrests as juveniles. They were also more like the adult offenders and exhibited the greatest offense specialization by juveniles. Significant specialization was found in all offenses for both races, except personal injury for white offenders. The pervasiveness of specialization in this sample of persistent juvenile offenders is illustrated in Table 48; it suggests that the juvenile-adult differences in specialization found in the other juvenile samples may be due to sample selection, particularly the presence of large numbers of less specialized offenders among juveniles who desist early from offending and thus are less prevalent in adult samples.

Smith and Smith (1984) used a different approach to analyze specialization by juvenile offenders; they examined other crime-mix attributes in addition to diagonal transition probabilities between adjacent arrests. Conditioning on the offense type of the first arrest, they found that the mean number of arrests and the probability of any arrests were both highest for repeating the offense type of the first arrest. Within a sample of incarcerated juveniles, such specialization was especially evident for of-

fenders first arrested for robbery and injury offenses. The tendency to repeat these serious offenses, however, may have been overestimated because the arrest leading to the sampled incarceration was not excluded from the analysis. Compared with arrests generally (Smith and Smith, 1984:Table 1), robbery and injury arrests were overrepresented among offense types leading to incarceration for offenders first arrested for these offense types (Smith and Smith, 1984:Table 4).

Summarizing, there are differences in the levels of specialization by juvenile and adult offenders. Specialization is evident and strong in all offense types among adult offenders, but it is more sporadic and somewhat weaker among juvenile offenders. Among adults, specialization is strongest for drugs, fraud, and auto theft—all offenses that play a role in organized illicit markets. It is weakest, although still significant, for the more impulsive, violent crimes of murder, rape, and weapons violations.

Offense Clusters. Closely related to specialization, in which the same offense type is repeated on successive arrests, is the concept of specialization within "offense clusters." Clusters represent natural partitions of offense types such that offenders display an increased tendency to switch among offenses within a cluster and a corresponding decreased tendency to switch to offenses outside a cluster. For adult offenders and incarcerated juveniles, violent and property offenses form distinct clusters; for other juvenile offenders, there is a sharp partition between common law crimes and juvenile status offenses.

Clusters can be identified by examining patterns among ASRs for switching between individual offense types. Significantly positive ASRs indicate greater switching between offense types than would be expected if switching was independent of prior offense type; significantly negative ASRs indicate less switching between offense types than expected. To avoid swamping interoffense tendencies when there is strong intraoffense specialization, a model of quasi independence is used, which excludes diagonal elements (Haberman, 1973, 1979). The analysis thus looks for systematic patterns of offense switching only among transitions that are not specialized.

In the analysis of offense switching among juveniles, individual offense types were aggregated into larger offense categories based on a priori conceptual similarities among the offenses. A richer array of offense types is available in the analyses of adult samples from Washington, D.C., and Michigan. These data can be examined to identify offense clusters empirically based on observed offender switching patterns.

The ASR values obtained in the Detroit SMSA (Table 49) exemplify the results found in other adult samples when specialized switching found in the diagonals is excluded from the analysis of offense switching. Only ASRs reaching a minimum significance level of .10 or better (two-tailed test) are reported in the table. In addition to ASRs for switches between pairs of offense types, the χ^2 value for all switches combined is reported in the table. This χ^2 value for the "incomplete" table of frequency counts after the diagonals are excluded is highly significant, and the hypothesis that switching among different offense types is independent of prior offense type is easily rejected in all adult samples examined.

Two distinct clusters of violent and property offenses are evident for all adult offender samples examined. Regardless of jurisdiction or race, adult offenders exhibited definite tendencies toward increased switching *within* these offense clusters (positive ASRs) and decreased switching *between* the two clusters (negative ASRs). This tendency for offense types to cluster varied somewhat by race—the partition between violent and property offenses was stronger among black offenders. In all Michigan jurisdictions, but not in Washington, D.C.,[30] there was also a limited ten-

dency for increased switching between the clusters of violent offenses and robbery, and decreased switching between the clusters of property offenses and drugs.

The clear tendency toward distinct clusters for violent offenses and property offenses provides empirical support for the use of these aggregate categories in other studies of offense switching. Not only are these offense types conceptually similar, they are also behaviorally related, that is, offenders are more likely to switch among offenses within a cluster on successive arrests.

The same approach just used to identify offense clusters among reasonably disaggregated offense types for adults can also be used to examine the patterns of switching among the more aggregate offense categories used in studies of juvenile offenders. After excluding specialization in the same offense category, one would like to know whether switching among the remaining offense categories is systematic or whether it is independent of prior offense. On the basis of a visual inspection of similarities in the rows of transition matrices, Wolfgang, Figlio, and Sellin (1972:188–189) concluded that other than a limited tendency to repeat the same offense type, offense switching appeared to be generally independent of prior offense type. Examination of ASRs in a model of quasi independence (i.e., omitting diagonal switches) permits a more rigorous test of independence of prior offense type. Bursik (1980) is the only study reviewed here to employ such a test. Sufficient data are available in the published studies, however, to perform this analysis for all the juvenile samples.

As was found in the adult samples, the χ^2 for switches among different offense types (diagonals excluded) are highly significant for juvenile samples (except nonwhites in Cook County), and the hypothesis that switching is independent of prior offense

---

[30]Because some nonstationarity in offense switching was observed across successive arrests in Washington, D.C., the analysis of offense clustering was performed separately for each of the first three

transition matrices. While there were some variations in the results for individual offense types across these transitions, the same general clustering pattern was observed for separate transitions.

type can be rejected. The differences across rows of a transition matrix are sufficient that knowledge of the prior offense type can be useful in predicting the next offense type.

The particular nature of dependencies on prior offense type is indicated by significant ASRs, as illustrated in Table 50 for juvenile offenders in Pima County, Arizona. A strong partition between violent and property offenses—reflected in significant negative ASRs for switches between these offense categories—was found among adults and incarcerated juveniles, but the partition was generally not as sharp among juveniles. Aside from incarcerated juveniles in New Jersey, only nonwhite offenders in Philadelphia and white offenders in Cook County (data not presented) displayed a tendency *not* to switch between the injury and theft offense categories. In addition, there is evidence of a tendency by some juveniles to switch between violent and property offenses. Offenders in Pima County, for example, exhibited higher-than-expected switching between offenses against persons and property, as indicated in Table 50, by significant positive ASRs for switches between these offense categories.

The Pima County study provides the only data that separately identify juvenile status offenses (runaway and "other status"). The results reported in Table 50 indicate a sharp partition between status offenses and traditional crimes.[31] First, a tendency not to switch from status offenses to the traditional crime categories is evident. Also evident is a tendency not to switch from the traditional crime categories to desistance; desistance is more likely after a juvenile status offense. Interestingly, running away is distinct from other status offenses; the negative ASRs indicate a tendency not to switch between the two juvenile status categories.

To summarize, offense switching does not appear to be independent of the prior offense type. Instead, knowledge of the

prior offense type provides information useful in predicting the next offense type for both repeated and nonrepeated offenses. The analysis of offense switching by adults and incarcerated juveniles provides behavioral support for the frequently used partition between violent and property offenses. Adults and incarcerated juveniles exhibited definite tendencies to switch among offenses within clusters of violent or property offenses and a tendency not to switch between those two clusters. This partition between violence and theft, however, is not as sharp among juvenile offenders generally. Moreover, based on one study of juveniles, there appears to be a sharp partition between traditional crime categories and juvenile status offenses: switching from a status offense to a traditional crime on the next arrest is less likely than would be expected if switching was independent of prior offense type. This partition may reflect a difference in the offending patterns of males and females represented in the data, i.e., females may have been more heavily represented in status offenses and males in traditional crimes.

Escalation. Escalation, a tendency for offenders to move to more serious offenses as offending continues, is probably the most widely held, commonsense view of criminal offending. Data on offense transitions provide an opportunity to investigate offense escalation empirically. Various approaches are used to study escalation in offense seriousness.

Rojek and Erikson (1982) searched for long-term trends based on the results of the test for stationarity across transitions. On the basis of their finding of stationarity in offense-switching patterns across transitions for juveniles in Pima County, they concluded that there was no support for a process of escalation to more serious offenses (1982:17).

The conclusion of no escalation for Pima County juveniles was not confirmed in the reanalysis conducted for this report. On the basis of the published data, nonstationarity was found for switching from runaway and

---

[31]Only the results for all offenders in Pima County are reported here. Similar results were also found in each racial-ethnic group.

TABLE B-49 Test for Offense Clusters in Switching by Adults in the Detroit SMSA--Significant Adjusted Standardized Residuals (ASRs) when Diagonal Switches Are Omitted

Offense Type on $\underline{k}$ + 1st Arrest

Offense Type on $\underline{k}$th Arrest	Violent				Robbery	Drugs	Property			
	Murder	Rape	Aggravated Assault	Weapons			Burglary	Larceny	Auto Theft	Fraud
Violent										
Murder	--	7.700						-2.168		
Rape		--	1.814							
Aggravated assault	3.763		--	5.975		2.323	-3.792	-2.038	-2.707	
Weapons	3.243	1.928		--		1.650				
Robbery	2.010		3.548		--			-2.433		
Drugs						--		3.365	-1.966	
Property										
Burglary							--	2.830		
Larceny		-3.073					1.721	--		-1.823
Auto theft				-2.264		-2.501	5.305	2.013	--	
Fraud										--

White Offenders: χ^2 = 263.59*** (71 d.f.)

Black Offenders: χ^2 = 351.56*** (71 d.f.)

	Murder	Rape	Aggravated assault	Weapons	Robbery	Drugs	Burglary	Larceny	Auto theft	Fraud
Violent										
Murder	--		2.702	6.219	-1.894					
Rape		--	3.368						-2.800	
Aggravated assault	3.006	3.659	--	4.727	4.448		-2.818		-3.474	-1.832
Weapons	4.163			--	2.846		-2.340		-3.216	-2.133
Robbery	2.353	5.976		2.966	--					
Drugs						--				
Property										
Burglary	-2.028	-1.676			-1.759	-1.713	--	4.492	2.729	-2.456
Larceny		-3.164			-2.872		4.046	--		3.022
Auto theft	-1.972				-2.611	-2.618	4.140		--	-1.953
Fraud	-1.883					-1.648		1.753		--

NOTE: Only ASRs significant at the .10 level or better (two-tailed test using standard normal distribution) are reported.

***χ^2 is significant at .001 level or better.

TABLE B-50 Test of Independence of Switching Among Offense Types for Pima County Juveniles: Observed and Expected Transition Probabilities and Adjusted Standardized Residuals (ASRs) When Diagonal Elements Are Omitted (all offenders)

Offense Type of kth Contact	Offense Type of k + 1st Official Contact					
	Persons	Property	Other Crimes	Runaway	Other Status	Desist[a]
Persons						
Observed	--	.375	.117	.158	.125	.150
Expected	--	.232	.094	.146	.168	.285
(ASR)		(3.9)***				(-3.4)***
Property						
Observed	.036	--	.110	.157	.163	.182
Expected	.028	--	.084	.131	.151	.255
(ASR)	(2.1)*		(4.2)***	(3.7)***	(1.7)	(-7.9)***
Other Crimes						
Observed	.034	.287	--	.140	.185	.227
Expected	.031	.235	--	.148	.170	.288
(ASR)		(2.6)**				(-2.8)**
Runaway						
Observed	.015	.167	.048	--	.107	.251
Expected	.022	.169	.068	--	.122	.207
(ASR)	(-1.7)		(-3.0)**		(-1.8)	(4.3)***
Other Status						
Observed	.028	.205	.084	.119	--	.431
Expected	.034	.256	.103	.161	--	.314
(ASR)		(-4.0)***	(-2.0)*	(-3.7)***		(8.1)***

x^2 = 136.4*** (15 d.f.)

[a]Offenders were characterized as desisting when no further official juvenile contacts were observed. Since the data were limited to juvenile official contacts, however, offenders who appeared to desist as juveniles may have had subsequent arrests as adults.

*Significant at the .05 level.
**Significant at the .01 level.
***Significant at the .001 level.

SOURCE: Derived from data in Rojek and Erikson (1982:Table 2). ASRs for an incomplete table (excluding diagonal values) are calculated using the program provided in Haberman (1979:Appendix). Only ASRs significant at the .10 level or better (two-tailed test using a standard normal distribution) are reported.

from other status offenses. On the basis of the analysis of ASRs for switches on successive transitions, switches from runaway and status offenses to person offenses and to the category of "other crimes" were less likely on early transitions and more likely on later transitions. Conversely, switches from juvenile status offenses to desistance were more

likely on early transitions and less likely on later transitions. This suggests possible escalation in seriousness for juvenile status offenders who remain criminally active. These results, however, must be regarded cautiously because of possible imprecisions in the reanalysis.[32]

An alternative approach to detecting escalation makes use of a seriousness scale to weight arrests differentially by offense type. The average seriousness on successive arrests can then be compared for upward or downward trends. The average seriousness (Sellin-Wolfgang scale) of police contacts for Philadelphia juveniles is shown in Figure 3.[33] A distinctive upward trend is evident; average seriousness increased by about 4.3 on each police contact, from an average level of 100 on the first contact up to an average of 165 on the fifteenth. Seriousness scores in this scale can vary over a very large range—from values under 100 to over 2,600. An increase in the average from 100 to 165 might arise, for example, if all first contacts had scores of 100 (associated with such offenses as forcible entry and thefts of under $10) and later contacts had a mixture of scores with 89 percent at 100 and 11 percent at 700 (associated with offenses involving injuries that require hospitalization of the victim or thefts of over $80,000). In race-specific analyses, a similar upward trend in seriousness was found only for nonwhite offenders; average seriousness for white offenders was far more variable over successive arrests.

The analysis of escalation by Wolfgang, Figlio, and Sellin (1972:165–168) focused on changes in seriousness within individual offense types. Focusing on theft offenses, for example, revealed very little change in the seriousness of theft offenses on successive arrests. Thefts on the tenth police contact were of about the same average seriousness as thefts occurring on the first police contact. Only injury offenses exhibited a

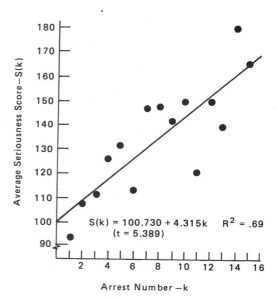

FIGURE B-3 Trends in average seriousness on successive police contacts for offenders in Philadelphia birth cohort (all offenders). Data from Wolfgang, Figlio, and Sellin (1972:Table 10.4 and Figure 10.2).

significant positive trend on successive arrests. That trend, however, can be attributed completely to very high seriousness scores on the last two observations. No trend was observed when these later police contacts, which were based on very small numbers of offenders, were excluded.[34] On the basis of the general absence of strong upward trends in seriousness for individual offense types, the authors concluded that "the notion that offense severity is positively related to the number of offenses that one commits is not strongly substantiated by these data" (p. 167).

This is a narrow view of escalation. While changes in seriousness within an offense type are certainly one component of escala-

---

[32]The replication results may be distorted by errors in the frequency counts used in the reanalysis arising from (1) imprecision in estimating frequency counts from published transition probabilities and (2) possible typographical errors in the published data, which are suggested by inconsistencies in frequency counts calculated from the various published tables.

[33]The Sellin-Wolfgang seriousness scale (Sellin and Wolfgang, 1964) was used to weight the seriousness of every police contact. The scale was extended here to include scores for non-index offenses, and all scores were multiplied by 100 to avoid decimal values.

---

[34]Using average seriousness-of-injury offenses, $S(k)$, on the first 15 police contacts ($k = 1,2, \ldots , 15$), the regression results are,

$$S(k) = 313.20 + 17.81k, R^2 = .28.$$
$$(t = 2.256)$$

Excluding the last two observations,

$$S(k) = 395.48 + 2.05k, R^2 = .01.$$
$$(t = .354)$$

tion, increases in the seriousness of offending may also result from changes in the mix of offense types on successive arrests. The increase in average seriousness on successive police contacts evident in Figure 3 reflects a combination of shifts to more serious offense types on later police contacts and any increases in seriousness within individual offense types.

Overall, offense-switching patterns in the Philadelphia sample were generally stationary over successive transitions. A more detailed look at switching for individual offense types using ASRs, however, revealed some isolated shifts toward more serious offenses on later transitions. The tendency for non-index offenses to be followed by another non-index offense on the next police contact decreased on later transitions, and the tendency to switch from non-index to injury offenses increased. Likewise, the tendency to switch from "combination" to injury offenses increased on later transitions, and switches from combination to damage offenses decreased. In all cases, there were increases in switches to more serious offenses and decreases in switches to less serious offenses on later transitions. Just as was found in the reanalysis for Pima County juveniles, there appears to be some escalation in seriousness for Philadelphia juveniles, especially for nonwhite offenders in that sample.

All the adult samples reviewed here were also examined for changes in average seriousness on successive arrests. In contrast to the increases in seriousness found among juveniles, average seriousness declined on successive arrests in all adult samples. When the same seriousness scale was used on all samples, small but statistically significant downward trends were found over successive arrests for all adult samples, except for black offenders in Detroit (Table 51).[35] Even in this latter subgroup, average

seriousness generally declined except for the last observation, which was anomalously high. When this last observation is excluded from the regression, the negative trend coefficient becomes significant [$S(k) = 3.11 - .0329k$, with $t = 3.295$]. To ensure that the results on seriousness were not sensitive to the particular seriousness scale used, a number of alternative scales were compared in the analysis of Washington, D.C., adults (Moitra, 1981), and significant declines in seriousness were observed for all scales used.

The analyses of adults also reveal a potentially important confounding selection effect in the observed trends of seriousness. Because offenders had different numbers of arrests, the same offenders were not observed over the full sequence of arrests. For early arrests, average seriousness reflects the contributions of a mixture of offenders, some with only a few arrests and some with long records of arrests. As the arrest number increases, however, average seriousness is increasingly restricted to offenders with large numbers of arrests. Thus, the decline in seriousness observed in Table 51 could reflect differences among offenders rather than a trend toward less serious offenses as individual offending continues. To control for this potential selection effect, offenders were partitioned by the number of arrests in their arrest records, and the analysis of trends was restricted to the common sequence of arrests for a subset of offenders. Thus, in comparing average seriousness on each arrest up to the sixth, for example, only offenders who had at least six arrests were included.

As illustrated in Figure 4 and Table 52, when record length was controlled, average seriousness was generally stable over successive arrests within all offender subgroups, except white offenders in Detroit. Moreover, in a simple regression, average seriousness was always lower for offenders who had longer records, and there was a significant negative effect of record length

---

[35]The seriousness scores are directly comparable across the various samples. Public order and "other" offenses, which were excluded from most of the analyses of Michigan samples, were included in computing average seriousness. The scale scores ranged from 0 to 12. Homicide was assigned a score

of 12, rape 9, robbery 7, aggravated assault 5.5, drugs 4.4, burglary 3.4, larceny 2.6, auto theft 2.1, weapons 1.5, fraud 1.1, public order 0.7, and "other" 0.3.

TABLE B-51 Changes in Average Seriousness, $\underline{S}(\underline{k})$, on Successive Arrests (k) for Adult Offenders: Regression Results of $\underline{S}(\underline{k}) = \underline{a} + \underline{bk}$

Value of $\underline{k}$	Detroit SMSA			Southern Michigan SMSA			Washington, D.C.
	All Races	Blacks	Whites	All Races	Blacks	Whites	
1	2.72	3.10	2.35	2.41	2.72	2.17	3.37
2	2.74	3.10	2.38	2.39	2.79	2.07	3.27
3	2.70	3.14	2.28	2.34	2.74	2.01	3.26
4	2.62	2.96	2.53	2.27	2.61	1.97	3.09
5	2.53	2.87	2.27	2.40	2.86	1.99	3.16
6	2.45	2.84	2.17	2.34	2.66	2.06	3.13
7	2.38	2.73	2.14	2.36	2.77	1.99	3.07
8	2.43	2.83	2.18	2.21	2.70	1.81	2.95
9	2.41	2.57	2.30	2.47	2.88	2.12	2.98
10	2.45	2.84	2.22	2.28	2.56	2.05	2.91
11	2.40	3.02	2.06	2.08	2.38	1.82	--
12	2.41	2.76	2.21	2.06	2.42	1.73	--
13	2.39	2.87	2.13	2.35	2.91	1.79	--
14	2.08	2.44	1.87	2.01	2.21	1.84	--
15	2.34	3.18	1.82	2.27	2.39	2.15	--
$\hat{a}$	2.74	3.03	2.42	2.43	2.85	2.09	3.38
$\hat{b}$	-0.0335	-0.0188	-0.0299	-0.0179	-0.0258	-0.0142	-0.047
	(-6.42)	(-1.58)	(-5.20)	(-2.59)	(-2.40)	(-1.83)	(-9.20)

NOTE: The $\underline{t}$-statistics of estimates are reported in parentheses.

SOURCE: Blumstein, Cohen, and Das (1985:Table 19).

in all samples except white offenders in southern Michigan. These results illustrate the importance of controlling for potential selection effects. Without adequate controls, systematic differences in the mix of offenders who are compared can be incorrectly interpreted as reflecting developmental changes during individual criminal careers.

A similar negative relationship between record length and offense seriousness was also noted in Frum (1958) and in Soothill and Gibbons (1978). The lower average seriousness for adult offenders who have long records may be due to differences in incarceration experiences for offenders. Incarceration is routinely imposed on offenders convicted of serious offenses, and a record of serious offenses further increases the likelihood of long prison terms at sen-

tencing (Blumstein et al., 1983). The expected reductions in time free in the community that accompany serious offenses would make it more difficult for offenders to accumulate large numbers of arrests for serious offenses.

Just as the apparent decline in seriousness for adult offenders results from differences in seriousness across offenders, differences among offenders may also account for the increases in seriousness on successive police contacts for juveniles. As the number of police contacts increases, average seriousness measures depend increasingly on offenders with large numbers of contacts. If more serious offenses are more common in the records of these more active juvenile offenders, perhaps because of a more limited use of incarceration for juvenile offenders, the changing mix of offend-

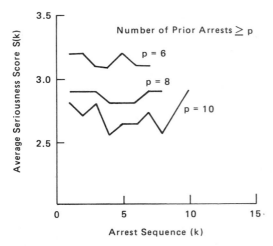

FIGURE B-4 Average seriousness on successive arrests, *k*, for arrestees with at least *p* arrests, Washington, D.C., adults. Source: Moitra (1981:Figure 2.4).

ers alone could produce the observed increases in average seriousness on successive contacts.

The analyses in Bursik (1980) and Smith and Smith (1984) explicitly controlled for record length among juvenile offenders. The analysis in Bursik (1980) was restricted to the first four switches for juveniles with five or more contacts. Bursik (1980:856) reported that the aggregate switching process was stationary over those four transitions. Unfortunately, the data necessary to replicate the analysis and to examine switching for individual offense types were not published. Smith and Smith (1984:Table 6) examined offense patterns for offenders who had at least six arrests as juveniles. Their data indicate a trend toward increased probabilities of robbery and injury offenses on later arrests for these recidivistic offenders. Since all offenders have at least six arrests, only the sixth arrest is potentially biased toward more serious offense types by including the last arrest that led to the sampled incarceration in the analysis. While these results (with appropriate controls for record length) are consistent with escalation in seriousness on successive arrests for

TABLE B-52 Changes in Average Seriousness, $\underline{S}(\underline{k})$, on Successive Arrests ($\underline{k}$) for Adult Offenders with $\underline{m}$ Prior Arrests When Sampled: Regression Results of $\underline{S}(\underline{k}) = \underline{a} + \underline{b}k + \underline{c}m$

Parameter Values	Detroit SMSA		Southern Michigan		Washington, D.C.
	Blacks	Whites	Blacks	Whites	
$\hat{a}$	3.14	2.55	2.84	2.13	3.7
$\hat{b}$	-.0058	.0341	.0188	-.0079	-.0014
	(-.52)	(3.94)	(1.45)	(-1.03)	(-.14)
$\hat{c}$	-.0300	-.0581	-.0279	-.0087	-.0640
	(-2.31)	(-6.7)	(-2.15)	(-1.14)	(-6.44)
Degrees of freedom	117	117	117	117	63
R^2	.072	.28	.04	.04	.50

NOTE: The $\underline{t}$-statistics of estimates are reported in parentheses.

SOURCE: Blumstein, Cohen, and Das (1985:Table 21).

juveniles, the authors interpret the results as reflecting increased diversification for offenders first arrested for nonindex or property offenses and increased specialization for those first arrested for robbery or injury offenses.

Markov Property. Markov processes are distinguished by the fact that transitions at any point depend, at most, on the current state of the process. In a Markov process, knowledge about the sequence of previous states leading to the current state provides no useful information in predicting the next state. Characterizing offense-type switching as a Markov process involves assuming that, with the exception of the offense type of the current arrest, the offense type of the next arrest is independent of all other previous arrests.

Markov processes are particularly useful analytic devices for predicting various future attributes of a switching process. If offense switching on successive arrests can be adequately represented as a Markov chain, it is a relatively easy matter to estimate the chance that some future arrest will be for a specific offense type. The chance of a robbery charge on the third arrest, for example, can be obtained directly from the estimated transition matrix and the initial distribution of offense types. The expected distribution over different offense types can also be estimated for any anticipated number of future arrests. With respect to specialization, one can estimate the expected number of arrests in other offense types between returns to an offense specialty, or the expected number of successive arrests within an offense specialty. If the transition process includes transitions to desistance associated with real termination of offending or with truncation of observation periods, it is possible to estimate the expected number of arrests before desistance will be observed. Similar predictions of future offending are usually possible if offense switching is not Markovian, but they are typically more difficult to estimate.

While Markov processes are very useful from an analytic perspective, they are not particularly satisfying substantively or operationally. Markov processes are "memory-less" in that dependence on prior history is limited only to the current offense type. If offense switching were to be adequately represented as a Markov process, then prior history of offense types would not usefully distinguish future offending. An offender with a long sequence of arrests for some offense type, say robbery, would be no more likely to repeat with robbery on the next arrest than would an offender with no other prior arrests for robbery other than the current arrest.

All the studies of juvenile offenders reviewed here invoked the Markov property in characterizing offense switching. The limited manner in which this property was applied, however, suggests a failure to recognize that the Markov property is not essential for estimation and analysis of transition matrices. While the Markov property was invoked, it was tested in only a limited fashion or not at all, and, with the exception of Smith and Smith (1984), none of the useful predictions that derive from the Markov property was explored in the analyses.

The one study of juveniles reporting a limited test of the Markov property is Wolfgang, Figlio, and Sellin (1972). Here a second-order transition matrix was considered in which the offense type on the next arrest depended on the offense types of both the current and the immediately preceding arrest. A χ^2 test was performed on the estimated transition matrix for the first three police contacts to assess the adequacy of this dependency structure against a null hypothesis that switching is dependent only on the current offense type. The resulting χ^2 value was significant at the .07 level ($\chi^2 = 100.03$, 80 d.f.), and thus there is a reasonable basis for rejecting the null hypothesis of first-order independence. However, using a .05 threshold of significance, the authors accepted the null hypothesis of independence, but they advised caution with respect to this analysis because of the small number of cases available to generate some of the transition estimates (1972:186–187).

Aside from the problem of small sample sizes, the aggregate χ^2 test is not sufficiently sensitive to violations of independence for individual offense types. A more sensitive test of the Markov property is available. This test relies on the well-known property of Markov chains: the j-step transition matrix, P_j, for offense-type switches between arrests separated by $j - 1$ intervening arrests should be given by the product of the j intervening one-step matrices, $P(k)$, with

$$P_j = \prod_{k=1}^{j} P(k).$$

In comparing offense types on the first and fourth arrests, for example, offense switching would be represented by a three-step matrix, P_3. The independence of Markov processes means that this three-step matrix can be obtained directly by successively applying the transition matrix from the first to second arrest, $P(1)$, and then the transition matrix from the second to third arrest, $P(2)$, and finally the transition matrix from the third to fourth arrest, $P(3)$. In this example, the three-step matrix is given by

$$P_3 = P(1) \times P(2) \times P(3).$$

For a stationary Markov process, where $P(k) = P$ for all k, $P_3 = P^3$.

Moitra (1981) was the only study reviewed that explicitly applied this test of the Markov property to offense-type switching. Using data on offense switching between arrests for adults arrested in Washington, D.C., Moitra (1981:Table 2.11) compared the two-step transition matrix to the product of the two intervening one-step matrices. As is commonly observed in analyses of other social processes (e.g., residential migration, social mobility), greater specialization (indicated by larger diagonal values) was found in the observed two-step matrix, P_2, than was expected from the product of the one-step matrix, P^2. This tendency toward greater specialization over successive arrests was a basis for rejecting the simple Markov characterization of no dependence on prior history in offense switching. Ordinarily, failure of the Markov property introduces unacceptable errors into long-term predictions, but short-term pre-

dictions based on the Markov property are reasonably accurate. The failure of the Markov property in the short term, represented by a two-step matrix, however, substantially limits the usefulness of any predictions of offense switching based on a simple Markov model.

Rather than offense switching being independent of prior history, it appears that offenders may in some way be distinguishable in terms of their accumulated record of prior offense types. In particular, offense switching appears to be more specialized than expected under a simple first-order Markov assumption. This failure of the Markov property has both analytic and substantive consequences. The Markov model is most useful as an analytic tool for making projections about future offending patterns based on available estimates of one-step switching patterns. These projections—e.g., the expected distribution of offense types for future arrests—are less reliable when the process violates the basic Markov assumption. While often useful for the insights they provide, such projections are not necessary, and empirically based transition matrices can still be estimated from observed offense switching and their structure analyzed without satisfying the Markov property. Any substantive insights into offense-switching patterns that emerge from such analyses, however, are limited by their failure to go beyond the immediately preceding offense type when characterizing the influence of prior criminal history on future offending. Offenders whose histories include many instances of the same offense type, for example, may exhibit greater specialization in future arrests than is found when the analysis is restricted to only the current offense type. When the Markov property fails, analyses that do not rely on transition matrices may be more appropriate.

Methodological Issues in Analyzing Offense Seriousness

Studies of offense seriousness during criminal careers attempt—to varying degrees—to characterize both the mix and sequence of offense types found during careers. Two general approaches are available, one that attempts to summarize entire careers, and another that focuses on successive arrests. Included among the summary approaches are various statistical measures, such as a simple percentage distribution of the offense types found in a career, the geometric scaling proposed by Shannon (1968) to capture the mix of different offense types during a career, and an actuarial technique of risk assessment proposed by Robins and Taibleson (1972) to assess the effect of one offense type on the probability that another offense type subsequently occurs. The approach focusing on changes over successive arrests includes, primarily, analyses of transition matrices of switching between offense types first introduced in Blumstein et al. (1967) and Blumstein and Larson (1969).

A number of methodological concerns have emerged in this review of empirical research on offense seriousness. Since most recent analyses of offense seriousness have relied on transition matrices, the various problems are discussed below primarily in relation to this technique. The same problems, however, are sometimes of equal concern for other, simpler descriptive techniques.

Requirement for Large Sample Size

The data requirements for analyses of offense switching are greater than those for analyses of other aspects of individual offending. While participation, frequency, and duration can be partitioned by single offense categories, analysis of offense switching is based on pairs of successive offense types. Thus, the collection of all robbery events that together form the datum for estimates of participation, frequency, and duration is partitioned into smaller subsets depending on the offense type of the next event when estimating offense-switching patterns.

Even a reasonably large number of arrests often reduces to unreliably small numbers of observations for offense pairs when offense switching is analyzed by individual

transitions and for a reasonable number of distinct offense types. Compared with a simple linear growth in data needs for other analyses, data needs grow multiplicatively in analyses of offense-type switching.

Lack of sufficient data often limits the usefulness of analyses of offense-switching patterns. Data limitations are especially a problem when there is extensive variability in individual offense-switching patterns as a result of population heterogeneity (i.e., differences across individuals) or nonstationarity (i.e., variability in the switching process on different transitions). By using transition matrices, transition probabilities can be estimated from the proportions observed for various offense pairs in samples of offenders. The adequacy with which these probability estimates characterize offense-switching patterns depends on the extent to which the collection of offense pairs used results from a reasonably homogeneous switching process. As variations in the switching process increase, the estimates of transition probabilities are a less accurate reflection of offense-switching patterns. When there is high variability in the switching process, it is desirable to partition the data, by population subgroup or by transition number, to form subsets that are more homogeneous with respect to offense switching. Such partitions, however, greatly increase data requirements.

While the results varied across data samples, the studies reviewed here indicate some important differences in switching patterns for different population subgroups (especially race and sex) and some nonstationarity on successive transitions (especially for adults). Analyses on separate subgroups and for different transitions are thus important in any study of offense-switching patterns. Ensuring the capacity to partition the data adequately puts increased demands on the sample size required for analysis. When the sample size is inadequate to the task, transition matrices should not be used; other, simpler techniques that describe the changing mix of offense seriousness are more appropriate. These might include differences in the percentage repeating an offense type based on the number of prior arrests for that same type found in a career, or using some weighted statistic for that offense type that gives greater weight to more recent occurrences of the offense type.

Reliance on Official Records

All of the studies of offense switching reviewed here relied on official-record data on sequences of police contacts or arrests for samples of offenders. This dependence on official-record data arises from the requirement for data that document the exact sequences of offense types over time—information that is readily available in official records.

The picture of offense switching that emerges from analyses of official-record data, however, confounds patterns of offense switching by offenders with patterns of law enforcement, especially by the police. As noted earlier, the offense types observed on successive police contacts or successive arrests will vary with the levels of police effectiveness in apprehending offenders for different offense types. Offense types with higher detection and apprehension rates will be overrepresented among official contacts compared with their representation in successive crimes committed. If enforcement rates vary substantially for different offense types, the patterns of switching observed in official-record data will provide a distorted view of offense switching between actual crimes committed. This confounding effect is recognized in virtually all studies of offense switching, and the studies are careful to note that the reported results apply to successive official contacts for offenders.

The variability in arrest risk for different offense types is illustrated in Table 53. Based on data for the United States, the ratio of arrests to reported crimes (in column 3) varies from a low of .12 for auto theft to a high of .42 for aggravated assault. The ratio of arrests to reported crimes alone, however, is an inadequate estimate of the chance of arrest for a crime for an individual. Crimes committed but not reported to the police are not included, and arrests

sometimes include arrests of more than one individual for the same crime incident.

The number of reported crimes can be adjusted for nonreporting by using the reporting rates for various offense types available from national surveys of criminal victimization. A further adjustment for multiple offenders per crime incident is also available in these national surveys.[36] The adjusted estimates of the probability that any individual offender is arrested for a crime committed, whether reported to the police or not, are shown in the last column in Table 53. The risk of arrest is highest for offenses involving direct contact between offenders and victims (robbery and aggravated assault) and lowest for property offenses without contact.

The final arrest risk for the various offense types is generally low, averaging only 1 arrest for every 20 crimes committed. Despite the reduction in arrest risk after the adjustments, there is still a threefold difference between the highest risk (aggravated assault) and the lowest risk (larceny and auto theft). Variability in arrest risk for different offense types is thus a very real concern in analyses of offense switching that rely on official contacts only.

Two strategies are available for dealing with distortions in offense-switching patterns that arise from use of official-record data. The first is to expand the scope of self-reports of offenses committed to include data on the actual sequence of different offense types. To date, such data on sequences of crimes actually committed have been unavailable. It is only recently that self-report studies have begun to collect data on frequency of offending during a reporting period. Collecting data on the sequence of offense types will require

---

[36]The adjusted arrest risk for a crime of offense type k, q_k, is given by

$$q_k = \frac{\text{Arrests of Type } k}{\text{Reported Offenses of Type } k} \times \frac{r_k}{O_k},$$

where r_k is the rate of reporting offenses to the police by crime victims and O_k is the average number of offenders per crime incident.

TABLE B-53 Probability of Arrest for a Crime, Adjusted for Nonreporting to the Police and Multiple Offenders per Crime

Offense Type	Reported Offenses in U.S., 1980[a]	Arrests in U.S., 1980[b]	Ratio of Arrests to Reported Offenses	Proportion of Total Offenses Reported to Police[c]	Number of Offenders per Crime Incident[d]	Probability of Arrest for a Crime, q, for Individual Offenders
Robbery	548,809	146,270	.27	.57	2.3	.07
Aggravated assault	654,957	277,470	.42	.54	2.6	.09
Burglary	3,759,193	513,300	.14	.51	1.6	.04
Larceny	7,112,657	1,191,900	.17	.27	1.6	.03
Auto theft	1,114,651	138,300	.12	.69	1.8	.03

[a]Federal Bureau of Investigation (1981:Table 1).
[b]Federal Bureau of Investigation (1981:Table 24).
[c]Bureau of Justice Statistics (1982a:Table 89).
[d]Reiss (1980b:Table 2).

panel designs that include data collection from the same sample of offenders at frequent intervals. Depending on the anticipated rates of individual offending, monthly or perhaps even weekly reports may be required.

Given that the focus of the research is offense seriousness, the strategy of repeated and frequent self-reports is best limited to samples of known offenders. Those offenders might be identified from self-reported offenses in a more widely used screening instrument, or through arrest or police contact associated with an offense. As noted earlier, self-report studies involving repeated and frequent reporting will be costly, will require a reasonably long-term commitment—of at least several years—to data collection, and will involve difficult logistics in order to maintain contact throughout the study with samples whose members are likely to be uncooperative and mobile. While the self-report approach is certainly possible, the various implementation problems—in addition to the large sample sizes required to estimate switching patterns—make pursuit of this research strategy all the more difficult. The data requirements are somewhat less demanding if repeated self-reports are used to estimate

changes in offense mix during successive reporting periods. Such analyses would not require data on the exact sequence of offense types and smaller samples of offenders would be adequate.

An alternative strategy for analyzing the actual sequence of crimes committed builds on the current reliance on official-record data, extending it to address offense switching between crimes actually committed. As we learn more about the links between individual offending and the criminal justice selection process, we will be better able to model the selection process. By incorporating models of the selection process with readily available official-record data, we can begin to draw inferences about the switching process for undetected crimes that intervene between official-record events. This inferential strategy has begun to be employed with some success in studies of individual crime rates based on official-record data.

Biases Associated with Sample Selection

The most obvious biases arising from the sampling process are distortions introduced by the sampling event itself. These are most likely to arise when sampling is based on some threshold of seriousness in offense types. The analyses of criminal histories for a sample of prison inmates by Frum (1958) and incarcerated juveniles by Smith and Smith (1984) are excellent illustrations of this problem. The samples were drawn from among inmates in state correctional facilities. Since all sample members were incarcerated for the last arrest in their records, that last event was likely to be for a serious offense type or to follow a record of repeated convictions for serious offense types. The sampling strategy of using incarcerated offenders, and the failure to exclude the last offense type from the analysis, were no doubt major factors contributing to the findings of escalation toward more serious offense types over the course of criminal careers and of the tendency for some offenders to specialize in serious offense types.

When sample selection is based on a seriousness threshold, it is essential that the sampling event be excluded from analysis of offense-switching patterns. Failure to exclude the necessarily more serious sampling event will bias estimates of offense-switching patterns toward these more serious events. It was precisely to avoid such biases that the more serious sampling event was excluded from analyses of adult arrestees by Moitra (1981) and Blumstein, Cohen, and Das (1985).

Sample selection in Rojek and Erikson (1982) and Bursik (1980) was based on either processing by the juvenile court or an adjudication as a delinquent in the juvenile court. Given that the discretion to resolve juvenile cases informally is available to both the police and to intake officers at juvenile court, the formal involvement of the juvenile court likely increases the seriousness of the sampling event in both samples. The sampling event was not excluded from either analysis. The sampling event, however, was not restricted to the last event in the record; it could appear anywhere in the record, depending on the age of the offender during the sampling period. This distribution of the sampling event over different points in a record limits the biasing effect toward more serious events at the end of the record. On the other hand, it may be responsible for findings of stationarity over transitions as intermittent escalations in seriousness associated with the sampling event are randomly distributed over individual arrest histories, obscuring any patterns over time that may otherwise exist.

Two strategies are available to control for distortions arising from the sampled event. First, the sampled event can be excluded from the analysis entirely. This strategy is especially appropriate when the sampled event falls at the end of arrest history data. The alternative is to include the sampled event in the analysis, but to limit the analysis to similar events. Thus, in the two juvenile court samples, analysis of offense switching would be limited to contacts processed by juvenile court (in the case of Rojek and Erikson, 1982) or to offenses that were adjudicated delinquent (in Bursik, 1980). In this way, the sampling event is indistinguishable from other events in the analysis. This strategy of only analyzing events similar to the sampling event was employed in the study of offense switching by juveniles in the Philadelphia cohort (Wolfgang, Figlio, and Sellin, 1972). Like the adult analyses, this study of juveniles is free of biases associated with the sampling event.

Aside from biases introduced into the switching process by the sampling event, the sampling process itself selectively limits the population of offenders who are studied. All analyses of offense switching require at least one official-record event (police contact, arrest, juvenile court processing, juvenile court adjudication, conviction, or incarceration). Those that exclude desistance require at least two contacts for each offender. The switching patterns observed thus apply most accurately to subsets of offenders with official records. Even if the criminal justice selection process was completely random, offenders with official contacts would be a random sample of all offenders only if all offenders are homogeneous in offending. Any variability in offending (e.g., higher frequency rates for some offenders compared with others, or longer criminal careers) would increase the representation of more active offenders in the sample. Because their greater criminal activity increases their exposure to risk, offenders with higher frequencies and longer criminal careers are more likely to experience an official contact and thus are more likely to be found in samples.[37] Most analyses of offense-switching patterns, therefore, reflect offense switching for the more active offenders who are found in the sample and may not apply to all offenders.

Role of Frequency Rates, Career Length, and Incapacitation in Switching Patterns

Frequency rates, career length, and time spent incarcerated vary for different offense types. As reported in the review of frequency rates above, individual crime rates are higher for property crimes and lower for violent crimes. Analyses of the length of criminal careers (Blumstein and Cohen, 1982) report an opposite relationship: shorter average careers in property crimes and longer average careers in violent crimes. Time spent incarcerated is also likely to be longer for violent crimes than for property crimes. These differences can affect the switching patterns observed, especially when observation periods are limited in length. In particular, offense types that occur at high rates, and thus involve short intervals between events and short periods of incarceration, are likely to be more prevalent as switching destinations. Conversely, switching to offense types that involve longer average intervals between events and longer periods of incarceration is likely to be underrepresented, especially when observation periods are short.

The possible distorting effect of the dis-

tribution in the various offense types was evident in the analysis of specialization for adults. Without controlling for differences in the distribution of offense types, burglary and larceny have the largest diagonal switching probabilities of all offense types for adults, which suggests greater specialization in these offense types by adult offenders. Examination of the column marginals for these offense types, however, reveals that switching to these offense types is higher generally. Thus, the tendency to specialize in burglary or larceny is not especially great relative to the generally higher frequency of switching to burglary and larceny as the next offense type. Conversely, even apparently small diagonal values may reflect significant specialization when switching to an offense type is generally quite rare. The distribution in different offense types is explicitly controlled in all analyses in which the observed frequency of switches is tested against a model of complete independence in switching. Differences in the distribution of the offense types are reflected directly in the frequency of switches expected in an independent process.

Variations in the number of events in a criminal history are one indication of different levels of offending and differences in incapacitation experiences. Most directly, differences in the number of events will reflect variations in individual frequency rates and in career length. High-rate offenders are more likely to accumulate large numbers of events, as are offenders who remain criminally active for long periods of time. Extended periods of incarceration during careers, by contrast, will limit the number of events in a career. Because levels of offending and incapacitation experiences may also be associated with the offense types found in a record, differences in the number of events can affect analyses of offense-switching patterns.

This potential source of bias in analyses of switching was illustrated most dramatically in the earlier examination of escalation effects. Without controls for differences in the number of arrests for different individuals, average seriousness appeared to de-

---

[37]This tendency to oversample more active offenders holds under a variety of conditions. The only exception is those instances in which selection risk per offense committed is strongly inversely related to individual offending patterns with high-rate or long-career offenders having a much lower risk of official contact per offense than low-rate or short-career offenders.

cline with each additional arrest for adults. The analysis, however, was not based on the same sample of individuals at each arrest. Offenders with only a few arrests contributed to the average seriousness of early arrests, but seriousness on successive arrests was increasingly based on offenders with larger numbers of arrests. Thus, the observed decline in seriousness could reflect differences among offenders, and not a change as individual offending progresses. The key role of population heterogeneity was confirmed when controls for this sample-selection effect were introduced. Controlling for the number of arrests in a history, average seriousness was generally stable on successive arrests for adults. Average seriousness, however, was lower for adult offenders who had larger numbers of arrests.

Variations in record length among offenders is a similar concern in estimating switching probabilities more generally. More active offenders, with their larger numbers of arrests, will contribute disproportionately to estimates of a single, summary transition matrix that combines all offense switches together. To the extent that switching patterns vary with record length among offenders, the combined matrix estimate will be biased to reflect the pattern of offenders who have long records. This potential bias is partially controlled by estimating separate transition matrices for each offense switch; variations in switching with record length will be evident in the variability (nonstationarity) across the separate matrices. These separate matrices, however, are subject to the same sample-selection biases affecting average seriousness. Successive matrices are based on an increasingly more selected sample of offenders—those with larger numbers of arrests. Thus any trends in switching observed over successive matrices may reflect population heterogeneity and not a progression in switching during individual criminal careers.

The potential role of selection effects in successive transition matrices was illustrated in the reanalysis above of the data on juvenile offenders in Pima County. The reanalysis found nonstationarity in switching probabilities from juvenile status of-

fenses, with more desistance on early transitions compared with later transitions, and more switches to personal and "other" crimes on later transitions compared with early transitions. This pattern suggests an escalation in seriousness for status offenders.

The successive transition matrices, however, were not estimated using the same sample of offenders on each transition. Offenders with only a few police contacts were selected out of the analysis through early desistance. Thus, the apparent trend to more serious offending for status offenders may reflect a selection effect in which status offenders with a small number of contacts were also less serious offenders. These less serious offenders, however, only entered the estimates of early transition matrices. Later transition estimates were based increasingly on status offenders who had larger numbers of police contacts. If these more active status offenders were also more serious offenders generally, the trend to more serious offending observed on successive transitions would reflect this population heterogeneity and not a tendency to move to more serious offenses for individual status offenders.

As in the analysis of trends in average seriousness, the effects of this form of population heterogeneity can be explored by estimating successive transition matrices after controlling for the number of arrests in a history. This, however, places increased demands on the sample size necessary for analysis.

Population heterogeneity, especially with respect to record length, represents a strong competing hypothesis in accounting for differences in offense patterns observed in the studies reviewed here. In comparing adult and juvenile offenders, for example, greater specialization was observed for adult offenders than for juvenile offenders. In the juvenile years, offender samples may consist of some casual offenders whose offending is exploratory and ends quickly and of other more committed offenders who are specialized in their offending. As exploratory offenders leave offending in the juvenile years, adult samples would consist more heavily of committed, specialized offenders. In this event, the difference in specialization for adults and juveniles might arise from differences across offenders and not from a developmental process toward greater specialization as offenders get older. Sorting out these rival hypotheses requires analyses of offense-switching patterns for a common sample of offenders who begin offending as juveniles and persist into adulthood.

Aside from the potential distortions associated with variations in the number of events in criminal histories, variations in the length of observation periods may also affect the switching pattern observed. Offenders' frequency rates and career lengths, as well as their incarceration experiences, all affect the length of intervals between events. Inter-arrest intervals, as noted, will be short when individual arrest rates are high. When individual arrest rates are low, by contrast, or when long periods of incarceration are likely to substantially reduce the time at risk for subsequent arrests, inter-arrest intervals are more likely to be long, and these intervals will only be observed in longer careers. To the extent that frequency rates, career length, and incarceration risk vary across different offense types, the associated differences in intervals between events for different offense types can affect the mix of offense types observed in switching data. In particular, offense types characterized by short inter-event intervals are more likely to be observed when observation periods are short. Correspondingly longer observation periods are required if offense types characterized by longer inter-event intervals are to be adequately represented.

Variations in inter-arrest intervals for different offense types may affect the estimates of transition matrices. All the analyses of offense switching reviewed here have suppressed differences in the time intervals between events. Switching events were defined by the occurrence of a next arrest (or police contact), and switching events were aggregated regardless of the differences in the time interval to that event. The pattern of switching among offense types, however, may vary with the length of inter-arrest intervals.

Building on the differences in frequency rates and career lengths observed for different offense types, for example, it might be expected that switches to property offenses—with their higher individual frequencies and short careers—would be more likely when the intervals between events are short. Conversely, when intervals are long, greater switching to violent offenses—with their lower frequencies and longer careers—would be expected.

The data on offense switching between arrests for adults in Washington, D.C., and Michigan are used here to explore these potential differences. The estimated transition probabilities for selected offense types for Washington, D.C., arrestees are presented in Table 54. The significance of differences in switching was assessed using the ASRs of Goodman's (1962, 1968) contingency table approach. Taking one offense type at a time, a test was made of whether switching patterns from that offense were independent of the length of the interval to the next arrest. Although not presented here, results similar to those for Washington, D.C., arrestees were also found for both whites and blacks in the Detroit and southern Michigan samples.

Systematic variations in switching were found with differences in the length of intervals between arrests. Consistent with the lower frequency and longer careers in aggravated assault, the most persistent difference was an increased tendency to switch to aggravated assault as the length of the interval between arrests increased (indicated by a shift from negative to positive ASRs). Switches to robbery, with its higher frequency rate and shorter careers, were more likely after short intervals (indicated by a shift from positive to negative ASRs). A decline in specialization as intervals increased was also observed for robbery and burglary (indicated by a shift from positive to negative ASRs).

Alternatives to Simple Markov Models

A simple Markov property was invoked in several analyses of offense-switching patterns. Under this Markov assumption, offense switching depends, at most, on the

TABLE B-54 Variations in Offense-Type Switching with Length of
Interval Between Arrests for Washington, D.C., Arrestees

Offense Type on kth Arrest	Length of Interval Between Arrests	Probability of Offense Type on k + 1st Arrest			Prevalence of Offense Type on kth Arrest (percent)
		Aggravated Assault	Robbery	Burglary	
Aggravated assault	≤1 year	.300 (NS)ᵃ	.086 (2.7)**	.059 (NS)	11.6
(χ^2 = 51.03,* 33 d.f.)	>1 year and ≤2 years	.269 (NS)	.070 (NS)	.065 (NS)	16.9
	>2 years and ≤4 years	.259 (NS)	.026 (-2.1)*	.043 (NS)	18.5
	≥4 years	.385 (3.0)**	.049 (-1.8)	.045 (NS)	19.3
Robbery	≤1 year	.109 (-2.7)**	.312 (3.7)***	.074 (NS)	10.4
(χ^2 = 57.03,** 33 d.f.)	>1 year and ≤2 years	.133 (NS)	.301 (NS)	.062 (NS)	10.3
	>2 years and <4 years	.143 (NS)	.214 (NS)	.071 (NS)	8.9
	≥4 years	.195 (3.0)**	.134 (-4.4)***	.101 (NS)	10.8
Burglary	≤1 year	.071 (-3.8)***	.083 (NS)	.316 (4.8)***	10.7
(χ^2 = 68.96,*** 33 d.f.)	>1 year and ≤2 years	.113 (NS)	.056 (NS)	.185 (-2.6)**	11.3
	>2 years and <4 years	.067 (NS)	.067 (NS)	.225 (NS)	14.2
	≥4 years	.180 (4.7)***	.087 (NS)	.174 (-3.5)***	12.5

ᵃOnly ASRs significant at the .10 level or better (two-tailed test using standard normal distribution) are reported in parentheses. All other nonsignificant values are indicated by NS.

*Significant at the .05 level.
**Significant at the .01 level.
***Significant at the .001 level.

offense type of the current arrest. The limited tests available for assessing the adequacy of the Markov assumption suggest that offense switching is not adequately modeled as a first-order Markov chain. Dependence on prior offense types appears to extend beyond the current offense type and results in greater specialization than would be expected in this simple Markov model.

The tendency for observations to bunch on the diagonals of transition matrices has been observed in a variety of social processes, most notably residential migration and status mobility. Failure of simple Markov models in these processes is often attributed to population heterogeneity, and a variety of alternative modeling strategies have been proposed (see, for example, Singer and Spilerman, 1978, for a discussion of the various approaches). In its most common form, the population is presumed to vary in its tendency to stay in the same state on successive transitions. In the case of offense switching, offenders would vary with respect to offense specialization. At one extreme, some offenders might be highly specialized and thereby have a high likelihood of repeatedly engaging in the same offense type. At the other extreme would be generalists, whose offending would vary randomly over many different offense types.

Various alternative models have been proposed to address population heterogeneity satisfactorily. Many of these models preserve the Markov property for switching within different population subgroups, but specify different transition matrices for each subgroup. The non-Markov aggregate transition matrix reflects the combined effect of these separate Markov transition processes. The simplest, and one of the earliest, approaches to population heterogeneity was the "mover-stayer" model first introduced by Blumen, Kogan, and McCarthy (1955).[38] If this model is applied to offense switching, the population of offenders would be

---

[38]Various later extensions and tests of the mover-stayer model are available in the research literature; see, for example, Goodman (1961), White (1970), and Spilerman (1972b).

TABLE B-55 Distribution of Youths with Over Half of Their Police Contacts in a Single Offense Category

Offense Type	White (percent)	Nonwhite (percent)
Personal injury	1.5	1.5
Personal property	1.5	0.9
Impersonal property	34.3	32.5
Other	28.4	14.9
No "specialization"	34.3	50.1
Total	100	100
	(N = 134)	(N = 335)

NOTE: Cook County Juvenile Court sample of youths with at least five police contacts.

SOURCE: Bursik (1980:Table 5).

---

divided into two groups—the "stayers," who would always repeat the same offense type, and the "movers," who would switch among offense types according to a common Markov transition process. Switching by both groups can easily be combined and various predictions of expected future switching patterns for the aggregate population are available.

The finding of specialization in a variety of offender samples suggests that this partition of offenders into specialists and generalists may be a fruitful approach to modeling offense switching. While there is evidence of specialization in all samples, some offenders seem to be more likely to specialize than others. As indicated in Table 55, specialization within aggregate offense categories was widespread among Cook County juvenile offenders. For offenders with at least five police contacts as juveniles, one-half of the nonwhites and two-thirds of the whites in the sample had over 50 percent of all their contacts in a single offense category. The distribution of specialists in different offense categories reflects the relative distribution over these offense categories generally.

On the basis of data on adult arrestees in Washington, D.C., the proportion of specialists varies considerably for different offense types. As indicated in Table 56, spe-

TABLE B-56 Proportion of Specialists Found Among Adult Arrestees in Washington, D.C.

Offense Type of Arrest in 1973	Number of Arrestees	Percent with Prior Arrests for Index Offenses	Percent Specialists Among Those with Prior Index Arrests	Percent Specialists Among All Arrestees
Murder	277	65.0	21.1	13.7
Rape	253	63.3	22.0	13.9
Robbery	1,230	65.2	53.4	34.8
Aggravated assault	1,930	59.6	57.0	34.0
Burglary	902	55.5	44.5	24.7
Auto theft	496	52.4	35.7	18.7

NOTE: "Specialists" are arrestees with prior arrests for the same charge as the sampled arrest in 1973. For arrestees with only one prior arrest for an index offense, that one prior index arrest is for the same charge as the sampled arrest. With two or more prior index arrests, the preponderance of the prior arrests are for the same charge as the 1973 arrest. Under the "predominance" criterion, about one-half of all index arrests in a record--including the 1973 sampled arrest-- must be for the current charge. For a record with a total of 3, 4, or 5 index arrests, including the sampled arrest, at least 2 must be for the current charge. For a total of 6 or 7 index arrests, at least 3 must be for the current charge. More generally, if n is equal to the number of prior index arrests of any type, and m is equal to the number of prior index arrests of the same type as the current arrest, a person satisfies the "specialist" criterion if for $n > 3$, $m \geq (n - 1)/2$ for n odd or $m \geq (n - 2)/2$ for n even, and for $n = 2$, $m \geq n/2 = 1$.

SOURCE: Derived from data in Cohen (1982:Table 3-3).

cialists within an offense type were most often found among offenders arrested for robbery and aggravated assault. One-third of all arrestees in these offense types had prior records and a predominance of arrests for the same offense type. Specialists in robbery and aggravated assault represented over one-half of those arrestees who had any prior arrests for index offenses. Specialists were least prevalent in murder and rape, accounting for only 14 percent of all arrestees for these offense types. This lower prevalence of specialists was not due to a lower likelihood of any prior arrests. Two-thirds of the arrestees for murder and rape had prior arrests for index offenses, but less than one-quarter of those recidivistic arrestees were specialists in those offense types.

A similar mix of specialists and generalists was evident among respondents to the second Rand inmate survey. As indicated in Table 57, diversity in offending was very common; most inmates indicated that they committed several different offense types during the observation period. Nevertheless, more than one-quarter of all respondents reported that they committed only one offense type. Only robbery was rarely committed as a sole offense type. Even among the category of "low-level robbers," 64 percent of the respondents (N = 153) also reported that they committed burglary and theft crimes during the 1- to 2-year observation period.

The simple mover-stayer model and variations of the model that permit a continuous distribution of differences among offenders (see, for example, Spilerman, 1972b) rest on an assumption of population heterogeneity.

The transition process varies across the population, but within any subgroup the transition process is invariant over time. An alternative explanation offered for the tendency of switching processes to bunch on the diagonals explicitly incorporates variability in the process with time. This is most often done by allowing for duration dependence in the switching process.

In analyses of residential migration and status mobility, duration dependence reflects a phenomenon of cumulative inertia (McGinnis, 1968), whereby the probability of remaining in the same state increases as

TABLE B-57 Combinations of Offense Types Committed by Respondents to the Second Rand Inmate Survey

Combinations	Offenses Reported During Observation Period					Number of Respondents	Percent
	Robbery	Assault[a]	Burglary	Theft[b]	Drug Deals		
Violent predators (robbery-assault-drug deals)	+	+	?	?	+	306	15.0
Robber-assaulters	+	+	?	?	0	160	7.8
Robber-dealers	+	0	?	?	+	188	9.2
Low-level robbers	+	0	?	?	0	240	11.8
Mere assaulters	0	+	0	0	0	105	5.1
Burglar-dealers	0	??	+	?	+	199	9.8
Low-level burglars	0	0	+	0	0	171	8.4
Property and drug offenders	0	??	0	+	+	128	6.3
Low-level property offenders	0	0	0	+	0	168	8.2
Drug dealers	0	0	0	0	+	112	5.5
Total[c]						1,777	87.1

NOTE: + Respondents commit this crime by definition. 0 Respondents do not commit this crime by definition. ? Respondents may or may not commit this crime; analysis shows that nearly all in this category do. ?? Respondents may or may not commit this crime; analysis shows that most in this category do not.

[a]Assault includes homicide arising out of assault or robbery.
[b]Theft includes auto theft, fraud, forgery, and credit card crimes.
[c]The remaining 12.9 percent did not report committing any of the offense types surveyed. Respondents with missing data (150 out of 2,190) were excluded in calculation of the percentages.

SOURCE: Chaiken and Chaiken (1982a:Table 2.5).

time already spent in that state increases. Switches to a different state are more likely the shorter the duration in any state. In offense switching, duration dependence is reflected in variations in switching patterns with increases in the length of the intervals between arrests. The preliminary analysis of the role of different intervals (Table 54) suggests that duration dependence may be a factor in offense switching. Contrary to the cumulative inertia observed in studies of mobility, however, repeating the same offense type seems to be more likely when intervals between arrests are short. The tendency to specialize appears to decrease for longer intervals.

A variety of modeling strategies have been proposed for incorporating duration dependence. These include expanding the state space to include duration explicitly as a defining attribute (Cox and Miller, 1965; McGinnis, 1968), introducing independent variables into Markov chain models (Coleman, 1964; Spilerman, 1972a), and semi-Markov processes (Ginsberg, 1971). (See Hoem, 1972, for a review of various models that incorporate duration depen-

dence.) These approaches may be fruitfully applied to analyses of offense switching as well.

The analytic treatment of offense switching is currently in the earliest stages of development. Only the simplest first-order Markov models have been explored, and then in very limited ways. Analysis in this area may gain substantially from the many developments in modeling already available in other fields, especially the treatment of mobility processes in demography and sociology. Attempts to model offense switching may also benefit from expanding the process to include consideration of the role of intervening, but undetected, offenses in the observed switching process between arrests. Such models would characterize switching between arrests in terms of the basic switching process between offenses committed and the selection process that transforms some offenses into observed arrests. Alternatives to Markov formulations, with their limited focus on successive events, might also be fruitfully explored to accommodate the role of prior history in future offense seriousness.

Appendix C

Workshop on Research on Criminal Careers: Program and Participants

Woods Hole, Massachusetts
July 23–25, 1984

JULY 23

"Characterizing the Offending Sequence: Prevalence, Duration, and Desistance"

Jeffrey Roth, National Research Council

Christy Visher, National Research Council

Discussants: David Farrington, Institute of Criminology, Cambridge University, England

Robert Gordon, Department of Sociology, Johns Hopkins University

Lee Robins, Washington University Medical Center, St. Louis

"Characterizing the Offending Sequence: Individual Crime Rates, Crime Mix, and Crime-Type Switching"

Jacqueline Cohen, School of Urban and Public Affairs, Carnegie-Mellon University

Discussants: Arnold Barnett, Massachusetts Institute of Technology

David Farrington, Institute of Criminology, Cambridge University, England

"Alternative Approaches to Observing the Individual Offending Sequence"

Joseph Weis, Center for Law and Justice, University of Washington

Discussants: Delbert Elliott, Behavioral Research Institute, Boulder, Colorado

Albert Reiss, Department of Sociology, Yale University

NOTE: Affiliations listed are those at the time of the workshop.

"Measuring Criminal Career Parameters in Recidivism Studies"

Jan Chaiken, Rand Corporation, Santa Monica, California
Marcia Chaiken, Rand Corporation, Santa Monica, California

Discussants: Arnold Barnett, Massachusetts Institute of Technology
Daniel Smith, Department of History, University of Illinois at Chicago Circle

"Dynamic Models of Criminal Careers"

Christopher Flinn, Department of Economics, University of Wisconsin

Discussants: Jan Chaiken, Rand Corporation, Santa Monica, California
Arthur Goldberger, Department of Economics, University of Wisconsin

"Random Parameter Stochastic Process Models of Criminal Careers"

John Lehoczky, Department of Statistics, Carnegie-Mellon University

Discussants: Jan Chaiken, Rand Corporation, Santa Monica, California
Arthur Goldberger, Department of Economics, University of Wisconsin

JULY 24

"Methodological Issues in Making Predictions"

John Copas, Department of Statistics, University of Birmingham, England
Roger Tarling, Home Office Research and Planning Unit, London, England

Discussants: Rolf Loeber, Western Psychiatric Institute and Clinic, University of Pittsburgh
Charles Manski, Department of Economics, University of Wisconsin

"Accuracy of Prediction Models"

Stephen Gottfredson, Department of Criminal Justice, Temple University
Don Gottfredson, School of Criminal Justice, Rutgers University

Discussants: John Monahan, School of Law, University of Virginia
Franklin Zimring, Earl Warren Legal Institute, University of California, Berkeley

"Empirical Comparisons of Prediction-Based Selection Rules with Decisions Made in Current Practice"

William Rhodes, INSLAW, Inc., Washington, D.C.

Discussants: Stephen Gottfredson, Department of Criminal Justice, Temple University
Albert Reiss, Department of Sociology, Yale University

"The Rand Inmate Survey: A Reanalysis"

Christy Visher, National Research Council

Discussants: Jan Chaiken, Rand Corporation, Santa Monica, California
Peter Greenwood, Rand Corporation, Santa Monica, California
Arthur Goldberger, Department of Economics, University of Wisconsin

"Juvenile and Criminal Court Influences on Criminal Careers"

Peter Greenwood, Rand Corporation, Santa Monica, California
Franklin Zimring, Earl Warren Legal Institute, University of California, Berkeley

Discussants: Lloyd Ohlin, Department of Sociology (emeritus), Harvard University
James Q. Wilson, Department of Government, Harvard University

"The Relationship of Alcohol Abuse to Criminal Career Parameters"

James Collins, Research Triangle Institute, Research Triangle Park, North Carolina

Discussants: John Kaplan, School of Law, Stanford University
Lee Robins, Washington University Medical Center, St. Louis
Marvin Wolfgang, Center for Studies in Criminology and Criminal Law, University of Pennsylvania

"The Relationship of Drug Use to Criminal Career Parameters"

Eric Wish, Narcotic and Drug Research, Inc., New York
Bruce Johnson, Narcotic and Drug Research, Inc., New York

Discussants: John Kaplan, School of Law, Stanford University
Lee Robins, Washington University Medical Center, St. Louis
Marvin Wolfgang, Center for Studies in Criminology and Criminal Law, University of Pennsylvania

JULY 25

"Interactive Effects Between the Criminal Justice System and Criminal Career Parameters"

Marcia Chaiken, Rand Corporation, Santa Monica, California
Jan Chaiken, Rand Corporation, Santa Monica, California

Discussants: Harold Rose, Department of Urban Affairs, University of Wisconsin
Franklin Zimring, Earl Warren Legal Institute, University of California, Berkeley

"Group Influences on Criminal Career Parameters"

Albert Reiss, Department of Sociology, Yale University

Discussants: Robert Gordon, Department of Sociology, Johns Hopkins University
Lloyd Ohlin, Department of Sociology (emeritus), Harvard University

"Operational Effects of Introducing Prediction-Based Decision Rules"

> Jonathan Casper, Department of Political Science, University of Illinois

> *Discussants*: Allen Andrews, Director of Public Safety, Peoria, Illinois
> Andrew Sonner, State's Attorney, Montgomery County, Maryland
> Reggie Walton, Associate Judge, Superior Court of the District of Columbia

"The Justice of Assessing Dangerousness in Criminal Justice System Operations"

> Mark Moore, Kennedy School of Government, Harvard University

> *Discussants*: John Monahan, School of Law, University of Virginia
> Norval Morris, School of Law, University of Chicago

Appendix *D*

Biographical Sketches, Panel Members and Staff

ALFRED BLUMSTEIN is J. Erik Jonsson professor of Urban Systems and Operations Research and director of the Urban Systems Institute in the School of Urban and Public Affairs, Carnegie-Mellon University. He also serves as the chair of the Pennsylvania Commission on Crime and Delinquency, the state criminal justice planning agency for Pennsylvania. He served as director of the Task Force on Science and Technology for the President's Commission on Law Enforcement and the Administration of Justice (1966–1967), as chair of the National Research Council's Committee on Research on Law Enforcement and the Administration of Justice (1981–1984), and as chair of that committee's panels on research on deterrent and incapacitative effects (1976–1978) and on sentencing (1980–1982). He is a fellow of the American Association for the Advancement of Science and of the American Society of Criminology and is a member of the Scientific Committee of the International Society of Criminology. He has been president of the Operations Research Society of America (1977–1978) and was recently awarded its Kimball Medal. He is an associate editor of several journals in operations research and in criminology. He received a bachelor's degree in engineering physics and a Ph.D. degree in operations research, both from Cornell University.

ALLEN H. ANDREWS, JR., is superintendent of police of Peoria, Illinois. He has served on many professional advisory panels, including the Law Enforcement Assistance Administration's National Advisory Committee on Criminal Justice Standards and Goals, the Bureau of Justice Statistics' Advisory Panel on the National Crime Survey Redesign, and the Advisory Panel to the Federal Bureau of Investigation on the Uniform Crime Report redesign. He was also appointed by the governor to serve as executive director of the Illinois Law Enforcement Commission, and he was a U.S. delegate to the Fifth United Nations Congress on the Prevention of Crime and Treatment of Offenders. He is a member of the Illinois Association of Chiefs of Police, the Central Illinois Police Training Center Board of Directors, and the Police Executive Research Forum and is vice-chair of the YMCA Board of Directors in Peoria, Illinois.

423

He received an A.B. degree in political science from the University of Illinois and an M.S. degree in law enforcement and public safety administration from Michigan State University.

DELBERT S. ELLIOTT is director of the Behavioral Research Institute and professor of sociology at the University of Colorado. His research concerns adolescent problem behavior (delinquency, drug use, runaway, mental health problems), domestic violence, and the evaluation of delinquency prevention and treatment programs. He is coauthor of *Delinquency and Dropout* (1974), *The Social Psychology of Runaway* (1978), and *Explaining Delinquency and Drug Use* (1985). He served as chair of the Crime and Violent Behavior Review Committee for the National Institute of Mental Health (1984–1986). He is a member of the American Society of Criminology and the American Sociological Association. He received a B.A. degree from Pomona College and M.A. and Ph.D. degrees from the University of Washington, all in sociology.

DAVID P. FARRINGTON is lecturer in criminology at Cambridge University, England. His major research interest is in the longitudinal study of delinquency and crime, and he has also published empirical research on victimization and police recording of crime, observing shoplifting, prison overcrowding, magistrates' sentencing, juvenile diversion, and the experimental study of stealing. He has authored or edited eight books, the most recent being *Prediction in Criminology* (1985), *Reactions to Crime* (1985), *Aggression and Dangerousness* (1985), and *Understanding and Controlling Crime* (1986). In 1984 he received the Sellin-Glueck Award of the American Society of Criminology. He is chair of the Division of Criminological and Legal Psychology of the British Psychological Society and a member of the National Parole Board of England and Wales. He was on the organizing committee of the British Society of Criminology and is currently on the editorial boards of several journals. He received B.A., M.A., and Ph.D. degrees in experimental psychology from Cambridge University.

JOHN KAPLAN is the Jackson Eli Reynolds professor of law at the Stanford University Law School. His fields are criminal law, evidence, and criminology. He has written on a variety of topics in the criminal justice system, including work on drug control. He is the author of *Marijuana: The New Prohibition* (1970), *Criminal Justice* (1973, with Jerome Skolnick), *The Hardest Drug: Heroin and Public Policy* (1983), among other works. He received an A.B. degree in physics and an L.L.B. degree, both from Harvard University.

ROLF LOEBER is assistant professor in psychiatry at the Western Psychiatric Institute and Clinic, School of Medicine, University of Pittsburgh. He is also codirector of the Child Conduct Problem Program. His research and publications reflect his interest in the early part of criminal careers, the development of conduct problems in children, familial influences, and the predictability of delinquent behavior over time. He received an M.A. degree from the University of Amsterdam in Holland in clinical psychology and a Ph.D. degree in clinical psychology from Queen's University, Kingston, Ontario, Canada.

CHARLES F. MANSKI is professor of economics at the University of Wisconsin. His research concerns econometric methods and empirical economics, with emphasis on the analysis of individual-choice behavior. He is coauthor of *College Choice in America* (1983, with D. Wise) and coeditor of *Structural Analysis of Discrete Data* (1980, with D. McFadden). He is a fellow of the Econometric Society. He received B.S. and Ph.D. degrees in economics from the Massachusetts Institute of Technology.

NORVAL MORRIS is Julius Kreeger professor of law and criminology at the University of Chicago, and he previously served as dean of the Law School. His research concerns the criminal justice system. He is the author of *The Future of Imprisonment* (1974) and *Madness and the Criminal Law* (1982). He is a fellow of the American Bar Foundation, a member of the American Academy of Arts and Sciences, of the Police Board of the City of Chicago, and of the Board of Governors of the Chicago Bar Foundation. He received L.L.B. and L.L.M. degrees from the University of Melbourne, Australia, and a Ph.D. degree in law and criminology from the University of London.

ALBERT J. REISS, JR., is the William Graham Sumner professor of sociology at the Institution for Social and Police Studies and a lecturer in law at Yale University. He has served as a consultant to the President's Commission on Law Enforcement and the Administration of Justice (1966–1967), the National Advisory Commission on Civil Disorders (1967–1968), and the National Commission for the Protection of Human Subjects in Biomedical and Behavioral Research (1976). Under presidential appointment, he served as a member of the National Advisory Commission on Juvenile Justice and Delinquency Prevention (1975–1978). He is a past president of the American Society of Criminology and is serving as president of the Scientific Commission of the International Society of Criminology. He is a fellow of the American Academy of Arts and Sciences, the American Statistical Association, and the American Society of Criminology. He has authored or edited 12 books including *Social Characteristics of Urban and Rural Communities* (1950, with O. Duncan), *The Police and the Public* (1971), *Indicators of Crime and Criminal Justice: Quantitative Studies* (1980, with S. Fienberg), and *Communities and Crime* (1986, with M. Tonry). He received a Ph.D. degree in sociology from the University of Chicago, an L.L.D. (honoris causa) degree from the City University of New York, and a Docteur Honoris Causa from the Université de Montréal.

LEE N. ROBINS is professor of sociology in psychiatry at the Washington University School of Medicine, St. Louis. Her research has centered on childhood predictors of antisocial personality, alcohol and drug abuse, and on the rates of mental disorder in the community. She is a fellow of the American College of Epidemiology and a member of the American College of Neuropsychopharmacology, the American Psychopathological Association, and the Institute of Medicine. She received B.A., M.A., and Ph.D. degrees in sociology from Radcliffe College (Harvard University).

HAROLD M. ROSE is professor of geography and urban affairs at the University of Wisconsin, Milwaukee. His research is concerned with the black homicide risk in urban environments and patterns of black residential change. He is a member of the Association of American Geographers and the Population Association of America, and he is on the editorial boards of *Urban Geography* and *Urban Affairs Quarterly*. He received a B.S. degree from Tennessee State University and M.A. and Ph.D. degrees in geography from Ohio State University.

DANIEL SCOTT SMITH is professor of history at the University of Illinois, Chicago. His research involves historical demography, social history, and quantitative methods. He is the editor of *Historical Methods* and is a member of the Social Science History Association, the Population Association of America, and the American Historical Association. He received a B.A. degree from the University of Florida and M.A. and Ph.D. degrees in history from the University of California at Berkeley.

ANDREW L. SONNER is State's Attorney for Montgomery County, Maryland, now serving his fourth elected term. He is a past vice-president of the National District Attorneys' Association and has also served as a member of the executive committee of the board of directors. He has been president of the Maryland State's Attorneys' Association and is currently a member of its board of directors and he has served as a member of the Governor's Commission on Law Enforcement and the Administration of Justice. He designed and implemented "Operation Last Chance," an alternative sentencing program for juvenile offenders that received the National Association of Counties Achievement Award in 1984. He has held a number of positions in the American Bar Association and is currently a member of the Criminal Justice Section Council. He is the author of several articles on criminal law and procedure. He received B.A. and J.D. degrees from the American University.

REGGIE B. WALTON is an associate judge of the Superior Court of the District of Columbia. Previously, he was an Assistant U.S. Attorney for the District of Columbia and a staff attorney with the Philadelphia Defender Association. He is a member of the Joint Committee on Judicial Administration for the District of Columbia Courts, a member of the executive committee of the District of Columbia Counsel for Court Excellence, and a member of the D.C. Bar Association Criminal Instructions Committee. He received a B.A. degree in political science from West Virginia State College and a J.D. degree from Washington College of Law, the American University.

JAMES Q. WILSON is the Shattuck professor of government at Harvard University and the Collins professor of management at the University of California, Los Angeles. He is the author of several books on crime and law enforcement, including *Crime and Human Nature* (1985, with Richard J. Herrnstein), *Thinking About Crime* (revised edition, 1983), *The Investigators* (1978), and *Varieties of Police Behavior* (1966), and is editor of *Crime and Public Policy* (1983). He is chair of the board of directors of the Police Foundation and has served as a member of the Science Advisory Committee to the President's Commission on Law Enforcement and Administration of Justice (1966), chair of the National Advisory Council for Drug Abuse Prevention (1972–1973), and member of the Attorney General's Task Force on Violent Crime (1981). He received a B.A. degree from the University of Redlands and a Ph.D. degree in political science from the University of Chicago.

MARVIN E. WOLFGANG is professor of criminology and law and director of the Sellin Center for Studies in Criminology and Criminal Law at the University of Pennsylvania. He is currently the president of the American Academy of Political and Social Science. He has been president of the American Society of Criminology; associate secretary general of the International Society of Criminology; a consultant to the President's Commission on Law Enforcement and Administration of Justice; a member of the Panel on Social Indicators of the Department of Health, Education, and Welfare; director of research, Commission on the Causes and Prevention of Violence; member, Advisory Committee on Reform of the Federal Criminal Law; and member, National Commission on Obscenity and Pornography. He has authored or edited 11 books, including *Patterns in Criminal Homicide* (1958); *The Measurement of Delinquency* (with T. Sellin, 1964); *Delinquency in a Birth Cohort* (with R. Figlio and T. Sellin, 1972); and *Criminal Violence* (with N. Weiner, 1982). He received M.A. and Ph.D. degrees in sociology from the University of Pennsylvania.

JEFFREY A. ROTH, who served as the panel's study director, is the senior staff officer of the Committee on Research on Law Enforcement and the Administration of Justice. His interest is in the policy use of social research, especially in the areas of criminal careers, taxpayer compliance, and pretrial release. He is a member of the American Society of Criminology, the Law & Society Association, the American Economic Association, and the American Statistical Association. He received B.A., M.A., and Ph.D. degrees in economics from Michigan State University.

CHRISTY A. VISHER, who worked with the panel as a National Research Council Fellow, is research associate with the Committee on Research on Law Enforcement and the Administration of Justice. Her research is concerned with criminal careers, juror decision making, police arrest decisions, and public policy issues in criminal justice. She is a member of the American Sociological Association, the American Society of Criminology, and the Law & Society Association. She received a B.A. degree from Trinity University and M.A. and Ph.D. degrees in sociology from Indiana University.

JACQUELINE COHEN, who served as consultant to the panel, is associate director of the Urban Systems Institute and research associate in the School of Urban and Public Affairs, Carnegie-Mellon University. Her research concerns quantitative methods (including econometrics and stochastic processes), criminal careers, and incapacitation. She is a member of the Law & Society Association, the American Society of Criminology, the American Sociological Association, and the Academy of Criminal Justice Sciences. She received B.S. and M.A. degrees from the University of Pittsburgh and a Ph.D. degree in urban and public affairs from Carnegie-Mellon University.

References

Adler, F.
1975 *Sisters in Crime.* New York: McGraw-Hill.
Ahlstrom, W.M., and Havighurst, R.J.
1971 *400 Losers.* San Francisco, Calif.: Jossey-Bass.
Akers, R.L.
1964 Socio-economic status and delinquent behavior: a retest. *Journal of Research in Crime and Delinquency* 1:38–46.
Akers, R.L., Krohn, M.D., Lanza-Kaduce, L., and Radosevich, M.
1979 Social learning and deviant behavior: a specific test of a general theory. *American Sociological Review* 44:636–655.
Alexander, J.F., and Parsons, B.V.
1973 Short-term behavioral interventions with delinquent families: impact on family process and recidivism. *Journal of Abnormal Psychology* 81:219–225.
Anglin, M.D., and McGlothlin, W.H.
1984 Outcome of narcotic addict treatment in California. Pp. 106–128 in F.M. Tims and J.P. Ludford, eds., *Drug Abuse Treatment Evaluation: Strategies, Progress and Prospects.* Research Monograph No. 51. Rockville, Md.: National Institute on Drug Abuse.
Ares, H.M., Rankin, A., and Sturz, H.
1963 The Manhattan Bail Project. *New York University Law Review* 38:67–92.
Arnold, W.
1965 Continuities in research: scaling delinquent behavior. *Social Problems* 13:59–66.

Austin, R.
1978 Race, father-absence, and female delinquency. *Criminology* 15:487–504.
Avi-Itzhak, B., and Shinnar, R.
1973 Quantitative models in crime control. *Journal of Criminal Justice* 1:185–217.
Bachman, J.G., Kahn, R.L., Mednick, M.T., Davidson, T.N., and Johnston, L.D.
1967 *Youth in Transition: Volume I, Blueprint for a Longitudinal Study of Adolescent Boys.* Ann Arbor, Mich.: Institute for Social Research.
Bachman, J.G.
1970 *Youth in Transition: Volume II, The Impact of Family Background and Intelligence on Tenth-Grade Boys.* Ann Arbor, Mich.: Institute for Social Research.
Bachman, J.G., Green, S., and Wirtanen, I.D.
1971 *Youth in Transition: Volume III, Dropping Out: Problem or Symptom?* Ann Arbor, Mich.: Institute for Social Research.
Bachman, J.G., O'Malley, P.M., and Johnston, J.
1978 *Youth in Transition, Volume VI, Adolescence to Adulthood: Change and Stability in the Lives of Young Men.* Ann Arbor, Mich.: Institute for Social Research.
Bahr, S.J.
1979 Family determinants and effects of deviance. Pp. 615–643 in W. Burr, R. Hill, F.I. Nye, and I.L. Reiss, eds., *Contemporary Theories About the Family.* New York: Free Press.
Ball, J.C., Ross A., and Simpson, A.
1964 Incidence and estimated prevalence of re-

corded delinquency in a metropolitan area. *American Sociological Review* 29:90–93.

Ball, J.C., Rosen, L., Flueck, J.A., and Nurco, D.N.
1981 The criminality of heroin addicts when addicted and when off opiates. Pp. 39–66 in J.A. Inciardi, ed., *The Drugs-Crime Connection.* Beverly Hills, Calif.: Sage Publications.

Ball, J.C., Shaffer, J.W., and Nurco, D.N.
1983 The day-to-day criminality of heroin addicts in Baltimore: a study in the continuity of offense rates. *Drug and Alcohol Dependence* 12:119–142.

Barnett, A., and Lofaso, A.J.
1985 Selective incapacitation and the Philadelphia cohort data. *Journal of Quantitative Criminology* 1(1):3–36.

Baron, R., Feeney, F., and Thornton, W.
1973 Preventing delinquency through diversion. *Federal Probation* 37:13–18.

Barton, R.
1978 Exoffender Post-Release Performance Evaluation with Related Theoretical Topics in Variable Selection and Followup Intervals for Regression Models Using Grouped Censored Survival Data. Unpublished Ph.D. dissertation. School of Operations Research and Industrial Engineering, Cornell University.

Barton, R.R., and Turnbull, B.W.
1979 Failure rate regression models for evaluation of recidivism data. *Evaluation Quarterly* 3:629–641.
1981 A failure rate regression model for the study of recidivism. In J.A. Fox, ed., *Models in Quantitative Criminology.* New York: Academic Press.

Bases, N.C., and McDonald, W.F.
1972 Preventive Detention in the District of Columbia: The First Ten Months. Georgetown Institute of Criminal Law and Procedure, Washington, D.C.

Belkin, J., Blumstein, A., and Glass, W.
1973 Recidivism as a feedback process: an analytical model and empirical validation. *Journal of Criminal Justice* 1:7–26.

Berg, I., Consterdine, M., Hullin, R., and Tyrer, S.
1978 The effect of two randomly allocated court procedures on truancy. *British Journal of Criminology* 18:232–244.

Berg, I., Hullin, R., and McGuire, R.
1979 A randomly controlled trial of two court procedures in truancy. In D.P. Farrington, K. Hawkins, and S.M. Lloyd-Bostock, eds., *Psychology, Law, and Legal Process.* London: Macmillan.

Berger, A.S., and Simon, W.
1974 Black families and the Moynihan report: a research evaluation. *Social Problems* 22: 145–161.

Berk, R.A., Lenihan, K.J., and Rossi, P.H.
1980 Crime and poverty: some experimental evidence from ex-offenders. *American Sociological Review* 45:766–786.

Bernal, M.E., Klinnert, M.D., and Schultz, L.A.
1980 Outcome evaluation of behavioral parent training and client-centered parent counseling for children with conduct problems. *Journal of Applied Behavior Analysis* 13:669–676.

Bernstein, I.N., Kick, E., Lehng, J.T., and Schultz, B.
1977 Charge reduction: an intermediary stage in the process of labelling. *Social Forces* 56: 362–384.

Berntsen, K., and Christiansen, K.O.
1965 A resocialization experiment with short-term offenders. In K.O. Christiansen, ed., *Scandinavian Studies in Criminology, Volume 1.* London: Tavistock.

Berrueta-Clement, J.R., Jr., Schweinhart, L.J., Barnett, W.S., Epstein, A.S., and Weikart, D.P.
1984 *Changed Lives: The Effects of the Perry Preschool Program through Age 19.* Ypsilanti, Mich.: High/Scope Press.

Betsey, C.L., Hollister, R., Jr., and Papageorgiou, M.R., eds.
1985 *Youth Employment and Training Programs: The YEDPA Years.* Committee on Youth Employment Programs, Commission on Behavioral and Social Sciences and Education, National Research Council. Washington, D.C.: National Academy Press.

Binder, A.
no   Pre-Trial Intervention and Diversion
date   Project: 1973–1976. Final Report. California Council on Criminal Justice, Grant No. 1426. University of California, Irvine.

Binder, A., Monahan, J., and Newkirk, M.
1976 Diversion from the juvenile justice system and the prevention of delinquency. In J. Monahan, ed., *Community Mental Health and the Criminal Justice System.* New York: Pergamon.

Black, D.
1971 The production of crime rates. *American Sociological Review* 35:733–748.

Black, D., and Reiss, A.
1970 Police control of juveniles. *American Sociological Review* 35:63–77.

Bloom, H.S.
1979 Evaluating human service and criminal justice programs by modeling the probability and timing of recidivism. *Sociological Methods and Research* 8:179–208.

Blumen, I., Kogan, M., and McCarthy, P.J.
1955 The Industrial Mobility of Labor as a Probability Process. No. 6, Cornell Studies in Industrial and Labor Relations. Ithaca, N.Y.

Blumstein, A., and Cohen, J.
1979 Estimation of individual crime rates from arrest records. *Journal of Criminal Law and Criminology* 70:561–585.
1982 Analysis of Criminal Careers from an Incapacitative Perspective. Work in progress under grant from National Institute of Justice. (Grant 79-NI-AX-0121.) Unpublished results available from authors. School of Urban and Public Affairs, Carnegie-Mellon University, Pittsburgh, Pa.

Blumstein, A., and Cohen, J., with Hsieh, P.
1982 The Duration of Adult Criminal Careers. Final report submitted to National Institute of Justice, August 1982. School of Urban and Public Affairs, Carnegie-Mellon University, Pittsburgh, Pa.

Blumstein, A., and Graddy, E.
1982 Prevalence and recidivism in index arrests: a feedback model. *Law and Society Review* 16:265–290.

Blumstein, A., and Larson, R.
1969 Models of a total criminal justice system. *Operations Research* 17:199–232.
1971 Problems in modeling and measuring recidivism. *Journal of Research in Crime and Delinquency* 8:124–130.

Blumstein, A., and Moitra, S.
1980 The identification of "career criminals" from "chronic offenders" in a cohort. *Law and Policy Quarterly* 2(3):321–334.

Blumstein, A., Christensen, R., Johnson, S., and Larson, R.
1967 An analysis of crime and the overall criminal justice system. Chapter 5 in *Task Force Report: Science and Technology*. Report of the President's Commission on Law Enforcement and Administration of Justice. Washington, D.C.: U.S. Government Printing Office.

Blumstein, A., Cohen, J., and Das, S.
1985 Crime-Type Switching in Criminal Careers. Unpublished paper. Urban Systems Institute, School of Urban and Public Affairs, Carnegie-Mellon University, Pittsburgh, Pa.

Blumstein, A., Cohen, J., Martin, S., and Tonry, M., eds.
1983 *Research on Sentencing: The Search for Reform.* 2 vols. Panel on Research on Sentencing, Committee on Law Enforcement and the Administration of Justice, Commission on Behavioral and Social Sciences and Education, National Research Council. Washington, D.C.: National Academy Press.

Blumstein, A., Cohen, J., and Nagin, D., eds.
1978 *Deterrence and Incapacitation: Estimating the Effects of Criminal Sanctions on Crime Rates.* Panel on Research on Deterrent and Incapacitative Effects, Committee on Research on Law Enforcement and Criminal Justice, Assembly of Behavioral and Social Sciences, National Research Council. Washington, D.C.: National Academy of Sciences.

Blumstein, A., Farrington, D.P., and Moitra, S.
1985 Delinquency careers: innocents, amateurs, and persisters. Pp. 187–222 in N. Morris and M. Tonry, eds., *Crime and Justice: An Annual Review of Research, Volume 6.* Chicago, Ill.: University of Chicago Press.

Bock, E.W., and Frazier, C.E.
1977 Official standards versus actual criteria in bond dispositions. *Journal of Criminal Justice* 5:321–328.

Boland, B., and Wilson, J.Q.
1978 Age, crime and punishment. *The Public Interest* 51(Spring):22–34.

Boland, B., Brady, E., Tyson, H., and Bassler, J.
1983 *The Prosecution of Felony Arrests, 1979.* Bureau of Justice Statistics. Washington, D.C.: U.S. Department of Justice.

Bonger, W.A.
1916 *Criminality and Economic Conditions.* Boston, Mass.: Little, Brown.

Booth, E.
1929 *Stealing Through Life.* New York: Knopf.

Bordua, D.
1958 Juvenile delinquency and anomie: an attempt at replication. *Social Problems* 6:230–238.

Bradburn, N.M., and Sudman, S.
1979 *Improving Interviewing Method and Questionnaire Design.* San Francisco: Jossey-Bass.

Brosi, K.B.
1979 *A Cross-City Comparison of Felony Case Processing.* Washington, D.C.: Institute for Law and Social Research.

Bry, B.H.
1982 Reducing the incidence of adolescent problems through preventive intervention: one- and five-year follow-ups. *American Journal of Community Psychology* 10:265–276.

Bry, B.H., and George, F.E.
1979 Evaluating and improving prevention programs: a strategy from drug abuse. *Evaluation and Program Planning* 2:127–136.
1980 The preventive effects of early intervention on the attendance and grades of urban ado-

lescents. *Professional Psychology* 11:252–260.

Bureau of the Census
1981 *Statistical Abstract of the United States: 1981*. Washington, D.C.: U.S. Department of Commerce.
1983 *Statistical Abstract of the United States 1983*. Washington, D.C.: U.S. Department of Commerce.

Bureau of Justice Statistics
1979a *Census of Jails and Survey of Jail Inmates 1978*. Preliminary report, National Prisoner Statistics Bulletin. Washington, D.C.: U.S. Department of Justice.
1979b *Profile of State Prison Inmates: Sociodemographic Findings from the 1974 Survey of Inmates of State Correctional Facilities*. National Prisoner Statistics Bulletin. Washington, D.C.: U.S. Department of Justice.
1980a *Criminal Victimization of New York State Residents*. Washington, D.C.: U.S. Department of Justice.
1980b *Prisoners in State and Federal Institutions on December 31, 1978*. National Prisoner Statistics Bulletin. Washington, D.C.: U.S. Department of Justice.
1981a *Census of Jails 1978, Volumes I-IV*. Washington, D.C.: U.S. Department of Justice.
1981b *Criminal Victimization of California Residents*. Washington, D.C.: U.S. Department of Justice.
1981c *Survey of Inmates of State Correctional Facilities, 1979*. U.S. Department of Justice. Ann Arbor, Mich.: Inter-University Consortium for Political and Social Research.
1982a *Criminal Victimization in the United States, 1980*. Washington, D.C.: U.S. Department of Justice.
1982b *Prisons and Prisoners*. Bureau of Justice Statistics Bulletin. Washington, D.C.: U.S. Government Printing Office.
1983 *Criminal Victimization in the United States: 1973–82 Trends*. Bureau of Justice Statistics Special Report. Washington, D.C.: U.S. Department of Justice.
1984a *Criminal Victimization in the United States, 1982*. Bureau of Justice Statistics. Washington, D.C.: U.S. Government Printing Office.
1984b *The Prevalence of Guilty Pleas*. Report NCJ-95111. Washington, D.C.: U.S. Department of Justice.
1984c *Prison Admissions and Releases, 1981*. Washington, D.C.: U.S. Department of Justice.
1984d *Returning to Prison*. Special Report. Washington, D.C.: U.S. Department of Justice.
1984e *Time Served in Prison*. Special Report. Washington, D.C.: U.S. Department of Justice.

1985 *State Criminal Records Repositories*. Bureau of Justice Statistics Technical Report, October 1985. Washington, D.C.: U.S. Department of Justice.

Burgess, E.W.
1928 Factors determining success or failure on parole. In A.A. Bruce, E.W. Burgess, A.J. Harno, and J. Landeseo, eds., *The Workings of the Indeterminate Sentence Law and the Parole System in Illinois*. Springfield, Ill.: Illinois State Board of Parole.

Burkett, S., and Jensen, E.
1975 Conventional ties, peer influence, and the fear of apprehension: a study of adolescent marijuana use. *Sociological Quarterly* 16:522–533.

Bursik, R.J., Jr.
1980 The dynamics of specialization in juvenile offenses. *Social Forces* 58:851–864.

Byles, J.A., and Maurice, A.
1979 The juvenile services project: an experiment in delinquency control. *Canadian Journal of Criminology* 21:155–165.

Bynum, T.
1976 An Empirical Exploration of the Factors Influencing Release on Recognizance. Unpublished Ph.D. dissertation, School of Criminology, Florida State University.

Cadoret, R.J., and Cain, C.
1980 Sex differences in predictors of antisocial behavior in adoptees. *Archives of General Psychiatry* 37:1171–1175.

California Department of Corrections
1980 *California Prisoners—1980: Summary Statistics of Felon Prisoners and Parolees*. Sacramento, Calif.: California Department of Corrections.

California Department of Justice
1980 *Criminal Justice Profile 1979: Santa Clara County*. Bureau of Criminal Statistics and Special Services. Sacramento, Calif.: California Department of Justice.

Cantor, D., and Land, K.C.
1985 Unemployment and crime rates in the post-World War II United States: a theoretical and empirical analysis. *American Sociological Review* 50:317–332.

Carr-Hill, G.A., and Carr-Hill, R.A.
1972 Reconviction as a process. *British Journal of Criminology* 12:35–43.

Carroll, J.S., and Payne, J.W.
1977a Crime seriousness, recidivism risk, and causal attribution in judgments of prison terms by students and experts. *Journal of Applied Psychology* 62:592–602.
1977b Judgments about crime and the criminal: a model and a method for investigating parole

decisions. In B. Sales, ed., *Perspectives in Law and Psychology, Volume I: Criminal Justice System*. New York: Plenum.

Cernkovich, S., and Giordano, P.
1979 A comparative analysis of male and female delinquency. *Sociological Quarterly* 20: 131–145.

Cernkovich, S.A., Giordano, P.C., and Pugh, M.D.
1983 Chronic Offenders: The Missing Cases in Self-Report Delinquency Research. Paper presented at annual meeting of the American Society of Criminology, Denver, Colo. Department of Sociology, Bowling Green State University, Bowling Green, Ohio.

Chaiken, J.M., and Chaiken, M.
1982a *Varieties of Criminal Behavior*. Rand Report R-2814-NIJ. Santa Monica, Calif.: Rand Corporation.

Chaiken, J.M., and Chaiken, M., with Peterson, J.
1982b *Varieties of Criminal Behavior: Summary and Policy Implications*. Rand Report R-2814-1-NIJ. Santa Monica, Calif.: Rand Corporation.

Chaiken, J., and Rolph, J.E.
1983 Self-Reported Commissions of Crimes: Comparison of Two Questionnaire Formats. Unpublished paper. Rand Corporation, Santa Monica, Calif.
1985 Identifying High-Rate Serious Criminal Offenders. Draft report. Rand Corporation, Santa Monica, Calif.

Chaiken, M.R., and Chaiken, J.M.
1984 Offender types and public policy. *Crime and Delinquency* 30(2):195–226.

Challinger, D.
1974 A predictive device for parolees in Victoria. *Australian and New Zealand Journal of Criminology* 7:44–54.

Chelimsky, E., and Dahmann, J.
1981 *Career Criminal Program National Evaluation*. Final Report. National Institute of Justice. Washington, D.C.: U.S. Department of Justice.

Chi, K.S.
1983 Offender risk assessment: the Iowa model. *Innovations*, pp. 1–12. Lexington, Ky.: Council of State Governments.

Chilton, R.J.
1964 Continuity in delinquency area research: a comparison of studies for Baltimore, Detroit and Indianapolis. *American Sociological Review* 29:71–83.

Christensen, R.
1967 Projected percentage of U.S. population with criminal arrest and conviction records. Pp. 216–228 in *Task Force Report: Science and Technology*. Report to the President's Commission on Law Enforcement and the Administration of Justice, prepared by the Institute for Defense Analysis. Washington, D.C.: U.S. Government Printing Office.

Christiansen, K.O., Elers-Nielsen, M., LeMaire, L., and Stürup, G.K.
1965 Recidivism among sexual offenders. Pp. 55–85 in K.O. Christiansen, ed., *Scandinavian Studies in Criminology, Volume 1*. London: Tavistock.

Clark, J., and Harvek, E.
1966 Age and sex roles of adolescents and their involvement in misconduct: a reappraisal. *Sociology and Social Research* 50:495–508.

Clark, J., and Wenninger, E.
1962 Socioeconomic class and area as correlates of illegal behavior among juveniles. *American Sociological Review* 27:826–834.

Clarke, S.H.
1974a Getting 'em out of circulation: does incarceration of juvenile offenders reduce crime? *The Journal of Criminal Law and Enforcement* 65(4):528–535.
1974b Juvenile offender programs and delinquency prevention. *Crime and Delinquency* 6(3): 377–399.

Clelland, D., and Carter, T.J.
1980 The new myth of class and crime. *Criminology* 18:319–336.

Cline, H.F.
1980 Criminal behavior over the lifespan. Pp. 641–674 in O.D. Brim, Jr., and J. Kagan, eds., *Constancy and Change in Human Development*. Cambridge, Mass.: Harvard University Press.

Coates, R., Miller, A., and Ohlin, L.
1978 *Diversity in a Youth Correctional System*. Cambridge, Mass.: Ballinger.

Cohen, A.K.
1955 *Delinquent Boys: The Culture of the Gang*. New York: Macmillan.

Cohen, J.
1978 The incapacitative effect of imprisonment: a critical review of the literature. In A. Blumstein, J. Cohen, and D. Nagin, eds., *Deterrence and Incapacitation: Estimating the Effects of Criminal Sanctions on Crime Rates*. National Research Council. Washington, D.C.: National Academy Press.
1981 Racial Differences in Individual Arrest Patterns. Working paper, presented at annual meeting of American Society of Criminology. Urban Systems Institute, School of Urban and Public Affairs, Carnegie-Mellon University, Pittsburgh, Pa.

1982 Patterns of Adult Offending. Unpublished Ph.D. dissertation. School of Public and Urban Affairs, Carnegie-Mellon University, Pittsburgh, Pa.

1983 Incapacitation as a strategy for crime control: possibilities and pitfalls. Pp. 1–84 in M. Tonry and N. Morris, eds., *Crime and Justice: An Annual Review of Research, Volume 5*. Chicago: University of Chicago Press.

1984a Categorical Incapacitation Effects: Empirical Issues. Paper presented at the 1984 meeting of the American Society of Criminology, Cincinnati, Ohio. Urban Systems Institute, School of Urban and Public Affairs, Carnegie-Mellon University, Pittsburgh, Pa.

1984b Selective incapacitation: an assessment. *University of Illinois Law Review* 1984(2): 253–290.

1985a Alternative estimates of the incapacitative effect of increased criminal penalties. In *Proceedings of the Attorney General's Crime-conference 85*. Sacramento, Calif.: California Department of Justice.

1985b Empirical Estimates of the Incapacitative Effect of Imprisonment. Working Paper. Presented at annual meeting of American Association for the Advancement of Science, Los Angeles, Calif. Urban Systems Institute, School of Urban and Public Affairs, Carnegie-Mellon University, Pittsburgh, Pa.

Coleman, J.S.
1964 *Models of Change and Response Uncertainty*. Englewood Cliffs, N.J.: Prentice Hall.

Collins, J.J., and Allison, M.
1983 Legal coercion and retention in drug abuse treatment. *Hospital and Community Psychiatry* 14:1145–1149.

Collins, J.J., Hubbard, R.L., Rachal, J.V., and Cavanaugh, E.R.
1984 *The Effects of Legal Involvement on Drug Abuse Treatment Outcomes*. Research Triangle Park, N.C.: Research Triangle Institute.

Collins, J.J., Rachal, J.V., Hubbard, R., Cavanaugh, E.R., Craddock, S.G., and Kristiansen, P.L.
1982a *Crime and Crime Indicators in the Treatment Outcome Prospective Study*. Research Triangle Park, N.C.: Research Triangle Institute.

1982b *Criminality in a Drug Treatment Sample: Measurement Issues and Initial Findings*. Research Triangle Park, N.C.: Research Triangle Institute.

Consortium for Longitudinal Studies
1983 *As the Twig Is Bent . . . Lasting Effects of Preschool Programs*. Hillsdale, N.J.: Lawrence Erlbaum.

Cook, P.J.
1975 The correctional carrot: better jobs for parolees. *Policy Analysis* 1:11–34.

Coombs, R.H.
1981 Back on the streets: therapeutic communities' impact upon drug users. *American Journal of Drug and Alcohol Abuse* 8(2):185–201.

Cooper, C.S., Kelley, D., and Larson, S.
1982 *Judicial and Executive Discretion in the Sentencing Process: Analysis of State Felony Provisions*. Washington, D.C.: The American University.

Cooper, J.R., Altman, F., Brown, B.S., and Czechowicz, D.
1983 *Research on the Treatment of Narcotic Addiction: State of the Art*. Rockville, Md.: National Institute on Drug Abuse.

Copas, J.B.
1983 Regression, prediction, and shrinkage. *Journal of the Royal Statistical Society, Series B* 45:311–354.

Cox, D.R.
1972 Regression models and life tables. *Journal of the Royal Statistical Society, Section B* 34:187–220.

Cox, D.R., and Miller, H.D.
1965 *The Theory of Stochastic Processes*. London: Methuen.

Datesman, S.K., and Scarpitti, F.R.
1975 Female delinquency and broken homes: a re-assessment. *Criminology* 13:33–55.

Davidson, W.S., Seldman, E., Rappaport, J., Berck, P.L., Rapp, W.A., Rhodes, W., and Herring, J.
1977 Diversion program for juvenile offenders. *Social Work Research and Abstracts* 1:47–56.

Davies, M.
1969 Offense behavior and classification of offenders. *British Journal of Criminology* 9:39–50.

DeLeon, G.
1984 *The Therapeutic Community: Study of Effectiveness, Social, and Psychological Adjustment of 400 Dropouts and 100 Graduates from the Phoenix House Therapeutic Community*. DHHS Publication No. ADM 84-1286. Rockville, Md.: National Institute on Drug Abuse.

Dentler, R., and Monroe, L.
1961 Social correlates of early adolescent theft. *American Sociological Review* 26:733–743.

Douglas, J., Ross, J., and Simpson, H.
1968 *All Our Future*. London: Peter Davies.

Duncan, O.D., Ohlin, L.E., Reiss, A.J., and Stanton, H.R.
1953 Formal devices for making selection decisions. *American Journal of Sociology* 58:573–584.

Dunford, F.W.

1981 *National Evaluation of Diversion Projects: Final Report.* Office of Juvenile Justice and Delinquency Prevention, Washington, D.C.: U.S. Department of Justice.

Dunford, F.W., and Elliott, D.S.

1984 Identifying career offenders using self-reported data. *Journal of Research in Crime and Delinquency* 21:57–87.

Ebbesen, M.D., and Konecni, K.

1975 Decision making and information integration in the courts: the setting of bail. *Journal of Personality and Social Psychology* 32(5):805–821.

Elion, V., and Megargee, E.I.

1979 Racial identity, length of incarceration, and parole decision making. *Journal of Research in Crime and Delinquency* 16:232–245.

Elliott, D.S., and Ageton, S.A.

1980 Reconciling race and class differences in self-reported and official estimates of delinquency. *American Sociological Review* 45:95–100.

Elliott, D.S., and Huizinga, D.

1983 Social class and delinquent behavior in a national youth panel: 1976–1980. *Criminology* 21:149–177.

1984 *The Relationship Between Delinquent Behavior and ADM Problems.* The National Youth Survey Project Report No. 28. Boulder, Colo.: Behavioral Research Institute.

Elliott, D.S., and Voss, H.L.

1974 *Delinquency and Dropout.* Lexington, Mass.: Lexington Books.

Elliott, D.S., Huizinga, D., and Ageton, S.S.

1985 *Explaining Delinquency and Drug Use.* Beverly Hills, Calif.: Sage Publications.

Elliott, D., Ageton, S., Huizinga, D., Knowles, B., and Canter, R.

1983 *The Prevalence and Incidence of Delinquent Behavior: 1976–1980.* National Youth Survey, Report No. 26. Boulder, Colo.: Behavioral Research Institute.

1985 *The Social Correlates of Delinquency Behavior.* Project Report No. 30. Boulder, Colo.: Behavioral Research Institute.

Empey, L.T., and Erickson, M.L.

1966 Hidden delinquency and social status. *Social Forces* 44:546–554.

1972 *The Provo Experiment.* Lexington, Mass.: Lexington Books.

Empey, L., and Lubeck, S.

1971 *The Silverlake Experiment.* Chicago, Ill.: Aldine.

Ensminger, M.E., Kellam, S.G., and Rubin, B.R.

1983 School and family origins of delinquency: comparisons by sex. Pp. 73–97 in K.T. Van Dusen and S.A. Mednick, eds., *Prospective Studies of Crime and Delinquency.* Boston, Mass.: Kluwer-Nijhoff.

Erickson, M.

1973 Group violations, socioeconomic status, and official delinquency. *Social Forces* 52:41–52.

Farrington, D.P.

1979a Delinquent behavior modification in the natural environment. *British Journal of Criminology* 19:353–372.

1979b Environmental stress, delinquent behavior, and convictions. Pp. 93–107 in I.S. Sarasan and C.D. Spielberger, eds., *Stress and Anxiety, Volume 6.* Washington, D.C.: Hemisphere.

1981 The prevalence of convictions. *British Journal of Criminology* 2(2):173–175.

1982 Randomized experiments on crime and justice. M. Tonry and N. Morris, eds., *Crime and Justice: An Annual Review of Research, Volume 4.* Chicago, Ill.: University of Chicago Press.

1983a Further Analyses of a Longitudinal Survey of Crime and Delinquency. Final report to the National Institute of Justice, Washington, D.C.

1983b Offending from 10 to 25 years of age. Pp. 17–37 in K.T. Van Dusen and S.A. Mednick, eds., *Prospective Studies of Crime and Delinquency.* Boston, Mass.: Kluwer-Nijhoff.

1983c Randomized experiments on crime and justice. Pp. 257–308 in M. Tonry and N. Morris, eds., *Crime and Justice: An Annual Review of Research, Volume 4.* Chicago, Ill.: University of Chicago Press.

1984 Measuring the natural history of delinquency and crime. In R.A. Glow, ed., *Advances in the Behavioral Measurement of Children, Volume 1.* Greenwich, Conn.: JAI Press.

1986 Age and crime. In M. Tonry and N. Morris, eds., *Crime and Justice, Volume 7.* Chicago, Ill.: University of Chicago Press.

Farrington, D.P., and Tarling, R.

1985 *Prediction in Criminology.* Albany, N.Y.: SUNY Press.

Farrington, D.P., and West, D.J.

1981 The Cambridge study in delinquent development. Pp. 137–145 in S.A. Mednick and A.E. Baert, eds., *Prospective Longitudinal Research: An Empirical Basis for the Primary Prevention of Psycho-Social Disorders.* Oxford: Oxford University Press.

Farrington, D.P., Gundry, G., and West, D.J.

1975 The familial transmission of criminality. *Medicine, Science and the Law* 15:177–186.

Farrington, D.P., Ohlin, L., and Wilson, J.Q.

1986 *Understanding and Controlling Crime:*

Toward a New Research Strategy. Report commissioned by the MacArthur Foundation, Chicago, Ill. New York: Springer-Verlag.

Federal Bureau of Investigation
1966 *Crime in the United States—1965*. Uniform Crime Reports. Washington, D.C.: U.S. Department of Justice.
1971 *Crime in the United States—1970*. Uniform Crime Reports. Washington, D.C.: U.S. Department of Justice.
1974 *Crime in the United States—1973*. Uniform Crime Reports. Washington, D.C.: U.S. Department of Justice.
1977 *Crime in the United States—1976*. Uniform Crime Reports. Washington, D.C.: U.S. Department of Justice.
1981 *Crime in the United States—1980*. Uniform Crime Reports. Washington, D.C.: U.S. Department of Justice.
1982 *Crime in the United States—1981*. Uniform Crime Reports. Washington, D.C.: U.S. Department of Justice.
1984 *Age-Specific Arrest Rates 1965–1983*. Federal Bureau of Investigation Uniform Crime Reporting Program. Washington, D.C.: U.S. Department of Justice.

Feeney, F.
1983 Prosecutorial selectivity: a view of current practices. In McGillis et al., eds., *Dealing with Dangerous Offenders, Volume 2*. Cambridge, Mass.: J.F. Kennedy School of Government.

Feeney, F., Dill, F., and Weir, A.
1983 *Arrests Without Conviction: How Often They Occur and Why*. National Institute of Justice. Washington, D.C.: U.S. Department of Justice.

Feldhusen, J.F., Thurston, J.R., and Benning, J.J.
1973 A longitudinal study of delinquency and other aspects of children's behavior. *International Journal of Criminology and Penology* 1:341–351.

Figueira-McDonough, J., Barton, W., and Sarri, R.
1981 Normal deviance: gender similarities in adolescent subcultures. M. Warren, ed., *Comparing Female and Male Offenders*. Sage Research Progress Series in Criminology, Volume 21. Beverly Hills, Calif.: Sage Publications.

Fischer, D.R.
1983 Better public protection with fewer inmates? *Corrections Today* (December):16–20.
1984 Prediction and Incapacitation: Issues and Answers (An Overview of the Iowa Research on Recidivism and Violence Prediction). Paper presented at the annual meeting of the

American Society of Criminology, Cincinnati, Ohio. Statistical Analysis Center, Des Moines, Iowa.

Fisher, F., and Kadane, J.
1983 Empirically based sentencing guidelines and ethical considerations. In A. Blumstein, J. Cohen, S. Martin, and M. Tonry, eds., *Research on Sentencing: The Search for Reform, Volume 2*. Washington, D.C.: National Academy Press.

Folkard, M., Smith, D.E., and Smith, D.D.
1976 *IMPACT, Volume 2*. London: Her Majesty's Stationery Office.

Forbes, A.F.
1971 Markov chain models for manpower systems. In A.R. Smith and D.J. Bartholomew, eds., *Manpower and Management Science*. Lexington, Mass.: D.C. Heath.

Forst, B., and Brosi, K.
1977 A theoretical and empirical analysis of the prosecutor. *Journal of Legal Studies* 6:177–191.

Forst, B., Lucianovic, J., and Cox, S.J.
1977 *What Happens After Arrest: A Court Perspective on Police Operations in the District of Columbia*. PROMIS Research Publication No. 4. Washington, D.C.: Institute for Law and Social Research (INSLAW).

Forst, B., Rhodes, W., Dimm, J., Gelman, A., and Mullin, B.
1982 Targeting Federal Resources on Recidivists. Unpublished final report of the Federal Career Criminal Research Project. Institute for Law and Social Research, Washington, D.C.

Fowles, A.J.
1978 *Prison Welfare*. London: Her Majesty's Stationery Office.

Freeman, R.B.
1982 Crime and the Labor Market. NBCR Working Paper No. 1031. National Bureau of Economic Research, Cambridge, Mass.

Friedrich, R.L.
1977 The Impact of Organization, Individual, and Situational Factors on Police Behavior. Unpublished Ph.D. dissertation, Department of Political Science, University of Michigan, Ann Arbor.

Frum, H.S.
1958 Adult criminal offense trends following juvenile delinquency. *Journal of Criminal Law, Criminology, and Police Science* 49:29–49.

Gandossy, R.P., Williams, J.R., Cohen, J., and Harwood, H.J.
1980 *Drugs and Crime: A Survey and Analysis of the Literature*. National Institute of Justice. Washington, D.C.: U.S. Department of Justice.

Garber, S., Klepper, S., and Nagin, D.
1983 The role of extralegal factors in determining criminal case dispositions. In A. Blumstein et al., eds., *Research on Sentencing: The Search for Reform, Volume 2.* Washington, D.C.: National Academy Press.

Garrison, S.R., and Stolberg, A.L.
1983 Modification of anger in children by affective imagery training. *Journal of Abnormal Child Psychology* 11:115–130.

Gay, W.G., and Bowers, R.A.
1985 *Career Criminal Initiative Projects: Issues and Practices.* Deliverable No. 11 to National Institute of Justice. Washington, D.C.: University City Science Center.

Gerstein, D.R., ed.
1981 *Guidelines for Studies on Substance Abuse Treatment.* Committee on Substance Abuse and Habitual Behavior, Commission on Behavioral and Social Sciences and Education, National Research Council. Washington, D.C.: National Academy Press.

Gibbons, D.C.
1965 *Changing the Lawbreaker.* Englewood Cliffs, N.J.: Prentice Hall.
1975 Offender typologies—two decades later. *British Journal of Criminology* 15:140–156.

Gibson, H.B.
1969 Early delinquency in relation to broken homes. *Journal of Child Psychology and Psychiatry* 10:195–204.

Ginsberg, R.B.
1971 Semi-Markov process and mobility. *Journal of Mathematical Sociology* 15:233–262.

Glaser, D.
1964 *The Effectiveness of Prison and Parole.* Indianapolis, Ind.: Bobbs-Merrill.

Glaser, D., and Rice, K.
1959 Crime, age, and employment. *American Sociological Review* 24:679–686.

Glueck, S., and Glueck, E.T.
1930 *500 Criminal Careers.* New York: Alfred A. Knopf.
1934 *One Thousand Juvenile Delinquents.* Cambridge, Mass.: Harvard University Press.
1937 *Later Criminal Careers.* New York: The Commonwealth Fund.
1940 *Juvenile Delinquents Grown Up.* New York: The Commonwealth Fund.
1943 *Criminal Careers in Retrospect.* New York: The Commonwealth Fund.
1950 *Unraveling Juvenile Delinquency.* Cambridge, Mass.: Harvard University Press.

Gold, M.
1966 Undetected delinquent behavior. *Journal of Research in Crime and Delinquency* 3: 27–46.
1970 *Delinquent Behavior in an American City.* Belmont, Calif.: Brooks/Cole Publishing Company.

Gold, M., and Reimer, D.
1975 Changing patterns of delinquent behavior among Americans 13 through 16 years old: 1967–72. *Crime and Delinquency Literature* 7:483–517.

Goldkamp, J.S.
1979 *Two Classes of Accused: a Study of Bail and Detention in American Justice.* Cambridge, Mass.: Ballinger.

Goldkamp, J.S., and Gottfredson, M.R.
1981a *Bail Decisionmaking: A Study of Policy Guidelines.* Washington, D.C.: National Institute of Corrections.
1981b *Bail Decisionmaking: Appendices.* Washington, D.C.: National Institute of Corrections.
1984 *Policy Guidelines for Bail: An Experiment in Court Reform.* Philadelphia, Pa.: Temple University Press.

Goodman, L.A.
1961 Statistical methods for the mover-stayer model. *Journal of the American Statistical Association* 56:841–868.
1962 Statistical methods for analyzing processes of change. *American Journal of Sociology* 68:57–78.
1968 The analysis of cross-classified data: independence, quasi-independence, and interactions in contingency tables with and without missing entries. *Journal of the American Statistical Association* 63:1091–1131.

Gordon, R.A.
1973 An explicit estimation of the prevalence of commitment to a training school, to age 18, by race and sex. *Journal of the American Statistical Association* 68:547–553.
1976 Prevalence: the rare datum in delinquency measurement and its implications for the theory of delinquency. Pp. 201–283 in M. Klein, ed., *The Juvenile Justice System.* Beverly Hills, Calif.: Sage Publications.

Gordon, R.A., and Gleser, L.J.
1974 The estimation of the prevalence of delinquency: two approaches and a correction of the literature. *Journal of Mathematical Sociology* 3:275–291.

Gottfredson, D.M., and Ballard, K.B.
1965 *The Validity of Two Parole Prediction Scales.* Vacaville, Calif.: Institute for the Study of Crime and Delinquency.

Gottfredson, D.M., and Bonds, J.A.
1961 A Manual for Intake Base Expectancy Scoring (Form CDC-BE 61A). Research Division, California Department of Corrections, Sacramento, Calif.

Gottfredson, D.M., Cosgrove, C.A., Wilkins, L.T., and Wallerstein, J.
1978 *Classification for Parole Decision Policy.* Washington, D.C.: U.S. Department of Justice.

Gottfredson, D.M., Wilkins, L.T., and Hoffman, P.B.
1978 *Guidelines for Parole and Sentencing: A Policy Control Method.* Lexington, Mass.: Lexington Books.

Gottfredson, M.R.
1974 An empirical analysis of pre-trial release decisions. *Journal of Criminal Justice* 2:287–303.

Gottfredson, M.R., and Adams, K.
1980 Prison Behavior and Parole Performance: Empirical Reality and Public Policy. Unpublished manuscript. Criminal Justice Research Center, Albany, N.Y.

Gottfredson, M.R., and Gottfredson, D.R.
1980 *Decisionmaking in Criminal Justice: Toward the Rational Exercise of Discretion.* Cambridge, Mass.: Ballinger.

Gottfredson, M.R., Mitchell-Herzfeld, S.D., and Flanagan, T.J.
1982 Another look at the effectiveness of parole supervision. *Journal of Research in Crime and Delinquency* 19:277–298.

Gottlieb, B.
1985 *Public Danger as a Factor in Pretrial Release: A Comparative Analysis of State Laws.* Washington, D.C.: Toborg Associates, Inc.

Gould, L.C.
1969 Who defines delinquency: a comparison of self-reported and officially-reported indices of delinquency for three racial groups. *Social Problems* 16:325–336.

Greenberg, D.F.
1975 The incapacitative effect of imprisonment: some estimates. *Law and Society Review* 541–580.

1977a Delinquency and the age structure of society. *Contemporary Crises* 1:189–224.

1977b The correctional effect of corrections: a survey of evaluations. In D.F. Greenberg, ed., *Corrections and Punishment.* Beverly Hills, Calif.: Sage Publications.

1978 Recidivism as radioactive decay. *Journal of Research in Crime and Delinquency* 24:124–125.

1983 Crime and age. Pp. 30–35 in S.H. Kadish, ed., *Encyclopedia of Crime and Justice.* New York: Macmillan.

Greene, M.A.
1977 The Incapacitative Effect of Imprisonment Policies on Crime. Unpublished Ph.D. thesis, School of Urban and Public Affairs,

Carnegie-Mellon University, Pittsburgh, Pa. (University Microfilms, Ann Arbor, Mich.)

Greenwood, P.
1985 The incapacitative/deterrent role of increased criminal penalties. In *Proceedings of the Attorney General's Crimeconference 85.* Sacramento, Calif.: California Department of Justice.

Greenwood, P., with Abrahamse, A.
1982 *Selective Incapacitation.* Report R-2815-NIJ. Santa Monica, Calif.: Rand Corporation.

Greenwood, P.W., and Zimring, F.
1985 *One More Chance: The Role of Rehabilitation in Reducing the Criminality of Chronic Serious Juvenile Offenders.* Report R-3214-OJJDP. Santa Monica, Calif.: Rand Corporation.

Greenwood, P.W., Abrahamse, A., and Zimring, F.
1984 *Factors Affecting Sentence Severity for Young Adult Offenders.* Report No. R-3173-NIJ. Santa Monica, Calif.: Rand Corporation.

Greenwood, P.W., Petersilia, J., and Zimring, F.E.
1980 *Age, Crime, and Sanctions: The Transition from Juvenile to Adult Court.* Report R-2642-NIJ. Santa Monica, Calif.: Rand Corporation.

Gropper, B.A.
1985 *Probing the Links Between Drugs and Crime.* National Institute of Justice, Research in Brief. Washington, D.C.: U.S. Department of Justice, National Institute of Justice.

Haberman, S.J.
1973 The analysis of residuals in cross-classified tables. *Biometrics* 29:205–220.

1979 *Analysis of Qualitative Data, Volume 2.* New York: Academic Press.

Hackler, J.C., and Hagan, J.L.
1975 Work and teaching machines as delinquency prevention tools: a four-year follow-up. *Social Services Review* 49:92–106.

Hagan, J., and Bumiller, K.
1983 Making sense of sentencing: a review and critique of sentencing research. In A. Blumstein et al., eds., *Research on Sentencing: The Search for Reform, Volume 2.* Washington, D.C.: National Academy Press.

Hamparian, D., Schuster, R., Dinitz, S., and Conrad, J.
1978 *The Violent Few: A Study of Dangerous Juvenile Offenders.* Lexington, Mass.: Lexington Books.

Hannan, M.T.
1971 *Aggregation and Disaggregation in Sociology.* Lexington, Mass.: Lexington Books.

Harris, C.M., and Moitra, S.D.
1978 Improved statistical techniques for the mea-

surement of recidivism. *Journal of Research in Crime and Delinquency* 15:194–213.

Harris, C.M., Kaylan, A.R., and Maltz, M.D.
1981 Recent advances in the statistics of recidivism measurement. In J.A. Fox, ed., *Models in Quantitative Criminology.* New York: Academic Press.

Hart, H.
1923 Predicting parole success. *Journal of Criminal Law and Criminology* 14:405–413.

Hart, H.L.A.
1968 *Punishment and Responsibility.* Oxford: Oxford University Press.

Harvard Law Review Student Note
1982 Selective incapacitation: reducing crime through predictions of recidivism. *Harvard Law Review* 96:511–533.

Hathaway, S.R., and Monachesi, E.D.
1963 *Adolescent Personality and Behavior.* Minneapolis: University of Minnesota Press.

Hausner, J., Mullin, B., and Moorer, A.
1982 The Investigation and Prosecution of Concurrent Jurisdiction Offenses. INSLAW, Inc. Washington, D.C.

Havighurst, R., Bowman, P., Liddle, G., Matthews, C., and Pierce, J.
1962 *Growing Up in River City.* New York: John Wiley and Sons.

Heckman, J.K.
1979 Sample selection bias as a specification error. *Econometrica* 47:153–161.

Hennessey, M., Richards, P.J., and Berk, R.A.
1978 Broken homes and middle class delinquency: a reassessment. *Criminology* 15:505–527.

Hinde, R.A.
1980 Family influences. In M. Rutter, ed., *Scientific Foundations of Developmental Psychiatry.* London: Heinemann.

Hindelang, M.J.
1971 Age, sex, and the versatility of delinquent involvements. *Social Problems* 18:522–535.
1976 With a little help from their friends: group participation in reported delinquent behavior. *British Journal of Criminology* 16:109–125.
1978a Race and involvement in common law personal crimes. *American Sociological Review* 43:93–109.
1978b *Victims of Personal Crime: An Empirical Foundation for Theory of Personal Victimization.* Cambridge, Mass.: Ballinger Press.
1980 Sex differences in criminal activity. *Social Problems* 27:143–156.

Hindelang, M.J., Hirschi, T., and Weis, J.G.
1979 Correlates of delinquency: the illusion of discrepancy between self-report and official measures. *American Sociological Review* 44:995–1014.
1981 *Measuring Delinquency.* Beverly Hills, Calif.: Sage Publications.

Hirschi, T.
1969 *Causes of Delinquency.* Berkeley: University of California Press.
1972 Social class and crime. Pp. 503–520 in G.W. Thielbar and S.D. Feldman, eds., *Issues in Social Inequality.* Boston, Mass.: Little, Brown.
1983 Crime and the family. Chapter 4 in J.Q. Wilson, ed., *Crime and Public Policy.* San Francisco, Calif.: ICS Press.

Hirschi, T., and Gottfredson, M.
1983 Age and the explanation of crime. *American Journal of Sociology* 89:552–584.

Hirschi, T., and Hindelang, M.J.
1977 Intelligence and delinquency: a revisionist view. *American Sociological Review* 42:571–587.

Hirschi, T., and Selvin, H.C.
1973 Description and prediction. Pp. 235–256 in *Principles of Survey Analysis.* New York: Free Press.

Hoem, J.
1972 Inhomogeneous semi-Markov process, select actuarial tables, and duration-dependence in demography. In T.N.E. Grevelle, ed., *Population Dynamics.* New York: Academic Press.

Hoffman, P.B.
1983 Screening for risk: a revised Salient Factor Score (SFS 81). *Journal of Criminal Justice* 11:539–547.

Hoffman, P.B., and Beck, J.L.
1974 Parole decision-making: a Salient Factor Score. *Journal of Criminal Justice* 2:195–206.
1976 Salient Factor Score validations: a 1972 release cohort. *Journal of Criminal Justice* 4:69–76.
1980 Revalidating the Salient Factor Score: a research note. *Journal of Criminal Justice* 8:185–188.

Hoffman, P.B., Stone-Meierhoefer, B., and Beck, J.L.
1978 Salient Factor Score and release behavior: three validation samples. *Law and Human Behavior* 1:47–62.

Hubbard, R.L., Allison, M., Bray, R.M., Craddock, S.G., Rachal, J.V., and Ginzburg, H.M.
1983 An overview of client characteristics, treatment services, and during-treatment outcomes for outpatient methadone clinics in the Treatment Outcome Prospective Study (TOPS). Pp. 714–751 in J.R. Cooper et al.,

eds., *Research on the Treatment of Narcotic Addiction: State of the Art.* Rockville, Md.: National Institute on Drug Abuse.

Hubbard, R.L., Rachal, J.V., Craddock, S.G., and Cavanaugh, E.R.
1984 Treatment outcome prospective study (TOPS): client characteristics and behaviors before, during, and after treatment. In F. Tims and J. Ludford, eds., *Drug Abuse Treatment Evaluation: Strategies, Progress, and Prospects.* Monograph No. 56. Rockville, Md.: National Institute on Drug Abuse.

Hurwitz, J.I.
1965 Three delinquent types: a multivariate analysis. *Journal of Criminal Law, Criminology, and Police Science* 56:328–334.

Hutchings, B., and Mednick, S.A.
1975 Registered criminality in the adoptive and biological parents of registered male criminal adoptees. Pp. 105–116 in R.R. Fieve, D. Rosenthal, and H. Brill, eds., *Genetic Research in Psychiatry.* Baltimore, Md.: Johns Hopkins University Press.

Inciardi, J.A.
1979 Heroin use and street crime. *Crime and Delinquency* 25:335–346.

Jabine, T., Straf, M., Tanur, J., and Tourangeau, R.
1984 *Cognitive Aspects of Survey Methodology.* Report of the Advanced Research Seminar on Cognitive Aspects of Survey Methodology. Committee on National Statistics, Commission on Behavioral and Social Sciences and Education, National Research Council. Washington, D.C.: National Academy Press.

Jacoby, J., Mellon, L.R., and Smith, W.
1982 *Policy and Prosecution.* National Institute of Justice. Washington, D.C.: U.S. Department of Justice.

Janus, M.G.
1985 Selective incapacitation: Have we tried it? Does it work? *Journal of Criminal Justice* 13:117–129.

Jensen, G.F.
1972 Parents, peers, and delinquent action: a test of the differential association perspective. *American Journal of Sociology* 78:562–575.
1976 Race, achievement, and delinquency: a further look at delinquency in a birth cohort. *American Journal of Sociology* 82:379–387.

Jensen, G., and Eve, R.
1976 Sex differences in delinquency. *Criminology* 13:427–448.

Jesness, C., DeRisi, W., McCormick, P., and Wedge, R.
1972 *The Youth Center Research Project.* Sacramento, Calif.: American Justice Institute.

Johnson, R.E.
1980 Social class and delinquent behavior: a new test. *Criminology* 18:86–93.

Johnson, B.D., Goldstein, P., Preble, E., Schmeidler, J., Lipton, D.S., Spunt, B., Duchaine, N., Norman, R., Miller, R., Meggett, N., Kale, A., and Hand, D.
1983 The Economic Behavior of Street Opiate Users. Final report to the National Institute on Drug Abuse and the National Institute of Justice. Narcotic and Drug Research, Inc., New York City, N.Y.
1985 *Taking Care of Business: The Economics of Crime by Heroin Abusers.* Lexington, Mass.: Lexington Books.

Johnson, D.L., and Breckenridge, J.N.
1982 The Houston parent-child development center and the primary prevention of behavior problems in young children. *American Journal of Community Psychology* 10:305–316.

Johnston, L.D., O'Malley, P.M., and Eveland, L.
1978 Drugs and delinquency: a search for causal connections. Pp. 137–156 in D. Kandel, ed., *Longitudinal Research on Drug Use.* New York: John Wiley and Sons.

Johnstone, J.W.C.
1978 Juvenile delinquency and the family: a contextual interpretation. *Youth and Society* 9:299–313.

Kamin, L.J.
1985 Letter to the Editor: criminality and adoption. *Science* 227:983.

Kandel, D.B.
1978 *Longitudinal Research on Drug Use.* New York: John Wiley and Sons.

Kaplan, E., and Meier, P.
1958 Nonparametric estimation from incomplete observations. *Journal of the American Statistical Association* 53:457–481.

Kaplan, J.
1983 *The Hardest Drug: Heroin and Public Policy.* Chicago, Ill.: University of Chicago Press.

Karlin, S., and Taylor, H.M.
1975 *A First Course in Stochastic Processes.* 2nd ed. New York: Academic Press.

Karoly, P., and Rosenthal, M.
1977 Training parents in behavior modification: effects on perceptions of family interaction and deviant child behavior. *Behavior Therapy* 8:406–410.

Kellam, S.G., Ensminger, M.E., and Simon, M.B.
1980 Mental health in the first grade and teenage drug, alcohol, and cigarette use. *Drug and Alcohol Dependence* 5:273–304.

Kemeny, J.G., Snell, J.L., and Thompson, G.L.
1966 *Introduction to Finite Mathematics.* 2nd ed. Englewood Cliffs, N.J.: Prentice Hall.

Kettlewell, P.W., and Kausch, D.F.
1983 The generalization of the effects of a cognitive-behavioral treatment program for aggressive children. *Journal of Abnormal Child Psychology* 11:101–114.

Kinch, J.W.
1962 Continuities in the study of delinquent types. *Journal of Criminal Law, Criminology, and Police Science* 53:323–328.

Kirby, B.C.
1954 Parole prediction using multiple correlation. *American Journal of Sociology* 59:539–550.

Klepper, S., Nagin, D., and Tierney, L.
1983 Discrimination in the criminal justice system: a critical appraisal of the literature. In A. Blumstein et al., eds., *Research on Sentencing: The Search for Reform, Volume 2.* Washington, D.C.: National Academy Press.

Knapp, K.
1982 Impact of Minnesota sentencing guidelines on sentencing practices. *Hamline Law Review* 5:237–256.

Krasker, W., and Welsch, R.
1982 Efficient bounded-influence regression estimation. *Journal of the American Statistical Association* 77:595–604.

Kratcoski, P., and Kratcoski, J.
1975 Changing patterns in the delinquent activities of boys and girls. *Adolescence* 10:83–91.

Krohn, M.D., Akers, R.L., Radosevich, M.J., and Lanza-Kaduce, L.
1980 Social status and deviance: class context of school, social status, and delinquent behavior. *Criminology* 18:303–318.

Kvaraceus, W.C.
1944 Juvenile delinquency and social class. *Journal of Educational Sociology* 8:51–54.

LaFave, W.R.
1965 *Arrest: The Decision to Take a Suspect into Custody.* Boston, Mass.: Little, Brown and Co.

LaFree, G.D.
1985 Official reactions to Hispanic defendants in the Southwest. *Journal of Research in Crime and Delinquency* 22:213–237.

Lamb, H., and Goertzel, V.
1974 Ellsworth House: a community alternative to jail. *American Journal of Psychiatry* 131:64–68.

Lander, B.
1954 *Towards an Understanding of Juvenile Delinquency.* New York: Columbia University Press.

Langan, P.A., and Farrington, D.P.
1983 Two-track or one-track justice?: some evidence from an English longitudinal survey.

The Journal of Criminal Law and Criminology 74(2):501–527.

Lerman, P.
1975 *Community Treatment and Social Control.* Chicago, Ill.: University of Chicago Press.

Lichtman, G.M., and Smock, S.M.
1981 The effects of social services on probation recidivism: a field experiment. *Journal of Research in Crime and Delinquency* 18:81–100.

Lipton, D., Martinson, R., and Wilks, J.
1975 *The Effectiveness of Correctional Treatment: A Survey of Treatment Evaluation Studies.* New York: Praeger.

Little, A.
1965 The "prevalence" of recorded delinquency and recidivism in England and Wales. *American Sociological Review* 30:260–263.

Locander, W.B., and Burton, J.P.
1976 The effect of question form on gathering income data by telephone. *Journal of Marketing Research* 13:189–192.

Loeber, R.
1982 The stability of antisocial and delinquent child behavior: a review. *Child Development* 53:1431–1446.

1984 Experimental Studies to Reduce Antisocial Delinquent Child Behavior: Implications for Future Programs and Optimal Times for Intervention. Unpublished paper. Western Psychiatric Institute, University of Pittsburgh.

1985 The Prevalence, Correlates, and Continuity of Illegal Conduct Problems of Elementary School Children. Unpublished paper. Western Psychiatric Institute, University of Pittsburgh.

Loeber, R., and Dishion, T.
1983 Early predictors of male delinquency: a review. *Psychological Bulletin* 94(10):68–99.

Loeber, R., and Stouthamer-Loeber, M.
1986 Models and meta-analyses of the relationships between family variables and juvenile conduct problems and delinquency. In N. Morris and M. Tonry, eds., *Crime and Justice: An Annual Review of Research, Volume 7.* Chicago, Ill.: University of Chicago Press.

London Home Office
1985 *Criminal Careers of Those Born in 1953, 1958, and 1963.* Home Office Statistical Bulletin. London: Home Office Statistical Department.

Lukoff, I.F.
1974 Issues in the evaluation of heroin treatment. Pp. 129–157 in E. Josephson and E. Carrol, eds., *Drug Use: Epidemiological and Socio-*

logical Approaches. New York: John Wiley and Sons.

1976 Consequences of use: Heroin and other narcotics. Pp. 195–227 in J. Rittenhouse, ed., The Epidemiology of Heroin and Other Narcotics. NIDA Research Monograph Series. Rockville, Md.: National Institute on Drug Abuse.

Lundman, R.J.
1984 Prevention and Control of Juvenile Delinquency. New York: Oxford University Press.

Lundman, R.J., McFarlane, P.T., and Scarpitti, F.R.
1976 Delinquency prevention: a description and assessment of projects reported in the professional literature. Crime and Delinquency 22:297–308.

Mallar, C., Kerachsky, S., Thornton, C., and Long, D.
1982 Evaluation of the Economic Impact of the Job Corps Program, Third Follow-Up Report. Princeton, N.J.: Mathematica Policy Research, Inc.

Maltz, M.
1984 Recidivism. New York: Academic Press.

Maltz, M., and McCleary, R.
1977 The mathematics of behavioral change. Evaluation Quarterly 1(3):421–438.

Mannheim, H., and Wilkins, L.T.
1955 Prediction Methods in Relation to Borstal Training. London: Her Majesty's Stationery Office.

Marquis, K.H., with Ebener, P.A.
1981 Quality of Prisoner Self-Reports: Arrest and Conviction Response Errors. Santa Monica, Calif.: Rand Corporation.

Martin, J.B.
1952 My Life in Crime: The Autobiography of a Professional Thief. New York: Knopf.

Martin, S.
1984 Catching Career Criminals: An Evaluation of the Repeat Offender Project. Paper presented at the annual meeting of the American Society of Criminology, Cincinnati, Ohio. The Police Foundation, Washington, D.C.

Matsueda, R.
1982 Testing control theory and differential association: a causal modeling approach. American Sociological Review 47:489–504.

McCord, J.M.
1977 A comparative study of two generations of native Americans. In R. Meier, ed., Theory in Criminology. Beverly Hills, Calif.: Sage Publications.
1978 A thirty-year follow-up of treatment effects. American Psychologist 32:284–289.
1979 Some child-rearing antecedents of criminal behavior in adult men. Journal of Personality and Social Psychology 37(9):1477–1486.
1981 Consideration of some effects of a counseling program. Pp. 394–405 in S. Martin, L. Sechrest, and R. Redner, eds., New Directions in the Rehabilitation of Criminal Offenders. Washington, D.C.: National Academy Press.
1982 A longitudinal view of the relationship between paternal absence and crimes. Pp. 113–128 in J. Gunn and D. Farrington, eds., Abnormal Offenders, Delinquency, and the Criminal Justice System. Chichester: John Wiley and Sons.

McCord, J.M., and McCord, W.
1959 A follow-up report on the Cambridge-Somerville Youth Study. Annals of the American Academy of Political and Social Science 322:89–96.

McDonald, W.F., ed.
1978 The Prosecutor. Beverly Hills, Calif.: Sage Publications.

McGahey, R.M.
1982 Labor Market Segmentation, Human Capital and the Economics of Crime. Unpublished Ph.D. dissertation. Graduate Faculty of Political and Social Science, New School for Social Research, New York City.

McGinnis, R.
1968 A stochastic model of social mobility. American Sociological Review 33:712–721.

McGlothlin, W.H., and Anglin, M.D.
1981 Shutting off methadone: costs and benefits. Archives of General Psychiatry 38:885.

McGlothlin, W.H., Anglin, M.D., and Wilson, B.D.
1977 An Evaluation of the California Civil Addict Program. Services Research Issues Series, No. 78–558. Rockville, Md.: National Institute on Drug Abuse.
1978 Narcotic addiction and crime. Criminology 16:293–315.

Mednick, S.A., Gabrielli, W.F., Jr., and Hutchings, B.
1984 Genetic influences in criminal convictions: evidence from an adoption cohort. Science 224:891–894.
1985 Response to letters from L.J. Kamin and L.E. Moses regarding Mednick's criminality and adoption paper. Science 227:984.

Mednick, S.A., Pollock, V., Volavka, J., and Gabrielli, W.F.
1982 Biology and Violence. Pp. 85–158 in M.E. Wolfgang and N.A. Weiner, eds., Criminal Violence. Beverly Hills, Calif.: Sage Publications.

Menard, S., and Morse, B.J.
1984 A structuralist critique of the IQ-delin-

quency hypothesis: theory and evidence. *American Journal of Sociology* 89:1347–1378.

Merton, R.K.
1938 Social structure and anomie. *American Sociological Review* 3:672–682.

Michigan State Police
1983a CCH—A Closer Look: Update. Internal document. Michigan State Police, East Lansing.
1983b Michigan's Computerized Criminal History System: A Closer Look. Internal document. Michigan State Police, East Lansing, Mich.

Miller, F., Court, S., Knox, E., and Brandon, S.
1974 *The School Years in Newcastle-Upon-Tyne.* London: Oxford University Press.

Miller, S., Dinitz, S., and Conrad, J.
1982 *Careers of the Violent.* Lexington, Mass.: Lexington Books.

Minnesota Sentencing Guidelines Commission
1984 *The Impact of the Minnesota Sentencing Guidelines: Three-Year Evaluation.* St. Paul: Minnesota Sentencing Guidelines Commission.

Mitchell, S., and Rosa, P.
1981 Boyhood behavior problems as precursors of criminality: a fifteen-year follow-up study. *Journal of Child Psychology and Psychiatry* 22:19–33.

Moitra, S.D.
1981 Analysis of Sentencing Policies Considering Crime Switching Patterns and Imprisonment Constraints. Unpublished Ph.D. dissertation. School of Urban and Public Affairs, Carnegie-Mellon University.

Monahan, J.
1981 *Predicting Violent Behavior: An Assessment of Clinical Techniques.* Beverly Hills, Calif.: Sage Publications.
1982 The case for prediction in the modified just desert model of criminal sentencing. *International Journal of Law and Psychiatry* 5:103–113.

Monahan, T.P.
1960 On the incidence of delinquency. *Social Forces* 39(October):66–72.

Moore, J.W., Garcia, C., Garcia, R., Cerda, L., and Valencia, F.
1978 *Homeboys: Gangs, Drugs and Prison in the Barrios of Los Angeles.* Philadelphia, Pa.: Temple University Press.

Moore, M., Estrich, S.R., McGillis, D., and Spelman, W.
1984 *Dangerous Offender: The Elusive Target of Justice.* Cambridge, Mass.: Harvard University Press.

Morash, M.
1984 Establishment of a juvenile police record:

the influence of individual and peer group characteristics. *Criminology* 22:97–111.

Morris, N., and Miller, M.
1985 On "dangerousness" in the judicial process. Pp. 1–50 in M. Tonry and N. Morris, eds., *Crime and Justice: An Annual Review of Research, Volume 6.* Chicago, Ill.: University of Chicago Press.

Moses, L.E.
1985 Letter to the Editor: criminality and adoption. *Science* 227:983.

Moynihan, D.
1965 *The Negro Family: The Case for National Action.* ("The Moynihan Report") Washington, D.C.: U.S. Department of Labor.

Mrad, D.F.
1979 The effect of differential follow-up on rearrests: a critique of Quay and Love. *Criminal Justice and Behavior* 6:23–29.

Nagel, I.
1983 The legal/extra-legal controversy: judicial decisions in pretrial release. *Law and Society Review* 17:481–515.

Nagel, I., and Hagan, J.
1984 Gender and crime: Offense patterns and criminal court sanctions. In N. Morris and M. Tonry, eds., *Crime and Justice: An Annual Review of Research, Volume 4.* Chicago, Ill.: University of Chicago Press.

Nash, G.
1976 An analysis of twelve studies of the impact of drug abuse treatment upon criminality. Pp. 231–271 in *Appendix to Drug Use and Crime: Report of the Panel on Drug Use and Criminal Behavior.* Research Triangle Park, N.C.: Research Triangle Institute.·

National Council on Crime and Delinquency
1970 Hidden crime. *Crime and Delinquency* 2:1–49.

Nuffield, J.
1982 *Parole Decision-Making in Canada.* Ottawa: Supply and Services Canada.

Nye, F.I.
1958 *Family Relationship and Delinquent Behavior.* New York: John Wiley and Sons.

Nye, F.I., Short, J.F., and Olson, V.J.
1958 Socioeconomic status and delinquent behavior. *American Journal of Sociology* 63:381–389.

O'Donnell, C.R., Lydgate, T., and Fo, W.S.O.
1979 The "buddy system": review and follow-up. *Child Behavior Therapy* 1:161–169.

Ohlin, L.E.
1951 *Selection for Parole.* New York: Russell Sage Foundation.

Ohlin, L.E., and Duncan, O.D.
1949 The efficiency of prediction in criminology.

American Journal of Sociology 54:441–445.

Olweus, D.
1979 Stability of aggressive reaction patterns in males: a review. *Psychological Bulletin* 86:852–857.

Osborn, S.G., and West, D.J.
1979 Conviction records of fathers and sons compared. *British Journal of Criminology* 19:120–133.

Ouston, J.
1984 Delinquency, family background, and educational attainment. *British Journal of Criminology* 24:2–26.

Palmer, J., and Carlson, P.
1976 Problems with the use of regression analysis in prediction studies. *Journal of Research in Crime and Delinquency* 13(1):64–81.

Palmer, T.B.
1971 California's community treatment program for delinquent adolescents. *Journal of Research in Crime and Delinquency* 8:74–92.
1974 The youth authority's community treatment project. *Federal Probation* 38:3–14.

Palmore, E.B., and Hammond, P.E.
1964 Interacting factors in juvenile delinquency. *American Sociological Review* 29:848–854.

Parker, W.
1972 Parole: Origins, Development, Current Practices, and Statutes. Research Document 1. American Correctional Association, College Park, Md.

Patterson, G.R.
1980 Treatment for children with conduct problems: a review of outcome studies. Pp. 83–132 in S. Feshback and A. Fraczek, eds., *Aggression and Behavior Change: Biological and Social Process.* New York: Praeger.
1982 *A Social Learning Approach, Volume 1: Coercive Family Process.* Eugene, Ore.: Castalia.

Patterson, G.R., and Stouthamer-Loeber, M.
1984 The correlation of family management practices and delinquency. *Child Development* 55:1299–1307.

Patterson, G.R., Chamberlain, P., and Reid, J.B.
1982 A comparative evaluation of parent training programs. *Behavior Therapy* 13:638–650.

Penick, B., and Owens, M., eds.
1976 *Surveying Crime.* Panel for the Evaluation of Crime Surveys, Committee on National Statistics, Assembly of Mathematical and Physical Sciences. Washington, D.C.: National Academy of Sciences.

Petersilia, J.
1983 *Racial Disparities in the Criminal Justice System.* Report No. R-2947-NIC. Santa Monica, Calif.: Rand Corporation.

Petersilia, J., Greenwood, P.W., and Lavin, M.
1977 *Criminal Careers of Habitual Felons.* Santa Monica, Calif.: Rand Corporation.

Petersilia, J., Turner, S., Kahan J., and Peterson, J.
1985 *Granting Felons Probation: Public Risks and Alternatives.* Report No. R-3186-NIJ. Santa Monica, Calif.: Rand Corporation.

Peterson, M.A., and Braiker, H.B.
1980 *Doing Crime: A Survey of California Prison Inmates.* Report R-2200-DOJ. Santa Monica, Calif.: Rand Corporation.

Peterson, M.A., and Braiker, H.B., with Polich, S.
1981 *Who Commits Crime.* Cambridge, Mass.: Oelgeschlager, Gunn, and Hain Publishers, Inc.

Peterson, M., Chaiken, J., Ebener, P., and Honig, P.
1982 *Survey of Prison and Jail Inmates: Background and Methods.* A Rand Note. Santa Monica, Calif.: Rand Corporation.

Peterson, R.A., Pittman, D.J., and O'Neal, P.
1962 Stabilities in deviance: a study of assaultive and non-assaultive offenders. *Journal of Criminal Law, Criminology and Police Science* 53:44–48.

Peterson, R.D., and Hagan, J.
1984 Changing conceptions of race: towards an account of anomalous findings of sentencing research. *American Sociological Review* 49:56–70.

Piliavin, I., and Briar, S.
1964 Police encounters with juveniles. *American Journal of Sociology* 70:26–214.

Polk, K., Alder, C., Basemore, G., Blake, G., Cardray, S., and Coventry, G.
1981 *Becoming Adult: An Analysis of Maturational Development from Age 16 to 30.* Final report, Grant No. MH 14806, Center for Studies of Crime and Delinquency, National Institute of Mental Health. Washington, D.C.: U.S. Department of Health and Human Services.

Polk, K., Frease, D., and Richmond, F.L.
1974 Social class, school experience, and delinquency. *Criminology* 12:84–96.

Pollack, O.
1950 *The Criminality of Women.* Philadelphia: University of Pennsylvania Press.

Pond, E.
1970 *The Los Angeles Community Delinquency Control Project: An Experiment in the Rehabilitation of Delinquents in an Urban Community.* Los Angeles: California Youth Authority.

Porterfield, A.L.
1946 *Youth in Trouble.* Fort Worth, Tex.: Leo Potishman Foundation.

Pulkkinen, L.
1983 Search for alternatives to aggression in Fin-

land. In A.P. Goldstein and M. Segall, eds., *Aggression in Global Perspective*. New York: Pergamon.

Quay, H.C., and Love, C.T.

1977 The effect of a juvenile diversion program on rearrests. *Criminal Justice and Behavior* 4:377–396.

1979 Effects of a juvenile diversion project on rearrests: a reply to Mrad. *Criminal Justice and Behavior* 6:31–33.

Quetelet, A.

1984 *Research on the Propensity for Crime at Different Ages*. (Originally published 1831.) Translated by S.F. Sylvester. Cincinnati, Ohio: Anderson Publishing Co.

Rankin, J.H.

1983 The family context of delinquency. *Social Problems* 30:466–479.

Reckless, W.C., and Dinitz, S.

1972 *The Prevention of Juvenile Delinquency*. Columbus: Ohio State University Press.

Reckless, W.C., Dinitz, S., and Kay, B.

1957 The self component in potential delinquency and potential non-delinquency. *American Sociological Review* 22:566–570.

Reid, J.

1983 *Home-Based Treatment for Multiple Offending Delinquents*. Final Report to the National Institute of Mental Health. Grant No. R01MH37939, Rockville, Md.

Reiss, A.J.

1971 *The Police and the Public*. New Haven, Conn.: Yale University Press.

1973 Survey of Self-Reported Delicts. Unpublished paper. Department of Sociology, Yale University, New Haven, Conn.

1980a Crime rates and victimization. In S.E. Fienberg and A.J. Reiss, eds., *Indicators of Crime and Criminal Justice: Quantitative Studies*. Bureau of Justice Statistics. Washington, D.C.: U.S. Department of Justice.

1980b Understanding changes in crime rates. In S.E. Fienberg and A.J. Reiss, eds., *Indicators of Crime and Criminal Justice: Quantitative Studies*. Bureau of Justice Statistics. Washington, D.C.: U.S. Department of Justice.

Reiss, A.J., and Rhodes, A.L.

1959 *A Socio-Psychological Study of Adolescent Conformity and Deviance*. Washington, D.C.: U.S. Department of Education.

1961 The distribution of juvenile delinquency in the social class structure. *American Sociological Review* 26:720–732.

Research and Forecasts, Inc.

1980 *The Figgie Report on Fear of Crime: America Afraid*. Willoughby, Ohio: Figgie International, Inc.

Rhodes, W.

1980 Investment of prosecution resources in career criminal programs. *The Journal of Criminal Law and Criminology* 71:118–123.

1984 Empirical Comparisons of Prediction-Based Decision Rules with Decisions Made in Current Practice. Unpublished paper. Presented at the Workshop on Research on Criminal Careers, Woods Hole, Mass. U.S. Sentencing Commission, Washington, D.C.

1985 The adequacy of statistically derived prediction instruments in the face of sample selectivity: criminal justice as an example. *Evaluation Review* 9:369–382.

Rhodes, W., Tyson, H., Weekley, J., Conly, C., and Powell, G.

1982 *Developing Criteria for Identifying Career Criminals*. Washington, D.C.: U.S. Department of Justice.

Robins, L.N.

1966 *Deviant Children Grown Up: A Sociological and Psychiatric Study of Sociopathic Personality*. Baltimore, Md.: Williams and Wilkins.

1975 Discussion of genetic studies of criminality and psychopathy. *Proceedings of the American Psychopathological Association* 63:117–122.

1979 Addict careers. Pp. 325–336 in R. DuPont, A. Goldstein, and J. O'Donnell, eds., *Handbook on Drug Abuse*. Rockville, Md.: National Institute on Drug Abuse.

Robins, L.N., and Lewis, R.G.

1966 The role of the antisocial family in school completion and delinquency: a three generation study. *Sociological Quarterly* 7(4):500–514.

Robins, L.N., and Taibleson, M.

1972 An actuarial method for assessing the direction of influence between two datable life events. *Sociological Methods and Research* 1(2):243–270.

Robins, L.N., and Wish, E.

1977 Childhood deviance as a developmental process: a study of 223 urban black men from birth to 18. *Social Forces* 56(2):448–473.

Robins, L.N., Gyman, H., and O'Neal, P.

1962 The interaction of social class and deviant behavior. *American Sociological Review* 27:480–492.

Robins, L.N., West, P.A., and Herjanic, B.L.

1975 Arrests and delinquency in two generations: a study of black urban families and their children. *Journal of Child Psychology and Psychiatry* 15:125–140.

Robinson, W.S.

1950 Ecological correlations and the behavior of

individuals. *American Sociological Review* 15:351–357.

Roebuck, J., and Quinney, R.
1967 *Criminal Behavior Systems: A Typology.* New York: Holt, Rinehart & Winston.

Rojek, D.G., and Erickson, M.L.
1982 Delinquent careers: a test of the career escalation model. *Criminology* 20(1):5–28.

Rolph, J.E., Chaiken, J.M., and Houchens, R.L.
1981 *Methods for Estimating Crime Rates of Individuals.* Santa Monica, Calif.: Rand Corporation.

Rossi, P.H., Berk, R.A., and Lenihan, K.J.
1980 *Money, Work, and Crime: Some Experimental Results.* New York: Academic Press.
1982 Saying it wrong with figures: a comment on Zeisel. *American Journal of Sociology* 88:390–393.

Roth, J., and Wice, P.
1978 *Pretrial Release and Misconduct in the District of Columbia.* PROMIS Research Project Publication No. 16. Washington, D.C.: INSLAW.

Ruppert, D.
1985 On the bounded-influence regression estimator of Krasker and Welsch. *Journal of the American Statistical Association* 80: 205–208.

Rutter, M.
1977 Separation, loss, and family relations. Pp. 47–73 in M. Rutter and Littersov, eds., *Child Psychiatry: Modern Approaches.* Oxford: Blackwell.
1981 Epidemiological/longitudinal strategies and causal research in child psychiatry. *Journal of the American Academy of Child Psychiatry* 20:513–544.

Rutter, M., and Giller, H.
1984 *Juvenile Delinquency: Trends and Perspectives.* London: Guilford Press.

Schmidt, P., and Witte, A.
1980 Evaluating correctional programs: models of criminal recidivism and an illustration of their use. *Evaluation Quarterly* 4:585–600.

Schuessler, K.F.
1954 Parole prediction: its history and status. *Journal of Criminal Law and Criminology* 45(November):425–431.

Schweinhart, L.J., and Weikart, D.P.
1980 *Young Children Grow Up: The Effectiveness of the Perry Preschool Program on Youths Through Age 15.* Ypsilanti, Mich.: High/Scope Press.

Scott, J.E.
1974 The use of discretion in determining the severity of punishment for incarcerated offenders. *Journal of Criminal Law and Criminology* 65(2):214–224.

SEARCH Group, Inc.
1982 *Criminal Justice Information Policy: Privacy and Juvenile Justice Records.* Report of work prepared under BJS Grant No. 81-BJ-CX-0012. Bureau of Justice Statistics. Washington, D.C.: U.S. Department of Justice.

Sechrest, D.K.
1979 Methadone programs and crime reduction: a comparison of New York and California addicts. *The International Journal of the Addictions* 14(3):377–400.

Sechrest, L., White, S.O., and Brown, E., eds.
1979 *The Rehabilitation of Criminal Offenders: Problems and Prospects.* Panel on Research on Rehabilitative Techniques, Committee on Research on Law Enforcement and Criminal Justice, Assembly of Behavioral and Social Sciences, National Research Council. Washington, D.C.: National Academy of Sciences.

Sellin, T.
1958 Recidivism and maturation. *National Probation and Parole Association Journal* 4:241–250.

Sellin, T., and Wolfgang, M.
1964 *The Measurement of Delinquency.* New York: John Wiley and Sons.

Sells, S.B.
1979 Treatment effectiveness. Pp. 195–218 in R.L. DuPont, A. Goldstein, and J. O'Donnell, eds., *Handbook on Drug Abuse.* Rockville, Md.: National Institute on Drug Abuse.

Sells, S.B., Stimson, D.D., Joe, G.H., Demaree, R.G., Savage, L.J., and Woyd, M.R.
1976 A national follow-up study to evaluate the effectiveness of drug abuse treatment: a report on cohort I of DARP five years later. *American Journal of Drug and Alcohol Abuse* 3:545–556.

Severy, L.J., and Whitaker, J.M.
1982 Juvenile diversion: an experimental analysis of effectiveness. *Evaluation Review* 6:753–774.

Shannon, L.W.
1968 Scaling juvenile delinquency. *Journal of Research in Crime and Delinquency* 5:52–65.
1978 A longitudinal study of delinquency and crime. In C. Wellford, ed., *Quantitative Studies in Criminology.* Beverly Hills, Calif.: Sage Publications.
1981 *Assessing the Relationship of Adult Criminal Careers to Juvenile Careers.* Final Report to National Institute of Juvenile Justice and Delinquency Prevention. Iowa Urban

Community Research Center. University of Iowa.

1982a *Assessing the Relationship of Adult Criminal Careers to Juvenile Careers.* Office of Juvenile Justice and Delinquency Prevention. Washington, D.C.: U.S. Department of Justice.

1982b *Assessing the Relationship of Adult Criminal Careers to Juvenile Careers: A Summary.* Office of Juvenile Justice and Delinquency Prevention. Washington, D.C.: U.S. Department of Justice.

Shaw, C.R.

1930 *The Jack Roller: A Delinquent Boy's Own Story.* Chicago, Ill.: University of Chicago Press.

1931 *The Natural History of a Delinquent Career.* Chicago, Ill.: University of Chicago Press.

Shaw, C.R., and McKay, H.D.

1969 *Juvenile Delinquency and Urban Areas.* Revised Version. Chicago, Ill.: University of Chicago Press.

Shaw, M.

1974 *Social Work in Prison.* London: Her Majesty's Stationery Office.

Sherman, L.

1980 Causes of police behavior: the current state of quantitative research. *Journal of Research in Crime and Delinquency* 17:69–100.

Sherman, L.W., and Glick, B.D.

1984 *The Quality of Police Arrest Statistics.* Police Foundation Reports No. 2. Washington, D.C.: The Police Foundation.

Shinnar, R., and Shinnar, S.

1975 The effect of the criminal justice system on the control of crime: a quantitative approach. *Law and Society Review* 9:581–612.

Shore, M., and Massimo, J.

1979 Fifteen years after treatment: a follow-up study of comprehensive vocationally oriented psychotherapy. *American Journal of Orthopsychiatry* 49:240–245.

Short, J.F., and Nye, F.I.

1957 Reported behavior as a criterion of deviant behavior. *Social Problems* 5:207–213.

1958 Extent of unrecorded juvenile delinquency: tentative conclusions. *Journal of Criminal Law and Criminology* 49:269–302.

Sickles, R.C., Schmidt, P., and Witte, A.D.

1979 An application of the simultaneous Tobit model: a study of the determinants of criminal recidivism. *Journal of Economics and Business* 31:166–171.

Simon, F.H.

1971 *Prediction Methods in Criminology.* London: Her Majesty's Stationery Office.

Simpson, D.D., Savage, L.J., Lloyd, M.R., and Sells, S.B.

1978 Evaluation of drug abuse treatments based on first year follow-up. In *Evaluation of Drug Abuse Treatments.* DHEW Publication No. ADM 78–701. Rockville, Md.: National Institute on Drug Abuse.

Singer, B., and Spilerman, S.

1978 Some methodological issues in the analysis of longitudinal surveys. In K.E. Taeuber, L. Bumpass, and J.A. Sweet, eds., *Social Demography.* New York: Academic Press.

Slocum, W., and Stone, C.

1963 Family culture patterns and delinquent type behavior. *Journal of Marriage and Family* 25:202–208.

Smith, D.A.

1982 Invoking the Law: Situational, Community, and Organizational Determinants of Arrest Decisions. Unpublished Ph.D. dissertation, Department of Sociology, Indiana University. (University Microfilms, Ann Arbor, Mich.)

1986 The neighborhood context of police behavior. In A. Reiss and M. Tonry, eds., *Crime and Justice: An Annual Review of Research, Volume 8.* Chicago, Ill.: University of Chicago Press.

Smith, D.A., and Klein, J.R.

1984 Police control of interpersonal disputes. *Social Problems* 31:468–481.

Smith, D.A., and Visher, C.A.

1981 Street-level justice: situational determinants of police arrest decisions. *Social Problems* 29:167–177.

Smith, D.R., and Smith, W.R.

1984 Patterns of delinquent careers: an assessment of three perspectives. *Social Science Research* 13:129–158.

Sonquist, J.A., Baker, E.C., and Morgan, J.N.

1973 *Searching for Structure.* Ann Arbor: Institute for Social Research, University of Michigan.

Soothill, K.L., and Gibbens, T.C.N.

1978 Recidivism of sexual offenders: a reappraisal. *British Journal of Criminology* 18:267–276.

Spelman, W.

1984 A Sensitivity Analysis of the Rand Inmate Surveys. Paper presented at the 1984 meeting of the American Society of Criminology, Cincinnati, Ohio. Police Executive Research Forum, Washington, D.C.

Spilerman, S.

1972a The analysis of mobility processes by the introduction of independent variables into a

Markov chain. *American Sociological Review* 37:277–294.

1972b Extensions of the mover-stayer model. *American Journal of Sociology* 78:599–627.

Springer, F., and Phillips, J.
no   The Career Criminal Prosecution Program: An Examination of Program Results. Draft report submitted to Law Enforcement Assistance Administration, U.S. Department of Justice. MetaMetrics, Inc., Washington, D.C.

Statistical Analysis Center
1984 Risk Assessment in Iowa: An Overview. Office for Planning and Programming, Des Moines, Iowa. April 25, 1984.

Stollmack, S., and Harris, C.
1974 Failure rate analysis applied to recidivism data. *Operations Research* 22:1192–1205.

Stryker, R., Nagel, I., and Hagan, J.
1983 Methodological issues in court research: pretrial release decisions for federal defendants. *Sociological Methods and Research* 2:469–500.

Stuart, R.B., Jayaratne, S., and Tripodi, T.
1976 Changing adolescent deviant behavior through reprogramming the behavior of parents and teachers: an experimental evaluation. *Canadian Journal of Behavioral Science* 8:133–144.

Sutherland, E.
1937 *The Professional Thief.* Chicago, Ill.: University of Chicago Press.

Sutherland, E.H., and Cressey, D.R.
1978 *Criminology.* 10th ed. New York: Lippincott.

Thornberry, T.P., and Christensen, R.L.
1984 Unemployment and criminal involvement: an investigation of reciprocal causal structures. *American Sociological Review* 49:398–411.

Thornberry, T.P., and Farnworth, M.
1982 Social correlates of criminal involvement: further evidence on the relationship between social status and criminal behavior. *American Sociological Review* 47:505–518.

Tittle, C.R.
1980 *Sanctions and Social Deviance: The Question of Deterrence.* New York: Praeger.

Tittle, C.R., Villemez, W.J., and Smith, D.A.
1978 The myth of social class and criminality. *American Sociological Review* 43:643–656.

Tracy, P.E., Wolfgang, M.E., and Figlio, R.M.
1985 *Delinquency in Two Birth Cohorts.* Chicago, Ill.: University of Chicago Press.

U.S. Department of Justice
1979 *Evaluation of Treatment Alternatives to Street Crime.* National Evaluation Program, Phase II Report, Law Enforcement Assistance Administration. Washington, D.C.: U.S. Department of Justice.

U.S. Parole Commission
1981 Federal Parole Commission's Guidelines for Decisionmaking. Washington, D.C.: U.S. Department of Justice.

Van Alstyne, D.J., and Gottfredson, M.R.
1978 A multidimensional contingency table analysis of parole outcome. *Journal of Research in Crime and Delinquency* 15:172–193.

Van Dusen, K.T., Mednick, S.A., Gabrielli, W.F., and Hutchings, B.
1983 Social class and crime in an adoption cohort. *Journal of Criminal Law and Criminology* 74:250–269.

Venezia, P.S.
1972 Unofficial probation: an evaluation of its effectiveness. *Journal of Research in Crime and Delinquency* 9:149–170.

Vera Institute of Justice
1977 *Felony Arrests: Their Prosecution and Disposition in New York City's Courts.* New York: Vera Institute of Justice.

Viscusi, W.K.
1983 Market Incentives for Criminal Behavior. Paper prepared for the Conference on Inner City Black Youth Unemployment in Cambridge, Massachusetts, August 11–12. National Bureau of Economic Research, Inc., Cambridge, Mass.

von Hirsch, A.
1985 *Past or Future Crimes: Deservedness and Dangerousness in the Sentencing of Criminals.* New Brunswick, N.J.: Rutgers University Press.

von Hirsch, A., and Gottfredson, D.
1984 Selective incapacitation: some queries on research design and equity. *New York University Review of Law and Social Change* 12(1):11–51.

Wadsworth, M.E.J.
1976 Delinquency, pulse rates, and early emotional deprivation. *British Journal of Criminology* 16(3):245–255.
1979 *Roots of Delinquency.* London: Barnes and Noble.

Walberg, H., Yeh, E., and Patton, S.
1975 Family background, ethnicity, and urban delinquency. *Journal of Research in Crime and Delinquency* 11:80–87.

Waldo, G.P., and Chiricos, T.G.
1972 Perceived penal sanctions and self-reported delinquency: a neglected approach to deterrence research. *Social Problems* 19:522–540.

Wallerstein, J.S., and Wyle, C.J.
1947 Our law-abiding law-breakers. *Probation* 25:107–112.

Walters, H.I., and Gilmore, S.K.
1973 Placebo versus social learning effects in parental training procedures designed to alter the behavior of aggressive boys. *Behavior Therapy* 4:361–377.

Ward, P.F.
1968 The comparative efficiency of differing techniques of prediction scaling. *Australian and New Zealand Journal of Criminology* 1:109–112.

Warren, M.Q.
1971 Classification of offenders as an aid to efficient management and effective treatment. *Social Problems* 19:522–540.

Wechsler, H., and McFadden, D.
1976 Sex differences in adolescent alcohol and drug use. *Journal of Studies on Alcohol* 37:1299–1301.

Weis, J.
1973 Delinquency Among the Well-to-Do. Unpublished Ph.D. dissertation, School of Criminology, University of California, Berkeley. (University Microfilms, Ann Arbor, Mich.)
1976 Liberation and crime: the invention of the new female criminal. *Crime and Social Justice* 1(6):17–27.

West, D.J.
1969 *Present Conduct and Future Delinquency.* London: Heinemann.
1982 *Delinquency: Its Roots, Careers, and Prospects.* London: Heinemann.

West, D.J., and Farrington, D.P.
1973 *Who Becomes Delinquent?* London: Heinemann.
1977 *The Delinquent Way of Life.* London: Heinemann.

White, H.C.
1970 Stayers and movers. *American Journal of Sociology* 76:307–324.

Wilkins, L.T., and MacNaughton-Smith, P.
1964 New prediction and classification methods in criminology. *Journal of Research in Crime and Delinquency* 1:19–32.

Wilkinson, K.
1980 The broken home and delinquent behavior. Pp. 21–42 in T. Hirschi and M. Gottfredson, eds., *Understanding Crime.* Beverly Hills, Calif.: Sage Publications.

Williams, J.R., and Gold, M.
1972 From delinquent behavior to official delinquency. *Social Problems* 20(Fall):209–229.

Wilson, H.
1975 Juvenile delinquency, parent criminality, and social handicap. *British Journal of Criminology* 15:241–250.

Wilson, J.Q.
1968 *Varieties of Police Behavior.* Cambridge, Mass.: Harvard University Press.

Wilson, J.Q., and Herrnstein, R.J.
1985 *Crime and Human Nature.* New York: Simon and Schuster.

Winslow, R.
1967 Anomie and its alternatives: A self-report study of delinquency. *Sociological Quarterly* 8:468–480.

Witte, A.D.
1980 Estimating the economic model of crime with individual data. *Quarterly Journal of Economics* 94:57–84.

Wodarski, J.S., and Pedi, S.J.
1978 The empirical evaluation of the effects of different group treatment strategies against a controlled treatment strategy on behavior exhibited by antisocial children, behaviors of the therapist, and two self-rating scales that measure antisocial behavior. *Journal of Clinical Psychology* 34:471–481.

Wodarski, J.S., Filipczak, J., McCombs, D., Koustenis, G., and Rusilko, S.
1979 Follow-up on behavioral interventions with troublesome adolescents. *Journal of Behavior Therapy and Experimental Psychiatry* 10:181–188.

Wolfgang, M.E.
1977 From Boy to Man—From Delinquency to Crime. Paper presented at the National Symposium on the Serious Juvenile Offender, Minneapolis, Minnesota. Center for Studies in Criminology and Criminal Law, University of Pennsylvania.

Wolfgang, M.E., and Collins, J.
1978 *Offender Careers and Restraint: Probabilities and Policy Implications.* Final report to National Institute of Juvenile Justice and Delinquency, April 1978. Center for Studies in Criminology and Criminal Law, University of Pennsylvania.

Wolfgang, M.E., Figlio, R.M., and Sellin, T.
1972 *Delinquency in a Birth Cohort.* Chicago, Ill.: University of Chicago Press.

Wolfgang, M.E., Thornberry, T., and Figlio, R.
1985 *From Boy to Man—From Delinquency to Crime.* Sellin Center for Studies in Criminology and Criminal Law, Wharton School, University of Pennsylvania, Philadelphia.

Wright, W.E., and Dixon, M.C.
1977 Community prevention and treatment of juvenile delinquency: A review of evaluation studies. *Journal of Research in Crime and Delinquency* 14:35–67.

Zatz, M.S.
1984 Race, ethnicity, and determinate sentencing: a new dimension to an old controversy. *Criminology* 22:147–171.

Zeisel, H.
1968 *Say It with Figures.* New York: Harper and Row.
1982a Disagreement over the evaluation of a controlled experiment. *American Journal of Sociology* 88:378–389.
1982b Hans Zeisel concludes the debate. *American Journal of Sociology* 88:394–396.

Index